THIS BOOK BELONGS TO:

BIOFEEDBACK

Principles and practice
for clinicians

Third Edition

BIOFEEDBACK

Principles and practice for clinicians

Third Edition

Edited by

John V. Basmajian, M.D.

Professor Emeritus of Medicine and Anatomy
and
Former Director of Rehabilitation
Chedoke-McMaster Hospitals
McMaster University
Hamilton, Ontario, Canada

WILLIAMS & WILKINS
BALTIMORE · HONG KONG · LONDON · MUNICH
PHILADELPHIA · SYDNEY · TOKYO

Editor: John P. Butler
Associate Editor: Linda Napora
Copy Editor: Judith F. Minkove
Design: Norman W. Och
Illustration Planning: Wayne Hubbel
Production: Charles E. Zeller

Copyright © 1989
Williams & Wilkins
428 East Preston Street
Baltimore, Maryland 21202, USA

Accurate indications, adverse reactions, and dosage schedules for drugs are
provided in this book, but it is possible that they may change. The reader is
urged to review the package information data of the manufacturers of the
medications mentioned.

Printed in the United States of America

First Edition 1979
Second Edition 1983

Library of Congress Cataloging-in-Publication Data

Biofeedback : principles and practice for clinicians / edited by John
  V. Basmajian.—3rd ed.
      p.   cm.
    Includes bibliographical references and index.
    ISBN 0-683-00357-7
    1. Biofeedback training.   2. Therapeutics.   I. Basmajian, John
V., 1921-   .
    [DNLM: 1. Biofeedback (Psychology)   WM 420 B6147]
  RC489.B53B56 1989
  615.8'51—dc19
  DNLM/DLC
  for Library of Congress   88-20562
                                                        CIP

                                                         92
                              4 5 6 7 8 9 10

Preface to the Third Edition

In a new field of science and therapy that is rapidly changing, significant books become either collectors' items or important landmarks that measure progress. The first and second editions of this work served well as landmarks, and we are grateful for their generous reception by reviewers and readers. But, as before, we cannot ignore the passage of time. So this third edition records ideas and results that are new and provocative or new and accepted, while retaining and consolidating whatever is older and acceptable. As noted in the second edition, "old" is really not very old, for biofeedback as a widely recognized discipline is barely a young adult. But in its short life, it has been documented in some ten thousand professional articles, and its practitioners and scientists number in the many thousands around the world.

Perhaps the greatest success is the major impetus it has given to the growing field of behavioral medicine. By dramatically revealing the extent of self-regulation possible with suitable training techniques, biofeedback showed physicians, rehabilitation therapists, behavioral scientists, and clinical psychologists that they all had responsibilities in the same health camp—at least those who were not sure that their current practices were perfect.

In this new edition, many of the old chapter headings have been retained, but the contents have been changed quite markedly to reflect progress in the field and to achieve greater succinctness. The space-saving results permitted the inclusion of seven important new chapters: Chapter 2 by the "dean" of psychophysiology, Neal Miller; related Chapters 5 by G. Richard Smith and 6 by Patricia Norris; related Chapters 9 by Debbie LeCraw and 10 by myself; Chapter 23 by Charles Stroebel; Chapter 25 by Dugal Campbell, and Chapter 26 by Brent Carman and Gary Ryan. In addition, there has been massive reorganization, integration, and refurbishing of most older chapters. This present work is, I fervently believe, the most comprehensive, scientifically sound, and up-to-date book on the subject for psychophysiologists, clinical psychologists, physicians, rehabilitation and/or biofeedback therapists, and all who are interested in behavioral medicine. We invite their suggestions for further improvements that may someday reflect the best of biofeedback theory and practice in a fourth edition. Meanwhile, this book is the state of the art and science today.

Acknowledgments for this book are most deserved by the chapter authors. They responded to my urgent requests with easy grace and reasonable promptness. The publishers continued to be cooperative and responsive, making my editorial role as simple as that complex task can be. To earlier authors, present authors, and all who contributed to the success of previous editions and the preparation of this third edition, my warmest thanks.

McMaster University
1989

J. V. BASMAJIAN

Preface to the First Edition

Practical biofeedback in medicine and psychotherapy has come of age. In its embryonic period during the 1960s and early 1970s, some doubts as to its legitimacy and future prospects were widely expressed. As one of its putative fathers, I was deeply concerned that biofeedback—particularly myoelectric biofeedback—should get a fair start. Thus, along with many students, colleagues, and with growing numbers of workers in other centers, we struggled to provide the research which nourished its growth. During the late 1960s, this healthy growth was threatened by a popular sweep of interest in biofeedback and the accompanying host of entrepreneurs who began exploiting it—especially "alpha feedback"—for a variety of purposes.

Alpha feedback, after its glamourous and confused flirtation with the public press, has returned now to research where it needs to mature. Serious clinicians emerged from the early popularization phase relatively safely, and the popular press is beginning to understand that biofeedback is a medical methodology. The more directly useful clinical applications have matured through validating research projects to the point where clinicians can safely apply some aspects to the treatment of well-defined conditions while they continue research in other aspects of biofeedback applications.

The authors of the various chapters all have had a commitment to research and/or application of research results in biofeedback. Several have been doing basic research in the field of electronic recordings of biological phenomena for many years; others moved from related clinical fields into biofeedback research and therapy with ease because of their strong clinical backgrounds. They are generally recognized as leaders in their special fields. Most important, they are expert therapists and diagnosticians who employ biofeedback techniques judiciously and selectively, not as a shotgun treatment.

We offer this book as a timely summary and explication of the best applications of biofeedback treatment techniques to neurological, psychosomatic, and psychological disturbances. The techniques are not final and complete, but the underlying principle is quite clear and substantiated. Provided with various electronic instrumental displays of covert responses, patients can acquire substantial voluntary control of them. Where the responses are exaggerated, they can be reduced by an effort of will; where reduced (e.g., paresis), they sometimes can be restored or reinforced by retraining. Treatment of patients with stroke, cerebral palsy, severe recurring headaches, all distressingly difficult (sometimes hopeless) in the past, offers new hope to many patients. Other conditions not so impressive to an observer, but very important to the sufferer, also respond to biofeedback techniques. This book brings together in one volume the present state of the art.

Hamilton, Canada   J. V. BASMAJIAN
1978

Contributors

Charles Spencer Adler, M.D. *Assistant Clinical Professor of Psychiatry, University of Colorado School of Medicine; Chief of Psychiatry and Psychophysiology, Colorado Neurology and Headache Center, Denver, Colorado.*

Walter F. Baile, M.D. *Assistant Professor of Psychiatry, The Johns Hopkins University School of Medicine and Director of Liaison Psychiatry, Department of Psychiatry, Francis Scott Key Medical Center, Baltimore, Maryland.*

John V. Basmajian, M.D., F.A.C.A., F.R.C.P.(C.), F.A.C.R.M. (Austral.), F.A.C.B.M.R. *Director of Rehabilitation, Chedoke-McMaster Hospitals, and Professor of Medicine, McMaster University, Hamilton, Ontario, Canada.*

Stuart A. Binder-Macleod, P.T., Ph.D. *Assistant Professor, School of Life and Health Sciences, University of Delaware, Newark, Delaware.*

Robert Blumenstein, Ph.D. *Senior Instructor, Department of Anatomy, Hahnemann Medical College, Philadelphia, Pennsylvania.*

D. Michael Brown, O.T.R. *Owner and Director, Hand Rehabilitation Center of Atlanta, Inc., Atlanta, Georgia.*

Thomas H. Budzynski, Ph.D. *St. Luke's Medical Center, Bellevue, Washington.*

Dugal Campbell, Ph.D. *Professor, Department of Psychiatry, McMaster University, Hamilton, Ontario; Director, Canadian Mental Health Association, Toronto, Ontario, Canada.*

Andrew J. Cannistraci, D.D.S., F.A.C.D. *Associate Professor, Department of Prosthedontics, Myofacial Pain Dysfunction Syndrome Clinic, Fairleigh Dickenson University School of Dentistry, Teaneck, New Jersey.*

Brent Carman, Ph.D. *Manager, Division of Speech-Language Pathology, Calgary General Hospital, Calgary, Alberta, Canada.*

Charles S. Cleeland, Ph.D. *Director Biofeedback Clinic; Associate Professor, Department of Neurology, Center for Health Sciences, University of Wisconsin—Madison, Madison, Wisconsin.*

Bernard A. Cohen, Ph.D. *Successful Software Inc., Wawautosa, Wisconsin; Formerly Associate Professor of Neurology, Pediatrics and Physical Medicine & Rehabilitation, The Medical College of Wisconsin, Milwaukee, Wisconsin.*

Gary DeBacher, Ph.D. *Private Practice of Psychology and Former Assistant Professor of Rehabilitation Medicine and Senior Investigator, Regional Rehabilitation Research and Training Center, Emory University School of Medicine, Atlanta, Georgia.*

Bernard T. Engel, Ph.D. *Chief, Laboratory of Behavioral Sciences, National Institute of Aging, Gerontology Research Center, Francis Scott Key Medical Center, Baltimore, Maryland.*

Paul L. Fair, Ph.D. *Private Practice of Psychology, ACTS Inc.; Formerly Senior Investigator, Regional Rehabilitation Research and Training Center, Emory University School of Medicine, Atlanta, Georgia.*

C. Kumarlal Fernando, M.A., R.P.T. *Director, Forest Hill Therapy Center, Downers Grove, Illinois; Associate Professor, University of Illinois, Chicago, Illinois.*

George Fritz, Ed.D. *Director of Research, Princeton Biofeedback Institute and Clinic; Co-director, Biofeedback Clinic of Lehigh Valley, Allentown, Pennsylvania.*

Alyce M. Green, Ph.D. *Research Department, The Menninger Foundation, Topeka, Kansas.*

Elmer E. Green, Ph.D. *Director, Voluntary Controls Program, Research Department, The Menninger Foundation, Topeka, Kansas.*

Virgil Hockersmith, R.P.T. *Director of Program Development and Former Director of Biofeedback Services, Comprehensive Back Services, Casa Colina Hospital for Rehabilitation Medicine, Pomona, California.*

Herbert E. Johnson, M.D. *Medical Director, Comprehensive Back Services, Casa Colina Hospital for Rehabilitation Medicine, Pomona, California, and Associate Clinical Professor, University of California, Irvine, California.*

Debbie E. LeCraw, R.P.T. *Research Therapist, Center for Rehabilitation Medicine, Emory University, Atlanta, Georgia.*

Joel F. Lubar, Ph.D. *Professor of Psychology, University of Tennessee College of Liberal Arts, Knoxville, Tennessee.*

Neal E. Miller, Ph.D. *Professor Emeritus, Rockefeller University; Research Affiliate, Yale University, New Haven, Connecticut.*

Sheila Morrissey-Adler, Ph.D. *Private Practice of Psychology, Denver, Colorado (Deceased).*

Foad Nahai, M.D., F.A.C.S. *Assistant Professor of Surgery (Plastic and Reconstructive), Emory University School of Medicine, Atlanta, Georgia.*

Patricia Norris, Ph.D. *Director, Biofeedback and Psychophysiology Center, The Menninger Foundation, Topeka, Kansas*

David A. Paskewitz, Ph.D. *Assistant Professor, Department of Psychiatry, University of Maryland School of Medicine, Baltimore, Maryland.*

Kirk E. Peffer *Clinical Psychologist, Porter Memorial Hospital; University of Colorado School of Medicine and Biofeedback Institute of Denver, Denver, Colorado.*

Gary Ryan, B.Sc., M.H.Sc. *Manager, Rehabilitation Department, York County Hospital, Newmarket, Ontario, Canada.*

Marvin M. Schuster, M.D., F.A.C.P., F.A.P.A. *Professor of Medicine and Assistant Professor of Psychiatry, The Johns Hopkins University School of Medicine; Director, Division of Digestive Disease, Francis Scott Key Medical Center, Baltimore, Maryland.*

Gary E. Schwartz, Ph.D. *Professor of Psychology and Psychiatry, Yale University, New Haven, Connecticut.*

Keith Sedlacek, M.D. *Medical Director, Stress Regulation Institute, New York, New York.*

G. Richard Smith, Jr., M.D. *Associate Professor of Psychiatry and Medicine, University of Arkansas for Medical Sciences, Little Rock, Arkansas.*

Johann Martin Stoyva, Ph.D. *Associate Professor of Psychiatry, University of Colorado School of Medicine, Medical Center, Denver, Colorado.*

Charles F. Stroebel, Ph.D., M.D. *Professor, University of Connecticut Medical School, and Director, Institute for Advanced Studies in Behavioral Medicine, Hartford, Connecticut.*

Steven L. Wolf, Ph.D., R.P.T. *Professor of Rehabilitation Medicine and Anatomy; Director of Research, Regional Rehabilitation Research and Training Center, Emory University School of Medicine, Atlanta, Georgia.*

Contents

PART 1
INTRODUCTION AND NEUROSCIENCE

CHAPTER 1

Introduction: Principles and Background

JOHN V. BASMAJIAN

Biofeedback may be defined as the technique of using equipment (usually electronic) to reveal to human beings some of their internal physiological events, normal and abnormal, in the form of visual and auditory signals in order to teach them to manipulate these otherwise involuntary or unfelt events by manipulating the displayed signals. This technique inserts a person's volition into the gap of an open feedback loop—hence the artificial name *biofeedback*, a name that some scientists and clinicians abhor for linguistic and other reasons. Unlike conditioned responses, the animal involved, here necessarily a human being, must want to voluntarily change the signals because they meet some goals.

Teaching patients to control a wide range of physiological processes occasionally has amazing therapeutic results, but legitimate clinical use of biofeedback as described in this book must be differentiated from the fad which caught the popular imagination in the late 1960s. While many self-serving promoters of general biofeedback are still at work, true clinical biofeedback has quietly taken a place as a genuine treatment for a growing number of neurological and psychosomatic ailments. Both scientific and practical studies provide us with sufficient concrete evidence that objective neurological signs and symptoms can be altered, particularly in patients with upper motor neu-

ron paralysis and spasticity due to brain damage. The easiest form of do-it-yourself biofeedback—alpha brain wave biofeedback—is still not understood scientifically. "Alpha feedback" is still a mystery, and it is not a definitive treatment method. Other forms of EEG feedback have shown considerable promise in the experimental situation (Chapter 7).

Biofeedback control of cardiac rates and blood pressure has emerged slowly from research-oriented clinical studies. Whether it will have great practical usefulness with large numbers of hypertensive patients remains to be seen. Reports of patients who maintain continued lower blood pressure over months and other patients who can willfully elevate their blood pressure (to prevent, for example, orthostatic hypotension) provide striking evidence that biofeedback may have very practical results in changing cardiovascular function.

Among the most striking areas of biofeedback treatment has been the alleviation of migraine by teaching subjects to elevate the temperature of fingertips. While some of the results may arise from "placebo effect," the evidence is growing that the link between peripheral blood flow and cranial blood flow provides a clear explanation of the phenomenon.

Another area in which placebo effects provide considerable underpinning of the results

1

is in the treatment of chronic tension headaches with myoelectric biofeedback, which is aimed at reducing general muscle tension. Deep relaxation strikes directly at the cause, i.e., muscle tension. There are other ways in which relaxation can be taught effectively, but biofeedback gadgets are useful in accelerating the treatment, and good psychotherapists quickly wean their patients from the gadgets. They teach their patients self-control as part of their long-term treatment. General or total body relaxation also has proved to be very useful in the rehabilitation clinic along with targeted relaxation of specific muscles in spasm. Thus, in patients with dyskinesias (e.g., spasmodic torticollis) and cerebral palsy, and for patients who have suffered stroke and have spasticity, relaxation therapy enhances their subsequent training of improved motor performance.

In rehabilitation, the most useful feedback has been myoelectric or "electromyographic" (EMG). "Electromyographic" is probably not a good adjective to apply to this form of biofeedback because the patient and the clinician both do not view electromyograms or an electromyograph. Instead, the myoelectric signals from the muscle are translated into acoustic and visual signals that are very simple to understand—buzzing sounds and lights. A premise of myoelectric biofeedback has always been that patients can respond to a physician's request during an EMG examination to alter the coarse level of activity of individual muscles as they are displayed as spikes on a cathode ray oscilloscope and also heard as popping noises on a loudspeaker. Indirectly, this knowledge (gained in the period following the Second World War in many clinics, including mine) led to my early studies. In the 1950s and 1960s, we were advocating the possible application of tiny sources of muscle potentials for the development and control of myoelectric prostheses. This led to more intense studies of how this control is exerted and its exquisite nature.

Several streams springing from widely separated sources came together in the 1960s to form the broad but shallow river that was to become the clinical biofeedback technology of today. This river is becoming deeper as scientists and clinicians add controlled research results to the wide scattering of case reports. One of the early sources was the work done by Jacobson (1) in the 1920s and 1930s. He devel-

oped and became an enthusiastic proponent of relaxation therapy in which he employed rather primitive electromyographic equipment to monitor the level of tension in the muscles of his patients. Limited by the apparatus available at that time, Jacobson developed methods of electrical measurement of the muscular status of tension, and with these measurements, he facilitated progressive somatic relaxation for a variety of psychoneurotic syndromes. Meanwhile, in Germany, Shultz (2) developed his related technique, autogenic training, which was most widely popularized in Canada by his pupil Luthe (3). Although autogenic training employed no specific EMG equipment, nevertheless it was one of the early sources of much of today's biofeedback application in the treatment of psychosomatic and neurotic symptoms.

While medical specialists and psychologists who knew of these relaxation techniques kept them alive and growing, the field of diagnostic electromyography was spreading equally slowly. Electromyography grew out of studies of neuromuscular and spinal cord functions. It began with the classic paper in 1929 by Adrian and Bronk (4) who showed that the electrical responses in individual muscles provided an accurate reflection of the actual functional activity of the muscles. In subsequent years, only a scattering of research papers kept the flow of the stream that was to become myoelectric biofeedback alive. Thus, in 1934, Olive Smith (5) reported observations on human conscious control of individual motor unit potentials, their general behavior, and their frequency. She showed that normally there is no proper or inherent rhythm acting as a limiting factor in the activity of motor units. Shortly after, Lindsley (6) confirmed Smith's findings and seems to have been the first scientist to emphasize that at rest "subjects can relax a muscle so completely that . . . no active units are found." Relaxation sometimes requires conscious effort and, in some cases, special training.

Lindsley found that complete relaxation was not difficult in any of his normal subjects. This finding has since been confirmed by thousands of investigators using modern electrical apparatus. Gilson and Mills (7), Harrison and Mortensen (8) and I (9) continued this type of work. Using fine-wire electrodes that we had recently developed for other purposes, I was able to train normal subjects to isolate many separate motor units and to activate them consciously. This was a form of single spinal motor neuron training. Then, a long series of studies with my students and colleagues led progressively towards a confluence with the other streams that were to form the modern biofeedback river.

The influence of the single motor unit research projects on the development of therapeutic techniques was not dramatic. As early as 1960, Marinacci and Horande (10) presented various case histories and discussed the effectiveness of the display of the EMG to patients in an effort to restore function for various neurological conditions. Later, Andrews (11) trained stroke patients to flex and extend a paralyzed elbow region. Then, a growing number of investigators began to concentrate on the treatment of stroke patients with myoelectric biofeedback (12-14). The myoelectric control "stream" joined the muscle relaxation "stream" in the mid-1960s. Following my publications on single motor unit controls (9, 15), Budzynski et al. (16) developed a technique for inducing generalized body relaxation for the relilef of tension headaches. This type of application of myoelectric feedback has grown to dominate the entire field. While medical rehabilitation groups emphasize targeted relaxation or targeted retraining of semiparetic muscles, clinical psychologists and specialists in psychosomatic medicine almost limit their clinical work to general deep relaxation, often combining Jacobsonian techniques and autogenic training along with instrumental relaxation.

Two other streams arrived in the mid-1960s. One of these was the increasing use of operant conditioning in animal psychological research. Thus, the cardiovascular conditioning of Miller and his colleagues (17) caught the imagination of many scientists and clinicians (18). At the same time, experts in EEG began to report interesting correlations between the state of emotional set and consciousness on the one hand and the amount of alpha waves generated by the subject on the other hand. By the end of the 1960s, all of the various streams had joined, leading to the formation in 1969 of the Biofeedback Research Society—renamed in 1976 the *Biofeedback Society of America*, and in 1988, the *Association of Applied Psychophysiology and Biofeedback*.

In the 1970s, the shape of biofeedback changed dramatically. The most dominant form, which received the greatest publicity in the late 1960s, alpha feedback, virtually dried up as a scientifically defensible clinical tool. Where it is still used by serious clinicians, it is combined with other techniques to achieve relaxation. However, it has also returned to the research laboratory from which it probably should not have emerged prematurely. Through the next generation of scientific investigation, it may return as a useful applied technique.

Temperature and/or peripheral blood flow control of the extremities has become one of the major tools of clinical psychologists and their scientific associates. Considerable controversy continues as to whether direct blood flow measurements, photoplethysmography or skin-temperature sensing devices are preferable. These matters are considered elsewhere in this volume as are the possibilities for altering blood pressure and general tension.

The most dramatic application of biofeedback to large numbers of severely handicapped patients has been in the area of myoelectric biofeedback. Both for general relaxation, which alleviates many symptoms due to anxiety or excess muscular tension (e.g., tension headache, general anxiety, stress pain such as low-back pain, etc.), and for the treatment of neurological handicaps, myoelectric biofeedback has gained a solid following of clinical scientists. In the physical rehabilitation field, biofeedback has made its greatest medical strides. For example, we reported that 64% of our patients wearing a short leg brace for footdrop following stroke could discard the device after several weeks of biofeedback training (19). This confirmed our earlier control studies, which were performed more rigidly (14). We have also gained considerable experience with the retraining of patients with tendon transfers and surgery in the hand (20), and with spasticity control (19). These matters will be discussed in subsequent chapters.

To conclude this chapter, a quotation from my 1976 paper in *Modern Medicine* is still appropriate (21):

... a cautiously optimistic view of clinical biofeedback is justified.... By acquiring sound knowledge, physicians and therapists can ensure that the uses of biofeedback in treatment of patients are both scientifically correct and ethical.

References

1. Jacobson. E. Electrical measurements concerning muscular contraction (tonus) and the cultivation of relaxation in man: studies on arm flexors. Am. J. Physiol. *107*: 230–248, 1933.
2. Schultz, J. H. and Luthe, W. *Autogenic Training.* Grune & Stratton, New York, 1959.
3. Luthe, W. (ed.) *Autogenic Therapy,* vols. 1–6. Grune & Stratton, New York, 1969.
4. Adrian, E. D. and Bronk, D. W. The discharge of impulses in motor nerve fibres. Part II. The frequency of discharge in reflex and voluntary contractions. J. Physiol., *67*: 119–151, 1929.
5. Smith, O. C. Action potentials from single motor units in voluntary contraction. Am. J. Physiol., *108*: 629–638, 1934.
6. Lindsley, D. B. Electrical activity of human motor units during voluntary contraction. Am. J. Physiol., *114*: 90–99, 1935.
7. Gilson, A. S. and Mills, W. B. Activities of single motor units in man during slight voluntary efforts. Am. J. Physiol., *133*: 658–669, 1941.
8. Harrison, V. F. and Mortensen, O. A. Identification and voluntary control of single motor unit activity in the tibialis anterior muscle. Anat. Rec. *144*: 109–116, 1962.
9. Basmajian, J. V. Conscious control of individual motor units. Science. *141*: 440–441, 1963.
10. Marinacci, A. A. and Horande, M. Electromyogram in neuromuscular re-education. Bull. Los Angeles Neurol. Soc., *25*: 57–71, 1960.
11. Andrews, J. M. Neuromuscular re-education of hemiplegic with aid of electromyograph, Arch. Phys. Med. Rehabil., *45*: 530–532, 1964.
12. Johnson, H. E. and Garton, W. H. Muscle re-education in hemiplegia by use of electromyographic device. Arch. Phys. Med., *54*: 320–322, 1973.
13. Brudny, J., Grynbaum, B. B. and Korein, J. Spasmodic torticollis: treatment of feedback display of EMG. Arch. Phys. Med. Rehabil., *55*: 403–408, 1973.
14. Basmajian, J. V., Kukulka, C. G., Narayan, M. G. and Takebe, K. Biofeedback treatment of footdrop after stroke compared with standard rehabilitation technique: effects on voluntary control and strength. Arch. Phys. Med. Rehabil., *56*: 231–236, 1975.
15. Basmajian, J. V. Muscles Alive: Their functions Revealed by Electromyography, 4th ed. Williams & Wilkins, Baltimore, 1979.
16. Budzynski, T. H., Stoyva, J. M., Adler, C. S. and Mullaney, D. J. EMG biofeedback and tension headache: a controlled outcome study. Psychosom. Med., *35*: 484–496, 1973.
17. Miller, N. E. and Bunuazizi, A. Instrumental learning by curarized rats of a specific visceral response, intestinal or cardiac. J. Comp. Physiol. Psychol., *65*: 1–7, 1968.
18. Schwartz, G. and Shapiro, D. Biofeedback and essential hypertension: current findings and theoretical concerns. Semin. Psychiatr., *5*: 493–503, 1973.
19. Basmajian, J. V., Regenos, E. M. and Baker, M. P. Rehabilitating stroke patients with biofeedback. Geriatrics, *32*: 85–88, 1977.
20. Basmajian, J. V., Kukulka, C. G. and Brown, D. M. Biofeedback training for early finger joint mobilization following surgical repair of tendon lacerations in the hand: preliminary report. Am. J. Occupational Ther., *29*: 469–470, 1975.
21. Basmajian, J. V. Biofeedback: the clinical tool behind the catchword. Modern Med., *44*: 60–64, 1976.

CHAPTER 2

Biomedical Foundations for Biofeedback as a Part of Behavioral Medicine[a]

NEAL E. MILLER

Most clinicians should and do use biofeedback in combination with other techniques. A solid foundation for biofeedback and the rest of behavorial medicine is provided by the role of the brain in the health of the body. Different levels of the brain control functions that range from release of hormones, modulation of the immune system, heart rate, blood pressure, and breathing, through emotional responses and motor skills, up to learning and the highest intellectual functions.

HIERARCHICAL CONTROLS

The system is a hierarchical one with automatic regulations at local levels being modified and orchestrated into adaptive patterns at progressively higher levels. For example, the flow of blood needed to supply oxygen and nutrients to a particular tissue, like a skeletal muscle, and to remove waste products from it, is under local autoregulatory control. In direct response to chemical conditions indicating local need for more blood, the muscles narrowing the size of the blood vessels relax, allowing more blood to flow. But appropriate flow depends also on appropriate blood pressure. The baroreceptor reflex in a lower center of the brain helps to hold blood pressure at a constant appropriate level. When the receptors, primarily in the carotid sinus, indicate that pressure is too high, this reflex automatically elicits a number of responses, such as a slowing of heart rate, that lower the pressure.

But in a state of emotional excitement likely to lead to violent activity, the baroreceptor reflex is inhibited by impulses from higher centers, so that blood pressure can go up. This is an example of an important fact, namely that lower reflexes cannot be fully understood if studied only in complete isolation, but are determined by the state of the individual as mediated by higher centers of the brain. This is also true of reflexes involved in the skeletal muscles, like those in the arms and the legs. A spinal reflex contributes to the efficiency of most movements by causing the muscles that extend the arm to relax when those that flex the arm are stimulated. But impulses from the brain can inhibit this reflex so that the arm can be held rigid by the contraction of both sets of muscles.

At the same time the baroreceptor reflex is inhibited, impulses from the brain via the sympathetic nervous system (and a decrease in those via the parasympathetic one) increase blood pressure in other ways, such as by causing the heart to beat harder and faster. But in situations that may require intense muscular activity, the mere general increase in blood pressure may not be enough; there is a need to override the local autoregulatory mechanisms and change the priorities for delivery of blood to different parts of the body. Messages from the brain do this in a number of ways, such as by causing the adrenal glands to release adrenaline, which stimulates receptors in the blood vessels of the stomach, intestines, kidneys and skin to constrict and different ones in the muscles of the body to dilate. Thus, the blood supply is shifted to where the need will be most urgent. This can mean that some tissues get less blood than they need.

[a]Work on this chapter was supported by office facilities supplied by Yale University Department of Psychology, and funds for clerical work and supplies by Rockefeller University and the Health and Behavior Network of the John D. and Catherine T. MacArthur Foundation.

The state of emotional arousal is in turn affected by what the individual has learned about the dangerousness or safety of the situation and even by the highest mental processes of the brain. Thus, if the navigator of a plane over the ocean has just used mathematics and sophisticated reasoning to discover that he is encountering exceptionally strong headwinds so that he will run out of fuel before he can reach land, his stomach may feel nauseous, his heart may pound rapidly, and his face and hands may grow pale and cold as the blood drains out of them (1).

Fight-Flight and Freezing-Vigilant Patterns

What we have described so far is one part of what Cannon (2) studied as the *fight-or-flight response*. Some other parts, discovered since then, are chains of neural and hormonal events initiated by the brain that cause widespread changes throughout the body—(a) an increased tendency of the blood to clot that is useful in stopping a wound from bleeding but may eventually contribute to the buildup of clots in arteries; (b) release into the blood of fatty acids that will be needed as fuel for intense activity, but if not used in this way, will be reprocessed by the liver to increase the level of cholesterol that can contribute to plaques, which eventually can block arteries; (c) release of blood sugar from the liver as a source of energy and blocking of the actions of insulin that would take sugar out of the blood and put it into storage, a sequence that can aggravate diabetes; and (d) release from the adrenals of corticosteroids that reduce the effects of injury, but also tend to suppress parts of the immune system. There are other such mechanisms, and more are being discovered. But we know enough already to establish that there is no mystery about the fact that the brain, including its highest functions, can affect the health of the body (3).

During the dangerous conditions under which our ancestors evolved, the need for immediate survival in an emergency apparently had to be met at the expense of certain disadvantages, especially ones whose effects may not show up till after reproduction has occurred. Various types of behavioral therapy, including biofeedback, have been found useful in reducing stress responses under modern conditions in which preparation for violent physical activity is no longer necessary. Some

of these are described in greater detail in other chapters.

More recent research has found that, in addition to the fight-flight response to a dangerous situation, there is at least one other—becoming both inconspicuous and highly vigilant. This *freezing-vigilant response* involves a different pattern of internal responses—decrease in heart rate but increase in blood pressure from an increase in peripheral resistance (4). While it has not been studied in complete detail, it also involves some differences in glandular response (5). Yet other research is showing that the sympathetic nervous system is capable of a considerably larger number of specific responses than had been realized (3) and that the same is true for different patterns of glandular responses (6). Such advances will allow us to understand a greater variety of ways in which the brain affects the health of the body and will be a guide to more specific types of treatment.

In addition to nerves from the brain to the internal organs, there are others, like those from the carotid sinus, that run from sensory receptors in the organs back to the brain. Many of the messages via these nerves are perceived dimly, if at all. But special training can teach animals and people to discriminate many of them (7). The anatomy of the sympathetic and parasympathetic systems that carry both motor and sensory nerves is described in Chapter 4.

EXPERIMENTAL PROOF OF PREDICTED EFFECTS

Proof that mechanisms like those described do actually have a variety of clinically relevant effects on health is evident in an increasingly impressive number of rigorously controlled experiments on animals. The results are in line with clinical and epidemiological observations on people in which confounding factors prevent completely convincing proof. But the combination of experimental and clinical results is indeed convincing. Some illustrative examples follow.

Role of Psychological Factors in Stomach Lesions

Observations after bombing raids and in a variety of other stressful situations suggest that fear can produce ulcers. But many other factors, such as changes in diet and exposure to infections, are involved in such situations.

Studies in combat have indicated that being able either to learn to discriminate when it is dangerous and when it is safe or to perform a coping response (even if it does not appreciably reduce the danger) can reduce fear. But there are many confusing factors in combat (8).

The foregoing observations were confirmed by a rigorously controlled series of experiments by Dr. Jay Weiss (9) in my laboratory. He tested rats in groups of three, each partially restrained in a separate soundproof box with an electrode on its tail. One was a control rat that received no electric shocks. The other two experimental rats received exactly the same shocks because the electrodes on their tails were wired in series. In one study, one of each pair of rats with tails wired in series had a tone signaling each shock so it could learn the discrimination of when it was dangerous and when it was safe. The other rat heard similar tones, but they were unrelated to the shocks so that it could not learn the discrimination. After this treatment, the stomachs of the control rats were virtually perfect. The stomachs of the rats that could not learn discrimination showed extensive lesions. This showed that the stressor of electric shocks could produce stomach lesions. But the rats that could learn the discrimination had only a fifth as extensive stomach lesions. This showed that, subject to exactly the same physical stressor of electric shocks, the purely psychological variable of being able to learn a discrimination could produce a great reduction in the amount of stomach lesions.

In a similar experiment, one of the experimental rats could turn the electric shock off by rotating a little wheel as a coping response. His partner could rotate a similar wheel, but since it was disconnected, his shock was determined exclusively by what his partner did; he had no control. In this case the purely psychological variable of the control by a coping response reduced the extensiveness of stomach lesions by a factor of three. But if the coping response was a conflict-inducing one, because rotating the wheel caused both rats to receive an initial brief shock, the result was completely reversed; the rats that controlled the shock had by far the most lesions. A similar reversal was produced by requiring the coping response to involve a lot of effort. This type of reversal indicates the need for caution in ap-

plying conclusions to complex situations that have not been throughly investigated.

Cardiovascular Effects

Clinical and epidemological evidence suggest that stressors can have an adverse affect on various aspects of the cardiovascular system, but that some people are much more affected than others. Experimental studies confirm these observations. A variety of strong stressors can lead to high blood pressure but are more likely to do so if combined with factors such as a genetic susceptibility or a high salt intake, even when neither of these two factors would produce high blood pressure without the stress. Similarly, arteriosclerosis can be produced experimentally by combining high stress with a high-fat diet.

If the heart has been damaged by tying off a coronary artery (a condition similar to that produced by a heart attack), cardiac arrhythmias leading to fatal fibrillation can be induced by either direct electrical stimulation of the sympathetic nerves from the stellate ganglion or exposure to a situation in which the animal has learned to expect shocks but is not presently receiving them. In this connection, it is interesting to note that a study found that patients recovering from heart attacks in an intensive care unit were five times as likely to go into fatal fibrillation when an unfamiliar group of doctors and residents were making ward rounds than at any other time of the day (1).

EFFECTS VIA IMMUNE SYSTEM

Yet another mechanism for the brain to affect the health of the body is via the immune system. A large number of experiments on animals and observations on people show that emotional stress can depress the function of various components of the immune system and that the ability to exert control over a stressor can significantly reduce such depressing effects (10,11). Part of these depressing effects are mediated via the corticosteroids, but experiments in which the adrenal glands releasing these hormones have been removed show that other mechanisms must be involved, and indeed potential ones exist such as receptors for neurotransmitters on circulating cells of the immune system. As would be expected from the foregoing results, stressors have been found to decrease the resistance to experimental infections and implanted tumors in animals and also are related to increased probability of diseases in people (12).

There is, however, need for additional research on the relation of stress to the immune system. While the vast majority of studies show a depression and a greater susceptibility to disease, there are a few studies that show the opposite effect of an increased level of immune function or resistance to disease. Perhaps the answer is to be found in a few studies that indicate an initial depression followed by a rebound above baseline. The immune system is extremely complex, and more detailed and analytical research on its relationships to functions of the brain is recommended (13). Chapters 5 and 6 of this book consider these issues more thoroughly.

BRAIN CONTROL OF PAIN

Pain is an important medical problem, and abundant clinical evidence indicates that it can be influenced by psychological factors. In some people, major surgery can be performed under hypnosis with pain apparently completely inhibited. Recently, tracts have been discovered in the brain the electrical stimulation of which can relieve pain in unanesthetized animals so effectively that they can be operated on without evidence of discomfort. Similarly, people who have been completely devastated by incessant and excruciating pain with no other hope of relief have secured merciful relief by stimulation via chronic electrodes of similar tracts in their brains. Some of these tracts have been found to use opiate-like substances as neurotransmitters; others seem to use something else that has not yet been identified (14).

Such research suggests mechanisms that may be involved in behavioral treatments of pain and hold out hope for more effective and less addictive pain-killing drugs. Unfortunately, some of the research on pain, brain-body control mechanisms, stress, and the effects of stress on the immune system could not have been done without subjecting some animals to pain and stress. But it would be highly immoral and inhumane not to conduct the research that has relieved a far larger number of animals and people from severe distress (15,16).

POSITIVE EMOTIONS

Clinical and epidemiological evidence shows that people who have more social support and have feelings of self-efficacy have better health. There is suggestive evidence that the will to live is beneficial. But there are many possibilities for confounding factors, such as better personal hygiene. Unfortunately, virtually no rigorous experimental work has been done on the possible beneficial effects of positive emotions such as hope, love, joy, and mirth.

An opening wedge to the investigation of positive emotions is the phenomenon of counterconditioning. Consider Pavlov's experiment where a stimulus that elicits mild pain or fear is made the signal for some desirable event (such as preferred food for a very hungry dog), and during a series of trials each such stimulus is reinforced by food but is also progressively changed so that it ordinarily would elicit stronger pain or fear. All of the signs of the stronger pain or fear will be eliminated (17). The possible role of opiate-like neurotransmitters in counterconditioning has not yet been determined. It has been reported that soldiers for whom a serious wound means the end for them of further dangerous combat show far less signs of pain and request far less pain-killing drugs than do similarly injured civilians (18). In this example, as well as in counterconditioning, higher functions of the brain involving learning and meaning determine the reaction of pain.

EFFECTS OF LEARNING ON VITAL FUNCTIONS

One of the higher functions of the brain that can affect vital processes in the body is learning. Research is showing that such effects are considerably more extensive than previously realized (19).

Classical conditioning is a simple type of learning situation. In it a stimulus becomes able to elicit a new response after it has been followed a number of times by another stimulus, called an unconditioned one that already elicits that response. The various components of the fight-flight response, as well as those of the freezing-vigilance one, can be conditioned to new situations. In the digestive system, the response to a food, be it nausea, a pleasant sense of well-being, or rapid satiation, can be conditioned to whatever flavor is associated with that food. This enables the individual to react appropriately to what the effects of the food will be before too much is swallowed (19). Similarly, the secretion of saliva, stomach acid, pancreatic juice and bile, and contractions of the stomach, gall bladder and intestines, all can be conditioned (20). This enables different portions of the digestive tract to be prepared for the arrival of food. Many other internal responses are subject to conditioning.

Besides being conditioned to neural impulses from sense organs like the eye and ear, responses can also be conditioned and/or generalized to the impulses in the brain that are involved in images and thoughts (21). For example, thinking about and vividly imagining the sight and taste of a lemon can cause people to salivate. Vividly imagining details of a relaxing scene from a pleasant, carefree vacation can induce relaxation and counteract fight-flight or freeze-vigilant reactions. Therapeutic use of imagery and thoughts (cognition) is described in Chapters 5 and 6.

Behavioral medicine makes use of the detailed, experimentally verified principles of classical conditioning to eliminate maladaptive and to establish adaptive responses (22, 23).

Another type of learning situation is called instrumental learning or *operant conditioning*. In it the responses that are rewarded (i.e., reinforced) are strengthened, and those that are not rewarded or are punished tend to be weakened. It is more flexible than classical conditioning because it does not depend on an unconditioned stimulus that already elicits the response to be learned. When a novice is trying to learn to shoot baskets from the foul line, there is no unconditioned stimulus that the coach can use to elicit a perfect shot on the first trial. Based on innate responses modified by past learning, the novice shoots in the general direction of the basket. When he comes nearer, he is rewarded by the partial success and is more likely to repeat that response. When the ball goes farther from the basket, he feels frustrated and is less likely to repeat that response. He also may make use of the direction of the miss to guide the next trial. When the ball goes swishing through the net, this success serves as a strong reward. In this way, the novice gradually learns better control over making the ball go into the basket.

Another source of greater flexibility of instrumental learning is the fact that a variety of rewards—success, praise, or reduction in pain or fear, to name only a few—can be used to strengthen a given response, and a given reward can be used to strengthen any one of a considerable variety of responses.

BIOFEEDBACK

The information about where the ball went on each shot is called feedback. If both the coach and the novice were blindfolded, there would be no feedback, and the novice would not learn to improve. Some tense patients may not be aware of the fact that certain muscles are tense, and patients with neuromuscular disorders, or even their therapists, may not be able to discriminate small increases in the activity of paralyzed muscles or decreases in the contractions of spastic ones. They are like a blindfolded basketball novice and coach. But a display of a measurement of the electrical activity of the muscles (the EMG) can remove the blindfold and give them better feedback about what the muscles are doing. This feedback might be in the form of a series of auditory clicks that gets faster the more the muscle contracts, or a tracing of the activity of one or more muscles as a dot draws the curve of a graph on a TV screen. Feedback from a measuring instrument that yields moment-to-moment information about a biological function is called biofeedback.

One of the advantages of biofeedback is that it allows small changes in the correct direction to be noticed and rewarded as success so that they gradually can be built up into larger changes. Eventually, patients learn to perceive these changes without the measuring instrument so that they can practice by themselves. Biofeedback should be especially effective in those cases where the patients cannot perceive their initial small correct responses or even may have the wrong perception of what they are doing.

Other advantages of biofeedback are that by making the early signs of slight progress conspicuous, it can encourage and motivate the patients, relieve their sense of helplessness, and serve as a coping response to reduce symptoms of stress. Instead of having something done to the patients, it teaches them to do something for themselves, increasing their confidence, or what has been called self-efficacy. This factor is particularly important when biofeedback is being used to treat symptoms that are elicited or aggravated by stress.

Treatment of Neuromuscular Disorders

Often, the effects of paralysis or spasticity produced by a stroke or other injury to the brain are greatest at first; recovery of different muscle groups may occur at different rates over considerable periods. During this time patients may learn some bad habits such as learned nonuse of temporarily paralyzed muscles (24) and the use of other nonparalyzed muscles, or early recovering muscles that produce an awkward and extremely inefficient response. These bad habits may prevent the patients from relearning the much better response after potentiality for using it has recovered. They may be in the position of a tennis player who has learned bad habits as a result of starting out with the wrong grip on the racket. When such players attempt to use the proper grip and learn the correct habits that ultimately will improve their game, they experience a frustrating period of playing much more poorly, which may cause them to return to their earlier bad habits. Thus, the patients may not try or not practice the use of the correct muscles. But if the nature of the task is radically changed to that of moving a spot on a TV screen by contracting the correct muscles, this different task will avoid eliciting the bad habit. By clearly displaying even small contractions, the patient will see progress and will not become discouraged. The patient will relearn to contract the correct muscle and to strengthen it if it has atrophied. He can then be taught easily to use it in daily life. Furthermore, it is possible that the plasticity of the nervous system may allow learning to use alternative pathways that bypass the injured tissue (25,26). Therapeutic applications are described in Chapter 8.

Aid to Diagnosis: Patient's Recognition of the Problem

Yet another use of biofeedback is to help in the therapist's diagnosis and the patient's own recognition of the problem. For example, during a test session the therapist may use sensitive electrical recording to determine whether any motor units in a paralyzed muscle are present and whether the patient can begin to learn some slight control over them. This can be useful in deciding whether it is worthwhile to initiate biofeedback training. Similarly, EMG may be used to convince the patient about the nature of the problem. For example, some patients with bruxism, grinding of the teeth, report a tension in the head region that is relieved by clenching the jaws. Recording from muscles of the jaw can convince them that they are really increasing tensions in this area and perhaps relieving mental tension by distraction. This is explained further in Chapter 27. Moment-to-moment recording of blood pressure of one patient who had episodes of dangerously high blood pressure convinced her that these were elicited by episodes of anger. Convincing patients of the relationship between their emotional reactions to specific situations and their symptoms can be an important first step toward treating their condition by biofeedback or by other psychotherapeutic procedures. How biofeedback can be used as part of a more extensive psychotherapeutic process is well-illustrated in Chapter 16.

RELAXATION AND BIOFEEDBACK

Muscular tension that prepares a person for quick action is a part of stress responses such as the fight-flight one. Thus, training in relaxing muscles is useful in the treatment of symptoms that are elicited or aggravated by stress. Some examples are headaches and Raynaud's disease, which is a vascular constriction in response to emotional stress or cold, causing the hands to become white and painfully cold; this is considered further in Chapter 29.

Many patients can learn to relax by fairly simple means, such as by systematically paying attention to sensations in various parts of the body that are produced when patients tense their muscles and when they relax them and by trying to increase the latter sensations. Jacobson (27) initiated this procedure and called it progressive relaxation. In addition, imagery of warmth, heaviness, and pleasant tranquil situations helps. This procedure is called autogenic training. For some patients, attention to biofeedback signals is a distraction, but to others it helps, especially those who find it hard to become aware of all of their sources of muscle tension. The use of relaxation is described in Chapters 16, 17, and 22.

Biofeedback from the EMG can be useful also as a diagnostic indication for the therapist. For example, some patients may proceed nicely with progressively deeper relaxation only suddenly to stop their progress and even reverse it. If the therapist asks the patient what is happening at that time, the patient may report that he is frightened by feeling out of control, by some fantasy, or by the feeling that he might die. Then this problem can be dealt with by reassurances and other therapeutic means.

Some patients can be completely relaxed but yet be extremely anxious. In such cases, it may be useful to employ biofeedback to reduce other signs of general stress, such as cold hands by rewarding hand warming, the galvanic skin response elicited by sympathic activity by rewarding increases in skin resistance, slower heart rate, or a combination of these. Different patients may have different responses that are their particular reactions to stress (28). In cases like Raynaud's disease and hypertension where the symptom that is aggravated by stress can itself be directly measured, the combination of relaxation and biofeedback for reducing the symptom can be better than either one of these procedures by itself.

LEARNED MODIFICATION OF VISCERAL RESPONSES

Many visceral responses, such as blood pressure, heart rate, and vasomotor responses that are controlled by the autonomic nervous system are perceived poorly, if at all. Thus, it is not surprising that they are not ordinarily modified by instrumental learning, but that biofeedback can enable such modification by instrumental learning to occur. Research on biofeedback has shown clearly that it can modify such responses and thus open up new therapeutic possibilities. The only question remaining is whether instrumental learning affects such responses directly or only indirectly, for example, by producing learned increases in muscular tension that increase heart rate and blood pressure, or conversely decreases that reduce them (29). The possibility that the effects of learning are direct would allow these effects to be more specific, more flexible, and to play a greater role in maintaining normal homeostasis or in producing pathophysiology.

Direct Control

To date, some of the best evidence for a direct effect of learning on visceral responses comes from patients paralyzed by high spinal lesions. Some such patients completely paralyzed from the neck down had suffered such severe postural hypotension that they fainted whenever they were helped to sit up. Various procedures to adapt them to a vertical posture had failed. Therefore, they had been confined to a horizontal position in bed for more than 2 years. When such patients were given moment-to-moment information about their systolic blood pressure, they learned to increase

it by 20 to over 70 mm of mercury. After training, they were able to perceive the large changes in blood pressure so that they could practice by themselves. This enabled them to be helped to sit up, to ride in wheelchairs or cars, and to go to plays and other such events. At first, both their heart rate and blood pressure increased, but with further practice, the response became specific to the increase in blood pressure that was needed to produce the desired result. In fact, the heart rate often went down as the blood pressure went up, as might be expected from the sinocardiac reflex.

When they were instructed to contract all of their nonparalyzed muscles as strongly as possible and even to try to contract their paralyzed ones, this produced obvious signs of extreme effort, huge activity of the EMG, and, as would be expected, some indirect effect of a modest increase in blood pressure and heart rate. When they were instructed to breathe faster than normal or breathe slower than normal, or to perform a valsalva maneuver to increase pressure in the chest and abdominal cavity, none of these produced more than moderate changes in blood pressure. But when they were instructed to produce their learned increases in blood pressure, they produced considerably larger increases with no evidence of physical effort, of increased EMG from their nonparalyzed muscles or of changes in breathing. When asked how they changed their blood pressure, they reported using various emotional strategies during early stages of learning, such as getting angry by thinking about the unfairness of their condition, getting excited by thinking about sexual intercourse, or imagining an exciting horse race with their blood pressure being one of the horses; they did not mention any responses of the skeletal muscles. Furthermore, after considerable practice, they reported that they no longer had to imagine things that aroused their emotions, but that their blood pressure went up when they wanted it to just like their hand used to go up before they were paralyzed whenever they wanted to raise it (30).

CONCLUDING GENERAL CONSIDERATIONS
Need for Sufficient Training

Learning skills, such as playing the violin or tennis, require considerable amounts of practice. Thus, it is not surprising that learning to control neuromuscular disorders, undesirable visceral responses, or even to achieve the deepest levels of muscular relaxation may also require considerable practice, some of which may have to continue after the formal therapy sessions have produced a promising start in the right direction. Refresher sessions may be desirable. The positive side of this is that, although progress may have slowed down, patients may not have reached their full potentialities.

Certain experiments on biofeedback are relatively irrelevant to therapy because they use such a short period of training.

Transfer from Clinic to Life

The greater the change in the stimulus situation, the greater is the reduction in the performance of a learned response. Often, the situations of performing in the clinic are considerably different from those in life. Thus, after the patient has learned under the most favorable situations, the therapist must gradually introduce conditions like those that will be encountered in life and, where this is not completely possible, must help the patients to practice their new skills in their lives. Examples of this will be found in later chapters.

Reward for Sickness Behavior

In the clinic the patient is rewarded for reducing a symptom of sickness, such as a headache. But sometimes the symptom that the therapist is trying to treat is rewarded outside of the clinic. This fact causes difficulty for progress in the clinic and adds special difficulty to transfer of therapy from the clinic to life. For example, the family of an unusually submissive woman may be incessantly imposing unreasonable demands on her so that having a sick headache is the only way she can get relief by a rewarding moment of peaceful quiet. With the rewards for having the headache stronger than those for losing it, the patient will fail to improve, or after a punishing period of improvement, relapse. In many cases, the patient may not be deliberately doing this; effects of the reward may be automatic. The task of the therapist is to discover the conditions rewarding the headache and to change these by teaching the patient a better coping response. In this case, assertiveness training might be used to teach the patient to demand some free time for herself. But as Wolpe (31) points out, in this kind of therapy another factor, in fact possibly the major one, could be

that the provision of the coping response has reduced the symptom via reducing the emotional responses to the impositions.

Often, sickness behavior starts with an organic cause but when strongly rewarded, persists after all organic cause has disappeared. Common rewards (technically called *reinforcements*) for sickness behavior are release from difficult duties or responsibilities, sympathy, attention, special privileges, and administration of sleeping pills or pain-killing drugs. It has long been known that it is difficult to cure patients who are receiving large payments as conpensation for their continuing disabilities (32).

Interface with Medical Profession

Practitioners of biofeedback need to be aware of sickness behavior; they also need to be knowledgeable about the particular medical conditions that they are treating. An introduction to these topics can be gained from books on behavioral medicine (23). Information is also given in other chapters in this book.

Practitioners working in a medical setting likewise need to understand the medical terminology and culture (33). Finally, it is important that the patients, either in a medical setting or private practice, have had an adequate physical examination to rule out conditions, such as a brain tumor, that require prompt medical treatment or a chronic infection that can be corrected by antibiotics.

Exploiting Electronic Advances

Remarkable advances in miniaturized electronic technology are providing new opportunities for giving patients more extensive training and for achieving some of this at home rather than in the clinic. Uses of this kind are already being made of devices such as cheap, sensitive electronic thermometers for temperature training and of equipment for home measurement of blood pressure. Equipment for plugging sophisticated displays of EMG recording into TV sets have been developed but are not yet generally available for home use.

For recording blood pressure periodically on a magnetic tape, small Halter monitors that can be carried around by the patient are available. These rely on the rather awkward method of pumping up a cuff on the arm at periodic intervals, which requires the patient to remain motionless for several seconds.

They have been used in research to supply valuable information on the fluctuations in blood pressure during a day's activities (34). There is an urgent need for them to be used in research to determine how well patients are transferring their skills in reducing blood pressure measured in the clinic to maintaining it low during life.

A similar device could be used to discover the situations that precipitate incidents of especially high blood pressure in a patient. The device could be made to give a signal, such as a vibratory stimulus on the skin, when pressure is unusually high and a control signal at random times when it is low. At each signal, the patient should dictate what the situation was and what his responses to it were at that time. The device should enable the investigators to place each dictation at the proper point on the records of blood pressure. Then the patient could be taught how to cope with or avoid the situations inducing the increases in pressure.

Training Devices That Can Be Worn

Electronic advances are providing opportunities for inventing training devices that can be worn by the patient and provide a solution to the two problems of providing sufficient practice and doing this in the daily life situation. One example is a posture-training device for use with children who have scoliosis, which is an s-shaped lateral curvature of the spine, or kyphosis, which is a pronounced forward curvature (35). This device is much more benign than either the cosmetically disfiguring and physically restraining braces or the electric shocks to contract the muscles that currently are used. It is worn inconspicuously under the clothes and does not restrain movement. Whenever the person has been out of good posture for more than twenty seconds, a barely audible tone is sounded. If the subject does not respond with an additional 20 seconds, a louder tone sounds. Responding with a better posture immediately turns off any tones. As the subject learns, the device automatically adjusts the difficulty of the criterion of good posture. Studies using x-rays taken and measured by orthopaedists have shown that the use of an early model of the posture-trainer during the preadolescence growth spurt can be useful in cases of idiopathic scoliosis and kyphosis (35). This device does not replace, but rather extends the effectiveness of

a suitably trained coach-therapist. It is not effective if it is not worn, and so psychological skills are required to ensure compliance and to adjust the rate of automatic advancement of the criterion. If this is too fast, the child becomes discouraged; if it is too slow, valuable time is wasted.

Need for Evaluation

Many medical procedures were adopted in the past without rigorous evaluation (36). But increasing concern for soaring medical expenses is producing increasing demands for better evaluation, especially of cost-effectiveness. I believe that some of our behavioral techniques will prove to be especially cost-effective. Additional research on the evaluation of behavioral packages that include biofeedback will benefit patients by helping them to get better types of treatment and will help therapists by preventing them from wasting their time by using an inferior technique of therapy, or by using a generally superior technique on an inappropriate kind of patient. Proof of the cost-effectiveness of good types of therapy will be increasingly important in securing payment for their use (37).

The difficulty of adequate evaluation indicates the desirability of initiating rigorous case registries, of analyzing the results obtained from them, and also of initiating extensive cooperative studies (37).

Need for Basic Research

Parts of this chapter have illustrated how clinical problems can provide exciting leads for significant basic research on, for example, effects of stress and coping on stomach lesions and on the immune system, and how such research can lead to valuable clinical applications. Other examples are given elsewhere (38). In behavioral medicine, including biofeedback, there is a continuing need and challenge to use powerful new techniques to conduct the basic research that provides the foundation for radical improvements in therapy. We need research to increase our understanding of the principles for facilitating difficult types of learning such as those involved in the treatment of neuromuscular disorders and the modification of visceral responses. Too much of the present research is limited to ridiculously short periods of learning.

We need detailed, analytic research on how learning, stress, and positive emotions affect the immune system. We need research to increase our understanding of the role of learning in homeostatic mechanisms. In short, we need to learn more about all of the mechanisms by which the brain, including its highest mental processes, affects the health of the body.

References

1. Miller, N. E. How the brain affects the health of the body. In *Prevention and Early Intervention: The Bio-Behavioral Perspective*, edited by K. D. Craig and S. M. Weiss. Springer, New York: (in press).
2. Cannon, W. B. *Bodily Changes in Pain, Hunger, Fear and Rage,* 2nd. ed. C. T. Branford, Boston: 1953.
3. McCabe, P. M., Schneiderman, N. and Tapp, J. T. Psychophysiologic reactions to stress. In *Behavioral Medicine: The Biopsychosocial Approach*, edited by N. Schneiderman and T. Tapp. Lawrence Erlbaum Associates, Hillsdale, New Jersey: 1985, pp. 99–131.
4. Williams, R. B. Neuroendocrine response patterns and stress: behavior mechanisms in disease. In *Perspectives on Behavioral Medicine: Neuroendocrine Control and Behavior*, edited by R. B. Williams. Academic Press, New York: 1985, pp. 71–101.
5. Corson, S. A. and Corson, E. O'L. Constitutional differences in physiologic adaptation to stress and disease. In *Psychopathology of Human Adaptation*, edited by G. Serban. Plenum Press, New York: 1976. pp. 77–94.
6. Mason, J. W. Specificity in the organization of neuroendocrine response profiles. *Frontiers in Neurology and Neuroscience Research.* University of Toronto Press, Toronto: 1974, pp. 68–80.
7. Adam, G. *Interoception and Behaviour.* Budapest: Akademiai Kiado, 1967.
8. Dollard, J. and Miller, N. E. *Personality and Psychotherapy.* McGraw-Hill, New York: 1950.
9. Weiss, J. M. Psychological and behavorial influences on gastrointestinal lesions in animal models. In *Psychopathology: Experimental Models*, edited by J. D. Maser and M. E. P. Seligman. Freeman, San Francisco: 1977, pp. 232–269.
10. Ader, R. (ed.) *Psychoneuroimmunology.* Academic Press, New York: 1981.
11. Jankovic, B. D., Spector, N. H., Markovic, B. M. (eds.) *Neuroimmune Interactions: Proceedings of 2nd International Workshop on Neuroimmunomodulation.* Ann. N. Y. Acad. Sci., Vol. 496, New York: 1987.
12. Miller, N. E., Effects of emotional stress on the immune system. Pavlov. J. Biol. Sci., *20:* 1985. 47–52.
13. Miller, N. E. A perspective on the effects of stress and coping on disease and health. In *Coping and Health*, edited by S. Levine and H. Ursin, Plenum Press, New York: 1980, pp. 323–353.
14. L. Karger and J. C. Liebeskind (eds.), *Advances in Pain Research and Therapy, Vol. 6.* Raven Press, New York: 1984.
15. Miller, N. E., The value of behavioral research on animals. Am. Psychol., *40:* 1985, 432–440.
16. Miller, N. E., The morality and humaneness of animal research on stress and pain. In *Stress-Induced Analgesia*, Ann. N. Y. Acad. Sci., *467:* 1986, 299–314.
17. Pavlov, I. P. *Conditioned Reflexes.* (G. V. Anrep, Transl.). Oxford Univ. Press, London: 1927. (Reprinted by Dove, New York, 1960).
18. Beecher, H. K. Relationship of significance of wound to pain experienced. J.A.M.A., *61:* 1956. 1609–1613.
19. Miller, N. E. Learning: Some facts and needed research relevant to maintaining health. In *Behavioral Health: A Handbook of Health Enhancement and Disease Prevention*, edited by J. D. Matarazzo, S. M. Weiss, J. A. Herd, N. E. Miller and S. M. Weiss. Wiley Interscience, New York, 1984, pp. 199–208.
20. Bykov, K. M. *The Cerebral Cortex and the Internal Organs*, edited and translated by W. H. Gantt. Chemical Publishing, New York: 1957.
21. Miller, N. E. Learnable drives and rewards. In *Handbook of Experimental Psychology*, edited by S. S. Stevens, John Wiley & Sons, New York: 1951. pp. 435–472.
22. Melamed, B. G. and Siegel, L. J., *Behavioral Medicine. Practical Applications in Health Care.* Springer, New York: 1980.
23. Prokop, C. K. and Bradley, L. A. (eds.) *Medical Psychology: Contributions to Behavioral Medicine.* Academic Press, New York: 1981.
24. Taub, E. Somatosensory deafferentation research with monkeys: Implications for rehabilitation medicine. In *Behavioral Psychology in Rehabilitation Medicine: Clinical Applications*, edited by L. P. Ince. Williams & Wilkins, Baltimore; 1980, pp 371–401.
25. Goldsmith, M. F. Computerized biofeedback training aids in spinal injury rehabilitation. J.A.M.A., *253,* (issue 8): 1985, pp. 1097–99.
26. Brucker, B. Biofeedback in rehabilitation. In *Current Topics in Rehabilitation Psychology*, edited by C. Golden. Grune & Stratton, San Diego, 1984.
27. Jacobson, E. *Modern Treatment of Tense Patients.* Charles C. Thomas, Springfield, Ill., 1970.
28. Lacey, J. I. and Lacey, B. C. Verification and extension of the principle of autonomic response stereotypy. Am. J. Psychol., *71:* 1958, 50–73.
29. Miller, Neal E., Biofeedback and visceral learning. Ann. Rev. Psychol., *29:* 1978, 373–404.
30. Miller, N. E. and Brucker, B. S. A learned visceral response apparently independent of skeletal ones in patients paralyzed by spinal lesions. In *Biofeedback and Self-Regulation*, edited by N. Birbaumer and H. D. Kimmel. Lawrence Erlbaum Associates, Hills, New Jersey, 1979, pp. 287–304.
31. Wolpe, J. *The Practice of Behavior Therapy*, 3rd ed. Pergaman Press, New York, 1982.
32. Fordyce, W. E. Back pain, compensation and public policy. In *Prevention in Health Psycholo-*

gy, edited by J. Rosen and L. Soloman University Press of New England, Hanover, Vt: pp. 390–400, 1985.

33. Miller, N. E., Education for a lifetime of learning. In *Health Psychology: A Discipline and a Profession*, edited by G. C. Stone, S. M. Weiss, J. D. Matarazzo, N. E. Miller, J. Rodin, C. D. Belar, M. J. Follick. and Singer, J. E. Health Psychology: Univ. of Chicago Press, Chicago: 1987.

34. Pickering, T. G., Harshfield, G. A., Kleinert, H. D., Blank, S. and Laragh, J. H. Blood pressure during normal daily activities, sleep, and exercise. J.A.M.A., 247, 992–996, 1982.

35. Dworkin, B., Miller, N. E., Dworkin, S., Birbaumer, N., Brines, M. L., Jonas, S., Schwentker, E. P. and Graham, J. J. Behavorial Method for Treatment of Idiopathic Scoliosis. Proc. Natl. Acad. Sci. USA, 82: 1975, 2493–2497.

36. Committee for evaluating medical technologies in clinical use, Institute of Medicine, Fredric Mosteller, Chairman. *Assessing Medical Technologies*. National Academy Press, Washington, D. C., 1955.

37. Miller, N. E. Some professional and scientific problems and opportunities for biofeedback. Biofeedback Self Regul, 10: 3–23, 1985.

38. Miller, N. E., Behavioral Medicine: Symbiosis Between Laboratory and Clinic. Ann. Rev. Psychol., 34: 1983, 1–31.

CHAPTER 3

Neurophysiological Factors in Electromyographic Feedback for Neuromotor Disturbances

STEVEN L. WOLF AND STUART A. BINDER-MACLEOD

Significant strides have ben achieved in both clinical and experimental biofeedback applications governing several anatomical systems. These advances may be considered remarkable in light of the relatively short time in which investigators have been examining the far-reaching implications of biofeedback training. From a clinical perspective, instances demonstrating appropriate physiological performance in patients or laboratory subjects have become known to the clinician, who has been able to successfully implement such findings and thus improve the status of his client. Nevertheless, any new technique is bound either to fall by the wayside or to become easily labeled as a technology if its roots are not quickly and correctly planted in soil tempered by scientific merit and credence. As Brown (1) has correctly noted:

Laboratory procedures are developed and modified to probe and uncover elements critical to the phenomenon being studied, and relatively few research studies are directed toward evaluating elements critical to successful application. This has been especially true in biofeedback where it has been assumed, often with considerable error, that the essential aspects for optimal clinical effectiveness have been adequately defined.

Indeed, references in the biofeedback literature are filled with studies which clearly define variables and statistically or empirically analyze results. Seldom have investigators extrapolated information contained within the annals of basic scientific research to explain or hypothesize mechanisms to account for clinical observations. While systems analyses (2–4) to explain biofeedback and critical reviews (5, 6) about this modality have been provided, the purpose of this chapter is to provide (a) a general review of the essentially neurophysiological events underlying motor control and (b) mechanisms which might contribute to an understanding of reports supporting the efficacy of biofeedback treatments. It should be emphasized that the discussion which follows is not designed to unequivocally explain or interpret neural mechanisms invoked by virtue of biofeedback paradigms. Rather it is to encourage researchers and clinicians to think about and delve into the physiological bases of their observations. Discarding empiricism in favor of thought-provoking concepts can elevate the status and potential of biofeedback.

EMG FEEDBACK TO ACHIEVE MOTOR CONTROL

A primary objective of all electromyographic (EMG) biofeedback is to enable the patient to reacquire voluntary control over his striated musculature. Goals are directed toward an appropriate increase in activity of weak or paretic muscle and a reduction in activity levels of spastic muscles (7, 8). The anatomical and physiological factors underlying the processing of information from muscle feedback systems are complex and poorly understood. Yet, compared to feedback systems governing autonomic or behavioral functions, a measurement of treatment efficacy can be more easily assessed from muscle feedback. Ultimately, the acquisition of a motor skill can be manifest in any variety of ways—from the elimination of an assistive ambulatory device to the resumption of a vocation.

In clinical EMG feedback training, a patient is made aware of minute or overexaggerated muscle contractions through visual and auditory feedback from that muscle. The information provided instantaneously about this covert activity is readily processed by the patient. An examination of patient behavior as the training procedure progresses enables the observer to offer some speculations on the neural mechanisms contributing to reacquisition of motor control. In the case of the patient with neurological deficits, processing the informational content of a feedback signal is confounded by the disruption of supraspinal neural influences upon muscle. Patients at first rely upon visual and auditory representations of muscle activity quite extensively. As the patient improves in ability to initiate and terminate muscle contractions, he becomes less dependent on electronically generated cues and more reliant upon visual input from the moving limb segment.

Traditional Rehabilitation Procedures

EMG biofeedback as a muscle reeducation tool should not be employed at the expense of traditional therapeutic procedures, but it should, at least, serve as an adjunct. One should realize that rehabilitation personnel serve as exteroceptive stimulants for the patient. A therapist's ability, for example, to palpate a spastic muscle and instruct the patient to relax provides verbal feedback about motor behavior which the patient cannot adequately perceive. Specifically, most therapies are designed to provide appropriate proprioceptive input so that the patient may learn to make the proper motor response. While an EMG feedback machine can never substitute for a clinician, its advantages are obvious. Such a device provides exteroceptive cues which are accurate and instantaneous. Quantitatively, the information available is always proportionate to the magnitude of muscle force. Realistically, the feedback signal may substitute for inadequate proprioceptive signals and can be used to shape responses more precisely than signals generated by any clinician. This may enable the central nervous system to reestablish appropriate sensory-motor loops under the volitional control of the patient. A discussion of this issue has been well presented (4).

Clinical Efficacy Studies

The inclusion of EMG feedback applications among patients with purely musculoskeletal disorders has proven to be a valuable adjunct in treatment following meniscectomy (9) or chronic low back pain (10). In such cases, the neural circuitry necessary to adequately process feedback signals is intact. Loss of kinesthetic cues is nonexistent and, primarily, muscle weakness or reduced strength predominates. In such cases the patient uses visual and auditory representations of muscle activity in combination with increased motivational drive to accelerate corticospinal and parallel descending motor systems to induce increased motor neuronal drive.

The situation is exceedingly more complex among patients who are afflicted with central nervous system deficits. Not only must disinhibition of specific muscle groups be overcome through reduction of hypermotor responses, but a reappreciation of proprioceptive cues must be gained. Knowledge regarding the efficacy of feedback interventions to cause such improvements is inadequate primarily because of the limited number of controlled studies comparing feedback interventions to no treatment or other physical therapeutic procedures. Significant improvement in upper (11) and lower (10) extremity function in stroke patients exposed to EMG feedback paradigms has been reported. Results from these studies were based upon clinical grades rather than on concrete data and lack appropriate controls. Basmajian and colleagues (12) attempted to demonstrate that superior strength and range of motion around the ankle joint can occur among stroke patients who receive feedback and therapeutic exercise as compared with individuals receiving exercise alone. Unfortunately, this work has been criticized because, (despite randomization in group determinations) those individuals receiving feedback and exercise were comparatively more recent in stroke onset than the group receiving exercise exclusively. The results from that study, however, were substantiated by a controlled, blind study among a chronic stroke population, undertaken by Binder and colleagues (13). Patients receiving a standardized exercise program as well as chronic stroke patients receiving feedback in conjunction with exercise showed improvements.

On the other hand, the work of Lee and colleagues (14) focused attention on the deltoid muscle in only three experimental sessions among stroke patients with hemiplegia from 6 months to 7 years in duration. Results from that study indicated no differences with respect to changes in EMG levels among patients placed in a true feedback or false feedback group. Unfortunately, all patients were subjected to limited measurement trials of short duration. Of potential importance was the observation that older and less motivated patients did not do as well as younger patients.

Crossover designs which compared EMG feedback with physical therapy have been reported (15, 16). Inglis et al. (15) showed that an experimental group receiving EMG feedback plus physical therapy displayed greater improvements in upper extremity function than the control group which received only physical therapy. In addition, the EMG feedback was shown to be effective when the control patients switched over to the experimental treatment condition. Mroczek and colleagues (16), while studying wrist mobility, found that biofeedback after physical therapy appeared less effective than the reverse sequence. This suggests that the strategies used by the patient (or the therapist) may interact with the efficacy of the feedback treatment.

Wolf and colleagues (17, 18) have attempted to make exacting neurophysiological measurements of improvement among stroke patients subjected to feedback training exclusively. At the conclusion of their study and at 1-year follow-up, the results remained consistent, which suggests that improvements learned during feedback sessions were retained. Of significance was the fact that improvements among chronic stroke patients could occur without respect to age, side of the lesion, duration of stroke, or duration of previous rehabilitation. These findings have subsequently been corroborated by other investigators (18, 19).

In a more recent study, Wolf and Binder-Macleod (20) have shown that functional improvement with biofeedback was related to the amount of voluntary control the patient displayed prior to treatment. Patients who had greater active movement at all major upper extremity joints and less hyperactivity within typically "spastic" muscles showed greater functional gains than patients with less voluntary control. In fact, if a patient was unable to volitionally recruit a muscle or muscle group prior to training, no functional gains were ever made which utilized that muscle(s). Similar observations have been made by Skelly and

Kenedi (21). This suggests that a minimum of neural circuitry must remain intact for the patient to use this modality appropriately.

Few attempts have been made to explain changes in neuronal processing during feedback applications among patients with central nervous system pathology (22, 23). In fact, most information designed to provide explanations about how exteroceptive signals induce improved sensory-motor integration is exceptionally vague. This state of affairs is not terribly surprising, since neuronal circuitry for execution of simple placement movements among sub-human primates is uncertain. In summary, while feedback applications to neurological patients have appeared promising, further controlled clinical studies are required, and neurophysiological correlates of movement must be obtained in animal models that simulate clinical neurological conditions.

MOTOR CONTROL AND FEEDBACK LOOPS

How do patients process feedback information? What factors account for the patient's ability to gradually become less dependent upon artificially induced information signals? Why might patients gain motor control using EMG feedback after failing to achieve significant gains using conventional rehabilitation procedures? Answers to these questions and others form the basis for our understanding of EMG feedback. By exploring these issues, many of the anatomical and neurophysiological components necessarily associated with EMG feedback emerge. Even more questions are raised than answered. What follows below, then, is a discussion of several aspects of "feedback loops" involved with establishing motor control. It is indeed remarkable that a multitude of internal, modulatory neural networks exists, and, even more significant, that electronic feedback may evoke exteroceptive systems that ultimately engage these internal networks.

The information contained below, although broad in nature, relies heavily upon decades of intensive observations on motor control systems within subhuman primate models. Most of the neurophysiological data recorded from conscious animals have been acquired using operant conditioning paradigms.[a]

---

[a]Operant conditioning should not be confused with EMG biofeedback training techniques. The former refers to a condition in which a particular behavior

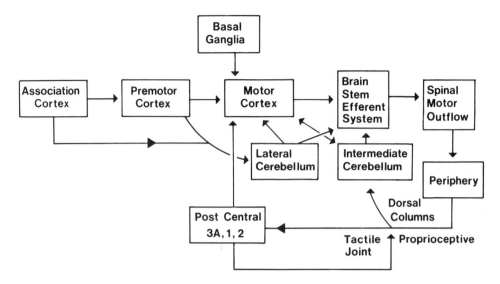

Figure 3.1. Essential central and peripheral nervous system components involved in the execution of a voluntary movement. Modified after Allen and Tsukahara (24). See text for details.

While one would be tempted to extract mechanisms from motor control studies that explain how feedback can restore motor function among neurological patients, such external validation must be excessively tempered. First, the simple act of executing a command, such as volitional grasp of an object, includes complex sensory and motor circuitry that has yet to be clearly elucidated. Second, changes in neuronal processing following experimentally induced central nervous system lesions very rarely mimic true pathology. The neuronal damage following a cerebral vascular accident is often poorly localized. Even a disruption of a specific cerebral arterial component can produce highly variable neuronal losses. Therefore, naturally occurring neuropathology can rarely be equated to specific experimental lesions. Caution must be exercised in transferring mechanisms underlying sensory-motor integration in the presence of experimentally induced pathology to clinical situations. Nonetheless, it is imperative to understand some conceptions regarding motor and sensory functioning during volitional activities and to speculate upon how exteroceptive cues might

contribute to improved fluidity of movement and function.

An Overview

The general scheme involving essential components to execute volitional movement is shown in Figure 3.1, derived and modified from the work by Allen and Tsukahara (24). Information about the formulation of a volitional motor act is conveyed from cortical association areas to the lateral cerebellum, basal ganglia, and the premotor cortex (including the posterior parietal lobe and frontal lobe premotor areas). This information is converted into a command for movement that is organized into neuronal discharge patterns at appropriate efferent areas of the motor cortex (25–27). In this case, the basal ganglia may reinforce motor cortical activity (28–30) or, if appropriate, cause a delayed motor response (31–33). The basal ganglia also function to integrate the motor command with appropriate visual, auditory, proprioceptive and other exteroceptive inputs. As a result, eye and body responses are oriented toward attention to a limb movement (28, 34, 35). The lateral cerebellum functions to provide appropriate temporal patterns of agonist-antagonist muscle activity so that the programmed movement is appropriate. In part, this comparator function of the lateral cerebellum is based upon prior motor learning (36, 37).

The neuronal patterns emerging from the motor cortex may activate brainstem and spi-

is selectively reinforced so that its frequency of occurrence may be augmented or reduced. Frequently the motivational component of an operant conditioning paradigm is difficult to evaluate. EMG feedback provides a precise and continuous signal proportional to the subject's response. Operant reinforcement is often discontinuous, delayed, or intermittent.

nal efferent systems for further elaboration on the execution of the desired movement as well as for provision of essential input to the intermediate cerebellum and somatic sensory areas. These areas subsequently may modulate their responses to sensory input that will be derived from the resulting movement (38–40). Motor output may also activate the lateral cerebellum by way of projections to reticulospinal and rubrospinal pathways. The resulting output from these subcortical systems may be used to control activity in axial and proximal muscles during movement. On the other hand, precise control over distal upper extremity musculature may be primarily accomplished through activation of neurons in both the precentral and postcentral areas of cortex (41, 42).

As a result of the impending movement, feedback from specific sensory systems may impinge upon structures in the pathways that generated the initial movement. This peripheral feedback to control motor programs may vary with the speed of the movement, the degree of accuracy required to execute the movement (43), and the amount of previous motor learning necessary to complete the specific act.

AFFERENT COMPONENTS
Auditory

Very little information is available about the function of different nuclei in the auditory pathway. Collaterals from the ascending auditory pathway (lateral lemniscus) are given off to the cerebellum and reticular formation, two areas known to be implicated in the transmission of proprioceptive information. The auditory cortex is tonotopically organized and located along the superior temporal convolution. On neurophysiological grounds, the auditory cortex can be divided into a short-latency and a long-latency area. The short-latency area is often called the primary auditory cortex (Areas 41 and 42) and the long-latency area is referred to as the secondary auditory cortex. From clinical observations, these two locations have been described as functioning to receive and interpret tonal patterns, respectively. The relationship between the long-latency, auditory interpretation area, and alterations in motor activity are undertermined. It should be noted, however, that auditory feedback about motor activity must be important and perhaps easier to process effectively than visual feedback signals. Patients undergoing EMG feedback training will frequently forsake visual feedback from instrumentation in favor of watching their limbs while listening to auditory signals.

Visual Components

It is known that rostral Area 4 contains numerous neurons responsive to visual input (44). In addition, the middle one-third to the caudal portion of the primary motor cortex contains neurons that are clearly receptive to inputs arising from visual stimuli, joint movements, and tactile presentations (45–47). Many of these neurons discharge before a movement begins and, therefore, are probably involved in its initiation. Area 7 of the posterior parietal cortex is known to be a site of convergence from a number of polymodal sensory association neurons (48, 49). Projections to this area arise from the intraparietal sulcus, which receives input from the visual parasensory association areas and from the superior temporal sulcus. The latter receives inputs from visual and auditory association areas. Numerous projections to Area 7 have been observed to originate from the cingulate gyrus and from the parahippocampal region (50). These areas are associated with emotional and motivational states (51, 52). Area 7 is thought to project directly to pretectal regions and to the middle and deepest portions of the superior colliculus (53). These structures, in turn, are probably involved in the control of eye movements and in directing visual attention (54). The relationships of various inputs to Area 7 are depicted in Figure 3.2.

Output from Area 7 may project to frontal cortical Areas 8 and 9 (49, 55). Area 8 appears to receive converging inputs from association areas dealing with visual, auditory, and somatic sensory systems as well as from frontal cortical regions thought to be associated with control of axial muscles. Therefore, possible oculomotor modulating functions in Area 8 may be influenced by major sensory projections and coordinated with axial orienting movements derived from the supplementary motor area. Visual inputs appear to be conveyed by way of Areas 7, 8, and posterior 9 to ultimately reach the motor cortex, possibly by way of connections within the arcuate sulcus.

As noted in Figure 3.2 (central portion) motor outflow may be directed by visual or audi-

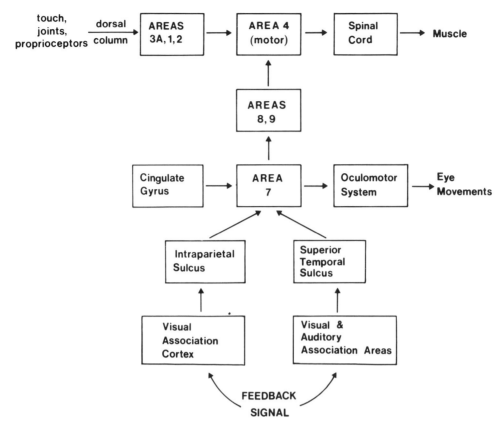

Figure 3.2. Possible neural substrates activated from a visual or auditory feedback stimulus. Ocular and striated musculature are engaged as a result of cerebral processing of the feedback signal, but cutaneous, joint, or proprioceptive inputs may be integrated at cortical levels to produce changes in movement.

tory inputs, possibly derived from a feedback signal. The pathways described, however, have been more closely associated with visual guidance of voluntary movements. Nonetheless, components of these pathways are possibly operative during feedback paradigms since patients often forsake direct visual attention to a feedback signal in favor of visual observation of voluntary movement in a limb segment. Of additional significance is the observation that hippocampal and cingulate inputs project to Area 7. Since these inputs govern attention and motivational aspects of behavior, it is possible that lesions disrupting this input may have a bearing on the efficacy of feedback training. Patients who display poor concentration or lack of motivation often respond poorly to feedback training (17). Whether this behavior is attributable to anatomical lesions or psychosocial factors is better left to speculation at present.

Cutaneous Receptors and Proprioceptors

Pressure, touch, and vibratory stimuli delivered to skin areas overlying muscles undergoing feedback training are usually facilitory to those muscles and provide an excellent method for reflexly evoking activity (56–58), thereby providing the patient with sensory feedback for further neuromuscular retraining. Neural pathways to the somatic sensory cortex (59) are also activated. Various classes of cutaneous afferent systems are relayed through the thalamus to specific locations within the postcentral gyrus.

Many of these cortical areas are arranged somatotopically. For example, afferent information derived from muscle spindles and joint receptors is known to project to Area 3a; those from slowly adapting cutaneous receptors project to Area 3b; input from rapidly adapting cutaneous receptors is directed to Area 1; and Area 2 receives input primarily from joint receptors. In addition, cutaneous inputs may be relayed to the caudal portion of the precentral gyrus, while afferent inflow from joint receptors may project to the middle to caudal portion of the precentral gyrus.

Quantitatively, neurons in the primary motor cortex responding to cutaneous inputs are at least twice as numerous as those responding to inputs from joint afferents. Yet, both types of inputs are organized somatotopically and the precentral cortical areas controlling a particular set of muscles tend to receive inputs principally from joint receptors activated through movement of those particular muscles or from cutaneous locations that would be stimulated as a result of a particular movement. More specifically, Humphrey (60) has provided an example of how the precentral area associated with hand movements may be related to cutaneous inputs. Neurons in the caudal hand area may be excited when skin overlying a moving digit makes contact with a specific object that is being retrieved. This act and the resulting neural circuitry constitute a positive excitatory feedback loop designed to promote further exploration and grasping. This loop may constitute part of a neural substrate for cortically mediated grasp reflexes (61). These reflexes, in turn, may be exceptionally hyperactive when released from control by virtue of a lesion within the supplementary motor area (62, 63).

Neurons in the caudal portion of the primary motor cortex responsive to cutaneous or joint inputs tend to discharge prior to movement onset and may be involved in the initiation of the movement. These neurons are known to respond intensely to input from joint receptors and may be involved in guiding movement based upon kinesthetic cues (45, 46, 64). This relationship tends to be highly specific for precision and rate of movement. Corticospinal cells in the caudal portion of the primary motor cortex are highly responsive to feedback from joint receptors during controlled movements: however, during ballistic movements, these cells may be comparatively unresponsive to sensory input from the same location (65, 66).

Many neurons in the precentral gyrus are responsive to joint inputs as part of a negative feedback control system. These neurons may be part of a reflex arc that would tend to stabilize joint position and assist voluntary joint movements in a servo-like manner by causing

an increased discharge in corticospinal cells when a joint is moved by external forces in a direction opposite to the intended contraction (67, 68). As noted in the upper portion of Figure 3.2, inputs from touch or joint receptors tend to traverse through the dorsal columns to the somatic sensory cortex.

Muscles are specially equipped with structures (muscle spindles and Golgi tendon organs) capable of sensing varying magnitudes of change in muscle length. Activation of these organs is controlled by the motor system directly or by descending influences capable of altering the transmission of proprioceptive sensory input within the central nervous system. In patients with central nervous system pathology, an imbalance in neuronal activity can render proprioceptor innervation to specific muscles hyperactive or inactive. Such disruption leaves musculature in a spastic or flaccid state, respectively. Without question, the key to reacquiring motor control in neurological patients rests in reestablishing proper proprioceptive behavior; it is this goal that EMG biofeedback training attempts to achieve.

The anatomy and physiology of muscle proprioceptors have been well documented in texts (69–71), and for years, clinicians have known that man can exert precise control over his proprioceptive system (72). Primate research performed during the last three decades has demonstrated that information about muscle position and length can project to the motor cortex, whose output is adjusted by way of a servo-loop as impedance to movement undergoes changes (68, 73–77). In addition, corticospinal neurons located in Area 3a, which lies between the classical motor and somatic sensory cortical locations, respond to muscle stretch in a velocity-dependent manner (78, 79). Such neurons may be involved in cortical reflex arcs which guide movement based upon sensory inputs. According to Humphrey (60), little information is available regarding the timing of neuronal discharges in this area relative to voluntary movements. Therefore, the importance of proprioceptive input to the activation of cells located in Area 3a as a mechanism for central control of movement is still vague.

Ablation studies have enabled researchers to determine that the postcentral gyrus (Areas 3, 2, 1) and the posterior parietal lobe play a vital role in assessing the weight and roughness of objects. Furthermore, from indirect evidence (80), it has

been ascertained that the so-called "motor areas" may subserve discriminative functions and
are, in fact, sensory motor areas. Lesions of the
medial lemnisci, tracts which convey proprioceptive information at the midbrain level, do not
result in complete loss of proprioceptive function. Impairment of proprioceptive function is
increased if the dentatorubrothalamic tract is le-
sioned. From this and other observations, it has
been deduced that the cerebellum plays a key
role in conveying proprioceptive input to the
cerebral cortex.

The possibility that proprioceptive information is imparted to the motor cortex either directly or through relays from the somatic sensory cortical areas is not difficult to appreciate. Pyramidal cells of the motor tract extend
posteriorly into the anterior lip and surface of
the postcentral gyrus where they lie intermin-
gled with many granule cells of the somatic
sensory cortex. Similarly, granule cells of the
somatic sensory cortex extend anteriorly into
the precentral (motor) cortex. Electrophysiological observations are in accord with those
made anatomically. Frequently, stimulation of
the motor cortex will induce sensory experiences rather than muscle contractions, while
electrical activation of the anterior sensory
cortex will cause a muscle response in the absence of sensory reports.

CEREBELLUM

As shown in Figure 3.3, the cerebellum received considerable proprioceptive information by way of the spinocerebellar tract. Neurons located in the cortex and deep nuclei are
activated vigorously during voluntary movement of the trunk or limbs (81). Transmission
along the spinocerebellar pathways tends to be
faster than the tract conveying proprioceptive
input through the length of the neuroaxis to
the cortex. The frequency of discharge in cerebellar neurons, as well as the time of occurrence of these discharges, depends upon
whether the neuron lies within the intermediate or lateral cerebellum. Output from neurons
activated in the lateral cerebellum travels to
the dentate nucleus and ultimately to the thalamus and motor cortex (Figure 3.3). This pathway suggests a premovement function for this
cerebellar area. Discharge from neurons lying
within the intermediate cerebellar cortex activates the nucleus interpositus and subsequently the red nucleus and the medullary reticular formation. These latter structures then

project to the spinal cord. As a result, it would
appear that the intermediate cerebellum may
be part of a motor execution component
whose outputs are modulated by cortical inputs as well as by somatic sensory feedback.

Neurons in the lateral cerebellum alter their
frequency of discharge before motor cortical
cells are activated during voluntary movements (82). This discharge may be correlated
with the activity of a particular set of muscles.
Evidence (83) indicates that the dentate nucleus within this cerebellar location contains specific cells that discharge in relation to the pattern of activity in flexor or extensor muscles,
the direction of a subsequent movement, or
the direction of the immediate movement.
Those neurons in the lateral cerebellum appear to be unaffected by somatic sensory input. Therefore, the lateral cerebellum appears
to serve a vital function in programming the
direction, duration, and sequences of specific
voluntary movements, which may persist in a
modified fashion after cerebellar ablation.

Neurons located in the intermediate cerebellar cortex appear to be strongly affected by somatic sensory input, and these cells are
known to discharge after the onset of motor
cortical activity.

Figure 3.3 also suggests that the cerebellum
functions in association with activities initiated elsewhere in the nervous system, such as
the spinal cord, reticular formation, and basal
ganglia. As motor impulses are transmitted
from the cortex to voluntary muscles by way
of the corticospinal tract, collaterals are given
off to the anterior cerebellum and cerebellar
hemispheres. Therefore, muscle and cerebellar
structures receive motor information concurrently. When muscle proprioceptors are acti-

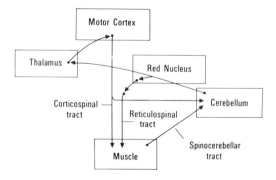

Figure 3.3. Essential pathways for cerebellar
modification of voluntary movement.

vated, information is conveyed to the anterior cerebellum by way of the spinocerebellar dorsal column pathways. Anatomically, it has been ascertained that the cerebellar locations for nerve fiber terminals in the collateral descending motor system and in the ascending spinocerebellar tract are closely approximated. The output from cerebellar cortex to the motor cortex by way of the ventrolateral thalamic nuclei, as suggested above, represents a feedback loop starting and terminating in the motor cortex. Therefore, it is suggested that the cerebellum may serve as a comparator between motor cortical (commands) and muscle (performance). Errors in the proper relationship between command and performance are determined by the cerebellum so that appropriate corrections can be made. Usually, the cerebellum functions to inhibit excessive motor activity. This function is revealed by the gradual reduction (damping) in "overshooting" of an intended movement.

The importance of the cerebellum to the control of movement has been demonstrated by Terzuolo and colleagues (84–87). Their primate and human studies indicate that the cerebellar cortex affects the timing of motor output and is responsible for generating intentional motor commands. Since cerebellar neurons may discharge before motor cortical cells as an animal prepares to execute an arm movement, the cerebellum may be able to modulate motor command signals in an attempt to maintain or even restore normal efferent activity.

The efferent flow from the cerebellum, noted in Figure 3.3, traverses the red nucleus and the reticulospinal tract. Since outputs from these two brainstem structures are capable of modifying motor neuronal activity at the spinal cord level, the relative activation of extensor and flexor or axial and limb muscles may be directly controlled through these output systems.

EFFERENT COMPONENTS

Red Nucleus and Reticular Formation

The left portion of Figure 3.4 depicts essential components of the corticorubrospinal system. A portion of this system projects from the arm and leg areas of the primary motor cortex to the magnocellular component of the red nucleus. Output from this component is directed to the spinal cord as the rubrospinal tract. Another projection stems from Areas 4, 5, and 6 to the parvocellular component of the red nucleus. Outflow from this component is directed to the cerebellum by way of the inferior olive of the medulla oblongata. The rubrospinal tract neurons synapse upon interneurons that may mediate components of volitional control in a manner similar to that exercised by the corticospinal tract. This control is capable of existing even after pyramidotomy (88).

Apparently, the rubrospinal tract axons impinge upon spinal motor neurons whose outflow is directed toward contractions of more proximal rather than distal musculature. The projection from the magnocellular component in man appears to be underdeveloped. The true effect of parvocellular projections from the red nucleus to the cerebellum on control of proximal or distal limb movements is not clear.

The cortical projection to the reticular formation is derived primarily from the medial and dorsolateral components of Area 6. Projections through the medullary reticular formation to the spinal cord appear to activate motor neurons that control trunk and proximal limb musculature (89, 90).

Basal Ganglia

The anatomy and neurophysiology of the basal ganglia are poorly understood. That portion of the basal ganglia involved with motor control includes the caudate nucleus, the putamen, and globus pallidus along with portions of the thalamus, subthalamus, red nucleus, and substantia nigra. From neurophysiological data, it is known that the basal ganglia are operative in a number of feedback loops between: (a) the thalamus and cortex, (b) cortex to basal ganglia to thalamus to cortex, (c) cortex or basal ganglia to cerebellum, then back to thalamus, and finally once again to the cortex or basal ganglia. The primary descending influences of the basal ganglia are thought to be made through the reticular formation. It is known that the striate body (caudate nucleus and putamen) component of the basal ganglia controls intentional movements which are normally relegated to unconscious levels. Since these structures are capable of influencing components of the neuroaxis (thalamus, cerebellum, red nucleus) which, in turn, provide input or feedback to the motor cortex, the basal ganglia must be considered as possessing the ability to influence motor responses. In fact, DeLong (91) has demonstrated that fol-

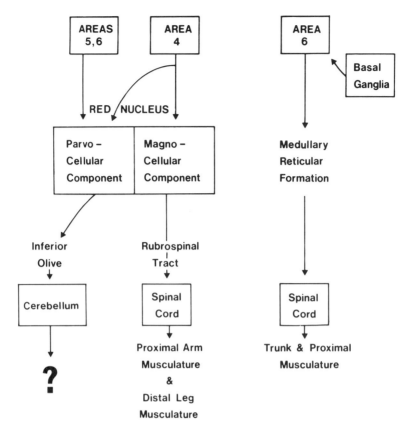

Figure 3.4. Parallel descending pathways through the red nucleus and medullary reticular formation that will activate output to specific limb or trunk segments.

lowing individual cues signaling an intent to move, basal ganglia cells become active prior to the muscular contraction.

Our knowledge of neuroanatomy suggests that the cerebellum and basal ganglia receive information from the somatic sensory, visual, and auditory cortices, process this information, and then send a new set of information to the motor cortex. Inputs to the cerebellum and basal ganglia may be coded in a more abstract manner than those going to the motor cortex.

Motor Cortex

The work of Basmajian and his colleagues (92, 93) demonstrated that human subjects are capable of controlling the activity of single motor units located within the recording range of a percutaneous electrode. This behavior pattern implies that man can volitionally control the discharge of a single anterior horn cell while actively inhibiting supraspinal input to other portions of a specific spinal cord motor nucleus (94, 95). Because individuals could be trained to perform this task with visual and auditory cues about muscle activity, the procedure actually represented a preliminary form of EMG biofeedback which has served as an impetus for the clinical work of other investigators (11). Complementing this clinical work is the finding that activation of supraspinal structures results in a specific recruitment order for activation of motor units (96). Motor units appear to be recruited in order of increasing size with tonic, smaller units recruited first and larger phasic units activated secondarily. Thus, there appears to exist a functional organization of motor neurons at the spinal level.

Our understanding of conscious control over voluntary movement could be enhanced if more were known about the temporal relationship between motor command neurons of the cerebral cortex and the characteristics of movement which these neurons influenced. The work of Evarts and colleagues (97–101) and others (102, 103) have dealt with this issue extensively using an operant conditioning paradigm on primates.

Such information has revealed that: (a) activity of neurons in the motor cortex is related to the magnitude and pattern of the muscle contraction but not the joint displacement produced by the contractions; (b) motor cortical activity precedes a movement; (c) motor cortical cells may be inhibited during antagonist movements; (d) from recordings in the sensory cortex, activity in this region occurs after the initial muscular contractions (thus the sensory cortex may aid in guiding the movement by a supraspinal transmission of proprioceptive information, but it does not participate in the initiation of the movement); and (e) cortical units in the precentral area respond to perturbations with a shorter latency than they respond to auditory or visual stimuli. Most cells from which records were obtained could be identified as pyramidal tract cells. Since it is known that these cells make direct and indirect synapses upon alpha and gamma motoneurons of the spinal cord (104, 105), a linkage between the motor cortex and muscle and the activation of this motor system by visual and auditory stimuli has been established.

The fifth finding noted above suggests that perturbations or resistance to intended movements facilitate efferent cortical activity so that descending input onto spinal motor neurons may occur more quickly than during intended movements which are preceded by visual or auditory cues. The application of this neurophysiological finding to an EMG feedback paradigm predicated upon resisted exercise to facilitate muscle activity is indeed inviting. With respect to the second observation above, that is, motor cortical activity preceding movement, it is interesting to note that when a similar operant paradigm was attempted in human subjects (106), a visual cue preparing the subject to make a Jendrassik maneuver resulted in augmented H reflex responses prior to the actual movement.

More recently, the relationship between motor cortical areas and muscles governed by outflow from these locations has been further elucidated and appears to be even more complex. For example, the work of Wise and Evarts (107) indicates that numerous cortical fields are involved in motor control to an extent greater than previously observed. In fact, Humphrey (108) has identified precentral motor cortical neurons that are capable of activat-

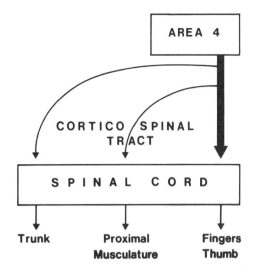

Figure 3.5. Schematic representation of corticospinal tract outflow to the spinal cord and subsequently to striated musculature. Note the predominant representation of efferent components to the spinal cord for activation of motor neurons to the thumb and fingers.

ing synergistic muscles independently or antagonist muscles reciprocally. The location for such cortical cells appears to be restricted to specific areas.

Figure 3.5 indicates a summary of existing information regarding corticospinal outflow from Area 4 to the spinal cord. In contrast to brainstem efferent systems, a primary outflow from the descending corticospinal tract is to motor neuronal pools governing digital movements with fewer contributions destined to motor neurons innervating trunk and proximal musculature. If Figure 3.5 is contrasted to Figure 3.4, the existing information would suggest that cortical output to the red nucleus and reticular formation parallels that of the corticospinal tract; and that the former is as equal a primary source of cortical outflow as the latter. Therefore, rubrospinal and reticulospinal projections activated by cortical areas to ultimately engage spinal motor neurons act selectively upon proximal musculature. The corticospinal system in primates, on the other hand, may be a more specialized component developed principally for fine guided control of the hand and fingers.

Considerable physiological information relevant to EMG feedback training mechanisms could be obtained through animal operant conditioning experiments. For example, it would be interesting to determine the temporal and qualitative (movement characteristics) relationships between motor cortex and limbs before and following a lesion simulating a cerebrovascular accident rather than one destined to disrupt one and only one specific subset of neurons.

The preceding account probably represents an oversimplification concerning the influence of motor cortical activity on skeletal muscle behavior. Fetz and his colleagues have used cross-correlation techniques to demonstrate that during operant conditioning experiments in primates, single cortical cells are capable of influencing several synergistic muscles and, depending upon behavioral circumstances, can increase or decrease their activity levels.

Furthermore, a recent biofeedback study completed by Wolf and coworkers (110) suggests that the schematics depicted above may be incomplete. Among a group of chronic head-injured and stroke patients, a motor copy procedure requiring matching EMG outputs from homologous upper extremity muscle groups was compared with conventional (targeted) feedback training procedures in which dual channel monitoring of antagonist muscle pairs was restricted to the plegic upper extremity. Surprisingly, both groups improved in comparable fashion with respect to EMG changes, active ROM, and functional scores. One would have expected more profound improvements in proximal rather than distal muscles from the motor copy group because bilateral descending motor systems appear to be more numerous emanating from brainstem structures that have substantially more input onto motorneurons innervating proximal muscles. Yet, improvements in distal muscle functioning appeared almost as numerous as with proximal muscle groups!

Some Explanations

As the central nervous system matures, motor activities assume purposeful goals. In the sensory and sensory association areas of the cortex, memories of different motor patterns are established. These patterns are frequently referred to as "sensory engrams."[b] To successfully initiate a motion, one need only activate an engram and the chain of events leading to activation of the motor system is set

---

[b]The concept of an "engram" is not new. Taub (111) has suggested the presence of engrams entirely on the basis of repetitive centrifugal impulses in totally deafferented monkeys. These animals learned to reestablish controlled movement in the apparent absence of feedback.

forth. From previous comments, it should be apparent that proprioceptive (or even exteroceptive) activity can affect motor activity. Proprioceptive systems are capable of activating sensory engrams directly or through cerebellar relays. Once the appropriate pattern has been "learned" by the sensory cortex, the memory engram can be used to initiate motor responses which lead to the performance of the same sequential pattern whenever called upon. Each portion of an engram for a specific movement (involving one or more muscles) is projected according to a time sequence.

Thus, the motor system actually acts as a servomechanism which completes a loop (Fig. 3.6A). If, as in the case of cerebral dysfunction, the motor system fails to follow the pattern, some sensory signal must be fed back to the cerebral cortex to apprise the sensorium of this failure. Should the proprioceptive system become disrupted, the responsibility for providing corrective information must then be relegated to other sensory systems.

EMG feedback achieves its effectiveness because of its *immediacy* in providing the sensorium with pertinent information and because the prime contributor to the established engram, the proprioceptor, can be temporarily replaced by visual and auditory systems. These systems are known to project to the cerebellum and to the motor cortex. Thus, it is efficacy in timing and alternatives in sensory processing that make EMG feedback a plausible training tool.

Most patients with central nervous system deficits are aware of the tasks they should accomplish, but fail to execute them. This implies that the sensory engram is intact, but the pathology must lie either within the motor system or between the sensory cortex and the motor command system, that is, the sensory association cortex (Fig. 3.6B). Ostensibly then, the feedback loops within the brain would be incapable of successfully modifying (inhibiting spasticity, facilitating controlled movement) the temporal-spatial requirements for appropriate motor behavior.

A patient's ability to regain varying degrees of voluntary motor control using visual and auditory sensory processing must rest upon the capability of these inputs to activate subsidiary functional sets of motor cells—either directly or through reflex loops (Fig. 3.6C). Such mechanisms should not be

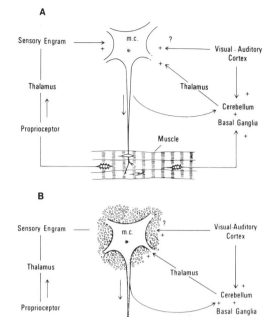

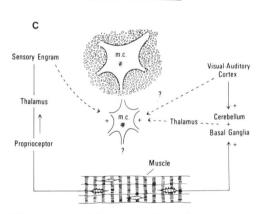

Figure 3.6. Schematic view of components in the servo-loop which is activated under normal conditions (A) and may be disrupted as a result of central nervous system insult (B). The use of muscle biofeedback may activate a subset of cells which function to activate muscle or other cellular elements (C) [M.C.—motor cell].

construed as a demonstration of true neuronal plasticity. There is virtually no evidence to indicate that motor neurons which have remained nonfunctional for long periods following central nervous system trauma are capable of regaining useful activity (112, 113);

however, there seems to be the possibility of activating central synapses previously unused in executing motor commands (114). How this process is accomplished remains uncertain. Nevertheless, it is interesting to speculate that as the visual or auditory input of EMG activity is continually processed by the cerebellum and/or sensory and motor cortices directly, available and responsive motor cells are called into play (Fig. 3.6C). With continued training, patients are capable of improving performance while eliminating one form of feedback. This behavior pattern suggests that either only one feedback mode is sufficient or, more likely, the sensory engram has established an increasing reliable linkage with functional transmitting cells, thus making the patient more reliant upon proprioceptive feedback and less dependent upon artificial (visual or auditory) feedback. This possibility resembles what Bach-y-Rita and Balliet refer to as "unmasking" (115).

These cells may represent any or all of the following: connections to lower motor centers, unoccupied or unused entities, neurons that were previously "depressed" but functionally intact, or nerve cells which serve a multitude of functions. Identification of such cellular elements must be left to speculation at this time. Whether pathways developed or recruited during EMG feedback training can be considered as "learned" must be defined by clinicians appraising the competence and reliability of muscle activity during patient performance of a functional goal.

The content of the information contained herein is purely speculative. An attempt has been made to identify physiological activity patterns obtained primarily from primate models subjected to experiments designed to clarify neuronal components underlying motor control. Whether these findings are clearly applicable to normal human motor control systems can be questioned. Clearly, the section addressing possible explanations is purely speculative. The reader must once again be cautioned of the inherent dangers in ascribing basic, animal neurophysiological findings to humans. For example, any one of multiple locations for cerebral vascular accidents can lead to clinical symptomotology of stroke. Some of these loci and concomitant problems are noted in Table 3.1. A cerebral lesion can have varifying effects that differ in magnitude from one patient to the next. This occurrence

Table 3.1.
Functional deficits following stroke

Deficit	Categories	Locus of pathology
Thinking and communi- cation	Stupor-coma	Bilateral cortical lesions; subarachnoid or subdural bleeding; intracranial hemorrhage; lesions of midbrain reticular formation or septum
	Confusion	Nondominant parietal lesion; temporal lobe lesion; prefrontal lesion
	Aphasia	Sylvian fissure of dominant hemisphere
Strength and coordina- tion	Opposite lower extremity muscle impairment; bowel and bladder dysfunction	Anterior cerebral artery
	Opposite arm and face muscle impairment	Occluded surface branches of middle cerebral artery
	Entire opposite side	Penetrating arterial branches of middle cerebral artery to internal capsule and basal ganglion
	Loss of coordination	Cerebellar arteries
Sensation	Impaired perception of touch, pressure, pain, temperature, and proprioception	Primary sensory cortex (parietal lobe)
	In leg	Anterior and posterior cerebral arteries
	In arm	Surface branches of middle cerebral artery
	Impaired sense of vibration, joint position, texture, localization of objects	Remainder of parietal lobe
	Loss of awareness of sensory deficit on affected side	Parietal cortex, nondominant side
Vision	Monocular blindness (with contralateral hemiparesis)	Occlusion of internal carotid, ophthalmic and middle cerebral arteries
	Binasal or bitemporal visual field deficits	Aneurysm of internal carotid artery
	Hemianopsia	
	Recognizable by patient	Lesions of optic tracts without occlusive vascular disorder
	Without awareness by patient	Acute parieto-occipital infarction
	Head and eyes deviate away from blind visual field	Lesion of middle cerebral artery in either hemisphere
	Visual pursuit halted at midline	Lesion of middle cerebral artery in either hemisphere
	Absence of optokinetic nystagmus from blind side	Lesion of pretectal area
	Paralysis of upward gaze	Lesion in basis pontis (pons)
	Paralysis of upward gaze	Lesion in tectum of pons
	Paralysis of abduction in one eye and hemiparesis of contralateral abduction movement	Basilar and posterior cerebral artery occlusions
	Facial weakness and paresis of lateral gaze	ʼʼ
	Ptosis and pupillary dilatation	ʼʼ

is a function of the amount of neural disruption accompanying the loss of blood supply.

Unfortunately, computerized axial tomography (CAT) scans reveal only the size of the lesion and not the physiological deficit. The only statement that can be made with certainty is that the amount of lost cerebral tissue following a cerebral vascular accident *may* relate to the severity of functional loss. No matter how extensive this loss may be, the neural substrates involved in the processing and integration of feedback signals are, at best, complex and speculative, but still require the clinician's attention if the potential benefits derived from this modality are to be eventually understood.

A novel alternative consideration for integrating biofeedback within a neurophysiological construct has been provided by Mulder (116), who draws a clear distinction between feedback to control EMG and transfer of this motor learning to function (Fig. 3.7). The latter requires multiple inputs for numerous muscles, their afferents, and other sensory systems governing perception. These multiple inputs produce movements which, in turn, can be re-organized into precise actions. When these actions become smooth and virtually automatic, a series of them become a routine. Feedback (and other therapeutic interventions) often progress to the stage of relearned isolated movements that fail to progress toward actions. Accordingly, Mulder has suggested that feedback be oriented toward goal-directed behaviors rather than for isolated movements.

More recently, Wolf, Edwards and Shutter (117) introduced the notion of concurrent assessment of muscle activity (CAMA), a redirection in thinking regarding feedback applications based upon casual observations noted by Basmajian and coworkers (118). CAMA requires that clinicians use feedback as much or more than patients as a vehicle to: 1) transcend visual and palpatory guidance both of which are neither descriptive nor quantitative; 2) quantify "on-line" muscle activity as it is being fed back; and 3) enable clinicians to modify a therapeutic approach, be it either function (routine)-oriented as per Mulder's model or directed toward a specific neuromuscular retraining technique that would be restricted to shaping muscle or move-

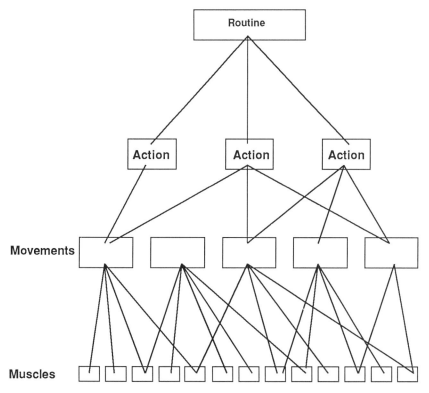

Figure 3.7.   Units of control to achieve function. Most therapeutic intervention progress only to the level of muscle or movement retraining. (Modified after Mulder.)

ment responses rather than routines. More discussion on this subject appears in Chapter 9 by LeCraw.

FUTURE CONSIDERATIONS

From a clinical perspective, gaps in our knowledge concerning the effect of electromyographic feedback are obvious. Methodologies and procedures demonstrating the time course over which measurable functional gains can be obtained with this therapeutic tool must be forthcoming. In addition, specific evidence to suggest which aspect of training is most important needs to be elucidated. For example, does the key to restitution of function with EMG feedback reside in training patients to reduce hyperactive stretch reflexes, to facilitate the recruitment of motor activity in weak antagonist muscles, or in both?

If the cerebellum is an important entity in comparing sensory and motor neuronal pathways during feedback training, then application of this modality in patients with cerebellar dysfunction might reveal important information; yet no reports of this nature have appeared. Similarly, no concrete data on the effect of vestibular or labyrinthine influences on motor learning using EMG biofeedback have been reported. On an even more elementary level, training strategies regarding duration or magnitude of contractions have failed to consider the predominating physiological typing (tonic vs. phasic) of the target muscle. The paucity of information available on how this modality might affect motor behavior in several diagnoses such as multiple sclerosis, Parkinson's disease, and Huntington's chorea, is both a testimony to the infancy of this therapeutic tool and a challenge to the clinician.

Since the magnitude of proprioceptive loss may be a primary deterrent to the rehabilitation process in neurological patients using any therapeutic approach, attention should be focused on discriminative training and relearning of finite kinesthetic tasks. From a different perspective, the use of positron-emitting tomography may enable us to determine which neural substrates are most directly responsible for incorporation of feedback information to effect appropriate motor responses.

Several clinicians have noted vast improvements in head and limb tremor among patients with demyelinating disease when head position feedback has been employed. The validity of these findings and mechanisms to explain how this presumed vestibular control can profoundly influence intention tremor must be explored.

Additionally, it remains to be determined whether feedback training that is totally goal-oriented produces better function than single movement-directed training or individual muscle training, especially among patients with neurological deficits. What role does perception or timing play in movement or routine reacquisition? Should clinicians be training muscles or joint movement characteristics such as velocity or acceleration? These avenues of basic and clinical research interest await the explorations of interested scientists and practitioners.

References

1. Brown, B. *Stress and the Art of Biofeedback.* Harper and Row, New York, 1977.
2. Brener, J. A general model of voluntary control applied to the phenomena of learned cardiovascular change. In *Cardiovascular Psychophysiology*, edited by P. A. Obrist, A. H. Black, J. Brener and L. V. DiCara. Aldine Atherton, Chicago, 1974.
3. Gaarder, K. R. and Montgomery, P. S. *Clinical Biofeedback: A Procedural Manual.* Williams & Wilkins, Baltimore, 1977.
4. Mulder, T. and Hulstyn, W. Sensory feedback therapy and theoretical knowledge of motor control and learning. Am. J. Phys. Med., 63: 226–244, 1984.
5. Wolf, S. L. Electromyographic biofeedback applications to stroke patients: A critical review. Phys. Ther., 63: 1448–1455, 1983.
6. Wolf, S. L. and Fischer-Williams, M. The use of biofeedback in disorders of motor function. In *Biofeedback: Studies on Clinical Efficacy*, edited by J.P. Hatch, J.G. Fisher and J.D. Rugh. Plenum Press, New York, 1987, pp. 153–178.
7. Wolf, S. L. Essential considerations in the use of EMG biofeedback, Phys. Ther., 58: 25–31, 1978.
8. Kelly, J. L., Baker, M. P. and Wolf, S. L. Procedures for EMG biofeedback training in involved upper extremities of hemiplegic patients. Phys. Ther., 59: 1500–1507, 1979.
9. Sprenger, C. K., Carlson, K. and Wessman, H. C. Application of electromyographic biofeedback following medial meniscectomy. Phys. Ther., 59: 167–169, 1979.
10. Wolf, S. L., Basmajian, J. V., Russe, T. C. and Kutner, M. Normative data on low back mobility and activity levels. Am. J. Phys. Med., 58: 217–229, 1979.
11. Brudny, J., Korein, J., Levidow, L., Grynbaum, B. B., Lieberman, A. and Friedmann, L. Sensory feedback therapy as a modality of treatment in central nervous system disorders of voluntary movement. Neurology (N.Y.), 24: 925–932,

1974.

12. Basmajian, J. V., Kukulka, C. G., Narayan, M. G. and Takebe, K. Biofeedback treatment of foot-drop after stroke compared with standard rehabilitation technique: Effects on voluntary control and strength. Arch. Phys. Med. Rehabil., 56: 231–236, 1975.

13. Binder, S. A., Moll, C. B. and Wolf, S. L. Evaluation of electromyographic biofeedback as an adjunct to exercise in treating the lower extremities of hemiplegic patients. Phys. Ther., 61: 886-893, 1981.

14. Lee, K. H., Hill, E., Johnston, R. and Smiehorowski, T. Myofeedback for muscle retraining in hemiplegic patients. Arch. Phys. Med. Rehabil., 57: 588, 1976.

15. Inglis, J., Donald, M. W., Monga, T.N., Sproule, M. and Young, M.J. Electromyographic biofeedback and physical therapy of the hemiplegic upper limb. Arch. Phys. Med. Rehabil., 65: 755–759, 1984.

16. Mroczek, N., Halpern, D. and McHugh, R. Electromyographic feedback and physical therapy for neuromuscular retraining in hemiplegia. Arch. Phys. Med. Rehabil., 59: 258–267, 1978.

17. Wolf, S. L., Baker, M. P. and Kelly, J. L. EMG biofeedback in stroke: effect of patient characteristics. Arch. Phys. Med. Rehabil., 60: 96–102, 1979.

18. Middaugh, S. J. Electromyographic feedback: effect on voluntary muscle contractions in paretic subjects. Arch. Phys. Med. Rehab., 61: 24–29, 1980.

19. Hurd, W. W., Pegram, V. and Nepomuceno, C. Comparison of actual and simulated EMG biofeedback in the treatment of hemiplegic patients. Am. J. Phys. Med., 59: 73–82, 1980.

20. Wolf, S. L. and Binder-Macleod, S.A. Electromyographic biofeedback applications to the hemiplegic patient: changes in upper extremity neuromuscular and functional status. Phys. Ther. 63: 1404–1413, 1983.

21. Skelly, A.M. and Kenedi, R.M. EMG biofeedback therapy in the re-education of the hemiplegic shoulder in patients with sensory loss. Physiotherapy, 68:34–38, 1982.

22. Brudny, J., Korein, J., Grynbaum, B. B. and Sachs-Frankel, G. Sensory feedback therapy in patients with brain insult. Scand. J. Rehabil. Med., 9: 155–163, 1977.

23. Wolf, S. L. EMG biofeedback applications in physical rehabilitation: an overview. Physiotherapy (Canada), 31: 65–72, 1979.

24. Allen, G.I. and Tsukahara, N. Cerebrocerebellar communication systems. Physiol. Rev., 54: 957–1006, 1974.

25. Anderson, P., Hagan, P. J., Phillips, C. G. and Powell, T. P. S. Mapping by microstimulation of overlapping projections from area 4 to motor units of the baboon's hand. Proc. R. Soc. London (Biol.). 188: 31–60, 1975.

26. Asanuma, H. and Rosen, I. Topographical organization of cortical efferent zones projecting to distal forelimb muscles in the monkey. Exp. Brain Res., 14: 243–256, 1972.

27. Rosen, I. and Asanuma, H. Peripheral afferent inputs to the forelimb area of the monkey motor cortex: input-output relations. Exp. Brain Res., 14: 257–273, 1972.

28. Denny-Brown, D. and Yanagisawa, N. The role of the basal ganglia in the initiation of movement. In The Basal Ganglia, edited by M.D. Yahr. Raven Press, New York, 1976, pp. 114–149.

29. Liles, S. and Davis, G. D. Interaction of caudate nucleus and thalamus in alteration of cortically induced movement. J. Neurophysiol., 32: 564–573, 1969.

30. Purpura, D. P. Physiological organization of the basal ganglia. In The Basal Ganglia, edited by M. D. Yahr. Raven Press, New York, 1976, pp. 91–114.

31. Dean, W. and Davis, G. Behavior following caudate lesions in rhesus monkeys. J. Neurophysiol., 22: 524–537, 1959.

32. Goldman, P. S. and Rosvold, H. E. The effects of selective caudate lesions in infant and juvenile rhesus monkeys. Brain Res., 43: 53–66, 1972.

33. Teuber, H.-L. Complex functions of basal ganglia. In The Basal Ganglia, edited by M. D. Yahr. Raven Press, New York, 1976, pp. 151–168.

34. Buerger, A. A., Gross, C. G. and Rocha-Miranda, C. E. Effects of ventral putamen lesions on discrimination learning by monkeys. J. Comp. Physiol. Psychol., 68: 440–446, 1974.

35. Cohen, S. M. Electrical stimulation of cortical-caudate pairs during delayed successive visual discrimination. Acta Neurobiol. Exp. (Warsz.), 32: 211–233, 1972.

36. Brooks, V. B. Roles of cerebellum and basal ganglia in initiation and control of movements. Can. J. Neurol. Sci., 2: 265–277, 1975.

37. Schwartzman, R. J., Gran, B. and Marcos, J. A functional analysis of cortical motor sensory convergence areas in the monkey. Trans. Am. Neurol. Assoc., 100: 114–117, 1975.

38. Ghez, C. and Pisa, M. Inhibition of afferent transmission in cuneate nucleus during voluntary movement in cat. Brain Res., 40: 145–151, 1972.

39. Coulter, J. D., Maunz, R. A. and Willis, W. D. Effects of stimulation of sensorimotor cortex on primate spinothalamic neurons. Brain Res., 65: 351–356, 1975.

40. Allen, G. I., Gilbert, P. F. C., Marini, R., Schultz, W. and Yin, T. C. T. Integration of cerebral and peripheral inputs by interpositus neurons in monkey. Exp. Brain Res., 27: 81–100, 1977.

41. Brinkman, J. and Kuypers, H. G. J. M. Cerebral control of contralateral and ipsilateral arm, hand and finger movements in split brain rhesus monkeys. Brain, 69: 653–674, 1973.

42. Lawrence, D. G. and Hopkins, D. A. The development of motor control in the rhesus monkey: evidence concerning the role of corticomotoneuronal connections. Brain, 99: 235–254, 1976.

43. Bizzi, E. and Polit, A. Characteristics of the motor programs underlying visually evoked movements. In Posture and Movement, edited by R. E. Talbot and D. R. Humphrey. Raven

Press, New York, 1979, pp. 169–176.

44. Mountcastle, V. B., Lynch, J. C. and Georgo-poulos, A. Posterior parietal association cortex of the monkey: command functions for operations within extrapersonal space. J. Neurophysiol., 38: 871–908, 1975.

45. Fetz, E. E., Finocchio, D. V., Baker, M. A. and Soso, M. J. Sensory and motor responses of precentral cortex cells during comparable active and passive joint movements. J. Neurophysiol., 43: 1070–1089, 1980.

46. Lemon, R. N. and Porter, R. Afferent input to movement related precentral neurons in conscious monkeys. Proc. R. Soc. London (Biol.), 194: 313–339, 1976.

47. Wong, Y. C., Kwan, H. C., MacKay, W. A. and Murphy, J. T. Spatial organization of precentral cortex in awake monkeys. I. Somatosensory inputs. J. Neurophysiol., 41: 1107–1119, 1978.

48. Divac, I., LaVail, J. H., Rakic, P. and Winston, K. R. Heterogeneous afferents to the inferior parietal lobule of the rhesus monkey revealed by the retrograde transport method. Brain Res., 123: 197–208, 1977.

49. Pandya, D. P. and Kuypers, H. G. J. M. Corticocortical connections in the rhesus monkey. Brain Res., 13: 13–36, 1969.

50. Mesalum, M.-M., Van Hoesen, G. W., Pandya, D. N. and Geschwind, N. Limbic and sensory connections of the inferior parietal lobule (area PG) in the rhesus monkey: a study with a new method for horseradish peroxidase histochemistry. Brain Res., 136: 393–414, 1977.

51. MacLean, P. D. Psychosomatic disease and the "visceral brain": recent developments bearing on the Papez theory of emotion. Psychosom. Med., 11: 338–353, 1949.

52. Watson, R. T., Heilman, K. M., Cauthen, J. C. and King. F. A. Neglect after cingulectomy. Neurology (Minneap.), 23: 1003–1007, 1973.

53. Kuypers, H. G. J. M. and Lawrence, D. G. Cortical projections to the red nucleus and the brain stem in the rhesus monkey. Brain Res., 4: 151–188, 1967.

54. Mohler, C. W. and Wurtz, R. H. Role of striate cortex and superior colliculus in visual guidance of saccadic eye movements in monkeys. J. Neurophysiol., 40: 74–94, 1977.

55. Jones, E. G. and Powell, T. P. S. An anatomical study of converging sensory pathways within the cerebral cortex of the monkey. Brain, 93: 793–820, 1970.

56. Hagbarth, K.-E. Excitatory and inhibitory skin areas for flexor and extensor montoneurones. Acta Physiol. Scand., 26: 1–58, (Suppl. 94), 1952.

57. Hunt, C. C. The reflex activity of mammalian small nerve fibers. J. Physiol. (Lond.), 115: 456–469, 1951.

58. Wolf, S. L. The effect of a specific cutaneous cold stimulus on underlying gastrocnemius muscle motor activity. Dissertation Abstr., 34: 299, 1974.

59. Carpenter, M.B. and Sutin J. Human Neuroanatomy, 8th ed. Williams & Wilkins, Baltimore, 1983.

60. Humphrey, D. R. Corticospinal systems and their control by premotor cortex, basal ganglia and cerebellum. In The Clinical Neurosciences. Section 5: Neurobiology, edited by W. D. Willis, Jr., section editor. Churchill Livingstone, New York, 1982.

61. Asanuma, H. Recent developments in the study of the columnar arrangements of neurons within the motor cortex. Physiol. Rev., 55: 143–156, 1975.

62. Humphrey, D. R. On the cortical control of visually directed reaching: contributions by nonprecentral motor areas. In Posture and Movement, edited by R. E. Talbot and D. R. Humphrey. Raven Press, New York, 1979, pp. 51–112.

63. Travis, A. M. Neurological deficiencies following supplementary motor area lesions in Macaca mulatta. Brain. 78: 155–173, 1955.

64. Kwan, H. C., MacKay, W. A., Murphy, J. J. and Wong, Y. C. Spatial organization of precentral cortex in awake primates. II. Motor outputs. J. Neurophysiol., 41: 1120–1131, 1978.

65. Evarts, E. V. and Fromm, C. Sensory responses in motor cortex neurons during precise motor control. Neurosci. Lett., 5: 267–272, 1977.

66. Fromm, C. and Evarts, E. V. Relation of motor cortex neurons to precisely controlled and ballistic movements. Neurosci. Lett. 5: 259–265, 1977.

67. Evarts, E. V. and Fromm, C. Transcortical reflexes and servo control of movement. Can. J. Physiol. Pharmacol., 59: 757–775, 1981.

68. Phillips, C. G. Motor apparatus of the baboon's hand. Proc. R. Soc. Lond. (Biol.), 173: 141–174, 1969.

69. Creed, R. S., Denny-Brown, D., Eccles, J. C., Liddell, E. G. T. and Sherrington, C. S. Reflex Activity of the Spinal Cord. Clarendon Press, Oxford, 1972.

70. Granit, R. Receptors and Sensory Perception. Yale University Press, New Haven, 1955.

71. Matthews, P. B. C. Mammalian Muscle Receptors and Their Central Actions. Williams & Wilkins, Baltimore, 1972.

72. Hefferline, R. F. The role of proprioception in the control of behavior. Trans. N.Y. Acad. Sci., 20: 739–764, 1958.

73. Arezzo, J. and Vaughan, H. G., Jr. Cortical potentials associated with voluntary movements in the monkey. Brain Res., 88: 99–104, 1975.

74. Lucier, G. E., Ruegg, D. C. and Wiesendanger, M. Responses of neurones in motor cortex and in area 3a to controlled stretches of forelimb muscles in cebus monkeys. J. Physiol. (Lond.), 251: 833–853, 1975.

75. Murphy, J. T., Wong, Y. C. and Kwan, H. C. Distributed feedback systems for muscle control. Brain Res., 71: 495–505, 1974.

76. Phillips, C. G., Powell, T. P. S. and Wiesendanger, M. Projections from low-threshold muscle afferents of hand and forearm to area 3a of baboon's cortex. J. Physiol. (Lond.), 217: 419-446, 1971.

77. Wiesendanger, M. Input from muscle and cutaneous nerves of the hand and forearm to neurones of the precentral gyrus of baboons and monkeys. J. Physiol. (Lond.), 228: 203–

219, 1973.

78. Hore, J., Preston, J. B., Durkovic, R. C. and Cheney, P. V. Responses of cortical neurons (areas 3a and 4) ramp stretch of hindlimb muscles in the baboon. J. Neurophysiol., *39:* 484–500, 1976.
79. Wise, S. P. and Tanji, J. Neuronal responses in sensorimotor cortex to ramp displacements and maintained positions imposed on hindlimb of the unanesthetized monkey. J. Neurophysiol., *45:* 482–500, 1981.
80. Sjoqvist, O. and Weinstein, E. A. The effect of section of the medial lemniscus on proprioceptive functions in chimpanzees and monkeys. J. Neurophysiol., *5:* 69–74, 1942.
81. Thach, W. T. Discharge of cerebellar neuron related to two maintained postures and two prompt movements. II. Purkinje cell output and input. J. Neurophysiol., *33:* 537–547, 1970.
82. Thach, W. T. Timing of activity in cerebellar dentate nucleus and cerebral motor cortex during prompt volitional movement. Brain Res., *88:* 233–241, 1975.
83. Thach, W. T. Correlation of neural discharge with pattern and force of muscular activity, joint position, and direction of next intended movement in motor cortex and cerebellum. J. Neurophysiol., *41:* 654–676, 1978.
84. Soechting, J. F. Modeling of a simple motor task in man: motor output dependence on sensory input. Kybernetics, *14:* 25–34, 1973.
85. Soechting, J. F., Ranish, N. A., Palminteri, R. and Terzuolo, C. A. Changes in a motor pattern following cerebellar and olivary lesions in the squirrel monkey. Brain Res., *105:* 21–44, 1976.
86. Terzuolo, C. A., Soechting, J. F. and Viviani, P. Studies on the control of some simple motor tasks. I. Relation between parameters of movements and EMG activities. Brain Res., *58:* 212–216, 1973.
87. Terzuolo, C. A., Soechting, J. F. and Viviani, P. Studies on the control of some simple motor tasks. II. On the cerebellar control of movements in relation to the formulation of intentional commands. Brain Res., *58:* 217–222, 1973.
88. Shapovalov, A. I., Karamyan, O. A., Kurchayvi, C. G. and Repina, Z. A. Synaptic actions evoked from the red nucleus on spinal alpha motoneurons in the rhesus monkey. Brain Res., *32:* 325–348, 1971.
89. Catsman-Berrevoets, C. E. and Kuypers, H. G. J. M. Cells of origin of cortical projections to dorsal column nuclei, spinal cord and bulbar medial reticular formation in the rhesus monkey. Neurosci. Lett., *3:* 245–252, 1976.
90. Woolsey, C. N., Settlage, D. R. and Meyer, W. Patterns of localization in precentral and "supplementary" motor areas and their relation to the concept of a premotor area. In *Patterns of Organization in the Central Nervous System.* Res. Publ. Assoc. Res. Nerv. Ment. Dis., *30:* 238–264, 1951.
91. DeLong, M. R. Activity of basal ganglia neurons during movement. Brain Res., *40:* 127–135, 1972.
92. Basmajian, J. V. *Muscles Alive: Their Func-*

tions Revealed by Electromyography, 4th ed. Williams & Wilkins, Baltimore, 1978.
93. Basmajian, J. V. Learned control of single motor units. In *Biofeedback: Theory and Research,* edited by G. E. Schwartz and J. Beatty, Academic Press, New York, 1977.
94. Basmajian, J. V. Motor learning and control: a working hypothesis. Arch. Phys. Med. Rehabil., *58:* 38–41, 1977.
95. Smith, H. M. Jr., Basmajian, J. V. and Vanderstoep, S. F. Inhibition of neighboring motoneurons in conscious control of single spinal motoneurons. Science, *183:* 975–976, 1974.
96. Henneman, E., Somjen, G. and Carpenter, D. O. Functional significance of cell size in spinal motoneurons. J. Neurophysiol., *28:* 599–620, 1965.
97. Evarts, E. V. Relation of pyramidal tract activity to force exerted during voluntary movement. J. Neurophysiol., *31:* 14–27, 1968.
98. Evarts, E. V. Changing concepts of central control of movement. Can. J Physiol. Pharmacol., *53:* 191–201, 1975.
99. Evarts, E. V. Activity of motor cortex neurons in association with learned movement. Int. J. Neurosci., *3:* 113–124, 1975.
100. Evarts, E. V. and Tanji, J. Reflex and intended responses in motor cortex pyramidal tract neurons of monkey. J. Neurophysiol., *39:* 1069–1080, 1976.
101. Tanji, J. and Evarts, E. V. Anticipatory activity of motor cortex neurons in relation to direction of an intended movement. J. Neurophysiol., *39:* 1062–1068, 1976.
102. Schmidt, E. M., Jost. G. and Davis, K. K. Cortical cell discharge patterns in anticipation of a trained movement. Brain Res., *75:* 309–311, 1974.
103. Smith, A. M., Hepp-Reymond, M.-C. and Wyss, U. R. Relation of activity in precentral cortical neurons to force and rate of force change during isometric contractions of finger muscles. Exp. Brain Res., *23:* 315–332, 1975.
104. Kuypers, H. G. J. M. Central cortical connections to the motor and somatosensory cell groups. An experimental study in the rhesus monkey. Brain, *83:* 161–184, 1960.
105. Porter, R. Early facilitation at corticomotoneuronal synapses. J. Physiol. (Lond.), *207:* 733–745, 1970.
106. Kawamura, T. and Watanabe, S. Timing as a prominent factor of the Jendrassik maneuver on the H reflex. J. Neurol. Neurosurg. Psychiatr., *38:* 508–516, 1975.
107. Wise, S. P. and Evarts, E. V. The role of the cerebral cortex in movement. Trends Neurosci., *4:* 297–300, 1981.
108. Humphrey, D. R. Separate cell systems in the motor cortex of the monkey for the control of joint movement and of joint stiffness. Kyoto Symposia (EEG Supp. No. 36), edited by P. A. Buser, W. A. Cobb, T. Okuma. Elsevier, Amsterdam, 1982, pp. 393–408.
109. Fetz, E. E. Biofeedback and differential conditioning of response patterns in the skeletal motor system. In *Biofeedback and Behavior,* edited by J. Beatty and H. Legewie, Plenum Press,

New York, 1977.

110. Wolf, S. L., LeCraw, D. E., Barton, L. A. and Rees, B. J. A comparison of motor copy and targeted feedback training techniques for restitution of upper extremity function among neurologic patients. Phys. Ther., 1988, submitted for publication.

111. Taub, E., Goldberg, I. A. and Taub, P. Deafferentation in monkeys: pointing at a target without visual feedback. Exp. Neurol., 46: 178–186, 1975.

112. Guth, L. Axonal regeneration and functional plasticity in the central nervous system. Exp. Neurol., 45: 606–654, 1974.

113. Pettegrew, R. K. and Windle, W. F. Factors in recovery from spinal cord injury. Exp. Neurol., 63: 815–829, 1976.

114. Brudny, J., Korein, J., Gyrnbaum, B. B., Friedmann, L. W., Weinstein, S., Sachs-Frankel, G. and Belandres, P. V. EMG feedback therapy: review of treatment of 114 patients. Arch.

Phys. Med. Rehabil., 57: 55–61, 1976.

115. Bach-y-Rita, P. and Balliet, R. Recovery from stroke. In Stroke Rehabilitation: The Recovery of Motor Control, edited by P. W. Duncan and M. Badke, Year Book Publishers, New York, 1987, pp. 79–107.

116. Mulder, T. From movement to action: Perspectives for future research. In The Learning of Motor Control Following Brain Damage: Experimental and Clinical Studies, by T. Mulder, Swets and Zeitlinger, Lisse, 1985, pp. 104–112.

117. Wolf, S. L., Edwards, D. I. and Shutter, L. A. Concurrent assessment of muscle activity (CAMA): A procedural approach to assess treatment goals. Phys. Ther., 66: 218–224, 1986.

118. Basmajian, J. V., Gowland, C., Brandstater, M. E., Swanson, L. and Trotter, J. EMG feedback treatment of upper limb in hemiplegic stroke patients: A pilot study. Arch. Phys. Med. Rehabil., 63: 613–616, 1982.

CHAPTER 4

Anatomical and Physiological Basis for Biofeedback of Autonomic Regulation

JOHN V. BASMAJIAN

Two systems control the smooth muscles, secreting glands and cardiac muscles. They modify these effector organs in maintaining the stability of the body's *milieux interieur*—the autonomic nervous system and endocrine glands. A healthy autonomic nervous system (composed of the sympathetic and parasympathetic divisions) supplemented by hormones secreted by the endocrine glands are essential. All parts of the body's regulatory mechanisms are tuned to produce optimal responses both during repose and during activities and emotions ranging up to maximum arousal of many systems.

AUTONOMIC NERVOUS SYSTEM

The peripheral part of the autonomic nervous system (ANS) is well described in standard textbooks. Also, the gray matter of the brainstem and spinal cord is quite well known. The major problem lies in describing the connections that we now know must exist between the human cortex and the peripheral outflow to smooth muscles, cardiac muscles, and secreting glands. The ANS is not so much autonomic as it is automatic and semi-autonomous. Conscious voluntary and unperceived cortical and subcortical neural impulses do influence the control of those effector organs. This fact was well known by neurophysiologists long before the growing interest in biofeedback and operant conditioning. Perhaps the discrete nature and size of the two sympathetic trunks running parallel to the central nervous system (CNS) overimpressed others (e.g., clinical psychologists) into believing that the sympathetic nervous system was functionally autonomous.

The ANS consists of gray matter in the CNS, nerves and ganglia. Its nerves supply motor impulses to (a) the heart, (b) smooth muscle, wherever situated, and (c) glands. Accompanying the motor fibers are sensory (afferent) ones carrying impulses into the CNS.

The ANS has two parts: (a) the sympathetic system, and (b) the parasympathetic system.

The *sympathetic system* (Fig. 4.1) has its outflow from the CNS at the thoracolumbar part of the spinal cord from all levels between the 1st thoracic to the 2nd (or 3rd) lumbar segments.

The *parasympathetic system* has (a) a cranial part and (b) a sacral part; it has central connections with the brain through cranial nerves III, VII, IX, and X, and with the spinal cord at sacral segments 2, 3, and 4.

The *cerebral "cortex"* of the ANS appears to be localized in the hypothalamus with connections to many parts of the CNS. More details will be given later in this chapter.

Sympathetic System

In the sympathetic system there are neurons corresponding to the efferent, connector, and afferent neurons of the voluntary system. The efferent cells occur (a) in the *paravertebral ganglia* or ganglia of the sympathetic trunk and (b) in the *prevertebral ganglia* (or visceral ganglia—cardiac, celiac, intermesenteric, hypogastric, and subsidiary ganglia), which are but detached parts of paravertebral ganglia, and (c) in the medulla of the suprarenal gland.

The gray matter of the spinal cord from segments T.1-L.2 possesses an intermediolateral column (horn), and it is in this intermediolateral column that the sympathetic connector cells are lodged (Fig. 4.2). Their

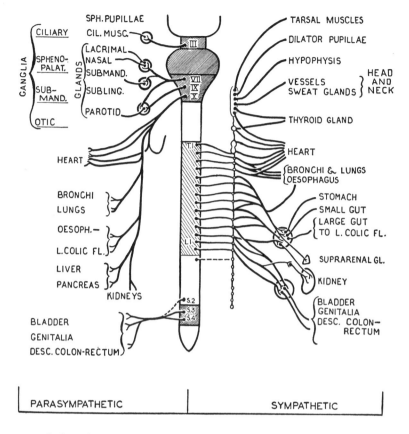

Figure 4.1. General plan of autonomic nervous system. (From Basmajian, J. V. *Grants' Method of Anatomy*, 10th ed. Williams & Wilkins, Baltimore, 1980.)

axons pass as fine, medullated *preganglionic fibers* via the ventral nerve roots and white rami communicantes (T.1-L.2) to the paravertebral ganglia, and there synapse with the excitor cells.

Some preganglionic fibers, however, ascend and descend in the sympathetic trunk to form synapses with the cells in the ganglia at various levels, whereas other preganglionic fibers pass through the paravertebral ganglia without synapsing to form *splanchnic nerves* (Figs. 4.2 and 4.3).

The *postganglionic fibers*, or axons of the excitor cells, are mostly nonmyelinated and therefore gray. These gray fibers, carried in a short nerve, a *gray ramus communicans*, pass laterally from the ganglia of the sympathetic trunk to each and every spinal nerve. They reach the blood vessels, sweat and sebaceous glands, and tiny arrectores pilorum muscles (which pull on the hair roots) of the entire cutaneous surface of the body and of somatic structures (limbs and body wall). Other postganglionic fibers are relayed from the superior

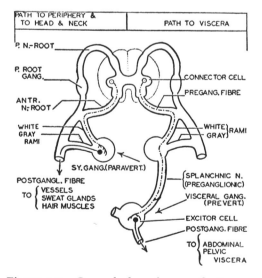

Figure 4.2. General plan of sympathetic ganglion and its connections. (From Basmajian, J. V. *Grant's Method of Anatomy*, 10th ed. Williams & Wilkins, Baltimore, 1980.)

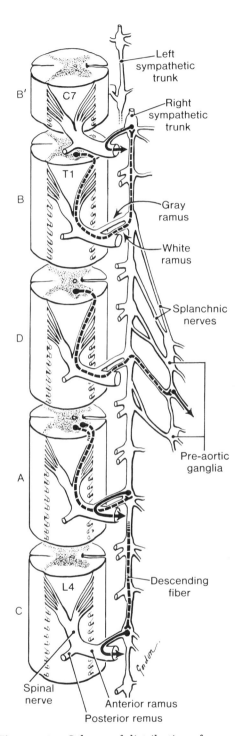

cervical ganglion to the face, which is the territory of the trigeminal nerve (Fig. 4.2).

The thoracic and lumbar *splanchnic nerves* carry elongated preganglionic fibers which have passed without interruption through paravertebral ganglia (T.5-L.2). They synapse with excitor cells in prevertebral ganglia.

The greater (T.5-T.10), lesser (T.10, T.11) and lowest (T.12) thoracic splanchnic nerves and the four lumbar splanchnic nerves end in the celiac and other prevertebral ganglia, whence they are relayed almost entirely as perivascular branches to the abdominal and pelvic viscera (Fig. 4.3).

The *suprarenal gland* is supplied from cord segments T.10-L.1 (or 2). Branches of the splanchnic nerves ramify among the cells of its medulla, because they develop from sympathetic neurons.

The cervical and upper thoracic sympathetic ganglia, although paravertebral in location, represent both para- and prevertebral ganglia of more caudal levels; that is to say, the postganglionic fibers of the excitor cells in these ganglia pass, on the one hand, (a) in rami communicantes to the spinal nerves and so to somatic structures; and, on the other hand, (b) as visceral fibers to such structures as the eye, salivary glands, heart, and lungs.

The *visceral afferent* (sensory) fibers of the sympathetic system travel with the visceral efferent fibers. They pass via the white rami communicantes to the spinal ganglia (dorsal root ganglia) where, like the afferent fibers of the voluntary system, they have their cell stations. They enter the spinal cord through the dorsal roots, mainly of T.1-L.2, and synapse with the conector cells in the intermediolateral column of gray matter. Many, however, first ascend or descend in the sympathetic trunk.

Sympathetic Trunk

This long "nerve" running bilaterally alongside of the whole length of the spinal column is composed of ascending and descending fibers. Some of these are preganglionic efferent, others postganglionic efferent, and still others are afferent fibers. The paravertebral ganglia (ganglia of the trunks) are formed by synapses between preganglionic efferent neurons and the cell bodies of postganglionic neurons. The influence of a single preganglionic neuron is diffused over a wide area because each preganglionic fiber synapses with a number of postganglionic neurons.

Figure 4.3. Scheme of distribution of sympathetic outflow up and down the sympathetic trunk to ganglia that send impulses to the vessels and glands of the limbs (at *A, B,* and *C*) and to abdominal organs (at *D*). (From Basmajian, J. V. *Primary Anatomy*, 8th ed. Williams & Wilkins, Baltimore, 1982.)

Sympathetic Supply of Individual Regions and Organs

Upper Limbs. Preganglionic fibers from cord segments T.3-T.6 ascend bilaterally in the sympathetic trunk to the upper thoracic, inferior cervical, and middle cervical ganglia. Thence, a dozen or so postganglionic gray rami pass to the roots of the right and left brachial plexuses to be distributed to the limbs. Most of these fibers travel in the lower trunk of each plexus and in the median and ulnar nerves.

Lower Limbs. Preganglionic fibers from cord segments T.11, T.12, and L.1 and L.2 descend in each sympathetic trunk to ganglia L.2-S.3. Thence, the postganglionic fibers pass in gray rami to the nerves of the lumbar and sacral plexuses. The upper part of each femoral artery is supplied by an extension from the aortic plexuses along the common and external iliac arteries; but as in the upper limb, so in the lower, most of the femoral artery and the arteries distal to it are supplied locally by the motor and sensory somatic nerves.

Head and Neck. Cord segments are mainly T.1 and T.2, i.e., connector cells are situated in segments T.1 and T.2, though some may extend lower. The excitor cells lie mainly in the superior cervical ganglion. Postganglionic fibers pass to the arrectores pilorum (smooth muscles that make the hairs stand up), sweat glands, and vessels of the skin; to the heart; and, via the internal carotid nerve, to the vessels of the nasal cavity (through the deep petrosal nerve), to the dura mater, to the cerebral vessels, and to the smooth muscles of the orbital cavity (tarsal muscles, dilator pupillae, and vasoconstrictors). The orbital fibers arise mainly in cord segment T.1, pass to the 1st thoracic ganglion, and ascend to the excitor cells in the superior cervical ganglion.

Thorax. Cord segments are mainly T.2, T.3, and T.4. For the *heart*, the cord segments are T.1-T.5. From relay stations in the cervical and upper 4 or 5 thoracic ganglia, cardiac nerves pass to the cardiac plexus (Fig. 4.4). Pain impulses travel in the afferent fibers (but apparently not by way of the superior cervical ganglion) and have their cell stations in the upper 4 or 5 thoracic spinal (dorsal root) ganglia.

For the lungs, the cord segments are T.2-T.6; for the esophagus, T.4-T.6.

Abdomen and Pelvis. Cord segments are T.5-L.2. For the stomach, liver, and pancreas they are T.6-T.9, and for the gall bladder, T.4-T.9.

For the small intestine the cord segments are T.9 and T.10; for the cecum and appendix, T.10-T.12; for the colon to left colic flexure, T.12 and L.1; and for the left colic flexure to rectum, L.1 and L.2.

For the kidney, cord segments are T.12 and L.1; for the ureter, L.1 and L.2; and for the bladder, L.1 and L.2.

From the cord segments, connector fibers pass through the thoracic and lumbar *paravertebral (trunk) ganglia*, as the thoracic and lumbar splanchnic nerves, to be relayed in the celiac, renal, mesenteric, and superior and inferior hypogastric ganglia.

For other pelvic viscera, see Figure 4.1.

Parasympathetic System

Parasympathetic nerve fibers (efferent) are contained in cranial nerves III, VII, IX, and X and in sacral nerves 2, 3, and 4. Many branches of the trigeminal nerve (cranial nerve V) are accompanied in the terminal parts of their courses by efferent parasympathetic fibers from other nerves (e.g., the lingual nerve by the chorda tympani).

Oculomotor Nerve

This nerve (cranial nerve III) sends fibers to the *ciliary ganglion* in the orbit, whence they are relayed by short ciliary nerves to the sphincter pupillae and the ciliary muscle, mediating contraction of the pupil and accommodation of the lens to near vision.

Facial Nerve

The nervus intermedius (pars intermedia of the facial or seventh cranial nerve) carries secretomotor and vasodilator impulses to the lacrimal, nasal, palatine, and salivary glands.

Glossopharyngeal Nerve

This cranial nerve (IX) carries blood pressure regulating sensory fibers from the *sinus nerve*, and transmits motor fibers to the *otic ganglion*, which supplies the parotid salivary gland.

Vagus Nerve

This nerve (X) supplies the digestive and respiratory passages and the heart (Fig. 4.1). The relay stations of the efferent fibers of the

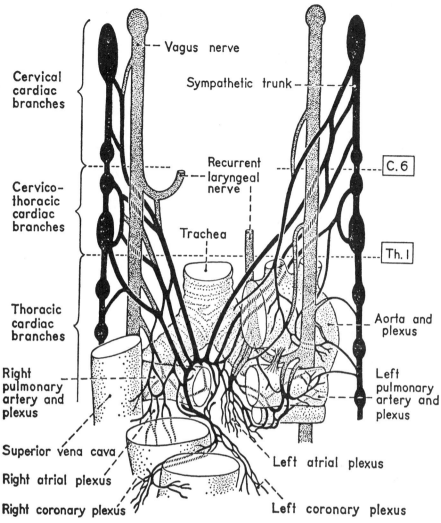

Figure 4.4. Cardiac plexus received fibers from both the vagus and the sympathetic trunks. (From Basmajian, J. V. *Grant's Method of Anatomy*, 10th ed. Williams & Wilkins, Baltimore, 1980.)

vagus are in terminal ganglia, situated in (or near) the walls of the organ or part it supplies. The vagus causes hollow organs to contract and their sphincters to relax. It is also secretomotor. Its efferent fibers do *not* carry pain impulses from the heart or from abdominal organs.

Pelvic Splanchnic Nerves

These nerves (S.2, 3, and 4) behave just like vagal fibers. While the vagus supplies the gastrointestinal tract as far as the left colic flexure, the pelvic splanchnic nerves supply the gut distal to that point and the genitourinary organs in the pelvis. Their afferent fibers are conductors of pain impulses.

Dual Innervation

Many of the autonomic effectors (e.g., heart, gut, spleen, kidney) receive innervation from both sympathetic and parasympathetic components while other effectors (e.g., adrenal medulla, vascular supply to skin or muscle) gain only a sympathetic supply. In dually innervated structures, the action of each autonomic division upon the effector is usually antagonistic. For example, parasympathetic supply to the heart will cause deceleration, and sympathetic stimulation will accelerate cardiac activity. The functional state of any dually innervated organ will be the resultant balance between the continuous activity delivered both over sets of nerves. However, some effectors receive a dual innervation from which a synergistic rather than antagonistic action results. Secretory cells in salivary glands will produce secretions when either system is activated, but the composition of secretory materials may differ.

ENDOCRINE GLANDS

An endocrine or ductless gland is one that produces an internal secretion or hormone, i.e., a secretion carried off in the venous blood stream to influence the activities of another part of the body.

Hypophysis (Pituitary Gland)

This small gland (about the size of a pea) "hangs" by a stalk—the infundibulum—from the hypothalamus, which forms the floor of the third ventricle of the brain. It is made up of two lobes that are entirely different from one another functionally.

The *anterior lobe (adenohypophysis)* produces several hormones which, because of their influence on other endocrine glands, have caused the hypophysis cerebri to be referred to as the "master gland." Disturbances of this lobe result in dwarfism, giantism, infantilism, excessive obesity, and other manifestations associated with growth and sex.

The *posterior lobe (or neurohypophysis)* is a downgrowth from the brain and produces secretions that stimulate contractions of the uterus and the production of urine by the kidneys and which influence the production of insulin by the pancreas. This lobe also affects blood pressure. It is possibly associated with sympathetic and (or) parasympathetic functions because of its connections with the hypothalamus. Its portal system of veins carries the secretions first to the hypothalamus before the blood is returned to the systemic veins that drain that part of the brain.

Pineal Gland or Body

The pineal body is placed deep within the brain, where it is attached to the roof of the 3rd ventricle. Little is known about its status as an endocrine gland.

Thyroid Gland

This neck gland produces the hormone (thyroxin), which affects a great many bodily functions. When produced in excessive quantities, it disturbs the basal metabolic rate at which the cells of the body function.

Parathyroid Glands

The parathyroid glands—two attached to the thyroid gland on each side—regulate the relative amounts of calcium in the blood and in the bones. Certain distressing diseases in which the bones become soft or extremely brittle are the result of a malfunctioning of the parathyroids.

Thymus Gland

This gland lies behind the manubrium sterni (the upper part of the breast-bone) and in front of the great vessels above the heart. Its period of greatest functional activity is in fetal life. After birth, it gradually shrinks. Though there is no general agreement on its endocrine function, there is no question that the thymus is an important production center for lymphocytes before puberty. Lymphocytes play a critical role in immunity.

Suprarenal (Adrenal) Glands

These cap the top of the kidneys, but they are not functionally related. The *cortex* of each (a thick outer layer) produces a group of hormones—among them cortisone. Some are essential for life because they regulate various metabolic processes, e.g., salt metabolism, production of sex hormones, and production of collagen fibers of fibrous tissue throughout the body. The adrenal *medulla* is closely associated in developmental origin with the sympathetic ganglia. It is in the medullary part of the gland that *adrenalin* is produced.

Chromaffin Bodies

Scattered along the line of the sympathetic chain and the abdominal aorta are many tiny bodies identical in structure with the suprarenal medulla. They are known as para-aortic bodies or paraganglia or chromaffin bodies and, like the suprarenal medulla, are associated with the activity of the sympathetic system.

Pancreas

The pancreas has both an exocrine and an endocrine function. The hormone *insulin* is vital to the proper metabolism of carbohydrates, and its production is partly regulated by the hypophysis.

Testes and Ovaries

The gonads have important endocrine functions. Specialized cells release the male and female sex hormones. These regulate the sexual function of the adult and determine the secondary sexual characteristics, including all aspects of maleness and femaleness.

In women, the monthly cycle of ovulation followed by menstrual bleeding is regulated by a balance of hormones produced by the ovaries and other endocrine glands, especially the hypophysis. These various hormones interact in such a way as to cause: (a) a sloughing off of the uterine mucosa if the ovum is not fertilized by a sperm within a few days of its release, or (b) an embedding and protection of a fertilized ovum in the mucosa. The placenta of a developing embryo itself produces hormones which interact with hormones of the ovaries and hypophysis to prevent premature expulsion of the child.

GASTROINTESTINAL MOTILITY

As noted before, both the sympathetic and parasympathetic systems supply the esophagus, stomach, and small and large bowel. Esophageal branches of the upper and lower thoracic sympathetic ganglia blend with a plexus of nerves formed from the vagus nerves to supply the smooth musculature which predominates in the lower half of the esophagus. The upper half of the esophagus has much more striated (voluntary) muscle in its walls. The parasympathetic fibers of the vagus nerve supply the smooth (involuntary) musculature while its somatic motor fibers innervate the striated esophageal muscles.

Within the submucosa of the stomach and intestines, both sympathetic and parasympathetic fibers, accompanied by sensory fibers, form a plexus. The vagal postganglionic fibers function to stimulate peristalsis and gastrointestinal secretions while stimulation of postganglionic sympathetic fibers from the thoracic ganglia and splanchnic nerves causes vasoconstriction of visceral blood vessels and inhibition of peristalsis. Secretion of the hormonal agent (adrenalin or epinephrine) is caused by direct preganglionic innervation of the adrenal medulla. This compound has specific sympathomimetic actions in man and can cause constriction of arterioles, acceleration of

heart rate, and increase in systolic blood pressure.

Gastric secretion operates through two mechanisms—neural (vagus nerve) and humoral (adenohypophysis and adrenal cortex). Lowered blood sugar activates the secretion of gastric acid in preparation for the intake of food. Indeed, emotional stress and prolonged hypothalamic stimulation may cause gastric hyperacidity and, ultimately, peptic ulcers. Clinicians wishing to control for excessive gastric motility probably should sample blood sugar levels and circulating epinephrine before and after feedback training. Perhaps relaxation procedures should be a method used to quiet excessive hypothalamic activity and thus reduce gastric hyperactivity.

The *external anal sphincter* is composed of striated muscle and is innervated by the fourth sacral spinal nerve and the inferior rectal branch of the pudendal nerve. It is *not* supplied by the autonomic nervous system; but the less important *internal anal sphincter* of smooth muscle is.

HEART RATE

Impulses generated in the *sinoatrial* (SA) *node* of special tissue in the wall of the right atrium establish the rate at which the heart beats. Changes in heart rate are dictated by the balance between the "slowing" influence of the heart's parasympathetic innervation from the vagus nerve and the cardioaccelerator function of sympathetic fibers supplying the pacemaker cells and the entire atrial and ventricular myocardium. During physical exertion, for example, heart rate accelerates because of the simultaneous increase in sympathetic activity and decrease in general discharge from vagal nerve fibers supplying the SA node. Cardiac output may be compensated during elevated heart rates by reductions in stroke volume. Thus, the total output from the heart can remain fairly constant over variations in heart rate between 70 and 150 beats per minute.

At any one instant, sympathetic outflow can be influenced by neural pathways subserving spinal and medullary reflexes or higher control centers within the central nervous system. A primary locus from cardioaccelerator function resides in the medulla oblongata, but its specific location is unclear.

The vagus nerves are distributed to the SA and *atrioventricular* (AV) *nodes*, as well as to atrial muscle. When the medullary motor nucleus and its surrounding areas are stimulated, the heart rate is slowed. Thus, this region has been termed the "cardioinhibitory" center. Both cardioaccelerator and inhibitor areas function reciprocally; when one set of fibers is excited, the others are inhibited. The higher brain centers are capable of exerting powerful effects upon the entire cardiovascular system.

Changes in heart rate may provide valuable information about the present physiological state of the cardiovascular system. Heart rate is influenced by stress, exercises or muscle tension (1-6), personality (7-8), motivation, emotion (9), and organic pathology. Heightened levels of arousal, anticipation and muscular tension are intimately linked to increased heart rate activities. Mounting evidence suggests that other basic autonomic functions, such as respiration (2, 10), show activity levels that do not correspond to changes in heart rate. Although it is held by

some (11) that arousal activities tend to increase heart rate while relaxation techniques can be used to lower heart rate, more details about these and other cognitive strategies must be sought.

BLOOD PRESSURE

Arterial blood pressure tends to fluctuate within a narrow range despite changes in posture. Usually only a remarkable change in activity can produce a significant alteration in arterial blood pressure. Regulation of blood pressure is ascribed to specific anatomical entities (Fig. 4.5). Receptors are localized at the bifurcation of the carotid artery (carotid sinus and carotid body) and on the aortic arch and its main branches. These receptors are acutely sensitive to blood pressure changes. Nerve impulses from the carotid sinus receptors ascend in the carotid sinus nerve, which joins the ninth cranial

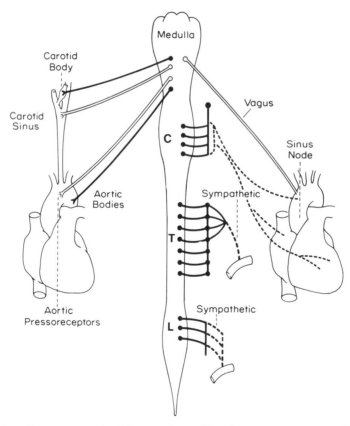

Figure 4.5. Automatic components of the regulatory blood pressure system. (After Scher, A. M., Chapter 34, in *Physiology and Biophysics*, edited by T. C. Ruch and H. D. Patton, W. B. Saunders, Philadelphia, 1966).

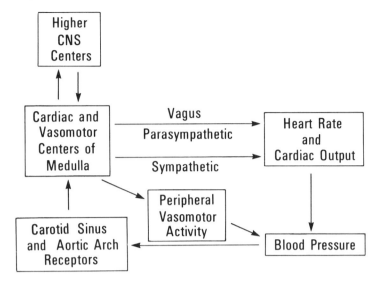

Figure 4.6.   Servo-control system for heart rate and blood pressure regulation.

nerve (glossopharyngeal); those from receptors near the aortic arch travel in the vagus nerve. These sensory fibers in the glossopharyngeal and vagus nerves enter the medulla oblongata and terminate at the *vasomotor* or *cardiac center*. Through synaptic relays in this region, afferent input from carotid or sinus receptors are capable of changing the discharge rate in the appropriate motor nerves.

This servo-control system (Figure 4.6) dictates that when afferent input increases (in response to elevated blood pressure), efferent activity is reduced in the sympathic nervous system and augmented in the parasympathetic nervous system (vagal fibers). As a result, sympathetic drive to the heart is diminished and heart rate tends to decrease. An additional consequence of this particular reflex activity is a diminution of sympathetic tonus to the peripheral arteries, the smooth muscular walls of which relax, thereby reducing the peripheral resistance to blood flow.

Should arterial blood pressure become reduced, afferent input from carotid and aortic pressoreceptors to the medulla oblongata is diminished. Reflexly, an increase in sympathetic efferent activity and a decrease in vagal motor activity occur. This increased sympathetic flow tends to increase heart rate and constriction of peripheral arterial muscular walls—thus leading to increased blood pressure once again (Fig. 4.6). Stimulation of certain additional brainstem areas can modify blood pressure (12). When the *lateral reticular formation*

in the upper medulla is stimulated, an increased blood pressure occurs, i.e., it is a "pressor" center. Conversely, a lower and more central region of the medulla, such as the *area postrema* just lateral to the obex, is a "depressor" center.

The pressor area is believed to be tonically active; it constantly activates preganglionic vasoconstrictor neurons of the periphery, incurring some degree of vascular constriction. Heart rate may also become elevated as a result of pressor center activity. Tonic activity in vagal efferents to the heart suggests there is continuous activity in depressor centers.

Higher centers (hypothalamus and cortex) known to respond to environmental or psychogenic factors contribute to the regulation of the cardiovascular system through actions upon medullary neurons (13, 14). Wang and Borison (15) found that stimuli which activate parasympathetic efferents lead to a subsequent alteration in heart rate within one heartbeat. Activation of sympathetic efferents results in much slower changes in blood vessel constriction and heart rate—sometimes requiring more than 20 seconds.

In addition to pressure receptors, *chemoreceptors* send impulses to medullary centers. They lie in carotid and aortic bodies with their respective pressoreceptors, and they influence cardiovascular and respiratory rates. The most frequent responses of chemoreceptors are to conditions of anoxia and hypercapnea. Clinical situations of hypoxia, apnea, or hypercapnea are not principal concerns for biofeedback as yet (but see references 16 and 17), and the subject is covered well in physiology texts (18-20).

The hypertensive state may be caused by excessive hypothalamic stimulation which interrupts baroreceptor-controlled cardiac inhibition (21). A person's inability to handle stressful situations may well be a contributing factor to the disease. Relaxation techniques would appear to help lower blood pressure (22) and serum cholesterol levels (23). The mechanism contributing to these observations is still uncertain, but laboratory evidence has shown that a reduction in muscle proprioception is related to lowered hypothalamic responsiveness to sympathetic afferent input (24, 25).

With biofeedback, subjects learn to regulate heart rate and blood pressure functions in both the same and opposite directions (26), suggesting there is a multiphysiological dynamic system in self-regulating activities. The implications for the long-range clinical efficacy of biofeedback to control blood pressure and heart rate independently or concurrently are still unclear and remain to be demonstrated.

PERIPHERAL VASCULAR CONTROL

Research reports suggest that such factors as autogenic training, musculoskeletal activity, and hypnosis are not critical factors in biofeedback training for a control of skin temperature. Environmental temperature probably plays a key role in the successful control of digital temperature (see reference 27 for a review).

Digital temperature and cutaneous vasomotor tonus are intimately related. Generally, increased sympathetic outflow to peripheral vessels supplying muscle or skin will result in vasoconstriction, which results in a decrease in skin or muscle temperature, a reduction in peripheral blood flow or a decrease in peripherally recorded blood pressure.

The strategy employed by subjects has a strong psychogenic component, which is probably processed by the *limbic cortex* and hypothalamus to influence autonomic responses. The biofeedback signal helps the subject to assess the adequacy of his otherwise imperceptible afferent input (imagery), and helps to shape or delineate the strategy spectrum.

INTEGRATION OF CARDIOVASCULAR RESPONSES

The cerebral cortex provides the neural substrate necessary for learning to occur, and adequate evidence exists that cardiovascular changes can occur as a result of a conditioning paradigm (28). For example, a noxious stimulus can result in an increased heart rate and peripheral blood flow. If a light or tone precedes the painful stimulus, eventually this visual or auditory cue can produce the autonomic response in the absence of the pain input. Such conditioning of cardiovascular responses shows many of the principles of learning, including generalization, extinction and stimulus generalization (29). These responses differ from some forms of learning since they are slow to extinguish and have a gradient of generalization.

While the cerebral cortex probably works in concert with brainstem structures to bring about learned autonomic changes, ablation and stimulation studies suggest that specific areas of the cerebral cortex are capable of exerting direct influences upon the cardiovascular system. Early primate studies (30) proved that cortical areas adjacent to the motor cortex affect the systemic circulation. Therefore, conditioning of circulatory changes may be related to movement of somatic musculature, a strategy known to induce alterations in vascular activity.

Stimulation of the *rostral cingulate gyrus* on the medial side of the cerebral hemisphere can alter blood flow. Removal of this area in monkeys results in an increased heart rate and a reversal in blood pressure, perhaps due to a reduction in sympathetic tone, leading to a drop in blood pressure and a subsequent reflex tachycardia (31). A lesion in the *association area in the frontal lobe* can partially abolish conditioned circulatory responses. Cortical stimulation of the *insula* and *anterior temporal lobe* produces effects upon heart rate. Since the *limbic system* is active during emotional behavior, a linkage is thus established between patient strategy based upon emotional components and changes in cardiovascular activity.

Hypothalamus

Most subcortical regions involved with circulatory adjustments have specific connections to the cortical areas noted above. Perhaps the subcortical region most involved in cardiovascular adjustments is the *hypothalamus*. Variations in heart rate, contractility of arteries, and blood flow result from stimulation of different hypothalamic nuclear regions. The preoptic hypothalamic region receives input from the cerebral cortex over a pathway which, when stimulated, will produce dilatation of vessels in striated muscles (32). Direct activation of the preoptic nucleus is capable of inducing peripheral vasodilatory effects. The anterior hypothalamus, when subjected to a warm environment, will also produce dilatation in peripheral vasculature. Stimulation of the middle and posterior hypothalamus can effectively alter cardiovascular parameters and functions of the adrenal medulla. The importance of the hypothalamus as a regulator of cardiovascular function is further emphasized by the results from bilateral lesions which disrupt cardiovascular responses to exercise or eating (33).

The hypothalamus is accessible through afferent fibers from the optic tract by way of the *supraoptic* and *ventromedial nuclei*. Thus, visual input is capable of affecting hypothalamic activity. Additional afferent flow comes from the spinal cord and tegmental brainstem regions to the hypothalamus *via* the *mammillary nucleus*. Thus, peripheral sensory information from the periphery enters the hypothalamus. How this information is processed and the efferent pathways are matters of conjecture. Signals arising from the supraoptic, posterior, and tuberal hypothalamic nuclei descend in the *periventricular gray region* of the brainstem and mostly end in the *dorsal longitudinal fasciculus*. This structure projects to those cranial nerve nuclei having parasympathetic functions and also, via several synapses, to spinal cord sympathetic preganglionic cells. There is also evidence for a dorsolateral tract system from the hypothalamus to spinal levels.

Connections between the above-noted sensory and motor pathways and the hypothalamus may play an intimate role in the processing of feedback signals indicative of autonomic activity. The hypothalamus appears to be an integrator for somatic and autonomic aspects of different behavioral activities including temperature regulation, emotional patterns, and blood flow. At the level of the medulla oblongata, there is an interaction between afferents directed to the vasomotor centers and efferents from the cortical limbic system and hypothalamus, but the physiological ramifications of these synapses have not as yet been clarified.

The spinal cord is capable of producing intersegmental autonomic reflexes which can readily be demonstrated in paraplegic patients. Research demonstrates that thermoregulatory centers also reside within the spinal cord (34).

FEEDBACK TO CONTROL HEADACHE

Migraine headache has been characterized by periodic, localized, or general vasodilatations which may be associated with nausea and vomiting. The occurrence of distensions within the branches of the external carotid artery, particularly the superficial temporal, may be preceded by noticeable vasoconstriction. Reduction of circulating dopamine β-hydroxylase (an enzyme which mediates the conversion of dopamine to norepinephrine during sympathetic stimulation) correlates well with the alleviation of migraine (35). Thus, an overactive sympathetic system, possibly brought on by stress, may be implicated in the pathogenesis of migraine.

Tension headaches, on the other hand, are characterized by pain secondary to excessive activity in striated (voluntary) muscles about the scalp, forehead and neck. The relaxation techniques augmented by EMG feedback from striated musculature (36, 37) may be similar to those used by neurological patients to reduce hyperactivity in spastic musculature (see Chapter 3). Perhaps stress-related factors contribute to activation of descending cortical and bulbar motor systems whose final common pathway innervates head and neck muscles.

CONCLUSION

Future progress in clinical biofeedback to influence the autonomic nervous system must be based on clear understanding of neural and hormonal processes as much as it is on behavioral theory and practice outlined in the following chapters. Only through a growing clarification of the scientific principles involved can clinicians hope to advance the real progress of biofeedback.

References

1. Blanchard, E. B. and Young, L. D. Self-control of cardiac functioning: a promise as yet unfulfilled. Psychol. Bull., 79: 145–163, 1973.
2. Cohen, M. J. and Johnson, H. J. Relationship between heart rate and muscular activity within a classical conditioning paradigm. J. Exp. Psychol., 90: 222–226, 1971.
3. Engel, B. T., Gottlieb, S. H. and Hayhurst, V. F. Tonic and phasic relationships between heart

rate and somato-motor activity in monkeys. Psychophysiology, 13: 288–295, 1976.

4. Lynch, W. C., Schupi, U. and D'Anna, J. Effects of isometric muscle tension on vasomotor activity and heart rate. Psychophysiology, 13: 222–230, 1976.

5. Magnusson, E. The effects of controlled muscle tension on performance and learning of heart-rate control. Biol. Psychol., 4: 81–92, 1976.

6. Petro, J. K., Hollander, A. P. and Bouman, L. N. Instantaneous cardiac acceleration in man induced by a voluntary muscle contraction. J. Appl. Physiol., 29: 794–798, 1970.

7. Gatchel, R. J. Locus of control and voluntary heart-rate changes. J. Pers. Assess., 39: 634–638, 1975.

8. Ray, W. G. and Lamb, S. B. Locus of control and the voluntary control of heart rate. Psychosom. Med., 36: 180–182, 1974.

9. Germana, J. Central efferent processes and autonomic-behavioral integration. Psychophysiology, 6: 78–90, 1969.

10. Manuck, S. B., Levenson, R. W., Hinrichsen, J. J. and Gryll, S. L. Role of feedback in voluntary control of heart rate. Percept. Mot. Skills, 40: 747–752, 1975.

11. Blanchard, E. B., Scott, R. W., Young, L. D. and Edmundson, E. D. Effect of knowledge of response on the self-control of heart rate. Psychophysiology, 11: 251–264, 1974.

12. Uvnäs, B. Central cardiovascular control. In Handbook of Physiology, Section I: Neurophysiology, edited by H. W. Magoun. American Physiological Society, Washington, D.C., 1960, vol. 2.

13. Pitts, R. F., Larrabee, M. G. and Ronk, D. W. An analysis of hypothalamic cardiovascular control. Am. J. Physiol., 134: 359–383, 1941.

14. Wang, S. C. and Ranson, S. W. Descending pathways from the hypothalamus to the medulla and spinal cord. Observations on blood pressure and bladder responses. J. Comp. Neurol., 71: 457–472, 1939.

15. Wang, S. C. and Borison, H. L. An analysis of the carotid sinus cardiovascular reflex mechanism. Am. J. Physiol., 150: 712–728, 1947.

16. Feldman, G. M. The effect of biofeedback training on respiratory resistance of asthmatic children. Psychosom. Med., 38: 27–34, 1976.

17. Johnston, R. and Lee, K. H. Myofeedback: a new method of teaching breathing exercises in emphysematous patients. Phys. Ther., 56: 826–831, 1976.

18. Folkow, B., Heymans, C. and Neil, E. Integrated aspects of cardiovascular regulation. In Handbook of Physiology, Section II: Circulation, edited by W. F. Hamilton. American Physiological Society, Washington, D.C., 1965, vol. 3.

19. Guyton, A. C. Textbook of Medical Physiology, W. B. Saunders, Philadelphia, 1966.

20. Willis, W. D. Jr. and Grossman, R. G. Medical Neurobiology, C. V. Mosby, St. Louis, 1973.

21. Abboud, F. M. Relaxation, autonomic control and hypertension. N. Engl. J. Med., 294: 107–109, 1976.

22. Stone, R. A. and DeLeo, J. Psychotherapeutic control of hypertension. N. Engl. J. Med., 294: 80–84, 1976.

23. Patel, C. Reduction of serum cholesterol and blood pressure in hypertensive patients by behavior modification. J. R. Coll. Gen. Pract., 26: 211–215, 1976.

24. Bernhaut, M., Gellhorn, E. and Rasmussen. A. T. Experimental contributions to the problem of consciousness. J. Neurophysiol., 16: 21–30, 1953.

25. Gellhorn, E. Motion and emotion: the role of physiology and pathology of emotion. Psychol. Rev., 71: 457–472, 1964.

26. Schwartz, G. E. Biofeedback and patterning of autonomic and central processes: CNS-cardiovascular interactions. In Biofeedback: Theory and Research, edited by G. E. Schwartz and J. Beatty. Academic Press, New York, 1977.

27. Surwit, R. S., Shapiro, D. and Feld, J. L. Digital temperature autoregulation and associated cardiovascular changes. Psychophysiology, 13: 242–248, 1976.

28. Folkow, B. and von Euler, U. S. Selective activation of noradrenalin and adrenalin producing cells in the cat's adrenal gland by hypothalamic stimulation. Circ. Res., 2: 191–195, 1954.

29. Glickstein, M. Neurophysiology of learning and memory. In Physiology and Biophysics, edited by T. C. Ruch and H. D. Patton. W. B. Saunders, Philadelphia, 1966.

30. Green, H. D. and Hoff, E. C. Effects of faradic stimulation of the cerebral cortex on limb and renal volumes in the cat and monkey. Am. J. Physiol., 118: 641–658, 1937.

31. Smith, O. A. Jr. Cardiovascular integration by the central nervous system. In Physiology and Biophysics, edited by T. C. Ruch and H. D. Patton. W. B. Saunders, Philadelphia, 1966.

32. Eliasson, S., Kindgren, P. and Uvnäs, B. Representation in the hypothalamus and the motor cortex in the dog of the sympathetic vasodilator outflow to the skeletal muscles. Acta Physiol. Scand., 27: 18–37, 1952.

33. Rushmer, R. F., Smith, O. A. and Lasher, E. P. Neural mechanisms of cardiac control during exertion. Physiol. Rev., 40: 27–34, Supplement 4, 1960.

34. Simon, E. Temperature regulation: the spinal cord as a site of extrahypothalamic thermoregulatory functions. Rev. Physiol. Biochem. Pharmacol., 71: 1–76, 1974.

35. Kentsmith, D., Strider, F., Copenhaver, J. and Jacques, D. Effects of biofeedback upon suppression of migraine symptoms and plasma dopamine-β-hydroxylase activity. Headache, 16: 173–177, 1976.

36. Budzynski, T. H., Stoyva, J. M., Adler, C. S. and Mullaney, D. J. EMG biofeedback and tension headache: A controlled outcome study. Psychosom. Med., 35: 484–496, 1973.

37. Wickramaskera, I. E. The application of verbal instruction and EMG feedback training to the management of tension headache—preliminary observations. Headache, 13: 74–76, 1973.

CHAPTER 5

Intentional Psychological Modulation of the Immune System

G. RICHARD SMITH, JR.

For centuries, mankind has speculated about the interrelationship between health and the mind, the psyche, or the brain. One prominent area where much of the speculation is focused has been the relationship between the mind and the immune system. Recent scientific advances have developed what was previously only a speculation into a new developing field of scientific investigation called psychoimmunology or psychoneuroimmunology.

This new field, now quite large, will not be presented in its entirety. There are several excellent comprehensive presentations (1-4). Nor will this review cover the large literature relating the immune system to stress, to various psychiatric disorders such as depression and schizophrenia or to neurological disorders such as Huntington's disease and multiple sclerosis. Rather, it will be limited to empirical reports attempting intentional modulation of the immune system via some psychological mechanism. First, a brief overview of the immune system will be presented, followed by data from animal studies, which represent the bulk of the positive research findings. Finally, a discussion of the scientific data based on human studies will be discussed.

ORGANIZATION OF THE IMMUNE SYSTEM

The immune system provides the body's defense against infections and serves as a surveillance system against neoplastic disease. It is important in disease prevention (immunization) and organ transplantation. More recently, the immune system has been found to be susceptible to the human immunodeficiency virus (HIV), the prime etiological factor in acquired immunodeficiency syndrome (AIDS). Since the immune system is exceedingly complex, a thorough analysis as part of this pres-

entation is not possible; however, a brief overview follows.

There are molecular and cellular components of the immune system, which is usually divided into humoral, cellular, and phagocytic compartments. The humoral compartment refers to antibodies; the cellular refers to lymphocytes; and the phagocytic refers to cells which engulf and phagocytize foreign material such as viruses or bacteria.

Antibodies are made of polypeptide chains called immunoglobulin molecules. They are synthesized by cells called B-cells in response to molecules which are foreign to the body—antigens. Once made, they may circulate freely throughout the body or remain bound to the surface of various immunological cells. Antibodies have physical configurations that allow them to recognize circulating antigens and to bind to them. The antigen-antibody binding allows for the deactivation of the antigen and facilitates its removal by phagocytosis or other means.

Lymphocytes are the primary cells of the cellular component and are of two major types, B cells and T cells. B cells are lymphocytes that produce antibodies. T cells generally do not produce antibodies and circulate as small lymphocytes. They are the main effector of cell-mediated immunity. T cells can be subdivided further into helper, suppressor, and effector T cells (natural killer cells). Cell-mediated immunity, also called delayed-type hypersensitivity, is mediated principally by T cells that have been synthesized in response to antigen. Cell-mediated immunity plays an important role in the body's defense against infectious agents, the killing of tumor cells, and the rejection of allografts, such as organ transplants. One example of cell-mediated immunity is the delayed-type hypersensitivity skin test, such as the one used for tuberculosis testing where an intradermal injection of antigen results in a reaction consisting of redness (erythema) and the development of a small bump (induration), which reaches its peak at approximately 2 days. Various aspects of cell-mediated immunity may be assessed in the laboratory. One frequently used assay is lymphocyte transformation, where lymphocytes growing in tissue culture are exposed to a nonspecific stimulus (mitogen) or a specific stimulus (antigen); then the response of the cells is measured.

Phagocytosis is a function of neutrophils, often called PMNs, short for polymorphonucleocytes. These cells phagocytize bacteria or viruses which have been recognized as foreign, usually as a result of antigen-antibody complex formation. Once phagocytized, the foreign material is destroyed by intracellular mechanisms.

BRAIN-IMMUNE SYSTEM INTERACTIONS

There are several postulated mechanisms whereby the brain may interrelate with the immune system. The most obvious is via the hypothalamus-pituitary-adrenal system where input from the brain results in the production of cortisol in the adrenal gland. Lymphocyte and PMN function are known to be sensitive to corticosteroids administered in large doses from outside of the body. These hormones, produced inside the body, are responsible for mediating the effects of stress and are logical candidates for modulators of psychoneuroimmunology. Unfortunately, empirical data to support this are conflicting. At present, there is no convincing evidence that corticosteroids are the mediators (2-5). Recently, exciting work has demonstrated that there is direct autonomic nervous system innervation of aspects of the immune system such as lymph nodes and the thymus (6-7). While the functional significance of this is not known, this could be one mechanism where the central nervous system (CNS) may affect the immune system. Neurotransmitter receptors have also been found on circulating lymphocytes and in other lymphoid tissue (3). This could be another way that the CNS affects modulation of the immune system.

ANIMAL RESEARCH

The major positive findings in psychoimmunology have been in animal research. Psy-

chological processes in animals can be demonstrated using learning or behavioral conditioning. Psychoimmunology research was first developed by Russians who based their initial studies on Pavlov's work and found it was possible to condition specific immune responses (8). Their work in the 1920s and 1930s was frustrated by their failure to replicate their studies, by the political instability of the investigators, and by the difficulty of translation of their work from Russian. Consequently, this work went largely unnoticed. The pioneering work for psychoimmunology was by Ader and Cohen at the University of Rochester. They have led with numerous well-designed studies that have been confirmed by others. In this section, animal studies involving humoral immunity will be presented, followed by cell-mediated immunity studies, and finally, studies involving disease states will be discussed.

Ader and Cohen's first full report in 1975 demonstrated that conditioning can affect the humoral immunity of rats (9). They used a taste-aversion paradigm which involved pairing a novel drinking solution, in this case, saccharin with an immunosuppressive drug, cyclophosphamide (CY). After the rats recovered from the immunosuppressive effects of the CY, various groups of the rats were reexposed to saccharine alone. When these rats were challenged with an antigen, the conditioned rats did not develop the same level of antibody response as did the rats who were not conditioned. The conditioned rats, however, demonstrated more of a response than did the rats who were exposed to CY on a second occasion. The conditioning was therefore immunosuppressive but not to the extent that would be expected from a reexposure to the immunosuppressive drug. Ader and Cohen's work was rapidly confirmed by Rogers et al. (10), Wayner et al. (11), Gorczynski et al. (12), and Neveu et al. (13). Significantly, the effects of conditioning using this paradigm are relatively small; however, they are notably reproducible. This preciseness and large number of replicative studies have led to its broad acceptance.

Conditioning of cell-mediated immunity in animals has also been demonstrated and was first reported by Bovbjerg et al. (14, 15). They demonstrated a conditioned suppression of the graft-versus-host response that occurs in transplant rejection. Rats were conditioned by pairing saccharin and an injection of CY 48 days before the rats were given an immunological challenge. On the same day as the challenge, the conditioned rats were reexposed to saccharin and a low dose of CY. This was repeated on the next 2 days. As before, the use of conditioning produced an intermediate level of immunosuppression between rats which had exposure to regular doses of CY and those rats which were not conditioned.

The conditioned modulation of cell-mediated immunity has been confirmed by others. Gorczynski et al. demonstrated a conditioned enhancement of the cell-mediated immune response in mice with skin grafts (16). An invitro measure of cell-mediated immunity was demonstrated by Kusnecov et al. to also be sensitive to reconditioned suppression (17). Bovbjerg et al. observed a conditioned enhancement of delayed type hypersensitivity in mice (18). Neveu et al. demonstrated a behaviorally conditioned immunosuppression of mitogen induced lymphocyte stimulation as well as antibody production in mice (13). Recently, Kelly et al. have argued that conditioned test aversion suppresses delayed type hypersensitivity independently of the use of any immunosuppressive drug (19).

Ader and Cohen were the first to apply conditioning principles to the treatment of immunologically mediated disease states (20). They used a mouse model of systemic lupus erythematosus, where a hybrid mouse develops lethal glomerulonephritis, which can be delayed by treatment with CY. They hypothesized that conditioning stimuli could be substituted for some immunosuppressive therapy, thereby delaying the development of the disease and delaying mortality. They used four groups. A standard dose group who were conditioned using saccharin and were given 30 mg per kilogram of CY after every saccharin exposure. The two experimental groups were a nonconditioned group that received 50% less CY than the control group and a conditioned group that received 50% of the CY plus conditioning. The fourth group was an untreated control. Time was measured to the development of disease and to death. As predicted, the conditioned group with the 100% dose of CY had the longest time to development of disease and death. The control group had the shortest time. The two intermediate groups were the two groups with a 50% dose. As hypothesized, the conditioned group with the

50% dose developed disease later and survived longer than did the nonconditioned group with the same dose. Hence, these data demonstrate that conditioning can have a therapeutic immunosuppressive effect.

Further work was reported by Klosterhalfen and Klosterhalfen, who used conditioned immunosuppression to modify adjuvant-induced arthritis in rats (21). They have further extended this work with a different strain of rats and varying concentrations of adjuvant. Sato et al. used a paradigm of recovery from low doses of ionizing radiation to demonstrate that a conditioned psychological stress can impede the recovery from radiation exposure (22). Other confirmation of the effect on disease states comes from Gorczynski et al., who reported that repeated exposures to a conditioned stimulus, which was associated with CY, accelerated tumor growth and mortality in animals who were challenged with a tumor (23). Finally, Ghanta et al. demonstrated a conditioned enhancement of natural killer cell activity in mice with myeloma (24).

These animal data provide striking evidence that the immune system may be modulated by behavioral conditioning. To date, animal models have been used to demonstrate modulation of humoral immunity, cell-mediated immunity, and disease states. As stated above, the mechanisms for this modulation have not been elucidated. As will be seen in the next section, evidence supporting intentional modulation of the immune system is much further advanced in animal models than it is in human subjects.

HUMAN RESEARCH

Much of the psychoimmunology research involving humans has involved the study of stress and its immunological associations. This work has been developed extensively by Kiecolt-Glaser and Glaser. The reader is referred directly to their work (25-27). Another large body of research involves the association of immunological changes with bereavement or depression and decreased cell-mediated immunity. This was first reported by Bartrop et al. then confirmed with a prospective design by Schleifer et al. (28, 29). This latter group has further demonstrated the association of major depressive episodes with decreased cell-mediated immunity (30, 31). Other work has demonstrated immunologic abnormalities in schizophrenic patients as well as other psychiatric and neurological disorders (32-34). This chapter will not review these areas, but instead will concentrate on intentional efforts to mediate human immune function.

Obviously, more restraint is required in research designs involving humans. Additionally, it is more difficult to adequately control studies in humans. Work in this area has employed several psychological processes to modulate the immune system: hypnosis, relaxation and biofeedback, conditioning, and meditation/self-hypnosis.

Hypnosis

A pioneering series of papers by Black and colleagues published in 1963 demonstrated the effect of hypnosis on three aspects of human immunological functioning (35-37). They first demonstrated that 8 of 12 subjects could inhibit immediate hypersensitivity response after suggestion under hypnosis not to respond (35). Highly selected trained hypnotic subjects who showed an allergic response to various allergens were tested using a single-prick-through-drop technique. The skin tests were first applied to one arm as a control condition; the subject was then hypnotized, and the same procedure was applied to the alternate arm. Differences in immediate hypersensitivity were manifested by decrease in skin temperature and a decrease in skinfold thickness.

The Prausnitz-Kustner is an immediate hypersensitivity reaction elicted after transfer of skin sensitizing antibodies using the serum of an allergic subject. Twenty-four hours after the transfer, immediate hypersensitivity is elicited using the prick-through-drop method. When dilutions of the donor serum are placed separately on the arm, a series of decreasing responses is produced. The size of the reaction or wheal is a function of the dilution of the donor's serum and is therefore, a dose response curve. Black demonstrated a shift in the dose response curve for 14 subjects after suggestion under hypnosis not to respond (36).

Using an entirely different aspect of the immune system, Black et al. demonstrated that the delayed type hypersensitivity reaction to tuberculin could also be inhibited by hypnosis (37). This cell-mediated immune reaction is used widely in tuberculosis testing. They studied four highly selected hypnotic subjects

with a before and after comparison using direct suggestion not to respond to the skin test. They measured the erythema and induration at the skin test site, as well as obtaining skin biopsies. After suggestion under hypnosis not to respond, all four subjects' reactions converted from positive to negative. Three of the four subjects had no reaction, and one had only a slight reaction. Biopsies showed that there was the expected cellular infiltration; however, edema did not develop suggesting a vascular phenomenon. This latter study is particularly important, since the tuberculin test is used widely.

Dennis and Philippus reported supporting data of five hypnotized asthmatic patients, who were excellent hypnotic subjects, using intradermal skin tests to elicit immediate hypersensitivity reactions (38). They found that the patients could inhibit their responses when the suggestion was made to not react and that their arm was cold.

There are at least four reports of negative evidence involving hypnosis and its effect on the aspects of the immune system. The first by Zeller, before Black's work, studied five patients to determine whether immediate hypersensitivity skin test responses could be influenced by hypnotic suggestion (39). Suggestion failed to effect the usual response in passively sensitized skin areas and failed to alter skin test responsiveness in subjects sensitive to ragweed or animal dander.

Levine et al. reported an attempt to replicate Black's work using hypnosis to modify immediate hypersensitivity (40). Ten college students as a control group and two groups of 10 patients selected from clinical practices were studied. They performed skin tests using saline as a control, histamine, and ragweek extract using intradermal skin tests. These investigators used naive hypnotic subjects, trained them with only one practice session, followed by the experimental session. Under these conditions, they could not demonstrate an effect of hypnosis.

Beahrs et al. published the results of several pilot studies using five college students with normal skin reactivity and no history of allergies, but who were highly experienced subjects (41). They employed mumps antigen, which produces a delayed type hypersensitivity reaction, as well as trypsin and histamine, both of which produce immediate type hypersensitivity. In neither of their experiments could they demonstrate evidence of an effect of hypnotic suggestion.

In a dissertation, Crawford used hypnosis to modify the percentages of various lymphocyte subpopulations and the level of salivary IgA (42). A 1-hour hypnotic session was the intervening variable with measures 1 day before, immediately before, 1 hour afterward, and 8 days afterward. After the hypnotic session, subjects were asked to practice self-hypnosis and imagery twice daily for 1 week. Analysis produced no evidence to support the overall hypothesis that the experimental group could modify any of the measured immunological parameters.

Conflicting results are obviously present in this area. Zeller's report did not describe methods in detail; therefore, it is difficult to assess this study. Levine et al. used only two hypnotic sessions and hypnotically naive subjects compared with the two positive studies. Beahrs et al. did use highly trained subjects, and their mumps antigen is similar to Black's tuberculin. In their three studies they were unable to reproduce a positive effect of hypnosis. Crawford's approach was substantially different, since the outcome was the percentage of peripheral lymphocytes and salivary IgA. Here, there was only a 1-hour hypnotic session with presumably naive subjects. In this area, it is important to remember the old scientific adage that the "absence of evidence is not evidence of absence." In other words, the failure to replicate work by Dennis and Philippus and by Black does not contradict the work; rather, it simply fails to offer support for these findings.

Relaxation

Kiecolt-Glaser et al. reported a study assessing enhancement of immunocompetence using relaxation and social contact in a group of geriatric subjects who were randomly assigned to either relaxation training, social contact, or no contact (43). Subjects in the relaxation group and social contact group were seen three times weekly for a month. Blood was obtained for immunological studies at baseline, at the completion of the intervention and at 1-month follow-up. The relaxation group demonstrated an enhancement of natural killer cell activity at the end of the intervention. Further, they showed decreases in antibody titers to herpes simplex virus.

In a study of 34 medical student volunteers, Kiecolt-Glaser et al. attempted to modify the effect of examination stress (44). Students were assessed 1 month before examination and again on the second day of examinations. For the group as a whole, there were significant decreases between baseline and examination times in helper T lymphocytes, helper-suppressor cell ratio, and natural killer cell activity. Half of the students had been assigned randomly to a relaxation group which met regularly between sample times. In those students, it appeared that frequency of relaxation practice was a significant modulator of the immunological changes and helper cell percentages. In other words, relaxation may be a moderator of the adverse immunological effects of stress.

Myers attempted to have subjects use relaxation imagery to change the absolute numbers of peripheral lymphocytes (45). Two experimental groups and one control group were taught relaxation skills to criterion level on EMG and temperature biofeedback. The two experimental groups were then taught relaxation imagery. One group was instructed to increase their lymphocytes, while the second group was instructed to decrease absolute lymphocytes. No differences were demonstrated between groups in peripheral lymphocyte count across trials.

In the first report by Kiecolt-Glaser of relaxation in a geriatric population, it does appear that the subjects enhanced natural killer cell activity substantially. There was also a change in herpes simplex antibody titers. Their further finding that relaxation may serve as a moderating influence in stress-mediated immunosuppression is consistent with this finding. Myers' negative finding would indicate that peripheral lymphocyte ratios cannot be effected 2 hours after relaxation. These findings point toward a possible influence of relaxation on cell-mediated immunity, and call for replication.

Biofeedback

At present, biofeedback techniques cannot be directly employed in psychoimmunological research. There is no presently available technology to assess immune function and to provide instantaneous feedback. Many immune functions also appear to take place over days. Therefore, it is unlikely that direct biofeedback techniques can be applied in the near future. One study by Peavey et al. did use bio-feedback-assisted relaxation to modulate one type of immune phenomenon (46). Their study first investigated whether subjects who reported high levels of stress had lower phago-cytic capacity. Subjects received venipuncture for nitroblue tetrazolium tests of phagocytic function. Those who reported high levels of stress tended to have low levels of phagocytic function, while those with low levels of stress tended to have high levels of functioning. The second phase involved the 16 subjects who were in the high-stress, low-phagocytic capac-ity "category." These subjects were randomly assigned to experimental and control groups. Subjects in the experimental group were trained to specific criterion levels of relaxation using EMG and temperature biofeedback. Af-ter subjects who were trained on an individual basis two times a week met criteria levels, blood samples were again obtained to assess phagocytic capacity. As predicted, the experi-mental group showed a significant increase in phagocytic capacity. Thus, it appears that the functional ability of the neutrophils changed during the intervention. This study is impor-tant to replicate since reports to date have not used biofeedback as the modulator nor phago-cytic capacity as an outcome measure.

Behavioral Conditioning

Smith and McDaniel reported the use of be-havioral conditioning to modulate the delayed-type hypersensitivity reaction to tu-berculin (47). In this study, seven tuberculin positive hospital personnel were recruited for a study of the reproducibility of the tuberculin reaction. They used a conditioning paradigm, where subjects were skin-tested at 48 hours, after which they were paid $25. The antigen was drawn into the syringes in front of the subject with the contents of a green vial al-ways applied to the left arm and the contents of a red vial always applied to the right arm. They were told the vials contained varying concentrations of tuberculin and that they would receive the same concentration each month on each arm. Actually, one arm always received tuberculin and the other arm saline. This procedure was followed for 5 months (conditioning trials). On the sixth month (ex-perimental trial), the contents of the vials were switched so that the arm that had been receiv-ing tuberculin received saline and the arm that had been receiving saline received tuberculin.

On the seventh month (control trial) the sub-jects received a tuberculin skin test from an unaltered tuberculin vial on the arm that had received tuberculin during the experimental trial. As predicted, the response to tuberculin on the experimental trial was significantly less than the skin test reaction during the condi-tioning trials or the control trial.

This study demonstrated a behaviorally conditioned modulation of the cell-mediated immune system by conditioning in humans. To date, it is the only such published positive finding. One attempt was made by the same group to replicate this study using 20 tubercu-lin-positive subjects and a nearly identical protocol. No effects of conditioning could be demonstrated.

Meditation/Self-Hypnosis

A single case study was reported by Smith et al. demonstrating a psychological modula-tion of the cell-mediated immune response by an experienced meditator (48). This study uti-lized the cell-mediated immune response to varicella zoster, the virus which causes chick-en pox and shingles. The outcome measures were skin test response and invitro lympho-cyte stimulation to the antigen. The meditator was studied for 3 weeks of baseline with weekly skin tests and blood samples for lym-phocyte stimulation. During the second 3-week block, she was asked to inhibit her re-sponse using a meditative technique. During the final 3-week block, she was asked to re-lease this inhibition and to respond normally. This entire protocol was repeated 9 months later with the same subject. The results demonstrated that this meditator could inten-tionally inhibit her skin test response and sup-press the lymphocyte stimulation assay. The mechanism for this inhibition is not known. To date, there are no known attempts to repli-cate this study.

Recently, a study was undertaken by our same group to extend this line of research. Twenty-eight experienced meditators were randomized into two groups and instructed to either enhance or suppress their immunologi-cal responses to the varicella zoster. After ob-taining baseline blood samples for invitro lym-phocyte stimulation, the subjects were skin-tested. During the intervening 48 hours, the subjects attempted to enhance or suppress their responses using various meditative tech-niques, group meditation, and self-hypnosis.

At the end of 48 hours, the skin tests were read and blood was again obtained for lymphocyte stimulation. As predicted, the enhancer group had significantly larger skin tests compared with the suppressor group. The in vitro lymphocyte stimulation measures were blindly classified by an immunologist into three categories: a suppressed response, a no-change response, and an enhanced response. Again as predicted, the suppressor group had more suppressed responses, and the enhanced group had more enhanced responses. Both results support the overall hypothesis that humans can intentionally modulate their cell-mediated immunity to a viral antigen.

As is evident from the above presentation, there is still limited but promising work to indicate that humans can intentionally modify various immune responses by psychological mechanisms. However, the work is not as well controlled as the animal work, nor has it been confirmed using multiple designs by multiple groups, as has occurred in animal research.

CONCLUSION

As this presentation indicates, there is substantial evidence that various aspects of the immune system in animals can be modulated by behavioral conditioning. The mechanism for this modulation is not known; however, currently, investigators are pursuing these mechanisms actively. In humans, intentional modulation has only scattered reports of positive findings. Unfortunately, few of these reports have been confirmed. However, the reader is reminded that investigations in this area have been limited. If these can be replicated, the field of human psychological immunomodulation would have the scientific basis that the work in animals currently has. Following this, the next important step for the field is to evaluate the relationship of immune changes with disease states to understand whether these changes have clinical relevance. The field of intentional psychological modulation of the immune system is currently a new, struggling field. It is one, though, that offers great excitement and possible promise.

References

1. Ader, R. *Psychoneuroimmunology*, edited by R. Ader. Academic Press, New York, 1981.
2. Ader, R. and Cohen, N. CNS—immune system interactions: Conditioning phenomena. Behav. Brain Sci., *8*: 379–426, 1985.
3. Darko, D. F. A brief tour of psychoneuroimmunology. Ann. Allergy, *57*: 233–8, 1986.
4. Jemmott, J. B., Locke, S. E. Psychosocial factors, immunologic mediation and human susceptibility to infectious diseases: how much do we know: Psychol. Bull., *95*: 78–108, 1984.
5. Ader, R. Conditioned immune responses: adrenocortical influences. Prog. Brain Res., *72*: 79–90, 1987.
6. Bulloch, K. and Pomerantz, W. Autonomic nervous system innervation of thymic-related lymphoic tissue in wild type and nude mice. J Comp. Neurol., *228*: 57–68, 1984.
7. Felten, D. L., Felten, S. Y., Carlson, S. L., Olschowka, J. A. and Livnat, S. Nonadrenergic and peptidergic innervation of lymphoid tissue. J. Immunol., *135*: 755s–765s, 1985.
8. Ader, R. A historical account of conditioned immunobiologic responses. In *Psychoneuroimmunology*, edited by R. Ader. Academic Press, New York, 1981.
9. Ader, R., Cohen, N. Behaviorally conditioned immunosuppression. Psychosom. Med., *37*: 333–40, 1975.
10. Rogers, M. P., Reich, P., Strom, T. B. and Carpenter, C. B. Behaviorally conditioned immunosuppression: replication of a recent study. Psychosom. Med., *38*: 447–51, 1976.
11. Wayner, E. A., Flannery, G. R. and Singer, G. Effects of taste aversion conditioning on the primary antibody response to sheep red blood cells and brucella abortus in the albino rat. Physiol. Behav., *21*: 995–1000, 1978.
12. Gorczynski, R. M., Macrae, S. and Kennedy, M. Factors involved in the classical conditioning of antibody responses in mice. In *Breakdown in Human Adaptation of Stress Towards a Multidisciplinary Approach*, edited by R. Ballieuy, J. Fielding and A. L. Abibatte. Martinus Nighoff, Norwell, MA, 1983.
13. Neveu, P. J., Dantzer, R. and LeMoal, M. Behaviorally conditioned suppression of mitogen-induced lymphoproliferation and antibody production in mice. Neurosci. Lett., *65*: 293–298, 1986.
14. Bovbjerg, D., Ader, R. and Cohen, N. Behaviorally conditioned suppression of a graft-versus-host response. Proc. Natl. Acad. Sci. USA, *79*: 583–5, 1982.
15. Bovbjerg, D., Ader, R. and Cohen, N. Acquisition and extinction of conditioned suppression of a graft-vs-host response in the rat. J. Immunol., *132*: 111–113, 1984.
16. Gorczynski, R. M., Macrae, S. and Kennedy, M. Conditioned immune response associated with allogeneic skin grafts in mice. J. Immunol., *129*: 704–9, 1982.
17. Kusnecov, A. W., Sivyer, M., King, M. G., Husband, J. A., Cripps, A. W. and Clancy, R. L. Behaviorally conditioned suppression of the immune response by antilymphocyte serum. J. Immunol., *130*: 2117–20, 1983.
18. Bovbjerg, D. H., Ader, R. and Cohen, N. Long-lasting enhancement of the delayed-type hypersensitivity response heterologous erythrocytes in mice after a single injection of cyclophospha-

mide. Clin. Exp. Immunol., 66: 539–50, 1986.

19. Kelley, K. W., Dantzer, R., Mormede, P., Solmon, H. and Aynaud, J. M. Conditioned taste aversion suppresses induction of delayed-type hypersensitivity immune reactions. Physiol. Behav., 34: 189–193, 1985.

20. Ader, R. and Cohen, N. Behaviorally conditioned immunosuppression and murine systemic lupus erythematosus. Science, 215: 1534–1536, 1982.

21. Klosterhalfen, W. and Klosterhalfen, S. Pavlovian conditioning of immunosuppression modifies adjuvant arthritis in rats. Behav. Neurosci., 97: 663–666, 1983.

22. Sato, K., Flood, J. F. and Makinodan, T. Influence of conditioned psychological stress on immunological recovery in mice exposed to low-dose X irradiation. Radiat. Res., 98: 381–388, 1984.

23. Gorczynski, R. M., Kennedy, M. and Ciampi, A. Cimetidine reversus tumor growth enhancement of plaosmacytomao tumors in mice demonstrating conditioned immunosuppression. J. Immunol., 134: 4261–66, 1985.

24. Ghanta, V. K., Hiramoto, R. N., Solvason, H. B. and Spector, N. H. Neural and environmental influences on neoplasia and conditioning of NK activity. J. Immunol., 135: 848s–852s, 1985.

25. Kiecolt-Glaser, J. K., Garner, W., Speicher, C., Penn, G. M., Holliday, J. and Glaser, R. Psychosocial modifiers of immunocompetence in medical students. Psychosom. Med., 46: 7–14, 1984.

26. Kiecolt-Glaser, J. K., Speicher, G. E., Holliday, J. E. and Glaser, R. Stress and the transformation of lymphocytes by Epstein-Barr virus. J. Behav. Med., 7: 1–12, 1984.

27 Kiecolt-Glaser, J. K., Stephens, R. E., Lipetz, P. D., Specher, C. E. and Glaser, R. Distress and DNA repair in human lymphocytes. J. Behav. Med. (in press).

28. Bartrop, R. W., Lazarus, L., Luckhurst, E., Kiloh, L. G. and Penny, R. Depressed lymphocyte function after bereavement. Lancet, 16: 834–836, 1977.

29. Schleifer, S. J., Keller, S. E., Camerino, M., Thornton, J. C. and Stein, M. Suppression of lymphocyte stimulation following bereavement. JAMA, 250: 374–382, 1983.

30. Schleifer, S. J., Keller, S. E., Meyerson, A. T., Raskin, M. J., Davis, K. L. and Stein, M. Lymphocyte function in major depressive disorder. Arch. Gen. Psychiatry, 41: 484–6, 1984.

31. Schleifer, S. J., Keller, S. E., Siris, S. G., Davis, K. L. and Stein, M. Depression and immunity. Lymphocyte function in ambulatory depressed patients, hospitalized schizophrenic patients, and patients hospitalized for herniorrhaphy. Arch. Gen. Psychiatry, 42: 129–33, 1985.

32. DeLisi, L. E. Is immune dysfunction associated with schizophrenia? A review of the data.

Psychopharmacol. Bull., 20: 509–13, 1984.

33. Irwin, M. and Gillin, J. C. Impaired natural killer cell activity among depressed patients. Psychiatry Res., 20: 181–2, 1987.

34. Legros, S., Mendlewicz and Wybran, J. Immunoglobulins autoantibodies and other serum protein fractions in psychiatric disorders. Eur. Arch. Psychiatry Neurol. Sci., 235: 9–11, 1985.

35. Black, S. Inhibition of immediate-type hypersensitivity response by direct suggestion under hypnosis. Br. Med. J., 6: 925–929, 1963.

36. Black, S. Shift in dose-response curve of Prausnitz-Kustner reaction by direct suggestion under hypnosis. Br. Med. J., 13: 990–992, 1963.

37. Black, S., Humphrey, J. H. and Niven, J. S. F. Inhibition of Mantoux reaction by direct suggestion under hypnosis. Br. Med. J., 22: 1649–1652, 1963.

38. Dennis, M. and Philippus, M. J. Hypnotic and nonhypnotic suggestion and skin response in atopic patients. Am. J. Clin. Hypn., 7: 342–345, 1965.

39. Zeller, M. The influence of hypnosis on passive transfer and skin tests. Ann. Allergy, 515–517, 1944.

40. Levine, M. I., Geer, J. H. and Kost, P. F. Hypnotic suggestion and histamine wheal. J. Allergy, 37: 246–250, 1966.

41. Beahrs, J. O., Harris, D. R. and Hilgard, E. R. Failure to alter skin inflammation by hypnotic suggestion in five subjects with normal skin reactivity. Psychosom. Med., 32: 627–631, 1970.

42. Crawford, J. C. The effects of hypnosis and imagery on immunity. Dissertation Abstracts International, 46: 2800, 1986.

43. Kiecolt-Glaser, J. K., Glaser, R., Williger, D., Stout, J., Messick, G. and Sheppard, S. Psychosocial enhancement of immunocompetence in a geriatric population. Health Psychol., 4: 25–41, 1985.

44. Kiecolt-Glaser, J. K., Glaser, R., Strain, E. C., Stout, J. C., Tarr, K. L., Holliday, J. E. Modulation of cellular immunity in medical students. J. Behav. Med., 9: 5–21, 1986.

45. Myers, C. R. Relaxation imagery to facilitate endogenous control of lymphocytic function in humans. Dissertation Abstracts International, 45: 2353, 1985.

46. Peavey, B. S., Lawlis, G. F. and Goven, A. Biofeedback-assisted relaxation: Effects on phagocytic capacity. Biofeedback Self Regul., 10: 33–47, 1985.

47. Smith, G. R. and McDaniel, S. M. Psychologically mediated effect on the delayed hypersensitivity reaction to tuberculin in humans. Psychosom. Med., 45: 65–70, 1983.

48. Smith, G. R., McKenzie, J. M., Marmer, D. J. and Steele, R. W. Psychologic modulation of the human immune response to varicella zoster. Arch. Intern. Med., 145: 2110–2, 1985.

CHAPTER 6

Clinical Psychoneuroimmunology: Strategies for Self-Regulation of Immune System Responding

PATRICIA A. NORRIS

The mind operates according to its conception of itself.

. . . John Seaman Garns

Beyond the amelioration or healing of a physical disorder, biofeedback-assisted psychophysiologic therapy provides the experiential knowledge of self-regulation, self-mastery, and voluntary control, and an improved and empowered self-image. This has far-reaching consequences, for the image that we hold of ourselves influences everything that we are and everything we do. For centuries, physicians and healers have noted the relationships between psychological well-being and physical health, between various kinds of psychological stress and physical ailments and diseases. Quotes from great physicians, and the enduring medical literature from ancient times to the present, abound with stories and pronouncements about these relationships, some well documented, all reflecting the observations and thinking of their time.

In modern medicine, the relationship between stress and immune system suppression has been well established by both animal and human research; psychological, physiological, and environmental stress can lead to a breakdown in immune resistance, and many of the mechanisms and pathways of action are well understood. In the presence of stress, a large and complex number of mechanical, chemical, and immune changes take place as the body attempts to defend itself or restore homeostasis. Until recently, however, the relationship between stress management and enhancement of immune function was not as easily demonstrated in scientific, neurohumoral terms. Now, however, with the huge leap in technological medicine, in microchem-

istry and neurobiology, and immunology, the pathways of action of immune enhancement are coming into focus.

THE RATIONALE OF PSYCHONEUROIMMUNOLOGY

The role of the autonomic nervous system, of the limbic/hypothalamic/pituitary axis, and of the neuropeptides and other neurotransmitters and neuromodulators in mind-body interactions is being intensely studied, and is providing the rationale for self-regulation of the immune system. Many communication links between the central nervous system and the immune system exist. Whenever a unique neuropeptide is discovered, receptors are subsequently found for the new neuropeptide on immune system cells. Not only do immune system cells receive messages from the central nervous system via neuropeptides, but they actually manufacture these neuropeptides themselves, and send messages back to the central nervous system. The same chemicals in the brain that control moods, perceptions, and actions *are also made by the immune system.* Thus, the basis for a cybernetic feedback loop between the central nervous system and the immune system is clearly established. Not only do psychological states affect the immune system, but also the immune system influences brain, behavior, and mood states.

Elmer Green first proposed a rationale for psychophysiologic self-regulation in 1969 (see his Figure 19.1 in this book). According to this rationale, perception (or imagery) elicits mental and emotional responses, generating limbic, hypothalamic, and pituitary responses that bring about physiologic changes, which are again then perceived and responded to, completing a cybernetic feedback loop (1). This same rationale is also emerging as the *modus operandi* of *psychoimmunologic self-regulation*. In fact, clinical psychoneuroimmunology may be seen as a subcategory of psychophysiologic self-regulation.

At least two comprehensive, annotated bibliographies covering research on mind and immunity have been published by Locke and Hornig-Rohan (2) and Locke (3). As a cross-disciplinary field, psychoneuroimmunology is comprised of essentially all the sciences concerned with life processes, including psychology, psychiatry, biology, anatomy, endocrinology, biochemistry, neurology and neuroscience, and hematology, as well as immunology. This synergy can produce complexity: in January, 1988, a lecture I attended by endocrinologist Leonard Wisnesky was entitled "Psychoneuroimmunoendocrinology," a word with two more letters than antidisestablishmentarianism.

In the preceding chapter of this book, Richard Smith describes much of the research pertaining to psychoneuroimmunology, some of which is now demonstrating the marvelous specificity of visualization. Until recently, almost all the hundreds of research studies on mind and immunity have been directed toward demonstrating the effects of stress on immune system reactions, and little attention was given to proactive modification of this immune system behavior through self-regulation. Such modification of immune system responses through self-regulation—through gaining a measure of voluntary control over the physiological processes that affect the immune system—is the essence of clinical psychoneuroimmunology.

IMMUNE SYSTEM CORRELATES OF EMOTIONAL STATES

Of great interest for the biofeedback clinician is the fact that in animal research, the greatest modifier of the immune response to stress has been the amount of control the animal is allowed to exert over the stressor. In human research, *control* (or the absence of control) has appeared most often as the dominant factor in the outcome, or process, being measured. The *exceptional* cancer patient, the *hardy* personality, the *participative* patient, a *fighting* spirit, are some of the characteristics cited in study after study associated with positive outcome and enhanced immune function.

Conversely, *helplessness* and *hopelessness, passivity, depression,* inability to express emotion, the *uncomplaining* and *compliant* patient are characteristics often cited as associated with negative outcomes and lowered immune competence. Some variation of these themes can be found in essentially every cancer study, providing mounting evidence for the influence of emotional (limbic) factors in clinical psychoneuroimmunology.

Why is this of primary interest to biofeedback clinicians? Because control is associated with positive outcome; lack of control is associated with negative outcome; and self-control is what we teach. Peavy (4), Keicolt-Glaser et al. (5,6), Hall (7), Gruber et al. (8), and Velkoff (9) have all demonstrated, in one way or another, the capacity of the immune system to respond to intentional behavioral strategies, intentionality, and visualization.

We are gradually developing an understanding of how volitional mechanisms determine physiologic response, and of how mentation gets translated into action. Although the mechanisms of walking, talking, and serving a tennis ball via the sensory-motor cortex and the striate musculature are understood, the exact relationships between image, volition, and eventual behavioral response may be as yet undefined. Supported by the concepts of Claude Bernard, Flanders Dunbar, W. B. Cannon, and Hans Selye, an understanding of how the mind influences and controls the autonomic nervous system, affects cardiovascular behavior and gastrointestinal responses, is being recognized and systematically investigated. Only in the last decade, however, have specific mechanisms been discovered whereby visualization (volitional mental imagery) can have a direct physiological effect on the immune system. It is becoming evident that the central nervous system and the immune system are "hard-wired" together, and what some physicians and others have known intuitively—and empirically—for hundreds of years is being validated.

ADJUNCTIVE CANCER THERAPY—A WELLNESS MODEL

Since 1978, when I began treatment of a young boy with an inoperable brain tumor (10), we have used biofeedback and visualization in the Menninger Biofeedback and Psychophysiology Center as the mainstay of a multimodal adjunctive cancer therapy. We follow a *wellness* model rather than a sickness model, with all our patients, but this is particularly emphasized for cancer patients, and for patients with other immune system disorders. Our protocol is designed to help patients restore or maintain the greatest level of health possible, with the rationale that cancer will have less chance of taking over a healthy, optimally functioning body. To this end, our approach takes into account, as much as possible, each aspect of the whole person—physical, emotional, cognitive, and spiritual.

Adjunctive cancer therapy cannot be considered a *cure* for cancer. Of course, we still do not have any universal cure for cancer, despite extensive research on potential treatments and on viruses and other causative agents. Neither with chemotherapy nor radiation is the cancer cured and the patient free of disease. To be cured, the patient must be free of cancer and have an intact immune system that can protect against future cancer cells. As cancer is better understood in its environmental and psychosocial context, it is becoming clear that not only carcinogens, but also stress, poor immune functioning, and the biochemistry of helplessness and hopelessness play a very large role in outcome. Conversely, stress management, relaxation and eustress, enhanced immune functioning, and psychological well-being and empowerment together play important roles in positive outcomes. They are some of the dominant characteristics observed in cancer survivors, and have created considerable scientific interest in describing "the exceptional cancer patient." We believe that anyone can potentially learn to be an exceptional patient, and these are the goals of adjunctive cancer therapy.

Nutrition

Nutritional considerations are now being recognized by many experts, including the American Cancer Society as important in the prevention of cancer. It seems evident that nutritional factors become even more important once cancer is detected, to help to prevent its spread and to bolster host resistance factors. Our Biofeedback Center physician provides nutritional counseling for each cancer patient with the intent of optimizing the diet for pure, noncarcinogenic foods, recommending fresh vegetables, fruits and whole grains in abundance, fish, fowl, nuts and seeds, and dairy products in moderate to minimal amounts, and the elimination of refined and processed foods, fats and fried foods, and red meat. Extra vitamins and other nutritional elements that may be lacking are also prescribed. Although some cancer diets require drastic change, people need to be comfortable with what they eat, and enjoy their food; therefore, we generally tell patients to use as many aspects of the diet as they feel comfortable with, but not to feel a need to be austere or inflexible in order to succeed.

Exercise

Exercise is another important element of health in our wellness model. Recommendations for exercise are individually tailored to meet the preferences and comfort of the patient, but the emphasis is on improving flexibility, muscle tone, and general health. Prescribed exercise generally includes walking, and may include running, swimming, tennis, or racquetball if the person is able to participate. Yoga and Tai chi are good, and even karate or aikido are excellent choices for engendering a feeling of forcefulness and power. Even a completely bedridden patient can tense and relax various muscle groups, flex fingers and toes, and feel stronger. Symbolically, exercise gives a message to our bodies that we are building our strength, and moving toward health. Taking part in as many healthful things as possible gives the whole self a message, consciously and unconsciously, of the intention to get well, that the process of getting well is already occurring.

Diaphragmatic Breathing

Good breathing is an essential part of good health, and many books have been written about the healing aspects of breathing exercises. The science of breath has long been studied in Eastern systems such as yoga and chi gong (qi gong), and some Western medical researchers, seeking a unified theory of disease, are now looking at tissue *anoxia* as a basic underlying cause of ill health (11, 12). Proper *diaphragmatic* breathing promotes efficient gas exchange in the lungs and so rehabilitates oxygen deficiency disorders, balances the autonomic nervous system, reduces physiologic correlates of anxiety, massages the mesentery and splanchnic areas (promoting better blood flow), and pumps the lymphatic system, particularly the cisterna chyli. I have come to believe that I would choose correct diaphragmatic breathing if we had to share only one tool or technique for maximally improving physical health. The physiologic processes of respiration, and the critical role that breathing has in maintaining the body's metabolic processes, are covered comprehensively in *The Hyperventilation Syndrome: Research and Clinical Treatment,* by Fried (13).

Breathing also can have a profound effect on states of consciousness, and conversely, breathing styles are often a reflection of states of consciousness. Rapid, shallow breathing is often a sign of anxiety and has long been noted to be a secondary consequence of panic and fear. Almost everyone who does rapid shallow breathing for a few minutes experiences feelings of anxiety, and in agoraphobic patients, this procedure provokes symptoms identical to those of panic attacks. The breathing cycle is intimately connected to both sympathetic and parasympathetic actions of the autonomic nervous system. Conscious, deep diaphragmatic breathing is one of the best ways to quiet the autonomic nervous system. It has the effect of initiating a cascade of visceral relaxation responses. As yogis have long maintained, breathing, more than any other bodily activity, can be either voluntary or involuntary, can be either conscious or unconscious, and can therefore serve as a bridge between conscious and unconscious psychological and physiological processes.

Other elements of our therapeutic protocol include exploration of mental and emotional stresses preceding the onset of cancer, present life stresses, and psychological and psychotherapeutic issues such as denial and repression, hope, grieving, and attitude toward death. We use a theoretical model for psychological self-exploration based on Psychosynthesis (14). Goal setting, and participating as fully as possible in *living,* engaged in productive, enjoyable activities are encouraged. They constitute a conscious "vote for life." Last but not least, the central features of our program of adjunctive cancer therapy are acquisition of biofeedback-assisted psychophysiological self-regulation skills, and visualization and imagery directed toward the specific healing process, and as a vehicle for conscious-unconscious communication of psychological and physiological processes.

BIOFEEDBACK AND VISUALIZATION

From the beginning of therapy, we make it clear that there is an inextricable connection of visualized imagery with biofeedback. In simplest terms, visualization tells our bodies what to do, and biofeedback tells us how well the body carries out our instructions. Willful imagery, visualization, precedes action, and for success in learning or performing intentional action, feedback must follow. This is clinically demonstrated by having the patient perform a few simple movements. Visualizing *always* precedes willful action.

Some simple, relevant physiologic explanations provide a preliminary cognitive framework for learning biofeedback skills. Feedback, we tell the patient, is essential to the learning of *every* skill. Learning to walk, run, hop, and skip, for example, requires, at a minimum, proprioceptive feedback of the position of the body and limbs in space, and is enhanced by visual feedback as well. Although all voluntary physical activity is initiated by some form of image or visualization, it need not necessarily be conscious. Repetitive actions, like driving, can be performed with little or no conscious attention. *Learning* a skill, however, involves action and feedback; *practice* consists of repeating the action until outcome matches image. One definition of a skill is that it has become "unconscious" and automatic; the piano player no longer thinks of Every Good Boy Does Fine, and the typist no longer thinks of where the keys are, or which finger goes where.

I have found it particularly useful to introduce biofeedback and visualization *simultaneously*, without initially calling attention to this conjunction. Some examples are—

"if you visualize sucking on a lemon, at the same time feeling, being aware of, making *mental contact* with the sublingual parotid glands, the salivary glands under your tongue, you will probably become aware of increased salivation; if you imagine a hot wind blowing in your eyes, or visualize slicing an onion, while at the same time feeling the lacrimal glands, the glands that put tears in your eyes, you become aware of increased moisture to the eyes. These things are obvious. If, however, you imagine enthusiastic excitement and visualize your heart beating faster, you probably will not detect the change, and if you now imagine a relaxed, cozy scene with a calm, slow heartbeat, it may not feel any different. It is most likely, however, that your heart rate did indeed change in the direction you visualized, at least for a few beats; but in order to learn if your visualization did create a heart rate change, you will need feedback. This is useful for gaining control, to be able to bring about the desired change predictably. If you focus attention on exactly how your hands are feeling, and then imagine a feeling of *warmth*, they may very well begin to warm slightly, but in order to know what is happening, and then learn to make it happen any time you wish, you will need feedback. With biofeedback, you can get external, objective information about changes in your heart rate, and changes in the temperature of your hands."

These ideas are conveyed to all biofeedback patients, even small children, with appropriate wording, to establish clearly from the outset the links between visualization, physiologic behavior, and voluntary control.

In addition to emphasizing initially this link between visualization and action, we also provide an explanation of the biofeedback rationale, and discuss stress, distress, and eustress, and the usefulness of establishing voluntary control over the homeostatic "settings" of various autonomic processes. (A complete description is given by Green and Green in Chapter 19 on general and specific applications of thermal biofeedback.) This rationale is remarkably useful, satisfies the left cortex, and enhances believability and the willingness to *try*. Biofeedback clinicians everywhere have noted how much more easily children can accomplish various self-regulation tasks. This is primarily because their left cortex does not interfere with progress by countering with disbelief, with negative visualization—"That probably can't work," "I probably can't do it." These powerful negative visualizations make it hard for many adults to learn new things.

THE POWER OF BIOFEEDBACK

Biofeedback-assisted self-regulation plays three vital roles in clinical psychoneuroimmunology. First, it ameliorates stress, and for a cancer patient, there is a *triple* stress to deal with: (1) the stress that predated the cancer as a factor leading to its onset, (2) the stress of having cancer and dealing with the threats to self-image, identity, and personal security, and (3) the stress of a treatment that can be painful, frightening, and depleting of energy and healing resources.

On the other hand, the acquisition of volitional self-regulation modifies how stress is perceived, and modifies the physiologic responses to stress. Biofeedback helps provide skills and resources for dealing with stressors, for seeing stress as a challenge, and seeing cancer as a learning opportunity. Learning to control physiologic responses to stress generally leads to a sense of energy and exhilaration, as opposed to worry and despair, and this has a powerful healing effect.

Learning to control stress responses means learning to manage limbic system perturbations; and limbic arousal increases adrenergic and cholinergic responses, and has mutagenic effects such as decreased lymphocyte production, impaired natural killer cell activity, and decreases in phagocytosis. At the very least, learning to lower limbic arousal decreases these mutagenic effects, and may well reverse them.

Specific Biofeedback Techniques

The basic biofeedback strategy for stress management is to be able to achieve, and eventually maintain: (1) warm hands, accomplished by lowering sympathetic nervous system tone, promoting *quiet emotions*; and (2) relaxed muscles, promoting a *quiet body*. Often, a quiet body and quiet emotions are sufficient for promoting a quiet mind, but sometimes we use EEG alpha and theta training to reduce mental stress and achieve mental quietness. Similar to Schultz's state of "autogenic shift" (15), we have found that a quiet body, quiet emotions, and a quiet mind constitute the physiologic state that is most conducive for visualization to be effective (16). This stress management training is the "core" of biofeedback-assisted self-regulation training, and generally precedes specific visualization and imagery work, regardless of the disorder being treated—agoraphobia, cancer, rheumatoid arthritis, a gastrointestinal disorder, or any of the more common stress disorders, such as migraine or tension headache, or high blood pressure.

In addition to stress control, biofeedback training often helps patients to ameliorate many of the *side effects* of medical treatment, reducing pain, anxiety, nausea, fatigue. This promotes healing, and makes patients feel more in control of their own physiologic responses. This "benign circle," as opposed to the "vicious circle" of negative thinking and "feeling worse," helps patients stimulate, or direct, or reinforce, their healing processes.

Most important, acquiring skills of volitional control of many aspects of physiologic functioning enhances confidence and gives a strong sense of empowerment. For this reason, I have found it worthwhile to teach a number of extra self-regulation skills. One skill includes sequentially, or individually, warming hands, feet, knees, shoulders, neck, hip (at least a few of these areas), to feel and confirm self-mastery, and secondarily, to increase blood flow to an area of pain or diminished circulation if necessary. Another kind of skill includes deep muscle relaxation of several areas. Voluntary control of forehead muscle relaxation is always learned, and often, relaxation of trapezius, forearm, and other sites is learned as well. Other biofeedback skills may include increasing and decreasing heart rate at will, increasing and decreasing electrodermal response at will, moving back and forth at will between beta and alpha brain wave frequencies, and increasing theta. All these biofeedback tactics provide indispensable, experiential evidence of mind controlling body, of visualizations influencing physical processes. It is not a question of *believing*, or thinking, or feeling, or hypothesizing, that visualizations can effect healing, but of *knowing*, from the inside, that this is true.

EXPLORING IMAGES AND BUILDING VISUALIZATIONS

Before continuing, a crucial distinction must be made. It is necessary to differentiate between two complementary concepts, *visualization* and *imagery*. *Visualization* is the consciously chosen, intentional instruction to the body. *Imagery* is the spontaneously occurring, "appearing in consciousness" modifier, qualifier, or belief emerging from the unconscious. A two-way communication exists between visualization and imagery. Visualization acts as a message *to* the unconscious, which includes the subcortical parts of the brain, especially the limbic-hypothalamic-pituitary axis. On the other hand, spontaneously arising images are messages *from* the unconscious to the cortex, to consciousness, and, like dreams, carry insights and symbolic meanings.

In starting out with a patient, it is important and necessary to explore whatever conscious and unconscious imagery *already* exists regarding internal states of health and disease,

what they imagine is presently occurring in his or her own body. Ready-made visualizations on video and audio cassettes, however much touted, are of only limited value, or of value only as examples for forming individualized imagery that matches the patient's own unconscious beliefs and conscious knowledge, about what is actually happening in his or her own body. Often, it is necessary to help a patient modify, or reinterpret, seriously misunderstood imagery or fearful fantasies about what may be occurring. The goal of this first stage is to help the patient to be realistic about what the condition actually is, neither exaggerated or minimized, and to be optimistic about what can occur. In other words, a crucial part of self-regulation for cancer amelioration is the development of one's own *individual* visualization, using internal symbology that has deep, unconscious, personally unique meanings.

In working with many cancer patients, at all stages of their syndromes, it has been fascinating to see evidence of unconscious knowledge of their own physiologic conditions. Patients often have dreams that are physiologically accurate about a particular condition, even before symptoms appear. Carl Jung was expert at translating dream symbols into diagnoses even when the imagery was obscure, and many other clinicians have observed similar accurate unconscious knowledge appearing in dreams. Fortunately, the same knowledge often can be elicited from the unconscious by using active imagination in *guided imagery* trips into the body, and through *drawings*.

Guided Imagery

Generally, it is useful for the therapist to "set the scene" for the initial guided imagery trip in the body. A journey through the digestive tract, for example, might start out with

". . . imagine that you are extremely small, and can enter your body through the cave of your mouth. Walking across your tongue, you can observe the large shiny white stalactites and stalagmites of your teeth. Rosy light comes in through your cheeks, just as rosy light shines out from your cheeks if you put a flashlight into your mouth and puff out your cheeks, since our bodies are translucent . . ."

Occasionally, patients are unwilling or afraid to look inside their bodies. If possible, they must be helped to do so, and techniques similar to those used in systematic desensitization can be used effectively. The results of these exploratory imagery trips into the body are sometimes immediately confirmed. One patient who had injured his back, and had several hours to wait until an osteopathic appointment, got a clear mental picture of his third lumbar disk slipped out to the left. This happened while we were imaging his spine for reducing muscle tension and easing pain. This image was exactly confirmed by x-ray later that afternoon. Another patient received such a clear image of her pancreatic duct, while we were doing an internal dialogue with the body, that she was able to find it in an anatomy book and then go to her doctor with this image. This led to the correct diagnosis of a condition that had eluded diagnosis for over 2 years. In another case, a brain tumor patient beheld a "funny little white thing" where his tumor had been; 5 months later, x-rays revealed a small chunk of calcification in just that spot.

More often than not, in internal exploratory trips, there is no immediate confirmation of the accuracy of imagery, but nevertheless, the images often have important *symbolic* meaning for the individual, and form the basis for beginning the intentional visualization process. Gradually, through a reciprocal cyclic process of visualization and imagery, a bridge is built between conscious and unconscious processes, which includes cortical and subcortical processes, the "conscious" and "unconscious" portions of the brain. Gradually, a measure of *conscious* control of the unconscious is gained.

CHARACTERISTICS OF EFFECTIVE VISUALIZATION

1. The visualization must be *ideosyncratic*. Each of us has a whole panoply of ways of thinking, images based on our own experiences and knowledge. Imagery that would have meaning to a physicist or an engineer might not be useful to a space buff, and a musician might well employ different imagery from a football player. The best imagery fits one's own understanding of the world.

2. The visualization must be *ego-syntonic* to have power and energy behind it. It must conform with the patient's deepest desires and values, and it must be something the patient is *willing* to do, or allow to happen. Sometimes

patients need help here. Sometimes they may unconsciously identify with their cancer cells, feel sorry for them, unconsciously try to protect them, or feel that if their immune system is "good," it won't engage in killing. These attitudes initially surprised me, but I and many other clinicians have met them so often that I now am aware always of the necessity to watch for, and eventually modify with facts and education as well as other imagery, their existence in a satisfactory—and ego-syntonic—way. The imagery process must feel justified to the patient, must be proper, a correct action, in order to be sufficiently empowered to defeat the enemy.

3. Another important attribute of an effective visualization is the "sensation" that it is *taking place inside the body*. It must have kinesthetic and sensory as well as visual components. Making mental and sensory contact with the part of the body being visualized is essential. Internalization of the visualization is usually accomplished fairly easily during the first guided imagery trips into the body, when sensory as well as visual imagery is encouraged, and often, sensory information is the guide for understanding what is happening deep within the body.

4. The visualization must be *anatomically correct*. This does not mean that it need be technically and biologically accurate, but rather that it must contain the desired outcome, whether it is symbolic or strictly organic. Inexperienced critics often argue that visualization cannot work, since the visualizer would have to know too many details, which lymphocytes in what combinations of B cells and T cells, killer and suppressor cells, and macrophages, are needed. Sometimes, patients also believe, initially, that they need to understand *exactly* how to direct their immune system to be successful; but, in fact, trying to be scientifically and technically accurate leads to a feeling of frustration and helplessness. Being anatomically correct means correctly "telling" the body what is wanted, and letting the wisdom of the body take over the rebalancing of homeostasis, to accomplish the desired physiologic change.

Most patients eventually select symbolic visualizations rather than specific organic ones. I believe symbolic visualizations are often more powerful, precisely because they overcome the tendency (and associated doubt) of trying to know exactly what is going on at the cellular level. Symbolic visualizations of the immune system attacking a tumor can have many patterns: white knights slaying a dragon, armies of large white dogs eating raw hamburger with relish, soldier cells swarming over a tumor; but all resulting in its destruction and being carried away. These visualizations are all anatomically similar, involving destruction and removal of what is harmful to the body. Anatomically correct visualizations for healing injured tissue or mending a bone, are *building* visualizations, and might include scaffolding, smoothing on mortar, bringing fibers and nutriments to an area to build it up, not destroy it.

5. *Constancy* is another characteristic of effective visualization. We have used constancy or what we have termed "constant instant practice" in a variety of situations, and it can be especially effective in cases of cancer, autoimmune disorders, and other debilitating or life-threatening illnesses. The idea of constant instant practice is that it consolidates a skill, makes the required response an automatic reaction, helps to establish a new, healthier homeostatic balance, and promotes transfer of training (17). The patient is asked to repeat, as often as possible, a brief visualization of the physiologic action or response he or she wants to occur, such as warm hands, relaxed muscles, or a very specific change such as increased blood flow to an arthritic knee.

For cancer patients, this can be particularly useful in a number of ways. Patients are encouraged to respond to all the "hooks" (alerting signals from the body) with a very brief visualization. For example, every time they feel pain, they can respond with "thanks, body, for reminding me to send white cells there (or blood flow there, etc.) again" Every time their condition leaps into consciousness with a sinking emotional feeling, they can respond with "good, my mind is reminding me to repeat my visualization again." This technique not only assures that the practice continues frequently, but also takes some of the toxicity and resistance out of pain, confronting emotions, etc. and provides an opportunity to be an active participant rather than a *passive* sufferer.

6. An effective visualization is like a *blueprint*. The patient is encouraged to visualize the cancer being completely destroyed, and the battle being won, each time she or he

practices the visualization. Visualizing in this way constitutes a blueprint that expresses the intentionality of the healing process. Just as the blueprint for a house one intends to build is real even before the foundation is dug, and provides guidelines to be followed in the building, so this blueprint is a real description of the plan for the body, even though it takes time for the body to carry out the intention and the instructions. Seeing oneself as well, the outcome as successful, is an important part of this process.

7. Visualization must *incorporate the medical treatment* being given. A visualization of the medical treatment as a partner to the body's own healing process needs to be established. Visualization of the medical treatment being powerful and effective is of the utmost importance. Patients often have an ambivalent attitude toward their medical treatment, characterized by the unconscious dichotomous attitudes of "I must have this treatment to live," and "This treatment is killing me." The ways in which patients visualize their treatment, as well as the images, conscious and unconscious, that they have of treatment, is a major factor in how their bodies will respond to treatment. A positive attitude toward treatment, feeling it as a true helper to the body's well-being, even if it is temporarily very difficult, is important. Treatments often include the most powerful agents that medical science has to offer against each particular type of cancer, and although the whole system may temporarily suffer, the healthy cells are strong and can resist harm and repair themselves, whereas the cancer cells are weak and confused and cannot survive.

In addition, it is extremely helpful to have a positive visualization of the medical treatment right while receiving it. A visualization is developed that includes welcoming the treatment into the body, seeing it directed to the desired site of action, seeing all the healthy cells cooperating in its direction or deflection to a tumor site, and seeing the immune system *aiding* the treatment during the treatment itself. Again, the best visualizations are those that patients develop themselves, but I have found in general that patients often need particular help with this, probably because the chemotherapy or radiation is not an internally generated process, and therefore is not "familiar" to the unconscious parts of the brain.

PSYCHOLOGICAL ISSUES—IN BRIEF

It is beyond the scope of this chapter to discuss the very important psychological issues that directly affect the course of therapy, more than to briefly touch upon the most crucial— patient responsibility, denial, and issues of death and dying.

Patient Responsibility

Probably the most frequent criticism of adjunctive cancer therapy has to do with issues of patient responsibility. Some physicians and others have suggested that it is cruel and unethical to suggest to patients that they can assume some responsibility for their healing. One reason is that it seems to some people— and to some patients as well—that this implies that they are guilty of *causing* their disease. There is, however, a world of difference between the fixing of blame and the accepting of responsibility for a future outcome. To be consciously responsible for one's health does not imply that one is consciously responsible for one's illness.

The hypothetical objection to the concept of patient responsibility is that if patients try to affect the outcome of their illness and then are not successful, die anyway, or worsen, they will feel guilty for failing. In my experience, patients *never* feel this way, and their families seldom do either. Patients feel good about their efforts, whether for adjunctive cancer therapy, or for any treatment that *they choose and cooperate with*, including even the harshest of medical treatments. Physician Bernie Siegel (18) has pointed out that any treatment that a patient chooses, cooperates with, and believes will be effective has a much greater chance of succeeding. Perhaps the real failure of a patient is the failure to participate, to simply be passive and accept without any positive expectations, whatever "is done to" oneself. Accepting a role and participating in a healing process has benefits every single day, day by day, and these benefits are sufficient unto themselves.

Denial

Denial is a big factor in cancer outcome, and there are two major facets of it, and much confusion. Studies of personality and cancer have often shown that characteristics associated with survival are (1) a fighting spirit, and (2) denial—that one has an illness at all, that the

cancer exists. These may be useful, at least to the extent that they constitute a visualization that one is well, but I do not believe that this sort of denial is usually the case. More often, a positive attitude and a positive expectancy for healing in the face of drastic disease or poor statistical prognosis is called "denial." But this is a psychological error of inexperienced therapists. The opposite of this state in a patient would be hopelessness, and this is known to be a poor prognostic indicator, and possibly a carcinogenic attitude in itself. Applebaum (19), in discussing the failure to study adequately the psychological effects of emotions and beliefs on cancer, states that ". . . the options are few and clear. One can assume that one has a hopeless disease, that one's chances for survival are dictated irrevocably by the statistics attached to one's disease and its treatment, . . . or embrace the assumption that . . . if one works at it one may create a new set of statistics. It is a choice that the therapist, as well as the patient, must make."

I have learned that it is very useful to point out to patients that *they are not a statistic*, that statistics have nothing to do with individuals. It is as false to say that each individual has a 20% chance of surviving a particular cancer for 5 years, regardless of other factors such as their physical condition, or what they themselves do about their cancer, as it is to tell a particular individual that they have a 20% chance to run a 5-minute mile, regardless of their physical condition or what exercising they may have done. *What we do affects our chances.*

Death and Dying

No patient comes into adjunctive cancer therapy, or even receives a diagnosis of cancer, without coming face to face with feelings and beliefs about death and dying, and without confronting the possibility of their own imminent death. At the beginning of adjunctive cancer therapy, it is very useful to let the patient know that this is a healing process that can have being well as an outcome or may promote a "healing death." It is important to give a patient permission to explore attitudes and emotions about dying at the outset, and then to place all attention on wellness. Some patients are very fearful of dying, and I have found it useful to help patients feel more at ease, to "make friends" with their death in order to free them to concentrate on being well.

Far from being the enemy, death is the last great adventure that this life has to offer. Constant fearful thoughts about death are visualizations that make it more difficult to place energy and imagery on wellness. No one can postpone death forever, and a cure does not confer immortality on anyone, and yet this often seems to be an unconscious agenda of both therapist and patient.

References

1. Green, E. E., Green, A. M. and Walters, E. D. Feedback technique for deep relaxation. Psychophysiology, 6: 371–377, 1969.
2. Locke, S. E. and Hornig-Rohan, M. (eds.). *Mind and Immunity: Behavioral Immunology.* Institute for the Advancement of Health, New York, 1982.
3. Locke, S. E. (ed.). *Psychological and Behavioral Treatments for Medical Disorders: Volume 2, Disorders Associated with the Immune System.* Institute for the Advancement of Health, New York, 1987.
4. Peavey, B. S. Biofeedback Assisted self-regulation: Effects on phagocytic immune system. Unpublished doctoral dissertation, North Texas State University, Denton, Texas, 1982.
5. Kiecolt-Glaser, J. K., Glaser, R., Strain, E. C., Stout, J. C., Tarr, K. L., Holliday, J. E. and Speicher, C. E. Psychosocial enhancement of immunocompetence in a geriatric population. Health Psychol., 4: 25–41, 1985.
6. Kiecolt-Glaser, J. K., Glaser, R., Strain, E. C., Stout, J. C., Tarr, K. L., Holliday, J. E. and Speicher, C. E. Modulation of cellular immunity in medical students. J. Behav. Med., 9: 5–21, 1986.
7. Hall, H. R. Hypnosis and the immune system: A review with implications for cancer and the psychology of healing. Am. Clin. Hypn., 25: 92–103, 1983.
8. Gruber, B. L., Hall, N. R., Hersh, S. P. and Dubois, P. Immune system and psychologic changes in metastatic cancer patients while using ritualized relaxation and guided imagery. Paper presented at the 99th Annual Convention of the American Psychological Association, Washington, D.C., Aug., 1986.
9. Velkoff, D. [Patients with stress-related diseases initially showed repressed natural killer call activity that reversed once they established healthy homeostasis' with biofeedback self-regulation]. Unpublished raw data, 1988.
10. Norris, P. A. and Porter, G. *I Choose Life: The Dynamics of Visualization and Biofeedback.* Stillpoint Publishing, Walpole, Connecticut, 1987.
11. Jahnke, R. Immune enhancement and self-care. Presentation at the 21st Annual Medical Symposium, ARE Clinic, Phoenix, Arizona, 1988.
12. Pritikin, N. and McGrady, P. M., Jr. *The Pritikin Program for Diet and Exercise.* Grossett & Dunlap, New York, 1979.
13. Fried, R. *The Hyperventilation Syndrome: Research and Clinical Treatment.* Johns Hopkins University Press, Baltimore, 1987.
14. Assagioli, R. *Psychosynthesis: A Manual of Principles and Techniques.* Hobbs, Dorman & Company, Inc., New York, 1965.
16. Green, E. E. and Green, A. M. Biofeedback and states of consciousness. In *Handbook of States of Consciousness,* edited by Wolman, B. B. and Ullman, M. Van Nostrand Reinhold Company, New York, 1986.
17. Norris, P. A. and Fahrion, S. L. Autogenic biofeedback in psychophysiological therapy and stress management. In *Principles and Practice of Stress Management,* edited by Woolfolk, R. L. and Lehrer, P. M. The Guilford Press, New York, 1984.
18. Siegel, B. S. *Love, Medicine, and Miracles.* Harper & Row, New York, 1986.
19. Appelbaum, S. A. *Out in Inner Space.* Anchor Press/Doubleday, Garden City, New York, 1979.

CHAPTER 7

Electroencephalographic Biofeedback and Neurological Applications

JOEL F. LUBAR

PHYSIOLOGICAL BASIS OF EEG ACTIVITY

In 1875, Richard Caton of Britain recorded crude electrical activity from the cerebral cortex of rabbits, cats and monkeys (1). In 1890, Adolph Beck of Poland was able to record oscillations of 100 μV from the brain and stated that the generator was the cerebral cortex. He showed that it was not an artifact of movement or brain pulsations because its occurrence could be elicited in animals given the neuromuscular blocking drug, curare.

Other early investigators of brain wave activity include Fleischl Von Marxow (1883) and several European investigators, particularly in Germany, Vienna, Austria, and Poland. For example, in 1886, Danielvskey of Kharkov recorded evoked electrical activity to auditory stimuli (evoked potentials). However, it was not really until after 1925 that serious interest in the electrical activity of the brain began to appear.

Hans Berger had been interested in this phenomenon since 1900 and had recorded from the human scalp many times before the publication of his pioneer research in 1929. It is to him that we owe credit for the designation by Greek letters for various wave forms such as delta, theta, alpha, and beta and for the first observations of alpha blocking by stimulation. The modern viewpoint regarding the origin of the EEG is that it involves a complex series of electrical changes that occur both cortically and subcortically. The scalp recording of the EEG contains elements that are generated by thalamocortical relays, by connections between different cortical areas, and evoked potentials produced by specific sensory stimuli in the different sensory pathways. Berger, in 1933, insightfully proposed that thalamic inhibition blocks alpha rhythms during attention. Numerous other investigators, for example, Dempsey and Morison (2) and Adrian (3), all showed that significant EEG activity is generated by neuronal pools within specific thalamic nuclei. The evidence for this included studies of decortication, which did not eliminate the rhythmic activity of the thalamus but did show that it could occur independently of neocortical activity. Particular thalamic nuclei that seemed to be especially involved in the generation of rhythmic cortical electrical activity include the intralaminar nuclei, nucleus ventralis anterior, and the recticular nucleus of the thalamus. Significant electrical activity is generated by sensory nuclei such as the ventral posterolateral (VPL), ventral posteromedial (VPM), and the medial and lateral geniculate bodies.

A comprehensive recent theory for explaining the generation of electrical activity in the CNS was proposed by Andersen and Andersson (4). Assuming that rhythmic activity is an inherent property of cells within many thalamic nuclei, they presented evidence that specific thalamocortical fibers relay this rhythmic activity between subcortical nuclei and the cerebral cortex. Hence, the synchrony at the cerebral cortex can be linked directly to the rhythmic firing of single units or pacemakers within the thalamocortical relays. For example, Spencer and Brookhart (5) showed this by microelectrode studies in which electrodes were placed in specific thalamic nuclei. The correspondence between thalamic activity (i.e., activity at the cellular level) and EEG waves recorded at the surface of the scalp or from the cortical surface could be established.

The alpha rhythm, for example, is a rhythmic spindle between 8 and 13 Hertz (Hz) which can be recorded best from the posterior portion of the human or cerebral cortex and is more prevalent when the eyes are closed. According to the Andersen and Andersson model, rhythmic activity such as an alpha rhythm or perhaps other periodic activity including delta (0–3 Hz), theta (4–7 Hz), and beta spindles (14+ Hz) represented an " idling activity," that is, the activity of pools of thalamic neurons firing spontaneously, but in synchrony.

These various types of spindles are blockaded when specific barrages of sensory or motor activity override the idling frequency of thalamic pacemakers. Therefore, the common phenomenon of EEG activation when the eyes are open or when one is solving a complex problem is associated with the blocking of alpha spindles by desynchronized activity representing the recruiting of multiple cerebral cortical and subcortical areas simultaneously involved in more complex cognitive activity. The importance of this observation is perhaps that while the organism is in a relatively relaxed state, such as daydreaming in humans, then rhythmic activity appears at the cerebral cortex. Kamiya (6) and others have shown that there is a correspondence between theta activity and daydreaming. Alpha activity in the biofeedback literature has been linked to an alert but relaxed state. Slow delta rhythm is most prevalent during Stages 3 and 4 of deep sleep (7).

We do not have a clear behavioral state related to beta spindles since beta activity consists of infrequent desynchronized higher frequency and low amplitude activity as well as synchronized spindle bursts within the beta range.

In addition to the Greek letter-designated rhythms, there are special rhythms that also perhaps represent an idling of pools of subcortical neurons. One is the sensorimotor rhythm (SMR) described by Sterman and his associates, and recorded in mammals from the sensory-motor cortex while the organism is sitting quietly (8, 9). Movement causes a blockage of SMR. SMR in humans can be recorded over the central scalp and has a frequency of 12–15 Hz (10). A second motor rhythm described in humans by Kuhlman and Kaplan (11) is known as the MU rhythm. This is a 9- 11-Hz rhythm recorded from central scalp electrode

deviations and is blocked by clenching of the contralateral fist.

Another aspect of the EEG is that it represents oscillations or variations in dendritic excitatory and inhibitory postsynaptic potential (EPSPs and IPSPs) activity, primarily within the upper layers of the cerebral cortex. Thus, when there is no specific bombardment by incoming sensory relays or a specific motor outflow, idling in the form of synchronous shifts of ensembles or pools of cortical dendrites also generate significant EEG activity. Other changes in cortical potentials can occur at frequencies lower than EEG, such as slow wave shifts of less than 1 Hz. These are often caused by changes in the overall polarization of fields of cortical dendritics and are classified as slow potentials.

It is important for practitioners using biofeedback for altering EEG activity to realize that the EEG recorded with scalp electrodes in humans are the tip of an iceberg. We often make the mistake of thinking that EEG reflects unitary processes that define behavioral states. In recording the EEG from a particular location, for example, using bipolar electrodes placed over frontal and temporal lobes, we really see the *difference* between the electrical potentials at the two electrodes. This potential difference contains the following elements: dendritic activity from the upper cortical layers, direct current shifts occurring across large regions of the cortex, occasional evoked or event potentials (ERPs) elicited by sensory stimuli during the time the recording is taken, and relays of activity representing activation and inhibition from thalamocortical pools and pacemakers, which are in turn influenced by relays from the brainstem reticular formation. Thus, when we teach someone to alter a particular EEG component, such as alpha rhythm, beta spindles, or sensorimotor rhythm, we do not know which underlying processes are most related to the acquisition of the task. In some cases, it may be changes in dendritic potentials (EPSPs and IPSPs). In other cases, it may be direct activity from neuronal pools under the recording electrodes, and/or it might be activity of thalamic nuclei which are only remotely influencing the overlying cortical activity.

Conditioning a particular EEG pattern in one person might represent different processes than in another as a result of different kinds of subcortical and brainstem activity in different individuals. This may explain why subjective reports associated with alpha EEG biofeedback conditioning are quite variable (12). Some report increased relaxation; others report no change; and a few even find the experience unpleasant.

The degree of specificity for EEG biofeedback is more difficult to delineate than perhaps for other modalities of biofeedback. However, EEG biofeedback conditioning has become a very powerful modality for dealing with several severe neurologic and behavioral disorders including seizure disorders, management of hyperkinesis in children, and the diagnosis and treatment of specific learning disabilities. The last two disorders are now referred to as "attention deficit disorders," as defined in the DSM III (16).

METHODOLOGY FOR EEG BIOFEEDBACK CONDITIONING

We must briefly examine some of the techniques that have been used for extracting the critical information regarding frequency and amplitude from the raw EEG and processing this information in a manner that allows it to be readily understood by the client or patient in EEG biofeedback training or therapeutic intervention. A more detailed description has been presented in previous publications (13-15).

Because the EEG is a continuously varying signal, with a frequency distribution from less than 1 Hz to more than 40 Hz, and with amplitudes varying from less than 2 μV to over 150 μV, its analysis is complex. To extract specific frequency and sometimes specific amplitude information, several methods have been developed. These usually involve analog analysis, time-period or zero-crossing analysis, and dominant frequency analysis. More recently, the fast-Fourier spectral analysis has become of great interest, as a potential means of developing feedback for rapidly changing signals. An even newer technique, BEAM, or brain electrical activity mapping, is being used widely for neurologic diagnosis with possibilities in the near future for biofeedback applications (17). None of these methods are clearly superior to the others; all having advantages and disadvantages, with large differences in complexity and cost.

One problem in analyzing and extracting relevant data from the EEG is the relative "slowness" of the EEG signal. Compared with most electronic analysis systems that work in the kilohertz or even megahertz range, e.g., an AM-FM or television signals, the EEG is slow enough so that there may be a considerable lag between the specific EEG event and the time taken for the extraction and analysis of the relevant data and the initiation of feedback. Hence, the time required for recording and input has to be added to the inherent response time of a particular feedback analysis system. The total response time is important because in successful biofeedback, one must link the changes occurring within the organism with behavior involving sensations and perceptions. The extent to which feedback stimuli such as tones, clicks, visual displays, slide presentations, etc. relate directly, rapidly, and contingently to the behavior of the organism being trained is critical in bringing that behavior under operant or contingent control.

Components

Generally, a biofeedback system for EEG analysis involves the following components and interconnections: first, high quality electrodes including recording electrodes and reference or ground electrodes are inputted to an EEG preamplifier. This preamplifier may amplify anywhere from 5 to 20,000 times and must have a very high input impedance and common mode rejection. The input impedance and common mode rejection are both necessary parameters to reduce the probability that noise from much larger signals such as 60-Hz interference, radio frequency signals, movement artifacts, and so forth are minimized.

EEG recording may be monopolar or bipolar. One of the advantages of bipolar recording is that it looks at the difference between two signals recorded at different points on the scalp and allows the system to subtract any signal that is occurring in a "common mode" between the two points. If this common mode rejection is very high, i.e., 50,000:1 or greater, then common signals are rejected and differential activity remains. Fortunately, most common mode signals include 60 Hz or other tuned frequencies from interference sources and are easily rejected. Occasionally, body movements and eye movements are reduced by common mode rejection.

The advantage of high input impedances such as 10 megohms or greater is that they allow for clear signal reproduction even when the contact between the electrode and the scalp is not perfect. Actually, most systems today will function adequately when the impedance or resistance between the electrode and skin interface is less than 10,000 ohms. Although there is considerable distortion introduced by the skull and other tissues overlying the brain, with the extremely high quality EEG preamplifiers that are available today, the scalp EEG quite closely approximates EEG that can be recorded directly when subcranial electrodes on the dura mater, or skull using bone screws, or even from the cortical surface itself.

After EEG preamplification, the signal may be preprocessed with the use of digital and analog filters or other devices, and specific frequencies or specific amplitudes can be extracted. After these are extracted, criteria are set so that when specific frequency or amplitude combinations are present, a logic signal can activate a feedback device. At this point and providing that the delay is very short, the patient receives relatively contingent feedback based upon some EEG event in the form of light, tone or some other display parameter.

Filters

Analog methods of discrimination allow researchers and clinicians to use tuned active band-pass filters to extract specific frequencies from the raw EEG. These active filters incorporate operational amplifiers and have been developed in specific configurations such as the Butterworth, Bessel, elliptic, and others. These descriptors refer to the shape of the response curve of the filters within the selected band-pass. Analog filters have many advantages in that they respond relatively rapidly to the EEG signal. Usually, after delays of less than ½ sec, they begin to oscillate at their tuned frequency. Active filters, however, have problems so that a transient with a short rise or of high amplitude will cause the filter to "ring" or oscillate at its tuned frequency. The ringing of the tuned filter can give rise to false feedback, that is feedback which occurs in the absence of the actual frequency and/or amplitude parameters being met.

Various techniques have been devised to reduce filter ringing since the perfect filter that produces one cycle of output at the selected band-pass frequency from an input of one cycle of that frequency in the raw signal does not exist. The sharpness of tuned filters is determined by the number of poles of amplification

they possess. A minimal requirement for a good filter is that it have a roll-off of at least 24 decibels (db) per octave and preferably 48 db more. The latter requires an 8-pole filter. Although the addition of more poles of filtering increases the sharpness of the filter or its roll-off, it also increases the filter's capacity to ring. Hence there is a trade-off between sharpness and fidelity. One way to decrease ringing is to use amplitude-limiting or soft "clipping." These circuits preprocess the EEG before it enters the filter and are designed to round off and decrease high amplitude signals rather than abruptly clipping them. Abruptly clipped signals or square waves produce harmonics and considerable amount of transients and filter ringing. Clipping the signal does distort it, but usually reduces the amplitude due only to extracranial sources of interference.

Analog feedback involves additional circuits that translate filter outputs into their instantaneous voltage value. This is accomplished through rectification followed by analog integration of the output. In this manner, it is possible to drive a feedback signal that varies in an analog fashion to the frequency or amplitude of the original EEG; for example, a warbling tone that becomes higher in pitch as the EEG frequency increases and lower in pitch as the EEG frequency decreases, and also louder with higher amplitude and soft with lower amplitudes. This feedback can be made to closely follow the actual wavelets of the raw EEG.

Digital Zero-Crossing Analysis

Digital zero-crossing techniques for signal analysis are far more precise than analog techniques and much faster, but they are not without their own flaws. These techniques are based on the inverse relationship between the frequencies in the EEG signal and the time period of each cycle. Essentially, special devices measure the time between successive zero crossings in the same direction, i.e., positively going or negatively going.

Zero-crossing analyzers have an output that usually is a pulse whose amplitude is directly proportional to the period or inversely proportional to the frequency. Thus, the higher the frequency in the EEG, the shorter the pulse; the lower the frequency, the higher the pulse. These pulses are then fed into a device known as a *window discriminator*, which picks up all those pulses which lie between a certain prechosen minimal and maximal height. These heights define through the inverse relationship between frequency and period the frequencies that are selected. Since each time an EEG wave falls within the selected frequency the corresponding pulse will be chosen, these pulses can then be counted and provide direct feedback in the form of a count, or they can be accumulated, and when a certain number have occurred in a particular period of time, can activate a light display or some more elaborate type of feedback.

Although this type of digital or zero-crossing analysis is very precise, it makes the assumption that all EEG wave forms cross an imaginary zero line. This is not always true. In fact, complex wave forms often include high and low frequency components where high frequency components will ride as ripples on a slow wave background. These ripples, which may represent the desired wave form for training purposes, will be missed entirely by a zero-crossing analysis. An example is the sensorimotor (SMR), which often rides as a series of 12- to 15-Hz ripples on a background of slow, or even paroxysmal, wave forms in epileptic patients. Zero-crossing analysis would only pick up the low frequency component.

There are imperfect solutions to this problem, e.g., taking the first derivative of the EEG, which then requires that every relative or absolute maxima and minima to cross the zero line be taken; this allows for immediate detection of the higher frequency component but eliminates low frequency components.

Combined Technique

One solution to the problem of ringing filters for analog analysis and for zero-crossing analysis that is partial to either high or low frequencies is to combine both techniques. In our work in EEG biofeedback for seizures, we developed a system (14, 15), employing first an analog filter and then a zero-crossing analysis on the filter output rather than the raw EEG. The filter pre-selects the frequency of interest, and the zero-crossing analysis confirms the analog analysis by making it more precise and eliminating the possibility that either a low or high frequency component is favored.

Fast-Fourier Transform

A new method for EEG analysis is based on the fast-Fourier transform, which was first described by Bickford and Fleming (16) and may

be the ideal method for analyzing a complex wave form. Fourier analysis is superb for periodic wave forms such as those produced by musical instruments, oscillating strings, or organ pipes, but it is also highly applicable to nonperiodic complex biological signals such as the EEG, EMG, or EKG. Figure 7.1 provides an example of the fast-Fourier or spectral analysis of the EEG and shows designated areas in the EEG that might be of interest for feedback purposes. Abnormalities in the form of spikes, epileptic slow waves, or depressed electrical activity can be readily demarcated. The Fourier analysis also has the advantage that it is sequential and that epochs of different lengths can be analyzed and then displayed on a TV screen or on a graph as shown in Figure 7.1. The three-dimensionality of the display makes it possible to see changes over time.

The *somnogram* is an elegant technique for all night sleep analysis in which longer epochs, usually 20-80 sec, are analyzed, stored, and plotted for a period ranging from several hours to as many as 10 hours if neces-

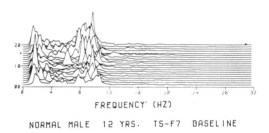

FREQUENCY (HZ)

NORMAL MALE   12 YRS.   T5-F7   BASELINE

POWER VS FREQUENCY

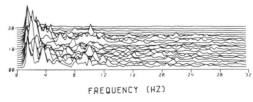

FREQUENCY (HZ)

NORMAL MALE   12 YRS.   T5-F7   READING

Figure 7.1. Fast-Fourier power spectral analysis of a normal EEG from the left hemisphere of a 12-year-old child during a resting baseline and a reading task. Each epoch represents 16 sec of EEG analysis. The ordinate represents time as measured by epoch number. The abscissa displays specific frequencies, with 0-3 Hz delta, 4-8 Hz theta, 8-12 Hz alpha, and greater than 13 Hz beta.

sary in order to obtain a clear picture of a full night's sleep. Somnograms have the advantage that it is possible to see the sleep stages and how they co-vary throughout the night and to readily discern events that might be unusual such as epileptic activity, abnormal EEG patterns, movement arousals, and so on.

The Fourier or spectral analysis based on the fast-Fourier transform technique must be carried out by computer. The first step is to digitize the data, so that the EEG signal is sampled at very high speed, often 128 times per second. Analog voltages are converted to binary numbers, representing the amplitude of the signal each time it is sampled. A sampling period such as the 16-sec epoch shown in the illustration is the number of required samples multiplied by the sampling rate. If the Fourier display is to be used for feedback directly, clearly the epochs have to be very short; otherwise a noncontingency develops between the display and the actual EEG events which led to the display. There are some limitations, so that the shortest period of time that can be used is about 1-2 sec. This delay therefore introduces some noncontingency between the event and the feedback.

Dynamic display. We have developed a dynamic Fourier display observed on a color TV monitor in which different portions of the display represent different regions of the EEG. For example, the delta regions may be shown in orange, the theta region in blue, the alpha region in green, and the beta region in red. The display looks like continuously undulating, ever-changing peaks and troughs with the lag time between the display and the actual EEG event of approximately ½ sec. The method for doing this is complex. It has the advantage that a subject viewing such a display can be told, "Make a mountain at 15Hz (red) and a valley at 8 Hz (blue)," which would mean essentially training the individual to enhance beta activity and suppress theta. As will be seen later, this is extremely important in working with certain types of epileptics and for children with specific learning disabilities.

This type of display may produce more rapid learning of the EEG task than has been possible before and may eliminate the disadvantages introduced by analog filtering or zerocrossing methods. The Fourier analysis also has the advantage that different frequency bands can be extracted and statistical analysis for differences or changes can be performed based on the percentage or absolute power measured in scaled picowatts of activity within the portion of the EEG spectrum.

COMPUTERIZED EEG TOPOGRAPHY— BRAIN MAPPING

The development of the Fourier analysis technique for analyzing EEG activity in the power and frequency domain provided neurosciences with a very accurate and important tool for a better description of electrical activity from the cerebral cortex. Conventional fast Fourier analysis as described and illustrated previously is essentially unidimensional, that is, it represents electrical activity of the brain at a single biopolar derivation. In order to obtain information about EEG activity from many brain surface locations, many channels must be utilized. Computers must have rapid computation times and large internal memories (RAM) to take advantage of multichannel Fourier analysis because the calculations are complex and involve the multiplication of very large numbers.

EEG topography or *brain mapping* is a new technique that has been pioneered by several instrument companies. One company, Nicolet Instrument Corporation, is currently distributing an instrument package known as BEAM (brain electrical activity mapping). BEAM systems are expensive and complex, but they allow investigators to represent the entire cortical surface in terms of either the frequency or amplitude domain. Looking at a BEAM map involves observing a monitor with a projection of the head from the top or from either the left or right side. Some brain mapping systems allow anterior or posterior views. The map is a multicolor display with the various colors representing Fourier analysis performed at many points; in some systems, as many as 32 channels are used simultaneously. Interpolation of activity is also performed between points so that the map contours are smooth. The multicolor map can be updated, depending on the epoch length, sometimes as rapidly as every 2 seconds or at longer intervals, if desired. In the amplitude domain, the map will display various colors representing the amplitude of a specific band of activity, for example: theta, alpha, delta, beta, or any desired band that is chosen. In the frequency domain, a particular amplitude region can be chosen, for example: 12–15 microvolts. Thus, brain activity can be displayed in different frequencies.

Already, a data base has been developed and is being used by neurologists in conjunction with BEAM. Some surprising findings have been obtained, e.g., there appears to be BEAM differences of normal populations matched for age with individuals experiencing manic-depressive psychosis or paronoid schizophrenia. Furthermore, the more conventional neurological disorders such as migraine headaches, tumors, aneurysms, and seizure disorders present different characteristic maps. Recently, Duffy and his colleagues have shown that attention deficit disorders also display BEAM patterns that are different from matched normal populations (17–19). In addition to EEG, evoked potential or event-related potential activity can also be portrayed in a BEAM format. Brain mapping in conjunction with nuclear magnetic resonance imaging (NMR), computerized axial tomography (CAT) scanning, or positron emission transaxial tomography (PETT) scanning provides an incredibly powerful set of measurements that allow for a detailed description of both the structural and functional integrity of the brain. With PETT scanning, inferences about neurotransmitter function and metabolism can be made. Correlation between these techniques allows for a rather detailed description of many types of neurologic and psychiatric disorders.

The connection requirements for brain topographic mapping are more stringent than for conventional EEG recording. Impedances must be less than 5000 ohms, and electrodes require very accurate placement. The patient has to be able to tolerate the measurements taken for periods up to 1 hour.

How can brain mapping be applied to biofeedback? Already, instruments are able to make computations and to display data almost on-line. In this case, the display of colors for a particular frequency or amplitude domain would be updated so rapidly that the pattern would look as if it were continuously changing, i.e., as if one were looking at an animated version of brain map activity. With this possibility, individuals could be taught to change the patterns from different parts of the cortex based on the feedback display. While the ultimate system does not yet exist, such a system would allow for both frequency and amplitude activity to be displayed simultaneously. One possible device would use different colors to represent different frequency domains, and changes in brightness would represent changes in amplitude, e.g., a bright red region might represent high amplitude and high frequency beta; a very desaturated blue region might represent low amplitude delta activity. Ultimately, for feedback purposes, such a brain map would have to be continuously updated with the lag of less than half a second between the recording of the information and the display. Although each epoch length can be longer, a sliding average technique would have to be used.

One problem in topographic analysis concerns artifacts. Movement artifacts can rapidly saturate the screen momentarily and block out other activity. Muscle activity shows up readily, and artifacts due to eye movements have to be controlled in the analysis. In doing a conventional BEAM, the technician scans the EEG for artifacts and removes them from storage before an interpretation is made—a tedious procedure. For biofeedback, however, such artifacts can be part of the feedback paradigm. That is, excessive muscle activity, eye movements, as in the case of blepharospasm or anxiety, or even excessive muscle activity from the scalp are all parameters that might be brought under behavioral control.

The main advantage of a topographic type of feedback system with continuous updating is that it would permit observations of regional changes in brain activity. We might speculate that beta activity over temporal lobe derivations might be useful in improving reading comprehension or perhaps visual memory based on what is currently known about the neuropsychology of that part of the cortex. Other inferences can be made about the importance of specific types of EEG activity recorded from other brain regions. Speculating even further: would biofeedback-induced changes in abnormal brain map patterns associated with psychiatric disorders help in conjunction with therapy and appropriate medication to ameloriate these problems? Perhaps within 10 years, topographic biofeedback of a very sophisticated nature will exist and that significant strides will be made. Perhaps EEG biofeedback based on these advanced technologies may play a more important role than other existing forms of biofeedback have at present.

A major drawback of BEAM and other topographic mapping systems is their cost. The computer software and amplifiers may range anywhere from $30,000 to several hundred thousand dollars. However, personal computer systems with several megabytes of internal memory and data storage systems involving hard discs holding 80 megabytes of memory or more now exist. Cycle times have reached 12 to 20 megahertz, and optical discs of both the read and write variety are just beginning to be developed. With these capabilities and cost reduced due to volume, more extensive software for brain topographic mapping and perhaps brain topographic feedback will be within the range of the small laboratory or moderately sized clinic within 5 years.

SELF-REGULATION OF EEG ACTIVITY EMPLOYING BIOFEEDBACK

It is somewhat difficult to pinpoint exactly when the first operant conditioning studies of the EEG were carried out, although since the 1940s changes in the EEG we believed to be associated with different states of consciousness such as the alpha blocking and activation of the EEG.

Alpha Rhythm

Kamiya and Kliteman were interested in the relationship between alpha rhythm and consciousness in early studies of the late 1950s at the University of Chicago. Later, at the Langley-Porter Institute, Kamiya in 1961 attempted to train subjects to control their alpha rhythm, although his first publication did not appear until 1969 (20). Individuals were provided auditory feedback (a tone that turned on and off when rectified and filtered alpha activity reached a preset criterion) like the amplitude discrimination techniques described earlier. This discrete information indicated that alpha activity above a certain microvolt level had been generated, but it did not provide continuous feedback so that the individual could learn to control the intensity or pitch of the tone, thus relating to the amount of filtered alpha activity. Subsequently, Kamiya employed more direct analog feedback (6).

These early studies showed that it was relatively easy to suppress alpha rhythm. In fact, visualizations, mental arithmetic, or other cognitive strategies were often used to block alpha rhythm and replace it with the faster beta activities. To this day, there is still controversy about whether it is possible to increase the amount of alpha rhythm in the eye-open condition over that which is normally present when the eyes are closed for a given individual, regardless of the feedback technique used. One problem in the conditioning of the alpha rhythm is that alpha will increase, sometimes to a marked extent, in subjects who are just sitting quietly. Since the physical setting for most feedback conditioning involves a comfortable chair and dimly lit surroundings, the enhancement of alpha due to this alone makes it difficult to assess any conditioning effect beyond those produced by relaxation or allowing this dominant cortical rhythm to "idle."

Some of the studies have employed an alternating sequence of trials in which one block of trials were designated as alpha-decrease trials followed by a block designated as alpha-increase trials. What usually happens in this paradigm is that subjects are able to block alpha successfully during alpha-decrease trials but subsequently rarely increased the amount of alpha activity above baseline. Kamiya and his associates discovered more recently that with varying analog feedback as opposed to on-off feedback, it is often possible to obtain increases in alpha rhythm above pretraining baseline levels (6). This is interpreted as support for the view that alpha can be conditioned and that learning to control alpha is a skill similar to controlling peripheral skin temperature or electromyographic activity.

Kamiya also reported that noncontingent feedback does not lead to an increase in alpha (6). Furthermore, after subjects had been given alpha increase trials and were interrupted in the middle of the session in order to relate what strategy they were using and what feelings were associated with the experience, upon resumption of training, the alpha percentage increased even further (although only temporarily). Kamiya believes that taking the break was not the cause of this increase, i.e., due to the "time-out." Instead, there seems to be an active process that occurs even in very highly trained subjects. There is a possibility that the increase in alpha after the break is an elicited phenomenon, similar to that which occurs in classical conditioning and that there may be a secondary reinforcer or conditioning stimulus imposed by the break period.

There has been considerable disagreement as to the subjective experience associated with increased alpha rhythm, although it has often been described as a relaxed but alert state. In a very well carried out study, Walsh (12) found that some persons experience no specific state associated with increased alpha production and occasionally report this being a negative or unpleasant experience.

Theta Rhythm

Theta activity, which is slower than alpha, can be recorded from many portions of the cortex or from the cerebrum in both awake and sleeping individuals. Green, Green, and Walters (21) and Brown (22) reported that theta is particularly abundant when individuals are drowsy, or entering the early stages of sleep, and is often associated with day-dreaming and vivid visualizations and imagery (21).

At the Southeastern Biofeedback Institute, we employ theta conditioning as a strategy for helping individuals with certain types of sleep onset insomnia. Those who tend to experience a "flood of thought," associated with tension and anxiety—thereby inhibiting sleep—are particularly helped by theta training. The patients often report that rather than a fading of pervasive thought patterns to a blank mind, there is a change in the thought content from disturbing and ruminating to more pleasant themes. Some, for example, have described the imagery of colors, forms, and pleasant places instead of images dealing with unpleasant work situations or negative family or other interpersonal interactions. We are now investigating systemic changes in the EEG based on Fourier analysis for subjects participating in autogenic training. Clearly, there is a shift toward theta and delta activity which is not due to eye movements and can occur in alert persons.

We have also seen increases in theta activity in patients who are provided a long sequence of autogenic phrases in the course of repeating autogenic formulae two or three times at a single setting according to the method of Luthe and Schultz (23). However, this effect is nonspecific, since for the vast majority of patients undergoing autogenic training there is an associated decrease in surface EMG recorded from frontal, forearm, trapezius, or masseter electrode locations and an increase in peripheral blood flow (as evidenced by increased hand temperatures and foot temperatures). We suspect that considerable drowsiness is associated with the change of thought patterns. The drowsiness, in turn, is responsible for the increase in theta activity, and changes in thought patterns may be secondary to this.

Migraine and Other Headaches

EEG biofeedback has also been employed as a means in dealing with a number of organic and psychophysiological disorders. For example, EEG alpha feedback was used by Andreychuk and Skriver (24) as an adjunct to treating migraine headaches, but reported only a 27% reduction in headache activity.

Tension headaches have been treated more successfully with alpha feedback, although it is not the primary modality used for this disorder. Alpha feedback was used as an alternative to EMG for muscle contraction headache feedback by McKenzie et al. (25), who reported an 80% reduction in headache frequency. However, their treatment program was contaminated by the fact that alpha was also combined with relaxation training. The control group receiving only relaxation training also improved, but there was neither an attention placebo group nor an alpha-only group for comparison.

Anxiety

In other contexts, Garrett and Silver (26) combined EMG and alpha feedback for individuals experiencing test anxiety. Both EMG and alpha feedback separately as well as when combined led to reduction in self-reports of anxiety, but there were no significant differences between the three groups. Glueck and Stroebel (27) with psychiatric inpatients at the Institute for Living in Hartford. Connecticut compared the effectiveness of transcendental meditation (TM), autogenic training and alpha feedback. Alpha feedback and autogenic training were not effective for this population, but patients receiving meditation training were somewhat improved. It should be noted, however, that meditation training also causes a shift of EEG toward lower frequencies from beta to alpha or theta (27a). They also obtained a negative report that some patients who became tense or frustrated elected to drop the treatment. This is similar to the findings that had been reported in some patients by Walsh (12).

Beta Rhythm

Of particular interest is the work of Bird et al. (28) involving the training of very high beta activity in human subjects. (This activity between 35 and 45 Hz has been described in the literature for a number of years in animals.) Previously, Sheer (29, 30) reported increases in power of 40-Hz activity in the visual cortex of cats during visual discrimination learning and in children (31) who were engaged in learning tasks involving short-term memory and attention. He cited a number of studies indicating that high beta activity is correlated with attentional or memory processes, e.g., studies done in the 1950s by Das and Gastaut (32). Bird et al. (28) trained 22 men to either increase or suppress either 40-Hz activity or lower beta 21- to 31-Hz activity. Eight demonstrated both increases and supression of 40-Hz activity even when feedback was no longer present.

One very serious technical problem which occurs in training high beta activity is that there is a total overlap of the high beta EEG frequency band with scalp EMG. Actually, scalp EMG can be recorded with frequencies as low as 15 Hz. How then is it possible to separate 40-Hz EMG activity from 40-Hz EEG activity, which (from the point of view of the amplifier) has identical characteristics? To overcome this problem, a *coincidence detector circuit* was employed in these 40-Hz studies. Since most of the EMG spectrum lies above 30 Hz, and may extend as high as 300 Hz or more, an EMG detector circuit employing a 70 Hz filter and a time window was used. Essentially, whenever 40 Hz and 70 Hz were detected almost simultaneously within a period 20 milliseconds before or 20 milliseconds after a 40-Hz response occurred, the coincidence circuit prevented the recording of the occurrence of the 40-Hz activity. Thus, 40-Hz activity, which occurred only when 70-Hz activity was *not* present, might more likely be due to EEG rather than contamination from EMG. A second control for EMG contamination involved 40-Hz detectors to monitor activity from trapezius muscles and temporal muscles on the same side of the head as the EEG recording. If 40-Hz activity was detected in these muscle groups, synchronous with 40-Hz detected over the scalp, that scalp activity was not counted.

These procedures are about the best that can be employed, but it is still possible that some 30- to 50-Hz activity generated by muscles could be counted as EEG activity. Perhaps more significantly, although the investigators were able to train individuals to both increase

and suppress 40-Hz activity without feedback, the ability to do this quickly extinguished after the training was discontinued.

Subjective Experiences

In order to determine what subjective experiences might be associated with different EEG states, Bird et al. (28) used a device known as a *Q-sort test*, which involves sorting different adjectives in response to different types of EEG experiences, with intriguing results.

The descriptors for theta activity involved the following terms: dreaming, drifting, drowsy, dull, floating, fuzzy, hazy, sluggish, and wandering. All of these correlate with random visual imagery, colors, forms, sleepiness, and very deep relaxation. The alpha descriptors included: at ease, calm, composed, passive-like, peaceful, placid, relaxed, tranquil, uncritical, and unfocused. These are immediately different from the theta descriptors.

The beta descriptors included: active, alert, anxious, energetic, excited, exhilarated, lively, restless, stimulated, and tense. Note that these have both positive and negative aspects.

The 40-Hz descriptors include: attentive, concentrative, effortful, focus, investigative, searching, scrutinizing, studying, thinking, and vigilance. None of these descriptors have much of an affective or emotional component. All of them seem to be intellectually oriented, that is, they are the types of descriptors that would be associated with complex learning such as processing complex information. It does seem that the high beta activity is more associated with complex cognitive tasks, the lower beta activity associated with anxious emotions, alpha with calm and peaceful, i.e., an uncritical relaxed state, and theta with the altered perception of the body itself.

Theta and alpha descriptors are also used by our patients who have undergone autogenic training, with the theta descriptors being favored over the alpha descriptors. It may be that if the EMG contamination problem could be solved, 40-Hz conditioning would be an ideal method for working with retarded and/or learning disabled individuals. It might also be ideal for both children and adults who are experiencing difficulties in concentrating independent of any learning problem, either due to boredom or interference with learning processes as a result of emotional or adjustment problems. Unfortunately, the

Bird et al. (28) studies don't appear to have any follow-up.

EEG FEEDBACK TRAINING FOR HYPERKINESIS AND SPECIFIC LEARNING DISABILITIES

One of the newest and most exciting applications of EEG biofeedback is in the context of working with children who experience the attention deficit disorder (ADD). This includes children who are hyperkinetic and/or learning disabled. Learning disability refers to a wide variety of problems in both children and adolescents of normal and above-normal intelligence who are not able to perform at their potential academic level.

In 1861, Broca observed linguistic difficulties that related to dysfunctional activity in certain regions of the brain. In 1896, Morgan (33) coined the term "dyslexia." Golden and Anderson (34) have reviewed concepts based on learning theory, attentional processes, ophthalmology, genetic disorders, emotional disturbances, perceptual disorders, perceptual and motor integration, and overall neurologic theories of dysfunction.

There does seem to be evidence that children who are learning disabled and/or hyperkinetic often demonstrate EEG abnormalities. For example, Muehl, Knott and Benton (35) noted that 63% of the learning disabled population that they studied had EEG abnormalities in contrast with less than 20% of the normal population. Schain (36) categorized the following abnormalities in children who experience what was then called the minimal brain dysfunction syndrome or the MBD, but it must be remembered that not all children experience all of these: paroxysmal spike wave discharges, paroxysmal polyspike complexes, repetitive focal spiking or slowing, amplitude asymmetries greater than 50% between the two hemispheres, and marked but diffuse dysrhythmias. Other abnormalities which are more questionable include 6- and 14-Hz positive spikes, occipital or parietal temporal slowing, excessive slowing of the EEG in many areas or diffuse dysrhythmias. The EEGs for many learning disabled children tend to fall more in the latter categories than the former, which are more characteristic of the epileptic person.

Many of these EEG abnormalities have been called "soft neurological signs." For example, Hertzig, Bortner and Birch (37) found a 29%

incidence of hard neurologic signs similar to those seen in epileptic populations and a 90% incidence of the "softer" neurologic signs. Overall, they found that 94% of their MBD population had some type of neurological impairment. This again is compared with approximately 20% of the matched normal population in terms of age and sex. In addition to the neurological signs, there are many behavioral signs that are found in children who experience hyperkinesis and/or learning disabilities. These include speech difficulties, problems in balance and coordination, abnormalities in muscle tone, and overall clumsiness in both athletic and nonathletic activities.

Satterfield and Dawson (38) and Satterfield (39) proposed that there are two populations of hyperkinetic children—one that responds positively to stimulant medication and perhaps suffers from a neurological defect and another that does not respond well to stimulant medication and for whom hyperactivity may be secondary to emotional or family problems. The medication-sensitive hyperkinetics they labeled as low-arousal hyperkinetics, also described in detail by Lubar and Shouse (40–43). One way of looking at the low-arousal manifestation of hyperkinesis, which may or may not be associated with an attendant learning disorder is that these children suffer from either a maturational lag (a delayed maturation of the nervous system), or from an inability to be sufficiently aroused by different sensory modalities.

These children may act as if they are in a state of partial sensory deprivation. Hence, light, sounds, olfactory and taste stimuli, touch stimuli, and vestibular stimulation, as well as muscle kinesthesis do not have the impact on these children that they do on the normal population. To compensate for this partial sensory loss, low-arousal hyperkinetic children increase their activity so as to increase the impact of stimulation. This behavior is exhibited in terms of excessive oral behavior, tactile stimulation, excessive motor activity, and distractability. Looked at in this way, the effects of stimulant drugs, which have been well established as helpful for dealing with hyperkinesis, increase the impact of various sensory channels and allow the stimulation to be equilibrated with the needs of the organism. In other words, stimulants increase the level of arousal so that the excessive arousal-seeking behaviors can decrease.

One would anticipate that barbiturates, which tend to decrease sensory impact, might make hyperkinetic children worse; in fact, because of this, barbiturates are an inappropriate medication for low-arousal hyperkinetic children (44).

Diagnostic Methods

Our EEG-based diagnostic method to help separate out learning disabled from nonlearning-disabled children involves three basic elements. Recordings are taken from left and right hemispheric derivations over the frontal and temporal lobes (F7-T5 and F8-T6) according to the international 10-20 system of EEG recording, first during a 5-minute resting baseline condition (alert with the eyes open) and while the child reads silently material which is appropriate for grade level and ability. During the reading task, a 5-minute block of EEG is recorded for both hemispheres. Next, the child is asked to draw figures reproduced from the Bender-Gestalt or the Berry test, to assess visual-motor coordination and right hemisphere functions.

Figure 7.1 (page 71 in this chapter) displays the power-spectral appearance of a left hemisphere recording in a normal child during a baseline and reading task. In the normal recording, the predominant features include some scanning eye movements at very low frequencies, between 0 and 3 Hz. There is a relatively sparsity of activity between 4 and 8 Hz, the appearance of alpha activity at 8 to 12 Hz, and then some scattered beta activity from 12 to 20 Hz. As mentioned previously, this represents a resting, idling condition of the normal cerebral cortex. During the reading task, however, the alpha rhythm blocks and there is an increase in higher frequency beta activity. There also may be an increase in eye movements, particularly since the reading task as well as the drawing task involves more eye movement activity than during baseline. The eye movements will appear as peaks between 0 and 4 Hz. The alpha blocking is represented by a decrease in activity between 8 and 13 Hz and usually increased beta activity from 14 to 20 Hz.

The learning disabled child shows a very different pattern from normal controls. Figures 7.2 and 7.3 show recordings taken from two learning disabled children, 1 year apart. Between the first and second recording, each child was provided an extensive period of EEG biofeedback training. First note the appearance of the EEG during both baseline and reading task (Fig. 7.2) or baseline, reading and drawing tasks (Fig. 7.3) on the left side of each figure. These were taken before biofeedback training. There are some notable differences between these and the normal recordings. First, there is often a lack of clear alpha activity. Most of the activity lies between 0 and 8 Hz.

These EEGs are relatively devoid of beta activity and represent an unfocused cerebral state probably consistent with daydreaming. Looking closer, one finds that for subject N.L. during baseline, the left hemisphere does display some alpha activity at approximately 10 Hz. However, during the reading task, the alpha activity disappears and is replaced by slower activity between 0 and 6 Hz. There is no significant beta activity at all.

During the drawing task, the same pattern is repeated. However, the right hemisphere for this child shows alpha activity at approximately 10 Hz, and during the reading task, there is some blockade of that alpha with some beta activity. However, during the drawing task, the EEG becomes very slow. The problem with this child is that the patterns are incorrect. Alpha should block and beta appear during the reading task for the left hemisphere. The right hemisphere, however, shows activation during reading, which indicates a cross-dominance in that the right hemisphere is trying to take over the left hemisphere's responsibility. The slowing of the right hemisphere during the drawing task shown in the lower left of that figure indicates that the right hemisphere is not participating in a task which is normally a right hemispheric task. (Both children were right-handed and left-dominant.)

Subject M.V. (Fig. 7.3) also showed slowing during the baseline and reading task for both the left and right hemisphere, except the right hemisphere lower left tracing showed some beta activation during reading, whereas the left hemisphere showed less beta. The biofeedback program initiated for both of these children has been described in detail elsewhere (45). Essentially, it involved the following elements: teaching the learning disabled child to simultaneously suppress slow activity between 4 and 8 Hz and to increase fast activity in the ranges of 12-15 Hz, 11-19 Hz, or 16-20 Hz. A good strategy for many children is to

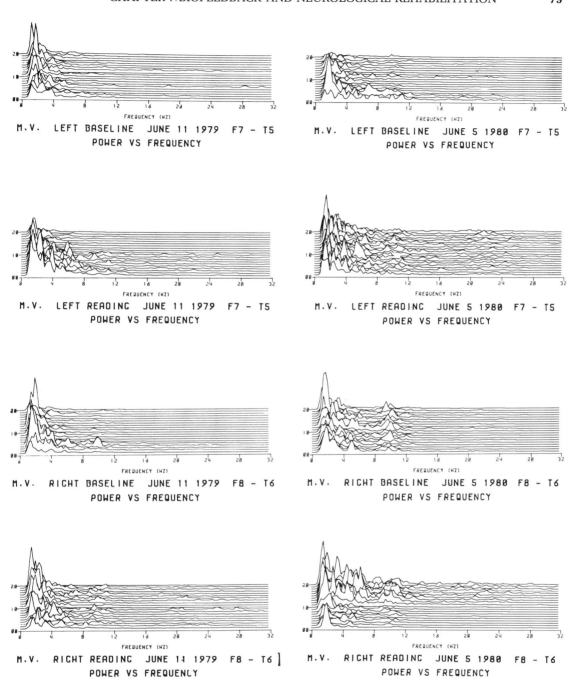

Figure 7.2. Changes in the power spectral analysis before and after biofeedback training for increasing SMR or beta activity and suppressing theta activity between 4 and 8 Hz for a 10-year-old learning disabled male. See text for detailed explanation.

begin with broad-band alpha and beta training between 11 and 19 Hz and then to concentrate on either increasing activity between 12 and 15 Hz, i.e., sensorimotor rhythm if there is hyperkinesis, or to increase beta activity between

16 and 20 Hz if there is a more pronounced learning disorder.

Examination of the right side of both Figures 7.2 and 7.3 displays that there are marked differences after EEG biofeedback training. For

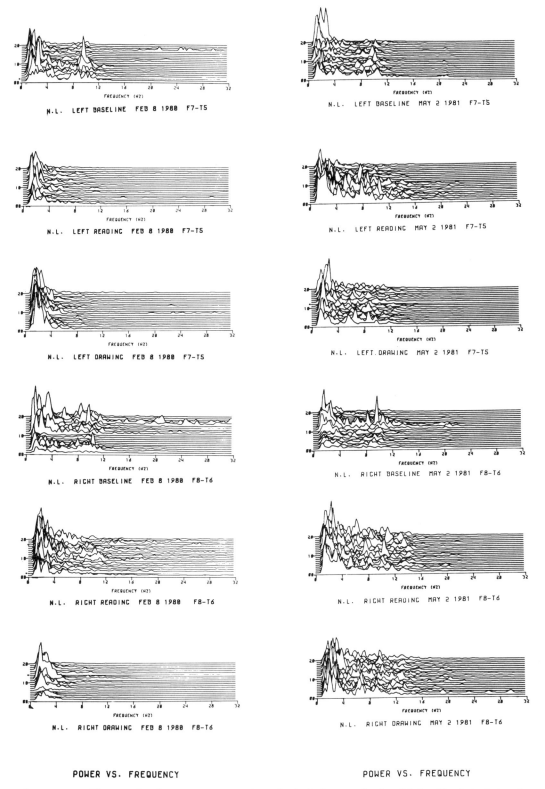

Figure 7.3. Changes in the power spectral analysis before and after biofeedback training for increasing SMR or beta activity and suppressing theta activity between 4 and 8 Hz for an 11-year-old learning disabled male. See text for detailed explanation.

example, during the baseline recording, both subjects N.L. and M.V. showed increased alpha and beta activity for the left hemisphere. During reading there is beta activation and alpha blocking for both children. This is also noted in N.L.'s left drawing spectral tracings. For the right hemisphere, the baseline recording for M.V. and N.L. show clear alpha, which now closely approximates the normal pattern, although alpha is somewhat diffuse for N.L. During reading, both right hemispheres show activation and during the drawing task which was carried out for subject N.L., the activation is very pronounced. The pattern shown on the right side of both tracings are now similar to the normal tracing in Figure 7.1 shown during the academic reading task. We have obtained data on many children before and after biofeedback training with similar results. These have been reported by J. O. Lubar (46, 47).

In 1985 we conducted a federally funded project to screen learning disabled children in their schools (48). This project consisted of using a portable 8-channel FM tape recorder to obtain recordings from six scalp locations in 69 learning disabled and 34 normal children. These data were obtained in the schools for five different counties in East Tennessee. The cerebral recording locations included frontal-temporal, parietal, and parietal-occipital for the left and right hemispheres. The data were then transferred to computer disk and subjected to power spectral analysis. Finally, multivariate statistical analysis programs were used to determine how learning disabled children differed from normal children with regard to their spectral distribution over eight frequency bands, six locations, and left vs. right hemispheres for a variety of academic tasks. These tasks included baseline recording, reading, arithmetic, and puzzle construction.

With this level of analysis, we have begun to develop a powerful and rapid diagnostic neurometric tool for separating learning disabled children from children who have academic difficulties not related to a neurophysiologically based learning problem. We found significant EEG power and percent differences for specific frequencies were obtained between the groups. Learning disabled children showed a predominance of 4 to 8 Hz activity in a variety of scalp locations including frontal, temporal, and central, particularly for the academic tasks. They also experienced increased muscle activity measured from many

scalp locations and had erratic, poorly organized eye movements compared with the control group. Using the technique of "discriminant function analysis" with 600 variables, we could predict with very high accuracy (over 95%) which children in the sample were learning disabled and which fell in the normal control group. When smaller discriminant analyses were carried out, the level of predictability fell, but even with eight variables, we could achieve predictability above 75%. With twenty variables nearly 80% accuracy was possible, based on frontal-temporal locations. Frontal-temporal locations on the left and right hemisphere were the best predictors based on power or frequency for specifically excessive 4 to 8 Hz activity.

Using this neurometric technique, we can now more easily assess a child as having a learning problem specific to a certain area of the cerebrum for a certain task in contrast with a learning disorder that may really be secondary to an emotional or an adjustment problem or dysfunction within the family. We can now identify children who are hyperkinetic vs. those children who have only a specific learning disability.

This neurometric method led to the second phase of our project, a demonstration project of biofeedback training programs in five schools for a period of 2 years. Using Autogen 120A EEG biofeedback instruments, we trained 37 selected children to increase first 12 to 15 Hz activity and then 14 to 20 Hz activity and to decrease 4 to 8 Hz activity. Training was carried out by resource teachers or school psychologists in 2-3 sessions each week. Most of the learning disabled children were able to increase the percentage of beta activity by 20% and some as much as 50%. The children in the learning disabled group showed a significant improvement in Metropolitan Achievement test scores as compared with controls.

Some of this work is described in more detail elsewhere (49). This demonstration project shows that EEG biofeedback training can be done in real school settings and that it has practical application.

Somewhat similar EEG feedback training is being carried out by J. Carter and H. Russell in the Houston and Galveston, Texas schools. Preliminary data from their work (50) indicates that increasing beta activity in the left hemisphere leads to a significant improvement in verbal IQ based on the Wechsler Intelligence Scale for Children-R (WISC), whereas increasing beta activity in the right hemisphere is correlated with a significant improvement on the performance IQ measure of the WISC. Furthermore, left hemispheric training does not affect the performance IQ, and right hemispheric training does not affect the verbal IQ.

Separate from work directed toward specific learning disabilities, a number of studies have investigated the effectiveness of biofeedback for helping hyperkinetic children (51-53), mostly with EMG or thermal biofeedback. Linn and Hodge (54) examined the effects of EMG biofeedback on attention span and locus of control for hyperkinetic children, and Carter (55) described a large study of 150 children employing relaxation training and EMG.

EEG biofeedback techniques for hyperkinesis began to be used following our studies (41-43) designed to determine whether low-arousal hyperkinetics and hyperkinetic children who are not characterized as low-arousal differ in terms of several physiological measures including the EEG. Our 1976 study (40) involved a single blind ABA crossover design to determine whether EEG biofeedback could be used to control hyperkinetic behavior both in the laboratory as well as home and classroom settings; 12 hyperkinetic children and eight normal controls were compared on four physiological measures: EMG activity recorded from muscles under the chin, galvanic skin reaction (GSR) conductance level, the number of SMR bursts per minute, and the amplitude of the auditory-evoked response (AER). The hyperkinetic children were subdivided into two groups, four of the low-arousal type, and eight of the high-arousal or nonmethylphenidate responders.

The four physiological measures did not discriminate between the hyperkinetic high-arousal children and the controls. However, it discriminated very effectively between the four low-arousal hyperkinetics, the hyperkinetic controls, and the normals. Low-arousal hyperkinetics who met the criteria of Satterfield and Dawson (38) were deficient in sensorimotor rhythm, indicating a deficit in inhibitory motor activity, and agreeing in terms of the hyperkinetic behavior. The low-arousal hyperkinetics had a lower electrodermal response level consistent with the concept of low arousal. Low-arousal hyperkinetics showed an increased amplitude of their AERs, as Satterfield and his colleagues also reported. We concluded that these children were

increasing the amplitude of this event-related potential in order to increase the impact or gain of stimuli or to increase their level of arousal.

Paradoxically, the EMG activity recorded from the low-arousal hyperkinetics was unusually low. This makes sense because the measures were taken in a very quiet setting, and it is known that low-arousal hyperkinetic children in a quiet setting after an initial burst of activity will often go to sleep. Their muscles become more flaccid, and their EMG activity declines.

After the initial baselines were taken both with and without medication, the four low-arousal hyperkinetics were trained to simultaneously increase 12- to 15-Hz sensorimotor activity recorded over the central cortex and to suppress 4- to 8-Hz slow-wave activity. This was done while they remained on their daily regimen of methylphenidate (Ritalin) medication. After this training was completed, reversal training was instituted in which the children were trained to increase slow-wave activity and inhibit their SMR. Neither the children nor their parents were aware of any change in the treatment paradigm. After this phase was completed, the initial A phase (that is, increasing SMR and inhibiting slow activity between 4 and 8 Hz) was reinstated, completing the ABA design. Finally, the training continued with the methylphenidate being gradually withdrawn. The entire training was prolonged over several months.

Three of the four children were able to complete this study. The child who did not was most distractible and was younger than the others (only age 6) and was unable to show significant acquisition during the initial training phase. The three children who learned the task demonstrated very clearly that they followed the contingencies of the ABA design precisely, i.e., they showed an increase in SMR activity with a decrease in theta during the initial SMR training phase, a decrease in SMR activity, and an increase in slow activity during the reversal phase, and finally, an increase in SMR activity again and a decrease in slow activity during the second A phase. Most important, when the medication was withdrawn, the increase in SMR and the inhibition of slow activity was maintained.

During all phases of this study, measures of behavior in school situations were obtained by independent observers. A large number of behavioral categories were analyzed, including 13 behavioral categories and six stimulus categories adapted from Wahler's category system (56). The behaviors were basically designated as desirable, undesirable, or social behaviors. The results were also strikingly clear. During the first SMR training phase, desirable behaviors improved by statistically significant levels, and undesirable behaviors increased significantly during the reversal phase, with a decrease in desirable behaviors. Finally, during both the reinstitution of the SMR training and the withdrawal phase for the medication, desirable and social behaviors improved with a concurrent decrease in undesirable behaviors.

We concluded that the SMR training was more powerful than previous studies with EMG training and were clearly more powerful than the effects of medication alone. The latter was shown in the final analysis of those behaviors by Lubar and Deering (45). In addition to a clear improvement in the positive behaviors associated with the SMR bursts increased and the evoked cortical potential of the low-arousal hyperkinetics approximated those of the normal and hyperkinetic controls. There was an approximately 50% normalization of the GSR conductance level measure, and there was a normalization of the auditory evoked potential.

Clinical Application

As a result of this initial study, we have employed SMR training as a clinical procedure for the past several years for helping low-arousal hyperkinetic children to achieve better control of the motor aspects of the hyperkinesis to decrease distractibility and improve attention span. This technique, combined with beta training and academic tutoring, does significantly facilitate reading and those other aspects of academic performance that have often been substandard in children who are experiencing hyperkinesis or hyperkinesis associated with learning disorder.

EEG biofeedback might become a more standard method of helping to remediate children who are experiencing the MBD syndrome. This technique is not in competition with pharmacotherapy, but is a means for helping children to decrease their amount of drug dependence or to eliminate drugs at an earlier age and develop self-confidence through the self-control procedures. Many children experiencing severe manifestations of the hyperkinetic syndrome would be untrainable without the use of medication, at least in the initial stages.

EVOKED POTENTIAL STUDY

We have recently completed a study to determine if there are differences in evoked potential activity in different populations of children. The study involved 45 children between ages 8 and 11. Fifteen were classified in the normal range, 15 as learning disabled (specifically attention deficit disorder without hyperkinesis), and 15 were in the borderline gifted population (I.Q. scores of 130).

Four types of evoked potential tasks were employed. The first was a simple auditory task in which an odd stimulus was presented 10% of the time, pseudorandomly, in comparison with a control stimulus. The control stimulus was a low-tone; the odd stimulus was a high tone, equated for loudness. The child was to signal the presence of the odd stimulus by pushing a small button. Evoked potentials were averaged, both to the control and the target stimulus, over a period from 180 millisecond (ms) before the stimulus presentation to 1000 ms after. Activity was recorded from three locations—frontally, centrally, and posteriorly.

Differences between groups indicated that in the learning disabled group, the P200 was well defined. This positive wave at about 200 ms indicates the detection of the stimulus. This was well defined for all three groups. However, in the learning disabled group, the P300 component, which indicates not only detection but also comprehension of meaning of the stimulus, was smaller, i.e., significantly lower in amplitude than the corresponding P300 in the normal or gifted groups. This was most evident in the central location. It could also be seen in the posterior location.

The second evoked potential task was an easy visual task. The common stimulus was the presentation of the letter O. The odd stimulus, or target stimulus, was the presentation of the letter Z. The child was asked to press a button whenever the Z appeared. Again, differences were obtained between the three groups, primarily in the 300 component as opposed to the 200 component of the evoked potential. This again indicated that in the learning disabled group, the meaning of the stimulus, as evidenced by the appearance of a well-defined 300 component was significantly poorer than in the normal or gifted group.

The third task involved a more difficult visual discrimination: the common stimulus was the small letter b, and the odd stimulus, or target stimulus, the small letter d. These letters are often confused by learning disabled children, who often write b's and d's backwards. Again, differences were obtained more in the 300 component than in the 200 component, both for central and posterior locations.

The final task involved a "semantic"-evoked potential. In this task, names of objects were presented, but approximately 10% of the time an animal's name would be presented, such as horse, cow, dog, etc. The task was to press the button when the animal name appeared. Here, differences were more striking. The learning disabled children had great difficulty with this task and although able to detect the stimulus as evidenced by the P200, they showed very little or no P300 response. The control children were able to discriminate many of the animal names. The gifted children showed a larger P300 than did the controls, indicating even better discrimination.

Applications

These findings are significant because they comprise one of the first demonstrations that complex stimuli can be used in an evoked potential paradigm. The evoked potential gives us information on the brain's immediate process of information, unlike the EEG which is more nonspecific and deals more with levels of alertness or consciousness. The evoked potential can be used to probe for the specific meaning of stimuli and how they are processed.

The use of the evoked potential might make it possible to develop more complex neurometrics in the future. These neurometrics could be based on the response to stimuli that are commonly used in intelligence tests, presented in such a form so as to observe the brain's immediate response. This adds one more dimension to the others described. The use of evoked potential can be extended not only to one dimensional EEG but also to two-dimensional brain mapping. Hence, evoked potentials can be followed with brain mapping devices across the cortex as they develop and propagate. As is the case with EEG, evoked potential feedback can be employed to help sharpen discriminations or to increase the responsivity of certain areas of the brain to discrete stimuli.

EEG BIOFEEDBACK APPLICATIONS FOR SEIZURE DISORDERS

Biofeedback has played a significant role in developing a methodology for helping epileptics to achieve better management of their seizure conditions. Of the 4 million epileptics in the United States, approximately 20%, or 800,000 individuals, are not adequately controlled by anticonvulsive medication (57). For patients with severe seizure disorders who also carry the burden of the side effects of anticonvulsive medications, there is clearly the need for interventions that might help significantly. The advent of biofeedback in the treatment of seizure disorders is relatively recent, but there has been considerable documentation in terms of double-blind studies, controlled outcome studies, and theoretical models for providing a rationale for how biofeedback methods can be applied.

Many animal studies provide a basis and rationale for using EEG feedback in human epileptics. Roth, Sterman and Clemente (9) noted that a specific rhythmic activity occurred in both waking and sleeping cats and designated this activity as sensorimotor rhythm or SMR. This activity is particularly prevalent during periods of inactivity or motor inhibition. Neurophysiologically, SMR is believed to be generated by neurons located within the ventrobasal complex of the thalamus. This region includes two important nuclei, the ventral posterolateral and ventral posteromedial nuclei, which receive inputs from both the lemniscal and spinothalamic systems. These systems receive afferents from exteroceptors and interoceptors and are responsible for the sensations commonly referred to as the skin senses, including touch, temperature, pain, and pressure sensations.

Harper and Sterman (58), using extracellular microelectrodes, showed that the firing patterns of single units within the ventrobasal complex exhibited recurrent bursting and inhibition which was synchronized with the cortical appearance of 12- to 16-Hz spindles recorded from the sensorimotor cortex. These SMR spindles were behaviorally associated with inhibition of movement and decreased muscle tonus. Sterman and Wywricka (59) and Sterman, Wywricka and Roth (60) trained cats to increase SMR in an operant conditioning paradigm using food reward. The animals had to learn to remain motionless or inhibit ongoing motor activity. In a series of publications, Sterman and his colleagues postulated that SMR is the brain's natural anticonvulsant rhythm and controls motor inflow and output from the motor cortex.

The motor cortex is involved in the generation of excessive activity in a variety of different seizure types, particularly tonic-clonic seizures, tonic seizures, clonic seizures and myoclonic seizures. Several other seizure types have certain motor components. The motor aspects of the seizure probably originate in pools of neurons located in the sensory and motor cortex or involve the activation or kindling of these neurons from epileptic activity occurring in other groups of cortical and subcortical neurons that project to these cortical regions.

In order to test the hypothesis that SMR is an anticonvulsant rhythm, Sterman, LoPresti and Fairchild (61) first trained cats to produce SMR spindles. They then injected these trained animals with a convulsant chemical, monomethylhydrazine (a component in rocket fuel). Normally this elicits a strong tonic-clonic seizure within a relatively well-defined period of time after its administration. However, in animals trained to produce SMR, these convulsions were diminished in intensity, and their latency was prolonged. This study has been repeated several times with larger numbers of animals, and it is quite clear that enhancement of inhibitory SMR seems to have an anticonvulsant effect.

Based on these and other animal studies, the first human study employing SMR training for epileptics was carried out by Sterman and Friar in 1972 (10). The very first attempt to use EEG biofeedback for human epileptics by Stevens in 1960 and 1962 had failed (62, 63). His patients were provided a feedback signal when abnormal spikes occurred in their EEG. Stevens, Milstein and Dodds in 1967 tried aversive conditioning (64). Pairing electric shock with paroxysmal EEG activity, they were able to obtain some minor decreases in seizures, but the effects were not sustained.

Sterman and Friar (10) first trained a 23-year-old woman with nocturnal and generalized motor seizures to increase 12- to 16-Hz SMR activity over the sensory motor cortex with a very striking outcome. The patient was able to reduce significantly the frequency of seizures, becoming almost free of them during the period of training. Unfortunately, long-term follow-up of this patient was never carried out, but this study initiated considerable interest in a further and more penetrating examination of this approach for dealing with epilepsy; many studies began to appear within the next few years. These are reviewed in detail by Lubar and Deering (45).

Sterman, McDonald and Stone (65) carried out a second study with four epileptic patients, again using SMR as the designated target frequency for training; but this time they also trained the patients to inhibit slow-wave activity between 6 and 9 Hz. These patients were trained for a long period of time, ranging from 6 to 16 months. Again, detailed statistical analyses were not presented, but there was an overall reduction of 66% in seizure frequency. An abrupt withdrawal of the training led to a rapid increase in seizure activity. Because of this, current treatment protocols employ gradual weaning from treatment for patients who are successful in reducing their seizures through biofeedback.

Another study by Kaplan (66) compared the effect of 12- to 14-Hz training with training for a rhythm known as the MU rhythm, which is also recorded from the Rolandic cortex and is associated with inhibition of movement. The MU rhythm is often described as a wicket rhythm because of its appearance and is designated as 7-9 Hz. Kaplan trained her patients for only 4 to 6 months, but she found a 52% reduction of seizures for the patients given MU rhythm training and no significant change for the SMR-trained patients. However, there was a problem with this study, particularly since the patients that improved most were those that had experienced stress associated with their seizures, and also no inhibit circuits for slow paroxysmal activity were used. It is well known that stress can exacerbate true epileptic seizures, and there are psychogenic seizures, i.e., seizure-like manifestations that patients sometimes use as a means of getting attention or controlling their social environment.

There are some valid theoretical issues raised by Kaplan's study in that she argued that SMR in cats does not have an analog in humans in the same frequency range and that the closest analog is MU rhythm. This issue has been debated but never resolved. In order to help to define the relationship of SMR with other rhythms more clearly, Shabsin, Bahler and Lubar (67) examined whether 12- to 15-Hz SMR activity is a unique independent brain rhythm or whether its occurrence coincides with occipital alpha rhythm. This study employed one female and five male nonepileptic university students who were trained for 9 months to produce SMR. Recordings were taken from both the sensorimotor cortex and from the occipital scalp. It was determined that the number of bursts of SMR activity per minute was not related to or coincident with alpha bursting. In fact, these two activities could occur randomly and independently of each other. The study has been described in more detail by Lubar and Deering (45).

In addition to studies by Sterman and by Kaplan, a series of studies by Finley (68, 69) replicated the original studies of Sterman. These were systematic case studies involving small numbers of patients trained to enhance sharply filtered 11- to 13-Hz activity and to suppress slow activity between 4 and 7 Hz. Not only was there an improvement in seizures, but also an increase in the proportion of SMR measured from the filter output and a decrease in epileptiform activity.

In his 1976 study (68), Finley described an increase of SMR from 10 to 70% and a decrease in slow activity from 45 to 15%. One of the greatest strengths of his research is that at one point he employed noncontingent reinforcement in a single-blind paradigm. During this "false feedback" period, there was a decrease in SMR, an increase in epileptiform activity, and an increase in seizures and seizure-related behavior. After the noncontingent feedback period was completed, SMR training with slow frequency inhibition was reinstituted, and the patient again experienced recovery. This represents the first use of the ABA design for epileptic biofeedback work in which the intermediate B period involved the introduction of the noncontingent or sham feedback. Studies of this kind help to argue strongly against placebo effects in explaining the improvement following EEG biofeedback training.

Cabral and Scott (70) used alpha conditioning for three epileptics and found an improvement in their seizure activity. All three patients decreased their seizures more than 92%. However, it must be emphasized that for alpha, even though its appearance does not coincide in any way with SMR, it does overlap

the SMR band since alpha is defined as 8-13 Hz, and SMR is 12-15 Hz. Furthermore, strong alpha rhythm can sometimes be reported from central locations and even from locations approaching the frontal portion of the scalp. It is possible that alpha conditioning might also condition SMR. It is also possible that alpha rhythm, which represents cortical idling in an intermediate frequency, being neither paroxysmal nor spike-like, helps to stabilize the EEG. Its conditioning could facilitate the normalization of the abnormal activity that is often either too slow or too fast in the EEG of the epileptic.

Our laboratory has been involved in the area of seizure control since 1972. Until 1975, our efforts were directed toward developing a highly reliable system for signal detection and analysis, involving both analog and zero-crossing (digital) techniques. This system, described in detail by Seifert and Lubar (71) and Lubar and Bahler (14), has the advantages over systems used in other studies in that precisely defined activity between 12 and 15 Hz can be reinforced, and slow activity between 4 and 8 Hz can be inhibited, with the added features that filter ringing is greatly reduced. A zero-crossing analysis is imposed on the output of the analog filter rather than the raw signal, which eliminates the problem of selective enhancement of either fast activity as would be obtained with differentiation of the signal, or slow activity which would be the case with the zero-crossing analysis. We also have incorporated additional inhibit circuits for gross movement and EMG activity defined between 30 and 300 μV recorded from the active scalp electrodes.

In our initial studies, we began monitoring anticonvulsant levels on a regular basis and asked patients to keep an accurate record of seizure events recorded each hour and daily over a long time period. In our more recent studies, progressively longer baseline periods have been employed. In the study carried out by Lubar and Bahler (14), eight patients were evaluated over a period of training of 6-8½ months. The results were reported as single case studies with correlational statistics. This study, and our previous one (71) which included some of the same patients as the 1976 study during their initial phases of training, involved both normal and retarded epileptics. The majority of the patients in these studies were able to produce more 12- to 15-Hz activity and less 4- to 8-Hz activity when provided feedback as compared with their baseline. Some of our patients who began training with seizures occurring daily were able to obtain seizure-free periods of greater than one month. We also concurred with Finley and Sterman that abrupt withdrawal of training leads to an exacerbation of seizures.

Single-blind and double-blind studies emerged at the end of the 1970s. Sterman and McDonald (72) used a single-blind study employing both SMR, 6-9 Hz, and beta training. Lubar et al. (73) in 1981 reported the first completely double-blind study of biofeedback in epileptics involving both noncontingent reinforcement as well as reversal training and employing several different treatment paradigms. In this double-blind study, eight patients with mixed and multiple seizure types who were refractory to medical treatment were included. Initially, seizures were recorded for a 4-month baseline period before any training was initiated, then all patients were provided with 2 months of false or noncontingent EEG biofeedback. However, a red light stimulus was presented contingently for gross movement and muscle activity. The purpose of this was to separate the effects of EEG from EMG relaxation training. The false feedback condition with the EMG feedback did not result in any significant increase or decrease in seizure frequency. This result helps to strengthen the contention that reduction of seizures using EEG biofeedback is specific and not due to placebo factors.

The patients were then divided into three small treatment groups and placed on different schedules of reinforcement. They were first trained to either suppress 3- to 8-Hz slow activity, enhance 12- to 15-Hz SMR, or to simultaneously suppress 3- to 8-Hz slow activity and increase broad-band 11- to 19-Hz activity. All training was over the left central cortex. The first condition, 3- to 8-Hz suppression, was employed to determine whether reduction of slow paroxysmal activity was sufficient to help control seizures. The second condition represented the traditional use of sensorimotor rhythm, and the third condition represented a normalization of the EEG. The goal was to reduce slow activity and increase intermediate and fast activity for this third condition, and represents an attempt to normalize that portion of the EEG spectrum which is often deficient in the epileptic.

Following 4 months of this A training phase, a B phase was initiated in which all patients were trained to enhance 3- to 8-Hz activity. Following this, the initial A phase was then reinstituted for all three groups, and then followed by 4 months of noncontingent training and follow-up.

The patients consisted of four males and four females between 13 and 52 years old. Only one had an IQ above 100, and four had IQ's of less than 60. The others had IQ's between 75 and 95. The extensive psychological testing was carried out as part of the initial baseline procedure. Anticonvulsant levels were monitored and maintained within the therapeutic range.

The overall results of this study were conservative but supportive of the notion that the EEG effects were specific. Five of the eight patients experienced a decrease in their mean monthly seizure rate as compared with their initial baseline level. Two followed the ABA aspects of the design quite precisely, that is they decreased their seizures during the A phase, showed an increase during the B phase reversal condition, and a decrease again during the reinitiation of the original contingencies in the second A phase.

All groups experienced a seizure decrease overall of 34.8% in comparing their initial baseline to their final A training phase. The patients in the group that were trained to decrease slow waves followed the contingencies best. The patients in the SMR group followed the contingencies worst but, unfortunately, these results were probably due to poor patient selection. The patients in the dual training condition, testing the normalization hypothesis, showed decreases in their seizures in all three training conditions and therefore did not follow the ABA aspects of the paradigm very closely. The spectral analytic data for some of the patients also showed changes that followed the ABA design of the study.

A more recent study dealing with the sleep EEG's of these patients throughout the entire double-blind investigation (74) has further shown that even some sleep EEG changes follow the ABA paradigm and were correlated with changes in seizures. Sterman's (72) study and this most recent study by Whitsett et al. (74) employed sleep analysis of the EEG as firm evidence that the changes that are experienced during EEG biofeedback in epileptics are specific and not due to placebo effects.

When reliable EEG changes can be obtained, while patients are sleeping, and these EEG changes mirror changes in their seizures correlated with daytime training contingencies, one is convinced that the EEG biofeedback must have some degree of specificity and this specificity is relevant and related to a decrease in seizure activity.

There is now an expanding interest in the use of EEG biofeedback for working with human epileptics. The questions that remain are primarily questions of practicality. Is such a complex technique, requiring special instrumentation and a minimum of at least 4 months of training with long-term follow-up and careful weaning, practical for dealing with the epileptic population? It could be argued, on one hand, that anticonvulsants have to be changed occasionally in any one epileptic and carefully monitored perhaps for the life of the patient. Based on this argument, it is reasonable that any treatment, whether it be behavioral or medical, may have to be applied over a very long time period. If large numbers of epileptics could achieve a decrease in their medication levels and improve their quality of life, then certainly biofeedback has a great deal to offer. This approach would have even more to offer if, after the initial intense training period, patients could be provided with home instruments (such as Sterman's group or as we have done), or if occasional booster sessions with very long-term follow-up are provided.

If EEG biofeedback training programs could be established throughout the country in regional epilepsy centers, or in certain hospitals so that patients would not have to come long distances for their booster training, then certainly EEG biofeedback could play an important role in working with the intractable epileptic. The factors that must be weighed are clinical short-term and long-term effectiveness, cost and the complexity of the treatment as compared with the use of drugs alone. Since no significant new anticonvulsant medications have become available, perhaps EEG biofeedback is the best adjunctive technique that is available at present. If studies continue to appear in this area and continue to validate the importance of this approach for epilepsy, then perhaps EEG biofeedback might make a significant contribution for many years to come. At least it is worth serious attention until the neurochemistry of epilepsy is well understood.

References

1. Caton, R. The electrical currents of the brain. Br. J. Med., 2: 278, 1875.
2. Dempsey, E. W. and Morison, R. S. The production of rhythmically recurrent cortical potentials after localized thalamic stimulation. Am. J. Physiol., 135: 292–300, 1942.
3. Adrian, E. D. Afferent discharges to the cerebral cortex from peripheral sense organs. J. Physiol. (Lond.), 100: 159–191, 1939.
4. Andersen, P. and Andersson, S. Physiological Basis of the Alpha Rhythm. Appleton-Century-Crofts, New York, 1968.
5. Spencer, W. A., and Brookhart, J. M. Electrical patterns of augmenting and recruiting waves in depth of sensorimotor cortex of cats. J. Neurophysiol., 24: 26–49, 1961.
6. Kamiya, J. Autoregulation of the EEG alpha rhythm: a program for the study of consciousness. In Mind, Body Integration: Essential Readings in Biofeedback, edited by E. Peper, S. Ancoli and M. Quinn. Plenum Press. New York, 1979, pp. 289–298.
7. Webb, W. B. and Cartwright, R. D. Sleep and dreams. Ann. Rev. Psychol., 29: 223–252, 1978.
8. Howe, R. C. and Sterman, M. B. Cortical-subcortical EEG correlates of suppressed motor behavior during sleep and waking in the cat. Electroencephalogr. Clin. Neurophysiol., 32: 681–695, 1972.
9. Roth, S. R., Sterman, M. B. and Clemente, C.D. Comparison of EEG correlates of reinforcement, internal inhibition, and sleep. Electroencephalogr. Clin. Neurophysiol., 23: 509–520, 1967
10. Sterman, M. B. and Friar, L. Suppression of seizures in an epileptic following sensorimotor EEG feedback training. Electroencephalogr. Clin. Neurophysiol., 33: 89–95, 1972.
11. Kuhlman, W. and Kaplan, B. J. Clinical applications of EEG feedback training. In R. J. Gatchel and K. P. Price (eds.) Pergamon General Psychology Series, Pergamon Press, New York, 1979.
12. Walsh, D. H. Interactive effects of alpha feedback and instructional set on subjective state. Psychophysiology, 11: 428–435, 1974.
13. Lubar, J. F. Electroencephalographic biofeedback methodology and the management of epilepsy. Pavlov. J. Biol. Sci., 12: 147–185, 1977.
14. Lubar, J. F. and Bahler, W. W. Behavioral management of epileptic seizures following EEG biofeedback training of the sensorimotor rhythm. Biofeedback Self Regul., 1: 77–104, 1976.
15. Lubar, J. F. and Culver, R. N. Automated EEG signal-detection methodologies for biofeedback conditioning. Behav. Methods Instrumentation, 10: 607–616, 1978.
16. Diagnostic and Statistical Manual of Mental Disorders, Third Edition (DSM-III), American Psychiatric Association, 1980.
17. Duffy, F. H. (ed.) Topographic Mapping of Brain Electrical Activity. Butterworths, London, 1986.

18. Duffy, F. H., Burchiel, J. L. and Lombroso, C. T. Brain electrical activity mapping (BEAM): A method for extending the clinical utility of EEG and evoked potential data. Ann. Neurol., 5: 309–321, 1979.

19. Duffy, F. H., Denckla, M. D., Bartels, P. H. and Sandini, G. Dsylexia: Regional differences in brain electrical activity by topographic mapping. Ann. Neurol., 7: 412–420, 1980.

20. Kamiya, J. Operant control of the EEL alpha rhythm and some of its reported effects on consciousness. In Altered States of Consciousness, edited by C. T. Tart, John Wiley, New York, 1969, pp. 507–517.

21. Green, E. E., Green, A. M. and Walters, E. D. Voluntary control of internal states: psychological and physiological. J. Transpersonal Psychol., 2: 1–26, 1970.

22. Brown, B. B. Awareness of EEG-subject activity relationships detected within a closed feedback system. Psychophysiology, 7: 451–464, 1971.

23. Luthe, W. and Schultz, J. H. Autogenic Therapy: Medical Applications, Grune & Stratton, New York, 1970.

24. Andreychuk, T. and Skriver, C. Hypnosis and biofeedback in the treatment of migraine headache. Int. J. Clin, Exp. Hyp., 23: 172–183, 1975.

25. McKenzie, R. E., Ehrisman, W. J., Montgomery, P. S. and Barnes, R. H. The treatment of headaches by means of electroencephalographic biofeedback. Headache, 13: 164–172, 1974.

26. Garrett, B. L. and Silver, N. P. The use of EMG and alpha biofeedback to relieve test anxiety in college students. In Biofeedback, Behavior Therapy and Hypnosis, edited by I. Wickramesekera. Nelson-Hall, Chicago, 1976.

27. Glueck, B. C. and Stroebel, C. F. Biofeedback and meditation in the treatment of psychiatric illnesses. Compr. Psychiatr., 16: 303–321, 1975.

27a. Wallace, R. K. Physiological effects of transcendental meditation. Science, 167: 1751-1754, 1970.

28. Bird, B. L., Newton, F. A., Sheer, D. E. and Ford, M. Biofeedback training of 40-Hz EEG in humans. Biofeedback Self Regul., 3: 1–12, 1978.

29. Sheer, D. E. Electrophysiological correlates of memory consolidation. In Molecular Mechanisms in Memory and Learning, edited by G. Ungar. Plenum Press, New York, 1970.

30. Sheer, D. E. Focused arousal and 40 Hz EEG. In The Neurophysiology of Learning Disorders, edited by R. M. Knights, and D. J. Bakker, University Park Press, Baltimore, 1976.

31. Sheer, D. E. Electroencephalographic studies in learning disabilities. In The Learning Disabled Child, edited by H. Eichenwald and A. Talbot, University of Texas Health Sciences Center, Dallas, 1974.

32. Das, N. N. and Gastaut, H. Variations de l'activité électrique du cerveau, du coeur, et des muscles squellettiques au cours de la meditation et de l'extase yogique. Electroencephalogr. Clin. Neurophysiol. 6 (Suppl): 281–306, 1955.

33. Morgan, W. P. A case of congenital word blindness. Br. Med. J., 2: 1612, 1896.

34. Golden, J. G. and Anderson, S. Learning Disabilities and Brain Dysfunction: An Introduction for Educators and Parents. Charles C. Thomas, Springfield, Ill., 1979.

35. Muehl, S., Knott, J. R. and Benton, A. L. EEG abnormality and psychological test performance in reading disability. Cortex, 1: 434, 1965.

36. Schain, R. J. Neurology of Childhood Learning Disorders, 2nd ed. Williams & Wilkins, Baltimore, 1977.

37. Hertzig, M. F., Bortner, M. and Birch, H. G. Neurological findings in children educationally designated as "brain damaged." Am. J. Orthopsychiatry, 39: 437, 1969.

38. Satterfield, J. H. and Dawson, M. E. Electrodermal correlates of hyperactivity in children. Psychophysiology, 8: 191–197, 1971.

39. Satterfield, J. H. Response to stimulant drug treatment in hyperactive children: prediction from EEG and neurological findings, J. Autism Childhood Schizophrenia, 1: 36–48, 1973.

40. Lubar, J. F. and Shouse, M. N. EEG and behavioral changes in a hyperactive child concurrent with training of the sensorimotor rhythm (SMR). A preliminary report. Biofeedback Self Regul., 1: 293–306, 1976.

41. Lubar, J. F. and Shouse, M. N. Use of biofeedback in the treatment of seizure disorders and hyperactivity. In Advances in Child Clinical Psychology, edited by B. B. Lahey and A. E. Kadzin. Plenum Press, New York, 1977.

42. Shouse, M. N. and Lubar, J. F. Physiological basis of hyperkinesis treated with methylphenidate. Pediatrics, 3: 343–351, 1978.

43. Shouse, M. N. and Lubar, J. F. Sensorimotor rhythm (SMR) operant conditioning and methlyphenidate in the treatment of hyperkinesis. Biofeedback Self Regul., 4: 299–311, 1979.

44. Walker, S. Help for the Hyperactive Child. Houghton Mifflin, Boston, 1977.

45. Lubar, J. F. and Deering, W. M. Behavioral Approaches to Neurology, Academic Press, New York, 1981.

46. Lubar, J. O. The use of EEG analysis for assessing the effectiveness of biofeedback for treating learning disabled and children with MBD syndrome. Paper presented at the 13th annual meeting of the Biofeedback Society of America, Chicago, Ill., March 5–8, 1982.

47. Lubar, J. O. and Lubar, J. F. Electroencephalographic biofeedback of SMR and beta for treatment of attention deficit disorders in a clinical setting. Biofeedback and Self Regul., 9: 1–23, 1984.

48. Lubar, J. F., Bianchini, R. J., Calhoun, U. H., Lambert, E. W., Brody, Z. H. and Shabsin, H. S. Spectral analysis of EEG differences between children with and without learning disabilities. Journal of Learning Disabilities, 7: 403–408, 1985.

49. Lubar, J. F. EEG biofeedback and learning disabilities. Theory into Practice, 24: 106–111, 1985.

50. Russell, H. and Carter, J. EEG and EMG hemi-

spheric specific biofeedback. Paper presented at the 13th annual meeting of the Biofeedback Society of America, Chicago, Ill., March 5–8, 1982.

51. Braud, I. W. The effects of frontal EMG biofeedback and progressive relaxation upon hyperactivity and its behavioral concomitants. Biofeedback Self Regul., 3: 69–90, 1978.

52. Hampstead, W. J. The effects of EMG-assisted relaxation training with hyperkinetic children: a behavioral alternative. Biofeedback Self Regul., 2: 113–125, 1979.

53. Hunter, S. H., Russell, H. L. and Russell, E. D. Control of fingertip temperature increases via biofeedback in learning-disabled and normal children. Percept. Mot. Skills, 43: 743–755, 1976.

54. Linn, R. T. and Hodge, C. K. Use of EMG biofeedback training in increasing attention span for internalizing locus of control in hyperactive children. Paper presented at the 11th annual meeting of the Biofeedback Society of America, 1980.

55. Carter, J. L. Effects of EMG/relaxation training on academic attainment of children. Paper presented at the 11th annual meeting of the Biofeedback Society of America, 1980.

56. Wahler, R. G., House, A. E. and Stanbaugh, E. E. *Ecological Assessment of Child Problem Behavior.* Pergamon Press, New York, 1975.

57. Masland, R. I. Epidemiology and basic statistics of the epilepsies: where are we? Paper presented at the Fifth National Conference on the Epileptics. Washington, D. C., 1976.

58. Harper, R. M. and Sterman, M. B. Subcortical unit activity during a conditioned 12-14 Hz sensorimotor EEG rhythm in the cat. Fed. Proc., 31: 404, 1972.

59. Sterman, M. B. and Wywricka, W. EEG correlates of sleep: evidence for separate forebrain substrates. Brain Res., 6: 143–163, 1967.

60. Sterman, M. B., Wywricka, W. and Roth, S. R. Electrophysiological correlates and neural substrates of alimentary behavior in the cat. Ann. N. Y. Acad. Sci., 157: 723–739, 1969.

61. Sterman, M. B., LoPresti, R. W. and Fairchild, M. D. Electroencephalographic and behavioral studies of monomethylhydrazine toxicity in the cat (Technical Report AMRL-TR-69-3). Air Systems Command, Wright-Patterson Air Force Base, Ohio, 1969.

62. Stevens, J. R. Electroencephalographic studies of conditioned cerebral response in epileptic subjects. Electroencephalogr. Clin. Neurophysiol., 12: 431–444, 1960.

63. Stevens, J. R. Endogenous conditioning to abnormal cerebral transients in man. Science 137: 974-976, 1962.

64. Stevens, J. R., Milstein, V. M. and Dodds, S. A. Endogenous-spike discharges as conditioned stimuli in man. Electroencephalogr. Clin. Neurophysiol., 23: 57–66, 1967.

65. Sterman, M. B., Macdonald, L. R. and Stone, R. K. Biofeedback training of the sensorimotor electroencephalographic rhythm in man: effects on epilepsy. Epilepsia. 15: 395–416, 1974.

66. Kaplan, B. J. Biofeedback in epileptics: equivocal relationship of reinforced EEG frequency to seizure reduction. Epilepsia, 16: 477–485, 1975.

67. Shabsin, H. S., Bahler, W. W. and Lubar, J. F. A comparison of 12-15 Hz Rolandic activity (SMR) during eyes-opened and eyes-closed conditions and its occurrence with occipital alpha. Paper presented at the annual meeting of the Southeastern Psychological Association, New Orleans, La., March 28-31, 1979.

68. Finley, W. W. Effects of sham feedback following successful SMR training in an epileptic: follow-up study. Biofeedback Self Regul., 1: 227–236, 1976.

69. Finley, W. W. Operant conditioning of the EEG in two patients with epilepsy: methodologic and clinical considerations. Pavlov. J. Biol. Sci., 12: 93–111, 1977.

70. Cabral, R. J. and Scott, D. F. Effects of two desensitization techniques, biofeedback and relaxation, on intractable epilepsy: follow-up study. J. Neurol. Neurosurg. Psychiatry, 39: 504-507, 1976.

71. Seifert, A. R. and Lubar, J. F. Reduction of epileptic seizures through EEG biofeedback training. Biol. Psychol., 3: 157–184, 1975.

72. Sterman, M. B. and Macdonald, L. R. Effects of central cortical EEG feedback training on seizure incidence in poorly controlled epileptics. Epilepsia, 19: 207–222, 1978.

73. Lubar, J. F., Shabsin, H. S., Natelson, S. E., Holder, G. S., Whitsett, S. F., Pamplin, W. E. and Krulikowski, D. I. EEG operant conditioning in intractable epileptics. Arch. Neurol., 38: 700–704, 1981.

74. Whitsett, S. F., Lubar, J. F., Holder, G. S., Pamplin, W. E. and Shabsin, H. S. A double-blind investigation of the relationship between seizure activity and the sleep EEG following EEG biofeedback training. Biofeedback Self Regul., 7: 193–210, 1982.

PART 2
NEUROMOTOR
REHABILITATION

CHAPTER 8

Electromyographic Biofeedback in the Physical Therapy Clinic

STEVEN L. WOLF
STUART A. BINDER-MACLEOD

Electromyographic (EMG) biofeedback requires the therapist to invest some time to learn effective applications. To apply feedback, the needs for changes in the physical set-up within a clinical environment are rather small. For the patient undergoing training for general relaxation or reduction of spasticity, a quiet room is useful. Noise should be held to a minimum, and visual distractions avoided. This effect may be achieved by scheduling patients when the clinician's patient load is not heavy. Ultimately, however, the patient will have to integrate what has been taught in this calm environment into everyday life; in that process, feedback training should meld into the mainstream of clinical activities, daily distractions, and functional goals.

So that biofeedback training can be performed in a variety of locations, the biofeedback equipment should be set up on an easily maneuvered cart. All the necessary supplementary items should be placed on the cart. These include: alcohol, cotton swabs, electrode gel, electrodes, adhesive disks, and a small trash receptacle. Alternately, many contemporary electromyographic units are small, battery-operated units that can be strapped to the patient or, under some circumstances, hung around the waist. These units are unobstrusive and often weigh less than 1 kg.

In acute cases of low-back or neck pain from noninvasive injuries or when patients must be immobilized, transportation of the patient to the physical therapy clinic for treatment may aggravate the condition. Biofeedback equipment on a cart can easily be transported to the patient's room for specific or general muscle relaxation, thus providing many advantages to the patient. The bed will already be adjusted comfortably, and there will be only a minimal amount of movement. After the relaxation session, the patient can remain in the comfortable position as long as desired, instead of having to leave the treatment plinth to be transported by wheelchair or stretcher.

For patients immobilized by skeletal traction, biofeedback can help maintain the patient's interest in doing isometric exercises by allowing goal-setting to reach and maintain specific values of muscle activity. Biofeedback can add some incentive and self-motivation for an exercise program that would otherwise be limited to simply performing a specific number of static contractions.

The list of uses of biofeedback in the patient's own room will continue to grow, just as its uses in the physical therapy clinic continue to expand. Table 8.1 presents some of the musculoskeletal applications amenable to biofeedback. This list should be used as a guide, but it

Table 8.1.
Musculoskeletal problems amenable to
biofeedback treatment

Prolonged immobilization
Myositis ossificans
Joint repair
Elevated activity following low back strain
Frozen shoulder
Muscle-tendon transfers
Substitution movements
Muscle strengthening and relaxation
Whiplash
Muscle shortening
Asymmetry in homologous trunk or back
  muscles

is not all-inclusive, a further appreciation of the numerous applications of EMG feedback to clinical conditions seen in the physical therapeutic clinic can be gained through inspection and review of the extended reference list at the end of this chapter.

BIOFEEDBACK EQUIPMENT AND HOW TO CHOOSE IT

Audiofeedback Alternatives

Many commercially available devices offer auditory feedback in the form of a tone, buzzer, or click, a combination of these possibilities, or the audio-amplified (raw) EMG itself. The tone is usually of variable pitch, which is related to the level of integrated EMG, i.e., higher pitched tones indicate a higher level of muscle activity. These audio signals can be presented in a variety of ways to help "shape" patient responses.

Some devices have a click rate meter that increases in frequency proportional to increases in EMG activity. Also available in commercial devices are short tones or "beeps" that indicate the change in EMG activity. For example, a beep is heard only as the integrated EMG increases; there is no feedback during relaxation. This alternative encourages the patient to work harder for another beep.

Conversely, with a different mode setting, as the EMG activity decreases, the beep is heard, with no feedback during periods of increased muscle activity. This alternative is useful for teaching patients to relax a spastic muscle and is presented as a form of positive reinforcement. Whenever the beep is heard, the patient should try to repeat whatever it was that caused the beep to occur. One disadvantage of this

mode is the fixed time constant for integration; i.e., the patient must demonstrate a reduction of muscle activity within a specific period of time. Many devices manufactured now have incorporated variable time constants that determine when a feedback tone or visual change is provided to the patient. Use of a short time constant will result in a shorter delay between a change in integrated EMG and the presentation of an audio or visual alteration in feedback. This shorter time constant is beneficial during training that necessitates dynamic muscle contraction. Selection of longer time constants means that a comparatively greater delay exists between the change in integrated EMG and presentation of this change to the patient. This alternative is often advisable when training for general relaxation in the absence of dynamic muscle action. In fact, a slight prolongation in an audio tone presentation following a change of only 1 or 2 microvolt-seconds may be beneficial; i.e., less distracting, to the client who is combining feedback with some form of relaxation instruction.

A monotone buzzer is found in some threshold devices. The buzzer is heard only when the patient generates a specific level of muscle activity that is preset by the therapist. Threshold settings refer to a specific level of integrated EMG below or above which an audio or visual feedback is provided, depending upon how the threshold is used. For example, if feedback is provided when integrated EMG exceeds a specific level, then a low-threshold setting may be used in training for recruitment of activity above a given level in a weak or paretic muscle. Once the patient reliably exceeds this level, the threshold is raised and the patient must engage in further recruitment and temporal summation of muscle activity to receive feedback. This procedure is often referred to as "shaping" muscle responses. In this case, the clinician is shaping activity "up" as opposed to the reverse strategy for which feedback may be used to reduce integrated EMG levels (i.e., reduction of resting hypertonus or elevated muscle responses during induced length changes in spastic muscles). In the latter situation, the clinician is attempting to shape "down" EMG activity.

Visual Feedback Alternatives

Visual displays available with EMG feedback devices include banks of lights, meters, video monitors, or oscilloscopes. The lights are activated sequentially with increasing levels of integrated EMG activity. Again, the threshold level can be set by the therapist or the patient, and the visual feedback will be provided when the threshold level is exceeded. A meter deflection is helpful in maintaining continuity and in giving both therapist and patient a more precise idea of how much activity is occurring. If the precautions described below are followed, the meter can be an excellent source of motivation for the patient. The most recent form of visual feedback employs a microcomputer and a video monitor. This allows the on-line presentation of more than one channel of EMG activity. This new technology lets the therapist develop new strategies for training that were not possible with many of the older devices. Desired patterns of EMG activity, either generated by the therapist or produced by the patient (perhaps by an uninvolved muscle), can be used as a template of targeted activity for the muscle being trained (1).

An oscilloscope tracing can be helpful to the therapist who is familiar with EMG. Local and extraneous EMG can be distinguished, and the therapist can then better analyze the training situation so as to optimize electrode placements. Both raw EMG displayed on an oscilloscope and integrated EMG displayed on the audio and video (meter deflection) components of a feedback device may be useful. The former is particularly valuable to the clinician wishing to detect possible artifacts or interference that could provide erroneous feedback. The majority of our patients prefer to watch a meter rather than an oscilloscope, because it gives them a clearer idea of just how much muscle activity is being produced.

The available sensitivity scales should be examined by the therapist. If the electrodes are properly applied, it is theoretically possible to obtain accurate readings of activity as low as 1 μ V. Such low integrated levels are particularly important during generalized relaxation training using frontalis or limb muscles. On the other hand, retraining patients with musculoskeletal weakness (for example, the quadriceps following meniscectomy) requires the use of a feedback device with comparatively low sensitivity since such patients often learn to generate several hundred microvolts of integrated EMG during isometric or isokinetic contractions.

Caution must be exercised, however, when comparing sensitivity scales or "gains" across feedback devices. Manufacturers choose to process the EMG signal differently, i.e., root-mean-square (RMS) integration, peak-to-peak integration, half-wave vs. full-wave rectification, etc. The consequence of using different options is that quantified values may appear substantially different between machines, irrespective of consistencies in skin preparation and electrode placements. This fact is important to the clinician wishing to document EMG readings between treatment sessions and across different feedback devices. To date, there has been no uniformity among manufacturers regarding some form of standardization for processing the EMG signal.

Electronic interfaces are available to allow use of both the biofeedback machine and an oscilloscope at the same time. These pieces of equipment are usually optional, but they must provide isolation of the battery-run biofeedback equipment from the AC current needed to drive the oscilloscope. This consideration is essential to insure patient safety against possible current leaks. For the clinic with a large rehabilitation patient population, this equipment offers tremendous value.

The final decision regarding the purchase of a muscle biofeedback machine must be based both on expense and on practicality. The most elaborate and expensive equipment is not necessarily the best suited for the physical therapy clinic. The types of patients seen in the clinic should also be given consideration. The equipment should be versatile enough to be meaningful to as many of the patients as possible. For example, if the therapist works primarily with a geriatric population, it would be advisable to use a visual feedback that is comparatively large, since many of these patients may have visual impairments. For some patients with neural deficits that compromise visual acuity and color discrimination, visual feedback that employs red light-emitting diodes (LEDs) may be inappropriate because interpretation of red visual stimuli is impaired. On the other hand, when primarily treating children, the size of visual feedback may not be as significant a consideration as the variety of audio or visual feedback alternatives needed to capture and maintain interest and motivation. Undoubtedly, such concerns have prompted the recent onslaught of multicolor displays and even video games as features of newer feedback devices.

ELECTRODES

Type

The basic types of electrodes are in-dwelling fine-wire, or concentric needles, or varying types of surface electrodes. The in-dwelling electrodes permit large amplitude, localized, and well-defined pick-up of muscle potentials. However, they must be inserted percutaneously and so are not practical for biofeedback training in most physical therapy clinics. The commercially available devices often do not provide the input jacks necessary for use with inserted electrodes. Special uses of inserted electrodes include attempts at training deep inaccessible muscles, paralytic muscles, muscles separated from the skin by considerable adipose tissue or muscles that are not easily isolated by surface electrodes (2). Often, needle electrodes can be used in cases where no sign of activity could be elicited. An EMG is done to determine if any viable motor units have survived. Other than for such limited applications, good results can be obtained with careful placement of surface electrodes.

Surface electrodes for electromyography are round disks, having silver/silver-chloride (or gold) recording surfaces which are recessed within a plastic cup. Commercial miniature electrodes, such as the type made by Beckman (which have recording surfaces measuring 4 mm in diameter) are very good for monitoring small areas, even muscles in the thenar eminence of the hand. Recording surface diameters are available in increasing diameters, up to 12.5 mm. Various manufacturers of biofeedback equipment supply similar electrodes. Disposable surface electrodes are also available. Many of these are made for EKG recordings, and so their recording area is large. This fact is important to keep in mind when deciding upon which electrode to use. The disposable electrodes are ready for application; disk-shaped surface electrodes require preparation before being applied to the skin. Many disposable silver-silver chloride snap-on electrodes are pre-gelled with conducting medium, which should be checked for dryness before application. Often, it is necessary to add a small amount of high salt-concentrated gel to these electrodes if the available gel has dried out.

Skin and Electrode Preparation

The removal of oils and dead skin from the skin surface helps to reduce high skin impedance. High skin impedance means attenuated EMG signals and increased noise levels. Rubbing the skin briskly with an alcohol-soaked gauze pad will remove the dead skin and oils and is an exercise in good hygienic skin care; if done well, no testing is required for the actual level because the impedance will become acceptable. The skin must be allowed to dry before applying the electrodes. In addition, input matching impedance of most contemporary feedback devices is so high compared with impedance at the skin electrode interface that the latter hardly presents the problem it did in the past.

Nondisposable surface electrodes require a washer with adhesive properties on both sides, one side being covered with paper. The washer is secured to the surface electrode, then the electrode is filled with high salt content electrode paste or gel, of sufficient quantity so that when the paper cover is removed from the washer, the paste is level with the washer. The electrode is then touched gently to the skin. The periphery of the washer should be lightly tapped down with fingertips before the body of the electrode is pressed. This procedure prevents the paste from oozing beneath the washer and destroying its adhesive properties. The ground electrode is prepared in a similar manner.

Before applying the larger disposable electrodes, only proper skin cleansing is necessary. Again, the periphery of the electrode should be secured before the center is pressed down. At times, the electrode check on the biofeedback equipment may indicate that the electrodes are not properly applied. If this occurs, any of the following simple procedures may help ensure adequate contact.

1. Add a bit more electrode paste or gel to the cup of the surface electrode. This procedure is often necessary when using the smaller surface electrodes. Occasionally, the pre-gelled disposable electrodes dry out. The addition of more gel to the gauze overlying the recording area will alleviate the problem.

2. Press down on the center of the electrode. At times, one can be too careful about pressing only on the periphery, and consequently the actual recording surface is not pressed into good contact. However, in pressing upon the

center of a disposable electrode, care should be taken to avoid gel leakage from beneath the recording surface.

3. Check to assure that the electrodes are properly connected. When using three disposable electrodes, the leads might get crossed, and a reference electrode might inadvertantly be connected to the ground input jack. This event is obvious to an experienced therapist as soon as the actual training session has begun, especially in retraining weak muscles.

The actual location of the electrode placement depends upon the muscle or action involved and upon muscle tonus. Widely spaced disposable electrodes are well-suited for recording from spastic muscles. The entire spastic muscle group, e.g., the forearm flexor group or the posterior calf muscles, should be monitored. In the latter example, electrodes placed over the medial and lateral heads of the gastrocnemius will pick up activity in most of the muscles of the posterior and lateral leg compartments. Feedback from wide electrode positioning gives the patient a more accurate picture of the amount of activity in all of the involved muscles.

Electrode placement for reeducation of weak muscles requires more care (3). The electrodes should be placed over the target muscles in an area of relative anatomical isolation from the surrounding musculature. This consideration is especially important in training the extensors of the fingers and thumb. The spacing of the electrodes is also of concern; widely spaced electrodes over the tibialis anterior, for example, will pick up from a spastic gastrocnemius, especially when using high sensitivity settings needed for feedback from weak muscles. Therefore, close spacing of reference electrodes over muscles to be recruited is recommended. (See Chapter 34.)

Skin preparation and electrode placement should be as consistent as possible since variations in the spacing lead to inconsistent meter readings. Widely spaced electrodes record from a larger area of the muscle; hence, the meter reading will be higher than when recording from closely spaced electrodes. The patients usually attend to the sensitivity scale and the meter reading quite intently and know immediately when they are not performing as well as previously. At times, it can be difficult to explain to the patient that the difference in the meter reading is due to the change in electrode placement. Consistent electrode placement allows smooth continuity from session to session, and also renders enough validity to the meter reading so that it can serve as an indication of general progress. Alternatively, changes in interelectrode distances and the resulting effect such changes will have upon the magnitude of integrated EMG fed back to the patient should be explained prior to treatment to avoid frustration or misunderstanding.

THERAPEUTIC EXERCISE

The use of therapeutic exercise for neuromuscular reeducation can, in many instances, be enhanced with the application of biofeedback techniques. Care must be taken in the application of the electrodes, both in securing the electrode to the skin and in placing the electrode leads so they will be least disturbed by movement. A few minutes in preparation will help avoid interruption once the exercises are underway.

In upper extremity exercises for the stroke patient, the use of bilateral exercises to engage the affected muscle can be enhanced a great deal by biofeedback. For example, with electrodes over the biceps, resistance to elbow flexion can be given to the unaffected side and the patient can be shown what the biceps on the involved side is doing, provided, of course, that the patient exhibits the synergist pattern. Then, the patient can focus attention on trying to generate as much activity from the muscle without reflexly activating it.

Dorsiflexion of the affected ankle is sometimes brought in by resistance to plantar flexion on the uninvolved side. Again, by appropriately placed electrodes and proper sensitivity settings, the patient can learn that the involved muscle is capable of activity.

As with traditional therapeutic techniques, biofeedback can be used in nearly all of the procedures involving bilateral exercises for stroke patients. Resistive exercises to certain body parts to facilitate weakened muscles in patients with spinal cord injuries (SCI) have also been reported.

Clinicians can also employ a variation on this theme through the application of efference or motor copy procedures. This technique necessitates dual channel monitoring of homologous muscles among patients with unilateral problems. The patient attempts to copy or match visual representations of EMG emanating from an uninvolved muscle with output from the involved homologous, contralateral muscle. Only the gains or sensitivities are controlled independently (4). With a little imagination, the clinician can think of numerous situations in which resisted movements can facilitate muscle activity at a distant site.

Patients with "frozen shoulders" who could benefit from Codman's exercises may need biofeedback to teach them to relax the shoulder muscles, thus allowing for free swinging of the arm. When using the wand for range of motion (ROM) exercises, properly placed electrodes will tell the patient and therapist whether the involved shoulder musculature is being used or if the ROM gained is due to an accompanying passive exercise program. Relaxation, reinforced by biofeedback, can help the therapist to gain more range during passive ROM by helping the patient avoid premature tightening of the muscle secondary to pain. To ensure that this procedure is successful, the patient must trust that the therapist will not exercise the shoulder far beyond the point of pain.

BIOFEEDBACK IN GAIT TRAINING

Along with several reports of biofeedback in gait training (5-9), we can add our favorable results (10–12). Small portable biofeedback machines lend themselves well to gait training. When electrodes are appropriately placed over the tibialis anterior, for example, the patient can carry with him the equipment necessary to reinforce dorsiflexion at the appropriate phase. In this example, care should be taken to ensure that the electrode placement is not picking up from the gastrocnemius. If a threshold device is used, the threshold should not be set too high. High threshold settings cause the patient to try so hard that unwanted muscle or movements (i.e., an exaggerated flexion synergy) could be recruited, thus causing frustration and confusion to the patient. Well-secured electrodes will not be pulled loose by the movement, and the wires should also be secured to guard against the distracting influence of movement artifact.

Because of the thin lateral intramuscular septum separating lateral and posterior compartments of the leg, hyperactivity from the triceps surae may be volume conducted to surface electrodes placed over the peroneals. An alternative placement to retrain for ankle eversion during the swing phase of gait would be to closely place reference electrodes at the dorsolateral foot below and anterior to the lateral malleolus over the well-isolated extensor digitorum brevis, an accessory evertor. As a consequence of this placement, however, the patient may not be able to wear shoes.

If the biofeedback equipment is on a movable cart, the patient can receive feedback from muscles during actual gait. However, this situation is usually awkward, and there may be considerable interference from motion artifact. If proper attention has been paid to the feeling accompanying spasticity, the patient may not need a great deal of biofeedback during gait.

With very weak muscles, as is the case with incomplete SCI patients, the biofeedback machine can be used to verify if these muscles are being used in gait. The quadriceps can be monitored even in a long leg brace, and the patient can actively try to bring on activity in these muscles during gait. This procedure gives the patient the benefits of standing and walking while allowing him a chance to exercise the appropriate muscles at the same time.

The hamstring muscle group is easily accessible and often needs to be monitored for spasticity or activity during inappropriate phases of gait. To do this, the patient must slow his gait considerably so that he may learn just when the muscles should and should not be active. The equipment used must not have too long a time constant for EMG integration, or it could lead to confusion for the patient. In this instance, interfacing the output from the raw EMG mode of a feedback device to an oscilloscope and audio amplifier might be advantageous.

A mirror is an excellent source of feedback to the patient. He can walk while watching himself in the mirror. Often, the stroke patient seems to lose some balance when looking in the mirror. In these cases, we have applied strips of masking tape to the floor (13). The tape is used as a guideline when attempting to remedy such problems as uneven stride length or circumducting and scissoring gait patterns in a cerebral palsied patient. Although we prefer not to train the patient by having him watch the floor, we find that this is sometimes a necessary starting point. Once the patient is better able to walk properly and is more comfortable with his gait, the emphasis is then placed on looking straight ahead while the therapist watches his gait in reference to the lines. In this way, the patient can get immediate feedback about his performance. Often, it is a good idea to ask the patient how he thought he did, since the goal is ultimately to walk properly without feedback.

While the emphasis in our clinical laboratories is to determine the effectiveness of biofeedback, we have had the opportunity to evaluate classical facilitation techniques in conjunction with biofeedback. Generally, the majority of such techniques may be integrated with feedback training procedures. The pros and cons of the techniques we have employed are discussed below.

VIBRATION

Vibration seems to have many favorable effects on the patient. It is a very good source of facilitation for flaccid muscles. Reciprocally, as the flaccid or weak muscles are facilitated, the spastic antagonists seem to be relaxed (14). We have had very good results using the vibrator over the extensor muscles of the wrist and fingers to both facilitate extensors and relax the flexors. Vibration over the tibialis anterior will help relax a spastic gastrocnemius and is a most beneficial technique during gait training. The emphasis in muscle reeducation is for the patient to gain conscious control of all his muscles, both spastic and flaccid. Therefore, the treatment of choice is teaching the patient to consciously control his spastic muscles. However, should the patient be unable to control the spasticity, rather than spend the entire session working on something that leads to frustration, the clinician should have an easy method to help the patient through the period of decreased control. There is a tremendous quantitative variation in spasticity seen in the same muscles at different training sessions. Even within a session, there have been instances of marked contrast in EMG activity. Keeping this point in mind, it is more advantageous for all concerned to downplay variability in control of spasticity by having an alternative method to gain essentially the same short-term results.

The vibrator we use is an inexpensive department-store model. We are avoiding here any statement as to the mechanisms involved in the facilitation and/or inhibition observed using vibratory stimuli concurrently with feedback training. We simply offer this technique and our observations to therapists for incorporation into their feedback training program.

The major disadvantage of the use of the vibrator is the 60-Hz interference it causes in the biofeedback equipment. At times, interference is minimal; at others, it actually confounds the treatment. Interference is minimal when the electrodes are placed fairly close together (less than 1 cm apart) and the electrode leads are as far from the vibrator as possible. The sensitivity of the equipment can be decreased so that the amount of 60-Hz interference will not cause the equipment to register any activity. This situation is one instance where the "raw" EMG audio mode is valuable—the therapist can easily distinguish the 60-Hz "buzz" from distinct electromyographic activity. At this point, the patient should be asked to concentrate on the task at hand (extending the wrist without bringing in the flexors), while the therapist listens for EMG from the antagonists (the flexors), despite the buzz heard from the vibrator applied to the prime movers (the extensors). Obviously, an oscilloscope, if available, is a valuable tool at such times. Alternatively, if 60-Hz interference confounds low levels of feedback, the vibrator should be quickly withdrawn so that the patient may build upon the developing tonic vibratory reflex. In either case, the therapist should be reminded that vibration is a facilitatory adjunct to muscle recruitment. To avoid extraneous noise that will be processed by most devices as erroneous EMG signals, the clinician is advised to withdraw the vibrator as soon as movement is initiated so that the patient can rapidly superimpose volitional effort while seeing a visual response truly indicative of his attempt.

STRETCH REFLEX

The stretch reflex is an effective facilitatory technique (15). This technique lends itself well to use with biofeedback. Stretch reflex activation also offers a quick check on the accuracy of the electrode placement. In trying to isolate the extensor digitorum from the remaining wrist extensors, for example, the wrist extensors can be quickly stretched. The finger extensors can then be stretched separately with the wrist maintained in a neutral position. The biofeedback equipment, set at the proper sensitivity or threshold, will pick up the EMG activity of the stretch reflex, which in this example would occur during stretch of the finger extensors but not during stretch of the wrist extensors. Successful isolation rests on accurate electrode placements. In this example, the clinician must recall that the most distal muscle fibers of extensor digitorum can be recorded from electrodes placed just proximal to the wrist joint where all wrist extensors are fully tendonous. Further details regarding specificity of electrode placements may be found elsewhere (Chapter 34).

We have used the stretch reflex to ensure that the muscle has sufficient tone to be more easily contracted by the patient. When we can elicit no stretch reflex and are confident that the electrode placement is correct, we then turn to techniques, such as vibration or working reflexes, that would help increase activity within the muscle. This procedure can save considerable time and avoid frustration on the part of the patient who is trying to contract a weak muscle.

The stretch reflex can be used to elicit a response from the biofeedback equipment preceding an attempt at contraction of a particular muscle. This technique helps emphasize to the patient the training goal awaiting him. Care must be taken not to confuse the patient by introducing false feedback due to movement artifact caused by stretch of the skin or movement of the electrode leads.

When placing the extremity in a position that stretches the muscle, extra care must be taken. The electrodes might become loosened or even dislodged if there is sufficient tension on the skin during the stretch.

REFLEXES

Normal or exaggerated reflexes can be facilitated in most patients. Biofeedback draws the patient's attention to the muscle and action set off by the reflex, and helps the patient gain a more concrete idea about what is expected of him. As we have noted previously (16), a noxious stimulus to the sole of the foot to evoke either a Babinski or withdrawal reflex is useful in helping a patient initiate a contraction in the tibialis anterior. Several quickly repeated stimuli to prolong the activity in the tibialis anterior gives the patient considerable feedback both from the biofeedback equipment and from seeing the movement at the ankle. The therapist might consider first using this procedure and then asking the patient to continue receiving feedback as the stimulus is removed. The audio feedback will probably drop to a lower level, but if the activity is prolonged, terminated upon command, and reproduced several times, the initial signs of

voluntary muscle control have been demonstrated. This demonstration can be offered to the patient as a positive sign of potential for further control. As another example, ankle dorsiflexion can be recruited through mass action by resisting hip flexion at the knee with the knee joint maintained in a flexed position.

In the previous examples, there is little worry of movement artifact. When working with thumb extension, this is not the case. Thumb extension can be facilitated by first quickly pronating and supinating the forearm several times, and secondly by holding it in supination while the patient's attention is focussed on observing what happens. Great care must be taken to avoid pulling the electrodes loose or causing movement artifact. After doing this procedure several times, the patient can be asked to assist. Relaxation should not be overlooked. Once the reflex is recruited, the patient might first learn to control the muscle by relaxing it. As soon as it is relaxed, and before the patient forgets which muscle he just controlled with relaxation, he should actively extend the thumb. The muscle the patient has just relaxed is the same one he now has to activate. Combining these two controls, one after the other, sometimes makes it easier for the patient to learn.

Application of the vibrator over the dorsum of the hand or on the dorsum of the wrist proximal to the joint sometimes reflexively activates finger extensor muscles. Electrodes placed over the extensor digitorum may be at a sufficient distance from the vibrator to minimize the 60-Hz interference, yet will show nicely the activity of the muscles that are being facilitated. The patient can then try to maintain that activity after the vibrator is removed.

Yawning and stretching frequently elicit finger extension in the stroke patient. While it is not always easy to get the patient to truly yawn and stretch several times during the session, as part of a home exercise program, he is encouraged to try to hold the fingers extended after the reflex has subsided. This helps the patient focus his attention on the proper movement and, it is hoped, on the proper muscle. This procedure is beneficial even if the patient is unable to prolong the finger extension.

SPASMS

Demonstration of voluntary control of a muscle is always an encouraging sign, whether the patient has suffered a stroke, spinal cord injury, cerebral palsy, or any other neurological damage. At times, it may be necessary to evoke a spasm to teach the patient control of a particular muscle. This particular method has worked especially well with our spinal cord-injured patients. Electrodes are placed widely over the quadriceps muscles, and spasm is set off in the muscle group. The patient is asked to think about the muscle and any feelings or sensations that he could associate with the contraction in the muscles. Once the spasm has subsided, he is asked to reproduce the activity. After several attempts, he can usually initiate minimal activity.

Several quick stretches to a muscle, such as the extensor pollicis longus, can set it off into spasm. The patient can try to learn to relax the spasm, then quickly reactivate the muscle before he forgets its activity pattern.

TACTILE STIMULATION

Properly placed electrodes that do not interfere with tactile stimulation can be of immense value to the patient in learning to initiate a contraction. Stroking the part of the body (for example, under the chin to aid in neck flexion) to facilitate movement in a particular direction is helpful. This technique works well with toe extension, particularly with stimulation over the last two toes to bring in the extensor digitorum brevis. After the patient can perform the motion with the stimulation, the contraction and/or motion is initiated without the benefit of tactile stimulation.

A combination of stroking and quick stretching is useful for finger extension in a stroke patient. With the hand lying flat on a pillow, and the forearm stabilized to prevent elbow movement, this stimulation is given to the dorsum of the hand and fingers. The patient is instructed to try to raise the fingers and wrist off the pillow. Along with stimulating the extensors, this technique seems to help relax the spastic flexors. Stroking and quick stretch can be performed with the hand hanging off the end of the pillow to allow more room for the patient to extend. This procedure was done with some of our stroke patients, but after each attempt at extension, time had to be devoted to relaxing the flexors. When starting from a neutral wrist and finger position, we did not have to take time to relax the flexors since they seemed to be quite relaxed in this comparatively shortened flexor muscle group position.

VERBAL COMMANDS AND INSTRUCTIONS

The proper use of verbal commands can greatly enhance the biofeedback training session. During relaxation sessions, a quiet soothing voice with references to relaxing, allowing the tension to drain away, and drawing attention to feelings of tension can be used with encouraging results. One must be careful, however, about how much verbal reinforcement to offer. Some patients might become annoyed at repeated commands to relax, when, in fact, they are trying to do just that. This verbal barrage may draw attention away from learning to control a spastic muscle. The patient might spend precious time being annoyed at the therapist and becoming frustrated when he cannot control the spasticity with the speed he thinks the therapist demands. Care must be taken to ensure that the patient is not fighting the biofeedback equipment. The patient should be introduced to the concept of biofeedback as an aid to learning control of the muscles, not as something that the patient must fight to beat. The patient will not learn to relax a spastic muscle if he feels he is competing against the machine.

When working with patients who have to learn to initiate activity in weak muscles while keeping the spastic antagonists relaxed, verbal commands play an important role. For example, after placing the wrist and fingers in extension, the therapist might ask the patient to "not let your hand fall," instead of "hold your hand in this position." The former command sounds easier. Thus, the patient will not have to try too hard to maintain the extension. The harder the patient tries, the quicker the flexors are activated. In trying to gain active extension, the patient might be asked to "let your hand and fingers float up," as opposed to "pull up your hands and fingers." Anything that will convey a message of easiness in executing the task might well be the best approach until the patient has good control of the extensors. Thumb movements must also be approached with an attitude of emphasizing ease in effort since any strong attempt will likely bring in flexion. This strategy is frustrating for the eager patient but, to avoid unwanted flexion activity, this seems to be a better approach.

Alternatively, we often ask patients with unilateral impairments to perform a given task by interfacing muscles of the uninvolved side with feedback. During this time, much verbal praise is offered, especially among patients who appear apprehensive or who have cognitive or receptive difficulties. This initial phase often makes compliance easier when feedback training is begun with involved muscles. At such time the therapist must temper verbalizations so that such "coaching" makes sense and is appropriate with respect to the gains achieved when efforts were directed to the uninvolved muscle group.

VARIABILITY

One of the most intriguing aspects of biofeedback training sessions is the variability in performance and muscles activity among neurologic patients. While stroke patients have always varied in the amount of spasticity present, up until the advent of biofeedback, this variability could be described only in subjective terms. Biofeedback offers a quantitative assessment of the amount of spasticity if electrodes have been placed in the same location as in previous sessions and if the patient is in the same position and asked to perform the same task. By employing the above standards, we have noted that our spinal cord-injured patients have demonstrated variability in spasticity, even within the training session.

We cannot determine if there is any pattern to variability in spasticity. Patients who are first learning control of spastic muscles may have a more dramatic amount of variability, but we have also seen this fluctuation in patients who have learned to control the spasticity fairly well. Upon questioning the patients about why they seem to be more spastic on any one particular day, we have received a variety of answers, including sudden changes in the weather, lack of sleep, too much sleep, fatigue from strenuous exercises, emotional factors such as family and financial problems, lack of concentration, changes or neglect in drug therapy, or simply, no explanation at all.

The patient is usually acutely aware of the change in his control. After doing well at learning to relax his spastic muscles, to find himself suddenly doing much more poorly is cause for a great deal of self-concern and anxiety. The therapist must treat this change sensibly so that the patient is prevented from becoming upset. The therapist should explain candidly that this happens often during the course of treatment and has been seen before in other patients. The therapist must then decide whether to work on control of the increased spasticity, which often can be done with encouraging results, or to work on another task until the spasticity has returned to more manageable levels. All patients have good days and bad days; the biofeedback can accentuate the bad days.

SUMMATED MUSCLE POTENTIALS

It is increasingly clear in our experience that reliance solely on the integrated output of a meter and varying pitch of the audio feedback can lead to misinterpretation of the actual muscle activity. We have found that most of our stroke patients and all of our spinal cord-injured patients can learn to relax the spastic muscle completely; yet, at some point, some patients seem to lose this control. This behavior can often occur within a relaxation session. According to the integrated output from the biofeedback equipment, one would expect that the entire muscle was becoming more active. This thought prevailed in our clinic when we reported some of our findings (15). We have since discovered otherwise. Often the visual feedback is held at an artificially high level because of the activity of what appears to be several motor units firing at a rapid rate. This observation has been made using surface electrodes at varying distances, over a variety of muscles, and with commercially available biofeedback devices coupled to an oscilloscope (17). This activity can be heard distinctly using the "raw" audio feedback mode, and is easily seen on an oscilloscope. There have been few reports of this phenomenon in the literature. Green (18) discusses his findings of a single motor unit (SMU) firing during training of normal subjects in deep relaxation. He used surface electrodes over the dorsal forearm muscles, and also used a very sensitive gain setting. The SMU he discusses appeared at a frequency of 6–7 per second and suddenly dropped to zero. The SMU appeared at the later stages of training when the subjects were becoming deeply relaxed. Gaarder and Montgomery (19) briefly mention their findings of a single spike. During treatment, there is a progressive decrease in the muscle activity. The last trace of muscle activity appears to be a rapidly firing single spike, detectable on the oscilloscope at medium sweep speed. This observation was made during their patient training for control of flexor spasticity of the upper extremity, using surface electrodes over both the flexors and extensor muscles.

Our considerable experience with persistently hyperactive muscle potentials grew from our concerns about why a patient who was doing well in controlling spasticity suddenly appeared to lose control, judging by a high unwavering visual representation. Switching to the "raw" audio mode of our equipment allowed us to recognize the sound of a single motor unit spike which was confirmed on an oscilloscope.

The apparent motor unit potentials we have seen have a very steady frequency, but their amplitudes are highly variable, ranging from very small (deflecting the meter to read 30 μV0 to very large (up to a reading of 300 μV) amplitudes. Of course, the peak values of raw EMG as well as integrated values will vary based upon the processing capabilities of the device. One may see two distinctly different potential configurations at the same time; when one falls out the other continues to fire. At times, when one potential is silenced, another will appear. On some days, patients will have the units, on others, they will not. There is no apparent explanation for these phenomena. These spontaneous muscle potentials have been seen in both the lower and the upper extremities. They can be recorded with varying distances between the surface electrodes, in patients with different neurological pathologies, and in the absence of all other muscle activity. At times, their amplitudes are clearly greater than that of surrounding units in the same muscle.

Whenever a persistent potential is observed during a relaxation session, we have initiated a kind of "reverse SMU training" (20) in order to train the patient to consciously control it. Some patients do well by thinking about slowing it down; others learn to control it by placing the spastic muscle on stretch. This technique usually stops the unit from firing or integrates it with the others brought on by the stretch. The patient then concentrates on inhibiting such activity when the limb is returned to the resting position.

At times, it is nearly impossible to consciously inhibit these persistent potentials. In such cases, we have the patient try any of a list of assorted "tricks" to inhibit them. The list includes: making a fist with the uninvolved hand, extending one knee or the other, changing position of the limb in which the unit was found, shifting position in the chair, turning the head to the uninvolved side and extending the uninvolved arm (the asymmetrical tonic neck reflex), sniffling, coughing, or tapping one foot or the other. Some of these maneuvers also help relax the spastic muscle when the entire muscle has activity in it. This list is not all-inclusive, and should be added to freely. Some days, one particular movement will work consistently well; then it may not work at all during the next session.

These potentials have been found mainly in the gastrocnemius and wrist and finger flexors of our stroke patients, perhaps because we have worked with those muscles most frequently. In patients with incomplete spinal cord injuries, these potentials have appeared in the quadriceps, tibialis anterior, and hamstring muscles, and they may occur even after the patient has learned to relax the spastic muscle quite well. At times, the potentials simply "refuse" to "drop out" like other muscle potentials. Often, when the limb is in the resting position and without placing the involved muscle on stretch, a potential appears quite spontaneously. While the etiology of these spontaneously occurring summated potentials remains elusive, it is interesting to speculate that they represent the outflow from descending disinhibited supraspinal activation of motorneurons. The influence is sufficient enough to cause these cells to discharge with resulting muscle fiber depolarization.

Obviously, the exclusive use of an integrated EMG biofeedback device can create great confusion for a novice treating spastic patients; the patient has done well learning to control a muscle, learning the difference of feelings associated with the activity in the muscle, and is sitting enjoying this relaxed feeling; suddenly, the machine tells him he is no longer relaxed! Worse still, the quantified activity can be quite high at times.

The spontaneous occurrence of muscle potentials is quite a distraction in the training session even when it is easily recognized, and the patient is asked to ignore it in continuing with the task at hand. We do not know if these potentials bias the whole muscle to set off more spasm. Nor do we yet know if it is worthwhile to spend time learning conscious control of them. The occurrence of prevailing muscle potentials may allow us on the one hand to train for quiescence of other "background" units and hence to facilitate relaxation. On the other hand, the frequent inability of our patients to eliminate the prevailing muscle potential often leads to frustration and can actually hinder additional biofeedback training. Therapists must be alert to this complication and be prepared to apply their professional training to its solution in individual patients.

References

1. Mulder, T., Hulstijn, W. and van der Meer, J., EMG feedback and the restoration of motor control. Am. J. Phys. Med., 65: 173–188, 1986.
2. Wolf, S. L., Essential considerations of the use of muscle biofeedback. Phys. Ther., 58: 25–31, 1978.
3. Wolf, S. L., Electromyographic biofeedback in exercise programs. Phys. Sports Med., 8: 61–69.
4. Wolf, S. L., LeCraw, D. E., Barton, L. A. and Rees, B. J. A comparison of motor copy and targeted feedback training techniques for restitution of upper extremity function among neurologic patients. Phys. Ther., 1988. Submitted for publication.
5. Basmajian, J. V., Kukulka, C. G., Narayan, M. G. and Takebe, K. Biofeedback treatment of foot drop after stroke compared with standard rehabilitation technique: effects on voluntary control and strength. Arch. Phys. Med. Rehabil., 56: 231–236, 1975.
6. Flom, R. P., Quast, J. E., Boller, J. D., Berner, M. and Goldberg, J. Biofeedback training to overcome post stroke footdrop. Geriatrics, 31: 47–51, 1976.
7. Johnson, H. E. and Garton, W. H. Muscle reeducation in hemiplegia by use of electromyographic device. Arch. Phys. Med. Rehabil., 54: 320–323, 1973.
8. Nafpliotis, H. EMG feedback to improve ankle dorsiflexion, wrist extension and hand grasp. Phys. Ther., 56: 821–825, 1976.
9. Spearing, D. L., and Poppen, R. The use of feedback in the reduction of foot dragging in a cerebral palsied client. J. Nerv. Ment. Dis., 159: 148–151, 1974.
10. Wolf, S. L., Baker, M. P. and Kelly, J. L. EMG biofeedback in stroke: effect of patient characteristics. Arch. Phys. Med. Rehabil., 60: 96–102, 1979.
11. Wolf, S. L., Baker, M. P. and Kelly, J. L. EMG biofeedback in stroke: a 1-year follow-up on the effect of patient characteristics. Arch. Phys. Med. Rehabil., 61: 351–355, 1980.
12. Wolf, S. L. and Binder-Macleod, S. A. Electromyographic biofeedback applications to the hemiplegic patient. Changes in lower extremity neuromuscular and functional status. Phys. Ther., 63: 1404–1413, 1983.
13. Jims, C. Foot placement pattern: an aid in gait training. Phys. Ther., 57: 286, 1977.
14. Bishop, B. Vibratory stimulation. Part 3. Possible applications of vibration in treatment of motor dysfunctions. Phys. Ther., 55: 139–143, 1975.
15. Harris, F. A. Facilitation techniques and technological adjuncts in therapeutic exercise. In Therapeutic Exercise, 4th ed., edited by Basmajian, J. V. Williams & Wilkins, Baltimore, 1984, pp. 110–178.
16. Baker, M., Regenos, E., Wolf, S. L. and Basmajian, J. V. Developing strategies for biofeedback: applications in neurologically handicapped patients. Phys. Ther., 57: 402–408, 1977.
17. Regenos, E. M. and Wolf, S. L. Involuntary single motor unit discharges in spastic muscles during EMG biofeedback training. Arch. Phys. Med. Rehabil., 60: 72–73, 1979.
18. Green, E. E., Walters, E. D., Green, A. M. and Murphy, G. Feedback technology for deep relaxation. Psychophysiology, 6: 371–377, 1969.
19. Gaarder, K. R. and Montgomery, P. S. Clinical Biofeedback: A Procedural Manual. Williams & Wilkins, Baltimore, 1977.
20. Basmajian, J. V. and Samson, J. Special review: standardization of methods in single motor unit training. Am. J. Phys. Med., 52: 250–256, 1973.

Supplementary Reading in Rehabilitation

Asato, H., Twiggs, D. G. and Ellison, S. EMG biofeedback training for a mentally retarded individual with cerebral palsy. Phys. Ther., 61: 1447–1451, 1981.
Beall, M. S. Jr., Diefenbach, G. and Allen, A. Electromyographic biofeedback in the treatment of voluntary posterior instability of the shoulder. Am. J. Sports Med., 15: 175–178, 1987.
Beckers, W. M., Jelsma, O., Huijing, P. A. and Van-Wieringen, P. C. Feasibility of single motor unit control in the m. abductor pollicis brevis and its relation to concentration ability and thumb tapping ability. Electromyogr. Clin. Neurophysiol., 24: 591–597, 1984.
Biedermann, H. J. Comments on the reliability of muscle activity comparisons in EMG biofeedback research with back pain patients. Biofeedback Self Regul., 9: 451–458, 1984.
Biedermann, H. J., McGhie, A., Monga, T. N. and Shanks, G. L. Perceived and actual control in EMG treatment of back pain. Behav. Res. Ther., 25: 137–147, 1987.
Bush, C., Ditto, B. and Feuerstein, M. A controlled evaluation of paraspinal EMG biofeedback in the treatment of chronic low back pain. Health Psychol., 4: 307–321, 1985.
Christie, D. J., Dewitt, R. A., Kaltenbach, P. and Reed, D. Using EMG biofeedback to signal hyperactive children when to relax. Except. Child., 50: 547–548, 1984.
Cox, R. J. and Matyas, T. A. Myoelectric and force feedback in the facilitation of isometric strength training: a controlled comparison. Psychophysiology, 20: 35–44, 1983.
Cummings, M. S., Wilson, V. E. and Bird, E. I. Flexibility development in sprinters using EMG biofeedback and relaxation training. Biofeedback Self Regul., 9: 395–405, 1984.
De Bakker, M. A., Bijlard, M. J., Kruse, F. T., Zantman, L. E., van Wieringen, P. C. and Huijing, P. A. Single motor unit control and variations of recruitment order of motor units in human m' abductor pollicis brevis and m' interosseus dorsalis

I. Electromyogr. Clin. Neurophysiol., *23:* 151–157, 1983.

Fields, R. W. Electromyographically triggered electric muscle stimulation for chronic hemiplegia. Arch. Phys. Med. Rehabil., *68:* 407–414, 1987.

Flor, H., Haag, G. and Turk, D. C. Long-term efficacy of EMG biofeedback for chronic rheumatic back pain. Pain, *27:* 195–202, 1986.

Flor, H., Haag, G., Turk, D. C. and Koehler, H. Efficacy of EMG biofeedback, pseudotherapy, and conventional medical treatment for chronic rheumatic back pain. Pain, *17:* 21–31, 1983.

Hijzen, T. H., Slangen, J. L. and van Houweligen, H.-C. Subjective, clinical and EMG effects of biofeedback and splint treatment. J. Oral Rehabil., *13:* 529–539, 1986.

Hirasawa, Y., Uchiza, Y. and Kusswetter, W. EMG biofeedback therapy for rupture of the extensor pollicis longus tendon. Arch. Orthop. Trauma Surg., *104:* 342–345, 1986.

Honer, J., Mohr, T. and Roth, R. Electromyographic biofeedback to dissociate an upper extremity synergy pattern: a case report. Phys. Ther., *62:* 299–303, 1982.

Ince, L. P. and Leon, M. S. Biofeedback treatment of upper extremity dysfunction in Guillain-Barre syndrome. Arch. Phys. Med. Rehabil., *67:* 30–33, 1986.

Ince, L. P., Leon, M. S. and Christidis, D. EMG biofeedback with upper extremity musculature for relaxation training: a critical review of the literature. J. Behav. Ther. Exp. Psychiatry, *16:* 133–137, 1985.

Ince, L. P., Leon, M. S. and Christidis, D. Experimental foundations of EMG biofeedback with the upper extremity: a review of the literature. Biofeedback Self Regul., *9:* 371–383, 1984.

Inglis, J., Donald, M. W., Monga, T. N., Sproule, M. and Young, M. J. Electromyographic biofeedback and physical therapy of the hemiplegic upper limb. Arch. Phys. Med. Rehabil., *65:* 755–759, 1984.

King, A. C., Ahles, T. A., Martin, J. E. and White, R. EMG biofeedback-controlled exercise in chronic arthritic knee pain. Arch. Phys. Med. Rehabil., *65:* 341–343, 1984.

Kleppe, D., Groendijk, H. E., Huijing, P. A. and Van Wieringen, P. C. Single motor unit control in the human mm. abductor pollicis brevis and mylohyoideus in relation to the number of muscle spindles. Electromyogr. Clin. Neurophysiol., *22:* 21–25, 1982.

Koheil, R., Sochaniwskyj, A. E, Bablich, K., Kenny, D. J. and Milner, M. Biofeedback techniques and behaviour modification in the conservative remediation of drooling by children with cerebral palsy. Dev. Med. Child Neurol., *29:* 19–26, 1987.

Large, R. G. Prediction of treatment response in pain patients: the illness self-concept repertory grid and EMG feedback. Pain, *21:* 279–287, 1985.

Large, R. G. and Lamb, A. M. Electromyographic (EMG) feedback in chronic musculoskeletal pain: a controlled trial. Pain, *17:* 167–177, 1983.

Lucca, J. A. and Recchiuti, S. J. Effect of electromyographic biofeedback on an isometric strengthening program. Phys. Ther., *63:* 200–203, 1983.

Morasky, R. L., Reynolds, C. and Clarke, G. Using biofeedback to reduce left arm extensor EMG of string players during musical performance. Biofeedback Self Regul., *6:* 565–572, 1981.

Mulder, T. and Hulstijn, W. Delayed sensory feedback in the learning of a novel motor task. Psychol. Res., *47:* 203–209, 1985.

Mulder, T., Hulstijn, W. and van der Meer, J. EMG feedback and the restoration of motor control. A controlled group study of 12 hemiparetic patients. Am. J. Phys. Med., *65:* 173–188, 1986.

Neilson, P. D. and McCaughey, J. Self-regulation of spasm and spasticity in cerebral palsy. J. Neurol. Neurosurg. Psychiatry, *45:* 320–330, 1982.

Nouwen, A. EMG biofeedback used to reduce standing levels of paraspinal muscle tension in chronic low back pain. Pain, *17:* 353–360, 1983.

Nouwen, A. and Bush, C. The relationship between paraspinal EMG and chronic low back pain. Pain, *20:* 109–123, 1984.

Pinchuk, D. Iu., Mikhailenok, E. L. and Bogdanov, O. V. [Procedure for functional biocontrol in severe forms of movement disorders in patients with infantile cerebral palsy]. Zh. Nevropatol. Psikhiatr., *85:* 1475–1479, 1985.

Poppen, R. and Maurer, J. P. Electromyographic analysis of relaxed postures. Biofeedback Self Regul., *7:* 491–498, 1982.

Robertson, D. W., Lee, W. A. and Jacobs, M. Single motor-unit control by normal and cerebral-palsied males. Dev.-Med. Child Neurol., *26:* 323–327, 1984.

CHAPTER 9

Biofeedback in Stroke Rehabilitation

DEBBIE E. LeCRAW

Survival following cerebrovascular accident has been improving. The death rate from cerebrovascular disease diminished from 79.7 per 100,000 residents to approximately 36 per 100,000 residents, from 1960 to 1982 (1), and 5-year survival has been reported for approximately 30% of victims following their first stroke (2). With the mean age of stroke victims now between 45 and 55 years (2) and increasing numbers of young persons affected by stroke (2), rehabilitative efforts are directed toward returning many affected individuals to a productive position in the workplace.

Restoration of function is a challenging clinical problem. Impaired cognition, receptive and/or expressive aphasia, neglect syndromes, sensory deficits, visual perception problems, as well as motor and coordination impairments may be present. Motor dysfunction may be characterized by alterations in muscle tone, muscle strength, and coordination. Frequently, a patient will present with mixed levels within these three areas, placing the burden on the therapist to assess these deficits accurately and to provide a thorough, concise rehabilitation program. Biofeedback is a tool by which additional information can be provided to the clinician and/or patient in an effort to improve outcomes from neuromuscular reeducation. The purpose of incorporating biofeedback into the rehabilitative process is to speed recovery and to maximize functional gains acquired. Recognized as a *component* of a comprehensive treatment approach, biofeedback is not regarded as a singular means by which comprehensive treatment is provided.

The three types of biofeedback discussed in this chapter are electromyographic biofeedback (EMGBF), force biofeedback (FBF), and joint position biofeedback (JPBF). The purpose of the chapter is to describe how EMGBF can be incorporated into the day-to-day clinical rehabilitation of stroke patients. Most of the emphasis will be placed on its use while treating impaired motor and coordination skills, but other impairments will also be addressed.

Strategies and techniques used by the author and colleagues at the Emory University Rehabilitation Research and Training Center for the neuromuscular reeducation of hemiplegic patients following stroke or head injury are emphasized, but the principles are applicable to most patients with neurological dysfunction.

In spite of the complexity of the problems, clinicians are being afforded less time in which to conduct a rehabilitation program. Traditional techniques, though widely used, generally lack verifying research (3–5). Biofeedback devices provide immediate, accurate, ongoing information concerning the muscle activity, joint position, or force produced through a limb segment and may help improve the rehabilitation outcome.

Although review articles have heralded biofeedback for neuromuscular reeducation when incorporated into a comprehensive treatment program (6–8), others regard its effectiveness with caution (9). Few studies have been designed adequately or controlled sufficiently to define the specific elements of the treatment that account for the reported improvement. More work needs to be done before definite conclusions can be made regarding the efficacy of specific training techniques and strategies.

SELECTION OF PATIENTS

In the study of stroke, many authors have used controlled group designs (11–18) documented clinical trials (10, 19–25) and case studies (26) to demonstrate the effectiveness of feedback. The extent of improvement between patients has varied widely even within reported studies; few reports have been designed to investigate the relationship between specific patient characteristics and the extent of improvement using feedback (24, 27). Wolf and colleagues investigated several patient characteristics that they felt may impact on outcome of EMG feedback training in hemiplegic patients (25). Age, sex, hemiparetic side, duration of stroke, previous rehabilitation, and number of training sessions could not be shown to have a significant effect. The presence of proprioceptive loss appeared to diminish the probability of making functional gains in the upper extremity. In general, patients showed greater functional improvements with lower extremity training than upper extremity training. The absence of a clear relationship between age and duration of hemiparesis is a common observation made by many authors (12, 15, 24). Thus, patients should not be excluded from feedback training based solely on their age or the time since their stroke. Similarly, the optimal time for introducing biofeedback has not been clearly elucidated.

Several significant factors do exist in determining if a patient is a candidate for treatment. First, the *potential for voluntary control* must exist before feedback training is begun. This is particularly relevant to patients who have sustained peripheral nerve and spinal cord injuries. The electromyogram can be used to help determine the extent of the injury or recovery. Next, *patient motivation and cooperation* are essential. Biofeedback places a great deal of responsibility upon the patient, for it is the patient who has to relearn the control of his muscles and practice this new control. Fortunately, the introduction of the feedback frequently serves to motivate patient and therapist alike. Related to patient cooperation is the ability of the patient to understand and follow commands.

TYPES OF FEEDBACK DEVICES AND SIGNALS

If a patient appears to be a candidate for feedback training, a *determination of the most appropriate mode of feedback* must be made. This same determination may need to be made many times as the patient progresses during his rehabilitation.

EMG feedback is certainly the most popular form of biofeedback utilized in rehabilitation.

In general we utilize EMG feedback whenever it is helpful for the patient or therapist to know what a specific muscle or muscle group is doing. EMG feedback iis often used with weak or poorly controlled muscles to help facilitate a contraction when the patient does not have the ability to produce any appreciable movement. EMG feedback is also particularly helpful in training relaxation of an overactive muscle both at rest and during active movements. The therapist can also use the EMG to help determine the patient's potential and need for training by helping to identify whether motor units are under volitional control and whether agonistic and antagonistic muscles are working appropriately during a volitional effort. The EMG contains little information regarding the actual movement produced by a muscle contraction and is not easily used when more than two muscles need to be monitored to guide a motion. Therefore, EMG feedback may not be the best form of feedback when we want to train a movement.

Position feedback is indicated when the goal of training is the regulation of movement, provided the patient is able to voluntarily recruit and relax the appropriate muscle groups. Position feedback is used to train the appropriate timing and coordination of the many muscle groups needed to control a movement. Examples of the application of position feedback in rehabilitation include: the training of head position control (28); coordination and control of hand movements in ataxia (29) and following hand surgery (30); and the training of knee joint position in cerebral palsied children (31), adult hemiplegia (32), and prosthesis wearers (33). In addition, position feedback may be used in stroke rehabilitation when the muscle(s) that need to be monitored are inaccessible or difficult to isolate.

Finally, *force feedback* may be indicated whenever information concerning the amount of force being transmitted through a body segment or assistive device is desired. For example, for the training of symmetrical standing or gait, several authors have used the Krusen Limb Load Monitor[a] (LLM) with hemiplegic adults (27) and children (33) to monitor the force transmitted through an extremity. In addition to its use as a feedback device, we are

[a]Krusen Research Center, Moss Rehabilitation Hospital, 12th Street and Tabor Road, Philadelphia, PA 19141.

encouraged in the LLM's potential as an inexpensive evaluative tool to analyze gait objectively (34). Also, Baker, Hudson and Wolf suggested the use of a "feedback" cane to help in the training of hemiplegic patients (35) to monitor the force being born on an assistive device.

In summary, EMG feedback trains muscles, position feedback trains movement, and force feedback trains weightbearing. In practice, combinations of devices can be used during training. Position feedback from a proximal joint can be used with EMG feedback from a distal muscle to help break up a synergy pattern. EMG or position feedback may be combined with force feedback during standing or walking to monitor muscle activity or joint position while simultaneously training weightbearing. These are just two examples of how different feedback devices can be combined.

The *selection of the most appropriate feedback signal* is generally straightforward. Most devices provide some form of both auditory and visual feedback. In addition, the therapist may have the ability to select either continuous or threshold feedback. Continuous feedback implies that the auditory signal (tone or pitch) is present and changes proportionately as any EMG activity is generated. The auditory signal from threshold biofeedback is altered in some manner as the level of EMG activity reaches a particular threshold established by the clinician. The feedback provided when the threshold is achieved may vary. A single tone may be produced only when the threshold is reached; the tone may be present prior to threshold and cease when it is reached; the signal may increase proportionately and change once threshold is reached, etc. Generally, the therapist and patient can decide together which signal is the most effective.

Clinically, we have found the following guidelines to be helpful: 1) a signal that increases proportionately will provide useful information as small changes of muscle activity are generated; 2) during relaxation training, a goal set such that the patient maintains silence while successfully relaxing the muscle with an error noted by the *onset* of an auditory signal is most conducive to relaxation; 3) with some guidance, the patient is usually able to decide the signal most easy to understand; and 4) the use of auditory feedback alone during relaxation training and gait training enables the patient's visual attention to be directed toward internal or environmental cues rather than upon the instrumentation.

PREPARATION OF THE CLINICIAN

Before implementing biofeedback effectively into a rehabilitation program, a clinician must have a reasonably strong knowledge base of 1) the patient's disabilities and goals; 2) the related anatomy and neurophysiology to be considered in the rehabilitation program; and 3) the biofeedback instrumentation. Limitations of any of these areas will adversely affect the clinical effectiveness of the program. A complete discussion of these areas is beyond the scope of this chapter and has been considered elsewhere (36–39). However, in light of recent reports in the literature and our experience concerning biofeedback applications in the stroke population, some discussion may be helpful.

Knowledge of Patient's Disabilities and Goals

Understanding the extent of the motor and sensory impairment *and* how that impairment relates to function is a critical prerequisite. With that foundation, the feedback training may incorporate functional activities in which the patient *applies* his developing abilities. Without such application, it will be most difficult, if not impossible, to see carryover of functional gains beyond the scope of the patient's performance in the clinic. As the patient is engaged in BF training, success in each session will tend to build confidence in the patient's ability to perform. Threshold levels that are somewhat challenging but less than frustrating tend to breed continued interest and enthusiasm.

Long-term goals must consider the impairments and their effect on realistic outcomes. The presence of proprioceptive deficits, the inability to follow commands, receptive aphasia, marked spasticity, or the inability to voluntarily initiate any exploratory (i.e., reaching) movements of an extremity tend to correlate with diminished functional improvements. These observations do not imply that patients may not make improvements; rather, that the patient and therapist must be realistic in the eventual outcome and relative success with feedback in these patients.

Knowledge of Related Anatomy and Neurophysiology

Anatomical understanding of those muscles to be directly monitored and those nearby influence decision-making. For EMGBF, electrodes are usually closely spaced (approximately 1 cm apart) for the majority of muscle groups monitored. Understanding the proximity of nearby muscle groups will enable the clinician to avoid electrode placements that pick up volume-conducted EMG activity from nearby muscle groups which contaminates the EMGBF signal and may confuse the patient. Understanding muscle tone, how it may be altered, and the goals related to changes in tone should be considered when deciding the appropriate electrode spacing to use. Rarely in neuromuscular reeducation of the stroke patient is the interelectrode spacing greater than 2-3 cm, usually to avoid contamination of the signal by volume-conducted activity.

Knowledge of Biofeedback Instrumentation and Its Use

The clinician must understand basic principles of BF instrumentation to appropriately interface the patient with equipment, accurately interpret the auditory and visual signals produced, and effectively progress the patient toward achieving functional goals. Earlier chapters provide detailed discussions.

GENERAL TRAINING PRINCIPLES

From the initial evaluation, the clinician may gain an appreciation of the patient's physical limitations, functional disabilities, and realistic goals. Specific muscle groups contributing to the limitations and disabilities are identified. Next, the nature of the muscle deficits—whether an inability to recruit or to relax muscle activity—is identified for the specified muscle group. Following this analysis of the problems and identification of goals, the training strategies are determined.

Included in these training strategies are such considerations as 1) the order of the progression of training; 2) goal selection; 3) dual versus single channel EMGBF selection; 4) progression of recruitment or relaxation; 5) use of supplemental techniques with feedback; 6) weaning the patient from the instrumentation; and 7) the training method to employ during the treatment session.

The progression of training will depend on the clinician's general treatment approach, the patient's specific problems, and the patient's response to training. At Emory University, we have generally moved from a proximal to distal direction, which is consistent with most popular treatment approaches (40–43). Most clinicians would agree that training should progress from isolated target muscle training to the more complex motor control displayed during functional activities. To date, no clear guidelines for the progression of training exist. Many of the earlier published studies used either targeted recruitment of a weak agonist (12, 14, 22) or relaxation of a spastic antagonist (17, 44). More recent reports tend to describe training for both relaxation and recruitment of the appropriate masculature (16, 20, 21, 24, 29, 38, 39).

In our experience with retraining a limb segment in which spasticity and weakness are present among muscles with opposing action, some cocontraction occurred as the patient attempted a functional activity. This occurrence was seen even after relaxation training of the spastic musculature and before recruitment of the paretic musculature. When dual channel monitoring was introduced, the patient would try to produce levels of the paretic muscle activity sufficient to overcome the hyperactivity of the opposing muscle in order to make functional gains.

Appropriate goal selection requires considerable clinical experience. Generally, we attempt to identify short-term goals that are difficult enough for the patient to feel challenged while at the same time are attainable during one or two treatment sessions to avoid frustration and to help realize progress. From an instrumental perspective, goals can be established with reference to 1) the threshold level, 2) the sensitivity or gain, or 3) by the electrode spacing.

When using the threshold level as the measure of success, the patient may either attempt to recruit or relax muscle activity or attempt to maintain increasingly longer muscle recruitment or relaxation times with respect to the threshold level. As the EMGBF instrumentation gain or sensitivity to detect EMG activity decreases, it becomes increasingly difficult for the patient to produce a visual or auditory signal. Consequently, for recruitment training, a decrease in the sensitivity used may be regarded as an improvement. Conversely, the patient who is able to relax at higher levels of instrument sensitivity is improving on an ability to reduce EMG activity.

Wide electrode spacing implies a larger area of muscle monitored. Hence, it is easier to detect some level of EMG activity with widely spaced electrodes, as compared with narrowly spaced electrodes over the same muscle. In relaxation training, however, it is easier to reduce the EMG signal when narrow spacing is used, as compared with wider spacing over the same muscle.

Dual-channel monitoring may be used to compare two muscle groups. We have used it to 1) reduce cocontraction of two antagonist muscle groups; 2) compare homologous, bilateral muscle groups for recruitment or relaxation; and 3) compare recruitment of two synergistic muscle groups.

Feedback can be used along with an isometric, isotonic, or isokinetic contraction, although the therapist should be aware of the differences in the EMG interference patterns associated with each type of contraction (45). In recruitment training, movement may not be seen initially. By increasing the targeted level of recruitment, overt movement eventually should become evident. Overt changes in movement are rarely observed during relaxation training. Consequently, one usually will rely largely on EMGBF outcomes and also will consider patients' comments and functional outcomes.

Just as the clinician will use supplemental techniques to augment treatment approaches, such techniques may be incorporated with EMGBF training. We have used a skateboard (Fig. 11.3 in Chapter 11) during the initial stages of movement training to reduce friction and make the task easier. As recruitment improves, resistance may be provided to encourage additional recruitment. As the patient increases strength and control, the skateboard is removed. Similarly, various supplementary techniques can be used to facilitate a poorly recruited muscle. Vibration (46), quick stretching, tapping, and resistance are available techniques (42).

During all stages of training, we attempt to wean the patient from the feedback. As the patient is able to master a task with feedback, we begin to remove the feedback, while continuing to monitor the patient's overt and electromyographic performance. If the performance deteriorates, or if we progress to a more difficult task, the feedback is reintroduced.

Two systematic training methods that have been studied include *targeted muscle training* and *motor copy*. Targeted muscle training involves a progression of training from relaxation of the spastic musculature around a joint to the training of targeted levels of recruitment of weak or paretic muscles before actual functional training. This progression is based partly upon earlier pilot work which suggested that the functional outcome of a treated extremity appeared related to the patient's ability to demonstrate notable reductions in resting spasticity. Relaxation of spastic musculature has generally progressed from relaxation at rest, to relaxation during distracting movements (such as moving an uninvolved extremity), to passive stretches, and to isometric concentric contractions of the antagonist. Attempts at training targeted levels of recruitment have generally progressed from contraction during an isometric hold, during an eccentric contraction and to recruitment during a concentric contraction. Mastery of all relaxation tasks does not have to be achieved prior to commencement of training for recruitment. Generally, the patient attempts to maintain relaxation of the spastic musculature while recruiting the weak or paretic muscle. Figures 9.1, 9.2, and 9.4 illustrate the application of targeted training in the upper and lower extremities.

Motor copy training consists of monitoring homologous muscle groups of the upper extremity with the intent to match the EMG output by superimposing the EMGBF signals. This "motor copying" is first performed on hyperactive musculature with the muscles at rest, then during active passive lengthening of the muscle. Next, the antagonist muscles are actively shortened simultaneously while patients maintain reduced levels of EMG activity in the hyperactive muscles. By varying the gain on each EMGBF amplifier, the output from each of the homologous muscle pair is matched. This enables the patients to most easily visualize "matching" EMG activity. Patients are progressed by making the amplifier gains more equal, thus requiring the patient to exhibit greater control while attempting to increase the EMGBF output to match that of the homologous muscle group (47).

As increasing levels of control are displayed by the patient, we attempt to integrate any in-

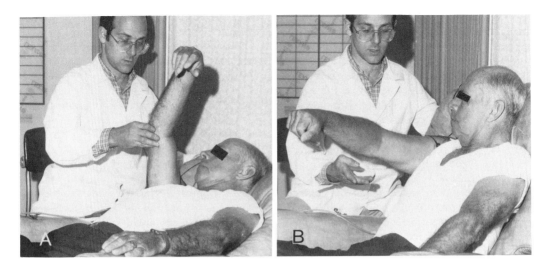

Figure 9.1. *A,* training shoulder flexion with patient fully reclined. *B,* patient progressed to sitting position. Patient is attempting to maintain shoulder flexion by recruiting activity from the anterior deltoid and simultaneously avoiding abduction of the arm by relaxing his middle deltoid.

creased control into functional activities and begin to wean the patient from the feedback. Specific exercises will be discussed in the sections on training of individual body segments.

MULTIPLE JOINT MOVEMENT TRAINING

Feedback modalities may be combined; position feedback from the forearm may be com-

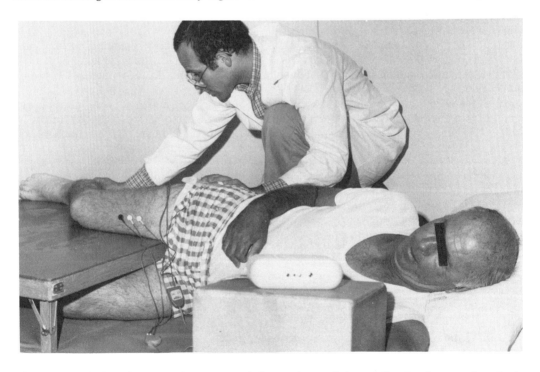

Figure 9.2. Patient is attempting to recruit hamstring activity while simultaneously relaxing quadriceps to produce active knee flexion. The patient's hip is progressively placed in greater hip extension to make the task more difficult.

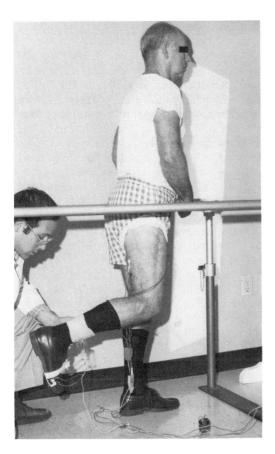

Figure 9.3. Patient is attempting to flex knee while simultaneously maintaining hip extension and actively dorsiflexing his ankle. An ankle goniometer with a auditory feedback mechanism is used to provide feedback from his ankle while dual-channel EMG monitoring is used to encourage recruitment from the hamstrings and relaxation of the quadriceps.

bined with EMG feedback from the elbow or shoulder. This is particularly helpful in the early stages of attempting to break up synergistic movement patterns. The patient begins to combine static and dynamic control of the forearm with active elbow and shoulder movement. As training progresses, once again we encourage greater use of the auditory rather than visual feedback signal. By the time the patient begins combining mulitple joint movements, such as reaching for an object, we may go to a simple auditory threshold signal from the forearm with EMG feedback from one elbow or shoulder muscle. For instance, the patient may be training to relax his biceps and maintain his forearm in a neutral or supinated

position while reaching for an object. Threshold feedback from the forearm, reminding the patient to avoid pronation, may be combined with EMG feedback from the biceps to encourage relaxation. If the patient pronates his forearm or tenses his biceps, the respective feedback signals are triggered. The patient can then use this feedback to help shape the appropriate response. (Figs. 9.1–9.3).

CLINICAL EXAMPLES

Wrist and Finger Extensors

We train the *wrist extensors* with the forearm resting on a table and the wrist flexed over a towel roll. As patients have problems contracting the wrist extensors when placed in the shortened position, we generally begin training with the wrist extensors placed on stretch. An isometric contraction against resistance appears to facilitate recruitment of the extensors. Targeted levels of EMG recruitment from the extensors are practiced while the patient maintains minimal levels of activity in the flexors. A point below the level of any active flexion is used as the EMG threshold for the flexors. The patient then progresses from an isometric contraction of the wrist extensors to active wrist extension. Facilitation techniques, such as tapping, quick stretches, or heavy resistance (42) may once again be used along with feedback. Synergistic movement patterns may be observed. Feedback as well as changes in the limb position can both be used to help reduce these synergistic patterns.

Initiating *finger extension* is often difficult for many patients. We have found that in working with chronic stroke patients (greater than 1 year after cerebrovascular accident), active finger extension was seldom attained if some active extension was not already present. In patients who do have some active finger extension, the results are much more encouraging. Marked improvements in movement and function have been noted with treatment. Training progressed as described for the training of wrist extension, except the wrist position also needs to be considered. Training is begun with the wrist and finger flexed and progresses by increasing the amount of wrist extension. As with the wrist, various limb positions and facilitation techniques can be used in conjunction with the biofeedback to train isolated finger extension.

Ankle Dorsiflexors

One of the first areas of biofeedback training was for the treatment of foot-drop (14), a common problem in hemiplegic patients. It may be caused by a combination of paralysis of the ankle dorsiflexors and spasticity of the plantar flexors. Both the dorsiflexors and the gastrocnemius are easy muscles to monitor with surface electrodes. A problem encountered when recording from the dorsiflexors is "cross-talk" from the spastic plantar flexors, and so a close spacing of the electrodes is used for the tibialis anterior. They are placed over the muscle belly just lateral to the anterior border of the tibia.

Depending upon the patient's specific problem, training may begin with either relaxation of the gastrocnemius or recruitment of the dorsiflexors. Control of gastrocnemius spasticity essentially follows a similar procedure, as described for other spastic muscles. Relaxation training is begun with the patient seated or semi-reclining and the ankle resting unsupported in plantar flexion. Relaxation training is then begun at rest, during passive lengthening, and during active dorsiflexion. Next, the knee is brought into progressively greater extension. This places the gastrocnemius on greater stretch and makes each of the relaxation tasks more difficult for the patient. The patient will ultimately attempt to maintain relaxation of the gastrocnemius during active dorsiflexion of the ankle with the knee fully extended, as is observed at heel strike.

Recruitment of the dorsiflexors during relaxation of the gastrocnemius may also need to be trained. Training for dorsiflexion is begun with the patient seated and the ankle again resting unsupported in plantar flexion. The patient is trained to recruit the dorsiflexors while maintaining relaxation of the plantar flexors.

Many patients will initially use a flexor synergy pattern to recruit the dorsiflexors by simultaneously flexing their knee and hip. The therapist may choose to allow the use of the synergy if this is the only method of activating the dorsiflexors. Resistance can be placed over the distal thigh and thus prevent the extremity from actually drawing into flexion, while still allowing the patient to generate a feedback signal. The goal is not to strengthen the synergy, but rather to learn how to recruit the dorsiflexors. Thus, the patient must quickly begin to work out of the synergy pattern.

As control of the dorsiflexors improves and the patient learns to dorsiflex the ankle without apparent hip and knee flexion, the patient begins exercising with greater knee extension. The next task is to attempt to recruit the dorsiflexors and relax the plantar flexors while the knee is passively held in progressively more extension. If any plantar flexor tightness exists, we would expect to see decreased active range of motion of the ankle as the knee reached full extension. In addition to the passive resistance, most patients generally have progressively more difficulty in recruiting the dorsiflexors as the knee nears full extension.

Also encountered with EMGBF training of dorsiflexion is inversion of the foot as dorsiflexion is attempted. To monitor the peroneals during static or dynamic dorsiflexion training frequently results in EMGBF signal contamination by the gastrocnemius-soleus group muscle activity. To avoid this possibility, we can monitor the extensor digitorum brevis (EDB) muscle located on the dorsolateral aspect of the foot. As the patient recruits the EDB, eversion is usually recruited as well.

Incorporation of neuromuscular stimulation (NMS) with EMGBF is relatively simple during dorsiflexion training. The EMGBF electrode placement for the dorsiflexors is sufficiently narrow to allow the placement of NMS electrodes proximally and distally to the EMGBF electrode pair. The EMGBF system is initially programmed to activate the NMS with minimal levels of EMG activity. As the patient gains strength and control over muscle recruitment, higher threshold levels may be required prior to NMS activation.

Furthermore, EMGBF with NMS training of dorsiflexion with eversion may be achieved by spacing the NMS electrodes over the peroneals and anterior tibialis muscles and using recruitment of the EDB as a measure of eversion.

Position Feedback of Ankle

The ankle joint lends itself well to the use of position feedback. If the patient has appreciable active dorsiflexion, we may combine position feedback with EMG feedback from plantar flexors. As opposed to the relatively complex electronic feedback signal that we use for training of the upper extremity, a simple auditory threshold signal is all that we use for the lower extremity. A relatively simple electrogoniometer developed by DeBacher works quite well (see Fig. 33.4). Its basic design ensures that only if the patient performs relatively pure sagittal-plane dorsiflexion will the threshold be reached. Significant amounts of undesired inversion, even if combined with dorsiflexion, tend to break the contact and thus withdraw the feedback. When the position feedback is combined with EMG feedback, the patient must pull his ankle into sufficient dorsiflexion to trigger the feedback signal while maintaining an appropriate level of relaxation of the plantar flexors.

Training is advanced by having the patient display control over both the distal and more proximal parts of the extremity. Starting in a sitting position, the patient first actively dorsiflexes his ankle and then begins to actively extend his knee. Position and/or EMG feedback from the ankle may be combined with EMG feedback from the knee flexors or extensor. The patient attempts to maintain dorsiflexion through complete knee extension.

Gait Training (Stance)

To encourage equal weight distribution onto both lower extremities, force feedback may be used from the very early stages of treatment while learning to rise from a chair, stand, and return to sitting. The feedback device we generally use is the previously mentioned Krusen Limb Load Monitor (LLM). Variable size force transducers the shape of an insole are worn in the patient's shoe. This footplate is connected by a coaxial cable to the amplifier and feedback unit, which is worn on the patient's belt. To train for symmetrical weightbearing during standing, the threshold of the device is set slightly above the patient's present force with the ultimate goal being 50% of the patient's body weight. The patient is then encouraged to remain above threshold while weightbearing. Quantification of the patient's actual weightbearing can be made either by simply having the patient stand on a scale or, if available, by feeding the analog voltage output of the LLM directly into an oscilloscope or strip chart recorder (34) for objective analysis.

The patient may next practice weight shifting onto each lower extremity while standing in place. The LLM threshold is manipulated to encourage the patient to shift progressively increasing amounts of weight for longer durations onto the involved extremity.

The force feedback is also used to train weight shifting during the stance phase of gait. Both the force and temporal components are again trained. To train the force component during stance phase, either the LLM or a feedback cane (35) can be used. Whereas the LLM monitors the force transmitted through the limb, the feedback cane monitors the force transmitted through an assistive device. By varying the threshold of either device, the peak force borne on the involved lower extremity can be shaped. For the training of the temporal component (that is, the duration of stance), we have used the LLM along with a time delay modification developed at Emory University (48) (Fig. 9.4). Though the LLM can be used without this modification, its addition helps to shape a more symmetrical gait by allowing the therapist to select the specific duration of stance required for feedback. Without this modification, no *specific* duration can be defined for the patient.

Several investigators have reported good results with the use of joint position feedback from the knee joint during stance phase (42). Our experience is limited to the addition of EMG feedback during the stance phase for the strengthening of the hip extensor, knee extensor, and hip abductor muscles. Exercises we have used include coming to standing and returning to sitting from a chair, weight shifting, climbing a step, and ambulation. EMG feedback from the appropriate targeted muscles are fed back to the patient along with the force feedback. Generally, patients are unable to shift weight onto the involved extremities if they are unable to recruit sufficient muscle activity from the targeted antigravity muscles. Conversely, as the recruitment from these targeted muscles increases, we begin to see increasing weight shifting onto the extremity. Thus, weight shifting is the goal, and the EMG provides feedback to help the patient reach this goal.

ELECTROMYOGRAPHIC BIOFEEDBACK AND NEUROMUSCULAR STIMULATION

In neuromuscular reeducation, the therapist is responsible for developing a treatment program that will incorporate appropriate motor and sensory input into a treatment program to achieve maximum functional outcome. We have already discussed the immediate, ongoing, accurate, and quantifiable information concerning muscle activity available via the

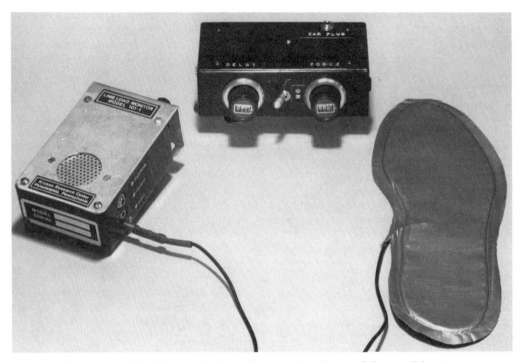

Figure 9.4. Limb Load Monitor, shoe insert and time delay modification.

use of EMGBF and how information regarding joint motion may be acquired.

Bowman et al. (49) documented one of the first attempts to incorporate feedback with neuromuscular electrical stimulation (NMS). By incorporating NMS and joint position feedback (JPF) of the wrist extensors, their experimental group subjects (compared with controls) realized statistically greater increases in wrist isometric extension torque, average change in wrist extension range of motion, and average wrist extension motion against resistance. Significant improvement in wrist extension force was also documented by Van Overeen (50) following treatment incorporating NMS and EMGBF of the wrist. Winchester et al. (51) used positional feedback stimulation training along with cyclical electrical stimulation to improve knee extension in hemiparetic patients. Control patients received an alternate plan of physical therapy. Although improvement differences were noted between the experimental and control groups in patterned knee extension ROM the second week of treatment, no significant differences between groups was noted for selective, isolated knee extension. Most recently, Fields (52) reported a study in which EMG-triggered NMS was combined with conventional physical therapy treatment to improve wrist extension and/or ankle dorsiflexion of 69 hemiplegic patients. Each patient served as his/her own control, and the total duration per patient varied as did the number of movement attempts per session (30-300). Improvements in ROM and ambulation were observed for the majority of patients, including those with poststroke intervals up to 14 years.

Automated incorporation of NMS with EMGBF in neuromuscular reeducation requires special equipment now commercially available.[b] The patient is prepared with EMGBF and NMS electrode placements and is interfaced with the equipment. The EMGBF unit is programmed to automatically activate the NMS once a certain level of EMG is produced by the patient and reaches a given threshold level. If such automated instrumentation is not available, the therapist may initiate the NMS as the desired level of EMG activity is recruited. The advantage to the automated method is the convenience it provides

[b]Verimed Myoexerciser. Medtronic Neuro Division, 7000 Central Avenue NE, P.O. Box 1250, Minneapolis, Minnesota, 55440.

as well as the potential for acquiring quantification of the EMG produced. Because joint position feedback (JPF) technology has not progressed to include the ability to interface with the NMS, therapist-initiated activation of NMS is required when JPF is used with NMS.

One precaution unique to the use of EMGBF with NMS concerns skin preparation. Skin preparation by some clinicians includes rubbing the skin with a saline-based electrode paste to help decrease skin resistance beneath the EMGBF electrodes. If done, care should be taken to avoid performing this preparatory technique over the skin where the NMS electrodes will be applied. Failure to do so could lead to skin irritation beneath the NMS electrodes.

CONCURRENT ASSESSMENT OF MUSCLE ACTIVITY (CAMA)

The traditional approach to incorporating EMGBF into the rehabilitation setting usually involved two key elements. First, the patient had to be trainable. The presence of cognitive dysfunction, receptive aphasia, neglect syndromes, etc, precluded the potential to incorporate EMGBF into the treatment plan. Motivation and cooperation were considered essential as well because the focus of the EMGBF intervention was toward *retraining the patient* to control his motor behavior in a more appropriate manner. Second, the EMGBF was measured in a relatively crude manner. Day-to-day performance in the clinic was usually measured by a change in the level of EMG generated when the patient was attempting a specified movement. Without EMGBF, the clinician serves as the sole 'interface' between the patient's efforts. The realization of the outcome of those efforts occurs by the clinician's palpation of muscle contractions, observation of movement, etc., and relaying these outcomes back to the patient. Other measures of outcome used included joint range of motion (ROM), measures of strength, descriptions of movement patterns or descriptions of functional outcomes—all of which may be affected by the subjectivity of the examiner.

Wolf et al. (53) proposed a new approach to treatment with EMGBF called concurrent assessment of muscle activity (CAMA). This approach "allows direct clinical data acquisition to demonstrate treatment efficacy." By implementing CAMA, a clinician breaks away from the traditional approach to incorporating EMGBF into the rehabilitation process in two related but virtually inseparable ways.

First, the muscle feedback is primarily used to inform *the clinician* about the "ongoing muscle activity as the patient responds to therapeutic interventions." A "trainable" patient no longer becomes the prerequisite to use EMGBF. As the clinician applies any given technique or therapeutic approach to modify motor control, information concerning how the clinician's intervention is affecting the muscle activity can be immediately ascertained, regardless of whether the patient is engaged in BF training. Consequent modifications of the intervention are based upon this immediate, objective, and accurate information. Second, with recent developments in EMGBF instrumentation, observed changes in muscle activity can now be *quantified* per unit time, thus enabling the clinician to *document* the effect of the therapeutic intervention most accurately and objectively.

The implications of this approach are fairly evident. Therapists attempting to improve a patient's motor control will often try a variety of approaches to determine which approach "works best." Now at their disposal is an objective and quantifiable means by which they can evaluate the patient's response to neuromuscular reeducation, compare the efficacy of two or more interventions, or assess a patient's changes in muscle activity over time with other clinical assessments (e.g., ROM functional gains, analyses of movement, etc).

To illustrate this concept, Wolf et al. (55) included in their article illustrations of CAMA applied during dynamic movements. The paraspinal muscles in the thoracic area of a 20-month-old child with cerebral palsy were monitored. The treatment approach of the pediatric therapist (who, incidentally, had no previous "expertise" in EMGBF) in charge of the child's rehabilitation program included techniques to increase spinal extension. The child had been observed to usually maintain a flexed posture and to demonstrate less trunk extension on the right. The child's paraspinal muscle activity was monitored during three activities (crawling, walking, and while being carried) as the therapist compared two treatment approaches in each activity to determine which approach to a given activity produced the most desired EMG activity.

CONCLUSION

To successfully incorporate EMGBF into stroke rehabilitation efforts, clinicians are required to understand the instrumentation, appropriate treatment strategies, and how to interpret and use the information gained. Unless each of these areas is within the clinician's scope of capabilities, success will be limited. If present, the clinician has available an effective tool with which to gain information that is specific, immediate, and quantifiable during rehabilitation strategies. Decisions may be made in a more timely manner concerning a patient's treatment progression, and progress may be made to a greater extent than possible with conventional therapeutic feedback.

References

1. Culler, S. D. and Van Veen Daigle. *The American Health Care System*. American Medical Association, Chicago, 1984.
2. Baum, H. M. and Robins, M. Survival and prevalence. Stroke, *12*: 59–68, 1981.
3. Basmajian, J. V. Neuromuscular facilitation techniques. Arch. Phys. Med. Rehabil., *52*: 40–42, 1971.
4. Stern, R., McDowell, F., Miller, J. et al. Effects of facilitation techniques in stroke rehabilitation. Arch. Phys. Med. Rehabil., *51*: 526–31, 1970.
5. Taft, L., Delagi, L. and Wilkie, O. Critique of rehabilitative techniques in treatment of cerebral palsy. Arch. Phys. Med. Rehabil., *43*: 238–43, 1962.
6. Keefe, F. J. and Surwit, R. S. Electromyographic biofeedback: behavioral treatment of nueromuscular disorders. J. Behav. Med., *1*: 13–24, 1978.
7. Fernando, C. K. and Basmajian, J. V. Biofeedback in physical medicine and rehabilitation. Biofeedback Self Regul., *4*: 435–455, 1978.
8. Basmajian, J. V. Biofeedback in rehabilitation: a review of principles and practices. Arch. Phys. Med. Rehabil., *62*: 469–475, 1981.
9. Manzuk, P. M. Biofeedback for neuromuscular disorders. Ann. Intern. Med., *102*: 854–858, 1985.
10. Brudny, J., Korein, J., Grynbaum, B. B., Friedmann, L. W., Weinsteinn, S., Sachs-Frankel, G. and Belandres, P. V. EMG feedback therapy: review of treatment of 114 patients. Arch. Phys. Med. Rehabil., *57*: 55–61, 1976.
11. Hurd, W. W., Pegram, V. and Nepomuceno, C. Comparison of actual and simulated EMG biofeedback in the treatment of hemiplegic patients. Am. J. Phys. Med., *59(2)*: 73–82, 1980.
12. Johnson, H. E. and Garton, W. H. Muscle reducation in hemiplegia by use of electromyographic device. Arch. Phys. Med. Rehabil., *54*: 320–322, 1973.
13. Mroczek, N., Halpern, D. and McHugh, R. Electromyographic feedback and physical therapy for neuromuscular retraining in hemiplegia. Arch. Phys. Med. Rehabil., *59*: 258–267, 1978.
14. Basmajian, J. V., Kukulka, C. G., Narayan, M. G. and Takebe, K. Biofeedback treatment of foot-drop after stroke compared with standard rehabilitation technique: effects on voluntary control and strength. Arch. Phys. Med. Rehabil., *56*: 231–236, 1975.
15. Binder, S. A., Moll, C. B. and Wolf, S. L. Evaluation of electromyographic biofeedback as an adjunct to therapeutic exercise in treating the lower extremities of hemiplegic patients. Phys. Ther., *61*: 886–893, 1981.
16. Santee, J. L., Keister, M. E. and Kleinman, K. M. Incentives to enhance the effects of electromyographic feedback training in stroke patients. Biofeedback Self Regul., *5*: 51–56, 1980.
17. Basmajian, J. V., Gowland, C. A., Brandstater, M. E. and Trotter, J. E. Integrated behavioral and physical therapy in the rehabilitation of the post-stroke arm. Int. J. Rehabil. Res. *8*: 89–90, 1985.
18. Mulder, T., Hulstijn, W. and van der Meer, J. EMG feedback and the restoration of motor control. A controlled group study of 12 hemiparetic patients. Am. J. Phys. Med., *65*: 173–88, 1986.
19. Brudny, J., Korein, J., Levidow, L., Grynbaum, B. B., Lieberman, A. and Friedmann, L. Sensory feedback therapy as a modality of treatment in central nervous system disorders of voluntary movement. Neurology (N.Y.), *24*: 925–932, 1974.
20. Brudny, J., Korein, J., Grynbaum, B. B. and Sachs-Frankel, G. Sensory feedback therapy in patients with brain insult. Scand. J. Rehabil. Med., *9*: 155–163, 1977.
21. Brudny, J., Korein, J., Grynbaum, B. B., Belandres, P. V. and Gianutsos, J. G. Helping hemiparetics to help themselves. J.A.M.A., *241*: 814–820, 1979.
22. Flom, R. P., Quast, J. E., Boller, J. D., Berner, M. and Goldberg, J. Biofeedback training to overcome poststroke foot-drop. Geriatrics, *31*: 47–51, December, 1976.
23. Shiavi, R. G., Champion, S. A., Freeman, F. R. and Bugel, H. J. Efficacy of myofeedback therapy in regaining control of lower extremity musculature following stroke. Am. J. Phys. Med., *58(4)*: 185–194, 1979.
24. Wolf, S. L., Baker, M. P. and Kelly, J. L. EMG biofeedback in stroke: effect of patient characteristics. Arch. Phys. Med. Rehabil., *60*: 96–103, 1979.
25. Wolf, S. L., Baker, M. P. and Kelly, J. L. EMG biofeedback in stroke: a 1-year follow-up of the effect on patient characteristics. Arch. Phys. Med. Rehabil., *61*: 351–355, 1980.
26. Marinacci, A. A. and Horande, M. Electromyogram in neuromuscular reeducation. Bull. Los Angeles Neurol. Soc., *25*: 57–71, 1960.
27. Wannstedt, G. T. and Herman, R. Use of augmented sensory feedback to achieve symmetrical standing Phys. Ther., *58*: 553–559, 1978.
28. Leiper, C. I., Miller, A., Lang, J. and Herman, R. Sensory feedback for head control in cerebral palsy. Phys. Ther., *61(4)*: 512–518, 1981.

29. Binder, S. A. Assessing the effectiveness of positional feedback to treat an ataxic patient: application of a single-subject design. Phys. Ther., *61(5)*: 735–736, 1981.

30. Brown, D. M., DeBacher, G. A. and Basmajian, J. V. Feedback goniometers for hand rehabilitation. Am. J. Occupational Ther., *33(7)*: 456–462, 1979.

31. Wooldridge, C. P., Leiper, C. and Ogston, D. G. Biofeedback training of knee joint position of the cerebral palsied child. Physiother. Can., *28*: 138–143, 1976.

32. Koheil, R. and Mandel, A. R. Joint position biofeedback facilitation of physical therapy in gait training. Am. J. Phys. Med., *59(6)*: 288–297, 1980.

33. Seeger, B. R., Caudrey, D. J. and Scholes, J. R. Biofeedback therapy to achieve symmetrical gait in hemiplegic cerebral palsied children. Arch. Phys. Med. Rehabil., *62(8)*: 364–368, 1981.

34. Wolf, S. L. and Binder-Macleod, S. A. Use of the Krusen Limb Load Monitor to quantify temporal and loading measurements of gait. Phys. Ther., *61*: 976–982, 1982.

35. Baker, M. P., Hudson, J. E. and Wolf, S. L. A "feedback" cane to improve the hemiplegic patient's gait. Phys. Ther., *59*: 170–171, 1979.

36. Wolf, S. L. Essential considerations in the use of EMG biofeedback. Phys. Ther., *58*: 25–31, 1978.

37. Wolf, S. L. EMG biofeedback applications in physical rehabilitation: an overview. Physiotherapy Canada, *31*: 65–72, 1979.

38. Kelly, J. L., Baker, M. P. and Wolf, S. L. Procedures for EMG biofeedback training in involved upper extremities of hemiplegic patients. Phys. Ther., *59(12)*: 1501–1507, 1979.

39. Baker, M., Regenos, E., Wolf, S. L. and Basmajian, J. V. Developing strategies for biofeedback: applications in neurologically handicapped patients. Phys. Ther., *57*: 402–408, 1977.

40. Rood, M. S. Neurophysiological mechanisms utilized in the treatment of neuromuscular dysfunction. Am. J. Occupational Ther., *10*: 220, 1956.

41. Bobath, B. *Adult Hemiplegia: Evaluation and Treatment*, 2nd ed., William Heinemann Medical Books, London, 1978.

42. Knott, M. and Voss, D. E. *Proprioceptive Neuromuscular Facilitation: Patterns and Techniques*, 2nd ed. Harper and Row, New York, 1968.

43. Brunnstrom, S. *Movement Therapy in Hemiplegia: A Neurophysiological Approach*. Harper and Row, New York, 1970.

44. Amato, A., Hermsmeyer, C. A. and Kleinman, K. M. Use of electromyographic feedback to increase inhibitory control of spastic muscles. Phys. Ther., *53*: 1063–1066, 1973.

45. Heckathorne, C. W. and Childress, D. S. Relationships of the surface EMG to the force, length, velocity, and contraction rate of the cineplastic human biceps. Am. J. Phys. Med., *60*: 1–17, 1981.

46. Bishop, B. Vibratory stimulation. Part III. Possible applications of vibration in treatment of motor dysfunctions. Phys. Ther., *55(2)*: 139–143, 1975.

47. Wolf, S. L., LeCraw, D. E., Barton, L., and Jann, B. B. Comparison of motor copy and targeted training techniques for restitution of upper extremity function among neurologic patients. 1988. Submitted for publication.

48. Wolf, S. L. and Hudson, J. E. Feedback signal based upon force and time delay. Phys. Ther., *60*: 1289–1290, 1980.

49. Bowman, B. R., Baker, L. L. and Waters, R. L. Positional feedback and electrical stimulation, automated treatment for the hemiplegic wrist. Arch. Phys. Med. Rehab., *60*: 497–502, 1979.

50. Van Overeen, H. G. EMG-controlled functional electrical stimulation of the paretic hand. Scand. J. Rehab. Med., *11*: 189–193, 1979.

51. Winchester, P., Montgomery, P., Bowman, B. and Hislop, H. Effects of feedback stimulation training on knee extension in hemiparetic patients. Phys. Ther., *63*: 1096–1103, 1983.

52. Fields, R. W. Electromyographically triggered electrical muscle stimulation for chronic hemiplegia. Arch. Phys. Med. Rehab., *68*: 407–414, 1987.

53. Wolf, S. L., Edwards, D. I. and Shutter, L. A. Concurrent assessment of muscle activity (CAMA). A procedural approach to treatment goals. Phys. Ther., *66*: 218–224, 1986.

CHAPTER 10

Combined Behavioral Therapy for the Hemiplegic Arm and Hand

JOHN V. BASMAJIAN

Of the half million survivors of strokes annually, some three out of four have either temporary or permanent loss of upper limb function. Studies (1) reveal that 71% showed no recovery, 12% moved from stage I to stage II on the Brunnstrom scale (2) (rather insignificant in activities of daily living), and 17% showed improvement beyond stage II.

Results of regular rehabilitation therapy for upper limb dysfunction in hemiplegic patients are acknowledged to be discouraging both for patients and the rehabilitation team. Gowland (1) summarized findings for 229 patients who had received intensive physical therapy for upper limb problems, but showed that only 5% regained functional use of their arm and hand during rehabilitation. This was in spite of very intensive efforts on an inpatient basis. These discouraging results, which agree with those of others (3), led to the introduction of biofeedback approaches.

Biofeedback was used in the treatment of the hemiplegia of the arm since the 1960s (4). Most of the early reports were case studies or clinical reports. Only a few systematically controlled experiments that purported to demonstrate the benefits of EMG biofeedback in rehabilitation of muscle function were reported (4). Flaws in methodology limited the validity of conclusions which had been generally very favorable.

Against this background, it is essential that improved techniques be developed for treatment of the hemiplegic upper limb if possible. Such study ideally should be double-blind and have some form of crossover with blinded objective rating of patient change. However, to do EMG feedback on a truly double-blind basis is almost impossible, and a crossover might be possible in at least one direction only; that is, the patient treated without experimental technique is later treated with it following regular treatment methodology.

CONTROLLED STUDIES

In a formal preliminary study, my group at the Chedoke Rehabilitation Centre treated the hemiplegic upper limb in 37 patients with a wide range of severity and durations after stroke (5). They were randomly assigned to either a 5-week, 15-session program of integrated EMG biofeedback (EMGBF) plus physical therapy (PT) or a standard exercise therapy (ET) program with the same time elements and intensity. In both groups, tested independently, some cases showed improved useful function. Patients' conditions were classified as early mild, early severe, late mild, and late severe. All in the early-mild group had substantial improvement, while those in the late-severe group did not improve. It became imperative to investigate the other two groups: early severe and late mild.

Meanwhile, reports of other independent controlled studies by Wolf and Binder-Macleod (6) and Inglis and associates (7) appeared; EMGBF plus PT had been tested against PT alone. Both studies found that in chronic stroke patients, EMGBF, when used as an adjunct to PT, resulted in improvement in upper limb range of movement and muscle strength. Though positive, these authors were more restrained in their enthusiasm for biofeedback for the upper limb than earlier uncontrolled clinical reports (8). Nevertheless, they brought new insights into the effects of both standard and biofeedback-behavioral approaches to the hemiparetic upper limb. They also emphasized that EMGBF is an adjunctive and not a total therapy.

At the start of a formal second study, we were impressed by the apparent importance of the elapsed time before therapy and the severity of the functional loss. In addition, the possible influence of behavioral factors in both groups appeared to require more careful attention. Hence, this study was fashioned as a comparison of "integrated" behavioral-physical therapy vs. a traditional physical therapy program.

Indirect evidence from several inpatient studies (9-15) strongly suggested that remedial therapies had clinically worthwhile outcomes. However, one less positive conclusion of the Smith (16) outpatient study warranted attention: only a minority of stroke patients (mostly men) are robust enough for vigorous intensive programs of outpatient rehabilitation; nevertheless, for that minority, such treatment "is effective and realistic." Since clinical experience supports that conclusion, we modified the patient selection criteria for our major follow-up study accordingly.

Our second study had four objectives, the most significant for this chapter being the one to determine whether the integrated behavioral therapy program including EMGBF is more effective clinically and statistically than the traditional program in the restoration of useful function in the arm and hand of a recovering stroke patient.

Extensive and intensive independent testing in a specially sheltered laboratory were conducted at the start and end of 5 weeks of therapy and 9 months thereafter. Patients were randomly assigned to treatments A and B, and the examiner was never aware of the specific assignments.

Both programs were restricted to 5 weeks with three sessions of exactly 45 minutes spread through each week on a fairly regular schedule. There were no current or related therapies for the manifestations of hemiplegia during the 5 weeks, and during the subsequent 9 months, patients were not controlled, and almost all had no further treatments by others.

To be included in the study, a patient had to demonstrate one of the following: mild motor involvement of the hemiplegic hand (a score of 20 or greater on the upper extremity function test (UEFT) (17) if 4 or more months poststroke—the late mild group; or less than 4 months poststroke with a score of less than 20 on the UEFT—the early severe group. To ensure therapist compliance with the maneuvers, a detailed program was prepared and adhered to, with a monitor therapist to act as an observer at random intervals.

Specific Outcome Measures

The primary objective was to demonstrate a clinically and statistically significant difference in upper limb function between the two groups at the end of therapy and at 9-month follow-up. Specifically, the objective was to show that a greater number of patients in treatment group A improved at least 10 points on the upper extremity function test (UEFT) (17) shown in our pilot study (5) to be a valid indicator by correlating well with ADL functions, being quantitative, valid, and reliable. It reveals the amount of change needed to demonstrate significant clinical improvement or regression, and is the most useful tool in predicting functional outcome. A second measure of physical ability, the finger oscillation test (18), measured speed of movement.

INTEGRATED BEHAVIORAL AND PHYSICAL THERAPY METHOD— TREATMENT A

Treatment A, developed and refined in our pilot study, was based on cognitive models that employ EMG feedback as an essential adjunct to therapy. This approach recognized the role of the patient's cognitions or thought processes during treatment and how they affect the recovery process. What the patient says to himself and how he appraises his status has a large influence on the responses. The cognitive behavioral model as put forth by Meichenbaum (19) consists of four phases: (1) conceptualization, (2) skill acquisition, (3) skill rehearsal, and (4) skill transfer.

Several strategies were used to achieve these skills; EMG feedback is pivotal for precise goal setting, e.g., the EMG output of lights and sounds may be fixed at a specific EMG level or bilaterally symmetric electrodes may be used for the patient to compare and match. The EMG feedback guides the identification of optimal strategies and goals during the skill acquisition phase. Only one or two clear and attainable goals are set for each session.

Using the Cyborg BL900 dual processor, the therapist attached pairs of standard surface biofeedback electrodes to the patient's skin over targeted muscles. At different times these may include many of the main muscle groups of the limb (See Chapter 9).

EXERCISE PHYSICAL THERAPY— TREATMENT B

This approach, based on neurofacilitatory techniques, is widely used for rehabilitation of stroke and depends directly on a physical therapist's technical ability. Techniques of facilitation and inhibition are used with selected sensory input to bring about automatic, high-quality motor output. The quality of the performance is stressed in all of the techniques. The process is iterative, i.e., the therapist is constantly reassessing and revising the therapeutic strategies based on the patient's response on a moment-to-moment basis. The approach used in treatment B strictly adhered to the principles described in detail in Bobath's text (20). Extensive literature and training in this neurodevelopmental treatment approach are widely available, and our treatment therapists were experts.

CONCLUSION

The evidence is clear that EMGBF is an effective form of therapy for restoration of range of motion and strength of the hemiplegic upper limb in select populations of stroke patients. It compares favorably with traditional exercise therapy based on Bobath techniques given over the same time periods. In selected stroke patients, the functional recovery following a formal behavioral approach (including biofeedback and cognitive therapy) is equal to, but not superior to, a matched program of Bobath-based physical therapy (PT). Both approaches were clinically effective, and significantly so, but our results do not tell us to advocate dropping one form of therapy in favor of the other. Instead, they dramatize that in a substantial but still poorly defined proportion of stroke patients with hemiplegic upper limbs, clinically useful improvement is achievable and worth the effort. But the specific patients who would benefit most from one or the other of these two approaches is still not clarified, and further study is essential to establish the physiologic basis of the functional changes.

"Motivation" enhancement is obviously needed in both our approaches, and in our study, the behavioral approach was not more successful than the PT approach in altering locus of control, mood, affect, etc. Thus, we cannot invoke superior psychologic changes as having come from the "psychologic" approach (21).

In conclusion, this behavioral technique by physical therapists (including EMGBF and cognitive therapy) rivals traditional neurophysiologic "hands-on" PT, both bringing about clinically worthwhile and lasting improvement in substantial numbers of patients. The time, costs, and required training are modest, and the treatments can be done on an outpatient basis. Of particular interest is the effectiveness of EMGBF on shoulder subluxation with or without a recovery of functional use of the hand. The latter presents a major problem compared with the relatively straightforward biomechanical principles, procedures, and good outcome of EMGBF for subluxation (22).

References

1. Gowland, C. Recovery of motor function following stroke: profile and predictors. Physiotherapy, 34: 77, 1982.
2. Brunnstrom, S. Movement Therapy in Hemiplegia: A. Neurophysiological Approach. New York, Harper and Row, 1970.
3. Joshi, J., Singh, N. and Varma, S. K., Residual motor deficits in adult hemiplegic patients. Proceedings of World Conference for Physical Therapy, Seventh International Congress, Montreal, June 1974.
4. Basmajian, J. V. Biofeedback in rehabilitation: review of principles and practices. Arch. Phys. Med. Rehabil., 62: 469, 1981.
5. Basmajian, J. V., Gowland, C., Brandstater, M. E., Swanson, L. and Trotter, J., EMG feedback treatment of upper limb in hemiplegic stroke patients: pilot study. Arch. Phys. Med. Rehabil., 63: 1982.
6. Wolf, S. L. and Binder-Macleod, S. A. Electromyographic biofeedback applications to hemiplegic patient: changes in upper extremity neuromuscular and functional status. Phys. Ther., 63: 1393, 1983.
7. Inglis, J., Donald, M. W., Monga, T. N., Sproule, M. and Young, M. J. Electromyographic biofeedback and physical therapy of hemiplegic upper limb. Arch. Phys. Med. Rehabil., 65: 755, 1984.
8. Basmajian, J. V., Regenos, E. and Baker, M. Rehabilitating stroke patients with biofeedback. Geriatrics, 32: 85, 1977.
9. Garraway, W. M., Akhtar, A. J., Hockey, L. and Prescott, R. J. Management of acute stroke in elderly: follow-up of controlled trial. Br. Med. J., 281: 827, 1980.
10. Garraway, W. M., Walton, M. S., Aktar, J. A. and Prescott, R. J. Use of health and social services in management of stroke in community: results from controlled trial. Age Ageing, 10: 95, 1981.
11. Lehmann, J. F., DeLateur, B. J., Fowler, R. S., Jr., Warren, C. G., Arnhold, R., Schertzer, C., Hurka, R., Whitmore, J. J., Masock, A. J. and Chambers, K. H. Stroke: does rehabilitation affect outcome? Arch. Phys. Med. Rehabil., 56: 375, 1975.

12. Logigian, M. K., Samuels, M. A., Falconer, J. and Zagar, R. Clinical exercise trial for stroke patients. Arch. Phys. Med. Rehabil., 46: 364, 1983.

13. Smith, M. E., Garraway, W. M., Smith, D. L. and Aktar, A. J. Therapy impact on functional outcome in controlled trial of stroke rehabilitation. Arch. Phys. Med. Rehabil., 63: 21, 1982.

14. Stevens, R. S., Ambler, N. R. and Warren, M. D. Randomized controlled trial of stroke rehabilitation ward. Age Ageing, 13: 65, 1984.

15. Strand, T., Asplund, K., Eriksson, S., Hägg, E., Lithner, F. and Wester, P. O. Non-intensive stroke unit reduces functional disability and need for long-term hospitalization. Stroke, 16: 29, 1985.

16. Smith, D. S., Goldenberg, E., Ashburn, A., Kinsella, G., Sheikh, K., Brennan, P. J., Meade, T. W., Zutshi, D. W., Perry, J. D. and Reeback, J. S. Remedial therapy after stroke: randomised controlled trial. Br. Med. J., 282: 517, 1981.

17. Carroll D., Quantitative test of upper extremity function. J. Chronic Dis., 18: 474, 1965.

18. Reitan, R. M. Davison, L. A. (eds). Clinical Neuropsychology: Current Status and Applications. Washington, Winston, 1974.

19. Meichenbaum, D. Cognitive-behavior Modification: Integrative Approach. New York, Plenum, 1977.

20. Bobath, B. Adult Hemiplegia: Evaluation and Treatment, 2nd ed. London, Heinemann, 1978.

21. Hyman, M. D. Social psychological determinants of patients' performance in stroke rehabilitation. Arch. Phys. Med. Rehabil., 53: 217, 1972.

22. Basmajian, J. V., Gowland, C. A., Trotter, J. E., Hall, A. L., Swanson, L. R., Finlayson, M. A. J., Stratford, P. W. and Brandstater, M. E. Stroke treatment: integrated behavioral-physical therapy vs. traditional physical therapy programs. Arch. Phys. Med. Rehabil., 68: 267–272, 1987.

CHAPTER 11

Biofeedback Strategies of the Occupational Therapist in Total Hand Rehabilitation

D. MICHAEL BROWN
FOAD NAHAI

To produce the best possible result, the hand surgeon and therapist must work as a team. Limitations of function may be due to a number of neuromuscular problems as well as mechanical problems involving adhesions of tendons and ligaments. Sensations of muscle contraction or tension may be so vague as to be almost useless as a guide.

ELECTROMYOGRAPHIC BIOFEEDBACK

A damaged muscle may have vestiges of activity, but in many instances, there is not enough strength to sense or see movement in the limb. To ask anyone who has not moved a paralyzed arm for several years to do so is not effective treatment. However, if his efforts produce a few motor units, then he may be able to assemble these into a workable limb. The majority of the biofeedback techniques utilized by today's therapist rely heavily on audiovisual facilitation.

Biofeedback equipment must be as simple as possible, reliable, and foolproof. We have been using small portable myotrainers for the past 15 years in our retraining of specific muscles and muscle groups. The myotrainer allows the patient and therapist to monitor a muscle and to achieve better control. The sensitivity of the myotrainer is of critical importance. Often, the output of the newly activated muscle is so slight that it requires a very sensitive instrument to pick up the electrical activity. Most myotrainers have threshold levels which can be preset by the therapist or patient. When the muscle activity exceeds this level, a tone or meter needle will register a response. In this manner, very specific and limited goals can be set.

With the central nervous system (CNS) patient, a complete sensory-motor evaluation is made with specific emphasis on motion (passive and active), strength, areas and degree of sensibility, subluxation, spasticity, splints, current medications, as well as medical history and overall functional evaluation.

EMG biofeedback is used as an adjunct rather than as a program in itself. Limb positioning is very important, not only for comfort, but also in trying to facilitate various forms of relaxation, e.g., often positioning the arm gives decreased activity. Positioning should precede all work on relaxation or facilitation (Fig. 11.1).

One must understand the anatomy of the area before attempting electrode placement. (Chapter 34). While initiating treatment, one should always try to obtain feedback from a normal extremity or muscle to give patients an idea of how it feels to relax and excite muscles.

Failure to find motor unit activity at the first session need not lead to complete defeat. Needle electrodes may be needed to obtain feedback from specific muscles and to eliminate crosstalk from surrounding muscles. The use of needle electrodes, however, is not generally acceptable for everyday treatment. Sometimes an oscilloscope is essential.

Our patients are encouraged to participate as much as possible in the educational process, relating any information that they feel might be helpful.

Relaxation

We have found it helpful to ask the patient to think of a relaxing scenario with the eyes closed and breathing slowly. Useful instructions are: "Think of a wave of water, slowly flowing

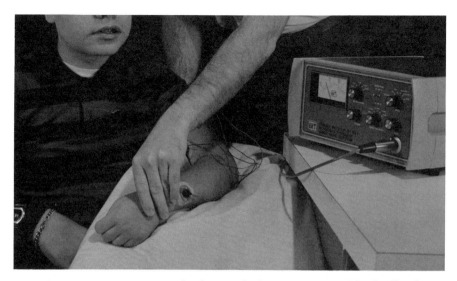

Figure 11.1. Positioning the forearm before starting EMG biofeedback.

down, or a rag doll, which when released, becomes floppy." Audio and/or visual feedback is necessary in the early achievement of this new feeling. Once training is initiated, relaxation may be limited to a few muscle groups (the biceps group is generally easy to work with). This aids in relaxation of the whole limb as well as relaxation of the part. We have also used bilateral contraction of muscle groups simultaneously. The patient is told to feel this tension and then to try to let it go out of the muscle. Various forms of general relaxation are useful also (1–3). (See Chapters 16–23.)

It is desirable to place patients in a very comfortable position, generally sitting, before attempting feedback training. When dealing with the forearm, one or two pillows are placed in the lap. The patient is allowed to place both upper and lower extremities in positions that feel most relaxing, and a room that has few distractions is ideal.

EMG feedback is not a muscle strengthener as much as it is an aid in reeducation. By gaining more appropriate feedback, the patient can then work on strengthening targeted muscles. Strength is certainly useful at the appropriate time, but patients have a tendency to want to work on strength too early and must be cautioned and guided through the entire treatment regime.

Splints

With the spastic upper extremity, relaxation is achieved in much the same way with the wrist,

fingers, and thumb. However, we occasionally use static extension splints. The patient begins working strictly with the EMG feedback, and later, we incorporate the use of the extension splint, which applies constant stress to the tendon by placing it in a lengthened position. By finding the proper tension, many times one can aid the muscle in relaxing (Fig. 11.2). Once some relaxation has been obtained, then work can be begun on increasing contraction in the paretic muscle while still maintaining relaxation of the agonist (4). This appears to aid in relaxation, and many patients can maintain this position for several hours after taking off the splint. The carry-over is not continuous, however, and must be followed by reapplication of the splint. Some patients have found that the splints tend to increase spasticity, and in these instances the splint is removed.

The thumb splint aptly positions the first metacarpal and proximal phalanx in extension abduction while leaving the distal phalanx free to aid in grasping prehension manuevers. Controlled flexion and extension of the digits may be possible without having to worry about interference from the thumb flexing across the palm and thereby getting in the way of grasping objects.

When working on wrist extension, it may be necessary to block the finger joints to eliminate as much of the finger movement as possible. When working on finger motions, the wrist can be splinted so that the individual does not use the tenodesis action of the wrist.

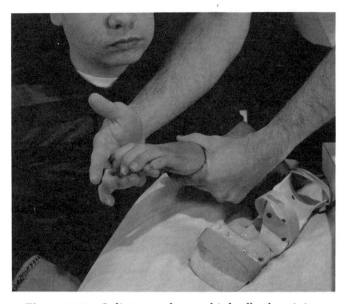

Figure 11.2. Splints supplement biofeedback training.

These same principles must be applied to the intrinsic action of metacarpophalangeal (MP) flexion and interphalangeal (IP) extension of the digits, as well as extension of the MPs by the extensor digitorum (5). A variation of a dorsal resting splint that incorporates a reflex-inhibiting movement pattern (6) is occasionally used in the hand dominated by flexor spasticity to aid in reducing tone.

Skateboard

Often helpful is the use of a skateboard (Fig. 11.3) made from a thin piece of wood and ball-bearing rollers to eliminate friction. A small raised pad allows palmar positioning of the hand in slight extension. It can be very helpful when working on elbow extension and, when combined with facilitation, it becomes even more meaningful. The electric vibrator has also been found to be helpful as an adjunct to other facilitation techniques. Specific patterns of motion can be outlined, with tape, on the top of the table. This allows the patient to pick up on visual cues while using the skateboard.

At home, the patient follows through with many of the same procedures learned earlier in the clinic.

Cerebral Palsy

Hemiplegic cerebral palsied patients with hand problems have been set up on programs with EMG biofeedback (7). Their problems include the need for general relaxation of the arm and hand, preoperative relaxation of the flexor group, and postoperative reeducation of transferred muscles, e.g., the flexor carpi ulnaris into the extensor carpi radialis longus tendon. When finger flexors have been released to give a stable wrist in extension for better functional use of the fingers, we have trained patients to get some active wrist extension by using the extensor digitorum communis and partial movement of the transferred flexor carpi ulnaris.

General relaxation of the arm and hand follows basically the same protocol as above, but all of our cerebral palsied patients are adolescents, and some are mildly retarded. With the postoperative tendon transfer, we are attempting to gain partial relaxation of the gross flexor groups, and at the point that there is evidence of relaxation, we begin to work for the initiation of reeducation of the flexor carpi ulnaris in an attempt to activate the wrist into some extension. We also work on the extensor digitorum as a wrist extensor. Postoperatively, one cannot spend too much time working on relaxation, as we must deal with a scar tissue problem. The tendon will begin to adhere to surrounding tissue almost immediately following surgery. Once the muscles have been reeducated to the point where they begin to obtain some excursion through the scar tissue and give active motion, then we have found it

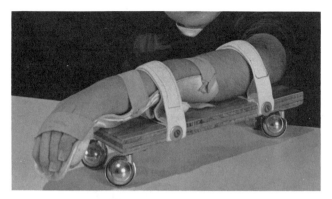

Figure 11.3.   Skateboard.

beneficial to switch to position or motion feedback discussed later in the chapter.

At this stage, we also incorporate specific activities to force the patient to use the hand in the proper reeducated motion.

Again, we use various static positioning splints for the various joints. The children are instructed in general body relaxation; the parents as well are educated to the total program. The children are seen by themselves without family members present because the presence of family can be distracting to the child. At the end of the session, the family members are brought in to be instructed, along with the child, to provide carry-over on the home program.

Peripheral Nerve Injuries

EMGBF has been found to be quite useful with peripheral nerve injuries including complete laceration and various forms of compression neuropraxia. One must search with the myotrainer in order to pick up areas that have motor unit activity when then can be reinforced.

With brachial plexus injuries, many of the problems are incomplete paralysis. Various fascicles have been damaged, which results in an incomplete return. Return many times will come quite rapidly in certain areas; others may reinnervate very slowly; while still others may not reinnervate at all. In the shoulder region, feedback by the use of surface electrodes can be used to counteract some of the problems with subluxation, by working on the deltoid and trapezius muscles. The triceps and biceps as well as hand musculature also may show good results. If there is no motor return, and sensation is protective, or if there appears

to be a poor chance of return, then tendon transfers may be appropriate. Transfers may be used to partially overcome the intrinsic-minus "claw hand": adduction, extension or opposition of the thumb; and wrist and finer extension as well as supination of the forearm.

Tendon Transfers

If the patient needs tendon transfers, several muscles may be used. After transfer, the person is started on EMG biofeedback for reeducation of the transferred muscle. Once the muscle is found to be pulling in the correct fashion, the patient is placed on specific functional activities to encourage this particular motion.

When dealing with reeducating specific muscles, as noted before, one must be very careful to avoid picking up activity from neighboring muscles. It is often helpful to use two sets of electrodes, one set for the muscle that is being reeducated while the other monitors the surrounding musculature to aid in decreasing or eliminating activity. Often, overflow is unavoidable, and all that can be done is to minimize it. An oscilloscope can often be useful in situations such as this. Once the specific motion has been learned with the transferred muscle, then EMGBF has not been found to be any more beneficial than other activities in regaining good function of the hand.

Various blocking splints and positioning splints will also aid in the early reeducation process. Splints also help to avoid the overstressing of scar tissue between the repaired tendon ends in the transferred position. It is extremely important to go from EMGBF and specific exercises to the use of specific activities to incorporate the newly learned motion.

We have found it beneficial to utilize a mirror to also aid in giving some form of position feedback along with the EMG biofeedback. As a general rule, the person will use EMG feedback during the first few sessions. This is carried over at home with specific exercises and activities to maximize the newly acquired motion to its optimum.

Tendon Repairs

EMGBF has been used at our Hand Center along with early motion following tendon repairs—either primary, delayed primary, secondary, primary graft, or two-stage tendon graft procedures. One has to be very careful that the electrodes are not over dense scar, as this interferes with electrical conduction. Following our initial observations (8) of the use of the EMGBF with tendon repairs, to follow-up over the ensuing years, several facts have become evident. During the first couple of weeks of treatment, the group utilizing EMG feedback had slight increases in the active range of motion as compared with the control group. Following 6 weeks of treatment, the control group had caught up, and at 3 months there was little or no significant difference between the groups in active range of motion. More recent investigations have shown EMG feedback to be of little use in this specific area and much inferior to joint position feedback (9).

Arthritis of the Hand

EMGBF plus isometric exercises has been helpful with arthritic patients, both preoperatively and postoperatively to increase function of the extrinsics as well as in retraining various intrinsic movements.

In the postoperative state, feedback allows the patient to gain the feeling of the newly centralized extensor tendons and their combined action with flexors as well as intrinsics. Here we are working with gross muscle groups as well as specific muscles. Reeducation has proven to be one of the areas in which EMGBF biofeedback has been most profitable.

Other Surgery

Reeducation following pollicization procedures has been aided through the use of EMGBF. Transfer of the index digit to the thumb position has been found to be very helpful in those individuals who are lacking a thumb (Fig. 11.4). The small Beckman miniature electrodes are placed over the reposi-tioned first dorsal interosseous muscle, which is now acting as an extensor/abductor. Once the individual has learned the new motion, one must quickly start working on functional activities to reeducate the sensory system to the new position while at the same time producing motion through the remodeling scar tissue.

Table 11.1 summarizes the uses of EMG feedback for hand rehabilitation.

ELECTROKINESIOLOGIC DEVICES

The use of electrokinesiologic devices in the treatment of upper extremity injuries (10) is a promising concept. It has been used with various injuries alone or with EMGBF (and various other activities and modalities) to increase hand function. The various devices are used as adjuncts to the normal treatment program. Improved designs and other treatment techniques may be found in Chapter 33.

Purposeful activity can be seriously limited due to one or more varying factors, e.g., newly healing scar tissue as a result of tendon and soft tissue lacerations, crushing injuries, burns, or corrective surgery as well as the shortening of various muscle units and tendons, and associated capsular and retaining

Table 11.1.
Effectiveness of electromyographic feedback (summary)

EMG feedback has been found most useful in treating:
- Paresis—spasticity (reeducation of specific musculature)
- Peripheral nerve problems (reeducation following reinnervation of muscle)
- Tendon transfers (relearning of new patterns of motion)
- Metacarpophalangeal implant arthroplasty (relearning proper use of intrinsics following recentralization of the extensor communis and adjustment of the lateral and medial fibers of the extensor and intrinsic tendons
- Fractures of the metacarpal head or shaft and proximal phalanx (use of the intrinsics to apply stress to the site of tendon and bone adherence to escalate early gliding and excursion)
- Occasional use with pollicization procedures involving an index-to-thumb transfer as well as with aggravating "extensor habitus" occasionally encountered

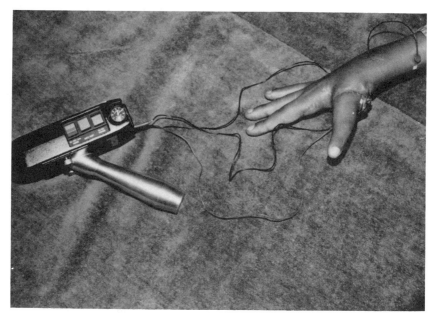

Figure 11.4.   Pollicization. EMG feedback training of muscles.

ligaments. The accepted method is through the controlled application of various stressors, such as dynamic splinting, active and passive exercise, massage, etc. The goal is to gradually induce remodeling with each of the various modes of treatment, by placing different patterns of stress on the various structures as well as scar tissue. (11).

We have to wait a certain period of time for the various phases in the healing process to take place. If intervention is made before this, possible damage can be done. Patients and even therapists have found it extremely difficult to judge the accuracy of how far they were flexing or extending the injured digit in their exercise programs.

Electrogoniometers can give accurate, objective measurements of motion (12). The devices have calibrated threshold settings that allow multiple goals to be set with very small increases of motion. This in turn produces variable amounts of stress applied to the remodeling scar tissue (Fig. 11.5). We have been using not only goniometers, which measure range of motion, but also various devices which incorporate pressure feedback when utilizing grasp and prehension movement activities (Fig. 11.6). When other activities are involved, one may use audio feedback rather than visual, as the latter may be distracting. Many devices have an accessory earphone.

Feedback Goniometry

To illustrate clinical application of feedback goniometers, the example of a patient recovering from tendon lacerations and consequent surgical repair is used. A trial of exercise with the goniometer can be made soon after bandages are removed. Swelling and inflammation should have substantially receded, and the patient should be able to produce small, active movements of the involved joints without significant discomfort. The patient's active and passive range of motion for involved joints is measured by the therapist with a conventional clinical goniometer and recorded in the chart. A joint is selected for goniometer application,

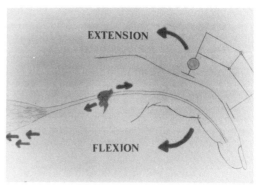

Figure 11.5.   Stress on healing scar tissue.

Figure 11.6. Newer lightweight version of finger goniometer.

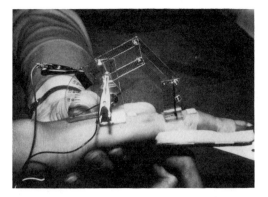

Figure 11.7. M.P. Arthroplasty in extension.

and the skin proximal and distal to it are cleaned with soap and water or alcohol. Excess hair is clipped short with scissors to improve goniometer adhesion. Adhesive washers are applied to both goniometer bases. The distal base is affixed first, positioned so that it does not overlap the skin folds at the knuckles. The proximal base is then affixed to the dorsal surface proximal to the joint. Positioning of goniometer bases is not critical to measurement accuracy, except that it must be such that goniometer linkage arms work without overextending or binding against one another as the patient exercises through the range of motion. Care is necessary when mounting goniometer bases over scleroderma, stitches, blisters, healing tissue, hypertrophic or keloid scars, and alternate attachment methods may be improvised as necessary.

Once baseline measures have been taken and the feedback goniometer is affixed over the joint, the initial exercise session lasts only 10 to 15 minutes, the patient working at his or her own pace and resting for about 30 seconds after every minute of exercise. The therapist is alert for physiological warning signs, especially pain, swelling, or inflammation, which suggest that the patient's exercise tolerance is being exceeded. If all goes well, subsequent daily sessions are increased in length to a maximum of 30 minutes, three times daily. The flexion or extension threshold is advanced by small increments (2 or 3 degrees) so that the patient's goal is always the most he or she can comfortably achieve

through a full session at that stage in recovery.

The first several sessions are carried out in the clinic so that the therapist can check frequently to see that the patient tolerates the exercises well and does them properly. Before patients take feedback goniometers out for home practice, they are thoroughly trained in the proper use of the devices.

When several joints are affected by trauma or surgery, the goniometer is rotated from joint to joint as necessary. For arthritic patients with metacarpophalangeal implant arthroplasties (artificial joint implants), the goniometer is used on all replaced joints, with effort focused on the joint lagging most behind the others in ROM (Figs. 11.7 and 11.8). These patients are usually asked to flex all MP joints together. With patients recovering from tendon or soft tissue injury, the goniometer is used more on the joints most limited by tendon excursion or ligamental tightness. Initially, such patients are usually asked to try to confine motion to the joint over which the goniometer is mounted, since flexing or extending several joints simultaneously might result in improper stress at other sites.

There are many varied capabilities of motion feedback. The elbow goniometer (Fig. 11.9) gives feedback to the hemiplegic patient as proprioception through auditory feedback. In the early phase, it is used only in placement exercises (e.g., touching the chin and then reaching out to touch the table). Activities are incorporated when the capable of telling where his extremity is in relation to space and movement. Greenberg and Fowler found that kinesthetic feedback was as beneficial as conventional occupational therapy in increasing

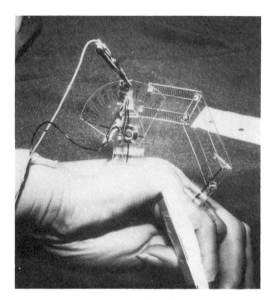

Figure 11.8.   M.P. Arthroplasty in flexion.

active elbow extension in 10 hemiplegic subjects (13).

Wrist goniometers (Figs. 11.10 and 11.11) give feedback on flexion and extension. They can be used with a standard form of feedback as with the elbow or in conjunction with a strip chart recorder, which gives the therapist and patient a more objective measurement of

motion by eliminating differences between the therapist's visual calculations with a standard goniometer.

For the fingers, a very small goniometer fabricated from highly durable, light, and inexpensive plastic (Fig. 11.12) employs a power pack and audiovisual feedback from either a small light or earphone. A threshold knob allows for numerical adjustment. The power pack is small enough to fit into the shirt pocket, and the small electrical cable runs down the sleeve to its attachment on the potentiometer. The device is small enough for the individual to go about various activities either in therapy or on the job and still obtain joint feedback. The newest designs by DeBacher (Chapter 33) result in devices which a therapist is capable of making within the clinic at a very small cost.

A multi-joint goniometer (Fig. 11.13) can be used to overcome intrinsic tightness, by giving feedback on extension of the proximal phalanx and flexion of the middle and distal phalanges as well as aid in "breaking up" the occasional problem of "extensor habitus."

Ten of our patients who had surgical procedures for MP joint implant arthroplasties received the same general treatment, but six used motion feedback goniometers as an added part of their program. MP joint ROM

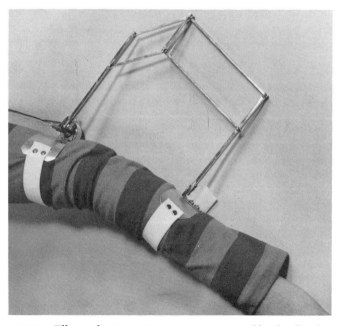

Figure 11.9.   Elbow electrogoniometer as source of biofeedback signal.

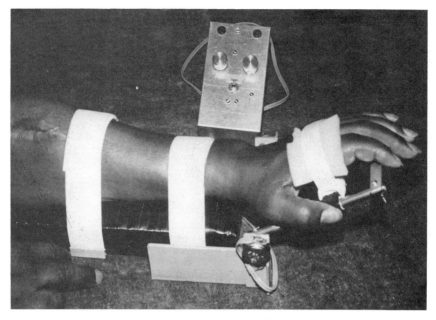

Figure 11.10. One form of wrist electrogoniometer.

increased an average of 14° at 3 weeks over the group that received no motion feedback. At 3 months, an increase of 8° was noted. Similar comparisons were noted for 14 patients recovering from joint and tissue trauma; however, the increases in motion were greater.

A forearm goniometer has been developed by DeBacher for troublesome problems with supination and pronation such as seen many times following a Colles' fracture (Figs. 11.14 and 11.15).

Goniometer biofeedback can give patients

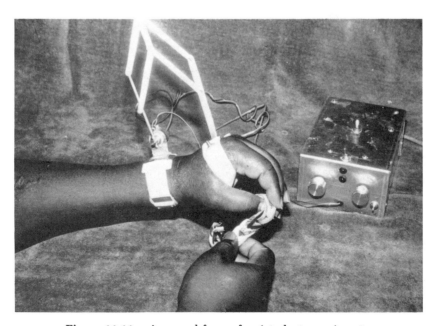

Figure 11.11. A second form of wrist electrogoniometer.

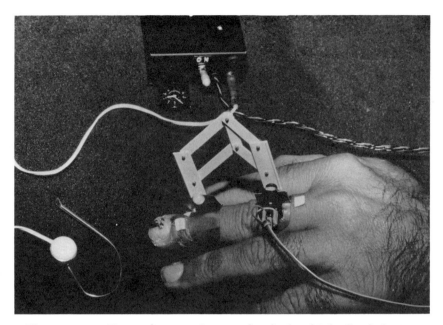

Figure 11.12. Finger electrogoniometer that feeds a biofeedback device.

independence in daily tasks and activities assigned by the occupational therapist (Fig. 11.16) while giving the supportive feedback needed in the various stages of upper limb rehabilitation.

The increments of movement can be more readily assessed from the goniometer than from the "naked eye" watching for perceptible increased motion in a joint (Table 11.2).

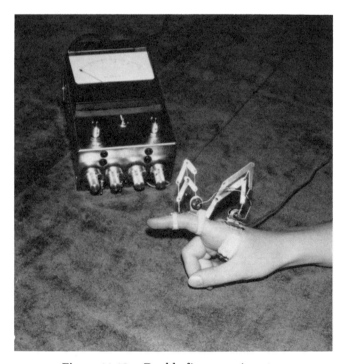

Figure 11.13. Double finger goniometer.

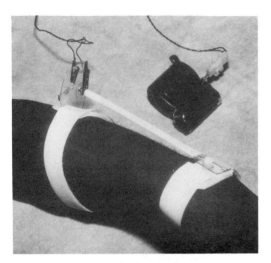

Figure 11.14. Forearm goniometer for supination and pronation.

Table 11.2.
Effectiveness of electrokinesiologic feedback (summary)

Motion feedback has been found most helpful in treating:

- Soft tissue, joint contracture, fractures and tendon anastomoses (refined control of stress to tissues while exercising)
- Resection implant arthroplasty: metacarpophalangeal and proximal interphalangeal joint (target on joints expected to be difficult or lag behind, i.e., fifth digit); following total wrist arthroplasty (useful in accentuating desired pattern of motion)
- Extensor habitus (helps focus on interphalangeal joint flexion)

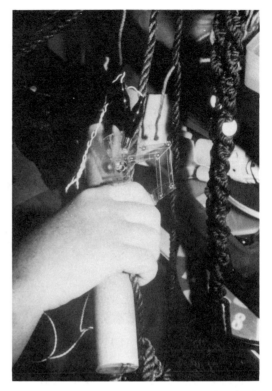

Figure 11.16. Activity with use of feedback for flexion of index interphalangeal joints.

OTHER FEEDBACK DEVICES

Pressure Biofeedback

When favorable motion has been obtained, other forms of feedback may be initiated such as: pressure feedback using pressure transducers, microswitches, or strain gauges. Through electronics, meaningful activities can be combined with immediate feedback. By grasping or pinching various types and sizes of compression cylinders (Fig. 11.17), the strength of the hand can be increased as well as applying stress to remodeling scar tissue in a longitudinal fashion. The decision as to which cylinder to use is based on the specific grasping pattern of the injured hand. At the base, there is a small shut-off valve that allows for air to be pumped into or extracted from the device. This small control knob along with a threshold switch will allow the therapist to control the amount of pressure exerted upon the pressure transducer or microswitch, the cadence at which the person will exercise, as well as the

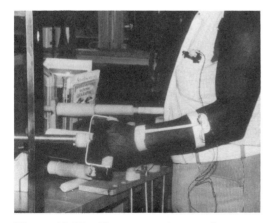

Figure 11.15. Forearm goniometer in use.

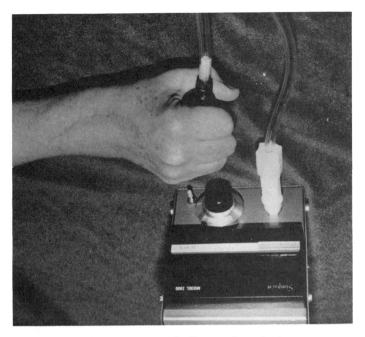

Figure 11.17. A compression bulb transducer to improve grasp.

length of time the switch will maintain clo-sure and thereby keep a desired electrical ap-pliance on.

The pressure of the various bulbs will main-tain closure of the switch, thereby completing an electrical circuit, and operating an appli-ance (110 V) such as: a radio for other patients in the hand clinic, TV, or a simple kitchen electric mixer. The devices not only give feed-back by turning on an appliance but also can allow for visual feedback via a small red light or digital readout. As strength, motion, and/or endurance increase, the level is adjusted.

Bioconverter

Another useful concept in biofeedback is our "bioconverter" (14), which works in con-junction with EMG feedback from a myo-trainer. The myotrainer picks up the electrical activity, then rectifies and integrates it. It is connected to the bioconverter by an electrical cable. An EMG signal strong enough to acti-vate the preset threshold of the myotrainer au-tomatically turns on the bioconverter by com-pleting the electrical circuit. The bioconverter is also capable of operating electrical appli-ances (110 V). The adjustable levels of the holding circuit are extremely important. A muscle that has been rendered inactive,

whether from paralysis or simple disuse atro-phy, is seldom capable of recruiting the neces-sary activity to show motion in the injured ex-tremity or joint. Children who have had ten-don transfers following nerve injury have used the bioconverter to allow them to gain feed-back on specific muscles while at the same time activating a radio or a slide projector that tells a children's story.

Another use for the bioconverter was found for a woman who was partially blind and deaf. Because she was unable to employ normal vis-ual and auditory cues, the bioconverter served as a missing link for EMG feedback training of denervated hand muscles. An oscillating elec-tric fan was plugged into the bioconverter, and when the proper motor units were activated, the fan came on and blew air into her face, giving her the needed cue. An electric vibrator also served well as a signal device.

THE FUTURE

Our treatment program is constantly being changed and updated. Many concepts in the first edition of this book are no longer consid-ered feasible or pertinent today. The areas of biofeedback and total hand management are relatively new and will continue to change. Feedback is extremely important in the early phases of the rehabilitation program but is only utilized as an adjunct to the ongoing treatment program.

One cannot ignore the necessary intimate relationships among hand surgeon, therapist and patient. So much of the hand program deals with a one-to-one relationship in the many transitions of treatment that it would certainly be detrimental to the patient to even consider doing away with this essential aspect of the program. Human relationships are a very vital part of our life and are paramount in our clinics.

References

1. Bernstein, D. A. and Brokovic, T. D. *Progressive Relaxation Training.* Research Press, Champaign, Ill., 1974.
2. Johnson, H. E. and Garton, W. H. Muscle reeducation in hemiplegia by use of an electromyographic device. Arch. Phys. Med. Rehabil., *54*: 320–323, 1973.
3. Basmajian, J. V. *Muscles Alive: Their Functions Revealed by Electromyography,* 4th ed. Williams & Wilkins, Baltimore, 1979.
4. Baker, M., Regenos, E., Wolf, S. L. and Basmajian, J. V. Developing strategies for biofeedback applications in neurologically handicapped patients. Am. J. Phys. Ther., *57*: 402–408, 1977.
5. Owen, S., Toomin, H. and Taylor, L. P. *Biofeedback in Neuromuscular Re-education.* Biofeedback Research Institute, Inc., Los Angeles, 1975, pp. 27–30.
6. Snook, J. Spasticity reduction splint. Am. J. Occupational Ther., *33:* 648–651, 1979.
7. Amato, A., Hermsmeyer, C. A. and Kleinman, K. M. Use of electromyographic feedback to increase inhibitory control of spastic muscles. Phys. Ther., *53:* 1063–1066, 1973.
8. Kukulka, G. G., Brown, D. M. and Basmajian, J. V. Biofeedback training for early finger joint mobilization. Am. J. Occupational Ther., *29:* 469–470, 1975.
9. Brown, D. M., DeBacher, G. A. and Basmajian, J. V. Feedback goniometers for hand rehabilitation. Am. J. Occupational Ther., *33:* 458–463, 1979.
10. Morris, A. F. and Brown, D. M. Electronic training devices for hand rehabilitation. Am. J. Occupational Ther., *30:* 376–379, 1976.
11. Arem, A., Madden, J. Effects of stress on healing wounds. I. Intermittent noncyclical tension. J. Surg. Res., *20:* 93–102, 1976.
12. Thomas, D. and Long, C. Electrogoniometer for the fingers: kinesiologic tracking device. Am. J. Med. Electronics, *3:* 96–100, 1964.
13. Greenberg, S. and Fowler, R. Kinesthetic biofeedback: a treatment modality for elbow range of motion in hemiplegia. Am. J. Occupational Ther., *34:* 738–743, 1980.
14. Brown, D. M. and Basmajian, J. V. Bioconverter for upper extremity rehabilitation. Am. J. Phys. Med., *57:* 233–238, 1978.

CHAPTER 12

Further Applications of Electromyographic Muscle Reeducation

FOAD NAHAI
D. MICHAEL BROWN

FACIAL MUSCLES

Surgical reconstruction of facial palsy includes repair of the facial nerve either directly or by nerve grafting, nerve transfers, muscle transfers, and dynamic and static sling procedures. It is in the area of nerve and muscle transfer that EMGBF techniques are applicable. On a limited scale, we have applied biofeedback techniques in reeducation of muscle following surgery for facial palsy (1, 2).

Facial Nerve Grafts

When direct repair or grafting of the seventh nerve is not possible, one alternative is to take the proximal portion of another nerve, most commonly the eleventh or twelfth nerve, and suture it to the divided distal end of the seventh nerve. Following a suitable interval of time, the muscles of facial expression are innervated by a foreign nerve. The motor nerve of the trapezius (eleventh nerve) or of the tongue (twelfth nerve) now innervates the muscles of facial expression, i.e., the brain center controlling tongue or shoulder motion now controls the muscles of facial expression and emotion. Through EMGBF, muscles of facial expression are retrained to respond to a foreign nerve.

Case Report. The patient had a resection of an acoustic neuroma 8 years previous to feedback training. At the time of surgery, the fifth, seventh, and eighth cranial nerves were sacrificed. Following the initial procedure, the patient had a transfer of the eleventh nerve to the distal portion of the seventh. There was evidence of facial reinnervation, but there was no voluntary or automatic control of the newly innervated muscles. Until EMG feedback treat-

ment was begun, the patient had remained at the same level of slight recovery.

The patient had neglected this side of her face and was found to be thoroughly frustrated in her efforts to use this side (Fig. 12.1). Treatment with the myotrainer was begun, initially using audio feedback and later progressing to visual feedback (Fig. 12.2). Use of a mirror to aid in visual cues was initiated during the 2nd week of training. Our treatment program also consisted of various activities, mainly those involved in smiling, blowing, and sucking. When performing other activities such as reading out loud or eating, the patient was told to concentrate on various other sensations from the face and mouth. Improvements were gained up to the 10th week following the initiation of treatment, at which time a plateau was reached. At this point, she was weaned off of EMG feedback. Upon plateauing, there was good facial symmetry and control with only minimal asymmetry during speech (Fig 12.3). The affected side of the face began to fill out, and she regained a much more pleasing facial appearance.

Masseter Muscle Transfers

The masseter muscle is most commonly used for transfer in facial palsy for animation of the lower face. The masseter, a muscle of mastication, is detached (usually only part of the muscle is used) from its insertion into the mandible and rerouted to the angle of the mouth on the paralyzed side. Thus, a muscle of mastication is now used to pull up the drooping angle of the mouth. EMG reeducation is useful in increasing control of this muscle in its new role.

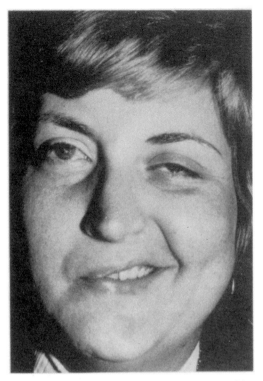

Figure 12.1. Patient 8 years following ablative facial nerve palsy and nerve graft, before biofeedback. (Reprinted with permission from Brown *et al.* (2).)

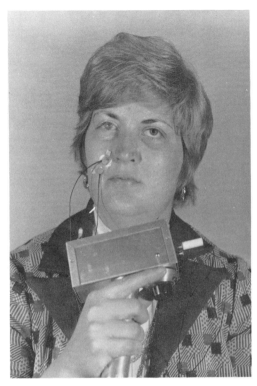

Figure 12.2. EMG biofeedback training of right facial muscles. (Reprinted with permission from Brown et al. (2).)

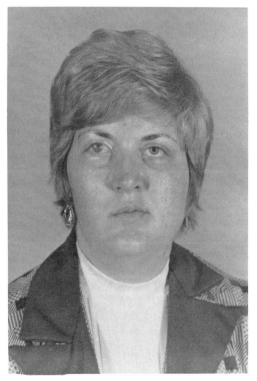

Figure 12.3. After biofeedback training. In later follow-up (2 years), patient was able to close eyelids. (Reprinted with permission from Brown et al. (2).)

Figure 12.4. Surgical left facial nerve palsy before treatment. (Reprinted with permission from Brown et al. (2).)

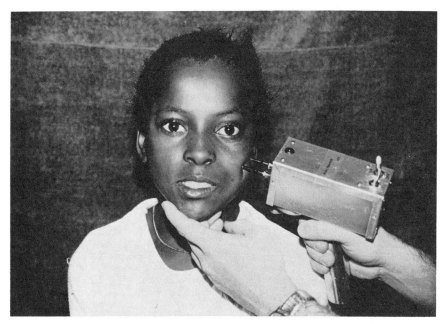

Figure 12.5. Biofeedback training of masseter transfer. (Reprinted with permission from Brown et al. (2).)

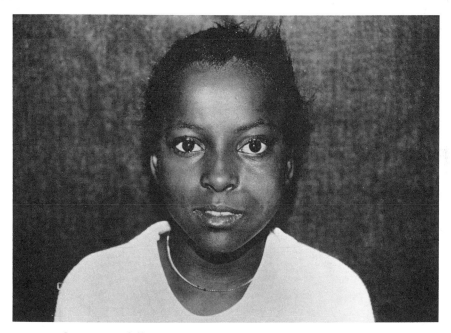

Figure 12.6. Facial symmetry following treatment. (Reprinted with permission from Brown et al. (2).)

Case Study. An 8-year-old child suffered seventh nerve damage during surgery to the middle ear. This subsequently left her with a left-sided facial palsy, which was treated surgically with a masseter muscle transfer and a static fascia lata sling. Several months after surgery, she was referred for muscle training utilizing EMG biofeedback (Fig. 12.4). The goal was to retrain the masseter to become a muscle of facial expression (Fig. 12.5). Due to travel difficulties, the patient was followed at monthly intervals. A plateau was reached at 3 months of feedback training, and at this point, she had attained good facial symmetry and control in smiling (Fig. 12.6). It was noted, however, that when attempting a broad smile, the unaffected side would overcompensate slightly.

OTHER AREAS OF THE BODY

Muscle reeducation is not limited to the hand or face. In reconstructive surgery, muscles are routinely transferred to replace paralyzed muscles. The gracilis muscle of the thigh, either one or both, may be used to reconstruct the anal sphincter in patients with anal incontinence. In one patient, where both muscles were to be used, preoperative education was carried out as well as postoperative reeducation in the transferred position. The patient showed marked improvement with more forceful contractions of the gracilis muscle.

Future Applications

With refinements in technique and advances in instrumentation, transfer of whole muscles and nerves from one part of the body to another is now a real possibility. There have been reports of transfer of the gracilis muscle to the face for facial palsy and to the arm for Volkmann's ischemic contracture. In such cases, not only is the transferred muscle innervated by a foreign nerve, but also its actions are changed. The gracilis or adductor of the leg becomes a finger and wrist flexor. Undoubtedly, muscle reeducation with biofeedback will in the future play a part in the rehabilitation of such patients.

References

1. Booker, H. E., Robow, R. T. and Coleman, P. J. Simplified feedback in neuromuscular retraining an automated approach using electromyographic signals. Arch. Phys. Med. Rehabil., 50: 621–625, 1969.
2. Brown, D. M., Nahai, F., Wolf, S. and Basmajian, J. V. Electromyographic feedback in the reeducation of facial palsy. Am. J. Phys. Med., 57: 183–190, 1978.

CHAPTER 13

Biofeedback in Spasticity Control

GARY DeBACHER

Spasticity is a neurological disorder caused by central nervous system damage that weakens or interrupts the influence of descending corticospinal tracts on spinal cord systems. Narrowly defined, it consists of increasing resistance in a muscle to passive stretch (1). For example, one asks a patient to relax, and then one straightens the arm at the elbow; in a normal adult, no muscular resistance is encountered, but if the elbow flexors are spastic, they contract in response to being stretched and resist the examiner's efforts.

STRETCH REFLEX EFFECTS

This resistance typically increases with higher stretch velocities and may not occur at all below a certain threshold speed. When the patient is resting quietly with his limbs comfortably supported, the spastic muscles usually relax completely (2, 3).

Spastic resistance is stretch reflex activity. Other clinical methods of stimulating stretch receptors—tendon taps or vibration—also elicit abnormal responses in spastic muscles (4). The stretch receptors in question are of course the muscle spindles scattered among and connected in parallel with the fibers of the muscle. Each muscle spindle also contains a few muscle fibers the purpose of which is not to help contract the entire muscle, but to control the sensitivity of the muscle spindle to stretch. While other muscle fibers are activated by alpha motoneurons, the spindle fibers are controlled separately by gamma motoneurons (5). The more contracted the muscle spindles, the more sensitive they are to stretch.

Until recently, there were just two basic explanations for the hyperactive stretch reflexes in spasticity. One posited a hyperactive gamma efferent system that would put muscle spindles in a more contracted state, resulting in increased response to stretch (4). The other held that loss of corticospinal inhibitory control would leave alpha motoneurons with a lower firing threshold so that they would fire more easily in response to any sensory input impinging on them, including that from the monosynaptic input from stretch receptors (1). Delwaide (6) has offered a third explanation that would account for the majority of the evidence about as well as the older theories. He proposes that (a) spinal interneurons normally exert a primarily inhibitory *presynaptic* modulating influence on afferent connections just upstream of alpha motoneurons, and (b) damage to corticospinal paths weakens this influence. Hence, afferent impulses, whether from stretch receptors or from other sources, would be more likely to increase the rate of firing of alpha motoneurons, even if muscle spindles were not abnormally contracted.

Granit (5) has pointed out that cortical control of alpha and gamma motoneurons is so closely coordinated that it could be described as yoked. If so, it would seem unlikely that an injury interrupting corticospinal influences would selectively disinhibit one system and not the other.

Bishop (4) reviewed studies that seemed to indicate that the gamma efferent system is hyperactive in the majority of cases of spasticity. A method that purports to discriminate between cases of "alpha" and "gamma" spasticity by means of cold stimuli applied over the muscle has been developed (7, 8). But this apparent triumph of the "gamma" theory has been reversed by recent evidence obtained by direct recording from muscle spindle afferent axons (9, 10), which demonstrates that in the spastic subject at rest, the discharge of spindle endings and their response to passive stretch are not greater than are seen for spindle endings in normal subjects.

Spasticity is only one facet of a syndrome including deficits in voluntary strength and in control of movements. Some degree of paralysis is almost always present in spastic limbs. Selective control of muscles and discrete movements is replaced to varying degrees by primitive flexion or extension synergies. Reciprocal inhibition of spastic flexors and extensors is typically insufficient so that a muscle may be overpowered by its antagonist before any movement has occurred. The clinical appearance of the spastic patient and his difficulties with daily living are really due less to spasticity itself than to the related deficits in strength and control (11–13). Holt (11) argues that abnormal electromyographic (EMG) activity of "spastic" muscles in cerebral palsied children often cannot be reasonably attributed to exaggerated stretch reflex activity. K. Bobath (12) maintains that abnormal muscle tone in individual muscles should not be the focus of treatment efforts.

Historically, neuromuscular reeducation in physical therapies has moved steadily away from training of individual muscles to an increasing emphasis on patterns of posture and movement (14). There is usually no intent to train discrete control over individual muscles and muscle groups or to synthesize such control into movements.

LOGIC OF BIOFEEDBACK

Against this, EMG feedback is something of a throwback. It works quite well for training individual muscles, well for muscle groups such as knee or elbow extensors, but poorly for direct training of limb movements that involve numerous muscles. Why is the new training technique useful?

Half of the answer is fairly simple. If a particular muscle remains functionally paralyzed in response to the full array of facilitation strategies, and it is essential to the movement pattern, the result is failure. If EMG feedback can bring about some volitional control of the muscle, the therapist can then try again to integrate it into movement patterns with traditional therapy. The work of Johnson and Garton (15) and of Basmajian et al. (16) in overcoming paralysis of tibialis anterior illustrates this very well. Facilitation approaches often fail to activate this muscle in hemiplegic stroke victims. EMG feedback training will usually restore some degree of voluntary control.

But is there any merit to a "peripheral" approach to spasticity, e.g., training subjects to inhibit the condition in individual muscles? The experience of Khalili and Betts (17) in alleviating spasticity in selective muscles with phenol blocks is instructive: the smaller gamma motoneuron axons are blocked, relaxing the muscle spindles, and spasticity in the muscle immediately diminishes. Voluntary control of the muscle sometimes improves, and diminished spasticity and improved control may sometimes be observed throughout the limb, although only one muscle was treated. Some generalized improvement from treatment of just one muscle can also result from orthopaedic surgery to lengthen the tendon, hence reducing the degree of stretch to which the muscle is subjected (18). Improvement in the untreated muscles of a limb seems more plausible when we recall that the stretch receptors from that muscle have collateral connections to other muscles via interneurons (4). In particular, they influence alpha motoneurons of antagonists via inhibitory interneurons. Thus, if the spindles of a spastic muscle are hyperactive, an abnormal inhibitory influence bears on the antagonists. This may be one of the reasons that hemiplegic patients have a hard time activating finger, wrist, and elbow extensors as long as the flexors are spastic; and it is surely one reason that vibration of the agonist tends to inhibit the antagonist (19, 20). Reducing spindle tone in a spastic muscle by any means should make it easier for the patient to activate the antagonist.

STUDIES OF EMG FEEDBACK AND SPASTICITY

My colleagues at Emory University Center for Rehabilitation Medicine have conducted clinical research studies on a number of patients with spasticity, some results of which are summarized in Basmajian, Regenos and Baker (21) and in Baker, Regenos, Wolf and Basmajian (22). In other chapters of this book, detailed training procedures are given.

Brudny et al. (23) reported their experience with 39 cases of hemiparesis in retraining function of the affected arm. Assistive capacity or actual prehension was established in 27 patients. Of the remaining patients, four experienced some relief of spasticity without achieving assistive capacity in the limb, four showed no change, and four had insufficient exposure to therapy. In most cases, just a single "prime mover" muscle was trained.

An earlier report (24) gave some details of a case in which a girl was trained to inhibit spastic contraction of the fingers and thumb and regained a degree of prehensive ability.

Achieving general improvement in arm and hand control by training just one muscle or muscle group suggests that in such cases, the target muscle was a very spastic flexor from which hyperactive spindle afferents might be raining excitation on other flexors, touching off mass synergies and inhibition of extensors—preventing their selective activation. This parallels experiences with nerve blocks (17, 18) in which blocking one spastic muscle sometimes unmasks considerable latent control over patterned movements. Such patients probably constitute a small proportion of the total population of spastic hemiplegics. My own observations and those of colleagues (22) would indicate that training a number of different muscles is usually necessary to achieve a prehensive or assistive capacity in the affected arm.

Amato, Hermsmeyer and Kleinman (25) used EMG feedback to train a spastic hemiplegic to relax the spastic gastrocnemius following contractions and to dorsiflex the ankle while relaxing the gastrocnemius. After 2 months of training, some improvement in dorsiflexion and gait was observed. In a later study, Kleinman et al. (26) treated eight stabilized stroke patients who had chronic flexor spasticity and contracture of one arm. Of seven patients completing the intensive training, six were able during feedback training to decrease EMG activity below baseline, and all seven showed increased active range of elbow extension after training with a mean increase of 25°.

Maher (27) trained subjects to control spasticity while they rested supine. In a controlled study, the eight experimental subjects markedly reduced biceps and triceps activity; the difference between them and a matched control group was statistically significant at the 0.05 level. Apparently, some spastic subjects achieved EMG silence. The experimental group with EMG feedback took less time to approximate zero EMG activity in special interexercise rest periods than control subjects.

In assessing the significance of Maher's study, we must note that most spastics can relax *without* feedback by carefully positioning them in a quiet environment and instructing them properly (2, 3). Being better able to relax while at rest usually has little impact on the spasticity and dyssynergy that occur during movement. Hence, training in resting relaxation is of limited value except as a stepping stone to more difficult tasks.

Ladd et al. (28, 29) provided evidence that spastic subjects can control single motor units in spastic muscles. EMG from fine-wire intramuscular electrodes was displayed on an oscilloscope and presented through a loudspeaker.

Ladd, Oist and Jonsson (30) applied their special training technique to patients with spastic paraparesis from multiple sclerosis, using soleus muscle. Before administration of the antispasticity drug (Dantrium), 4 of the 8 subjects were able to isolate a single motor unit; with Dantrium, 7 of 8 patients could do so. Reviewing results from all four tests, the authors concluded that the ability of patients to establish voluntary control over fine neuromuscular activity in the spastic soleus was considerably inferior to that of normal subjects but that this ability was significantly improved to near that of normals by Dantrium.

Jonsson et al. (29) conducted a very similar study on 11 spastic hemiplegic patients, with similar findings.

Harrison and Connolly (31) trained four diplegic spastic subjects to discretely control very low amplitude spikes in spastic forearm muscles while inhibiting other EMG activity. Harrison (32, 33) later provided a particularly interesting series of experiments on the nature and limitations of control of spastic musculature and the effect of EMG feedback training. The spastic subjects were cerebral palsied adults. The spastic forearm flexor muscles were studied, and the five spastic subjects were compared with normals or with themselves after successive training interventions. Brief exposure to EMG feedback produced a marked improvement in scaling of muscular tension efforts in some subjects. Following a training program, the spastic patients were retested without any feedback on the scaling task. All five subjects now did quite well at scaling their efforts.

Normal subjects could maintain various levels of forearm activity without feedback for 10 seconds with little deviation. Spastic subjects deviated more and failed to check a gradual reduction in EMG activity during the 10-second period. The spastic subjects repeated this experiment using EMG feedback from a meter. There was a significant improvement in their accuracy.

Harrison preferred to give no feedback other than "knowledge of results," merely saying "too high," "too low" or "correct" after each trial was completed. She explained her reasons in a later article (33), maintaining that immediate, continuous EMG feedback may be too complex, too distracting, and likely to keep patients dependent on it.

Certainly, many types of muscle response can be trained successfully with knowledge of results alone—single motor unit control has been achieved in this way (34). There are instances, as in training inhibition of spasticity during rapid passive stretch, when the patient has no chance to appreciate and react to changes in the EMG integral; he must assess the net result of his effort at the end of each trial. The real issue, however, is whether it is better to always train from the start using only knowledge of results or to use immediate feedback as well, weaning the patient later to knowledge of results alone and then to no extrinsic feedback at all.

K. U. Smith et al. (35) steadfastly argued that concurrent, continuous feedback is vital for motor control and skill acquisition and were very critical of the view that knowledge of results, operant conditioning, or any form of learning by consequences can be an important determinant of motor learning. My view is the same as that of Howson (36), that whenever possible, *both* types of feedback should be provided, especially in the first stages of learning.

The reader may wish to consult the chapters on "Information Feedback" and "Supplementary Feedback and Instructions" in *Principles of Skill Acquisition* by Bilodeau and Bilodeau (37). Harrison's arguments should spur therapists to include procedures to wean subjects away from immediate feedback and knowledge of results in the course of therapy. By such procedures, patients can shift to reliance on internal cues and more efficient and automatic motor strategies. Basic research on pigeons by Terrace (38) on discrimination learning suggests that providing immediate, continuous feedback during acquisition and then removing it systematically could in fact be the best way to aid spastic subjects to discover and learn to use internal proprioceptive cues.

TRAINING HIERARCHY

Clearly, there are many facets to spasticity, and no single training task can possibly teach all the skills that would be required to inhibit spasticity and dyssynergy in activities of daily living. Basmajian and I (39–41) tested the effectiveness of EMG feedback for treating spasticity, and organized a number of potentially relevant training tasks into a hierarchy of gradually increasing difficulty.

We conceptualized this training hierarchy in three stages. In the first, the spastic muscles are at rest, factoring out stretch stimuli as much as possible, and subjects learn to maintain relaxation in spite of "overflow" caused by arousal, distracting stimuli, mental effort, or concurrent use of normal limbs. The second stage of training focuses on learning to inhibit spasticity occasioned by passive static and dynamic stretch of the spastic target muscles. Dynamic stretching is at first very slow and is increased gradually as the subject's ability to inhibit spasticity shows improvement. The third stage is directed at training a few of the skills prerequisite to active use of the spastic limb. Subjects learn to activate the antagonist while inhibiting cocontraction of the spastic target muscle. They work isometrically at first, to factor out spasticity caused by dynamic stretch of the spastic antagonist. If they progress acceptably, isokinetic motion at increasing rates is added later. Subjects may also be trained to contract and relax without abnormal delays, and to produce graded contractions.

This paradigm represents a natural, almost necessary order of attack on spasticity.

EQUIPMENT NEEDS AND TECHNICAL ASPECTS

The equipment needed to treat spasticity does not differ significantly from that required for other EMG feedback applications. Both large (16–20 mm) and small (7–11 mm) surface electrodes are needed, the latter for placements on small muscles of the hand or forearm. The feedback device should have a meter or some other visual, quantitative feedback mode as well as auditory feedback. An output connection through which "raw" EMG can be viewed on an oscilloscope is important. Having two feedback devices is very helpful when training a patient to contract a paretic muscle while inhibiting its spastic antagonist.

Electrode spacing is an important variable. Wide-spaced electrodes (3 cm or more apart) give better coverage of large muscles but tend to pick up extraneous, irrelevant EMG from other muscles, even from the antagonists. Close-spaced electrodes (2 cm down to as little as 8 mm) pick up much less extraneous EMG and usually provide a fair sample of activity in the target muscle. Bipolar concentric or fine-wire inserted electrodes provide the ultimate in close-spacing and recording selectivity, but are seldom necessary. There are sometimes good reasons for changing electrode spacing in the midst of training (22), but if you wish to use EMG measures as a valid gauge of progress over successive sessions, you must standardize placement and spacing for each subject and not change it later.

Monitoring the "raw" EMG action potentials on an oscilloscope is very helpful for assessing spasticity, and to improve electrode placements, identify 60-Hz noise, motion artifact, or equipment malfunction, distinguish local from distant extraneous EMG, and recognize single motor units. But the greatest value is for assessing the adequacy of relaxation. Microvolt readings on a feedback meter cannot be used validly to assess relaxation. A 50-μV reading can be due to several small motor units firing randomly throughout the muscle, or to just one large motor unit firing steadily right under the electrodes (22), or to extraneous activity in an antagonist muscle being trained to contract. This is easy to resolve with an oscilloscope but almost impossible with a meter.

If you monitor raw EMG on an oscilloscope, you may find that the patient's difficulty in relaxing a spastic muscle completely is due to persistent, repetitive firing of large action potentials with regular wave form (42). These "maverick" motor units are remarkably resistant to direct efforts at voluntary inhibition. However, some subjects learn to terminate their firing by moving the head or contralateral limb. Briefly stretching and shortening the spastic muscle may also silence these potentials.

PATIENT SELECTION

Spasticity can result from a variety of lesions with widely differing etiologies—stroke, cerebral palsy, spinal cord injury, accidental brain trauma, general anoxia, degenerative disorders such as multiple sclerosis, and brain surgery to remove tumors or for other reasons.

There are few a priori grounds for assuming that patients from any of the above categories would not benefit from EMG feedback therapy. Of course, if a spinal transection were known to be complete, there would be no way the patient could exert control over spasticity

below the level of the lesion. Actually, it is the patients with partial spinal transections who manifest more spasticity. And while EMG feedback cannot halt degenerative CNS disorders, it might enable victims of these disorders to temporarily reduce the degree of spasticity and loss of control.

Sensory loss in an affected limb does not seem to prevent subjects from learning to inhibit spasticity, although if it persists, it may limit the usefulness of an arm for prehension in spite of considerable rehabilitative efforts (18). Receptive aphasia, often seen to some degree in stroke victims, seldom prevents them from understanding feedback tasks. Children with spasticity may require tangible rewards to maintain motivation (43). Therapists just starting to use EMG feedback should avoid the sort of patients who are hard to manage in any therapeutic program. There is no lack of bright, motivated patients with mild to moderate spasticity, and with such patients, the therapist will learn more quickly.

RECOVERY AND TIMING OF FEEDBACK THERAPY

In the case of stroke, brain trauma, or spinal cord injury, the question arises as to when in the course of recovery EMG feedback training can be started. The Brunnstrom (44) six stages of recovery in stroke patients are widely accepted by therapists. When spasticity appears, EMG feedback can be tried to assist the patient in reducing it to help prevent complications such as contractures. At times, one "works with" a synergy using EMG feedback to get a particular paralyzed muscle functioning again (22, 45). We do not know when in the course of recovery a patient is neurophysiologically ready to use EMG feedback to learn inhibition of spasticity, or to work against synergies to inhibit cocontraction and achieve more discrete control.

Another question pertains to the spatial course of recovery. Normally, strength and control recover first in the trunk and around proximal joints and proceed distally. The hand recovers last and least in stroke patients. But this spatial rule does not hold for EMG feedback in that training distal muscles first often goes quite well. For spasticity, there is a good reason to start training distally: spasticity develops rather early in the wrist and finger flexors, often before it is prominent around the elbow or shoulder.

BASELINE ASSESSMENT

Baseline assessment allows decisions about which problems to attack first, the obtaining of some initial measures against which to gauge eventual progress, and permits the patient to get used to the therapist, the clinic, and the feedback equipment. Since his state of arousal will probably increase his hyperreflexia, it may be better to consider the first session a time for an overall qualitative assessment. By the second session, the patient will have relaxed enough that reliable and valid measures are possible.

Once electrodes are on the relevant muscles, assess EMG activity while the subject is at rest, limbs comfortably supported with no muscles stretched inordinately. It may be necessary to wait quietly for a few minutes, or to carefully reposition the limb, but in all likelihood, substantial periods of complete relaxation will be observed. If not, this is the first thing to train. Next, determine what stimuli (besides muscle stretch or an attempt to use the spastic limb) disrupt relaxation: conversation, distracting noise, mental arithmetic, use of the other limbs, etc.

Stretch stimuli are applied while the subject is asked to continue relaxing. First, try static stretch, repositioning the limb so that spastic muscles are almost fully flexed or extended and taking note of any EMG activity that does not very quickly die away. Next is dynamic stretching. Flex and extend the joint steadily through a controlled arc. A useful set of angular velocities might include 15°, 30°, 45°, 60°, and 90° per second. Start with the lowest velocity and make at least two back-and-forth passes at each velocity; more at the higher velocities. Note the maximum level of integrated EMG activity during successive passes, and have someone write them down. You will probably find a threshold velocity below which most patients will show no spasticity.

Pausing at the extremes of the ROM may leave motor units firing in the stretched muscle, which were not seen previously in static testing. You might measure how long it takes for these to become silent. Remember that spasticity may be altered markedly by the position of the limb and by overall posture.

Finally, the behavior of spastic muscles is measured during simple attempts at voluntary flexion and extension. Starting relaxed as much as possible, the patient should attempt brief (5- to 20-second) moderate isometric efforts at flexion or extension, avoiding, if he can, going into a flexor or extensor synergy with the whole limb. Observe and, if possible, quantify:

1. Does the activity build up promptly, or is there a lag?
2. Is the effort steady and controlled, or does it fluctuate wildly or spread into a general synergy?
3. If the antagonists cocontract significantly, make an estimate of the ratio of antagonist to agonist activity.
4. When told to relax again, can the patient do so promptly?

THERAPY SESSIONS: AIMS AND TECHNIQUES
Resting Relaxation in Spastic Muscles

A patient must first be able to relax spastic muscles thoroughly when the affected limb is at rest. Baseline measurements will show that most spastic patients can do this, although perhaps not quickly or consistently.

A spastic hemiplegic should be able, while seated, to place the affected limb(s) in a comfortable, supported position and converse, watch TV, read, or write with the good arm while keeping spastic muscles substantially relaxed. The therapist must be able to take hold of the limb and coach the subject without setting off hypertonicity. If these criteria are not met, take the patient to a comfortable chair in a quiet room, with a limb position that minimizes resting hypertonicity. Then, turning to the EMG feedback, explain how to use it. A trial on muscles in the normal limb will help to clarify the nature of the task. Explain that to try to force muscles to relax is counterproductive.

Spasticity may actually increase when the patient first tries to relax. Middaugh et al. (46) in a systematic study of the initial response of 12 stroke patients, found that the spastic muscle relaxed more rapidly under the baseline condition than when subjects deliberately attempted to relax, with or without feedback.

Patients will be encountered who are poor at relaxing even their normal muscles. Turning from individual muscles to training in progressive general relaxation is probably the best course of action (Chapter 17). General relaxation training may by itself bring benefits in motor control: Finley et al. (43) trained spastic cerebral palsied children in general relaxation using EMG feedback and reported subtle benefits in speech and motor control.

Training Control of Stretch Reflex Activity

Once the patient can relax the affected limb reasonably well at rest, passive stretch can be added. Simply flex or extend the limb by stages to lengthen the spastic muscles, allowing the patient to reestablish relaxation at each stage. When this is achieved, the patient is ready for dynamic stretching at various speeds. Start rather slowly and work up until the EMG feedback signal and your own observations indicate that spasticity is consistently present—but not to such a degree that much resistance is felt. If you feel spasticity but there is too little EMG feedback generated, move the electrodes father apart, or choose a better location.

The velocity must result in just enough feedback that the subject can judge when he is doing better or worse. Passively flex and extend the limb, pausing briefly at the extremes, while the patient strives to keep the EMG feedback signal down. When improvement is apparent, increase the velocity by about 15° per second. Use a threshold—a bit of tape over the meter scale will do—to give a readily perceivable target. Also a pause before reversing direction gives the patient extra time to assess and inhibit the spasticity.

Case Report. In a patient with left hemiplegia, electrodes were placed over brachioradialis, biceps, and triceps. The elbow was passively flexed and extended through a range of about 100°. We found velocity-dependent stretch reflex activity in biceps and brachioradialis with a threshold velocity usually around 48° per second. We also noted some position-dependent spasticity in brachioradialis when dynamic stretching was completed and the elbow was near full extension.

Training began at 48° per second, with the patient viewing a computer-generated display of integrated EMG from biceps (but not brachioradialis to see if generalization would occur). The first two training sessions were difficult, and the subject was at first unable to establish control. Then the patient tried a strategy that he had discovered to get his elbow flexors to relax reciprocally when he took advantage of some ability to activate triceps. Brachioradialis was not as consistently inhibited by this strategy, but it was a breakthrough in training.

He was soon able to just *think* about triceps extension, without any measurable triceps activity, and later to drop the strategy most of the time.

We increased stretch velocity within and between sessions as performance improved, and after 11 training sessions, he had excellent control of biceps spasticity, even at 96° per second. Generalization to brachioradialis was inadequate. We changed to supplying feedback from brachioradialis; it took the subject three sessions to achieve good control of that muscle. Biceps control deteriorated temporarily and then returned.

After a 3-week break (including home practice in the interim with a portable EMG feedback device), biceps control was better than ever.

When we changed the forearm and hand from midpronation to midsupination, spasticity increased drastically. This necessitated repeating the training sequence with the forearm 45° from supine. Supinating the forearm shortens biceps, which might be expected to reduce spasticity (47). However biceps is a supinator as well as a flexor, and may be facilitated by proprioceptive influences when the limb is passively supinated. This subject seemed to have a positive feedback problem with biceps when he walked, the forearm would gradually supinate, and then the elbow would flex by stages. He found that by using a portable EMG device, he could practice inhibiting biceps while walking, and this was the most functionally relevant form of training for him.

A total of eight patients have received computer-assisted EMG feedback training to inhibit spasticity elicited by passive stretch (39, 40). Three patients failed; two had some success; and only three acquired an ability to directly inhibit spasticity. One patient has been discussed already. A second was similar in that he relied on reciprocal inhibition of elbow flexors by triceps as a starting point for spasticity inhibition. But his performance was much less consistent. The remaining subject could not use reciprocal inhibition, but by a slower general relaxation approach, she could often relax elbow flexors so thoroughly that they remained silent even at extension speeds of almost 100° per second.

Clinicians may achieve a higher success rate than we did in the laboratory. It is likely that EMG feedback training can help patients reduce typical everyday spasticity levels considerably, without having any appreciable effect on the residual levels that persist under laboratory conditions.

Cocontraction and Dyssynergy

At this point, we are beginning to train skills that pertain to active use of the spastic limb. These skills include:

1. The ability to activate a muscle without delay or false starts;
2. To modulate the ensuing contraction for an appropriate force output;
3. To inhibit the tendency for the activation efforts to spread to the "antagonist" or to other muscles not needed for the desired improvement;
4. To inhibit spasticity in other muscles when they are stretched by the ensuing motion;
5. To relax the muscle promptly and completely to terminate the effort.

The training described previously (resting relaxation and inhibition of spasticity occasioned by passive stretch) pertains only to the last two skills listed, and, of course, maintaining relaxation in a resting muscle may be different in nature from relaxing it suddenly at the end of voluntary effort. The first two skills arise from training strength and control in a paretic muscle. The third skill, preventing the spread of activation to muscle irrelevant to the intended effort, is our present topic for discussion. That this is primarily an inhibitory skill, developed through learning and maturation, has been argued by Basmajian (48). It is almost always deficient in spastic patients, in that they usually lack reciprocal inhibition of "antagonist" muscles and tend to go into primitive mass synergies when they attempt more discrete movements.

Lack of reciprocal inhibition makes training strength and control in a paretic muscle more difficult for two reasons. First, the antagonists cocontract and overpower the paretic muscle, and second, surface electrodes pick up extraneous EMG from the antagonists, thus misleading the subject as to what the paretic muscle is doing. The latter problem can be overcome by close-spacing of surface electrodes and appropriate high-pass filtering, but the problem of the cocontraction of other muscles can confound the patient's attempts to focus attention on the feedback.

Below are some tactics familiar already to therapists to reduce antagonist activity and/or make the muscle under training more likely to contract:

1. Train inhibition of any spasticity caused by passive stretch of the antagonists (see previous section). The ability to inhibit antagonist muscles may transfer to the new training situation to some degree.
2. Put the muscle to be strengthened under static stretch, with the spastic antagonists shortened.
3. Choose a body posture that will tend to facilitate the muscle under training.
4. At first, train isometrically so that the antagonist is not passively stretched.
5. Stretch the agonist a little just as the subject starts his effort, to load the muscle spindles.
6. Brush the skin over the agonist, or "ice" the skin over the antagonist.
7. Vibrate the agonist or its tendon.

Vibration of the right sort will tend to inhibit the antagonist and facilitate the muscle under training. Unfortunately, the vibrators used by most therapists vibrate too slowly and with too large or too small an amplitude. Eklund (49) specifies 100–300 Hz and 1–2 mm amplitude. Too low a frequency may tend to inhibit rather than facilitate. Too large an amplitude causes excessive stimulation of the antagonist. Using vibration in conjunction with EMG feedback equipment poses certain technical problems. Most vibrators emit copious electromagnetic noise, and the physical vibration of the electrodes also induces an artifact in the EMG. Fortunately, the facilitating and inhibiting effects of vibration on the muscles persist for a short time after the vibrator is removed, so it is possible to alternate vibration with short periods of feedback training.

Case Report. The patient, a right hemiplegic, had already received some EMG feedback training to strengthen tibialis anterior as well as training in relaxation of forearm flexors. Flexing and extending the elbow at various rates revealed that the elbow flexors were only minimally spastic. Triceps was rather weak, and cocontraction of the elbow flexors and pectoralis drew the arm up against the chest. We positioned the hand high against the chest (thus prestretching triceps and shortening the other muscles) and found that the patient would generate much more triceps EMG in this position. So he was asked to push down isometrically and rest in alternation (12 seconds of each): after eight trials, there was a minute's rest.

Using our computer and feedback screen, we supplied a signal that simultaneously showed triceps and biceps activity, and the patient learned in a couple of sessions to push down quite hard with the triceps while inhibiting nearly all biceps activity. However, pectoralis major still contracted strongly; so to break up the synergy, we supplied simultaneous feedback from triceps and pectoralis. After five sessions, triceps output had increased markedly, and pectoralis was substantially inhibited. The arm was moved down and away from the chest by stages until after 25 sessions, he could push down and away quite forcefully without pectoralis cocontraction, an action he could not even approximate before training. After a 3-week interval, he was retested without feedback. Triceps was still strong, but pectoralis cocontraction was somewhat increased. Restoring the feedback caused an immediate recovery of pectoralis inhibition.

Three additional subjects were trained under similar conditions (41). All improved in recruitment of paretic agonist muscles over the course of training. But they enjoyed little or no success in learning to inhibit cocontraction of spastic antagonists. This was balanced, however, by their learning to greatly increase recruitment of paretic agonists without a proportional increase in antagonist cocontraction.

Combining EMG Feedback Training with Conventional Therapy

Once basic control of the desired neuromuscular response is achieved, the training task should be modified into one that the patient perceives as functionally meaningful. The training hierarchy that has been presented should not by any means be viewed as a total program for neuromuscular reeducation. As noted earlier, EMG feedback is primarily a muscle training technique. It can be integrated with movement training methods; it can never supplant them. The following sequence indicates in a very general way how EMG feedback training is integrated with conventional therapy—steps 3–5 often being intermixed:

1. During initial evaluation, the therapist maps out an overall plan of therapeutic exercise and neuromuscular reeducation.

2. Either at initial evaluation or after a trial of therapy, the therapist finds that certain muscles or muscle groups are too spastic or paretic, do not respond adequately to conventional inhibiting or facilitating strategies, and prevent further progress with conventional therapy.
3. EMG feedback training is used to reduce spasticity and/or increase strength and control in these muscles.
4. The resultant gains in neuromuscular control are integrated into the overall program of therapeutic exercise. Conventional therapy proceeds toward goals of improved strength, posture, movement patterns, etc.
5. Additional steps are usually necessary to obtain generalization from the therapy situation to activities of daily living.

Step 3 is often accomplished fairly easily. The problem is in obtaining generalization or transfer of training to the overall therapeutic exercise program and thence to everyday activities. While pharmaceutical or surgical inhibition of spasticity is constantly present without any effort on the patient's part, with feedback training the patient learns to do something (we do not yet know just what) to inhibit spasticity and must keep on doing it. To the extent that learned control fails to become automatic and consistent, the patient must either expend valuable attention to inhibit spasticity or put up with it.

Generalization

When generalization does not occur, three reasons must be considered:

1. Perhaps the damaged nervous system is simply incapable of overcoming the manifestations of spasticity except transiently in the protected clinic training environment. We know this to be true of some patients, but we cannot predict which ones, so the only course is to optimize training procedures as much as possible and let results speak for themselves.
2. Perhaps the patient had not truly mastered the key muscle responses in the initial training situation. In other environments, this imperfect control promptly breaks down. To get around this, the therapist must carry each stage of training to the point of overlearning so that acquired skills are reliable and nearly automatic.

3. Perhaps there is dissimilarity between the clinic training situation and the everyday conditions under which the patient must use the neuromuscular skills he has tried to acquire. The therapist can bridge this gap by modifying training tasks in the clinic so that they resemble everyday activities as much as possible, and by weaning the patient away from reliance on extrinsic feedback at each stage of training.

Difficulty in obtaining generalization is not a limitation or shortcoming of EMG feedback, but merely one instance of a difficulty encountered commonly in physical therapies and in diverse realms of remedial training such as speech therapy or reading instruction. These other fields have been significantly aided by rigorous training methods referred to as precision-teaching techniques or behavior modification. It is to be expected that, once the easy victories for EMG feedback have been accomplished, the full potential of this new therapeutic tool will await rigorous application of similar precision-teaching approaches.

References

1. Landau, W. M. Spasticity and rigidity. In *Recent Advances in Neurology*, edited by F. Plum. *Contemporary Neurology Series*, vol. 6, pp. 1–32. F. A. Davis, Philadelphia, 1969.
2. Hoefer, P. F. A. and Putnam, T. J. Action potentials of muscles in "spastic" conditions. Arch. Neurol. Psychiatr., 43: 1–22, 1940.
3. Basmajian, J. V. and Szatmari, A. The effect of largactil (chlorpromazine) on human spasticity and the electromyogram. A.M.A. Arch. Neurol., 73: 224–231, 1955.
4. Bishop, B. Spasticity: its physiology and management. Phys. Ther., 57: 371–401, 1977.
5. Granit, R. *The Basis of Motor Control*. Academic Press, New York, 1970.
6. Delwaide, P. J. Human monosynaptic reflexes and presynaptic inhibition. In *New Developments in Electromyography and Clinical Neurophysiology*, edited by J. Desmedt, vol. 3, pp. 508–522. Karger, Basel, 1973.
7. Knutsson, E. On effects of local cooling upon motor functions in spastic paresis. Progr. Phys. Ther., 1: 124–131, 1970.
8. Wolf, S. L., Letbetter, W. D. and Basmajian, J. V. Effects of a specific cutaneous cold stimulus on single motor unit activity of medial gastrocnemius in man. Am. J. Phys. Med., 55: 177–183, 1976.
9. Hagbarth, K.-E., Wallin, G. and Lofstedt, L. Muscle spindle responses to stretch in normal and spastic subjects. Scand. J. Rehabil. Med., 5: 156–159, 1973.
10. Burke, D. A reassessment of the muscle spindle

11. Holt, K. S. Facts and fallacies about neuromuscular function in cerebral palsy as revealed by electromyography. Dev. Med. Child Neurol., 8: 255–268, 1966.
12. Bobath, K. The motor deficit in patients with cerebral palsy. *Clinics in Developmental Medicine*, No. 23: *Spastics Society Medical Education and Information Units*. William Heinemann Medical Books, London, 1966.
13. Sahrmann, S. and Norton, B. The relationship of voluntary movement to spasticity in the upper motor neurone syndrome. Ann. Neurol., 2: 460–465, 1977.
14. Basmajian, J. V. Neuromuscular facilitation techniques. Arch. Phys. Med. Rehabil., 52: 40–42, 1971.
15. Johnson, H. E. and Garton, W. H. Muscle reeducation in hemiplegia by use of electromyographic device. Arch. Phys. Med. Rehabil., 54: 320–322, 1973.
16. Basmajian, J. V., Kukulka, C. G., Narayan, M. G. and Takabe, K. Biofeedback treatment of footdrop after stroke compared with standard rehabilitation technique: effects on voluntary control and strength. Arch. Phys. Med. Rehabil., 56: 231–236, 1975.
17. Khalili, A. A. and Betts, H. B. Peripheral nerve block with phenol in the management of spasticity. J.A.M.A., 200: 1155–1157, 1967.
18. Caldwell, C. and Braun, R. Spasticity in the upper extremity. Clin. Orthop., 104: 80–91, 1974.
19. Hagbarth, K. E. and Eklund, G. Tonic vibration reflexes (TVR) in spasticity. Brain Res., 2: 201–203, 1966.
20. Johnson, R., Bishop, B. and Coffey, G. Mechanical vibration of skeletal muscle. Phys. Ther., 50: 499–505, 1970.
21. Basmajian, J. V., Regenos, E. and Baker, M. Rehabilitating stroke patients with biofeedback. Geriatrics, 32: 85–88, 1977.
22. Baker, M., Regenos, E., Wolf, S. and Basmajian, J. V. Developing strategies for biofeedback: applications in neurologically handicapped patients. Phys. Ther., 57: 402–408, 1977.
23. Brudny, J., Korein, J., Grynbaum, B., Friedmann, L., Weinstein, S., Sachs-Frankel, G. and Belandres, P. EMG feedback therapy: review of treatment of 114 patients. Arch. Phys. Med. Rehabil., 57: 55–61, 1976.
24. Brudny, J., Korein, J., Levidow, L., Grynbaum, B., Lieberman, A. and Friedman, L. Sensory feedback therapy as a modality of treatment in central nervous system disorders of voluntary movement. Neurology (N.Y.), 24: 925–932, 1974.
25. Amato, A., Hermsmeyer, C. A. and Kleinman, K. M. Use of electromyographic feedback to increase inhibitory control of spastic muscles. Phys. Ther., 53: 1063–1066, 1973.
26. Kleinman, K., Riggin, C., Keister, M., Goldman, H. and Korol, B. Use of EMG feedback to inhibit flexor spasticity and increase active extension

in stroke patients. Biofeedback Self Regul., *1*: 327, 1977.

27. Maher, K. R. Auditory feedback of muscle action potentials: applications to spasticity and athetosis. In *Productivity and the Cerebral Palsied*. Sydney Conference, August 1972. Proceedings published by Centre Industries, The Spastic Centre of N.S.W., Allambie Heights, Sydney, N.S.W., 2100, Australia, 1972.
28. Ladd, H., Jonsson, B. and Lindgren, U. The learning process for fine neuromuscular controls in skeletal muscles of man. Electromyography, *12*: 213–223, 1972.
29. Jonsson, B., Ladd, H., Afzelius-Frisk, I. and Lindberg-Broman, A. The effect of Dantrium on spasticity in hemiplegic patients. Acta Neurol. Scand., *51*: 385–392, 1975.
30. Ladd, H., Oist, C. and Jonsson, B. The effect of Dantrium on spasticity in multiple sclerosis. Acta Neurol. Scand., *50*: 397–408, 1974.
31. Harrison, A. and Connolly, K. The conscious control of fine levels of neuromuscular firing in spastic and normal subjects. Dev. Med. Child Neurol., *13*: 762–771, 1971.
32. Harrison, A. Studies of neuromuscular control in normal and spastic individuals, and Training spastic individuals to achieve better neuromuscular control using electromyographic feedback. In *Movement and Child Development*, edited by K. S. Holt. Clin. Dev. Med., *55*: 51–101, 1975.
33. Harrison, A. Augmented feedback training of motor control in cerebral palsy. Dev. Med. Child Neurol., *19*: 75–77, 1977.
34. Lloyd, A. and Leibrecht, B. Conditioning of a single motor unit. J. Exp. Psychol., *88*: 391–395, 1971.
35. Smith, K. U. and Henry, J. P. Cybernetic foundations for rehabilitation. Am. J. Phys. Med., *46*: 379–467, 1967.
36. Howson, D. *Report on Neuromuscular Re-education*. Isis Medical Instruments, Inc., Dewitt Building P761, Ithaca, New York 14850, 1976.
37. Bilodeau, E. A. Supplementary feedback and instructions, and Bilodeau, I. M., Information feedback. In *Principles of Skill Acquisition*, edited by E. A. Bilodeau and I. M. Bilodeau, Academic Press, New York, 1969.
38. Terrace, H. S. Stimulus control. In *Operant Behavior*, edited by W. K. Honig. Appleton-Century-Crofts, New York, 1966.
39. DeBacher, G. and Basmajian, J. V. Implications of variability in spasticity observed during EMG feedback training. Proceedings of the Fourth Congress of the International Society of Electrophysiological Kinesiology, Boston, Mass., August 5–10, 1979.
40. DeBacher, G. Training inhibition of spasticity elicited by passive stretch using computer-generated EMG feedback. Proceedings of the Twelfth Annual Meeting of the Biofeedback Society of America, Louisville, Ky., March 13–17, 1981.
41. DeBacher, G. Simultaneous training of recruitment in a paretic muscle and inhibition of inappropriate co-contraction in a spastic muscle using computer-generated EMG feedback. Thirteenth Annual Meeting of the Biofeedback Society of America, Chicago, Ill., March 5–10, 1982.
42. Regenos, E. and Wolf, S. L. Involuntary single motor unit discharges in spastic muscles during EMG biofeedback training. Arch. Phys. Med. Rehabil., *60*: 72–73, 1979.
43. Finley, W. W., Niman, C., Standley, J. and Wansley, R. A. Electrophysiologic behavior modification of frontal EMG in cerebral-palsied children. Biofeedback Self Regul., *2*: 59–79, 1977.
44. Brunnstrom, S. *Movement Therapy in Hemiplegia: A Neuropsychological Approach*. Harper and Row, New York, 1970.
45. Owen, S., Toomin, H. and Taylor, L. P. *Biofeedback in Neuromuscular Re-education*. Biofeedback Research Institute, Inc., Los Angeles, 1975.
46. Middaugh, S., Foster, G., Miller, M. C., and Murphy, E. EMG feedback in neuromuscular re-education: effects on voluntary relaxation of spastic muscles. Proceedings of the Twelfth Annual Meeting of the Biofeedback Society of America, March 13–17, 1981, Louisville, Ky.
47. Burke, D. and Lance, J. W. Studies of the reflex effects of primary and secondary spindle endings in spasticity. In *New Developments in Electromyography and Clinical Neurophysiology*, edited by J. E. Desmedt, vol. 3, pp. 475–495. Karger, Basel, 1973.
48. Basmajian, J. V. Motor learning and control: a working hypothesis. Arch. Phys. Med. Rehabil., *58*: 38–41, 1977.
49. Eklund, G. Some physical properties of muscle vibrators used to elicit tonic proprioceptive reflexes in man. Acta Soc. Med. Uppsala, *76*: 271–280, 1971.

CHAPTER 14

Electromyographic Feedback for Spinal Cord Injured Patients: A Realistic Perspective

STEVEN L. WOLF

In the United States, more than 20 people per 1,000,000 population are involved in accidents that traumatize the spinal cord (1). In northern California, for example, the incidence reached 53.4 per 1,000,000 population (2). The Texas Institute for Rehabilitation and Research, in a review of 1164 cases, revealed that most cord injuries involve the cervical area in males during the third decade of life and were caused primarily by automobile injuries (3, 4). The Midwest Regional Spinal Cord Injury Care System's 1976 statistics showed that first hospitalization costs for each spinal cord injured person were $36,300 for a 136-day period (5). These costs continue to increase at an alarmingly rapid rate. Thus, medical and supportive costs become high while avenues leading toward potential gains in independence, employment, and an improved psychosocial milieu remain relatively unexplored.

Traditional physical rehabilitation programs include: progressive resistive exercise (with group "mat" exercise programs); wheelchair transfer training, ball gymnastics, hydrogymnastics, moist heat, massage, passive and active range of motion, revision of the home environment to facilitate activities of daily living, gait training, and orthotics.

Recently, muscle feedback has been incorporated into some rehabilitation programs for the spinal cord injured (SCI) patient. Unlike traditional therapies that necessitate a "delayed" feedback from therapist to patient, electromyographic (EMG) feedback is continuous and uninterrupted, thus enabling the patient to "internalize" the meaning of audio or visual signals representing muscle responses (6). Thus, the clinician may use appropriate feedback equipment to help shape muscle responses toward restitution of functional activity.

APPLICATIONS TO SPINAL CORD INJURED PATIENTS

A review of the literature indicates that reports on EMG feedback training applied to SCI patients are few, and they provide scanty information regarding technique and outcome. Success has been reported in applying EMG feedback techniques to one (7, 8) or more (9) paraplegics. Toomin's abstract described a case in which biofeedback was combined with other techniques to provide significant gains in a young female client (10) who subsequently described her own experiences with biofeedback training (11). The same group's monograph (12) suggests that any SCI patient capable of demonstrating some muscle activity below the level of the lesion can be "helped" by EMG feedback training.

Schneider and colleagues, in a detailed explanation of biofeedback application for SCI patients, discussed the outcomes of training procedures on one paraplegic and one paraparetic patient (13). They noted that EMG biofeedback devices could be used to: (a) identify muscles with low measurable potentials; (b) identify the types of reflexly induced movements capable of producing measurable muscle activity; (c) evaluate improvement in muscle strength; and (d) provide feedback to patients and therapists during exercise.

A detailed account of muscle feedback applications to a patient with incomplete paraplegia of 3 years' duration was provided by Seymour and Bassler (14). Using a clinical electromyographic unit, they were able to train the patient to increase muscle output and subsequently muscle strength; the feedback was combined with strengthening exercises and gait training. This patient progressed from total wheelchair dependency to ambulation with assistive devices. During the 2 months of training, concomitant increases in electromyographic activity from the quadriceps, tibialis anterior, hamstrings, and gastrocnemius muscles occurred.

More recently, Newton and Coolbaugh (15) demonstrated substantial increases in active range of motion and EMG output in the triceps brachii of a 25-year-old man with a fracture at the sixth cervical level. During feedback training, there was generalization to the flexor carpi radialis bilaterally. Dunn and coworkers (16) demonstrated that muscle feedback was beneficial for three quadriplegic patients who gained control over the amplitude of their spasms when feedback was introduced. Inevitably, the presentation of a feedback signal resulted in voluntary reduction of integrated EMG. Unfortunately, removal of the feedback signal resulted in increased levels of EMG.

In 1982, Nacht and colleagues (17) described a unique application of EMG feedback during the acute phase of spinal cord injury in a 22-year-old man with an injury at the lumbar level. During the acute phase and while he was immobilized in a body cast, skin electrodes were used to monitor the occurrence of voluntary muscle activity around the hip and knee. This enabled clinicians to determine the presence of innervation as well as providing the patient with an activity during immobilization. These investigators reported useful changes in electromyographic activity during the several months of treatment. This unusual use of feedback serves a dual purpose: monitoring muscle return and providing the patient with an opportunity to perform isometric contractions while on bed rest. Caution must be used in attempting this procedure because it will also reveal to the patient the lack of return in voluntary movement. The psychological strength of the patient is an important factor in determining whether feedback should be tried.

Taft and coworkers (18) have become one of the first groups to advocate the use of biofeedback in spinal cord injured children. Despite the paucity of controlled clinical research trials among this young population, these investigators suggested use of EMG feedback to control spastic muscles during functional movements and pressure feedback following the protocols established by Whitehead et al. (19) to facilitate regaining of fecal continence.

Much attention has been drawn to the work of B. Brucker and his colleagues in Miami who claim to successfully rehabilitate SCI patients using up to four channels of EMG feedback— see Goldsmith (20). These patients must have demonstrated some degree of paresis in muscles below the level of partial cord lesion. Training emphasizes selective recruitment of certain muscles and inhibition of others, often simultaneously and within the context of training toward functional goal rather than integration of feedback within a therapeutic exercise or neuromuscular facilitation plan.

TREATMENT PROCEDURES

During the past few years, rehabilitation researchers at Emory University have developed their own approach to treatment of spinal cord injured patients with EMG feedback. The principles embodied in the following discussion represent only one approach to interfacing patients with a modality. They are designed for patients with both acute and chronic spinal cord injuries at virtually any level of the spinal cord who have demonstrable voluntary activity in muscles innervated by motor neurons below (caudal to) the site of injury. Feedback may be beneficial for these patients because: (a) the modality may be easily incorporated into exercise programs with immobilized patients during the acute phase of injury; (b) it provides immediate information to the patient concerning the level of voluntary muscle activity; by so doing, (c) this modality may help patients to obtain spatial and temporal summation of muscle potentials leading toward increased contractility and hence preparing the patient for a more vigorous therapy program.

The primary goals for interfacing the SCI patient with EMG feedback are much the same as outlined previously for stroke patients. First and foremost, attempts are made at reducing hypermotor responses to induced length changes in spastic muscles. Such hyperactive behavior of spastic muscles may occur during spontaneous episodes of clonus or during induced clonic seizures when the lower or upper extremity responds to various tactile stimuli.

Once the patient is able to reduce such responses in supine, sitting, and ultimately standing postures, efforts are directed toward recruitment of weak muscles. In treating patients with paraplegia, attempts are made to reduce activity in the adductors of the thigh and the gastrocnemius-soleus complex. Attempts to recruit muscle activity with feedback are obtained from the abdominals, lumbar paravertebral musculature, gluteus maximus and medius, rectus femoris and sartorius, hamstrings, and tibialis anterior. Usually, recruitment of increased electromyographic responses are obtained in a proximal to distal manner.

In quadriparetic or quadriplegic patients, the same sequence and muscle groups are approached for the lower extremity. Increased output from the upper extremity depends on the amount of weakness and voluntary activity the patient is able to display; hence, there is a need for a comprehensive neurological examination that must be repeated periodically during the training intervals. Usually, efforts are made to recruit increased activity around the shoulder from the upper trapezius, middle deltoid, and anterior deltoid; the triceps, biceps, and pectoralis major in the upper arm; and the wrist and finger extensors in the forearm.

The clinician wishing to employ feedback among SCI patients needs special training and plans. In chronic cases, the magnitude of atrophy and the concomitant increased pliability of skin and connective tissue are important because electrodes must be positioned over the appropriate muscle or muscle group with respect to the activity to be undertaken rather than to the location of the muscle at rest. Loose skin causes displacement of electrodes during active movements. When examining a specific muscle group, dual-channel monitoring should be used so that both the spastic muscle and its antagonist can be observed.

Initially, the training environment should be one that permits the patient to concentrate most intensely upon the feedback signal with minimal external disruptions. Increasingly, feedback training should be incorporated into the normal everyday environment of the patient with appropriate distractors presented. It is advisable for the feedback to be integrated within an exercise program, thereby allowing the patient to monitor muscle responses during isometric, active, or resistive exercises as well as during use of facilitation techniques.

During training to reduce hypermotor responses to muscle stretch, the EMG activity should be fed back to the patient first during slow stretches and subsequently during more rapid stretches of spastic muscles. The patient's goal is to reduce the magnitude of the stretch response as well as the time required to return the EMG level back to the prestretch integral while the muscle is still held in a lengthened position. When recruiting antagonist muscles, this activity should be undertaken first with gravity eliminated by using a supine or reclining posture. As muscle strength and concomitant movement occur, the range of passive joint excursion during feedback should be increased, leading toward positioning of the patient so that movement is against gravity. With increased active movement, resistance may be added subsequently.

Fogel has demonstrated excellent application of these principles—see Goldsmith (20). His feedback approach to paretic SCI patients essentially requires rapid, controlled reversal of antagonists during functional upper or lower extremity activities. These goals may be accomplished through single or dual channel monitoring and necessitate that patients show an awareness of relative muscle tension as well as reciprocal inhibition.

PATIENT EVALUATION

Evaluations of patient responses to feedback training should be made before initiating feedback and at periodic intervals thereafter. Such intervals should not exceed more than 15 consecutive sessions. It is important to monitor specific parameters of muscle response and movement activities resulting from feedback interventions. One such scheme is presented in Figure 14.1. Equally important is to quantify improvement based upon a patient's ability to change the functional status for doing such things as movement in bed, transfers, hygiene, and wheelchair or independent locomotion. There are numerous ways in which activities can be measured; the Spain Rehabilitation Center (Birmingham, Alabama), the Texas Institute for Rehabilitation and Research (Houston) and Rancho Los Amigos Hospital (Downey, California) have exemplary models for such measurements. The clinician wishing to devise an independent functional evaluation must take into account the amount of assistance required by the patient, the time to perform a specific task, and, when appropriate,

NAME: _____   DATE: _____

| DEVICE | MUSCLE OR GROUP | TYPE OF ELECTRODE | ELECTRODE SIZE | PATIENT POSITION | STRATEGY | ROM | | EMG | PEAK VALUE | | RELAX TIME | MUSCLE GRADE |
						ACTIVE	PASSIVE	RESTING	VOLUNTARY	INVOLUNTARY		

COMMENTS: _____

Figure 14.1. Representation of one method to document important measurements when using EMG feedback with SCI patient.

the endurance of the patient in performing the tasks.

INTEGRATING ELECTRICAL STIMULATION FOR FEEDBACK TRAINING AMONG SCI PATIENTS

Within the past decade, considerable attention has been drawn to functional electrical stimulation (FES) as either an adjunct to therapeutic exercise or a primary source for initiating ambulation among SCI patients. Excellent but critical reviews of this approach have been provide by Petrofsky (21) and by Cybulski (22). Even if the apparent drawbacks in this approach, including cardiovascular taxation, personnel and equipment expenses, specialized training, limited demonstration of long-term efficacy, could be overcome, the undeniable fact is that the patient is still placed in a totally passive role; that is, the SCI client does nothing to initiate or to volitionally control any aspect of muscle contractibility.

An alternative approach to the use of FES for SCI patients demonstrating voluntary activation of paretic muscle is to interface FES with EMG feedback in a contingency mode. Electrodes are placed over a muscle to be stimulated, and stimulation parameters are set. The output from the stimulator muscle is then led to an EMG feedback unit. The same (or another) muscle is monitored electromyographically in "work" (on) and "relax" (off) modes. During the working time (predetermined by the clinician), the preset electrical output is activated once an integral of EMG has exceeded the preset threshold. This output will be delivered for the remainder of the work time. In this manner, a patient's voluntary activity can be shaped so that at first, stimulation (to completion of muscle contraction) can be achieved with little voluntary drive. With further training, threshold levels are progressively raised, thus requiring more voluntary activity before the stimulator is triggered. Such an approach can be totally relegated to one muscle or muscle group or played between two or more groups. For example, during the swing phase of gait, EMG integrals from the sartorius (hip flexor) would have to exceed threshold before stimulation would be delivered for a remaining on time to the hamstrings (one output) and the anterior leg compartment (second output) of a dual channel FES unit.

OUTCOMES FROM FEEDBACK TRAINING

During the past several years, it has become apparent that muscle feedback applications will not restore significant function among those patients who have limited sparing of spinal cord integrity. Among our quadriparetic and paraplegic patients with severe movement limitations, feedback has been a satisfactory intervention for the reduction of spontaneous or induced clonus. Patients are able to volitionally eliminate a clonic episode without the use of antispasmodic medication (23). This ability is significant for such patients because, from a cosmetic perspective, clonus becomes less obvious and, more importantly, patients are able to attend to tasks without disruption from total limb or segmental clonic episodes.

In our partial lumbar spinal cord injured patients, feedback training has enabled many to increase the speed at which they ambulate and to reduce the number of required assistive devices. For quadriparetic patients with obvious voluntary movement, feedback combined with an exercise program have facilitated active range of motion and improved upper extremity function. However, in cases where little activity could be observed among chronic SCI patients, feedback provided little or no significant benefit toward restoration of function.

References

1. Stern, P. H. and Slattery, K. Spinal cord rehabilitation: new approaches. N. Y. State J. Med., 75: 1029–1034, 1975.
2. Krause, J. F., Franti, C. E. and Riggins, R. S. Incidence of traumatic spinal cord lesions. J. Chronic Dis., 18: 471–492, 1975.
3. Carter, R. E. Traumatic spinal cord injuries due to automobile accidents. South. Med. J., 70: 709–710, 1977.
4. Carter, R. E. Etiology of traumatic spinal cord injury: statistics of more than 1,100 cases. Texas Med., 73: 61–65, 1977.
5. Midwest Regional Spinal Cord Injury Care System's Annual Progress Report: No. 5, 1976. Prepared for Office of Human Development, Rehabilitation Services Administration, D.H.E.W., July 1, 1977, p. 231.
6. Wolf, S. L. The anatomical and physiological basis of biofeedback. In *Biofeedback: Principles and Practice for Clinicians*, 1st ed., edited by J.V. Basmajian. Williams & Wilkins, Baltimore, 1979.
7. Marinacci, A. A. *Applied Electromyography*. Lea & Febiger, Philadelphia, 1974.
8. Toomin, H. and Johnson, H. E. Biofeedback in neuromuscular re-education. Discussion at the annual meeting of the Biofeedback Research Society, Colorado Springs, Colo., 1974.
9. Fernando, C. K. Biofeedback in neuromuscular conditions. *Proceedings of the Annual Meeting of the National Paraplegics' Foundation*, Chicago, Ill., 1975.
10. Toomin, H. Electromyometer feedback in paraplegia: a case study in neuromuscular re-education. In *Proceedings of the Annual Meeting of the Biofeedback Research Society*, Colorado Springs, Colo., 1974.
11. Owen, S. M. Biofeedback and rehabilitation, Rehabil. Gazette, 17: 46–49, 1974.
12. Owen, S. M., Toomin, H. and Taylor, L. P. *Biofeedback in Neuromuscular Re-education*, p. 73. Biofeedback Research Institute, Inc., Los Angeles, 1975.
13. Schneider, S., Scaer, R., Groenwald, D. and Atkinson, R. H. EMG techniques in neuromuscular rehabilitation with cord injured patients, pp. 4–10. *Proceedings of the Annual Meeting of the National Paraplegics' Foundation*, Chicago, Ill., 1975.
14. Seymour, R. J. and Bassler, C. R. Electromyographic biofeedback in the treatment of incomplete paraplegia. Phys. Ther., 57: 1148–1150, 1977.
15. Newton, F. A. and Coolbaugh, C. F. Bilateral EMG biofeedback training of the triceps brachii and generalization effects in a quadriplegic. Biofeedback Self Regul., 6: 434–435, 1981.
16. Dunn. M., Davis, J. and Webster, T. Voluntary control of muscle spasticity with EMG biofeedback in the three spinal cord injured quadriplegics. In *Proceedings of the Ninth Annual Meeting of the Biofeedback Society of America*, p. 122. Albuquerque, New Mexico, 1970.
17. Nacht, M. B., Wolf, S. L. and Coogler, C. E. Use of electromyographic biofeedback during the acute phase of spinal cord injury, Phys. Ther., 62: 290–294, 1982.
18. Taft, L. T., Matthews, W. S. and Molnar, G. E. Pediatric management of the physically handicapped child. Adv. Pediatr., 30: 13–60, 1983.
19. Whitehead, W. D., Parker, C. H., Marek, B. J. et al. Biofeedback of fecal incontinence in patients with myelomeningocele. Dev. Med. Child Neurol., 23: 313–322, 1981.
20. Goldsmith, M. F. Computerized biofeedback training aids in spinal cord injury rehabilitation. J. A. M. A., 253: 1097–1099, Feb. 22, 1985.
21. Petrofsky, J. S. and Phillips, C. A. The use of functional electrical stimulation for rehabilitation of spinal cord injured patients. Centr. Nerv. Syst. Trauma, 1: 57–74, 1984.
22. Cybulski, G. R., Penn, R. D. and Jaeger, R. J. Lower extremity functional neuromuscular stimulation in cases of spinal cord injury. Neurosurgery, 15: 132–146, 1984.
23. Wolf, S. L. Biofeedback rehabilitation of the incomplete spinal cord injured patients, Emory University Regional Rehabilitation Research and Training Center Final Report, Grant No. NIHR G008003042, 1982, pp. 83–91.

CHAPTER 15

Biofeedback and Other Behavioral Techniques in the Treatment of Disorders of Voluntary Movement

CHARLES S. CLEELAND

The clinical application of biofeedback usually rests on the premise that there is "too much" or "too little" of something physiological that is causing symptoms. Some of the more challenging therapeutic problems in the area of neurological disorder, however, cannot be categorized as consistently presenting "too much" or "too little" of the physiological dimension that is abnormal. Disorders of voluntary movement remain a major puzzle for neurological investigators. The expression of symptoms in a system so completely voluntary as somatic muscle has led many to theorize that such disturbances have a major psychological component. The disorder may be predominantly present in isolated muscle groups, such as the neck (spasmodic torticollis), jaw (oromandibular dystonia), muscles used in protective blinking (blepharospasm), writing (dystonic writer's cramp), or may only involve muscles on one side of the face (hemifacial spasm). Because of the interconnection of these muscle groups with the expression of action, changes in dispositional states such as excitement, anxiety, and depression are interlocked with the severity of the expression of the symptom. The symptom may also be aggravated by the patient's attempting purposeful action, such as in tasks involving hand-eye coordination, which may make working extremely difficult. These disorders (often referred to collectively as the dystonias) are often so bizarre in presentation that patients may first be referred for psychiatric help.

Most investigators who have looked at long series of patients with movement disorders now agree that the symptoms have an organic basis, most probably a disturbance of the func-tion of the nuclei at the base of the brain which normally coordinate movement (1). Marsden (2) points to the lack of evidence that the incidence of psychiatric disorders in dystonic patients is any greater than in the normal population, and also observes that few patients with these disorders improve with psychiatric treatment.

Disorders of movement or posture have proven extremely difficult to treat. Surgically, techniques such as rhizotomy (3) or the placement of stereotaxic lesions in the basal ganglia or thalamic nuclei (4) have been used. Studies on the outcome of surgical treatment vary from optimistic to bleak and the risk of complications may run high (5). Some medications are reported to have a beneficial effect for some of these disorders (6).

We have evolved a treatment approach to the dystonias using electromyographic (EMG) biofeedback and other behavioral control techniques that is often of substantial benefit for the patient. This chapter will present our approach to different types of disorders of movement in some detail.

We began our attempts to treat dystonia with spasmodic torticollis. Following the behavioral theory of the disorder suggested by Yates (7), we conceptualized a massive spasm of the neck muscle in torticollis as a "habit spasm" and associated its occurrence in the laboratory with a cutaneous shock. The patient wore a position-sensitive switch on a headband, which was activated by head deviation. The activated switch delivered a shock to the fingertips. In five patients studied, four showed some reduction of spasmodic activity when wearing this device. The reduction in spasm was only temporary, and of little clinical benefit for the patients. The temporary decrease in spasm, however, suggested to us that patients might be able to restore voluntary control given the right set of treatment circumstances.

The patients that we studied reported that they had little sense of what the involved spastic muscles were doing at any given time, although continual activity and stretching of them often produced pain. Because of this, we were attracted by the experimental studies of Basmajian (8) and Hefferline (9) demonstrating very precise control of single motor units when the subject was given information (biofeedback) about the firing of these units. We were also encouraged by the report of Budzynski and Stoyva (10) that feedback of surface electromyography was of benefit to patients with muscle contraction head pain. We thus added auditory feedback of the activity of the involved muscles to the experimental situation. Presentation of the shock was modified as well, so that the shock was pulsatile in nature and was triggered by EMG to be present only when actual muscle spasm (as opposed to head deviation) was present. Results were encouraging enough to continue studying torticollis and other variants of dystonia with a combination of these two techniques. Of the initial 10 patients studied, six showed moderate to marked improvement on follow-up (11). Trials with biofeedback alone, shock alone, and the combination of the two were studied in individual patients. Consistently, lower spasm frequency in trials using both shock and feedback led to the retention of the shock, although the relatively mild nature of the shock led us to begin to question its "aversive" effect.

PRETREATMENT EVALUATION OF THE PATIENT

As most movement disorders can be presumed to be on the basis of a deficit in the central nervous system, all patients should have a thorough neurological assessment prior to biofeedback treatment. Many movement disorders may be the symptomatic reflection of a progressive pathological process in the brain, which may be surgically correctable. For example, hemifacial spasm may reflect a neoplasm or aneurysm pressing on the seventh cranial nerve. Once assured that no pathological process is present, a careful history of the onset and course of the symptom is recorded. A special

emphasis should be placed on any events or positions that change the severity of the symptom. Occasionally, patients will report that they maintain a posture at work that exacerbates the symptom, such as work on an assembly line or as a typist, which in torticollis may maintain the head in the pathologically deviated direction. Often, a job reassignment or a modification of a job procedure will be called for. If such a vocational adjustment cannot be made, patients will have to learn to control spasm by approximating this position in the laboratory as treatment progresses. Video tapes are made of the patients at this time as a way of allowing both patient and therapists to monitor the progress of treatment.

If at all possible, surface electromyography using multiple channel recording should be performed. The muscles suspected to be involved in the movement disorder should be studied as well as muscle groups adjacent to them. Occasionally, one particular muscle group will lead others in the expression of a complex movement disorder. Our practice has been to work with this muscle group first. Recordings are made with the patient sitting at rest as well as attempting to suppress the activity by whatever means possible.

It is desirable to obtain baseline frequency counts of the spasm, both in the laboratory and in other settings. Although spasms may be counted electronically in the laboratory, the patient can be trained to monitor spasm in the mirror at home and record frequency for 5-minute periods at various times during the day. This monitoring also provides an additional type of visual feedback that the patient can begin to utilize as training continues. Occasionally, spasm frequency does not vary much but the amplitude of the spasm does. Patients can be trained to rate this variation in severity (we use a 0–10 scale) and maintain the record of spasm severity on an hour-by-hour basis.

Patients come to the laboratory taking a variety of medications. It has been our policy not to suggest an alteration of medication schedule during the initial phase of treatment. If the patient responds to treatment, the referring physician may elect to decrease or discontinue these medications. Once the patient begins to get some control of the movement disorder, it has been our experience that medications may be discontinued or reduced without a resultant increase in symptom severity.

ORIENTATION OF THE PATIENT TO BIOFEEDBACK

Patients with a presumed neurological disease frequently have difficulty accepting the fact that biofeedback may be of benefit to them. Great care must be taken to emphasize that the patient's active effort is involved in any symptom relief obtained. Most patients come to the laboratory expecting something to be done to them and that biofeedback will be applied much as the ultrasound or heat treatments they have received in the past. Patients can exert maximal effort only when they clearly understand the biofeedback display and what they must do to change it. Such an explanation must include a simple but clear explanation of the location and function of the muscles involved.

USE OF SPASM-CONTINGENT CUTANEOUS SHOCK

Based on our initial work with torticollis, we have continued to use spasm-contingent cutaneous shock in addition to EMG biofeedback as part of our training procedures. Using two electrodes, the shock is delivered to the first two fingers of either hand. Studies in individual patients reveal no difference in the spasm-reducing capability of the shock to the hand on the same side or the side opposite of the muscle and spasm. The shock is present during the spasm only, and is activated by a trigger receiving amplified EMG. The trigger is adjustable, allowing the therapist to choose the amplitude of spasm that will initiate the shock. Pulse trains of 10 per second are used, with a pulse duration of 10 msec. The current delivered per pulse ranges from 3 to 5 mA, with the level of shock being determined by the patient's report that the feeling is somewhat unpleasant but not particularly painful. Initially introduced as an aversive technique, the exact role of shock in facilitating spasm reduction remains unclear. Once patients note the spasm-reducing nature of the shock, they are often reluctant to have it discontinued. This would argue against a predominantly aversive effect of the shock.

Shock presented in this fashion, triggered by muscle activity, can be thought of as a type of tactile biofeedback. Such feedback may be more relevant for muscle control than information presented either visually or auditorily. A second possiblity is that shock may help lower spasm frequency on some complex reflex basis. Such a possibility was suggested by Podivinski (12), who found that cutaneous tactile stimulation applied to the affected side of the neck tended to block or decrease spasm in torticollis.

TREATMENT OF SPASMODIC TORTICOLLIS

Spasmodic torticollis is a disturbance of the activity of the muscles that move the neck and maintain head posture. The head is deviated to one side. The head may be in a fixed position with muscles on one side of the neck in constant spasm or spasms may force the head to the side several times a minute, requiring the patient to exert great force to resume a midline position. Four-channel surface EMG of the left and right sternocleidomastoid and trapezius muscle groups usually indicates that the sternocleidomastoid on the side of the neck opposite to the direction of head turning demonstrates the greatest spasmodic activity. This muscle, with a clavicular and mastoid attachment, turns the head away from its side of location. Although occasional variations occur, this muscle is typically picked as the one to use in training. Standard silver/silver chloride electrodes are placed approximately 1 cm apart along the belly of the muscle. Occasionally, movement is so severe that the electrodes must additionally be secured by surgical tape.

If the head is fixed in one position with continuous muscle spasm, no spasm-contingent shock is used initially. The patient is taught to gradually decrease the amount of muscle activity present until the head can begin to approximate the midline position. The auditory biofeedback display that we use has a fixed baseline tone above which additional increases in EMG amplitude will create an increase in the pitch of the tone. As in many EMG biofeedback applications, this baseline tone can be set as a threshold, allowing for shaping of the desired response. Since spasms may be well over 200 μV peak-to-peak, we initially set the baseline tone as a target for the patient with small decrements over time as the patient begins to be able to reduce activity. As a rough guide for setting the tone in shaping, we select a range where the patient is achieving the target tone approximately one-third of the time. Once patients with the head in the fixed position begin to bring their head to midline, spasm is evident. At this point, we introduce the cutaneous shock.

One of the major concerns of the biofeedback technician is to emphasize the patient's active role in spasm reduction and to encourage continued effort at the task. Patients report that the work in the laboratory is extremely fatiguing and that they often must rest for approximately an hour after each session. Many patients experience some discomfort with the training as they realign muscles that have been shortened due to the continued maintenance of a deviated head posture, and we point out this possibility early in the treatment.

Patients are trained intensively for a period of 2–3 weeks. During that time, they receive two 45-minute biofeedback training sessions daily, Monday through Friday. After a patient begins to show some reduction of the spasm (usually after four to six sessions) exercises aimed at spasm reduction and increased range are performed in front of the mirror twice a day for approximately 15 minutes. Since the degree of spasm is often increased by tasks involving hand-eye coordination, patients may spend time working on individualized projects that call for maximal control of the spasm and head position. This type of activity is *not* begun until the patient begins to obtain substantial head control.

The symptoms of movement disorders, especially torticollis, are often exacerbated by walking. With adequate portable EMG devices, patients may work on spasm control while walking. When patients have special difficulty with spasm while performing tasks involving hand-eye coordination, such tasks are introduced in the laboratory. Many patients have difficulty reading, sewing, or working on assembly projects.

After training, patients are seen on an outpatient basis on a decreasing schedule. Optimally, the patient will be seen for two sessions on each of 2 days per week for the 1st month. The patient is then seen 1 day a week for the 2nd and 3rd month. Our frequency of treatment schedule has been constructed empirically. Usually, substantial improvement is noted after the period of hospitalization. Plateaus in performance are noted throughout, which may be extremely discouraging to the patient. At these points, the patient must be reminded of the long duration of the symptom (mean of 25 months in our patient group). It is difficult for us to specify a point beyond which no improvement may be expected. (See Table 15.1.)

As with the group of torticollis patients studied by Korein and Brudny (13), all of our patients had received multiple physical, surgical, or drug therapies prior to biofeedback. Over half the patients had received traction for sustained periods of time (up to 2 weeks in the hospital). Three patients had rhizotomies, one a thalamotomy, and one received the implant of a cerebellar stimulator.

Table 15.1.
Results of combined treatment with contingent cutaneous shock and EMG biofeedback in 50 patients with torticollis and 2 with retrocollis[a]

	End of training ($\overline{X}$ = 26.7 sessions)	Follow-up ($\overline{X}$ = 30.5 months)
Minimal or no improvement	8	11
Moderate improvement	28	18
Marked improvement	16	8
Lost to follow-up		15
Totals	52	$\overline{52}$

[a]For criteria, see Cleeland (15).

The most dramatic improvement was shown in patients who had had the symptom for less than 12 months. Of those patients (N = 10), 70% showed moderate to marked improvement. As with other movement disorders studied, the more rapidly biofeedback and behavioral intervention can occur, the greater likelihood of a successful outcome.

HEMIFACIAL SPASM

Hemifacial spasm is a spasmodic contraction of facial muscles generally present only on one side. At a later stage of the disorder, the spasm may spread to the other side of the face as well. Rarely accompanied by pain, the disorder is nevertheless of substantial cosmetic concern, as the spasms may massively distort facial expression. Frequently, the spasm can be attributed to compression of the seventh cranial nerve in the region of the cerebellopontine angle due to a mass lesion, aneurysm, or by a loop of the anterioinferior cerebellar or internal auditory artery (14). While surgery is extremely difficult in this region of the brain, relief of pressure on the nerve may be accompanied by relief of the symptom. As with torti-

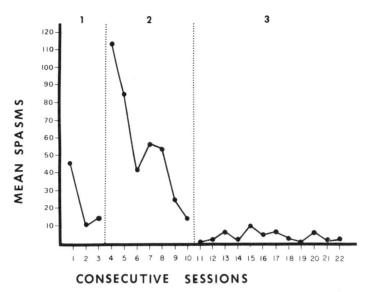

Figure 15.1. Hemifacial spasm. Mean spasm frequency for 5-minute presession baselines. Spasm-contingent cutaneous shock and EMG biofeedback used in all sessions: (1) patient relaxing, (2) arm movement present, (3) patient speaking.

collis and other disorders of movement, hemifacial spasm is aggravated by anxiety, stress and fatigue.

Hemifacial spasm presents a somewhat unique problem for a treatment approach based on biofeedback. The muscles involved in the spasm are often hypoactive between spasms (15), but asking the patient to increase the activity to match the unaffected side will increase the frequency of spasms.

We have treated five patients with hemifacial spasm, using biofeedback in conjunction with spasm-triggered cutaneous shock. With this particular disorder, the biofeedback display represented the presence of spasm only (Fig. 15.1). In one patient, by the end of 22 therapy sessions spasm was only occasionally present at rest and with arm movement and was markedly reduced while the patient attempted speech. Follow-up at 6 months indicated that spasm reduction was maintained outside of the laboratory.

Of the four other hemifacial spasm patients treated with biofeedback and spasm-contingent cutaneous shock, one patient, with symptom duration less than 6 weeks, demonstrated only an occasional twitching of the face after 22 training sessions and considered himself to be essentially symptom-free. Two patients demonstrated greater than 75% reduction in the spasm and were considered by themselves

and by us to be moderately improved. The fourth patient demonstrated only minimal reduction in the laboratory, with little generalization outside, and was considered by herself and by us to be not improved.

Two patients with blepharospasm have been studied using the combination of spasm-contingent cutaneous shock and biofeedback. As with hemifacial spasm patients, blepharospasm patients were instructed to attempt to suppress their spasm twice a day for periods of 20 minutes each while monitoring their progress in a mirror. One patient was able to reduce spasm rate to nearly zero with eight training sessions. Spasm frequency remained reduced at 3 months' follow-up. Another patient with blepharospasm of approximately a year's duration, was studied for 22 sessions. While she showed substantial reduction in the spasm when paired with shock in the laboratory, little generalization outside the laboratory was noted.

TREMOR

Tremor is a disorder of voluntary movement produced by a deficit in one or a combination of sites in the central nervous system. Like other disorders of movement, tremor displays a variability of intensity, and its amplitude is usually more pronounced during periods of emotional stress. While occasionally responsive to medication of surgery, many patients find tremor of both functional and cosmetic concern. One of our early successes with biofeedback is instructive.

Following almost complete recovery from a presumed CVA at age 11, this patient developed a movement disorder involving the right upper extremity characterized as a high amplitude tremor, with a rhythmic beat of 3 per second most prominent in the deltoid muscle. Its large amplitude caused the arm to flail (16). We first saw this patient when she was 15 years old. High levels of EMG activity were present in almost all muscle groups of the right arm, even at rest. Using EMG biofeedback, the patient was readily able to reduce resting activity by deep relaxation. After approximately 3 months of biofeedback training with step-by-step modifications, the patient was able to carry her tray in the school cafeteria, drink from a cup or glass without spilling, and shake hands in public with increased confidence.

Next seen 6 years later, she had maintained the progress made during the biofeedback sessions. She had become concerned with small tremor movements of the arm, which occurred in social situations. Following the techniques used in systematic desensitization, A. Dunn and I had the patient vividly imagine a variety of social situations while at the same time monitoring muscle activity from the deltoid and muscles of the upper arm. After having identified images provocative for the tremor, we asked the patient to imagine a given social situation as vividly as possible. As soon as the feedback tone indicated tremor, or even increased muscle activity, her instructions were to relax as deeply as she could. After approximately 10 sessions, she was able to imagine even the most stressful social situations with little electromyographic evidence of tremor. The training generalized to the social situations themselves.

Based on our experience with this patient, Dunn and I treated four other patients with tremor. Preliminary recording with multiple electrodes was used to determine the muscle site or sites most adequately representing changes in tremor amplitude. Once the site was determined, this site was used throughout training.

All patients were quite surprised with the occasional periods of control they demonstrated during the first or second sessions just by relaxing, and cooperation with the imagined situations as well as the training in general was easy to obtain.

All subjects demonstrated posttreatment reduction in tremor amplitude across all images as well as in the condition where they were instructed to relax. Another indication of possible control was that it took subjects only one-third of the time to bring the tremor to its minimal expression at the end of training.

Obviously, this pilot study included specific muscle relaxation, general muscle relaxation, as well as repeated presentation of the images that produced tremor. It is entirely possible that tremor reduction (presuming anxiety as a condition that exacerbates tremor) was due merely to habituation with the repeated presentations. Secondly, general relaxation presented in some other fashion than biofeedback may have been equally as effective as our training conditions in reducing tremor. These data do suggest, however, that behavioral treatment methods may be of some promise for the patient with tremor. Furthermore, the use of images related to stress appears to be quite an effective method of reliably reproducing tremor, and might be useful in the study of other physiological abnormalities for which stress may be presumed to be a factor.

PARKINSONIAN SYMPTOMS

G. Montgomery and I have applied multiple behavioral treatment strategies to patients with disordered movements. This can be illustrated by the application of biofeedback, progressive relaxation training, and stress management techniques to parkinsonian symptoms. Parkinson's disease is a degenerative neurological disease involving the loss of dopamine-producing cells, particularly of the substantia nigra. Principal symptoms of disordered movement include tremor at rest, rigidity, and slowness of movement or bradykinesia. The use of l-dopa, often in combination with a decarboxylase inhibitor, has provided dramatic symptom relief for many patients. Drug management, however, is not without serious side effects, and may become less effective over time. Because of these drawbacks, patients are often treated to a level of symptom reduction rather than to a level of total symptom relief.

The potential for behavioral intervention is suggested by the worsening of symptoms under conditions of emotional stress or high task demand. Symptoms are also exacerbated

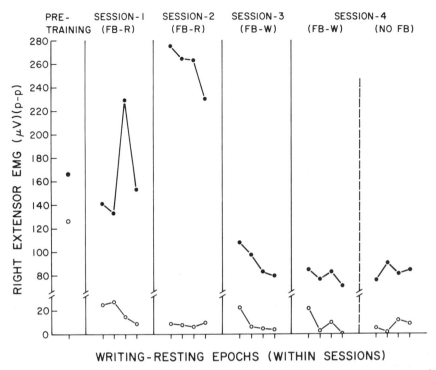

Figure 15.2.   Parkinson's disease. EMG activity from right forearm during baseline and 4 training sessions. ●, patient writing, ○, patient resting, over resting feedback (FB-R) and writing feedback (FB-W) sessions.

by fatigue. Prior studies, described above and elsewhere by us (17), offer some encouragement for the use of behavioral control with parkinsonian symptoms, although one report by Shumaker (18) found no significant changes in the performance of dexterity tasks by patients with Parkinson's disease after training in deep muscle relaxation via frontalis EMG biofeedback.

Our multibehavioral treatment strategy can be illustrated by a patient drawn from a project assessing the effects of behavioral treatment in parkinsonian symptoms of mild to moderate severity. The patient, a 52-year-old employed female, had developed parkinsonian symptoms 10 years earlier. She presented facial rigidity (masked facies) and handwriting difficulty (micrographia), which she believed affected her work and social activities. Other symptoms included resting tremor of the left hand, a shuffling gait, and loss of balance. She described her symptoms as typically exaggerated by fatigue or emotional arousal.

The patient received 12 sessions of frontalis EMG biofeedback training in response to her facial rigidity. Initial training was conducted with the patient relaxed with eyes closed. To facilitate transfer to more natural conditions, subsequent training was conducted with her eyes open, and under a moderate behavioral challenge (reading). She was instructed to monitor and relax her facial muscles at least hourly between sessions.

Excellent transfer of training to work and social settings occurred, with friends spontaneously commenting about her more "natural" appearance. Treatment for the improvement of the patient's handwriting was then conducted with four additional sessions of right extensor EMG biofeedback training (Fig. 15.2). Muscle activity was first reduced at rest between writing epochs (from more than 100 μV peak-to-peak), and later while writing (from more than 200 μV peak-to-peak), with markedly improved handwritten products and transfer of training.

Treatment for the reduction of tremor was conducted during five sessions. The patient was instructed to employ all of her arousal controlling skills (physiological and cognitive) to remain relaxed and with minimal tremor during recurring three-phase trials: rest, slowly-paced simple tasks, free speech on nonemotional topics (1 minute per phase). Over training sessions, left flexor EMG feedback was provided during rest, rest plus tasks, and rest plus tasks plus free speech, advancing patient response contingently. Reductions in tremor spike amplitude over training sessions were observed.

Positive transfer of training was reported by the patient, including several incidents (e.g., a near automobile accident) in which she was able to control markedly aggravated tremor (and rigidity) by conscious efforts to relax. While gait disturbances were never deliberately treated, the patient reported improving her gait and balance by employing relaxation techniques.

THE ROLE OF AUGMENTED FEEDBACK

When information back to the system about the operation of a given movement sequence is disrupted, the movement sequence itself may be disturbed. Hence, when internal feedback is disrupted, oscillatory or repeated movement may be present. Working with spasmodic torticollis, Podivinsky (12) has demonstrated the effects of modifying sensory input on the severity of the spasm, showing spasm reduction by an increase in tactile information at certain sites. Korein and Brudny (13) have also pointed to the disruption of sensory motor integration as a probable source of involuntary movements, using this postulate in attempting to explain improvements in dystonic patients following biofeedback therapy. If sensory deficit notions about the origin of disorders of movement are at least partially true, then biofeedback has great face validity as an appropriate treatment method. By the substitution of alternative types of feedback, the sensory-motor system might well be able to normalize itself.

One question is raised. What do patients learn that allows them eventually to be able to do without the ancillary biofeedback loop? Over time, the patient begins to receive cues about the effect of what he or she is thinking, feeling, or doing on spasm intensity. It may well be this type of cognitive mediation that allows the patient to generalize the reduction of the abnormal movement to situations outside the laboratory.

When biofeedback is used in isolation, the patient may not be getting the benefit of information concerning symptom alteration over larger blocks of time than is represented by the biofeedback session. Even with such an obviously discriminable symptom as pain caused by muscle contraction, patients may not notice its reduction unless specifically instructed to self-monitor presence or absence of pain on an hourly or a time-sampled basis. When this is not done, the clinician is also deprived of information that might be useful in redirecting the therapy if no change is noted. If symptoms are changing, and the patient is not fully aware of this change, an obviously very potent reinforcer of the effort involved in biofeedback training is lost. Self-monitoring provides yet another important feature relevant to the outcome of therapy. Often. the skills learned by the patient in biofeedback, for instance, focused concentration on muscle relaxation, cannot be practiced continuously by the patient. Self-monitoring of symptom intensity over time may allow the patient to identify particularly stressful times or events that occur on a regular enough basis to allow the patient to plan for relaxation when it will be of greatest benefit. Such association between stressor and symptom may also help the patient be more cognizant of certain physiological or psychological precursors of the symptom, which may come to serve as important signals that it is time for the patient to employ the strategies of physiological change learned through biofeedback.

TRAINING UNDER CHALLENGE

Once habituated to the laboratory, many symptoms that are present under the duress of stress in the patient's everyday life are absent. Only when the response is present can the patient use biofeedback to attempt new strategies for coping with the symptom. In addition, the hierarchical method of presenting stressors from least to most potent allows the patient to work with a manageable amount of symptom expression at any given time.

Another useful way to vary the intensity of the symptoms in the laboratory is to challenge the patient with simple, precisely intervalled tasks that vary in behavioral demand.

SOCIAL REINFORCERS AND BEHAVIOR CONTROL

While the biofeedback display itself provides an accurate rendition of moment-to-moment changes, the patient may well profit from the knowledge provided by the biofeedback technician providing comparative statements about performance based on smaller blocks than the entire biofeedback session—either verbally or by electronic summation.

Occasional steps backward (making the task easier) must be taken, and the whole process might be more accurately thought of as adjusting the biofeedback display so that the patient is achieving success in controlling the display a given percentage of the time. The percent of successful (on target) time that the display is adjusted to is an area in need of research.

CONCLUSION

The modification of movement and postural disturbances using behavioral techniques including biofeedback continues the demonstration that a symptom need not be "functional" to be treatable by such methods. Unfortunately, the bias against using the techniques of biofeedback or behavioral control in the treatment of organically based symptoms continues to be strong in some areas. As a result, such techniques have often been reserved for disorders not treatable by other methods, especially surgery or drugs. It is safe to assume that many symptoms now treated by more traditional medical intervention might actually be easier to treat using behavioral methods than some of the intractable disorders where behavioral methods have been typically employed. Behavioral treatment is being suggested for an increasing variety of neurologically related disorders. For a review, see Cleeland (19). It may be of some help to set aside the strong need to categorize a symptom as "functional" or "organic" at some point in the problem assessment, and instead develop a behavioral analysis of the symptom and potential modification of its conditions of expression, which might lead to symptom reduction or elimination.

References

1. Rothwell, J. C. and Obeso, J. A. The anatomical and physiological basis torsion dystonia. In *Movement Disorders 2*, edited by C. D. Marsden and S. Fahn. Butterworth, London, 1987.
2. Marsden, C. P. The problem of adult onset idiopathic torsion dystonia. In *Advances in Neurology*, vol. 14, edited by R. Eldridge and S. Fahn. Raven Press, New York, 1976.
3. Dandy, W. I. Operation for the treatment of spasmodic torticollis. Arch. Surg., *20*: 1021, 1930.
4. Cooper, I. S. Effect of thalamic lesions upon torticollis. N. Engl. J. Med., *270*: 967, 1964.
5. Meanes, R. Natural history of spasmodic torticollis and effect of surgery. Lancet, *2*: 149, 1971.
6. Fahn, S. and Marsden, C. P. The treatment of dystonia. In *Movement Disorders 2*, edited by C. D. Marsden and S. Fahn. Butterworth, London, 1987.
7. Yates, A. J. *Behavior Therapy*. John Wiley, New York, 1970.
8. Basmajian, J. V. Control and training of individual motor units. Science, *141*: 440, 1963.
9. Hefferline, R. F. The role of proprioception in the control of behavior. Trans. N. Y. Acad. Sci., *20*: 739, 1958.
10. Budzynski, T., Stoyva, J. and Adler, C. Feedback-induced muscle relaxation: applications to tension headache. J. Behav. Ther. Exp. Psychiatr., *1*: 205, 1970.
11. Cleeland, C. S. Behavioral technics in the modification of spasmodic torticollis. Neurology (N.Y.), *23*: 1241–1247, 1973.
12. Podivinsky, F. Torticollis. In *Handbook of Clinical Neurology*, vol. 6, edited by P. J. Vinken and G. W. Bruyn. North-Holland, Amsterdam, 1968.
13. Korein, J., Brudny, J., Grynbaum, B., Sachs-Frankel, G., Weisinger, M. and Levidow, L. Sensory feedback therapy of spasmodic torticollis and dystonia: results in the treatment of 55 patients. In *Advances in Neurology*. vol. 14, edited by R. Eldridge and S. Fahn. Raven Press, New York, 1976.
14. Haymaker, W. and Kalenbeck, H. Disorders of the brainstem and its cranial nerves. In *Clinical Neurology*, edited by A. B. Baker and L. H. Baker, chap. 30, p. 39. Harper and Row, Hagerstown, Md., 1976.
15. Coomes, E. N. Electrodiagnostic findings in clonic facial spasm and in facio-hypoglossal anastomosis. Ann. Phys. Med., *8*: 48, 1965.
16. Quaglieri, C. E., Chun, R. W. M. and Cleeland, C. S. Movement disorders as a complication of acute hemiplegia of childhood. Am. J. Dis. Child, *131*: 1009, 1977.
17. Netsell, R. and Cleeland, C. S. Modification of lip hypertonia using EMG feedback. J. Speech Hear. Disord. *38*: 131, 1973.
18. Shumaker, R. G. The response of manual motor functioning in parkinsonians to frontal EMG biofeedback and progressive relaxation. Biofeedback Self Regul., *5(2)*: 229–234, 1980.
19. Cleeland, C. S. Biofeedback as a clinical tool: its use with the neurologically impaired patient. In *Handbook of Clinical Neuropsychology*, edited by S. Filskov and T. Boll. John Wiley, New York, 1981.

PART 3
PSYCHOTHERAPEUTIC
APPLICATIONS

CHAPTER 16

Autogenic Training and Biofeedback Combined: A Reliable Method for the Induction of General Relaxation

JOHANN MARTIN STOYVA

It can be fairly said that electromyographic (EMG) feedback has become the clinical workhorse of the biofeedback area—this is true at least for the present. The practitioner, whether his discipline be clinical psychology, psychiatry or physical medicine, will find that knowledge of relaxation techniques will have many applications in his daily work.

The evidence that relaxation training has useful properties, particularly in alleviating symptoms of stress, has become substantial over the past two decades. Various types of relaxation procedures have been developed. Those with the most empirical documentation to date have been: progressive relaxation (1); autogenic training (2, 3); electromyographic feedback (4, 5); meditation, as for example, in Zen (6); and the modified transcendental meditation developed by Benson (7).

Some debate, however, has broken out over the question of whether biofeedback is necessary for inducing good relaxation. Thus, Tarler-Benlolo (8) questions whether biofeedback has demonstrated superiority over verbal instruction as a means of inducing relaxation. Similarly, Silver and Blanchard (9) state that

biofeedback is no better than other relaxation techniques in treating various stress-related or functional disorders. Nonetheless, it should be noted that the foregoing authors do affirm the usefulness of relaxation in general. The issue becomes: Which type of relaxation is most effective? Which is the least costly?

These questions are by no means totally settled, but a few comments are in order. To begin with, it may be noted that both autogenic training and progressive relaxation have been in existence for many decades, and were reported to be useful in a great variety of disorders; yet, one wonders why they were not widely adopted. One may conjecture that, although these techniques were highly effective in the hands of their originators, Schultz and Jacobson, the same was not generally true for their emulators. Simply reading a book about these methods is probably not enough to assure mastery of them. Much more is involved than merely giving the verbal instruction to "relax." Moreover, how does either patient or therapist know that a relaxed condition has been achieved? In our view, it is regarding this question that biofeedback methodology demonstrates great usefulness. In biofeedback training, the therapist takes measurements to determine whether EMG activity has decreased or not. And, if muscle tension has remained high, EMG feedback can be used to shape the patient's response in the proper direction. Thus, biofeedback techniques, despite their seemingly esoteric and even "science-fiction" flavor, should act to standardize relaxation training and to make it more reliable. In fact, criteria for what constitutes a relaxed condition are already beginning to develop. A particular set of such criteria have evolved in this laboratory (4) and have been described recently (5) (see Step 9 below, "Biofeedback in the Shaping of Low Arousal").

In previous work, we have emphasized that the individual's response to stress can be viewed as consisting of multiple components (10). These are manifested at the physiological, the behavioral, and the experiential levels. We have also conceptualized relaxation as a multiple-component phenomenon (10). In accordance with this conception, we have evolved a combination of biofeedback and autogenic training for use in relaxation training and stress management. The two techniques, complementing each other's strengths and weaknesses, focus on both cognitive and physiological aspects of relaxation training.

Autogenic training was developed in Germany prior to 1930 (2, 11). At its core are the six standard exercises (3). These enable the individual to shift voluntarily into a relaxed, low-arousal condition and consist of the limb heaviness exercise, the limb warmth exercise, the cardiac exercise, the respiration exercise, the solar plexus warmth exercise, and the "forehead cool" exercise. Fundamentally, the trainee practices cultivating sensations associated with good relaxation, an endeavor involving not only the musculoskeletal system, but autonomic and cognitive processes as well. We now regularly use the autogenic exercises in combination with biofeedback and find a sequence of four exercises especially useful. These are the heaviness, the warmth, the respiration, and the "solar plexus warm" exercises (see Step 10 below, "Autogenic Training and Biofeedback Combined.")

STRENGTHS AND WEAKNESSES OF BIOFEEDBACK IN RELAXATION TRAINING

As already noted, biofeedback and autogenic training have strengths and weaknesses which,

generally, are complementary, and are worth noting in some detail. A distinct advantage of biofeedback is that it helps to legitimize the intervention, quite an important matter for a new therapy. Is anything happening? How can you tell? In the case of the older relaxation therapies, it can be fairly easy for the skeptic to discount patients' reports as "airy nothings," the products of gullible imaginations.

Several specific characteristics of biofeedback contribute to its legitimization, and usefulness, as in intervention:

1. *Measurement of physiological parameters* offers definite advantages. Is there evidence of aberrant responding, either during rest or under stressful stimulation? Is the aberrant responding mainly autonomic or mainly muscular? Is the patient learning anything? Without monitoring, this can be difficult to tell, not only for the patient, but for the therapist as well. Often, patients are in fact making more progress than they think they are. Such knowledge can be encouraging news for the patient and acts to decrease the dropout rate—which in our clinic normally runs about 15%.

2. *New strategies for dealing with learning difficulties are made available.* Users of non-biofeedback relaxation techniques may mainly have to exhort the patient to "keep on trying." Biofeedback not only helps pinpoint the source of training problems, but opens up new intervention tactics. For example, it allows systematic use of shaping procedures; i.e., the trainee begins with an easy response and then proceeds to progressively more difficult ones—a technique we refer to as the *shaping of low arousal.* Thus, if frontal EMG is too difficult, we can shift back to the forearm extensor. If there are problems with the dominant arm, the patient nonetheless may do well with the nondominant arm.

3. Biofeedback provides a dramatic demonstration of what is meant by *passive volition*, of "letting go," of shifting into a nonstriving condition. Although the cultivation of this skill lies at the core of most relaxation therapies, it is a concept difficult to put into words. Biofeedback conveys the idea immediately in a direct and forceful way. "The 'old college try' drives up the tone! Learn to do the opposite!"

4. Instrumentation and measurement techniques assist in the task of placing biofeedback and self-regulation therapies within a scientific *explanatory framework.* Measurements are taken, and the therapist is stimulated to look for

relationships among the measurements. During relaxation, for example, changes occur in heart rate, peripheral temperature, and EEG patterns. How are these changes mediated? Several experiments (12–14) suggest that muscular relaxation reduces sympathetic activation, a phenomenon consistent with the broad "anti-stress" effects of good relaxation training.

The use of biofeedback does, however, suffer from certain *disadvantages*:

1. The patient may develop excessive reliance on the machine. There is also the related problem of "weaning" him from it, i.e., of effecting a transition from biofeedback control to self-control. And there is the danger, especially in the case of therapists without much clinical background, that training may become somewhat mechanical. Technique and measurement are overemphasized to the detriment of the human relationship. But these dampers can be circumvented. The therapist should make regular inquiries about a variety of issues. What are the patient's reactions to the biofeedback situation? How is his home practice going? What are the stresses in his or her daily life? How is he coping with them?

The other extreme must also be avoided. Therapists originally trained in experiential and psychodynamic therapies may bog down in the verbal aspects of the program. The aim of biofeedback and stress management techniques, however, is to produce change in reaction patterns. This task requires practice and lots of it, first in the clinic, then in the coping tasks of everyday life.

2. Sometimes the machines break down. What to do then? In this instance, the autogenic exercises can be valuable in maintaining continuity of training.

3. Biofeedback, with its physiological emphasis, is comparatively weak in generating cognitive strategies for producing relaxation.

4. With some patients, often those with severe anxiety symptoms, muscular relaxation has little effect on the autonomic components of the anxiety response. Here again, as noted below, the autogenic exercises offer some useful strategies.

STRENGTHS AND WEAKNESSES OF AUTOGENIC TRAINING IN A RELAXATION PROGRAM

The addition of autogenic training to the biofeedback program permits the therapist to cast a wider net over the various components of the stress response. Judiciously used, autogenic exercises can add the following strengths to a relaxation program:

1. The regular use of training phrases such as "arms and legs heavy and warm" offers a major strategy in coping with the critical *cognitive aspects of relaxation*. These phrases help keep the trainee's attention on the task at hand and are especially useful in dealing with the inevitable "stray thoughts." The phrases are a means of channelling and eventually quieting mental activity. "If stray thoughts come, as they surely will, go with them for a while; then let the phrase bring you back." Generally, too, we find that patients like the effect of the training phrases.

2. The autogenic exercises foster a type of *self-reliance*. Practically from the start, the patient has a procedure he or she can use independently. Moreover, the exercises foster a sensitivity towards one's bodily sensations—a skill integral to successful use of the training.

3. The autogenic exercises provide *strategies for dampening excessive autonomic activity*. One of these is the second standard exercise, "My arms and legs are warm." Another is the "solar plexus warm" exercise. Approximately 30% of our patients note epigastric warmth sensations, especially if they perform the exercises for 10-15 minutes. This exercise can be quite pleasant and is often associated with a marked reduction in anxiety. In this content, the reduction of anxiety attendant on the acquisition of a good warmth response has been noted in the autogenic training literature (3).

Also helpful for quieting autonomic symptoms is the respiratory exercise, in which the emphasis is on moderate, regular, and effortless breathing. This, too, is an exercise that patients frequently like. It is often useful in breaking up an excessive stress response, since in threatening situations, many patients show breathing irregularities—breath-holding, hyperventilation, irregular breathing—which contribute to autonomic disturbances.

An important additional strategy is regular use of the training phrases as a means of quieting cognitive activity, thus "short-circuiting" the cortical triggering of the defense-alarm reaction and its powerful attendant autonomic reactions. In this context, it is instructive to note the argument of Gellhorn and Kiely (15) that both CNS activity and musculoskeletal activity affect the autonomic nervous system, probably through their action on hypothalamic nuclei governing autonomic responses.

4. Autogenic exercises form a useful *bridge to other stress management techniques* such as the self-statements method of Meichenbaum (16). Although the latter procedure can be useful, it may strike some patients as gimmicky and superficial. "I've been telling myself for years to be 'calm, poised, and confident' with no particular effect at all! Sometimes it even makes me worse!" Patients familiar with autogenic training, however, will have noted the usefulness of the training phrases in dampening mental activity as well as their connection with physiological changes. Such persons will be more receptive than others to the self-statements approach as a method of altering reaction patterns under stress. (An intriguing possibility is that the mentally quiet condition induced by autogenic training may render the self-statements approach more effective by reducing "background noise." Note, too, that in autogenic therapy, the "intentional formulae," a type of self-statement, are employed after the patient has reached a mentally quiet condition by means of the standard exercises.)

Similarly, the autogenic exercises help prepare the ground for imagery techniques. As noted by Singer (17) and others, many imagery techniques involve an initial phase of relaxation—systematic desensitization, guided waking dreams, hypnotic imagery, and autogenic abreaction are examples. It appears that relaxation, perhaps by cutting down on competing stimuli (18) increases the vividness of imagery.

5. Autogenic training lends itself to the development of a *brief exercise* (1–2 minutes) that many patients find extremely valuable. This exercise can be practiced frequently—beginning each time with the phrase "My right arm is heavy"—so that the reaction becomes highly overlearned and virtually automatic. The training phrase has become a conditioned stimulus (CS) for good relaxation. The brief exercise can be worked into all sorts of situations: while waiting at a traffic light, before picking up a telephone, when tension becomes noticeable in a task such as studying for examinations, while waiting in a supermarket checkout line, during a pause in conversation and so forth. The patient has acquired a "portable anti-stress" response useful in breaking

up his previous habitual and maladaptive reaction to a variety of stressors.

Autogenic training has certain weaknesses, although these are minimized when the method is used in concert with biofeedback.

1. The idea of passive concentration, a central concept, can be quite difficult to convey accurately, especially to the habitually tense patient.

2. Is the patient learning anything or not? Without measurement, this can be hard to tell.

3. The training is very slow, and as Schultz (2) described it, took upwards of a year.

4. The process is not especially well tailored to producing muscle relaxation, which is probably a prelude to the later, more subtle aspects of relaxation. For example, it is doubtful whether a patient will develop arm heaviness sensations if his arm muscles remain tense. Our approach, accordingly, is not to begin the arm heaviness exercise until forearm EMG has reached fairly low levels in the laboratory (see Step 10 below, "Autogenic Training and Biofeedback Combined").

MAJOR STEPS IN THE TRAINING OF GENERAL RELAXATION

1. Psychological Preparation of Patient

This is a critical but often neglected phase of biofeedback treatment. In the self-regulatory therapies, of which biofeedback is one, this phase is especially important since, for the training to be of any benefit, the patient's cooperation must be enlisted. Thus, the training not only takes the time spent in the therapist's office—which typically ranges from 8 to 14 sessions—but the patient must practice the relaxation response frequently on his own. The response must become part of his habitual reaction to everyday stress situations. Such learning is not automatic; it must be acquired through diligent practice.

It is important that the patient understand the rationale for biofeedback training in his case. As already mentioned, it may be pointed out that the effects of relaxation training are opposite to those that occur when the individual feels under psychological stress. By utilizing the relaxation response frequently, the patient can learn to counter the effects of psychological stress and to lead a more tranquil and pleasant life. With regard to psychological stress, it is remarkable how many people are not aware that the head is connected to the body and vice versa, i.e., they do not realize how powerfully the interpretive activity of the brain can affect physiological reactions, as in its triggering of the defense-alarm reaction. Further details on the psychological preparation of the patient are given in the major section below, "Explaining Biofeedback Training."

2. Training Oneself

As in most therapies of a psychological nature, it is excellent advice first to undergo the training oneself. This not only allows the therapist to sample the experiential aspect of the training, but confronts him with some of the problems likely to be encountered by the patient and with ways of solving them. Moreover, if the therapist shows himself able to maintain a relaxed condition or looks like a relaxed person, then this will favorably influence the patient. A tense therapist is likely to produce a tense patient!

An added advantage is that by working with the feedback instruments the therapist becomes familiar with them and able to take care of much of the minor trouble-shooting that may be necessary. Thus, the therapist becomes familiar with such things as getting the units ready and attaching electrodes. (The latter we refer to as sensors since for many patients the word "electrodes" stirs up unfavorable associations.)

3. Experiential Correlates of Relaxation: Shift to a Nonstriving Mode

There are several prominent experiential aspects of relaxation training. These are particularly important in the retention of the relaxation response. The major experiential aspects of profound relaxation training are the following: *volitional aspects, bodily sensations*, and *shifts in the thought process*. These will be described in some detail.

A prominent dimension of most clinical biofeedback training is that the patient learns "*not to try.*" Instead of striving, or trying to achieve the objective by main force, he must learn to "*let go,*" after which an internal quieting gradually occurs. A similar phenomenon has been noted not only in various meditative disciplines, but also in progressive relaxation and in autogenic training. In autogenic training, the phenomenon is referred to as *passive concentration* as opposed to the active concentration required for most reality-oriented

tasks. It is worth noting that this *passive concentration*, or nonstriving condition, occurs not only in muscle relaxation training, but in the biofeedback training of alpha and theta rhythms, in diminishing galvanic skin response (GSR) activity, or in temperature training. Taub and Emurian (19) noted that this volitional aspect was the one consistent experiential correlate that emerged in temperature training.

A major advantage of providing the patient with information feedback is that it tells him immediately whether or not he is in the striving mode—and whether he is moving in the right direction. The lack of such information was probably an important reason for the difficulties that were sometimes encountered in the older relaxation therapies. Without physiological monitoring, it is hard to tell if the patient is proceeding in the right direction. Typically, too, patients with stress disorders are overresponders; they try too hard. This has frequently become a life-long pattern with them—to respond with a powerful activation response even though it is not called for. In biofeedback training, they must learn to do the opposite, to break up this pattern.

4. Bodily Sensations

A number of bodily sensations are likely to occur with profound relaxation. The patient may feel heaviness in the limbs, warmth in the limbs or in the epigastric region, tingling in the extremities, and salivation may occur. There may be sensations of drowsiness or floating, of changes in limb position or length. If the subject becomes drowsy, sleep-onset or hypnagogic imagery is likely to occur. These are perfectly natural experiences—peripheral warmth, for example, is the consequence of increased circulation resulting from diminished sympathetic outflow. These various changes in autonomic activity may be described as a shift from *sympathetic dominance towards parasympathetic dominance*. In the language of W. R. Hess (20), one would say that *ergotropic* activity has diminished; *trophotropic* activity has increased.

Although these various sensations are very common, they are not experienced by every individual—the profile varies from one person to another. For example, a particular individual may feel warmth and drowsiness, but nothing else. The sensations experienced by the patient in deep relaxation are very important for training purposes. When the individual is practicing on his own, he is able to use the presence of these sensations as a guide in recapturing the profoundly relaxed condition that he previously mastered with biofeedback.

5. Shifts in Thought Processes

Another prominent feature of a deeply relaxed condition is its *here and now* aspect. The profoundly relaxed individual is not ruminating about the past or worrying about the future; he is very much in the present. Equally noticeable when the individual shifts to a condition of profound relaxation, are changes in the thought process itself. Actually, it seems likely that profound relaxation probably does not occur unless there is this shift in conceptual processes. The latter involves a change from reality-oriented thinking—problem-solving, processing information, making decisions and so forth—to mental activity, which may be described as nonvoluntary, free-flowing, drifting. Should the patient become drowsy, hypnagogic imagery generally occurs—although many individuals fail to notice it. Sleep researchers have found that such imagery is extremely common (21). If subjects are roused at sleep onset, about 80% of the awakenings yield reports of imagery, usually visual in nature.

Generally, we do not dwell upon this hypnagogic imagery. But if the patient expresses great curiosity or concern about it, we reassure them this is very much a natural occurrence. With insomniacs, we try not to dwell on the hypnagogic imagery at all, since if the patient becomes preoccupied with it, this can be an impediment to sleep. (An interesting research project would be to examine the content of hypnagogic material in various kinds of patients; for example, to compare chronic anxiety patients with normal patients.)

6. Working with the Patient: Running Procedures

Seating

After the patient has been seated in a comfortable armchair, or lies down upon a couch, care should be taken that he is physically comfortable. Restrictive clothing such as ties, belts, and tight shoes should be loosened. A seated patient should not cross the legs, since this will interfere with circulation and will necessitate some movements in 15 minutes or less.

A reclining chair is a useful item of equipment. Many patients prefer to have the chair tilted to a semireclining position (about 45° from the vertical), so that they have a good head rest. For the patient who is lying on a couch, a pillow should be used—preferably a feather pillow because a foam rubber pillow is not nearly as comfortable. Also, some patients like a folded blanket placed under their knees. This helps in achieving thorough relaxation of the leg muscles.

Baseline Data

It is a good practice to obtain baseline data. For research purposes, we use the first three laboratory sessions, since it takes time for subjects to become accustomed to the laboratory. This many baseline sessions, however, may not be practical in a clinic setting in which patients pay for each session. A more practical procedure may be to use the first session and also the first half of the next session as baseline. In addition, the first 5 minutes of each session may be used to record baseline data. Among other things, this 5-minute segment can provide a useful guide as to whether the patient is learning to produce the relaxation response even in the absence of feedback. It may also be intimated to the patient that this period gives us an indication as to how the patient is doing in his home practice—and, by implication, whether he is working on his home practice!

Another important function of baseline data is to assess whether the patient is learning anything. Often a self-deprecating patient, who feels he is not learning anything, can be encouraged when the figures show that he has improved with feedback.

Instructions to Patients

Instead of requiring an immediate reduction of EMG activity, we tell the patient to make the feedback tone go in both directions, and then to try various maneuvers. For example, in the case of frontal EMG:

"What makes it go up? . . . What makes it go down? . . . What happens when you frown? . . . Now relax. . . . Now wrinkle your brow. . . . Again relax. . . . Now tense your jaw. . . . Now relax. . . . Now open your jaw a little bit."

Following this preliminary period, the patient is instructed to reduce the tone frequency (or the rate of the feedback clicks) as much as possible. A typical session lasts 20 minutes. At the end of the session, it is important to ask the patient what it was like.

Many therapists feel that this time may be the most fruitful part of the entire session. The patient discloses not only the personal strategies used to induce relaxation, but often reveals attitudes to the feedback situation, the therapist and to problems that may not have been expressed previously. (See Chapters 21 and 22 for fuller treatment of this point.)

7. Frequency of Training

A common question concerns the frequency of training. In our laboratory—for example, with tension headache patients—we typically employ two laboratory sessions per week for the first month, then one a week for the second. The actual time during which the patient receives feedback amounts to approximately 20 minutes. But when hookup time and "postfeedback" interviewing time are included, the sessions turn out to take about 50 to 60 minutes each.

In addition to the laboratory sessions, there is the important *home practice* part of the training—for which we employ the autogenic exercises. Many patients find a practical schedule of home practice to be as follows: three or four brief relaxation episodes a day and two longer periods of 5–10 minutes each. Preferably, the exercises are performed both at home and at work.

Sometimes, with patients who encounter difficulty in mastering the relaxation response, it is useful to have more than two laboratory sessions per week. This provides more intensive training. As the individual begins to master the relaxation response, the laboratory sessions may again, on the therapist's judgment, be cut back to twice weekly.

Occasionally, a patient finds it extremely difficult to come in twice a week, and we must fall back on one laboratory session per week along with extensive home practice of the autogenic exercises.

8. Developing a Stress Profile

An important feature often incorporated into our training is the development of a *physiological stress profile* of the individual. During the baseline sessions, the patient is subjected to some mental stressors such as performing mental arithmetic (subtracting serial 7's), or imagining either some fearful scene or an up-

setting experience. We then observe which system responds strongly under the "extra load." Typically, in tension headache cases, there is often a powerful muscle tensing response, especially in the head muscles. In migraine headaches, a vascular disorder, there is a strong peripheral vasoconstriction response. It should be noted that the disordered response may not be apparent unless some load is put on the system; i.e., the client may look normal under resting conditions.

The determination of a physiological stress profile is carried out as follows: an initial 10-minute period of relaxation is followed by a 6-minute period of stress (subtracting serial 7's). The latter, in turn, is followed by a 6-minute recovery period, during which the patient works at regaining relaxation. We normally monitor forearm extensor and frontal (forehead) EMG, finger temperature, and electrodermal response (EDR).

Sometimes clients will relax well during the first phase of the session, but then respond dramatically during the stress phase, and subsequently have difficulty recovering to relaxed baseline levels during the recovery period. It is our conviction that the *Relaxation-Stress-Recovery Profile* can provide useful information about the dynamics of the physiological systems measured and will become increasingly valuable in the future.

The training that follows is tailored to the patient's physiological stess profile. Its ultimate aim is to teach the patient to respond less maladaptively in the afflicted system, a task that normally involves learning a variety of relaxation skills and, frequently, the reshaping of coping skills as well (10).

On occasion, overzealous critics have accused us of maintaining that frontal EMG feedback is the only technique required for good relaxation. But this contention is actually close to the opposite of what we have been saying for at least the past 15 years (4, 22). We view relaxation as a phenomenon with many components (10). Consequently, feedback training of only a single parameter is likely to be too restricted in its effects to act as a robust "anti-stress response." The essence of our approach—in keeping with the idea of systematically shaping low arousal—has been to begin with an easy response; then, to proceed to more difficult ones.

In the interests of clarity, and partly to reflect the evolution of our procedures over the

Table 16.1.
Training general relaxation with EMG biofeedback.

Preparation phase
1. *Explain biofeedback* training and why it could be helpful in:
   a. Reducing localized muscle tension, or
   b. Counteracting the effects of psychological stress. Make certain your patient understands the reason for biofeedback training in his case.
2. Make sure the *physical setting* is a good one for relaxation training.
3. Make sure your *apparatus* is in working order and ready for use before the patient arrives.
4. *Obtain baseline data.*
5. *Obtain a stress profile.*
      This consists of three phases: *relaxation, stress and recovery.* A useful stressor is the subtraction of serial 7's. In what system does the patient respond too powerfully? For example, in EMG, peripheral temperature, or in GSR activity?

Training phase
1. Make sure the patient knows what the feedback signal is telling him.
2. *Step 1: Cultivating the muscle sense.* Do the *tense-relaxation* exercises in order to develop an awareness of muscle tension. These can be started at the end of the baseline session(s).
3. *Step 2: Forearm EMG training.* Give the patient a couple of minutes to experiment with the feedback. "What makes it go up? What makes it go down?"
   For a 20-minute period (±5 minutes), the patient practices letting the tone go to low levels (or on reducing the click rate). Afterwards, *discuss the session* with the patient. Train the patient on forearm EMG until he reaches an average level of 1.0 μV. Encourage patient to develop awareness of internal cues such as heaviness and warmth. Encourage home practice (see text).
4. *Step 3: Frontal EMG training.* Train the patient on frontal EMG till he reaches an average level of 3.5 μV. Encourage awareness of internal cues. Emphasize continuing importance of *home practice.* Is the patient mastering a thorough relaxation response? Is he having any difficulties? Work on correcting them.
5. *Step 4: Autonomic responses.* With patients who are strong autonomic responders under stress, hand temperature or GSR training can be useful. Note that the training's central focus is to promote a general relaxation response, so the therapist should be on the watch for remaining signs of high arousal. For example, is hand temperature low? If so, the patient should be taught the simultaneous mastery of peripheral temperature and profound muscle relaxation. Again, *encourage the patient to use the relaxation response frequently in everyday life.*

years, we will first confine our discussion to the biofeedback training of relaxation, as shown in Table 16.1. We will subsequently discuss the intergrated use of biofeedback and autogenic exercises as shown in Table 16.2.

9. Biofeedback in the Shaping of Low Arousal: A System of Sequential Criteria

One of the most common questions raised by the neophyte biofeedback therapist concerns the criterion to which the patient should be trained—what are satisfactory values of EMG activity? A helpful approach to this has been developed by Budzynski, details of which can be found in Budzynski, Stoyva and Peffer (5).

Sometimes, the question of using tapes as an aid to home practice is raised. Many therapists

have employed these to good advantage. In recent years, however, we have found that using a combination of biofeedback and autogenic training *without* tapes has definite advantages in systematic training of relaxation: self-reliance is encouraged; there is greater flexibility in the administration of the autogenic exercises—allowing for closer integration with the biofeedback phase of the program, and there is closer interaction with the patient during the session. (In fact, one might say that with the autogenic exercises, the patient develops his own tape.)

Step 1. Developing Awareness of Muscle Tension:

At the outset of training, we frequently use progressive relaxation techniques, especially

Table 16.2.
Autogenic training and biofeedback
combined

Note: Home practice consists of autogenic training exercises. Biofeedback is used only in the laboratory and as a prelude to autogenic training.

Forearm EMG training

Session 1. Begin autogenic heaviness exercise with training phrase: "My right arm is heavy." Repeat 5–7 times daily, 1–2 minutes per episode.

Session 2 (or thereabouts). Change training phrase to: "My right arm is heavy. My left arm is heavy. Both arms are heavy." Do 3 or 4 brief episodes a day, and add 2 longer episodes of 5–15 minutes each.

Frontal EMG training

Session 3. Change training phrase to: "My right arm is heavy. My left arm is heavy. Both arms are heavy. My right leg is heavy." Do 3 or 4 brief episodes daily, and 2 of 5–15 minutes each. Continue this regimen throughout training.

Session 4. Change training phrase to: "My right arm is heavy. My left arm is heavy. Both arms are heavy. My right leg is heavy. My left leg is heavy. Both legs are heavy." Same home practice regimen as above.

Session 5. Give summary training phrase: "My right arm is heavy. My arms and legs are heavy." Same home practice regimen.

Session 6 (or thereabouts). Introduce autogenic warmth exercise with training phrase: "My right arm is heavy. My arms and legs are heavy. My right arm is warm." Same home practice regimen.

Sessions 7–10. Add warmth phrases in a manner comparable to what was done for heaviness exercise. Then finish this part of at home practice with summary phrase: "My right arm is heavy. My arms and legs are heavy and warm." Maintain same home practice regimen.

Session 11. Add respiration exercise. "My right arm is heavy. My arms and legs are heavy and warm. Breathing." Schedule at home practice about the same as before.

Temperature or GSR feedback

Sessions 12–14. Add solar plexus exercise. "My right arm is heavy. My arms and legs are heavy and warm. Breathing. My solar plexus is warm."

For *brief exercise*, use: "My right arm is heavy, my arms and legs are heavy and warm"—then shift to paying quiet attention to breathing sensations (see text).

for individuals with high muscle tension. For example, with patients suffering from upper back and neck tension of functional origin, we teach them a set of four or five brief progressive relaxation exercises to practice at home even before they receive any biofeedback training. These exercises consist of hoisting the shoulders up to one's ears, tilting the head back, furrowing the brow, and clamping the jaw shut. Each exercise takes about 15 seconds and is to be practiced five to seven times daily. The exercises are designed to help the trainee become aware of what muscle tension feels like and to help break up persisting muscle tension (23) (24). They can be initiated at the end of the baseline session.

Step 2. Forearm EMG Training

At the next session, feedback training of the forearm extensor can be started. Low EMG levels at this site are related to proprioceptive cues such as heaviness and warmth. Developing awareness of such internal cues is important for transfer of learning to real-life situations.

On the basis of many observations over the past decade, we have adopted 1.0 microvolts as a suitable criterion for forearm relaxation training (i.e., the patient is able to reduce EMG activity to an average of 1.0 microvolts for a 10-minute period.)[a] Patients continue their training sessions with forearm EMG feedback until they meet this criterion, or until they have had three feedback sessions. If subjects meet the 1.0 microvolt criterion, the feedback is removed, and they are tested for their ability to retain low levels without feedback.

Step 3. Frontal EMG Feedback

To ensure transfer of forearm feedback training into the next phase, it is a good idea to monitor arm EMG. If the latter does not meet the 1.0 microvolt criterion, feedback from the arm is resumed for a few trials. When arm EMG activity has decreased sufficiently, then forehead EMG feedback is begun. Learning is generally slower during this phase compared with that occurring during forearm training. For most individuals, forehead EMG is a more

---

[a]These values are those obtained with EMG units having a bandpass filter of 95 to 1000 Hertz. EMG levels are a function of bandpass width—a wider bandpass gives a higher reading since it allows a wider range of EMG frequencies to pass through (see Chapter 31 for more details).

subtle response to master than is relaxation of the forearm. It is, however, especially useful since the forehead EMG placement is highly sensitive to the presence of thoughts, emotions, and mental effort. To reach a low forehead EMG, the patient must learn to shift to a "noneffort" or "nonstriving" condition.

Our criterion on this parameter is that the patient learn to keep EMG levels at 3.50 microvolts or less, a goal that may take two to five sessions. For the later nonfeedback condition, a criterion of 3.5 microvolts is also used.

Two additional stages of feedback training, depending on the patient's disorder, are frequently utilized in this laboratory. These are temperature training and systematic densensitization.

Step 4. Hand Temperature Feedback

This phase of training is intended to produce control of peripheral vasodilatation. In keeping with the idea of shaping low arousal, levels of both arm and forehead must be kept low as the subject practices with hand temperature feedback. If necessary, a brief period of feedback from arm or head is provided before temperature feedback is begun in each session. A criterion of greater than 89°F is set for the nonfeedback average. (For innovative suggestions about temperature feedback training, see Chapter 19 by Green and Green.)

Step 5. Systematic Densensitization of Anxiety

In this phase of training, which usually takes about three sessions, patients attempt to maintain relaxation while visualizing stressful situations from everyday life. This procedure is based on the behavior therapy technique of systematic desensitization (25), probably the most-used behavior therapy technique. Over the past two decades, much evidence has accumulated in support of its therapeutic usefulness, particularly for anxiety disorders (26). In our laboratory, we have employed "biofeedback-augmented-desensitization" for some years (4, 5, 27).

EMG criteria are set about 10–20% higher than for the preceding biofeedback sessions because patients are visualizing stressful situations. Each patient generates a hierarchy of scenes dealing with realistic problems in his or her daily life. The scenes are first ranked according to the amount of anxiety or stress that they provoke. The patient then attempts

to visualize the situations while remaining relaxed.

10. Autogenic Training and Biofeedback Combined

The integrated use of biofeedback and autogenic training is summarized in Table 16.2. This is an elaboration of the Training Phase portion of Table 16.1. Some comments on the successive steps are in order.

Step 1. Developing Awareness of Muscle Tension

As indicated in Table 16.1, this phase involves tense-relaxation exercises drawn from progressive relaxation.

Step 2. Forearm EMG Training

This step was also described in the Biofeedback Training section.

Usually at the end of the first forearm EMG session, we introduce autogenic training as part of a systematic program in learning an integrated set of relaxation skills. The *autogenic exercises are used for the vital home practice phase of training*. Ultimately, the patient masters a good brief relaxation response that he or she can independently utilize in a variety of stress situations.

The first autogenic exercise involves cultivating heaviness sensations in the limbs. For his first home practice exercise, the patient silently repeats to himself, "My right arm is heavy." The training phrase, which is repeated continuously—and *slowly*—during this exercise, helps one both to maintain passive attention on the arm and to keep out intruding cognitive activity. First, do one repetition out loud with the patient. Then, have the trainee do it silently by himself.

Note that most patients rattle through the phrase too quickly. Often they need to be reminded several times that they must say the phrase slowly. A rate of 1.0 second per syllable—or even slower—is usually satisfactory. Moreover, when the patient finds himself repeating the phrase too rapidly, he should deliberately moderate his tempo. Over the weeks of training, this slowing-down maneuver begins to have the effect of "pulling him into the deep relaxation." It needs also to be emphasized to the trainee that he must regularly bring his attention back to what the phrase is telling him to do. "When the intruding thoughts come, as they surely will, go with the thought for a little bit; but then detach from it—let it evaporate. Bring your attention back to your arm. The more you immerse your attention in the body part you are working on, the better you will find the effect of the exercise. With every word you say, shift your attention back to your arm. As you practice over the weeks, this skill becomes stronger and stronger."

Frequency of Home Practice

The first exercise is to be repeated five to seven times a day for one to two minutes each time. When home practice is beginning to go well—often this is after a week or two—the patient should take two episodes a day and "stay with it" from five to fifteen minutes. In addition, continue doing three or four brief episodes a day as well. Some patients seem to benefit most from the long episodes, others from the short ones.

Generally, at the end of the second biofeedback session we extend the exercise to: *My right arm is heavy. My left arm is heavy. Both arms are heavy.* Each phrase is repeated three to six times during the one-to-two minute home practice episodes. Usually, too, the trainee finds it best to spend one-third to one-half of each exercise on the new phrase that has been added.

Later, heaviness phrases are added for right leg, left leg, and both legs. Then, after adequate mastery of the heaviness exercise, the patient moves on to the final *summary phrase* for this exercise: *My arm and legs are heavy.*

Many trainees intially report that they do not feel much heaviness. This sensation, of course, cannot be forced any more than sleep-onset can be forced. But the trainee should persist in the exercise; first, because he or she will probably develop useful sensations in some of the later exercises; second, because the exercises are useful as a means to making relaxation an habitual and, later, a robust and overlearned response.

Note that the therapy is quite an active one. After each session, there is home practice to carry out, usually with some small increment in training. It must be emphasized to the patient that such home practice is critical in the reshaping of his maladaptive stress responding. It is important to ask, "How did it go with your home practice?" every time he visits the clinic. This tactic strengthens motivation and also alerts the therapist to the presence of training difficulties.

Step 3. Frontal EMG Feedback

We ordinarily introduce the autogenic warmth exercise after the patient has become proficient at lowering frontal EMG activity. Lowered frontal EMG is strongly associated with a mental shift to a nonstriving condition; i.e., there is a sharp reduction in effort signals from the CNS, a condition that seems to be at the core of various relaxation training procedures (10). Such a shift has been reported as the most distinct experiential correlate of hand temperature feedback training as well (19).

The foregoing considerations make it reasonable to introduce the warmth exercise after frontal EMG levels have become low. The beginning phrase is "My right arm is heavy. My arms and legs are heavy. My right arm is warm." Over several sessions—usually 2–3 weeks—the patient progresses with warmth training to both hands and feet in the same fashion as with the heaviness exercise. After he has mastered this exercise, the (permanent) summary phrase becomes, "My right arm is heavy. My arms and legs are heavy and warm."

Next, the respiration exercise is added. Here, we have modified the classical autogenic exercise, using the phrase "breathing" instead of the somewhat awkward phrase, "It breathes me" (3). The emphasis is on easy, regular breathing. Respiration should be effortless—as if something else were doing it! Since respiratory irregularities are very common in patients with anxiety and stress-related disorders, this is often a useful exercise. Trainees frequently indicate a marked liking for it.

The phrase sequence at this stage has become: "My right arm is heavy. My arms and legs are heavy and warm. Breathing." The new phrase, "Breathing" is used for about one-third to one-half of the exercise period.

Step 4: Thermal Feedback

As Table 16.2 indicates, hand temperature feedback is often introduced at this stage—especially if there is reason to believe that peripheral vasoconstriction is involved in the disorder—as in essential hypertension, migraine headache, or in Raynaud's disease. With many patients, however, we simply do not bother with temperature biofeedback since the three previous autogenic exercises appear to have been sufficient for the needs of the patient.

In any case, the next autogenic exercise becomes "My solar plexus is warm." This involves the cultivation of a warmth sensation in the epigastric region. To their frequent surprise, about 30% of our patients report noticing this sensation at least some of the time. When the exercise leads to perceptible warmth, patients report the condition to be strongly associated with tranquility, well-being, and absence of anxiety.

In about 50% of our patients, there is not much need to introduce either the solar plexus exercise, or temperature feedback—since the patient has already developed an adequate relaxation response. Individuals with performance anxiety or insomnia are cases in point: frequently, mastery of simply the heaviness, warmth, and respiration exercises prove sufficient for their purposes.

Brief Exercise

Often, we add another respiration-related exercise drawn from meditative disciplines. The trainee is instructed to pay attention to respiratory sensations. "Note the cool air flowing in, and the warm air flowing out." The training phrase is "Cool air in; warm air out." Should the patient find this a particularly agreeable exercise, he may wish to use it for longer episodes as well (i.e., for 5–20 minutes).

Patients may wish to drop this latter training phrase altogether. In its place, they can simply pay quiet attention to their respiratory sensations, a practice likely to produce the "emptying of consciousness" often referred to in the meditative disciplines. When introducing this exercise, we also point out the importance of abdominal breathing for profound relaxation. The stomach moves out on inhalation, then contracts on exhalation. Some patients find it useful—as a cognitive quieting device—to become aware of "cool air in" and "expanding stomach" at the same time. Often, patients have already made the shift from thoracic to abdominal breathing on their own. But, nonetheless, it is worthwhile to make them fully conscious of this valuable anti-stress maneuver—since this is perhaps the single most useful practical exercise to apply during the stressful situation itself, as for example, in an oral examination. "Check your res-piration frequently. This is something you can do even in the blink of an eye."

A variant of the foregoing exercise focuses on inner speech. For many and perhaps most individuals, a key obstacle to achieving mental quieting is the phenomenon of internal dialogue, a problem likely to be acute for patients in highly verbal professions such as law or journalism. This verbal "chatter" constitutes part of the unceasing flow of consciousness. A useful perspective on this problem comes from the progressive relaxation literature. In Jacobson's view (1), inner speech, or subvocalization, is accompanied by minute levels of EMG activity in the larynx, tongue, and other muscles associated with ordinary audible speech. To eliminate this inner speech, one must eliminate EMG activity in the muscles of vocalization, a task accomplished by good relaxation of the relevant muscles—which include the tongue, lips, jaw, laryngeal, and throat muscles. "Scan for signs of tension in these muscles. Then relax it out." A useful mental quieting device for many trainees is to combine the "cool air" exercise with relaxation of the speech muscles. This entire maneuver can be linked to respiration. "As you breathe in, notice the cool air; as you breathe out, scan for signs of tension in your speech muscles; and as your exhalation continues, let this tension dissipate. Simply perform this maneuver every time you inhale and exhale—cool air on the in-breath, then relaxation of the speech apparatus on the out-breath." For many, this maneuver proves extremely valuable in the critical but sometimes exasperating task of reaching a "mentally-quiet" condition. However, once patients begin to master the skill of "easing into" this state, they report it as pleasant and as having salutory aftereffects—some refer to it as being in a "mellow space."

Another type of breathing exercise, drawn from the Vipassana tradition of Buddhism, consists of having the trainee silently and slowly pronounce the words "rise" and "fall" in rhythm with his breathing. With the word "rise," one becomes aware of the rising abdomen and the accompanying muscular sensations—this is the inspiratory phase. In the expiratory phase ("fall"), the abdomen contracts.

As a concluding note to this section, we should point out that the trainee will not want to do regularly all the brief exercises we have just outlined. Rather, he should first experiment with several of these brief exercises in order to determine which works best for him—particularly with respect to producing a mental quieting effect. He may, moreover, wish to utilize some *combination* of brief exercises, as is described in the following paragraph. Once a choice of brief exercise (or combination exercise) has been made, it is best to stick with it. This practice results in a highly overlearned and robust response that can be successfully brought into play when circumstances are difficult.

Finally, as a practical condensed version of the autogenic and the breathing exercises, we often recommend the following combination: "My right arm is heavy. My arm and legs are heavy and warm." Then shift to paying attention to breathing sensations. Two merits of this brief exercise may be noted. First, as a result of much practice, "Right arm heavy" can become a CS for initiating a good relaxation response. Second, paying attention to breathing sensations dampens cognitive and volitional activity—critical components of good relaxation. Moreover, the nature of the exercise is such that the patient can himself estimate his proficiency. If he is not readily able to effect the cognitive shift of paying passive attention to breathing sensations, then frequency of practice should be increased. Frequent use of this brief exercise can be very helpful in preventing buildup of tension during the day.

11. Retaining What Has Been Learned

A critical transition point is the transfer of relaxation skills from the laboratory to everyday life. Here it is important to utilize the sensations the patient has become familar with during his laboratory sessions. It is in this regard that biofeedback techniques show definite advantages over the older approaches to relaxation. Some patients have difficulty in perceiving the bodily changes associated with profound relaxation; others have difficulty at first in maintaining low arousal for more than a few seconds. In the latter case, the trainee is not likely to experience many bodily sensations, since most of these seem to have a fairly slow time course (and are probably dependent on the rate at which autonomic activity changes). An advantage of biofeedback methodology is that the patient can be allowed to remain in a low arousal state for some time (5-10 minutes). During this more extended peri-

od, the experiential correlates of relaxation are likely to become perceptible to him.

Other aids in the cultivation of a proficient relaxation response are the following:

1. The Jacobson Progressive Relaxation Exercises

In these, the trainee is taught to tense and relax various muscle groups. The object of this is to become aware of muscle tension, and to be able to sense the difference between tension and relaxation. Specific information on the technique may also be obtained from Jacobson's various books (see references) or by writing to the National Foundation for Progressive Relaxation, Suite 311, 55 East Washington Street, Chicago, Illinois 60602.

2. Finding Time to Practice

Patients frequently complain that they lack time to do the home practice. They may promise to practice at home, yet not do it. Sometimes it is useful to go over the patient's schedule hour-by-hour in order to find time slots that may be available. This tactic helps to get the patient further committed to actually performing the home practice.

3. Technical Aids

The patient usually needs to be reminded to practice the relaxation response frequently. A colored tape on one's watch is a useful means of encouraging such behavior. The color of the tape should be changed every week to minimize habituation, since patients often become oblivious to a particular color. A related procedure is to perform the relaxation response every time prior to engaging in some frequently occurring behavior; for example, every time one looks at one's watch, or every time one picks up the telephone. Thus, the patient hears the telephone ring, does a brief relaxation response, then picks up the telephone receiver. Through association learning, the relaxation response begins to occur at a far higher rate as a consequence of its having been paired with a high probability behavior.

4. Discuss the Importance of the Home Practice

Emphasize how important it is for the relaxation response to be integrated into everyday behavior. Over the years, the patient has become a "hyperreactive" individual. This pattern takes time to change; but it can be done. It is chiefly a question of regaining a response that we have all had as children, but then gradually lost under the stresses and strains of everyday living.

5. Perform the Relaxation Response in the Presence of Graduated Stressors

In our laboratory, most of the biofeedback training is done with the patient in one room, and the therapist in an adjoining instrument room—since patients usually find it somewhat tension-producing to have the therapist right next to them. In the later phases of the training, however, the task can be made more difficult. In accordance with the shaping concept, the subject can be taught to relax under conditions of increasing difficulty. He first learns to relax under optimal conditions. Then, circumstances are gradually made more difficult. For example, the chair can be shifted from a semireclining to an upright position. Doors can be left open so that hall noises enter the subject's room. Similarly, lights can be left on, or a radio kept playing.

6. Use of a Cue Word

A particular phrase, such as "calm" or "I am at peace," can be paired with the relaxation response. The therapist first assures himself that the patient is mastering the relaxation response rather well; then he is asked to repeat to himself the cue word such as "calm," but only if he is actually quite calm. In this way, the relaxation response can become classically conditioned to the cue word; repeating the word "calm" will help to trigger the relaxation response.

EXPLAINING BIOFEEDBACK TRAINING

This is a critical, but often neglected, aspect of biofeedback treatment procedures. Unless the patient understands the rationale for biofeedback training and what it involves, he is unlikely to show much benefit. As Frank (28) has pointed out, there must exist a shared assumptive framework between the patient and the therapist. That is, both participants must agree on a course of treatment likely to be helpful and on the reasons as to why it might be helpful. Since it is so vital that the patient understand the rationale for biofeedback training, the following paragraphs are presented in a conversational manner, as if one were presenting the material to the patient.

What is Biofeedback?

"The basic idea in biofeedback training is to use sensitive detectors to tell you what is happening inside your own body—and to tell you right away. Ordinarily, this is a hard thing to do. Right now, for example, is my heart rate going up or down? And what about my blood pressure or muscle tension? It is difficult to know, but with the biofeedback instruments, we can tell immediately.

"Suppose we want to pick up muscle tension. What we do is to place sensors over the muscles we are interested in. These sensors pick up the tiny electrical signals that are generated by the muscles. What the biofeedback instrument does is to convert your muscle activity into sound, which you hear through your headphones. When the muscle is tense, you hear high-frequency tones. As soon as you relax, the tone frequency goes down. The tone tells you immediately whether you are going in the direction of relaxation or not. This is really the most important thing in any kind of learning—to know quickly whether you are going in the right direction. The tone tells you instantaneously if your muscle is tensing or relaxing. We have used this on a lot of people now, and it helps them to relax much faster."

Relaxation As an Anti-Stress Response

"Patients suffering from stress-related disorders typically show more than one symptom. In addition to tension headache, they may report indigestion, insomnia, anxiety, and so forth. In this regard, it can be emphasized to the patient that when he feels under stress, it is not just one part of the body that reacts; a whole cluster of processes is set in motion. This acts to energize the individual. Not only do the muscles become active, but heart rate increases, blood pressure goes up, and there is an increase in blood sugar. A great many reactions are triggered. At the same time, activities concerned with digestion and rest slow down. This emergency reaction is one that everybody has. We are all born with it, and it is a basic survival reaction.

"What becomes a problem, however, is that some people react too strongly, particularly with some component of this reaction. For example, somebody who has tension headaches—which are muscle contraction headaches—is a person in whom the muscle reaction is very strong when he is under stress. With such a person, there are generally a great many things that will set off this reaction—deadlines at work, emotional turmoil, meeting somebody he doesn't like, or being at a party where there are a lot of unfamiliar or annoying people.''

It is at this juncture that a rationale for biofeedback relaxation training can be developed. The fundamental idea behind this training is that, when people learn to become deeply relaxed, the effects are *opposite* to those produced by psychological stress. Things slow down. Patients first learn to relax with biofeedback, then learn to do it without biofeedback. All this involves a lot of practice on one's own.

Two additional points should be noted. In introducing biofeedback, we find it helpful to link it with the idea of relaxation, a concept known to almost everyone. Thus, what is not familiar becomes linked to something that is familiar. Additionally, patients are more ready to admit that what they have is a ''stress'' problem rather than a ''psychosomatic'' problem. Both on theoretical grounds, and for reasons of acceptibility, the idea of a stress response can be emphasized. We are dealing with disorders of adaptation.

During the intake session, we particularly emphasize to the patient: ''there are two main things we want you to learn. First, good physical relaxation—here, biofeedback is a big help. Second, we will help you to learn a good mental quieting reaction. The home exercises are especially tailored for this task, and are very helpful after you start to get the hang of them. Usually, people find that a beneficial result begins to occur after 3 or 4 weeks. It is a learned skill, and the more you practice, the stronger it becomes. So what we would like you to do is to give the thing a really good try for 1 month.''

COMMON PROBLEMS IN RELAXATION TRAINING

1. The Response Is Too Difficult

A good general rule in biofeedback training is that if a patient finds that a response is too demanding, shift him to an easier task. For example, instead of training to reduce frontal

EMG activity, the patient can change to the forearm extensors or the masseter. The latter are both muscles over which individuals generally have a high degree of voluntary control, and a thorough relaxation of them can typically be accomplished in a session or two. After this has been done, the patient can again return to the more subtle task of lowering frontal EMG activity.

The preceding approach is an important general strategy in biofeedback and autogenic training and has been incorporated into the technique we have termed *the shaping-of-low-arousal* (already described in #9). It may be noted that the shaping-of-low-arousal procedure draws upon extensive work in operant conditioning. The concept of shaping, and the idea of providing quick knowledge of results, constitute two of the major principles in operant conditioning. Both of these principles are readily incorporated into biofeedback training.

2. Inability to Achieve a Mental Quieting

Actually, the three most common difficulties encountered by the beginner is autogenic training bear directly on this matter. These difficulties are as follows: (a) saying the phrase too fast, (b) not keeping one's attention on the relevant body part, (c) not perceiving any heaviness or warmth.

The first two points were discussed in the preceding section. Should the patient not feel any heaviness or warmth, it is useful to do the home practice anyway. After a couple of weeks—and especially when guided into relaxation by the EMG feedback—the patient generally begins to notice some relaxation-related sensation. Most common is heaviness in the dominant arm. Moreover, the patient may discover sensations other than heaviness and warmth that he can use to guide his home practice.

For the 10% of patients (or fewer) who report no relaxation sensations at all, we often introduce one of the respiratory exercises earlier than usual—e.g., ''breathing,'' ''rise-fall,'' or ''cool air.''

3. Frequent Intruding Thoughts

This problem is really part and parcel of the one just discussed, ''How to achieve a good mental quieting?'' The three strategies already noted above should be encouraged. It is also worth emphasizing that the patient should not forcibly try to banish his thoughts. This maneuver involves effort and is thus self-defeating. "Instead, simply drift along with the stray thought for a few moments; then—in accordance with the phrase you have been repeating—swing your attention back to the body part you have been working on."

Another possibility is that the patient may not be as relaxed as he thinks he is. Consequently, it is a good idea for him to scan internally to see whether he can sense any residual muscle tension. If he does, then he should relax it away. Important areas to check include the face, the eye region, and the throat region. As Jacobson (1) has emphasized, there is a reasonably close association between many kinds of thinking and residual tension in the eye and laryngeal region. Thus, if subvocal (inner) speech is a problem, it is often useful to relax very thoroughly the muscles in the laryngeal area. Sometimes useful in this task is to begin softly humming to oneself, gradually reducing the level of the humming, until it finally disappears.

CONCLUDING REMARKS

At first glance, the training sequence we have outlined in this chapter may seem a little intricate. In practice, however, the procedure is comparatively straightforward—EMG feedback is utilized in the laboratory, the four autogenic exercises for the home practice part. Biofeedback aids especially in the acquisition of good physical relaxation, the autogenic exercises in the mastery of "mental quieting." At the end, a meditation-type exercise is often added, a procedure that further aids in the sometimes elusive task of reaching a "nonstriving," mentally quiet condition.

When the patient has mastered the skills necessary to attain the complementary goals of physical and mental relaxation, he or she will have made significant progress toward moderating a stress reaction that has become excessive or of too long a duration. Generally, appreciable headway begins to appear after 3 or 4 weeks of consistent practice. Although the integrated sequence of exercises we have outlined can be very useful in a variety of stress-related disorders, including: tension and migraine headaches, sleep-onset insomnia, situational anxiety—and sometimes as well for more generalized chronic anxiety, in essential hypertension, Raynaud's disease, and for chronic pain cases in which muscular tension and anxiety reactions are prominent compo-

nents. In general, it can be said that the combination of autogenic exercises and biofeedback described in this chapter is likely to prove useful for patients in whom an exaggerated stress reaction plays a conspicuous part in generating or maintaining their disorder.

References

1. Jacobson, E. *Progressive Relaxation*, 2nd ed. University of Chicago Press, Chicago, 1938.
2. Schultz, J.H. *Das Autogene Training: Konzentrative Selbstentspannung.* Georg Thieme Verlag, Stuttgart, 1932.
3. Luthe, W., ed. *Autogenic Therapy*, vols. I-VI, Grune & Stratton, New York, 1969.
4. Budzynski, T.H. and Stoyva, J.M. Biofeedback techniques in behavioral therapy. *Neuropsychologie der Angst*, Reihe Fortschritte der Klinischen Psychologie, bd. 3, edited by N. Birbaumer. Verlag Urban & Schwarzenberg, München, Berlin, Wien, 1973, pp. 248–270.
5. Budzynski, T.H., Stoyva, J.M. and Peffer, K.E. Biofeedback techniques in psychosomatic disorders. *Handbook of Behavioral Interventions*, edited by E. Foa and A. Goldstein. John Wiley & Sons, New York, 1980, pp. 186–265.
6. Hirai, T. *Psychophysiology of Zen.* Igaku Shoin, Tokyo, 1974.
7. Benson, H. *The Relaxation Response.* Morrow, New York, 1975.
8. Tarler-Benlolo, L. The role of relaxation in biofeedback training: A critical review of the literature. Psychol. Bull., 85, 727–755, 1978.
9. Silver, B.V. and Blanchard, E.B. Biofeedback and relaxation training in the treatment of psychophysiological disorders: Or are the machines really necessary? J. Behav. Med., 1, 217–239, 1978.
10. Stoyva, J.M. and Anderson, C.D. A coping/rest model of relaxation and stress management. In *Handbook of Stress: Theoretical and Clinical Aspects*, edited by L. Goldberger and S. Breznitz. Free Press/Macmillan, New York, 1982.
11. Stoyva, J.M. Wolfgang Luthe: In memoriam. Biofeedback Self Regul., 11, 91–93, 1986.
12. Davidson, D.M., Winchester, M.A., Taylor, C.B., Alderman, E.A. and Ingels, N.B. Effects of relaxation therapy on cardiac performance and sympathetic activity in patients with organic heart disease. Psychosom. Med., 41, 302–309, 1979.
13. Agras, W.S., Taylor, C.B., Kraemer, H.C., et al. Relaxation training: Twenty-four hour blood pressure reductions. Arch. Gen. Psychiatry, 37, 859–863, 1980.
14. Cooper, M.J., and Aygen, M.M. A relaxation technique in the managment of hypercholesterolemia. J. Human Stress, 5: 24–27, 1979.
15. Gellhorn, E., Kiely, W.F. Mystical states of consciousness: Neurophysiological and clinical aspects. J. Nerv. Men. Dis., 154: 399–405, 1972.
16. Meichenbaum, D. Cognitive factors in biofeedback therapy. Biofeedback Self Regul., 1, 201–216, 1976.

17. Singer, J.L. *Imagery and Daydream Methods in Psychotherapy and Behavior Modification.* Academic Press, New York, 1974.

18. Stoyva, J.M. Biofeedback techniques and the conditions for hallucinatory activity. *The Psychophysiology of Thinking,* edited by F.J. McGuigan and R. Schoonover. Academic Press, New York, 1973, pp. 387–414.

19. Taub, E. and Emurian, C. Feedback aided self-regulation of skin temperature with a single feedback locus: I. Acquisition and reversal training. Biofeedback Self Regul., *1,* 147–168, 1976.

20. Hess, W.R. *Diencephalon: Autonomic and Extrapyramidal Functions.* Grune & Stratton, New York, 1954.

21. Foulkes, D. *The Psychology of Sleep.* Scribner's, New York, 1966.

22. Stoyva, J.M. and Budzynski, T.H. Cultivated low arousal—an anti-stress response? *Recent Advances in Limbic and Autonomic Nervous Systems Research,* edited by L.V. DiCara. Plenum, New York, 1974, pp. 369–394.

23. Jacobson, E. *Modern Treatment of Tense Pa-tients.* Charles C. Thomas, Springfield, Illinois, 1970.

24. McGuigan, F.J. *Calm Down: A Guide to Stress and Tension Control.* Prentice-Hall, Englewood Cliffs, N.J., 1981.

25. Wolpe, J. *Psychotherapy by Reciprocal Inhibition.* Stanford University Press, Stanford, 1958.

26. Wolpe, J. Behavior therapy for psychosomatic disorders. Psychosomatics, *21:* 379–385, 1980.

27. Budzynski, T.H. and Stoyva, J.M. EMG-Biofeedback bei unspezifischen und spezifischen Angstzustanden. *Biofeedback-Therapie: Lernmethoden in der Psychosomatik, Neurologie und Rehabilitation (Fortschritte der Klinischen Psychologie,* vol. 6), edited by H. Legewie and L. Nusselt. Urban & Schwarzenberg, München, Berlin, Wien, 1975, pp. 163–185.

28. Frank, J.D. *Persuasion and Healing.* Johns Hopkins University Press, Baltimore, 1961.

29. Budzynski, T.H. Relaxation training program (set of three tape cassettes, Catalogue no. 2805). Guilford Press, New York, 1986.

CHAPTER 17

Biofeedback-Assisted Relaxation Strategies in Psychotherapy

PAUL L. FAIR

Psychotherapists with differing theoretical perspectives employ biofeedback (BF) techniques for monitoring and training physiological responses as an effective treatment component for a variety of emotional, behavioral, and psychosomatic disorders.

The use of BF technology to monitor physiological activity provides both therapist and client with an objective indicator of emotional arousal. For example, in the creation of anxiety imagery hierarchies in the systematic desensitization of phobic responses, BF instruments can be employed to detect differential physiological activation during imagery even when the client may give identical subjective ratings of anxiety intensity. During the desensitization process, increases in physiological activity typically precede the subjective experience of anxiety. Physiological monitoring can be used to terminate the imagery presentation and aid the client in returning to the relaxed state to be maintained during imagery.

The training of deep muscle relaxation using electromyographic (EMG) BF is perhaps the most common BF application in psychotherapy. In some cases, relaxation may be the major therapeutic goal as in the short-term treatment or it may provide the psychophysiological substrate that facilitates other psychotherapeutic techniques. Deep muscle relaxation may serve: (a) as a precursor to traditional psychotherapeutic procedures requiring a relaxed state to facilitate free association and visual imagery; (b) as a precursor for training control of autonomic nervous system parameters in psychosomatic disorders; or (c) as an antagonistic response to anxiety in the treatment of phobic states using systematic desensitization (1).

This chapter summarizes some general considerations and a variety of specific techniques for training deep muscle relaxation in both psychiatric and medical rehabilitation populations.

ORIENTING THE CLIENT

The first office session following intake is devoted to orienting the client about relaxation training. The session involves an open discussion of (a) the rationale for using relaxation training in the treatment program, (b) the role of biofeedback, (c) the client's expectations, and (d) the therapist's role.

We believe that it is important for the individual to fully understand what BF is, Many clients seek help from practitioners who offer BF as a treatment component. If this is known to the client and/or if it is the specific reason for the client's seeking treatment, it is sometimes important to question the client on his understanding and expectations of BF and how he sees it helping him. Often, clients are looking for quick remedies and misunderstand the "miracle powers" of BF so often portrayed in magazine and newspaper articles. We stress that BF is one of a number of equally important techniques that are used to teach self-regulation. A discussion of the advantages and limitations of BF treatment, and the necessity to adhere to office and home training procedures in a disciplined way is a more realistic view to convey.

PSYCHOPHYSIOLOGICAL PROFILE

In addition to generalized arousal, individuals will vary in their specific pattern of arousal to stress. Before relaxation training is begun, a psychophysiological profile is obtained in order to assess the stability and lability of physiological activity under resting and moderately stressful conditions. It is used to establish specific biofeedback training goals and provides baseline information necessary for evaluating the effectiveness of the treatment strategy.

Procedures

The profile should consist of continuous measures of EMG activity from three regions of the body, skin conductance, peripheral skin temperature from the nondominant hand, and respiration rate. In addition, pre- and postsession measures of heart rate and blood pressure are obtained.

The total recording period lasts about 45 minutes. The remainder of the 1-hour session is spent allowing the client to become familiar with the biofeedback instruments and various types of feedback that will be used in later sessions. During the profile session, EMG is simultaneously monitored at 1-minute intervals from three separate regions using commercial EMG biofeedback devices.

Skin temperature baselines are recorded from the middle finger of the nondominant hand. Skin conductance activity is recorded from the palm of the dominant hand.

Subjective Ratings

In order to obtain a quantitative assessment of the client's subjective experience of the symptoms, the specific symptoms are rated on an intensity scale of 1–10, with 1 being total absence, and 10 being the most intense experience of that symptom.

For the duration of the program, clients keep hourly or daily subjective ratings for each of the selected symptoms.

ESTABLISHING SPECIFIC BIOFEEDBACK RELAXATION TRAINING GOALS

The stress conditions of the psychophysiological profile session provide information about the reactivity of specific physiological responses and their rate of return to the baseline. The relaxation periods reveal which parameters appear to move most readily toward lower arousal levels and indicate the initial choice and sequence of physiological responses to be trained.

There is no hard and fast rule, however, for which physiological parameter should be employed for initial training. Clearly, if a particular parameter is functioning at higher than normal levels of arousal, and does not change with training in another system, then it must be specifically trained during the course of the treatment in order to assure generalized relaxation. It is noteworthy that—

1. It is rare to find a client with either a psychosomatic, psychological, or medical disorder that is appropriate for biofeedback training who does not manifest excessive muscle tension in some part of the body.

2. Clients readily accept the idea of deep muscle relaxation training.

3. The achievement of a deep muscle relaxation state generally results in unique and pleasurable experiential states that are highly motivating and reinforcing.

4. Deep muscle relaxation typically is accompanied by decreases in autonomic arousal levels.

5. Generalized muscular relaxation is often necessary before biofeedback training of autonomic parameters can be undertaken.

NONBIOFEEDBACK RELAXATION TECHNIQUES

In a typical relaxation program, biofeedback is used in combination with a number of other techniques including progressive relaxation, autogenic training, and meditation.

Berstein and Borkovec have developed a detailed manual for modified progressive relaxation with instructions on specific techniques and procedures and dealing with potential problems. This manual is recommended reading for practitioners desiring to use progressive relaxation (3).

Autogenic Training and Meditation

Autogenic training procedures consist of six standard exercises that combine both relaxation and autosuggestion. It may take many months, but can greatly increase the individual's ability to reach a deep state of psychophysiological relaxation through mental control of both neuromuscular and autonomic systems. (See Chapter 16.)

An effective meditation technique involves having the patient in a comfortable sitting position with eyes closed. Relaxation is produced by having the individual focus his attention on his breathing and say the word "one" to himself each time he exhales. Evidence suggests that this procedure, repeated in daily practice sessions, results in significant decreases in physiological arousal levels (4).

FIRST RELAXATION SESSION— PROGRESSIVE RELAXATION

The progressive relaxation instructions consist of a series of isometric tensions held for a period of 7–10 seconds followed by the instruction to "relax" for a period 20–40 seconds. The sequence of muscle regions proceeds from the dominant to the upper arm, followed by the nondominant hand, upper arm, right foot, lower leg, upper right leg, left foot, lower leg, upper leg, buttocks, abdomen, respiratory muscles, shoulder, neck, jaw, lips, eyes, and forehead. A complete transcript of our progressive relaxation instructions adapted from Berstein and Borkovec appears as an appendix to this chapter.

It is important to have the client describe the specific sensory experiences, thoughts, and fleeting images that may have occured during the session. The sensations of relaxation will vary from individual to individual. Should additional progressive relaxation sessions be required in the office (e.g., when there are problems in the home practice sessions), references to the unique experiences of the client can be introduced into the relaxation instructions. Further, it is helpful to determine any sites that were particularly difficult to relax. Interestingly, these areas are often associated with psychological conflicts and may require specific EMG biofeedback training.

The client is also questioned about: (a) the timing of the instructions, especially, whether the period following the "relax" instruction was sufficient to allow full relaxation of the region; (b) the pitch and voice quality of the therapist; and (c) any aspect of the exercise that was not conducive to success.

EMG BIOFEEDBACK SESSIONS

In the clinical feedback situation, the client reclines in a comfortable chair in a quiet semi-darkened room. In later sessions, differential relaxation may be trained, having the individual sitting upright or standing. Each session is 1 hour long with 20–40 minutes devoted to actual feedback training.

The three electrode placements we most frequently use in training general muscle relaxation are: forehead (frontalis region), neck (upper trapezius region), and forearm to forearm (forearm extensors).

Figure 17.1 shows several facial expressions of emotions that illustrate some of the complexity of possible underlying muscle patterns that may contribute but not be differentiated in the feedback signal using bilateral forehead placements.

From top to bottom on the oscilloscope insert, the following electrode pairs are shown: Channel "F" displays the activity recorded from the two topmost electrodes on each side of the forehead. This placement is analogous to the wide-spaced, bilateral forehead electrode placements used in biofeedback training; channel "rF" is recorded from the two topmost close-spaced electrodes over the right frontalis (right side of the forehead); channel "lF" is from the top two electrodes over the left frontalis; channel "lC" displays activity from the close-spaced electrode pair situated at the medial end of the left eyebrow; channel "lT" displays activity from the left temporalis muscle from the electrode pair lateral to the left eye; channel "lOc" displays activity from the left orbicularis oculi, derived from the electrode pair just below the left eye; and channel "lZ" displays the activity from the left zygomatic (smile muscle) from placements immediately below "lOc" EMG activity from the electrode pairs over the right corrugator and left masseter muscles are not displayed here.

Inspection of channel F across the four expressions reveals a magnitude differentiation between the happy expression and the other three. Of greater interest, however, are the differences in the patterns of activity across close-spaced electrode pairs which reveal some consistent differences between expressions. For example, visual observation reveals sad and anxious to be most similar in their patterns of muscle recruitment in both the upper face (rF, lF, lC, lT) and lower face (lOc, lZ). Anxiety is characterized by greater activity in the medial forehead (rF, lF, and lC) than is the sad expression. In contrast, the angry expression is most characterized by strong activity in the corrugators (lc) with relatively little activity in the individual frontalis. There is virtually no qualitative way to differentiate sad, angry, and anxious expressions based on the widespread forehead placement (F) alone.

The happy (smile) expression is most uniquely characterized by a virtual silence of activity in the medial forehead region (rF, lF, lC) with considerable activity in lT, lOc, and lZ. The observable activity in channel F is most likely attributable to volume-conducted

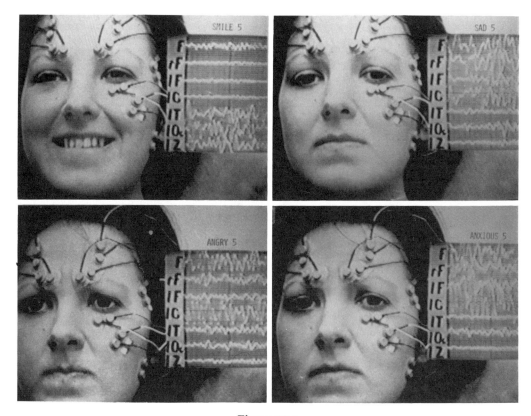

Figure 17.1

activity from the temporalis (see lT) muscles which reposition the jaw during maximum smiling.

Each expression shown is last expression in a five-step progressive series starting with a neutral face ("O") and increasing the magnitude of the expression at 2-second intervals. The instruction for Step 1 was to generate the expression without any noticeable change in observable facial features. The patterns of low-level EMG activity across the placements during the covert expressions were similar to those in the overt expressions. The smile expression is of particular theoretical and practical interest. With most individuals there is a noticeable progressive decrease in EMG activity in the medial forehead region with each step of the 1 to 5 count. We have consistently noted that when clients are instructed to relax after step 5 of the smile and drop their jaw, there is a virtual silence momentarily throughout the face which is clearly noticeable in the feedback signal from wide-spaced forehead placements. In most cases, after a few seconds,

there is a gradual increase in EMG activity. Our clients typically report that they are unaware of the gradual increase in muscle tension and are unable to voluntarily reduce it. These unique characteristics of the smile expression dramatically demonstrate the lack of awareness of low-level muscle tension prior to training and help to illustrate the intimate connection between emotional states and facial tension. Further, by noting the effects of jaw relaxation on the forehead signal, the clients are introduced to the concept of cross-talk and alerted to the possible contribution of jaw position and clenching to the forehead feedback signal.

Bilateral electrode placements on the back of the neck and on the forearm extensors are the other commonly used regions for EMG feedback-assisted general relaxation training.

The arm-to-arm placement consists of one active electrode placed over each forearm extensor mass (or flexor mass if the arms are hirsute) with the ground placement at roughl‧ equal distance from the active electrodes. This placement is sensitive to muscle activity in either arm as well as throughout the upper portion of the body including the shoulders. It is particularly useful as a monitor of upper trunk relaxation while specific feedback training is focused on the forehead region. One noticeable drawback of this placement is the presence of cardiac electrical (EKG) activity. The EKG is clearly audible in the feedback signal and may be disturbing to some subjects. On the other hand, we have found that an explanation of this biological artifact to the client can be turned to an advantage.

Shaping Relaxation

The strategy within the biofedback sessions involves shaping relaxation through a stepwise process that maximizes success. This is accomplished by having the therapist successively increase the gain of the EMG feedback loop as the client achieves lower levels of EMG activity.

Facilitating Internal Awareness

An important emphasis in the progressive relaxation instructions involves having the individual become aware of internal feedback cues signalling rising tension states. By focusing on the difference between feelings of tension and those of relaxation, the "muscle sense" is cultivated. During the tensing sequence, cues are very strong relative to the relaxation component.

No-feedback trials are interspersed with feedback trials, with the therapist monitoring the EMG levels and giving verbal feedback following each trial. If the sensory threshold begins to increase or relaxation is not maintained, the feedback is reintroduced. The individual is gradually shaped in detecting and releasing progressively smaller tension levels at higher feedback sensitivities.

Following relaxation of the initial site, the next muscle region is shaped in identical fashion.

There is a small group of individuals who experience feelings of anxiety, discomfort, and even panic as they begin to reach deep levels of muscle relaxation. These individuals often report feeling that they will lose complete control of themselves in some undefined way. Frequently, there are images or associations with personal death, and the problem may have to be dealt with psychotherapeutically. However, most of these people can be desensitized to muscle relaxation by merely instructing them to slightly tense their muscles if they begin to experience discomfort. With repeated trials, this obstacle can usually be overcome.

TRANSFER

The problem of facilitating transfer of relaxation skills to daily activities of living is structured into the very early stages of biofeedback training. This is accomplished by interspersing periods of feedback with no-feedback. The individual is instructed to maintain relaxation when the feedback tone is turned off by becoming aware of the internal sensations associated with the varying levels of feedback. Over the course of a number of sessions, the ratio of no-feedback periods to feedback periods is progressively increased until the individual is eventually responding only to internal cues as the feedback source. In addition, as the client becomes more skilled over time, the situation is varied to require relaxation while sitting upright and standing.

COGNITIVE STRATEGIES

Many persons are somewhat surprised at the changes in the biofeedback tone that occur with transient thoughts and images of an emotional or excitatory nature. This is especially true with EMG monitoring of the facial regions (forehead placement).

The role of cognitions and different cognitive strategies is discussed with the client in the early stages of biofeedback training. The effects of different emotions and images on muscle tension may be demonstrated using the forehead placement. In many disorders where obsessive or other forms of intrusive thoughts are especially difficult to control, considerable emphasis may be placed on training cognitive regulation. The effects of appropriate cognitive strategies being used play an important role, especially when approaching the achievement and maintenance of very deep levels of relaxation.

Cognitive Techniques

The following are some of the techniques that have been used successfully:

"Passive concentration," as used in meditation, is often a difficult notion to grasp. In describing this attitude, the client is told that it is a mental attitude characterized by a relaxation of active problem-solving or goal-orient-

ed thinking. Instead, it is necessary to become a passive observer of thoughts and feelings, to allow them to pass by without actively attending to them. Initial exposure to the feedback signal generally reveals to the person how difficult this passive attitude is to achieve. Many persons will, with practice, develop a passive attitude with a corresponding decrease in tension.

Benson's meditation procedure (4) is particularly useful when intrusive thoughts and/or a competitive attitude is the source of interference.

Visual imagery is effective for many individuals. The individual is instructed to create a scene of a quiet place.

It is the unsuccessful therapist who assumes that simply describing the technique automatically leads to its successful utilization by the client. All too frequently, clients in the early stages of training maintain misconceptions and nonverbalized negative attitudes towards different procedures. Constant monitoring of both the physiological response and the subjective experience of the client is necessary.

MONITORING

The early biofeedback sessions are of particular importance, and everything that can be done to maximize early success will greatly benefit long-term progress. Many individuals make rapid progress in reducing gross muscle tension levels during the initial phases of training. Therefore, constant monitoring in the early sessions allows EMG criteria changes to be adjusted to suit the rapid progress. The deepest levels of relaxation are most difficult to obtain, and relaxation criteria must be increased in progressively smaller steps. Only by constant monitoring can the therapist respond to the various stages of the client's progress.

HOME PRACTICE

Home practice sessions are of considerable importance to the success of the relaxation program. Clients are given a cassette recording of their progressive relaxation session and instructed to practice twice a day until the next session. In addition to the full progressive relaxation session taped in the initial session, one or more of the following tapes are used:

1. *Abbreviated Progressive Relaxation*
2. *Tense to Sensation*

3. *Breathe/Relax*

Variations of such tapes are used with individuals who experience an aggravation of their symptoms during the tensing component of progressive relaxation (e.g., low back pain syndromes, muscle cramping, and neuromuscular hyperarousal syndromes including spasticity, spasms, and athetoid movements resulting from cerebrovascular accident, cerebral palsy, and spinal cord injury).

PROGRESSIVE RELAXATION TAPE

Handout Instructions

This tape consists of a sequence of contractions of a number of muscles followed by relaxation of each muscle region. Each contraction lasts for a period of 7–10 seconds and should be strong enough so that you can feel the sensation of muscle tension in each particular region. Do not contract them so strongly as to produce muscle spasms or pain. If the instructions direct you to contract an affected muscle region and you are unable to voluntarily contract that group, then simply imagine the muscle contracting and relaxing. Try to imagine the same sensations that occurred in your nonaffected muscles for both the tensing and relaxing component. We have found that when individuals do this over time, they eventually become aware of slight increases and decreases in muscle tension in the affected muscle groups. Sensory awareness of the affected muscle regions is an important step in regaining voluntary control. Do not be discouraged if initially you are unable to feel any change in a particular region. It takes time. The important thing is to keep your attention on the task at hand each time you practice.

Practice Schedule

Initially, try practicing twice a day in a quiet place without interruptions such as telephone ringing, people walking by, or dogs sitting in your lap. Do not practice immediately after meals, and remember that coffee, tea, and soft drinks may act as stimulants and often make you feel jittery. Therefore, try to avoid these beverages before and after relaxing.

Posture

Make sure you are in a comfortable position—either sitting or lying down. If you are in a chair, make sure that your lower back and neck are supported using small pillows, rolled towels, etc. If lying in bed, place a pillow under your knees in order to keep your back comfortable. Also, make sure your head and neck are comfortably supported. Make sure that you are warm enough. Cover up with a blanket before you start, but make sure that the blanket does not press uncomfortable on your toes. Tight rings, watches, bracelets, and shoes will begin to annoy you when you get deeply relaxed, so remove them before starting. Socks help keep the feet warm.

Sensations of Relaxation

As people begin to learn to relax, they report certain sensations or feelings coming from their body. It is important that you begin to recognize these, for they are your feedback or information about your body and your growing success at beginning to relax deeply. Some people report feeling heaviness in the arms and legs; others have reported feeling lightness, tingling, warmth, and on occasion the feeling that the limbs or body have disappeared. These are all good signs, but don't worry if you don't feel them. They will come and may be unique to you. Make notes about the types of sensations you experience.

Distracting Thoughts

One of the biggest problems that many people have in the initial stages of relaxing is racing or intrusive thoughts. It may feel like you cannot turn off your brain. As you learn to relax, you will find that these thoughts begin to decrease automatically. However, in the initial stages, racing or stressful thoughts and fears interfere with your ability to learn relaxation and increase body tension. Here are some helpful hints:

1. Set a specific time and place for doing your relaxation. As you approach the session, mentally reflect on the types of stressful thoughts and feelings you are having. Are you thinking about such things as making dinner, scheduling an appointment, or paying a bill? Are you feeling angry, anxious, worried, depressed, or hurt? Be comfortable in acknowledging these thoughts and feelings to yourself and then tell yourself that you are going to place these thoughts aside for a half-hour. Create a visual image in which you take the thoughts out of your head, place them in a box and leave them outside the room. Remember— you can always pick them up again. There is always plenty of time to worry. Now it is time to begin cultivating your time to be worry-free and relaxed.

2. Assume a relaxed passive state of mind. This is difficult to explain. What is meant is that you stop goal-oriented thinking, planning, and trying to solve problems mentally. Instead assume a passive mental attitude where you simply notice or are aware of your thoughts. Learn to notice when your thoughts attract your attention and distract you from relaxing and attending to the bodily sensations. Learn to let the distracting thoughts float on by. Let them go and return your attention to relaxing.

Transfer of Relaxation Skills

As you get better at relaxing with the tape and become familiar with the instructions, try interspersing practice periods without the tape, relying totally on your own ability to self-instruct. Also, begin to do abbreviated practices when sitting in your chair or in the car. Even though these do not produce as deep a feeling of relaxation, they do help to bring the overall level of body tension down and will have the long-run effect of making you feel relaxed at the end of the day.

TEXT OF INSTRUCTIONS FOR HOME PRACTICE AUDIOTAPE

Adapted from Bernstein and Borkovec (3)

Now I want you to sit back in the chair and close your eyes. Keep your eyes closed throughout the session. Clear your mind of stray thoughts. Remember that the next half-hour is just for you. Spend a moment scanning through your body. Become aware of the sensations in your body. As you scan through your arms and legs, see if you detect any sensations or feelings of tension and allow yourself to relax those regions. Tune in to your breathing. Allow your breathing to become relaxed and calm.

Breathing

Now take a deep breath and hold it—just hold that for a moment. Notice the pressure. Feel the sensations in your chest. And now gradually relax and let the air slowly flow out. Allow your whole body to begin to relax as you breathe out. Allow your breathing to become relaxed and rhythmical.

And again, take a deep breath and hold it. Become aware of the sensations of tension— now relax, let the air slowly flow out of your lungs. Allow yourself to sink confortably into the chair, calm and relaxed.

Right Hand and Forearm

Now focus your attention on your right hand and forearm. Increase the tension very slowly by making a fist and gradually tensing tighter and tighter. Hold the tension in your right hand . . . [7 sec]. Notice the sensations from your fingers, your hand, wrist, and forearm. Become familiar with the feeling of tension . . . *relax* . . . Let all the tension dissolve. Allow the muscles of your fingers and hand to become smooth, loose, limp, and relaxed. When you feel as if your hand isn't going to relax any more, imagine that your hand is becoming even more relaxed. Allow relaxation to flow through the hand and forearm as they become very relaxed . . . [30–40 sec].

Upper Right Arm

Focus your attention on the upper part of your right arm. While allowing the lower part of your arm to continue relaxing, begin to tighten the muscles of the upper part of your arm by pressing your right elbow into the arm of the chair. As you make it tighter, notice the sensations of tension. Now hold the tension at a relatively strong level for a moment . . . *relax* . . . Let the muscles become relaxed. Allow relaxation to flow into the upper part of your arm. Allow the muscles in your upper arm to become loose and limp.

Allow your entire right arm to become very, very relaxed. And now imagine the relaxation being even deeper. Very, very relaxed.

Left Hand and Forearm

Focus on your left hand and forearm. Gradually make a fist and increase the tension in the left hand and forearm tighter and tighter. Be aware of the changes in tension. Hold that for a moment . . . *relax* . . . Let your left hand and forearm begin to relax. Allow your hand and forearm to sink into the chair, very, very relaxed. Allow all of your muscles to become loose, limp. Now imaging relaxation becoming even deeper—the muscles becoming very smooth, soft, and relaxed.

Upper Left Arm

Now, focus your attention on the upper part of your left arm. And begin to gradually tighten the muscles by pressing your elbow into the arm of the chair tighter and tighter. Hold

that tension for a moment. Be aware of it . . . *relax* . . . Let your left arm completely relax. Allow the entire left arm to become loose and limp. Very relaxed.

Now allow both arms to relax a little more.

Right Foot and Lower Leg

Now, focus your attention on your right foot. Increase the tension in your right foot by first pointing your toes away from your face and notice as you do, the tension in the top of the foot . . . *relax* . . . Imagine your right foot becoming even more relaxed.

Now focus on the lower part of your right leg, and increase the tension in that area by pointing your toes gradually toward your face. Notice the tension building up. Just hold that for a moment. Be aware of the sensations . . . *relax* . . . Allow the muscles to become soft, limp, and relaxed. Very relaxed. And now relax just a little bit more. Feel the sensations of relaxation.

Upper Right Leg

And now, focus on the upper part of your right leg. Gruadually begin to tense the muscles in the upper part of your right leg, tighter and tighter. Hold that for a moment. Notice the sensations of tension . . . *relax* . . . Allow your entire right leg to become very, very relaxed. Allow it to sink comfortably into the chair. Allow yourself to let go of all the tension in your right leg. Let your whole right leg become loose and very relaxed. Now allow it to become even more relaxed.

Left Foot and Lower Leg

And now, focus your attention on your left foot. Tense your left foot by pointing your toes away from your face, curling your toes down. Hold that for a moment . . . *relax* . . . Let your left foot begin to relax. Allow it to become as relaxed as your right foot . . . very, very relaxed. Feel the sensations in the muscles as your foot becomes relaxed.

And now, focus your attention on the lower part of your left leg, and increase the tension here by pointing the toes of your left foot toward your face. Notice the changes in tension. Hold that for a moment. Feel the tension . . . *relax* . . . Let the muscles become completely relaxed. Allow those muscles to become very loose, limp, and relaxed. Now, imagine your left leg becoming even more relaxed . . . very, very relaxed.

Upper Left Leg

Now focus your attention on the upper part of your left leg. Gradually increase the tension tighter, tighter. Hold that for a moment. Notice how it feels . . . *relax* . . . just let it go. Allow your entire left leg to sink comfortably and heavily into the chair. All the muscles becoming very loose, smooth, and relaxed.

And now imagine both legs becoming even more relaxed . . . sinking into the chair . . . very, very relaxed.

Buttocks

Now, focus on your buttocks. Begin to tighten up your buttocks, tighter and tighter. Hold that for a moment. Feel the tension . . . *relax* . . . Let it go. Let your hips and your buttocks become relaxed. Allow the whole lower part of your body to relax.

Abdominal Region

And now, focus your attention on your stomach, abdomen, and the lower part of your back. Begin to tense the muscles in your stomach; make it hard. Tighten it up. Notice the sensations in the stomach muscles, the abdomen, the lower part of the back. Just hold that for a moment . . . *relax* . . . let it go. Allow your back, your stomach, and your abdomen to become very relaxed . . . very, very relaxed.

Feel your entire body, now becoming more deeply relaxed.

Chest

Now take a deep breath and hold it. Notice the tension and pressure in your chest. Slowly let it out, allowing your muscles to relax. Allow your entire body to sink comfortably into the chair.

Shoulders

Now focus your attention on your shoulders and your shoulder blades. Increase the tension by pressing your shoulder blades back into the chair as if your shoulder blades want to touch behind your back. Notice the area where it is tense. And now, slowly, bring your shoulder blades up over the top of your chest as if your shoulders want to touch over the top of your body and hold that. Notice where it is tense . . . *relax* . . . Allow the shoulders and chest to relax . . . calm and relaxed . . . very relaxed.

Again, focusing on your shoulders, and leaving your arms relaxed, raise your shoulders up as if to touch your ears. Hold that for a moment. Notice the tension . . . *relax* . . . Let it go. Let your entire body sink into the chair as you allow all the muscles to become completely relaxed—very, very relaxed.

Now, imagine all the muscles in your body becoming even more relaxed.

Neck

Now focus on your neck. Tense the muscles in the front and the back of your neck as if your head were being pulled down towards your chest and pulled back at the same time. Hold that for a moment . . . *relax* . . . Let it go. Allow your neck muscles to begin to relax.

Allow that relaxation to spread down into your shoulders, into your back—very, very relaxed.

Jaw and Lips

While you continue to allow your other muscles to relax, focus on the muscles of your jaw and your lips. Gradually increase the tension by clenching your teeth, and simultaneously pull the corners of your mouth back into a very tight grimace. Feel the tension in your lips and your jaw. Hold that for a moment . . . *relax* . . . Let the muscles of your jaw and your lips become very relaxed. If you find that your mouth wants to drop open a little bit, that's okay. Your jaw muscles are beginning to relax. The tension is being smoothed away as the muscles begin to relax even more deeply—and then more deeply.

Eyes

Now focus on your eyes. Close your eyes tightly as if you were squinting. Notice the tension around your eyes, in your cheeks, and in your forehead. Hold that for a moment . . . *relax* . . . Let your eyes relax. Let your cheeks and your forehead relax. Feel the muscles become very smooth and relaxed.

Forehead

And now focus on your forehead and your scalp. Keeping your eyes closed, gradually raise your eyebrows up. Notice as you raise your eyebrows that your forehead and scalp muscles become very tense. You may feel a tightening band around your forehead and scalp. Hold that for a moment . . . *relax* . . . Let the muscles of your forehead and scalp become very, very relaxed. Allow the lines in your forehead to smooth away as all the muscles in your forehead, eyes, and scalp become very, very relaxed. Feel the relaxation spreading down through all the muscles of your face, through your neck, and down into your body.

Feel your entire body becoming very deeply, and comfortably relaxed.

I want you to think of this state of relaxation as the number 10. I'm going to start counting backwards from the number 10 down to 1. As I count each number, allow yourself to become noticeably more relaxed with each number I count. Starting at 10, 10 is the number that means the amount of relaxation that you feel right now. And now, relax even more at 9. And now, a little bit more at 8 ... 7 ... 6 ... 5 ... 4 ... 3 ... 2 ... one. Allow yourself to become completely relaxed. Just lie there for a moment. Feel the sensations of relaxation.

[3-5 minutes]

Now I am going to count forward from 1 to 5. As I count forward, let just enough energy flow back into your body to be alert, but calm and relaxed, just enough energy to be alert and refreshed and completely in control of your mind and body. One, two ... feeling more alert ... three, allow your eyelids to gradually open ... four, your eyes are open ... five, your eyes are open but remain quite still. ... Now begin to move your fingers. Move your hands and arms, stretch a little and move around.

References

1. Wolpe, J. *The Practice of Behavior Therapy.* Pergamon Press, New York, 1973.
2. Fuller, G. D. The organization and development of a multi-disciplinary biofeedback institute. In *Handbook of Physiological Feedback*, vol. 1. Autogenic Systems, Inc., Berkeley, 1976.
3. Bernstein, D. A. and Berkovec, T. D. *Progressive Relaxation Training: A Manual for the Helping Professions.* Research Press, Champaign, Ill., 1973.
4. Benson, H. *The Relaxation Response.* Academic Press, New York, 1975.

CHAPTER 18

Biofeedback Strategies in Headache Treatment

THOMAS H. BUDZYNSKI

Headache probably has plagued humankind for millions of years, although our more primitive ancestors perhaps were more successful at releasing tension through vigorous activity, thus alleviating or preventing a certain type of headache. Because of the necessary inhibition of many spontaneous, vigorous physical response patterns in modern societies, it is likely that headache is more prevalent today than ever before. For example, Ogden (1) found in a sample of 4634 individuals from a *nonclinical* population that 65% periodically suffered from headache. Some 48% had more than one headache per month. About 31% suffered more than two per month and over 1% had daily headaches.

Surprisingly, Waters and O'Connor (2) found that 46% of women with migraine never seek medical advice for their disorder, so that estimates of prevalence based on the number of patients seeking treatment would probably result in an underestimate. Since it is considered to be a less serious disorder, tension headache or muscle contraction headache is reported even less than migraine. Appenzeller (3), for example, showed that migraine patients constitute only 15–20% of those seen in headache clinics, the rest constituting a group identified as either tension headaches or those associated with depression.

The best estimates of headache incidence in the United States today indicate that there are about 20 million migraine and 100 million tension headache sufferers.

HEADACHE CLASSIFICATION

Sandoz Pharmaceuticals has an excellent publication, "Headache: The Commonest Symptom," in which is a list of the 15 categories of head pain:

1. Vascular headache of the migraine type, which includes classic and common migraine, cluster headache, hemiplegic and ophthalmoplegic migraine and lower-half headaches.
2. Muscle contraction headache (often referred to as muscle tension headache).
3. Combined headache (often referred to as mixed headache). These are headaches manifesting symptoms of both migraine and muscle tension headache.
4. Headache of nasal vasomotor reaction (often referred to as "sinus headache").
5. Headache of delusional, conversional, or hypochondriacal states: persistent headache without a demonstrable peripheral pain mechanism (sometimes referred to as "psychogenic headaches").
6. Nonmigrainous vascular headache (nonrecurrent dilation of cranial arteries).
7. Traction headaches: due to mechanical traction on intracranial structures by growing masses.
8. Headache due to overt inflammation of cranial structures (nonrecurrent inflammation, sterile, or infectious).
9. Referred pain from ocular structures.
10. Referred pain from aural structures.
11. Referred pain from nasal and sinus structures.
12. Referred pain from dental structures.
13. Referred pain from the neck and other structures of the cranium.
14. Cranial neuritides (nerve inflammation).
15. Cranial neuralgias: the most painful are the neuralgias of the fifth (trigeminal) and the ninth (glossopharyngeal) nerves.

For more detail on the differential diagnosis of head pain, see the excellent review by Andrasik and Baskin (4).

The biofeedback therapist who deals with headache disorders should be aware of these possible causes of head pain. Those categories to which biofeedback have been applied are: vascular headache of the migraine type, muscle contraction, combined and psychogenic.

Because of the possibility of organic involvement, it is important that a proper diagnosis be made before treatment begins. If the patient has not had recent and thorough neurological testing, especially if the headaches have been worsening, such tests may have to be carried out. Consultation with a neurologist is recommended.

DRUG TREATMENT

Almost all patients who are seen for biofeedback treatment for headache are taking some form of prescription medication. Many of these individuals are interested in a nondrug therapy because the medication no longer satisfactorily reduces the pain, because the side effects are too aversive, or because the medication costs are too high. If, however, the patient believes that the drugs are still useful in relieving pain or preventing headaches, then it is best to wait until the patient has achieved some degree of proficiency with the biofeedback learning before beginning a *gradual* withdrawal from the medications. In some instances where it appears that the drug may be interfering with the biofeedback learning, e.g., the patient is too tranquilized to focus on the feedback, reduction of the dosage may be necessary.

Medication Rebound

Medication rebound refers to a worsening of the headache in some cases as the medication wears off, or where medication is discontinued suddenly. Andrasik and Baskin (4) speak of analgesic abusers who start out having infrequent but severe headaches and who begin to use over-the-counter or prescription analgesics in increasing amounts. Relief is temporary and partial however, so they begin to use medication three to four times a day. Medication may be taken in anticipation of a headache as well. The frequent use of nonnarcotic analgesics such as aspirin and acetaminophen for chronic muscle-contraction headache often perpetuates and worsens head pain.

Patients do not come off favorite medications easily and may need to be systematically desensitized to slowly giving up the medication usage. One of our patients required three separate hierarchies: one for aspirin, one for diazepam (Valium), and one for ergotamine. The hierarchical scenes had her giving up the medications gradually. Following the completion of each hierarchy, she would begin to reduce the usage of that medication. All patients should be warned against giving up medications suddenly, and medication withdrawal should be coordinated closely with the physician.

Tension (Muscle Contraction) Headache Drugs

Tension or muscle contraction headaches are typically treated with an analgesic-sedative combination such as Fiorinal or Fiorinal with codeine. Overdosage is primarily manifested by drowsiness, although other side effects may include nausea, vomiting, constipation, dizziness, skin rash, and miosis.

Andrasik and Baskin (4) state that approximately 70%–80% of chronic scalp muscle-contraction headache patients obtain significant reductions in headache frequency with amitriptyline without daily analgesics. Dosage starts small and is built up gradually to 50 mg per day. One problem with amitriptyline is that it complicates EMG biofeedback training for muscle-contraction headache patients.

Vascular Headache Medication

In most instances, migraine headaches are treated with vasoconstricting drugs such as ergotamine tartrate (Cafergot and Gynergen, for example) for symptomatic relief and methoysergide maleate (Sansert) for prophylaxis. The side effects of the Cafergot and Gynergen types may include numbness and tingling in fingers and toes, muscle pains, weakness in the legs, precordial distress and pain, transient tachycardia or bradycardia, nausea, vomiting, localized edema, and itching. However, the side effects of Sansert can be particularly adverse. These include gastrointestinal symptoms, CNS symptoms (including insomnia, drowsiness, and unworldly dissociated symptoms), dermatological symptoms, edema, weight gain, and hematological manifestations.

The β-adrenergic blocking agent propranolol (Inderal) is sometimes effective for treatment of severe vascular headaches. In combination with Cafergot, Inderal appears to be quite useful in certain cases of cluster migraine.

When headache patients require hospitalization for their pain, they are often given Demerol. This drug is quite effective in reducing the pain; however, it can produce psychic as well as physical dependence. In some cases, the headaches diminish in intensity and/or frequency if Demerol is no longer available to the patient. Patients who abuse Demerol frequently resist its withdrawal, thus requiring skill on the part of the therapist in order to maintain the patient in therapy.

Antidepressants such as Elavil or Tofranil are sometimes effective if the headaches are associated with depression.

Tranquilizers may be prescribed for headache because these drugs tend to reduce the response to stress, a major cause of headache. Patients, however, often use too much of these medications and may appear to be quite drowsy and lethargic. In such a condition, they find it difficult to concentrate on the biofeedback. Additionally, these drugs and the anti-depressants have other side effects described in the *Physician's Desk Reference.*

MUSCLE CONTRACTION (TENSION) HEADACHE

By far the commonest type of headache, the muscle contraction headache, is usually described as a steady, dull pain located in the occiput or posterior region, often extending around to the forehead region. At times, the pain may be reported as located on one side only, but more often it has the "bandlike" quality of squeezing from all sides. Its frequency and duration are quite variable. It may occur daily and may last from a few hours to several months. This type of headache is believed to develop as a result of sustained contractions of the skeletal muscles about the face, scalp, neck, and shoulders (5–7).

VASCULAR HEADACHE OF THE MIGRAINE TYPE

The migraine headache, unlike the tension headache, usually is unilateral with the pain experienced as a sharp, throbbing sensation over the temple or back of the eye. The pain is quite severe, often requiring the client to lie down in a darkened room, avoiding noise and lights. Most migraine clients experience nausea and/or vomiting. The headache can last from 2 hours to several days, but typically is felt over an 8 hour period.

In *classic migraine*, which occurs in roughly 10% of migraine cases, there is a prodromal phase which lasts from 20–30 minutes and which is characterized primarily by visual disturbances such as scintillating flashing or sensations of flickering lights in the peripheral visual field. Zig-zag lines may appear in some cases. The head pain begins as the prodromal phase ends. It is thought that the prodromata are caused by the initial vasoconstriction of certain cerebral blood vessels. The pain begins as these vessels rebound into a vasodilative phase.

Common migraine, which occurs in 80–90% of all migraine cases, has little or no aura or prodromal phase. If there is a prodrome, it is more subtle and may last from several hours to several days before the headache begins. Some of these prodromal symptoms may include fatigue, water retention, nausea, and psychological changes.

Menstrual migraine is the term applied when the headache routinely appears during menses or within 3 days before or after cessation of flow. Women may experience a migraine-type headache after starting on birth control pills. Andrasik and Baskin (4) have suggested that the menstrual migraine is especially resistant to psychological approaches although relaxation and biofeedback training may help ease the pain. Medication is usually required in cases of this sort.

COMBINED MIGRAINE AND MUSCLE-CONTRACTION HEADACHE

Most biofeedback therapists see a great many individuals with combination headaches or, as they are sometimes called, *chronic mixed headaches.* These patients usually present with almost daily muscle-contraction headaches which, less frequently, will change into migraine. Typically, in the context of biofeedback training, the muscle-contraction headaches will decrease or be eliminated first, followed by the migraine condition.

CONVERSION HEADACHE

Andrasik and Baskin (4) note that a good portion of individuals classified as having "muscle-contraction headache" are actually conversion headache cases. In a personal communication, headache expert Dr. L. Kudrow suggested that although conversion headaches share many of the same characteristics as muscle-contraction headaches, one distinguishing feature of conversion headache is the presence of significant occupational and social dysfunction. Biofeedback would not be recommended in these cases.

CLUSTER MIGRAINE

The cluster headache is a vascular headache that occurs in clusters of one to three attacks a day for 4–6 weeks. They may not recur for 12 months and are often seasonal. The pain is quite excruciating and often described as, "an ice pick through my eyeball." It lasts for 30–45 minutes and is always unilateral and periorbital. There is a redness of the eye and excessive tears, and/or stuffiness or nasal discharge. The patient often paces and is unable to sit still. This type of headache typically occurs in men, and they usually possess a leonine appearance with a deeply furrowed face and ruddy complexion.

Biofeedback has not proven to be particularly useful for this type of headache, although instructing the patient in the RSA or diaphragmatic breathing pattern can help. A further strategy that is sometimes useful is teaching the patient to soften the facial musculature as much and as often as possible. This last goal may be assisted by frontalis EMG feedback.

HEADACHE PROCEDURES IN THE APPLIED SETTING

In clinical practice, it is very evident that biofeedback is not the sole therapy procedure. The actual type of therapy used to supplement the biofeedback training often depends upon the professional training of the practitioner. Thus, a medical clinic will rely heavily upon diagnostic procedures in order to rule out organic possibilities, and then augment the biofeedback with drug therapy. There will be little or no psychotherapy or behavior therapy. A psychiatric clinic will employ drug therapy and psychotherapy augmentation. The psychotherapy is often dynamic in nature. Psychology clinics often will focus on some form of behavior modification and stress coping as the augmenting type of therapy. Drug use is minimized.

Each type of clinic has both advantages and disadvantages. The medical clinic can, in more efficient fashion, rule out organic factors such as brain tumors and have an advantage in crisis intervention. On the other hand, the medical clinic is not suited for handling motivational problems, especially those which involve secondary-gain complications. This factor (a positive pay-off for manifesting a headache) is quite often associated with chronic migraine headache cases. If this confounding factor is not eliminated, there is the distinct possibility that the headaches will show only a temporary reduction, if indeed they are reduced at all. Thus, the headache patient may cycle through short periods of little or no headache (usually begun with the administration of a new drug) followed by long periods of increasing headache activity.

The psychiatric clinic probably lies on a continuum somewhere between neurology and psychology. Such a clinic however, is prepared to deliver crisis measures, and the psychiatric biofeedback milieu is also well suited to the handling of secondary-gain problems.

A psychologically oriented biofeedback clinic will often rely on psychometric testing to help define problem areas. There may be a heavy emphasis on cognitive as well as overt behavioral responses. Assertive training and role rehearsal are often used to augment the biofeedback and cognitive therapy. Behavior modification procedures are used to help transfer the stress-coping skills into everyday life situations. Clinics of this nature may enlist the consulting services of a neurologist or psychiatrist to aid in diagnostic and crisis intervention procedures.

Intake Interview

Headpain is multicausal, and the psychological factors are as diverse as the physical ones. Once you have ruled out organic possibilities, the job is to find out what are the psychological influences affecting this headache condition. I prefer to follow a chronological approach wherein I ask when the headaches began, when they worsened, if they did, and what was happening in the person's life at that point. Almost always, there was some stressful event taking place at the time of the headache onset, and possibly a second event at a time of worsening. I want to know all I can about the circumstances that occurred at the same time as headache onset or worsening. That includes the cognitive and behavioral as well as the emotional reactions to the situation. Often, an increase in job responsibility leads to an increase in stress and increased head pain. The patient is probably using many maladaptive cognitions at this time, which are triggering the headache stress reaction. Another possible factor is inappropriate or unassertive behavior on the job. Finally, the work environment itself may be inducing unusual stress in the patient and in other employees as well.

A careful cataloging of the various cognitive, behavioral, and emotional factors helps determine the therapy plan that will augment the biofeedback. Do not, however, underestimate the value of the biofeedback training itself because it not only helps change the physiology in a healthy direction, but instills in the patient a strong sense of control.

Another factor that often plays into this situation is the childhood environment. Did the mother or father role model head pain or other illness when crises occurred? Did the patient receive positive reinforcement for sick behavior when he/she was young? Was the patient given such negative scripting as, "you'll never amount to anything," or, "you are a sickly child?" Some patients try to compete with older, smarter siblings and find themselves suffering by comparison. In these cases, a chronic headache provides a reason for such performance.

POSSIBLE OUTCOMES OF BIOFEEDBACK TRAINING

When a patient with a severe headache problem receives biofeedback training, several outcomes are possible:

1. The patient learns to alter the response(s) voluntarily in the desired direction, and the headache gradually disappears.

2. The patient learns to alter the response(s) voluntarily in the desired direction, but the headaches do not diminish.

3. The patient cannot seem to learn to alter the response(s) in the desired direction, and yet the headaches disappear.

4. The patient cannot seem to learn to alter the response(s) in the desired direction, and the headaches do not diminish.

When outcome 3 is found, the clinician is alerted to a possible short-term placebo response. It is likely that the first major stressor to come along will bring back the headache activity. In these cases, the flexibility of a gradually increased spacing of training sessions over a 6-month period can handle "unexpected" headache breakthroughs.

Outcome 1 is ideal, of course, and usually requires no additional therapy. However, outcomes 2 and 4 do call for psychotherapy, behavior therapy, or holistic procedures. Thus, outcome 2 hints at a conscious or unconscious reluctance on the part of the patient to give up the headaches. Are the headaches self-serving in some way? Are unpleasant situations avoided by getting a headache? Are others manipulated by getting the headaches? Do the headaches bring sympathy and attention? These problems must be solved before the patient will give up the headaches. Life goals may need to be readjusted in keeping with reality. Acceptable alternative behaviors may have to be developed. In general, adaptive life-style changes need to be realized.

Outcome 4 may occur for the same reasons as in 2. However, the difficulty in learning with the biofeedback may also reflect a conscious or unconscious fear of deeply relaxing, letting go, or feeling vulnerable. This is especially likely to happen with patients who have, over a long period, adapted somewhat to a hyperaroused state. In these instances, the biofeedback can lead them momentarily to the "strangeness" of a truly relaxed state that may frighten them. The usual response is a sudden tightening up to restore the more familiar hyperstate. These clients may label the relaxed state as "painful," "frightening," "losing control," or "going to sleep." At times, the patient may report body image changes such as lengthening or shortening of limbs, bodily expansion, and/or rotating in space. Emotions may be brought close to the surface. In all of these instances, it is well to explain beforehand to the patient that any or all of these sensations may occur when the chronic hyperarousal pattern is broken, if only for a short period. Helpful also is the suggestion that the patient go ahead and "test the water" (relax deeply, if only momentarily) with the permission to voluntarily tighten up if necessary.

Some Difficulties with Deep Relaxation

A relaxed state may also free up forgotten memories often associated with emotional situations. More traditional therapy procedures can be used to deal with this material. The biofeedback is especially sensitive to such emotional cognitions when they arise out of a relaxed state. Thus, if a patient were relaxed and an intruding emotional or conflicting thought entered the mind, the biofeedback would reflect the physiological concomitant of that thought. The patient begins to develop the awareness that certain types of thoughts bring about distinct, possibly maladaptive physiological responses. Frontal EMG is very sensitive to these types of cognitions if they arise out of a relaxed level of low frontal EMG. On the other hand, in the presence of high frontal EMG, such thoughts may not be discriminated by the frontal EMG feedback.

In the early stages of biofeedback training, intruding thoughts often prevent the attainment of a relaxed state. Patients should be instructed to allow these thoughts to pass through rather than dwelling on them. Often, this instruction must be given not only at the beginning of each training session, but during the session as well. The "surging" frontal EMG pattern caused by intruding, arousing thoughts is a familiar one to experienced biofeedback clinicians.

Perhaps the commonest difficulty patients have with biofeedback is simply trying too hard to drive the feedback in the desired direction. This "active" striving mode is a difficult pattern to break for some individuals. Because there is the danger of frustrating the patient at this point, performance anxiety must be minimized. Gradually, the active striver learns that adopting a more passive strategy brings about the desired change. It appears that a patient experiencing difficulty in trying too hard to control should be asked to focus on breathing (from the abdomen, not the upper chest) and muscle relaxation. While doing so, the patient should simply observe the feedback and not try to control it. At the St. Luke Medical Center, Bellevue, Washington, we provide patients with the six-part cassette tape relaxation program. Often, they will use this program as a beginning strategy, refining it with the biofeedback.

The passive mode can be illustrated by a gentle manipulation of the patient's arm by the trainer. With the instruction to simply "Let go, let me do the moving; you just observe what it feels like," the trainer grasps the patient's arm by the wrist and elbow and guides it through a series of slow random movements until the arm is felt to free up. If there is extensor EMG feedback from that arm, it will dramatically decrease at the moment the arm "goes passive." Similarly, a tense jaw musculature can be freed by gentle manipulation, although this is more difficult than allowing the arm to "let go." Some patients may require that these manipulations be done several times during initial training sessions.

The active rather than passive striving may have its greatest effect during skin temperature feedback. This procedure, which is most commonly used for migraine conditions, requires a decrease in sympathetic tone specifically with regard to vasomotor control of peripheral blood flow. Some patients have great difficulty in "hand warming," as it is commonly labeled. The cassette tape program mentioned above is very useful for providing a successful warming strategy; however, there are others that may be effective as well. Here is a partial listing of additional strategies that have been successful for some individuals.

1. Visual imagery of hands warming, e.g., on a beach, near an oven, in warm water, warm family relationships.

2. Proprioceptive imagery of blood pulsing in fingers, feeling of warmth in the webbing between the fingers, the feel of hands heated by imagined battery-heated mittens.

3. Religious themes, e.g., "God's grace flows into my body down my arms and legs and warms my hands and feet."

4. Abdominal breathing—regular, rhythmic breathing with emphasis on the abdominal region. Instruction might be, "As you exhale, imagine the blood flowing into your hands and feet."

5. Ensuring very low forearm EMG levels with EMG feedback.

6. Massaging from the shoulders and working down to fingertips.

7. Whirling arms around to get a centrifuge effect of blood pooling in the hands.

8. Increasing room temperature. Many times, this will break loose a recalcitrant peripheral vasomotor response system.

A SYSTEMS APPROACH

In our work, we have employed a systematic sequence of biofeedback training. This procedure is detailed along with flow charts in the BioMonitoring Applications cassette called "Systems Approach to Biofeedback Training" (Cat. No. T-18). The biofeedback is augmented with the six-phase home practice relaxation cassette series. Training is carried out until certain criteria have been reached. Thus, a patient with high levels of forearm EMG will be given forearm EMG feedback until he can demonstrate less than 2.0 µV over the extensor muscle. He will next progress to frontal EMG until he is able to decrease this level to less than 2.5 µV in the case of tension headache or 4.0 μV in cases of migraine.

Since most tension headache patients find relief simply through muscle relaxation, it usually is not necessary to do temperature training with them; but mixed headaches and migraines usually do require the additional training of the skin temperature feedback, and such patients learn to produce hand temperatures greater than 90°F regularly. When transitioning from one type of feedback to another, it is important to ensure that in the effort of focusing on the new feedback, the previous learning is not ignored. Consequently, we use a mixer system (model AM200 from BioFeedback Systems of Boulder, Colorado). The mixer allows any combination of auditory feedback to be programmed through the patient's headphone set. Thus, in transitioning from frontal EMG to hand temperature feedback, the patient will hear a tone tracking both the frontal EMG and the hand temperature signal. This simultaneous feedback has proven invaluable with multiple response training. The systems flow charts provide a structure that details when transitions should take place.

Quantification of Headache Pain

For tension headache studies begun in the late 1960s at the University of Colorado Medical Center, we developed a rating scale for headache pain. As shown in Figure 18.1, the pain is quantified into five categories, ranging from "0" for no headache to "5" for an incapacitating headache. Patients rate their pain or lack of it once each waking hour. Various schemes can be used for data extraction from the daily chart. One can quantify headache frequency, intensity, or the average amount of pain per waking hours or per 24 hours. A formula for a 24-hour average (Id) is shown in Figure 18.1.

Medication information can be charted on the same daily graphs. The small arrows drawn on the graph indicate when the medication was taken and which category of medication was used. Thus, the patient took one capsule or pill from Category B at 10 a.m. and then another one at 4 p.m.

Therapy with Three General Systems

Although we may concentrate biofeedback on a peripheral vasomotor system or a skeletal muscle system, there are three more general response systems that we consider. These are the cognitive, the physiological, and the overt behavioral. We attempt in the initial sessions to assess where the maladaptiveness may lie. Thus, a patient may complain of headaches that occur daily. We may find that he believes in doing a 100% job at all times. This striving for perfection, which has become habitual, may derive from his need to have everyone like him all the time. This incorrect premise, "Everyone must love me all the time," can be challenged, or the patient can be led more gently to the conclusion that this premise first of all does exist for him, second, that it is in error, and third, that he can change it. Finally, the defeating self-statements or negative cognitions that derive from the wrong premise can be identified and eliminated with the subsequent substitution of positive self-statements.

In the session following the initial interview, we assess the physiological state of the individual under three conditions: relaxation, stress, and recovery. Often, someone can look very relaxed during the first phase but will then show great arousal during the stress (serial 7's) or recover slowly after the stress. On the other hand, some individuals may produce very normal responses in all three phases, i.e., heart rate, EMG, skin temperature, and electrodermal response (EDR) may show relaxed levels at first, then arouse moderately under stress only to recover quickly after the stress. Such a person most likely would not require biofeedback training. In most instances, patients will show evidence of maladaptive functioning in one or more of the phases. Quite often, they will produce high tension or autonomic arousal during the relaxation phase. In many instances, they show slow recovery of responses after being stressed. We have been gathering data with this "stress profile" procedure on large numbers of patients including those with cancer, essential hypertension, anxiety, migraine and tension headache, cardiac problems, and normals. These profiles may prove to be an important diagnostic tool.

SPECIFIC BIOFEEDBACK CONSIDERATIONS IN THE CLINIC SETTING

Most clinicians have their own paradigms for biofeedback applications to headache disorders; however, there are some commonalities. Relevant muscle groups are trained to relax with EMG feedback, and finger temperature feedback is almost always used to develop the skill of hand warming. Interest in

INTENSITY RATING SCALE

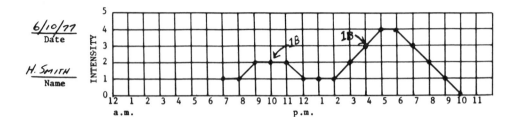

SYMPTOM INTENSITY

5 Unable to perform any work or social
   activities; confined to bed.
4 Unable to concentrate; can do simple tasks.
3 Pain moderate, can work however if
   necessary.
2 Pain irritating, can work and engage in
   social activities; pain can be ignored
   at times.
1 Pain there if attended to; otherwise ignored.
0 No pain.

MEDICATION RATING

A Aspirin, Tylenol, Datril, Excedrin.
B Darvon, Fiorinal, Midrin.
C Valium, Librium, Tranxene, Vistaril.
D Cafergot, Gynergen, Sansert.
E Alcohol (1 beer, glass of wine,
   highball, etc.).
F Codeine, Emperin w/codeine, Percodan.
G Elavil, Triavil, Etrafon, Sinequan,
   Aventyl, Trofanil, Norpramin.
H Demerol.
I Other_____.

$$Id = \frac{(1 \times 6) + (2 \times 5) + (3 \times 4) + (4 \times 2)}{24} = 1.50$$

Hourly average for this day.
This daily average can be
averaged over seven days to
get the weekly mean as
plotted in Figure

Figure 18.1. Pain intensity rating scale for patients and the formula for deriving an hourly average *(Id)*.

respiration patterns is increasing among clinicians. Of course, the biofeedback training is used in the context of an overall behavioral approach that includes cognitive skills training in most cases. Finally, the transfer of training to the real life situation outside the clinic environment is facilitated by a number of procedures including some variation of systematic desensitization and home practice cassette relaxation programs.

EMG Feedback

The muscle groups of the head, neck, and shoulders are to a great extent involved in cases of muscle contraction headache and to a slightly lesser extent, in migraine or vascular headaches. Over the years, the question has arisen as to the most effective site for the EMG feedback. A recent study by Hudzinski and Lawrence (8) sheds some light on this question. These researchers compared the effectiveness of three popular forms of EMG feedback for headache applications: the original bifrontal placement, the newer "Cram-Scan," and the more recent Schwartz-Mayo placement.

The Cram-Scan procedure (9) involves a hand-held preamplifier with two-post style, silver/silver chloride sensors that are set in a fixed distance of 2 cm, and a wrist sensor serving as a reference. The posts are touched to the left and right aspects of the frontalis, temporalis, masseter, sternocleidomastoid, and second cervical muscle regions. The bifrontal placement was simulated by taking the left and right frontalis activity from the Cram-Scan. (It should be noted that the traditional bipolar frontalis placement employs sensors set at a greater distance apart and usually has a bandpass of 100–1000 Hz, as contrasted with the 100–200 Hz used in this study).

The Schwartz-Mayo (10) procedure involves a bilateral placement with one active sensor placed over the frontalis, the second active on the ipsilateral posterior neck, and the reference on the side of the neck. This placement was best able to discriminate headache from nonheadache activity as compared with the Cram-Scan, which in turn discriminated better than the frontalis alone. Of note also was the fact that the left side registered higher readings than the right. One might conclude therefore that a single EMG placement, that of the Schwartz-Mayo model, situated on the left side could produce the most sensitive EMG arrangement for both diagnosis and feedback if one had only a single EMG biofeedback unit.

Another EMG site that can be used for feedback training is the bilateral trapezius/cervical spinalis muscle group. Besides static levels, this placement allows left/right neck rotational patterns to be monitored. These dynamic tests are detailed in Cram's manual on Clinical EMG (9).

Temporomandibular Joint (TMJ) Pain

The stresses prevalent in our fast-paced culture cause many individuals to clench their jaws during the day and even during sleep. Such mechanical stress applied to the TMJ can result in severe, lancing pain in the temporalis and masseter areas as well as tenderness over the joint itself. Although the Cram-Scan checks the EMG levels of the temporalis and masseter individually, another sensitive placement for this condition has one active sensor over the belly of the masseter and the other active on the temporalis. The reference sensor is placed over the mastoid process behind the ear. A bilateral placement is preferred because the left side can be compared with the right in a static and dynamic state. Opening the mouth and gently biting down often reveals assymetries. Biofeedback is used to train the patient to minimize and balance the left/right EMG readings. Biofeedback therapists can work with oral surgery specialists to ensure that the patient develops the skill to relax this musculature, thus enabling a better result whether or not surgery is performed. If the patient does not learn to relax these muscles, the postsurgical results can be very disappointing because the continued clenching will eventually undo the effects of the surgery. In the case of a secretary who suffered from severe head pain when she was overloaded at work, we found that her masseter EMG remained at normal levels until she reached a typing speed above 40 wpm, at which time the EMG began to increase in proportion to the typing speed. She received EMG biofeedback while typing and learned to keep the EMG low even while typing at her maximum rate of 90 wpm. She then practiced relaxing her jaw at work. Her TMJ pain ceased soon after. (See also Chapter 27.)

Thermal Training

Feedback of finger temperature remains one of the primary types of biofeedback, although some clinicians feel that this measure should be used more as a monitor of the state of the autonomic nervous system rather than used as a biofeedback source. Placement of the sensor, room air currents, varying room temperature, and seasonal temperature fluctuations complicate the problem of separating these factors from stress-induced peripheral vasoconstriction. However, in the hands of the experienced biofeedback trainer/therapist, thermal feedback is a sensitive enough indicator of the autonomic state to warrant its continued use in headache conditions. In the form of a temperature-sensitive liquid crystal element that can be taken home and worn on the finger, temperature feedback can be used to provide information to the therapist and patient as to the approximate degree of relaxation obtained during home practice as well as the degree of stress in the work environment.

The therapist in private practice often faces the dilemma of whether to attempt to train a given patient to meet the criterion of 92 or more degrees of finger temperature, even though his/her symptoms are significantly reduced or even eliminated and low EMG levels have been attained. It is probably true that the degree of skill required to reach such a criterion would help ensure a better long-term follow-up. However, economic and time considerations have to be taken into account. We believe that emphasizing the importance of the transfer skills and the cassette home training program can help ensure the long-term result even if certain biofeedback criteria have not been attained in a reasonable number of sessions. Our long-term follow-up data indicate that former clients tend to fall back on the home practice cassette program when and if the symptoms recur.

Respiratory Sinus Arrhythmia (RSA)

One of the most important skills that can be taught to the patient is proper breathing technique. The typical upper chest or thoracic breathing pattern, which most of us are taught from early childhood, is not conducive to deep relaxation. In contrast, diaphragmatic breathing facilitates relaxation and thus fosters the development of greater parasympathetic tone in the autonomic nervous system. When heart rate is presented in line graph form on a biofeedback computer screen, it can be seen to follow a sinusoidal pattern correlated with the respiration pattern when the patient is successfully breathing from the diaphragm. This pattern has been called respiratory sinus arrhythmia (RSA) (11).

If the patient is not breathing from the diaphragm, the RSA will not appear on the screen. With instructions to minimize upper chest and maximize "belly" breathing, most patients learn to produce the RSA in fairly short order. They are then advised to practice this type of breathing as much as possible. Many clinicians who have used this type of training are convinced that the production of RSA is a very important step in the reduction of stress-related symptoms, including headache.

Sequencing

Does one train on EMG first, then thermal, and then RSA? Should all of these be presented to the client simultaneously? Some time ago, when we first began our systematic approach to low-arousal training, we (11) proposed a specific sequence beginning with forearm extensor EMG because it is perhaps the easiest over which to gain control. After the patient met a certain criterion for this placement, the therapist proceeded to train the patient on frontalis EMG. Eventually, the patient met the criterion for relaxation level of the frontalis, and the patient was then sequenced to thermal training. A number of clinicians today feel that one can train on both EMG and thermal in the same session with both feedbacks available on a computer monitor or mixed together if auditory. Some clinicians prefer to pace the biofeedback sessions with the home practice program or vice versa. The question is, what sequence does the therapist feel comfortable using with a given patient? Ultimately, the patient's ability to control the EMG and the peripheral temperature can best dictate the most appropriate sequence. One patient will find it easier to control the temperature, while another will do much better with EMG. Generally, patients find that the EMG is the easier because it is at least partly under conscious control.

Transfer Skills

This term applies to all the procedures used to help generalize the stress-coping skills outside the clinic. This would include the liquid crystal temperature sensors in their many forms, home practice cassette programs, and reminder dots (brightly colored small stick-on dots that are placed on the watch face, telephone, steering wheel, refrigerator, mirror, and wherever else your gaze happens to fall. Get them in office supply stores). These dots, when noticed by the patient, remind her/him to check for maladaptive thoughts, behavior, physiology, and posture. They also remind the client to do the home practice, exercise, eat right, do a brief stress-coping procedure, etc.

Brief stress-coping techniques such as Stroebel's well-known "quieting response" can help during a busy day since it takes less than a minute to carry out (see Chapter 23). Less well known is a procedure we generated to help extremely busy Type A individuals. One of them had told us that the only time during the working day that he wasn't surrounded by people was when he went to the restroom. With his help, we devised a relaxation procedure that could indeed be carried out in a restroom. Going into the stall, the client first loosens his shirt collar and belt. Next, while sitting, he leans forward and allows his arms to hang down as he bends forward. The client lets gravity gently pull the head down a little more with each exhalation. After 10 breaths, he comes back upright slowly. This exercise relieves tension in the shoulders, neck, and back and is a real help with muscle-contraction headaches particularly.

There are any number of cognitive coping skills and behavioral change procedures that help facilitate the transfer of skills into the world of everyday living, but these are beyond the scope of this chapter. Suffice it to say that patients should be able to recognize and to handle maladaptiveness in thought, behavior, physiology, and even in the environment itself.

Systematic desensitization, when monitored with the biofeedback, can be one of the most effective transfer procedures (12). After the patient has acquired the relaxation skills in the clinic, he is asked to visualize himself in stressful situations as he maintains himself in a relaxed state with the biofeedback assisting. A variation on this procedure is to have the patient allow some buildup of stress as he visualizes and then attempts to relax as quickly as possible again. The patient thus gets practice at recovery from a stress response in his body. As with traditional systematic desensitization, the stressful scenes are arranged in a hierarchy with the less stressful scenes visualized first. During the scene visualizations, the patient sees himself thinking and behaving adaptively.

Mitchell and Mitchell (13) have reported that the use of systematic desensitization along with relaxation training could significantly augment the treatment effect of the relaxation alone. The patients treated with systematic desensitization showed a 76% reduction in migraine frequency and a 50% reduction in duration of each headache, compared with a 24% reduction in frequency and no reduction in duration of headache for those patients treated with relaxation alone.

Finally, perhaps the most important characteristic of biofeedback training is the subtle instillation in the client of the conviction that he or she can now control most aspects of life. This somewhat unrealistic attitude, a common phenomenon in biofeedback, nonetheless is quite helpful to the clients as they try out their new, healthier life-styles.

References

1. Ogden, H. D. Headache studies. Statistical data. I. Procedure and sample distribution. J. Allergy, *23*: 58–75, 1952.
2. Waters, W. E. and O'Connor, P. J. The clinical validation of a headache questionnaire. In *Background to Migraine*, vol. 3. William Heinemann Medical Books, London, 1970.
3. Appenzeller, O. Getting a sore head from banging it on the wall. Headache, *13*: 131–132, 1973.
4. Andrasik, F. and Baskin, S. Headache. In *Medical Factors and Psychological Disorders*, edited by R. L. Morrison and A. S. Bellack, Plenum Press, New York, 1987.
5. Bakal, D. A. Headache: a biopsychological perspective. Psychol. Bull., *82*: 367–382, 1975.
6. Martin, M. J. Muscle-contraction headache. Psychosomatics, *13*: 16–19, 1972.
7. Ostfeld, A. M. *The Common Headache Syndromes: Biochemistry, Pathophysiology, Therapy.* Charles C Thomas, Springfield, Ill., 1962.
8. Hudzinski, L. G. and Lawrence, G. S. Significance of EMG electrode placement models and headache findings. *Headache*, 28: 30–35, 1988.
9. Cram, J. *Clinical EMG: Muscle Scanning and Diagnostic Manual for Surface Recordings.* Clinical Resources and J & J: Seattle, Washington, 1986.
10. Nevins, B. G. and Schwartz, M. S. An alternative placement for EMG electrodes in the study and treatment of tension headaches. Paper presented at the 16th annual meeting of the Biofeedback Society of America, New Orleans. Wheatridge, Colorado: Biofeedback Society of America (April, 1985).
11. Fried, R. *The Hyperventilation Syndrome: Research and Clinical Treatment.* Johns Hopkins University Press, Baltimore, 1987.
12. Budzynski, T. H., Stoyva, J. M. and Peffer, K. E. Biofeedback techniques in psychosomatic disorders. In *Handbook of Behavioral Therapies*, edited by E. Foa and A. Goldstein. John Wiley & Sons, New York, 1978.
13. Mitchell, K. R. and Mitchell, D. M. Migraine: An exploratory treatment application of programmed behavior therapy techniques. *Psychosom. Res.,* *15*: 137–157, 1971.

CHAPTER 19

General and Specific Applications of Thermal Biofeedback

ELMER E. GREEN
ALYCE M. GREEN

Before considering applications of temperature training, it is useful to review some of the neuroanatomical and psychoneurological facts that make clear how it is possible to self-regulate an autonomic process.

Figure 19.1 (1) gives an idea of the mind-body synthesis in a somewhat different manner from preceding chapters. The diagram is a representation of processes that appear to occur simultaneously in two domains, the neurological domain (voluntary and involuntary) and the psychological domain (conscious and unconscious). The upper half of the diagram represents conscious-voluntary processes, that is, processes of which we normally have awareness when we wish it. The lower half of the diagram represents unconscious-involuntary processes. The neurological locus for conscious processes seems to be primarily in the cerebral cortex and the craniospinal apparatus.

The locus for unconscious processes seems to be primarily in the subcortical brain and spinal area and in the autonomic nervous system. Someone at a meeting of the American Medical Association called the cerebral cortex "the screen of consciousness." Then the subcortex and other normally involuntary parts of the nervous system might be called the screen of the unconscious. In any event, through proper training, the involuntary can often become voluntary, and one can become conscious, in a certain way, of what was previously unconscious.

Every perception of outside-the-skin (OUTS) events (see Fig. 19.1, upper left box) has associated with it (arrow 1) electrical activity in both conscious and unconscious structures, those involved in mental and emotional responses. The two boxes labeled *emotional and*

mental response . . . have been placed at the middle of the diagram, divided by the horizontal center line into conscious and unconscious parts, in order to indicate their two-part nature. The next box, called *limbic response*, is placed in the unconscious section of the diagram, although some neural pathways lead from limbic structures directly to cortical regions, implying that "information" from limbic processes can reach consciousness. Every bit of perceptual information that goes to the cortex also goes to the limbic brain and makes electrophysiological changes there, whether we are conscious of the stimulus or not.

The limbic system has been intensely studied in both animals and humans in the years since Papez' historic paper (2) outlined the possible functions of the limbic system in emotional responses. MacLean coined the phrase "visceral brain" for the limbic system (3), and others have referred to it as the emotional brain or the fight-or-flight brain, but the important point is that emotional states are reflected in, or correlated with, electrophysiological activity in the limbic system.

Of major significance to a satisfactory psychophysiological rationale is the fact that the limbic system is connected by many pathways (arrow 3) to the central "control panel" of the brain, the hypothalamus. Although the hypothalamus weighs only about 4 g, it regulates a large part of the body's automatic neural machinery. In addition, it controls the pituitary gland, the so-called master gland at the top of the hormonal hierarchy. Its action precipitates or triggers changes in the homeostatic levels of other glandular structures. In other words, limbic signals are converted to autonomic and hormonal signals through the transducing machinery of the hypothalamus

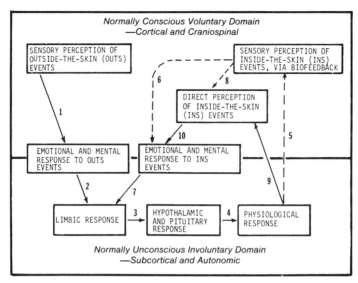

Figure 19.1. Simplified operational diagram of "self-regulation" of psychophysiological events and processes. Sensory perception of OUTS events, stressful or otherwise *(upper left box)*, leads to a physiological response along arrows *1* to *4*. If the physiological response is "picked up" and fed back (arrow *5*) to a person who attempts to control the "behavior" of the feedback device, then arrows *6* and *7* come into being, resulting in a "new" limbic response. This response in turn makes a change in "signals" transmitted along arrows *3* and *4*, modifying the original physiological response. A cybernetic loop is thus completed, and the dynamic equilibrium (homeostasis) of the system can be brought under voluntary control. Biofeedback practice, acting in the opposite way to drugs, increases a person's sensitivity to INS events and arrow *8* develops, followed by the development of arrows *9* and *10*. External feedback is eventually unnecessary because direct perception of INS events becomes adequate for maintaining self-regulation skills. Physiological self-control through classical yoga develops along the route of arrows *7-3-4-9-10-7*, but for control of specific physiological and psychosomatic problems, biofeedback training seems more efficient.

and pituitary. Left to themselves, the hypothalamus and pituitary maintain physiological balance in response to variations in internal feedback signals from tissues and organs, but they do not initiate change as far as we know. Change seems to proceed from the limbic level of the control hierarchy as implied, for example, by Masserman's work with sham rage in cats (4). And the limbic system, in turn, responds in animals to perception, as shown by several dozen ethological studies, and to both perception and *imagination* in humans. It is on this latter fact that *self*-regulation of autonomic processes rests. When a person watches a temperature feedback meter, it is not the movement of the needle that brings about self-regulation of blood flow; rather, it is the imagining and visualization of what the movement signifies to that person (e.g. increasing warmth in the hand) that leads to voluntary control.

These psychoneurological concepts make it easy to see how news from a telephone message can cause a person to faint, or, in some persons, to suddenly have a surge of high blood pressure. The perception of OUTS events leads to limbic-hypothalamic-glandular responses, and, of course, physiological change is the inevitable consequence. Both genetics and previous conditioning are factors in determining the specific nature of the response, but neither can be construed as voluntary, and neither is fully independent of the visualization factor in regulating effects.

FEEDBACK

Most of this was known by 1960, but what was not known was the fact that if we can detect what is going on inside our skin, we can often voluntarily change it in a direction we choose. If a physiological change from the box at the lower right in the diagram is "picked up" by a sensitive electrical transducer and displayed to the person with a meter (arrow 5) or made audible by a tone so as to feed back physiological information, then there ensues (arrow 6) a "new" mental-emotional response, a response to normally unconscious inside-the-skin (INS) information. The new mental-emotional response is associated with a "new" limbic response (arrow 7) that combines with, or replaces, or modifies, the original response (arrow 2). This modified limbic response in turn develops a "new" pattern of hypothalamic firing and pituitary secretion and changes the physiological state. It is this physiological perturbation that is revealed by the feedback monitor to the conscious cortex. Thus, a biocybernetic control loop is established as a result of providing the conscious cortex with information about normally unconscious INS processes.

This feedback loop is of profound significance. For the first time in human history, many unconscious and involuntary processes, having formerly sent feedback signals only to the hypothalamus, now give feedback signals to the cortex. Closing the biocybernetic loop means bridging the normal gap between conscious and unconscious processes, voluntary and involuntary, and, as already mentioned, it is accomplished in the case of voluntary self-regulation through imagination and visualization.

In learning voluntary control of normally unconscious processes, we do not become directly aware of the neural pathways and muscle fibers involved, any more than we become aware of what cerebral and subcerebral nerves are involved in playing tennis. When we get external objective feedback, we can learn to modify the internal "set-up" and bring about changes in the desired direction. Everything that is learned, without exception, is learned with feedback of some kind, whether it involves the corticostriate system or the corticosubcortico-autonomic system.

Biofeedback information (arrow 5) is sometimes not needed for more than a few weeks in learning to control a psychosomatic disorder, and we can deduce that biofeedback is not addictive because voluntary internal control is finally established, rather than dependence on an external agency. In this, biofeedback training differs considerably from drug use. Drug dosage often needs to be increased as time goes by in order to overcome the body's decreasing sensitivity through physiological ha-

bituation. With biofeedback, however, sensitivity (to subtle internal cues) is increased, and this increased sensitivity (arrow 8) is an essential step in closing the internal control loop, so that the use of external feedback devices need be only temporary.

With the above rationale in mind, it is easy to understand the purpose of procedures generally used in clinical temperature training and to discuss the effects of temperature training in preventive medicine, general medicine, and psychotherapy. Before turning to specific applications, it is useful to discuss, in addition to the rationale, some general indoctrination procedures that are particularly useful in all therapeutic applications.

We believe that one of the most effective aspects of clinical biofeedback training, whether it be temperature, muscle tension, or brain wave feedback, consists of giving the patient a thorough explanation of the rationale outlined above. We do this with physicians, psychologists, carpenters, ministers, homemakers—everyone. It provides a set within which physiological self-regulation is relatively easy to learn. In terms of a popular metaphor, it is as if the left cortex must be persuaded of, or at least tolerate the possibility of, the rational nature of neurological self-regulation before it can allow the right cortex to construct a psychophysiological visualization (pictorial, verbal, or kinesthetic).

Professional people and scholars tend to find the discussion of the rationale of considerable value in learning thermal control, and quite often, after two or three training sessions, they remark that they are beginning to understand how the entire process works, and are beginning to believe (correlated with a limbic process, in our view) that maybe they can make it work for them. This is in contrast to Johannes Schultz' observation that pedants and other scholarly types were the ones most difficult to work with in autogenic training. They could think of many reasons why warmth exercises could not work, and their consequent *attitude* (again correlated with a limbic response) interfered with learning.

The training set achieved by the rationale makes it possible for the patient to at least hypothesize that he or she can learn how to self-regulate normally involuntary physiological processes. If any of our educated trainees say that this may only strengthen a placebo effect, it is necessary to point out that there is an error in not realizing that the *placebo effect is merely the effect of unconscious visualization.* When increased blood flow is achieved through the use of a sugar pill, a placebo, the effect almost invariably goes away as time passes because it is attached to a sterile medical factor. But when the self-regulation effect is attached to one's own volitional effort, then a skill can be developed embodying genuine self-regulation of the autonomic nervous system. It does not fade away any more than knowing how to ride a bicycle fades away. The patient must thoroughly understand that self-regulation is not miraculous, merely practical.

Before beginning temperature training, we explain that the main reason we have not seen many examples of vascular self-regulation without biofeedback is because there is no sensitive sensory feedback system to make us conscious of vascular behavior (until we become sensitized to subtle internal cues that are generally ignored). From an evolutionary point of view, it was counterproductive. When a bear was coming into the cave at night, it would not have been useful for our ancestors to have to say, "blood pressure come up, heart rate come up, adrenalin increase," or try to regulate any other autonomic processes. Nowadays, however, we are not fighting the environment outside our skins as much as handling a psychosocial environment, and psychosocial stresses literally get under our skins. They strike directly through the perceptual apparatus, impinge on limbic, hypothalamic, and pituitary mechanisms.

We conclude the explanation of psychophysiological training to patients by pointing out that it is not stress that kills us, but our reaction to stress. Psychosomatic disease is, by definition, a medically undesirable physiological response to psychological stress. It is not in the head, but in the body, contrary to public opinion.

VISUALIZATION

Just as Johannes Schultz found that heaviness and warmth exercises were prerequisites in autogenic training to the successful use of the organ-specific "formulas" (5), so we have found that electromyographic (EMG) feedback and temperature self-control are useful as preliminary learnings for patients with *any* kind of problem—physical, emotional, or mental. If the body becomes quiet, both in the striate and autonomic domains, then it is often possible to extend control, through visualization, over organ systems for which no feedback is available. This has not been demonstrated in research, but has been merely observed in clinical situations such as follows.

A research assistant who helped in our weekly biofeedback workshop for professionals had been taking an inordinate amount of sick leave for a number of weeks. Her physician said she had an infection similar to a strep throat, but is was not responding to medication. She agreed to try the following self-regulation visualization, which we suggested she use three times a day, after relaxing into the heaviness and warmth state as a preliminary step: Shift the feeling of warmth from the hands to the throat and visualize a great increase in blood flow to the infected areas of the throat, bringing whatever biochemicals and immunoagents are needed to totally eradicate the problem and return the tissues to normal.

The next day, she came to work on time and said that the visualization had resulted in a noticeable throbbing and warmth in her throat, and now her throat felt normal for the first time in several weeks. All was well until the end of the day, when she suddenly appeared with a face that was pink from her upper lip to her hairline, and with bloodshot eyes. Alarmed, we asked what had happened. She explained that she had also had a virus infection in her eyes for the last 3 months and could not wear her contact lenses. And she thought that if the visualization helped her throat, it also would help her eyes. She tried it. Now what should she do?

Perhaps it was not wise for someone with such a strong psyche-soma response mechanism to use that visualization with something as delicate as the eye, but now that she had done it, the best thing was to modify the visualization and instruct the body first to complete what it had started and then to cool the eyes and the surrounding tissues to normal. The next day she arrived at work wearing her contact lenses and said that both her throat and eyes were fine. Neither trouble returned in the 10 months before she moved away.

For many patients, it is a new idea that the body must become quiet before it will respond to one's own visualized instructions. When explaining this concept for the first time, we sometimes say that trying to program the body while it is not quiet is like trying to make recordings with a tape machine while it is in "playback" mode. Unless the device is in "record" mode, it will not record. And our bodies seem to be almost always in playback mode, even when we are asleep. The limbic system appears to be almost always active rather than receptive, whether we are asleep or awake. In fact, it is possible to worry more while dreaming than when awake.

TEMPERATURE TRAINING PROCEDURES

Training procedures differ somewhat from clinic to clinic across the country, but most of them contain in one form or another most of the items outlined below:

1. After discussing the rationale and answering related questions, 15–30 minutes are spent identifying the patient's own treatment goals.

2. We explain what the feedback machine does, how it is used, and what the immediate temperature training goals are. Then we attach the thermistor to a finger of the dominant hand and conduct a 15-minute autogenic session with heaviness and warmth and inner quietness phrases. During this time, we record on the phrase sheet at the beginning of each phrase (Fig. 19.2) the deviations from starting temperature, 88.5°F in this example. (Our meters show zero at the center and go from $-2.5°F$, 25 divisions, at the left, to $+2.5°F$, 25 divisions, at the right. Starting temperature is read from a digital-dial potentiometer which is used to "zero" the meter at starting time.) Numbers at the left on the phrase sheet show decreases in tenths of a degree below the starting temperature of 88.5°F. In the same way, numbers at the right represent increases in temperatures.

We turn the machine away from the patient in this first session and suggest that usually it is easier to visualize the desired changes at first with the eyes closed. At the end of the autogenic session, patients write a short summary of body feelings, emotions and thoughts during the session, before being shown the temperature changes recorded during the session. Then their report is discussed and correlated, if possible, with the recorded temperature changes.

3. To conclude the first session, the machine is turned toward the patient, and he or she goes through the procedure of turning on and adjusting the machine and then using the phrases silently, in a true feedback situation. If the patient feels comfortable with procedures and with the machine, it is taken home for twice-daily practice. If not, a second practice session is given on another day. In the meantime, however, the autogenic phrases are used once in the morning and once in the evening, every day if possible.

4. Once a day at the end of a home session, a short report is made, as shown in Figure 19.3. This report is an important part of the training program and will be discussed below under applications in psychotherapy. For long-term evaluation of progress, we ask the patient to fill out, at home, a Spielberger State/Trait Anxiety Inventory and a Personal Orientation Inventory and return them at the next lab session. At termination of training, we ask for these questionnaires to be answered again. Whenever applicable, we ask the patients to keep records not only of temperature, but blood pressure, drug consumption, hours of sleep, etc.

5. After a week of home training, we suggest that trainees begin to discontinue the use of autogenic phrases and to replace them with their own personal visualizations relating to temperature control. For example, at first, some patients imagine lying on a warm beach, but later the control of temperature is often reduced to turning on an almost indescribable kinesthetic sensation that brings about vascular relaxation in a minute or two. Above all, we do not want patients to become bound by the idea that the use of phrases or any other procedures, such as listening to music or body-control suggestions on cassette tapes, are necessary to initiate a desirable kind of physiological behavior.

6. Within a week or two, we teach the patient a simple breathing exercise that we have used, and which was stressed by Swami Rama during psychophysiological testing at our laboratory (6). We call it "triangular breathing" because when wired up to a respiration gauge, the patient makes a triangular up-down pentracing on a polygraph record. The breathing pattern consists of deep, but not forced, inhalations and exhalations at a constant rate of flow with no pauses at the tops or bottoms of cycles. At first, each inhalation and exhalation cycle takes about 3 seconds, but as people learn to breathe deeply, the rate often slows to a comfortable six cycles per minute, or less.

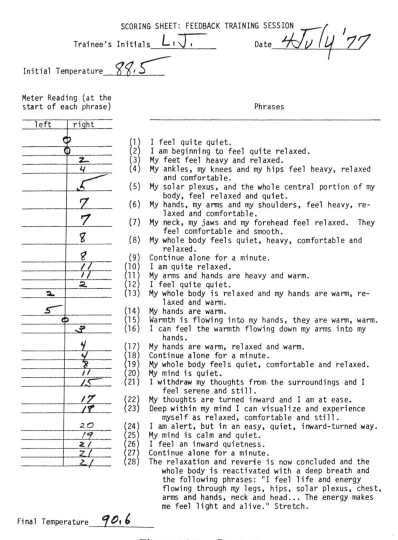

SCORING SHEET: FEEDBACK TRAINING SESSION

Trainee's Initials _L. J._   Date _4 July '77_

Initial Temperature _88.5_

Meter Reading (at the start of each phrase)

left	right	Phrases
	0	(1) I feel quite quiet.
	0	(2) I am beginning to feel quite relaxed.
	2	(3) My feet feel heavy and relaxed.
	4	(4) My ankles, my knees and my hips feel heavy, relaxed and comfortable.
	5	(5) My solar plexus, and the whole central portion of my body, feel relaxed and quiet.
	7	(6) My hands, my arms and my shoulders, feel heavy, relaxed and comfortable.
	7	(7) My neck, my jaws and my forehead feel relaxed. They feel comfortable and smooth.
	8	(8) My whole body feels quiet, heavy, comfortable and relaxed.
	8	(9) Continue alone for a minute.
	11	(10) I am quite relaxed.
	11	(11) My arms and hands are heavy and warm.
	2	(12) I feel quite quiet.
2		(13) My whole body is relaxed and my hands are warm, relaxed and warm.
5		(14) My hands are warm.
	0	(15) Warmth is flowing into my hands, they are warm, warm.
	3	(16) I can feel the warmth flowing down my arms into my hands.
	4	(17) My hands are warm, relaxed and warm.
	4	(18) Continue alone for a minute.
	8	(19) My whole body feels quiet, comfortable and relaxed.
	11	(20) My mind is quiet.
	15	(21) I withdraw my thoughts from the surroundings and I feel serene and still.
	17	(22) My thoughts are turned inward and I am at ease.
	18	(23) Deep within my mind I can visualize and experience myself as relaxed, comfortable and still.
	20	(24) I am alert, but in an easy, quiet, inward-turned way.
	19	(25) My mind is calm and quiet.
	21	(26) I feel an inward quietness.
	21	(27) Continue alone for a minute.
	21	(28) The relaxation and reverie is now concluded and the whole body is reactivated with a deep breath and the following phrases: "I feel life and energy flowing through my legs, hips, solar plexus, chest, arms and hands, neck and head... The energy makes me feel light and alive." Stretch.

Final Temperature _90.6_

Figure 19.2. See text.

7. Once or twice a week, most patients come to the Biofeedback Center for EMG training, and once a week, the accumulated home temperature reports are discussed.

8. At intake, we send to the patient's referring doctor a note saying that the patient is beginning a course of biofeedback training, and every 8 weeks thereafter, we send a progress note (with a copy to our staff physician with whose approval all patients are admitted to the Biofeedback and Psychophysiology Center). When the trainer and patient feel that the self-regulation gains have been maximized, the training is terminated and a final report summarizing what was accomplished is sent to the doctor.

Training schedules are set by patients to a major extent, and as they improve in health, they often reduce their lab visits to one per month, or less, before terminating. The temperature feedback machine is often not used for more than 4–8 weeks for migraine control, but for blood pressure control (in which case blood flow is increased in the legs as well as in the hands) 3–5 months of home practice with the machine may be necessary. In any event, after the use of the temperature machine is discontinued, regular home practice with relaxation, warmth, and breathing exercises is recommended for several additional months, until the newly developing skill at handling stress becomes

TEMPERATURE FEEDBACK TRAINING QUESTIONNAIRE

Your Initials _M.L.F._   Date _Jan. 19_   Time of Day _3:30 P.M._

Where did you practice _At home_   Starting Skin Temp. _90.2_

Highest Temp. Increase in Degrees F. _91.9_   _(It went all the way to cold at one point)._

Were you able to feel the following internal changes?
a. Warmth   Definitely   Moderately (underlined)   Slightly   Not at All
b. Flushing   Definitely   Moderately   Slightly   Not at All
c. Throbbing/Pulsating   Definitely   Moderately   Slightly   Not at All

How did the training session seem? _Frustrating at first because I did not understand the machine, since I had before had a very low starting temperature. I understand now._

Were you able to relax? YES (underlined) NO. If not, what seemed to interfere?
The machine measures what I do.

Physical sensations that occurred. _Complete relaxation — probably due to this morning's training session._

Emotional feelings that occurred. _At one point I looked at the machine and it was way down the left side. I was not doing as prescribed and found out — with good results._

Thoughts, fantasies, and imaginings. _This is wonderful! I've got it made. All I need do is apply what I've always known. But Fear — I can't stand prosperity. (Why?)_

Did your mind wander at all? YES NO. If so, A LOT MODERATELY SLIGHTLY
Did you have any tendency to fall asleep (or get drowsy)? YES NO
Did you have any dream-like experiences or mental pictures? YES NO

a. If so, did these experiences occur in a particular way? VISUAL AUDITORY
SPATIAL TOUCH (PRESSURE) SMELL TASTE

b. If so, were you aware of these experiences all of a sudden (very quickly) or in a gradual way? SUDDEN GRADUAL

Was there anything that you particularly liked or did not like about this training session? _The total relaxation. The truth — I must discipline myself!_

Further experiences you would like to share, or remarks you would like to make (if necessary please use reverse side of this sheet).

Figure 19.3. See text.

"a way of life." EMG training (and sometimes EEG) may continue for 4 or 5 months in the lab in conjunction with home temperature practice.

Before discussing applications, it is interesting to note that at three annual meetings of the Biofeedback Society (1985–1987) (7) a total of 52 papers on the research and clinical aspects of temperature training were distributed as follows: methodology and parametric studies, 16; migraine, 4; unclassified headache, 2; Raynaud's disease, 1; hypertension, 14; anxiety and tension reduction, 3; childbirth, 1; therapeutic situations, 2; arthritis, 2; gastrointestinal disorders, 2; sports, 1; hyperhydrosis, 1; tinnitus, 1; diabetic ulcers, 1; belief or set, 1.

PREVENTIVE MEDICINE

Biofeedback training for prevention may be the most promising latent medical procedure we have today, but we usually think of it as education. When school children learn that their minds and bodies work together and that through imagination they can easily affect the temperature of their hands, an indelible lesson has been learned. It is not easy, thereafter, for them to believe, as many of their parents do, that what we think and feel has nothing to do with our physiology, and that only the doctor can "cure" our illnesses.

After using a variety of feedback modalities over a period of several years, we feel that for educating people in prevention, no form of biofeedback is more useful than temperature training. This is because: (a) a temperature meter is easy to use, both for demonstration purposes and for self-administered practice; (b) large groups can be given a biofeedback experience using 15-cent thermometers attached with tape to a finger (8); (c) people know what temperature is, and the demonstration that it can be influenced and controlled is meaningful to them; (d) possible allergic reactions are avoided because no current is passed through the skin, and electrode paste is not used.

The sensitivity of most modern temperature feedback machines, as might be used in a biology class, is such that the smallest increment of temperature is 0.1°F. The average person cannot tell the temperature of the hands within 4 or 5 degrees, however, so the amplification of the machine provides a sensitivity much greater than that of the skin. This sensitivity is sufficient to provide information about very subtle changes in the activity level of the sympathetic nervous system, and yet it is not so sensitive that psyche-soma correlations are obscured by a plethora of minute responses.

As an example of the educational use of temperature feedback, consider the following. One of the psychophysiological therapists in the Menninger Foundation's Biofeedback and Psychophysiology Center recently was demonstrating the mind-body connection to a child and his mother, both of whom were wired to temperature trainers (with thermistors taped to a finger of the right hand). The child said, "Now say something that will make the temperature go down" and the trainer said, "Okay, what is two plus two? Come on now, hurry, give the answer." The child, flustered at the pressure, stammered, "Four," and his temperature dropped 1½ degrees. To his mother's surprise, her temperature dropped 5 degrees. She said afterward, "I'm beginning to realize how his learning problem has been tearing me up. I'm not going to let it do that to me anymore."

This temperature demonstration was not used to directly influence a psychosomatic problem, but to show both the child and the mother the tight relationship between psychological and the physiological processes. If blood flow in the hands is so easily affected by stress, we say in an educational setting, what about blood flow changes in the kidneys, the liver, the stomach? Is it possible that brain ar-

eas might be deprived of sufficient blood flow, on occasion, for psychogenic reasons? Along that line, what is psychogenic blindness? Or deafness? Are they neurological, or can they reflect vascular dysfunctions? The late Ward Halstead often pointed out that we have not adequately studied the behavior of "the vascular brain," and have focused inordinate attention on "the neurological brain" (9). These possibilities have not been adequately researched yet, but there is no reason to assume that the psychogenic influencing of blood flow is restricted to the peripheral parts of the body.

A beautiful example of self-regulation training in an educational setting has been provided by Loretta Engelhardt of Spearfish, South Dakota, where biofeedback was eventually introduced in the public school system from kindergarten through the twelfth grade (10). First, general information on the value of such a program was presented to school administrators and teachers, and to the school board; then, to the members of the community. This procedure ensured interest and commitment at the local level before the project was proposed for state funding.

The stated goal of the program (called "Awareness Through Biofeedback Training") was "the recognition and minimizing of stress and anxiety in individual everyday lives through the learning of relaxation skills." The techniques of progressive relaxation, autogenic training, and biofeedback training (EMG and temperature) were selected to teach stress reduction and to increase self-awareness through deep relaxation.

GENERAL MEDICINE: PSYCHOSOMATIC

If a disease is psychosomatic, then its alleviation can also be psychosomatic. That is, therapeutic physiological change can be psychogenically induced. Perhaps it is reasonable to say that if disease can be psychosomatic, so can health.

Our decision to conduct research in temperature training (1964) was a direct reflection of the previous choice made by Johannes Schultz in the 1920s. He chose warmth in the hands as one of the primary indications that the body was ready to accept psychogenic programming. The other indicator, as previously mentioned, was a feeling of heaviness in the limbs. This development in autogenic training originated from his observation that hypnotic subjects who were influenced most successfully by the doctor in overcoming psychosomatic disorders almost always reported a feeling of heaviness (striate relaxation) and warmth in the peripheral parts of the body (sympathetic relaxation).

Shortly after we noticed (1966) that recovery from an alleged migraine headache was accompanied by rapid vasodilation in the fingers (as shown by a photoplethysmographic tracing) and by a 10°F increase in hand temperature (dorsal and ventral thermistor placements), we were asked by the wife of a colleague to train her out of migraine. Without any promise of relief, the stress-limbic-hypothalamic-pituitary relationship was explained, she was given a short training session with the first two standard exercises of autogenic training, and was loaned a temperature feedback machine for twice-daily home practice. Within 3 weeks, she had recovered for her 5-year bout with weekly migraine, stopped taking drugs, and had no further trouble with migraine for the length of our follow-up, 11 years.

We seldom have a patient who is so quickly and completely successful. Fortunately, it was the first case and its striking results aroused the curiosity of Joseph Sargent, M.D., an internist at the Menninger Foundation. Eventually, he conducted a 5-year controlled-outcome research project with migraine and tension headache patients. Funded by NIMH, data (11) indicate that thermal feedback trainees "achieved more reduction in total headache and migraine frequency and intensity" than any control or comparison group. Follow-up showed, on the whole, that patients did not lose their skill in headache control, and on the contrary, tended to improve. Another 5-year follow-up of clinical findings with 58 patients who tried biofeedback training for headache control was reported by Charles and Sheila Adler (12). Their findings are quite similar to Sargent's.

OTHER CONDITIONS

Closely related to migraine headache is Raynaud's disease. These two health problems are conditions that differ in the fact that while migraine patients have cool or cold hands (in the seventies or low eighties) and an excess of blood in scalp arteries during attacks, Raynaud's patients have very cold hands (sometimes in the sixties, with almost no circulation in the fingers) and have only minor dysfunctions in cephalic circulation. In both cases, however, hand temperature training serves to ameliorate the condition because of its effects in the sympathetic nervous system. (See Chapter 29 for details.)

In order to significantly increase the temperature of the hands, it is necessary to reduce sympathetic firing, and this is controlled from the hypothalamus. Because of this neurovascular arrangement, temperature in the hands (ignoring slight evaporative cooling effects under the tape that holds a thermistor in place), is in main a one-variable indicator of general sympathetic tone.

In learning to warm the hands we must infer, therefore, that it is the hypothalamus and its associated machinery that are being trained. Recovery from migraine does not seem to be a simple hydraulic problem, merely shifting blood to the hands in order to get it out of the head. We have noticed that "skillful" patients can learn to warm their hands and at the same time maintain a migraine headache. We conclude that recovery from vascular problems is not so much the learning of a vascular "trick" as it is a normalization of hypothalamic homeostasis.

HYPERTENSION CONTROL

Concerning normalization of homeostasis, consider the following example of control of hypertension through biofeedback training, especially through temperature feedback from the hands and feet. A 39-year-old hypertensive woman was referred to us by a local physician. She had been treated intensively with hypertensive drugs for 16 years; yet her blood pressure ranged around 200/110 mm Hg. After discussing the general biofeedback rationale with both the patient and physician, we explained that the particular rationale for hypertension control had been derived to explain the puzzling fact that one of our *hand* temperature trainees had normalized her blood pressure in a few days. She turned out to be a generalizer, the kind of person who would warm both hands and both feet at the same time if she learned to warm one finger. She no doubt administered to herself "a reversible sympathectomy." In the days before a variety of drugs were available, surgeons often cut the sympathetic nerves to the legs in order to create massive vasodilation. This was accompanied by a significant blood pressure reduction.

We suggested a temperature feedback training program to be followed at home, first with the hands and then with the feet, accompanied by autogenic phrases for heaviness and warmth, a breathing exercise, and two EMG training sessions per week at the lab. Gradual improvement over 6 months permitted step-by-step elimination of all medication, and 12 years later her blood pressure remains normal without medication.

The hand-and-foot warming method described above has been tested with good results in group-outcome and follow-up research (13). In 77 patients with essential hypertension, significant reductions were seen in systolic and diastolic blood pressure (BP) and in hypotensive medication requirement. A multimodality biobehavioral treatment was used which included biofeedback-assisted training techniques aimed at teaching self-regulation of vasodilation in the hands and feet. Of the 54 medicated patients, 58% were able to eliminate hypotensive medication while at the same time reducing BP an average of 15/10 mm Hg. An additional 19 (35%) of the medicated patients were able to cut their medications approximately in half while reducing BP by 18/10 mm Hg. The remaining four (7%) medicated patients showed no improvement in either BP or medication requirement.

Similar reductions in BP were seen in initially unmedicated patients. Seventy percent of the 23 unmedicated patients achieved average pressures below 140/90 mm Hg, with an additional 22% of these patients making clinically significant reductions in pressure without becoming normotensive, and with 8% unsuccessful at lowering pressures to a clinically significant extent. Follow-up data available on 61 patients over an average of 33 months indicated little regression in these results, with 51% of the total patient sample remaining well controlled off medication, and an additional 41% partially controlled, and 8% unsuccessful in lowering either medications and/or blood pressures to a clinically significant extent.

Patients have been pleased with the reduction of medication, not only because it saves money, but because more than 20 undesirable side effects have been correlated with the use of standard medications for hypertension control (14).

There is not sufficient space to consider additional applications of temperature training for control of psychosomatic disorders, but it can be safely assumed that for every application of heaviness and warmth exercises mentioned by Luthe (15), there is also a potential application for EMG and temperature training.

GENERAL MEDICINE: NONPSYCHOSOMATIC

By applications of temperature training in nonpsychosomatic medicine, we mean application to such problems as infections, pain from physical trauma, neuromuscular damage from stroke, accident, or surgery, etc. Some physicians feel that infections, diabetes, and a host of other problems that might be thought to be nonpsychosomatic nevertheless have a psychosomatic component, strong or weak. In any event, it is clear that there is no sharp division between psychosomatic problems and problems that are purely somatic, and to us there is no significant difference in training procedures. We are not concerned with the genesis of the problem as much as with the "here and now" and what can be done.

If a dysfunction is congenital, the question is, "Can we go anywhere from here?" As in a clear-cut psychosomatic case, the biofeedback rationale is discussed, and the usefulness of temperature training for sympathetic turn-off is reviewed. This latter is explained in part as a useful step in preparing the body to receive instruction, even though it may appear at first glance to be unrelated to a problem such as congenital spasticity, for example. In some problems, the direct significance of temperature training is obvious to the patient, since blood brings almost all of the repair material to the site of tissue recovery.

Sometimes a patient says that he thought the body was supposed to know how to do this without help. In principle, that may be true, but the fact is that almost everyone who has a body-disrupting accident, or who undergoes surgery, unconsciously interferes with the body's recovery through a kind of visualization that can only be called "negative." A skier with a broken leg is likely to worry about a variety of problems, and induce in himself or herself a series of minor or major psychosomatic effects. We all know of patients in whom the physiological effects of anxiety were worse than the problem that aroused the anxiety.

To reduce the effects of negative visualization, we provide the patient with a positive visualization, and we also give them the old yogic instruction, "Do not fight negative thoughts, merely replace them with positive ones." The negative ideas and emotions such as fear, with its limbic correlates, inhibit the programming of the body. So rather than fight fear, it is better to construct the image of what body behavior is desired and return the thought to this positive program whenever it drifts into a fight or flight pattern.

We also emphasize the benefits of striate relaxation, of course, and as in psychosomatic cases, we include EMG feedback (usually of the forehead muscles) along with temperature training, autogenic phrases, and a breathing exercise. It is safe to say that research in this area has a host of fascinating problems to grapple with, especially (for theory) in the modification of congenital defects.

PSYCHOTHERAPY

It seems to us that a psychotherapeutic component is associated with almost every use of temperature training. It is not possible for a patient to realize that normally involuntary processes of the body can be controlled to some extent, without at the same time undergoing a modification of self-image. Sometimes, the revelation has overwhelming results.

This type of change in self-image is not uncommon in biofeedback trainees, though sometimes it might not be noticeable for several weeks. With many patients, temperature training serves to help reorganize their lives, not because it is necessarily good to have warm hands, for example, but because of the feeling of self-mastery they get. That feeling, if it could be put in mathematical terms, would be called "an enabling function." It enables the patient to take positive action in a variety of ways. In other words, the gains from temperature training as well as from other kinds of feedback training, are not merely physical.

Consider the comments shown in Figure 19.3, recorded after a home temperature training session. Patient M.L.F. was learning to use the temperature feedback machine and was frustrated at the beginning of her session because her starting temperature of 90.2°F seemed too high, in comparison with previous starts, and she thought she was doing something wrong. The frustration made her hands cool, and finally she understood (probably for the first time, even though she had been repeatedly informed) that the machine reflected her psychological state and that the high temperature at the beginning indicated that she was more relaxed than usual when the session started.

Under "Thought, fantasies, and imaginings," she revealed a basic fear: "I can't stand prosperity. (Why?)" At the bottom of the page she said she liked the total relaxation, but did not like "the truth. I must discipline myself."

A question which arises, of course, is, how can temperature training result in such significant insights? The answer seems to be quite similar to W. Reich's answer explaining how total striate relaxation can be accompanied by psychological insights (16). Continuous striate bracing, he said, was associated with defense against certain kinds of self-awareness. When the bracing (sometimes referred to as character armor) was removed through total striate relaxation, self-awareness often came to the surface because the information was needed and at the same time could be tolerated. In the same way, we seem to have a kind of "character armor" in the sympathetic nervous system, and when it is removed through hand warming (sympathetic turn-off), self-awareness can come to the surface. Autonomic character armor must logically derive from limbic armor, and when it is released, it signifies a change in the limbic response to stress.

Whether our patients practice with temperature, EMG, or EEG machines, the report form is essentially the same, and in almost every case, we find similar kinds of psychotherapeutic response. In our estimation, it is important that the patient understand how useful these reports are. They provide a kind of psychological awareness-sharpening that no machine can supply, and it is apparently this kind of information that bridges the gap in many patients between voluntary and involuntary, between conscious and unconscious. Without a report on body, emotions, and thoughts *to themselves*, the awareness that brings the body under voluntary control seems to develop more slowly. The crux of the matter here is self-awareness, although this is not true for conditioning, of course. For true, self-regulation, however, it is a "must."

After awareness and self-regulation are achieved, they can be relegated to the unconscious (preconscious might be a better word). After a bad psychophysiological habit is consciously replaced with a good habit, it need not remain in the forefront of consciousness.

CONTRAINDICATIONS

At a meeting of the Biofeedback Society in 1976, W. Luthe made a strong plea for caution in using biofeedback methods in manipulating the body's normal homeostatic mechanisms. He referred to the research of French et al. in which a group of men who first learned to increase blood flow in the hands during a month of temperature training, transferred the visualization of warmth to the scrotum after 5 days of training, with the effect of heating the sperm and temporarily lowering the sperm count to infertile levels. What might be the long-term effects of this, he asked. Can we "poke a hole in the homeostatic net?"

A few yogis whom we studied with psychophysiological equipment in India (6) warned against careless manipulation of the heart's firing patterns and named some of their brethren who now had defective hearts. Swami Rama in Topeka in 1971 demonstrated that it was possible to make one leg and foot become quite red while at the same time the other leg and foot become pasty white and clinically edemic. We asked him to perform more than once, but he warned against repeated manipulations of the involuntary nervous system without allowing the body at least half an hour to return to normal between trials. He said that the body could "get out of control."

Another warning concerns the use of biofeedback training with epileptics, hypertensives, and others whose disease syndrome is under drug control. Medical monitoring is essential in such cases. Fortunately, in using temperature training with patients, we are almost always in the position of helping the body return to normal, rather than deviate from normal.

FUTURE DIRECTION IN THERMAL TRAINING

One of the most interesting areas of research and application in temperature training may lie in the domain of organ-specific visualizations in internal medicine. As a teaching device in the use of such visualizations, for example, implanted temperature sensors whose readings are telemetered out of the body could well be used for feedback of internal vascular behavior. We know of an off-the-record case in which bleeding from a bladder cancer was inhibited and the growth reduced by hypnotically-induced circulatory starvation. Cancers usually have a well-developed vascular tree that automatically supplies their energy needs. The smooth muscles in the walls of this vascular system are under hypothalamic control, however, and if vasoconstriction can be self-programmed, such cancers might come under voluntary control.

In the case above, several metastatic growths disappeared while the bladder growth was being reduced. The above kinds of ideas could theoretically be extended to cover every organ and tissue problem in which blood flow is involved.

References

1. Green, E. E. and Green, A. M. Biofeedback: rationale and applications. In *International Encyclopedia of Neurology, Psychiatry, Psychoanalysis, and Psychology*, edited by B. B. Wolman. Van Nostrand Reinhold, New York, 1977.
2. Papez, J. M. A proposed mechanism of emotion. Arch. Neurol. Psychiatry, *38*: 725–743, 1937.
3. MacLean, P. D. Psychosomatic disease and the "visceral brain": recent developments bearing on the Papez theory of emotion. Psychosom. Med., *11*: 338–353, 1949.
4. Masserman, J. H. Is the hypothalamus a center of emotion? Psychosom. Med., *3*: 3–25, 1941.
5. Schultz, J. H. and Luthe, W. *Autogenic Training: A Psychological Approach in Psychotherapy*. Grune & Stratton, New York, 1959.
6. Green, E. E. and Green, A. M. *Beyond Biofeedback*. Delacorte Press, New York, 1959.
7. Proceedings of the Biofeedback Society of America can be obtained from: Francine Butler, Ph.D., Executive Secretary, 10200 W. 44th Ave., #304, Wheat Ridge, CO, 80033.
8. Small thermometers (PA 302) can be obtained from: Creative Materials, Inc., 5377 Michigan Avenue, Rosemont, Ill., 60018.
9. Halstead, W. C. *Brain and Intelligence: A Quantitative Study of the Frontal Lobes*. University of Chicago Press, Chicago, 1947.
10. Engelhardt, L. J. The application of biofeedback techniques within a public school setting. Presented at the seventh annual meeting of the Biofeedback Society of America, Colorado Springs, Colo., 1976.
11. Sargent, J., Solback, P., Coyne, L., Spohn, H. and Segerson, J. Results of a controlled, experimental, outcome study of non-drug treatments for the control of migraine headaches. Paper given at the Fourth International Symposium of The Migraine Trust, 22 September, London, 1982.
12. Adler, C. S. and Adler, S. M. Biofeedback-psychotherapy for the treatment of headaches: a 5-year follow-up. Headache, *16*: 189–191, 1976.
13. Fahrion, S., Norris, P., Green, A., Green, E. and Snarr, C. Biobehavioral treatment of essential hypertension: a group outcome study. Biofeedback Self Reg., *11*: 257–277, 1986.

14. Hosten, A. O. Hypertension: pharmacotherapy. Paper presented at a symposium on Psychosocial and Pharmacological Treatment Approaches: Issues and Interrelationships, sponsored by the Institute of Medicine (NAS), Washington, D.C., May 28, 1980.

15. Luthe, W. (ed.) *Autogenic Therapy*. Grune & Stratton, New York, 1969.

16. Reich, W. *Selected Writings*. Noonday Press, New York, 1961.

17. French, D. J., Leeb, C. S., Fahrion, S. L., Law, O. T. and Jecht, E. W. Self-induced scrotal hyperthermia in man followed by decrease in sperm output: a preliminary report. Andrologie, 5: 311–316, 1973.

CHAPTER 20

Behavioral Applications in the Treatment of Patients with Cardiovascular Disorders

BERNARD T. ENGEL
WALTER F. BAILE

INTRODUCTION

Practicing physicians have always known that some of the cardiovascular problems of their patients are mediated by the patients' behaviors. Few physicians are formally trained either to understand or to treat such problems. For example, three of the major American cardiology textbooks virtually ignore the role of patient behavior (1–3). The literature on high blood pressure is similar although there is somewhat greater interest in behavior among some investigators (4, 5).

This chapter will review a number of behavioral principles that the practicing physician can apply now in the treatment of his patients; and it will indicate some of the current behavioral research directed at improving the treatment of patients with cardiovascular disorders. The extensive literature on behavioral factors in cardiovascular diseases has been summarized in review articles (e.g., 6–8).

PRINCIPLES OF BEHAVIOR

The behavioral principles, investigated for more than 75 years (9), in general are well understood. Behavior is under the control of antecedent and consequent stimuli. The stimuli that precede the behavior of interest primarily function to signal the subject about the probable consequences of his behavior; the behavior itself is shaped by the consequent stimuli: thus antecedent stimuli are informative, consequent stimuli are (positively or negatively) reinforcing. An example of these principles in operation can be seen at any traffic signal.

We must emphasize the important distinction between learning and performance. Performance, of course, is behavior, whereas learning is one process by which behavior is modified, but it is not a perfect measure of learning since is is not only determined by the specific training of interest, but also by prior learning and existing incentives. Thus, a patient may have learned to take his antihypertensive medications but still may not do so because his prior experience with medications has been unpleasant, or because he simply does not perceive the seriousness of the consequences.

Antecedent stimuli serve the role of informing the subject about the potential consequences of his subsequent behavior. They acquire this informational property as a result of learning or because of their innate properties. One must know the factors that mediate such learning since only then is it possible to assess (i.e., diagnose) the environmental factors that are influencing a patient's behaviors. The elements that give antecedent stimuli their cue properties are: (a) temporal association; (b) frequency of association; and (c) differentiability of antecedent stimuli from other, coincidental, environmental stimuli. Response-contingent (i.e., consequent) stimuli control behavior since they are the environmental rewards or punishments. The important characteristics of stimuli that determine their reinforcing properties are: (a) the latency between the behavior and the occurrence of the consequence: (b) the potency of the consequence; (c) the reliability that the consequent stimuli will occur; and (d) the motivational status of the subject both at the time that the learning occurs and during subsequent performance.

Stimuli serve two behavioral roles: (a) informational and (b) reinforcing. The informational property of stimuli is determined by: (a) their temporal and repetitive associative histories with consequent stimuli; and (b) their discriminative characteristics. The reinforcing properties of stimuli are determined by: (a) their relationships to the preceding behavior; (b) their intensity; and (c) the motivational state of the patient. Next, we will consider how to determine these properties.

THE BEHAVIORAL ANALYSIS

Behavior can be reliably and validly measured and such measurements can be made relatively simply and economically. In contrast, the usual clinical method for obtaining behavioral data, the interview, may be unreliable, and unless done by highly trained experts, haphazard and unlikely to elicit valid information. The scientific analysis of behavior has three goals: (a) to measure the frequency and intensity of the aberrant behavior; (b) to identify the circumstances during which the response is more or less frequent; (c) to characterize the context (antecedent stimuli) and consequences (rewards and punishments) associated with the aberrant behavior. Several textbooks describe in detail how to implement behavioral analyses efficiently (e.g., 10).

An essential feature of a behavioral analysis is the formulation of relevant, answerable questions. The question one is most likely to ask during an interview—e.g., how do you feel?—often are ambiguous, may be misunderstood, and may not elicit useful information. A behavioral assessment should provide clinically relevant, unambiguous data about observable performance. Such data will be useful to both the primary physician who collected the data and to others who review the patient's chart.

Table 20.1 presents a questionnaire that we have used to evaluate the behavioral characteristics of angina pectoris in patients with so-called stable angina (11). Patients are given multiple copies of the questionnaire to fill out on an episode-by-episode basis and to mail to us daily. By the end of 2 weeks of such analysis, we have a clear picture of the typical anginal episode for that patient, and of his response to it. For following such a patient, this procedure could be repeated at regular intervals—e.g., annually. For determining the reliability of a patient's report, one could use these data as a basis for an interview with the patients' spouse. For assessing the effectiveness of a treatment regimen, one could compare the pretreatment data with the treatment changes. In any case, the investigator now has an objective, reproducible record of specific behavior.

Another form of behavior analysis cardiologists are using with increased frequency is the continuous monitoring of the electrical activity of the heart over a 24-hour period. Some of the more recently developed monitors provide two recording channels: one is for the electrocardiogram; the other permits the patient to describe activities and feelings at various moments during the monitoring period. Unfortunately, cardiologists who use their monitors have not yet formalized the subjective report data adequately.

Once one had succeeded in collecting orderly, relevant behavioral data from one's patient, one could develop a rational program of activities for the patient which is tailored to that patient's cardiac responses. If this were done, most physicians would find it no longer necessary to tell their patient to avoid "stress." Stress in an ambiguous term used by physician and patient to disguise the fact that neither knows what behavioral guidelines the patient should follow.

BEHAVIORAL APPLICATIONS

So far, we have considered behavior only as a coincidental risk factor in cardiovascular diseases. There is another way to look at behavior. If we consider the cardiovascular system as a motor system, then we can ask whether such motor responses can be brought under the control of consequent stimuli directly, and if so, whether such control can be implemented by the patient sufficiently reliably to have therapeutic potential, specifically clinical biofeedback.

Control of Behavioral Risk Factors

There are three behavioral risk factors especially relevant to patients with cardiovascular disorders; smoking, overeating, and treatment noncompliance. A fourth factor, usual daily living, may or may not be a risk factor. Every physician who treats patients who have high blood pressure or who have had myocardial infarctions must advise these patients about maintaining or changing their life-styles to reduce risk.

To change behavior, one first must understand the nature of the behavior and its relevance to the response of interest. Thus, every

Table 20.1.
Angina self-report checklist

Circle the correct response. Comment where asked.
Time: Morning Afternoon Evening Night
Activity at time of attack: Asleep Resting Walking Exercising or Working
Degree of pain: Mild Moderate Severe
Duration of pain: less than 1 3 5   more than 1 min.   minutes 5 minutes
Location of pain: Chest Neck Stomach Left arm Other
Relief of pain: Medicine Rest Other
                    (kind, amount)   Specify

Comments:
No pain attack
Date: _____ Name: _____

behavioral change program should begin with a behavioral analysis including relevant cardiovascular activity. One can collect behavioral and blood-pressure data. It is quite easy to train hypertensive patients to take their pressures throughout the day for a few weeks (12–14).

Blood pressure varies considerably throughout the day, and for some patients, the intradaily variations are so great that the patient would be considered hypertensive at some times and normotensive at other times (14, 15). Thus, before one can advise a patient about how to modify his behavior to reduce his cardiovascular risk, one must thoroughly understand the relationship between specific behaviors and specific cardiovascular responses for that patient.

An example will illustrate how we do this with patients recovering from myocardial infarctions. It is very difficult to provide patients with reliable advice on how to regulate their behavior during the immediate postinfarct period. In our program (16), we ask each patient while he is still in the Cardiac Care Unit (CCU) to develop a 10-step program of recovery for himself beginning with the time he is in the CCU. Usually, the first step is implemented in the CCU and involves various self-care activites and mild exercise such as moving around the unit. The last step is complete recovery (as the patient defines such recovery); usually, this is return to work, but many patients are content to retire and pursue other lifestyles. (It should be noted that one can jump to wrong conclusions about the patient's future plans, and that these conclusions can be avoided by asking him to identify his own goals.) Once the patient evolves his program, we review it

with him, and we ask the patient to include an ordered walking program in his rehabilitation protocol. We never try to change the final goal for the patient.

After the recovery protocol has been agreed upon, we teach the patient to take his pulse and to look for specific symptoms, e.g., shortness of breath or chest pain, and we provide the patient with worksheets (see Table 20.2) on which he is to enter his pulse rate before and after each activity, and any symptoms he many note during the activity. While on the CCU (or intermediate care unit) the patient reviews his worksheets daily with us. After discharge, we see the patient weekly (often with the spouse) and review the worksheets.

The decision to move to the next step in the recovery program is based on three criteria: the absence of symptoms, heart rate change from preactivity to activity of less than 20 beats per minute, and absolute heart rate during the activity of less than 110 beats per minute. With such a schedule as this—obviously

Table 20.2.
Cardiac rehabilitation program

Task/Time	Heart rate		Symptoms[a]	
	Before	After	Shortness of breath	Chest pain
1.				
2.				
3.				
4.				
5.				
6.				
7.				
8.				

[a]Indicate duration and severity; also note what you did to relieve the discomfort.

one can adapt the criteria to meet the specific needs of a given patient—we have found that patients at high risk for noncompliance with medical regimens readily agree to this self-regulated program of rehabilitation.

Our patients who had unrealistic ambitions about their ability to recover fully soon became aware of the fact that they could not progress beyond certain steps in their program. Rather than become discouraged, these patients revised their programs by setting new, more realistic goals.

The essential features of this program are: (a) the goals are patient-defined; (b) the decision to increase activity is based on data rather than intuition; (c) the patient is highly motivated because he is working within a framework of his own choosing, and because he can review his own record of progress in terms which he can easily understand. From a medical point of view, this program is useful because: (a) it provides data on which the physician can make rational decisions; (b) it permits the physician to control his patients's behavior much more closely, and therefore, it increases compliance.

SMOKING

Factors responsible for maintenance of the habit are unclear, but group influences and modeling are important, and social acceptability leads many to rationalize the adverse health consequences of smoking. In addition, continuing smokers tend to be extroverted and adventurous, and smoking behavior is more prevalent among nonwhites and those with lower income and educational status (17).

The risk is proportional to the number of cigarettes smoked, the amount inhaled, and increasing yield of tar and nicotine. The two principal components of cigarette smoke are nicotine and carbon monoxide (CO). A 20-cigarette-per-day smoker may inhale 50–100 mg of nicotine daily. Nicotine is an important factor in the genesis of atherosclerosis. In addition, it stimulates the heart to beat faster and work harder. In patients with recent heart attacks, it may interfere with wound healing and increase myocardial irritability (18). CO accelerates the atherosclerotic process, and having an extremely high affinity for hemoglobin, it can easily displace oxygen from this oxygen transport molecule. Thus, heavy smokers experience a decrease of up to 15% in the oxygen-carrying capacity of the blood.

There are several different methods available to assess smoking behavior objectively. Two of these involve measurements of products of cigarette combustion, CO in expired air, and cotinine, a breakdown product of nicotine which is assayed in the urine. Measurement of expired CO from the breath is probably the most commonly used assessment of smoking status. There is no universally agreed-upon cutoff level of CO that separates smokers from nonsmokers, but most investigators have used 7–9 ppm. In our experience, using a 9 ppm cutoff, there was a 78% agreement between self-reports of smoking and CO level. Cotinine is a breakdown product of nicotine, and its peak excretion in the urine occurs 2 hours after smoking. Cigarette smoke also contains trace amounts of thiocyanate, which can be measured in the serum and saliva.

Because cigarette smoking is the single greatest cause of preventable death (20), smoking cessation is directly linked to survival, morbidity, and mortality (21). Our data and those of others (20) have indicated that the patients at greatest risk are more likely to quit. However, there is a significant number of patients who resume the habit very quickly after a heart attack. For these patients, is there any strategy that will help? Several studies have shown that unequivocal advice to stop smoking can make a significant impact on cessation. Several strategies are thus suggested to increase the prevalence of smoking cessation in high-risk patients. These interventions might include: (a) environmental manipulation, e.g., closing the patient lounge to smoking; (b) educating visitors to the risk for the patient of resumption, and asking them to refrain from smoking in the patient's presence; (c) strategies to assist the patient in dealing with the powerful psychological withdrawal (e.g., relaxation, distraction); (d) the transmission of strong advice to quit early in the patient's hospital stay coupled with appropriate education.

Apart from these specific interventions, several principles may be kept in mind when seeking to implement smoking cessation programs in high-risk patients: (a) Patients are more motivated to change their smoking status following perceived deterioration in their health. The timing of health messages should be geared to clinic visits, hospitalizations, etc. (b) Advice should be coupled with information about the benefits of cessation and risks of continutation. (c) Patients should be surveyed about devices or mechanisms previously used in efforts to stop smoking and encouraged to employ devices that previously worked. (d) Family members should be encouraged to stop smoking because it will increase the probability of successful cessation on the part of the patient. (e) Verbal report seems to be a reliable indicator of smoking vs. nonsmoking status but may not accurately reflect the quantity of cigarettes smoked. (f) Practical noninvasive means of monitoring smoking (expired air CO, salivary thiocyanate and urinary cotinine) may be used to give direct or delayed feedback to the patient about his smoking status.

DIET

The behavioral research on weight control is extensive. We recommend several articles for the reader who wishes to pursue this literature. Foreyt (22) described his program for teaching patients to control their weight in detail. He also discussed some of the factors one needs to consider in a comprehensive weight control program. We strongly recommend the extensive review by Stunkard of the status of the research on the behavioral control of weight and on programs for getting people to lose weight (23).

BIOFEEDBACK

The underlying premises for the application of biofeedback to patients with cardiovascular disorders are first that cardiovascular responses are, in part, neurally mediated, and that through the use of behavioral training techniques, it is possible to bring these motor responses under control of antecedent or consequent stimuli. The second premise is that once such relationships have been learned, the patient can implement them himself. The final premise is that the patient can learn to recognize aberrant responses (or situations that are likely to elicit such responses), and he can then use the techniques he has learned to control directly and *in situ* autonomically mediated cardiovascular responses.

While there is considerable evidence that one can significantly change the cardiovascular responses of one's patients, and that once learned, these skills can be used by patients in natural settings, there have been no large-scale, controlled clinical trials of any of these methods. Furthermore, most studies have been done with relatively few patients so that the generality of the findings is not yet clear. Despite these very serious limitations, there is an impressive array of evidence that some patients can learn to control their cardiovascular responses, and that the skills acquired by some of these patients is sufficiently great to enable us to conclude that the effects are clinically significant.

From a behavioral point of view, biofeedback technique is a special instance of a procedure called operant conditioning. In operant conditioning one attempts to modify performance by making consequences of the performance contingent on the nature of the performance. In the applications of biofeedback to patients with cardiovascular disorders, the performance is a pathognomonic, cardiovascular response, and the consequence is success (or failure) in normalizing the response. Essentially then, all biofeedback studies of patients with cardiovascular disorders monitor some cardiovascular response, display the response to the patient (viz., feedback), define for the patient what the "correct" response is, and finally encourage the patient to control his response in such a way as to make it more "normal."

Heart Disease

Supraventricular Arrhythmias. A number of studies have shown that patients with supraventricular arrhythmias can be trained to control their heart rates. At least three different teams of investigators reported successful results in training one or more patients with sinus tachycardias to lower their heart rate (24–26). The patients were provided with beat-to-beat feedback about the nature of their heart rate, and they were able to lower their rates both during the laboratory sessions and away from the laboratories. The essential equipment was an EKG amplifier and a display device (such as an oscilloscope and a digital monitor). All of these patients were able to learn to regulate their heart rates, but all required a number of training sessions (ranging over a period of several weeks), as one would expect.

We have reported the results in two patients with paroxysmal atrial tachycardia (24), and one patient with intermittent Wolff-Parkinson-White syndrome (WPW) (27). All three learned to control their heart rates, and the patient with WPW also was able to learn to control her cardiac conduction pattern, i.e., she was able both to produce and to inhibit both normally and aberrantly conducted beats. In the case of the patient with WPW, and in the case of the other patients described below, these studies revealed another potential application of biofeedback: it may be possible to assess various pharmacotherapies or to diagnose potential pharmacological toxicities. Once a patient has been trained to control the arrhythmia—the patient with WPW learned both to increase and to inhibit aberrantly conducted beats—one can administer pharmacologic doses of various anti-arrhythmic agents and see what effect these have on the voluntarily produced arrhythmias. In our patient with WPW, we were able to show that propranolol had no effect on her ability to produce or inhibit her aberrant conduction patterns, but that atrophine abolished all aberrantly conducted beats.

We also have trained six patients with fixed atrial fibrillation (28). All had histories of rheumatic heart disease. They were able to increase and to decrease their ventricular rates reliably. One patient was especially interesting. When he increased his ventricular rate, he had a typical EKG pattern of atrial fibrillation, but when he slowed his rate, he consistently emitted an EKG pattern that included many junctional escape beats. Thus, it is possible that the biofeedback training exposed a latent digitalis toxicity (all patients in this series were maintained in well-established doses of digoxin).

Ventricular Ectopic Beats. Two laboratories first reported that it is possible to train patients with premature ventricular contractions (PVC) to control the prevalence of their ectopic beats (29–31). Apart from the potential clinical significance of such learned control, two additional findings of clinical importance are worth noting. In our laboratory, two patients were trained to slow their ventricular rates and to reduce frequencies of PVCs during periods when they were slowing their ventricular rates. Pharmacological studies revealed that in one case, this effect was associated with a reduction in sympathetic tone, whereas in the other, this effect was associated with an increase in vagal tone. Thus, once again, biofeedback was helpful in diagnosing the mechanism of PVC control. In one patient, propranolol would have had a beneficial effect, but in the other patient, this drug would not have been helpful, a vagally active drug being indi-

cated. In the second study (31), a patient was described who had a parasystolic, ectopic focus that became manifest whenever the patient increased her heart rate above 78 beats per minute. The patient was trained to speed her rate to about 106 beats per minute before she reached her ectopic threshold. This effect not only appeared during the conditioning sessions, but also occurred during exercise on a treadmill.

High Blood Pressure

Several investigators have reported that patients can learn to control their blood pressure in the laboratory. Our group reported that such skills, once learned, can be retained by the patients for at least 3 months (12). Another group reported that patients who were trained to lower their pressures showed improved performance in tests of cognitive function (32). These last findings also suggest this learned control of blood pressure may have an enduring effect, at least over the period of study.

Any consideration of behavioral interventions in patients with high blood pressure would not be complete without also considering the potential clinical value of so-called relaxation methods described in detail elsewhere in this book. Several investigators reported that such methods can lower blood pressure in hypertensive patients (33–36), and one group noted a concomitant reduction in plasma renin activity in their patients (37).

There is some evidence that biofeedback training and relaxation operate through different mechanisms. It had been reported that relaxation has a generalized effect in reducing sympathetic drive (38). These data suggest that relaxation may affect blood pressure at several levels, viz., through reduced cardiac output and through reducing plasma renin response. Our research (12) suggested that biofeedback worked primarily through vasomotor control since our patients were able to change their pressures in the laboratory, i.e., to increase and to decrease blood pressure—without changing their heart rates. This speculation subsequently was confirmed by Messerli et al. (39) who measured cardiac output directly, and who showed that diastolic blood pressure biofeedback was associated with a reduction in peripheral resistance but no change in cardiac output. These findings suggest that biofeedback and relaxation may be complementary rather than alternative methods in blood pressure control.

We have reported a large, controlled study of systolic blood pressure biofeedback and relaxation in the control of high blood pressure in "borderline" or "mild" hypertension (40, 41). We found that the two procedures are synergistic; and that patients who have been trained to lower their pressures using both procedures can achieve and sustain reductions in diastolic pressure of as much as 10 mm Hg (41) for more than 1 year. Furthermore, in a selected subset of patients receiving diuretic therapy, we found that we were able to withdraw their medication and to maintain these patients for at least 9 months without any drug therapy. On the basis of these findings, we have proposed a behavioral stepped care program for controlling blood pressure in mild or borderline patients (41). The main features of the program are: (a) self-monitoring in a context of proper professional supervision; (b) systolic blood pressure biofeedback; (c) relaxation. However, patients should only receive as much treatment as necessary to achieve adequate reductions in pressure. Thus, not all patients need to go through all three stages of treatment.

Patel has reported a series of studies using various relaxation procedures in conjunction with pharmacological therapy (42–45). In her first study (42) she treated a series of 20 patients with established hypertension. She taught them yogic relaxation and also used feedback procedures to improve the relaxation training (but she did not train the patients to control blood pressure directly). Sixteen of the 20 patients showed a significant reduction in mean arterial pressure (about 20 mm Hg) as well as a significant reduction in medication usage. In a second study (43), she reported a reduction in mean arterial pressure of about 16 mm Hg during treatment, which then persisted for 1 year. The second study included a matched control group that showed no change in pressure over a 9-month period. Finally, in a third study (44), she carried out randomized, controlled trials with a crossover procedure. The treated patients showed a fall in pressure; the controls did not. After 3 months, the control patients also were treated and their pressure then fell to the levels of the treated patients.

REPRISE

We cannot emphasize strongly enough that the biofeedback and relaxation procedures we have reviewed above are the subjects of intense investigation at the time of writing. Although there are sufficient data now available to warrant further study, and in some cases clinical trials, none of these procedures has been established with sufficient reliability to justify calling them established treatments. Nevertheless, the evidence does indicate that these methods have considerable potential as adjunctive therapies. This is an especially important consideration in patients with cardiovascular disorders because these are chronic, often progressive, diseases. The pharmacological treatments now available often have potent side effects that increase the risk of noncompliance. If such patients can develop behavioral strategies that enable them to regulate their aberrant cardiovascular responses, and if they can then function adequately on less potent drugs or on reduced dosages of such drugs, their chances of survival will be enhanced and their risk of morbid events will be reduced.

Although many behavioral *treatment* procedures are still under investigation, and still need to be verified, behavioral *assessment* procedures are well-established and should be used regularly. They provide a powerful tool for accurately appraising signs and symptoms as these manifest themselves in the everyday life of the patient. They provide the clinician with an objective means of evaluating a patient, and they provide a record that can be understood by anyone who follows the patient. Practicing physicians should incorporate the technique of behavioral analysis into their regular practice.

References

1. Bellet, S. *Clinical Disorders of the Heart Beat.* Lea and Febiger, Philadelphia, 1971.
2. Scherf, D. and Schott, A. *Extrasystoles and Allied Arrhythmias*, 2nd ed. Year Book Medical Publishers, Chicago, 1974.
3. Hurst, J. W., Logue, R. B., Schlant, R. C. and Wenger, N. K. *The Heart*, 3rd ed. McGraw-Hill, New York, 1974.
4. Pickering, G. *High Blood Pressure.* J. & A. Churchill, Ltd., London, 1968.
5. Weiner, H. Psychosomatic research in essential hypertension: retrospect and prospect. In *Psychosomatics in Essential Hypertension*, edited by M. Koster, H. Mosaph and P. Visser. Bibl. Psychiatr., No. 144, pp. 58–116. Karger, New York, 1970.
6. Lynch, J. J., Paskewitz, D. A., Gimbel, K. S. and Thomas, S. A. Psychological aspects of cardiac arrhythmias. Am. Heart J., *93*: 645–657, 1977.
7. Gutmann, M. C. and Benson, H. Interaction of environmental factors and systemic arterial

blood pressure: a review. Medicine, *50(6)*: 543–553, 1971.

8. Shapiro, A. P., Schwartz, G. E., Ferguson, D. C. E., Redmond, D. P. and Weiss, S. M. *Behavioral methods in the treatment of hypertension.* Ann. Intern. Med., *86*: 626–636, 1977.

9. Thorndike, E. L. Animal intelligence: an experimental study of the associative processes in animals. Psychol. Rev. Monograph Supplement No. 8, 1898.

10. Yates, A. J. *Theory and Practice in Behavior Therapy.* John Wiley & Sons., New York, 1975.

11. McCroskery, J. M., Engel, B. T., Gottlieb, S. M. and Lakatta, E. G. Operant conditioning of heart rate in patients with angina pectoris (abstract). Psychosom. Med., *40*: 89–90, 1978.

12. Kristt, D. A. and Engel, B. T. Learned control of blood pressure in patients with high blood pressure. Circulation, *51*: 370–378, 1975.

13. Letter to the Editor. Home blood-pressure recording. Lancet, Feb. 1, p. 259, 1975.

14. Engel, B. T., Gaarder, K. R. and Glasgow, M. S. Behavioral treatment of high blood pressure. I. Analyses of intra- and interdaily variations of blood pressure during a one-month, baseline period. Psychosom. Med. *43*: 255–270, 1981.

15. Sokolow, M., Werdegar, D., Perloff, D. B., Cowan, R. M. and Brenenstuhl, H. Preliminary studies relating portably recorded blood pressures to daily life events in patients with essential hypertension. In *Psychosomatics in Essential Hypertension*, edited by M. Koster, H. Musaph and P. Visser. Bibl. Psychiatr., No. 144, pp. 164–189. Karger, New York, 1970.

16. Baile, W. F. and Engel, B. T. A behavioral strategy for promoting treatment compliance following myocardial infarction. Psychosom. Med., *40*: 413–419, 1978.

17. Bigelow, C. E. and Stizer, M. Tobacco use and dependence. In *Textbook of Primary Care Medicine*, edited by L. R. Barker, J. R. Burton and P. D. Zieve, Williams & Wilkins, Baltimore, 1982.

18. Cryer, P. E., Haymond, M. W., Santiago, J. V. and Shah, S. D. Smoking, catecholamines and coronary heart disease. Cardiovasc. Med., *2*: 471–476, 1977.

19. Vogt, T. M., Selvin, S., Widdowson, G. and Hulley, S. B. Expired air carbon monoxide and serum thiocyanate as objective measures of cigarette exposure. Am. J. Public Health, *67(No. 6)*: 545–549, 1977.

20. *The Smoking Digest, Progress Report on a Nation Kicking the Habit.* U.S. Departments of Health, Education and Welfare, Public Health Service and National Institutes of Health, Washington, D. C., Oct. 1977.

21. Wilhelmsson, C., Vedin, J. A., Elmfeldt, D. Tiblin, G. and Wilhelmsen, L. Smoking and myocardial infarction. Lancet, *1*: 415–420, 1975.

22. Foreyt, J. P. Obesity. In *Behavioral Approaches to Medical Treatment*, edited by R. B. Williams, Jr. and W. D. Gentry, pp. 77–98. Ballinger Publishing Co., Cambridge, 1977.

23. Stunkard, A. J. From explanation to action in psychosomatic medicine: The case of obesity. Psychosom. Med., *37*: 195–236, 1975.

24. Engel, B. T. and Bleecker, E. R. Application of operant conditioning techniques to the control of the cardiac arrhythmias. In *Cardiovascular Psychophysiology: Current Issues in Response Mechanisms, Biofeedback and Methodology*, edited by P. A. Obrist et al., pp. 456–476. Aldine, Chicago, 1974.

25. Scott, R. W., Blanchard, E. B., Edmundson, E. D. and Young, L. D. A shaping procedure for heart-rate control in chronic tachycardia. Percep. Mot. Skills, *37*: 327–338, 1973.

26. Vaitl, D. Biofeedback—Einsatz in der Behandlung einer Patientin mit Sinustachykardie. In *Biofeedback Therapie*, edited by H. Legewie and L. Nusselt. Urban and Schwarzenberg, München, Berlin, Wien, 1975.

27. Bleecker, E. R. and Engel, B. T. Learned control of cardiac rate and cardiac condition in a patient with Wolff-Parkinson-White syndrome. N. Engl. J. Med., *288*: 560–562, 1973.

28. Bleecker, E. R. and Engel, B. T. Learned control of ventricular rate in patients with atrial fibrillation. Psychosom. Med., *35*: 161–175, 1973.

29. Weiss, T. and Engel, B. T. Operant conditioning of heart rate in patients with premature ventricular contractions. Psychosom. Med., *33*: 301–321, 1971.

30. Pickering, T. G. and Miller, N. E. Learned voluntary control of heart rate and rhythm in two subjects with premature ventricular contractions. Br. Heart J., *39*: 152–159, 1977.

31. Pickering, T. and Gorham, G. Learned heart-rate control by a patient with a ventricular parasystolic rhythm. Lancet, February, 252–253, 1975.

32. Kleinman, K. M., Goldman, H., Snow, M. Y. and Korol, B. Relationship between essential hypertension and cognitive functioning. II. Effects of biofeedback training generalize to non-laboratory environment. Psychophysiology, *14*: 192–197, 1977.

33. Benson, H., Rosner, B. A., Marzetta, B. R. and Klemchuk, H. M. Decreased blood-pressure in pharmacologically treated hypertensive patients who regularly elicited the relaxation response. Lancet, February, 289–291, 1974.

34. Benson, H., Rosner, B. A., Marzetta, B. R. and Klemchuk, H. P. Decreased blood pressure in borderline hypertensive subjects who practiced meditation. J. Chronic Dis., *27*: 163–169, 1974.

35. Blackwell, B., Bloomfield, S., Gartside, P., Robinson, A., Hanenson, I., Magenheim, H., Nidich, S. and Zigler, R. Transcendental meditation in hypertension. Lancet, January, 223–226, 1976.

36. Taylor, C. B., Farquhar, J. W., Nelson, E. and Agras, S. Relaxation therapy and high blood pressure. Arch. Gen. Psychiatry, *34*: 339–432, 1977.

37. Stone, R. A. and DeLeo, J. Psychotherapeutic control of hypertension. N. Engl. J. Med., *294*: 80–84, 1976.

38. Wallace, R. K. Physiological effects of transcendental meditation. Science, *67*: 1751, 1970.

39. Messerli, F. H., Decarvalho, J. G. R., Christie, B. and Frohlich, E. D. Systemic haemodynamic effects of biofeedback in borderline hypertension. Clin. Sci., *57*: 437s–439s, 1979.

40. Glasgow, M. S., Engel, B. T. and Gaarder, K. R.

Behavioral treatment of high blood pressure. II. Acute and sustained effects of relaxation and systolic blood pressure biofeedback. Psychosom. Med., 44: 155–170, 1982.

41. Engel, B. T., Glasgow, M. S. and Gaarder, K. R. Behavioral treatment of high blood pressure. III. Follow-up results and treatment recommendations. Psychosom. Med., 45: 23–29, 1983.

42. Patel, C. Yoga and biofeedback in the management of hypertension. Lancet, November, 1053–1055, 1973.

43. Patel, C. 12-month follow-up of yoga and biofeedback in the management of hypertension. Lancet, January, 62–64, 1975.

44. Patel, C. Randomised control trial of yoga and bioofeedback in management of hypertension. Lancet, July, 93–95, 1975.

45. Patel, C. Biofeedback-aided relaxation and meditation in the management of hypertension. Biofeedback Self Regul., 2: 1–41, 1977.

CHAPTER 21

Strategies in General Psychiatry

CHARLES S. ADLER
SHEILA MORRISSEY ADLER

"To hold as 'twere a mirror up to nature."
—William Shakespeare
Hamlet
"Despise no new accident in your body, but ask opinion of it."
—Francis Bacon
Of Regimen of Health

In nearly every treatment setting, the relationship between a therapist, a suffering patient, and a biofeedback instrument abounds with psychological issues. In some conditions, such as anxiety states and tension headaches, psychological issues may be dominant; in others, such as physical medicine, they may be subordinate. Yet, they are rarely absent. In physical medicine, for example, one's primary attention is directed towards helping a patient whose neuromuscular functioning is compromised. Meanwhile, that patient's body image, self-esteem, and capacity for optimism may also be impaired, or even broken. The degree to which psychological factors play a part in a particular case cannot be predicted by the nature of the disorder or the type of treatment facility in which the patient is seen.

Biofeedback facilitates the ability of many patients to communicate with a therapist and, aided by the mediation of psychophysiological insights, with their own bodies. The therapist should always recall how difficult it is for one human being to ask another for help, or to bare his psychological soul. Patients learning self-regulation will be as responsive to a therapist's capacity for empathy, and a sensitive to his inconsistencies as they are in any other form of therapy. They need time at the start of treatment to develop confidence in the therapist's motives and interest and time at the end of treatment, for a traditional working through of termination issues.

Patients judge a therapist not just by the questions he chooses to pursue, but also by his dress, bearing, and the overall tone of his of-fice. These factors determine how much the patient will be willing to reveal of himself. Moreover, such impressions can even influence which self-perceptions a patient's automatic protective mechanism will allow to reach consciousness. The patient who sees his therapist as only being interested in training people to perform physiological acrobatics, or as someone who "introduces" people to the instrument and then considers his job accomplished, is significantly more likely to leave intrapsychic problems repressed. A therapist's orientation influences what he sees, partly because he interprets things differently and partly because most patients are intuitive enough to notice only those problems they feel will be acceptable to their therapist's frame of reference.

Many patients presume that the person instructing them in biofeedback is conversant with the most up-to-date theories and treatments. As a result, they may ascribe unintended meanings to many offhand questions or comments, looking for clues to their illness, its causes, or prognosis. The reason for asking questions seemingly unrelated to presenting complaints should therefore be clarified.

SOME PRACTICAL CONSIDERATIONS

In psychiatry, biofeedback is most applicable as an adjunct in the treatment of anxiety states and in other conditions where anxiety is prominent. Nonspecific benefits of biofeedback make it useful with certain chronic and difficult patients. It offers potential for investigating and treating psychosomatic disorders. Neurotic conditions with somatization are especially amenable to biofeedback treatment as it can both alleviate anxiety and foster insight. Biofeedback can aid in revealing, confirming, or disconfirming areas of intrapsychic conflict. Psychotic and organic conditions are generally either non- or contraindications.

Character disorders are treatable only to the extent that anxiety plays a role in their maintenance.

Professionals continue to debate who is qualified to use biofeedback. This issue is especially important when treating the psychiatric patient, as the most frequent adverse reaction is a precipitous uncovering of repressed material the patient can't handle. A straightforward guideline is this: any therapist should be trained to evaluate and treat the patients and conditions in question without biofeedback and should also have training and experience with the biofeedback modality being used. In the case of psychiatric disorders, this means a therapist should have a professional level education in diagnosis and treatment of psychological disturbances by traditional means. Occasionally, particularly empathic individuals with lesser qualifications may administer biofeedback if they are actively supervised by a fully qualified professional within the facility. Although these are conservative standards, we have found that learning the technical aspects of instrumentation, while important, is less critical than understanding the patients and the disorders with which biofeedback will be used.

A biofeedback instrument continuously reflects to a patient the interaction between his stream of consciousness and some aspect of his physiology, allowing for a nonverbal "internal dialogue" which is absent from most therapies. Although this dialogue is present in some other self-regulatory therapies, it alone is magnified by biofeedback, as the others rely on proprioception for half of the conversation. Fantasies, misconceptions, and unrecognized attitudes towards one's body may be revealed through this process. Frequent hidden attitudes toward one's body are resentment, impatience, disgust, and fear.

BIOFEEDBACK AND PSYCHODYNAMIC THERAPY

Our work has focused attention on the exciting confluence of biofeedback with psychodynamic therapy (1–6), where we have observed biofeedback to act as a psychological barometer. A technique that we call biofeedback-psychotherapy maximizes the therapeutic potential of this tendency. We encourage a patient to allow his mind to drift "randomly" among images and associations that arise while he is in a state of biofeedback-assisted relaxation; and we then note which of these images repeatedly register physiological change on the feedback.

We came upon this technique serendipitously while treating a patient suffering from conversion headaches. Her lifelong hysterical personality was complicated by an acute conversion blindness, and this was in turn accompanied by a persistent conversion headache. Symptoms developed abruptly following an encounter with several intoxicated men whom she feared were planning to rape her. When first seen in the hospital, she was a study in contradictions: a fundamentalist minister's wife who dressed and acted seductively; a chief complaint of "I'm blind," but wearing sunglasses; insisting she was distressed in nearly ebullient tones.

One part of her treatment was frontal electromyographic biofeedback (EMGBF) for the continuous headaches, which showed high and unvarying tension levels for the first four sessions. During the fifth session, the readings suddenly dropped to low levels, rose, and abruptly dropped again. At this point, the patient laughed and remarked, "I know what's causing my headaches now, doctor, and don't think I need any more biofeedback." Asked to elaborate, she "confessed" that she had been struggling to suppress the wish to have an affair, "a sinful thought for a God-fearing person." While experimenting with trial and error on the feedback she allowed herself to picture the man and the imagined affair in detail, and an immediate decrescendo from the feedback tones greeted these initiatives. To confirm the connection, she again put the image out of her mind, again let it in. Her impression of cause and effect was confirmed. The headaches left from that point on, as did the blindness, and the underlying struggle was made available for therapeutic discussion. We realized that this patient had recognized more than she might ever have without EMGBF, but that biofeedback divorced from this insight also would not have helped her symptoms.

That was in 1970, and having been alerted to this process, we observed many other patients to report spontaneously that whenever a particular theme or image appeared, their peripheral temperature plummeted or their EMG skyrocketed. Curiosity was typically provoked because the image was not necessarily one they had associated with anxiety. After patients shared these correlations, we would seek through discussion to find a hidden element at the root of these reactions. The technique has since intrigued many patients who view feedback as an emotional divining rod, immediately tagging associations that trigger anxiety or anger.

DEVELOPMENT OF INSIGHT

Biofeedback-psychotherapy confronts a patient with his physiological reactions and gently insists that he reflect upon any discrepancies between how he is reacting and how he thinks he is consciously feeling. The inherent impartiality of an instrument reduced the patient's tendency to dismiss or disclaim the personal relevance of the direction the feedback takes. Since patients initially do not understand the meaning of unexpected shifts of the feedback, the therapist must clarify the significance of such fluctuations, and teach patients to carefully attend to their antecedents. If, following a sudden downturn in the feedback, the therapist asks about the thought content that preceded it, he should take care to avoid having his comments be overfrequent, so that the patient doesn't experience them as nagging or intrusive. It may require trial and error to find the right balance for each therapist and patient so points can be driven home without invading the sanctity of that inner world we call thought. One will often wish to discuss associations with the feedback running so that it can continue to "interpret" the content of the discussion. The patient is eventually better able to recognize situational antecedents to anxiety without the need for feedback, because he becomes increasingly aware of subtle proprioceptive signs that herald its onset.

Derivative thermal feedback is one good parameter to monitor for this purpose. The instrument is adjusted so that rapid changes in either direction will trigger a tone, but small fluctuations are filtered out.

It is an axiom of psychosomatic medicine that any change in mental-emotional functioning, big or small, conscious or unconscious, causes a corresponding shift in physiological functioning and vice versa (7). As professionals using biofeedback discover the pleasure, potential, and adventure of using biofeedback to deal with the "unconscious" part, even if they don't formally use "biofeedback-psychotherapy," they will become increasingly attuned to the appearance of unconscious nuances in their patients' productions.

When introspection is regularly blocked by anxiety, patients can be desensitized to the *process* of looking at themselves. The therapist may suggest that a patient scan internally for feelings related to a troublesome pattern of physiological reactivity. With "advice" from the feedback, the therapist can back off from further interpretation if physical signs of rising anxiety warn that resistance might soon reach a point at which the patient will defensively "not really hear" is pushed further. Guided by the feedback, self-reflection can be resumed or postponed according to the patient's response. In this way, otherwise inaccessible topics can be approached gradually.

We have observed that psychophysiological insights a patient gains from witnessing his reactions on a biofeedback instrument can increase his capacity for empathy for himself and others. While this seems an unexpected byproduct of biofeedback, perhaps we can make the connection less mysterious. As a result of interpersonal anxieties, many psychiatric patients behave in a masochistic, self-renunciating manner wherein "appearing" takes priority over "being." Biofeedback accentuates a patient's self-awareness, and he often comes to recognize that it is as if he were two people, an "inner" (or "true"—they are both "real") and a "public" him. The "public" him predominates in interpersonal relationships, and takes its behavioral cues from external rather than internal sources. Such a patient is unaware of how much this inner "self" differs from the "self" he presents to the world; that beneath a fixed smile and frequent laugh, his physiology is doing flipflops trying—unsuccessfully—to get his attention. And it always takes a migraine headache to finally catch that attention.

As one premise of biofeedback is that there can be a discrepancy between what a person believes he is feeling and how his body is reacting, it is an ally in pointing out self-deception. Once aware of this dichotomy, the patient can fight to let his outer self more accurately reflect his inner one. As a result of that personal battle, he often becomes more sensitive to comparable public-private splits in others. Less preoccupation with appearances also frees up attention that can be used to empathize with others in social situations.

Additionally, it is sometimes possible to direct the patient's attention centripetally back from an empathic awareness of emotional cues in others towards recognition of emotional cues in himself. The patient can be invited to pinpoint how he knows what other people are feeling. He can be asked to reflect upon how, as a child, he knew when his parents were worried or angry. He is often surprised at the number of subtle similarities present between his own affective manifestations and those he recalls seeing in his parents.

Many types of relaxation therapy can enhance free association in psychoanalytically oriented therapies. Any technique that reduces a patient's anxiety also decreases his resistance to free association. Glucksman (9) gives examples of the usefulness of the galvanic skin response (GSR) feedback when incorporating biofeedback-psychotherapy into the private practice of psychoanalysis. He has also outlined the direct effects of incorporating biofeedback-psychotherapy into an analytically oriented treatment (10), in a paper enriched by formal commentaries from six members of the biofeedback and the psychoanalytic communities.

Theta State

Physiological feedback of the theta state is being studied for its capacity to facilitate increased production of primary process associations. The theta EEG rhythm is associated with a twilight state flow of images and sensations similar to the hypnogogic imagery common immediately before dropping off to sleep. Preliminary work by Green (11) has indicated personality changes of a beneficial nature in normal students undergoing theta training. Budzynski (12) devised an instrument that teaches a subject to maintain theta for a prolonged period.

SOME CAUTIONS

It is advisable to try theta feedback with psychiatric patients only in a research setting. This causion is supported by findings of Luthe, Jung, Levendula, and others (13–15). Luthe, in his classic work delineating Autogenic Therapy (13), cites extensive experience with material similar to theta imagery. He has evolved a sophisticated technique called Autogenic Neutralization, which facilitates the release of these images and other sensations, motor discharges, etc., in a controlled and therapeutic manner. For selected conditions, the technique is one of the most dramatically effective in psychiatry. Experience in safely guiding this process is a prerequisite to its use. Jung (14) similarly cautioned against the dangers involved in abetting the verbalization of unchecked fantasy with the patient's eyes closed, which he studied while evolving a comparable but less refined process called "active imagination."

Other complexities must be understood before using biofeedback (3, 6, 16). An easily overlooked caution—a somewhat quixotic one—is that as biofeedback has been associated with so few serious side effects compared with most medical interventions, it's practitioners can become overconfident and underobservant (17). Most adverse reactions result from biofeedback's capacity to catalyze the release of more repressed psychological material than the patient can cope with.

Anxiety can be protective; it can help a patient defend against taking action. Some patients resist anxiety reduction—and therefore relaxation—from fear that it will lead to action of an aggressive or sexual nature. If these dynamics are suspected, the strength of the patient's impulse control should be assessed. Evidence of good impulse control in the patient's history is the most reassuring finding in this regard. Patients frequently do become more aware of aggressive and sexual impulses during relaxation, but as their defensive capacity is also paradoxically reinforced by the relaxed state, they can usually deal with these impulses verbally.

Most biofeedback professionals accept as a given that psychologically dysphoric states such as anxiety and depression have accompanying physiological changes. Like these dysphoric states, the psychological defenses against them also have somatic components. Many patients brace their striate musculature in defensive posturings. Tightening the abdominal muscles to prevent crying is one example. Autonomic and hormonal mechanisms can also function defensively. A migraineur's "holding" his peripheral vascular tone in an unvarying state of vasoconstriction (18) may be a physiological defense against the overswings that characterize the symptomatic migraine attack itself.

When biofeedback-assisted relaxation is being considered, one should try to discover which aspects of a patient's physiology are primary and which are defensive. It is important to make this distinction; the consequences of removing a patient's defenses are quite different from the consequences of removing symptoms.

In contrast to general relaxation therapy, a patient using biofeedback can be given a potent tool with which to change a specific physiological function without knowing what purpose that function serves. Fortunately, homeostatic mechanisms are usually even more powerful, and automatically disallow inappropriate or ill-timed change—but not always. In that case, there is a breakthrough of symptomatic affect or physiology. When the patient with chronically tensed abdominal muscles relaxes them, he may find himself suddenly and inexplicably sobbing.

Toomin (19) first noted that the GSR responded differently to arousal of conscious or preconscious affect than it did to the excitation of unconscious impulses or to the stimulation of psychological defenses. Conscious or preconscious anxiety raises the GSR. Defenses, on the other hand, are hallmarked by a drop or flattening of the GSR. Following the recognition and verbal release of such reactivated repressed material, GSR levels return to normal height and variability.

Indications that highly charged unconscious content is threatening to erupt during biofeedback include traditional signs of resistance, nonverbal evidence of discomfort, frequent spontaneous interruptions for seemingly superficial chatter, or intransigent turnabouts in relaxation. Such signs can be responded to with prompt queries that attempt further psychological evaluation.

Psychological problems we have observed to frequently interfere with relaxation have been (a) need for crying due to unresolved grief or masked depression, and (b) tenuously repressed rage or resentment. The full spectrum of repressed affects and impulses can be implicated, however, including erotic feelings, guilt, paranoia, strong dependent or regressive urges, painful childhood memories, feelings of physical vulnerability, and memories of physical trauma. Because of the stillness required during biofeedback, thanatophobia, fear of helplessness or passivity (especially in men), and even homosexual panic can be aggravated in susceptible individuals. The patient with a childhood history of chronic illness may be flooded with self-hatred when he focuses on his body. Those temporary distortions of body image consequent to decreased proprioception which normally accompany deep relaxation can stimulate anxiety in a patient with poor body boundaries; he may feel as though his body's spatial definition is growing vague and that his contact with it is fading as a result.

PATIENT SELECTION

All types of patients come for biofeedback. Patients who have been therapeutically frustrating and those who have not been helped by traditional approaches are often referred for treatment with any relatively new therapy; biofeedback is no exception. While certain patients refractory to previous therapies can be helped with biofeedback, the tendency for patients with high motivation and ego strength to have a better prognosis than their counterparts holds as true in biofeedback treatment as it does in traditional psychotherapy.

Adolescents having difficulty adjusting to the developmental tasks of their age can be helped for a variety of reasons peculiar to adolescence: (a) adolescents are curious; they may see biofeedback as a challenge and an adventure; (b) young adolescents are often too "grown up" for play therapy but too constricted for a gratifying verbal exchange; the feedback provides a compromise around which treatment can be structured; (c) rebellious tendencies so dear to adolescents can be safely acted out by doing poorly on the machine; their prized autonomy is guaranteed by the fact that only *they* can alter the feedback; (d) adolescents can save face with their peers by stating that they are learning an impressive skill, rather than coming in to "get shrunk;" similarly, any secret wishes to have dependency needs met can be gratified through "coaching"—and a coach is an acceptable image for a teenager to turn to for help; (e) at a time when he feels his body is growing too gangly, too sexual, and too fast, the feedback offers him a chance to experience some control over it and to put the reins to a sense of physiological anarchy.

Middle-aged and elderly patients can also be succesfully treated with biofeedback if existential problems mentioned in the last chapter are taken into account. We find that age requires some shift in style and duration of biofeedback-assisted treatment, but in no way precludes its usefulness (20).

It has been observed (21) that some patients view the feedback instrument as an idealized talisman that can magically confer uncommon powers to control their bodies. This type of person uses the feedback in an attempt to reconstitute narcissistic defenses. Improvement for these patients may be less durable, since it is in part maintained by elements of suggestion.

Patients who have wondered whether a mental health professional could help them with an emotional problem but are afraid, ashamed, or contending with an unsympathetic spouse, are sometimes able to justify starting biofeedback "for help with their physiology" and, while in treatment, "can see whether counselling is for them." Such a patient is often reassured after a few sessions, and starts to talk freely about long-standing problems.

Patients may also be sent by doctors who, for a variety of reasons, are uncomfortable about directly referring patients for psychotherapy. Some are unconvinced about the value of "talk;" others simply feel awkward about telling a patient that his problem may be psychological.

Biofeedback's concreteness and immediacy make it less frustrating than verbal therapy for certain inarticulate or concretely oriented patients. At the opposite pole, biofeedback is also tactically useful for the hyperarticulate person whose life is filled with superficial intellectual insights couched in jargon which bears little resemblance to the actual feelings underneath. Such patients find their rationalizations have been bypassed and disarmed by the nonverbal information from the feedback.

Some highly dependent people feel secretly and quietly bereft when away from their parents, spouse, sect, or even children. For such patient's, internalizing a protective image of the therapist is a vital but challenging goal of therapy. In classical psychotherapy, patients have little access to what is known as a "transitional object." A transitional object is like a child's teddy bear or Linus' blanket; it serves as a tangible symbol of the parent (also to be read as: therapist), one that comforts the child during a separation. In the normal developmental sequence, the child eventually develops a permanent internal image of the parents that stands in for them when they are away. Excessively dependent patients have progressed poorly if at all through this emotional ontogeny and may be fixated at a developmental stage in which they fell the need for a supportive person to be present constantly.

Biofeedback instructions (and at times, the instrument as well) are sometimes used spontaneously by a patient as a transitional object. Relaxation instructions can be a concrete link to the therapist when the patient remembers or incants them during home practice. When it is therapeutically indicated to enhance the transitional object value of the instructions as a supportive measure, the patient can be given a tape recording of the instructions. These tapes work best when they are specifically recorded during the patient's session, and when the therapist directly addresses the patient by name in them. (In contrast, the impersonality of a prerecorded tape can leave a psychiatric patient feeling less than unique.) Ideally, the therapist's predictability and interest will in time allow the patient to develop a stable internal image of him as a comforting and helpful figure, an image that obviates the need for a "transitional" recording. Biofeedback thus supplements psychotherapy by replaying one aspect of the childhood task of achieving autonomy.

For an occasional patient, the initial experience of using biofeedback is uncomfortable; it only seems to confirm his preconception that he has little control over his body, and this perception is followed by a corresponding drop in self-esteem. Other patients who fear they lack adequate self-control attempt to deny this helplessness by becoming preoccupied with atttempts to overcontrol the body's functions. Such endeavors are soon found to be impossible, impractical, and fatiguing.

Hysterical and obsessive-compulsive patients have divergent styles of relating to biofeedback. Hysterics get bored, neglect home practice, overreact with wide physiological swings, and have trouble cognitively integrating the feedback information in a usefully structured way. They are more frightened by their impulses, and at times will eroticize procedures such as the attaching of electrodes. A formal approach in a well-lighted room with the patient seated rather than reclining is helpful when treating this type of patient.

The obsessive-compulsive is often diligent about home practice, but strives too hard for results, experiencing the feedback as a pure success/failure situation. As opposed to the hysteric, he may be attentive to minute details, yet be unable to relinquish his attempts to make everything happen according to plan and on schedule. Passive concentration is a difficult state for these patients to achieve or even conceptualize. Compulsive patients approach the feedback task in a tightly ritualized manner; they feel constrained by an internal lack of freedom (self-imposed) to explore through trial and error, a lack evidenced by the constricted range of physiological fluctuations resistered on the instrument. Many obsessive-compulsives and certain depressed patients are both perfectionistic and self-critical; they project these strident superegos onto the instrument, experiencing its signals as criticism rather than as information. Before long, they become restless, angry, or despairing as each sound from the machine is interpreted as berating them for an imperfect performance. They compare each performance with the preceding one.

Patients with a serious, major depression or a primary obsessional state requiring hospitalization have been found by Stroebel (23) to be incapable of successfully using biofeedback. When treating less severly ill obsessive-compulsive patients, three things are helpful: (a) substituting highly supportive verbal coaching for direct feedback, guided by the therapist's silent monitoring of changing physiological levels; (b) shifting to a low sensitivity setting in the same or an easier feedback modality to the slightest maneuver in the right direction brings success, then only hiking the sensitivity very, very slowly; (c) finally, interrupting feedback for discussion of the patient's problematic view of his relationship to the instrument.

THE PATIENT AND THE INSTRUMENT
Tranference

As we have just seen, the style in which a patient undertakes to learn biofeedback typically recreates the way he approaches new situations outside the office. Attitudes toward the perceptions of both therapist and therapy that spring from a reenactment of important childhood relationships rather than from a realistic appraisal of the actual here-and-now situation are called transference reactions, and it is vital to recognize when they are intruding into any therapeutic encounter, including self-regulatory ones. The therapist using biofeedback is sometimes faced with a unique and fascinating form of transference: transference to the biofeedback instrument itself.

In previous papers (1, 3, 4, 6, 24), we have observed that patients frequently develop transference-like perceptions of the biofeedback instrument during the course of therapy. One patient may feel that the instrument is trying to frustrate him, and has a "will of its own." Others may experience the instrument as ridiculing them, teasing them, withholding its comfort from them, deceiving them, competing with them, invading them, or exposing them. The transference can also be "positive;" one patient developed erotic impulses towards a garden-variety EMG device and, leaning over only half-playfully, kissed it! More common is the patient who expects to be directly protected or soothed by the instrument. In fact, any of the distorted expectations about interpersonal relationships that people carry forward from childhood can be projected onto an instrument. The specific distortions usually reflects either attitudes important people held toward the patient during childhood or feelings the patient secretly harbors himself from that time.

Actually, the biofeedback instrument is symbolically in a very special relationship with the patient; it can be seen as nurturing or withholding mother, connected by an "umbilical cord" (electrode leads), and responding sensitively to his every shift in feeling. The form of this interaction is analogous to the infant's symbiotic relationship with his mother. It is in one sense the idealized symbiosis, as no actual mother could ever respond with the precise immediacy of the feedback. This allows the patient to experience the instrument as a functional extension of himself, just as the neonate normally experiences his mother. On the other hand, it is also a "frustrating mother" as it does not respond to the patient's agitation with soothing sounds; if anything, it responds in the opposite way, and sets up its own squall when he gets tense. This gives the therapist a chance to see how the patient responds to frustration, and information can sometimes be deduced about the qualitative tone of that earliest of relationships. Might the patient be helped to understand his reactions to frustration by this "symbolic mother"? Might this insight then alter characterologically inappropriate reactions to frustrations he feels as an adult?

As we have said, patients who never internalized an image of a protective parent grow into adults lacking adequate means to soothe themselves through times of loneliness and stress, and the corrective emotional experience for such a patient can come when they recognize that a therapist (or mother key figure) is providing consistent, relevant help. In this process, the instrument can function as a reminder of the availability of that help, one which is abstract enough to be nonthreatening.

Transference reactions to the instrument are sometimes displaced transference reactions to the therapist. Displacement to the instrument adds emotional "distance" from the therapist; it reduces the patient's fears of confronting his perceptions by putting things, so to speak, in the "third person." The instrument is also a convenient vehicle for interpretation. Few patients persist in the belief that a biofeedback instrument has "motivations;" the patient will usually recognize that the source of any feelings is within himself.

The therapist can be alert to indications that the patient is having transference-like reactions to the instrument; their presence is usually hinted at rather than announced outright. Jokes and offhand comments about the instrument are not always meaningless, but are a common way in which the patient gives clues to his reactions to the biofeedback instrument.

Areas for Biofeedback in Psychiatry

The neutrality of biofeedback as a tool allows it to find application in as many schools of psychological theory and practice as does a box of Kleenex. Historically, it has been primarily applied within the context of behavior therapy. Yet, it clearly blends well with psychodynamic psychotherapy also, and biofeedback can find a home in many other theoretical persuasions as well.

There are many areas of psychiatry to which biofeedback is currently applicable. Yet its eventual place in the armamentarium of psychiatrists and clinical psychologists is still evolving. A review of the biofeedback literature is of less help than might be expected in deciding whether to use biofeedback with a given patient or illness. Studies to date are most usefully read to extract underlying principles and practical techniques, rather than to pin down a precise list of indications.

Undoubtedly, research will eventually determine additional areas where biofeedback is

better than other potent means for learning generalized relaxation such as autogenic training or progressive relaxation or other means of affecting specific dysfunctional organs or attitudes (autogenic modification, hypnosis). In the clinical practice of mental health, the theoretical details of a technique should dovetail with a flexible, empirical, and intuitive commitment to the art of medicine even when prolific literature documents that technique. At present, the psychiatric applications of biofeedback are not backed by a voluminous or a time tempered literature. Unfortunately, research into psychiatric applications of biofeedback is handicapped because studies using biofeedback usually fail to replicate how biofeedback is actually used in practice, and may have unjustly disappointing results.

On the other hand, field research using biofeedback in conjunction with traditional therapies (used concomitantly) is both difficult and time-consuming, as one needs to control many variables.

Migraine Studies

The authors did an experiment that attempted to follow this latter paradigm. The work, which studied the effects of biofeedback on seriously impaired migraineurs, was presented in 1983 at the first International Headaches Society meeting in Munich, and published 2 years later. This controlled, 10-year study (25) compared the effectiveness of standardized thermal feedback to criterion, along with appropriate medications, dietary changes, and other life-style modifications, to the effect of this same treatment combined with psychotherapy of variable length (sometimes only a few sessions) and depth—these last factors were determined by patient-specific requirements. As can be seen in Figure 21.1, 10–12 years after treatment had ended, the experimental group (n = 53) dropped from a mean of 36 migraine attacks per year to 5.8 per year. The matched controls only fell from 35 per year to 20 per year, a difference significant at the p < .01 level using the chi^2 test with the Yates correction. Mean number of different medications taken by the experimental group fell from 5 to 1.1; the contols declined only from 5 to 3.7. Continued regular or intermittent use of self-regulatory techniques was 91% in the experimental group at the time of follow-up, while just 45% of controls still bothered to. Treatment proved slightly longer for

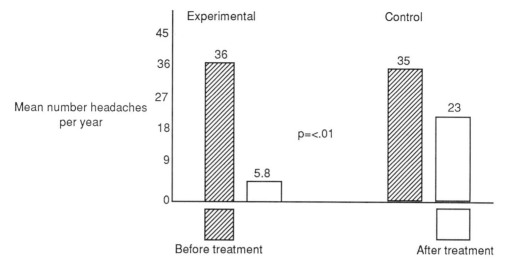

Figure 21.1   Mean number of headaches per year before and after treatment (25).

this more successful group—mean of 36 sessions compared with 20. The research indicated that the patients who did not get psychotherapy nevertheless usually found the intervention had been worthwhile, though considerably less so.

In 1984 we presented a paper at a conference on migraine in London which explored the presumed reasons for this difference in durability of outcome, and published it the following year (26). In short, there appear to be many areas of synergy, including but not limited to increased insight; these became manifest when the techniques were used conjointly, and are detailed.

Clinical Observations

For now, it is our candid belief that the practical observations of experienced clinicians can be trusted as much as, and sometimes more than, superficial and potentially deceptive data produced by many studies which look only at the effects of biofeedback. If the experience of many clinicians concurs, the evidence becomes more compelling. For example, although studies to support biofeedback's use in anxiety reduction are fragmentary, most experienced clinicians have found it useful for treating anxiety in selected patients—which is not to suggest that this criterion is ultimately sufficient, or should mark the end of our quest.

INDICATIONS FOR THE USE OF BIOFEEDBACK

Discussion of the psychiatric indications for biofeedback will begin with a review of its applications to anxiety states and the many specific manifestations and derivatives of anxiety, as this has been the most important psychiatric use to date. In the treatment of anxiety, biofeedback supplements more fundamental relaxation and homeostasis-enhancing treatments.

Use with Medication

For selected patients, biofeedback-assisted relaxation can supplement or supplant ataraxic drugs. When compared with tranquilizers, the method has greater functional specificity, as it does not need to subdue entire regions of the central nervous system to be effective. When ataraxic medication is still indicated, biofeedback can act synergistically to potentiate the drug's calming effects. Relaxation may be the best alternative for the patient allergic to available compounds, or with religious beliefs precluding drug use, or for the one who illogically believes that taking medication proves, and thereby creates, his psychiatric illness, an illness he wishes to deny. The frequent therapeutic dilemma of how to treat the anxiety-ridden yet chronically suicidal patient can be finessed by including relaxation therapy in his treatment program.

Addictions

Drug addiction, a problematic disorder, is often initiated by anxiety; its treatment can be fortified by using relaxation techniques. The crucial element is their capacity to provide an alternative to the anxiety-relieving but addictive substance. Many addicts cannot persevere in treatment programs that demand the addictive substance to be forsworn and replaced by nothing but the patient's tenuous willpower. Except with the anti-social personality, people who become addicted are usually attempting, through self-medication, to treat themselves in order to function better as well as to feel better (28). They are often trying to quell a deep sense of emotional or spiritual emptiness with roots in feelings of inadequacy and narcissistic injury; or they are trying to relieve an overwhelming anxiety and depression that results from this state. We have here a basic premise: that most addicts may, first and foremost, be trying to heal themselves, rather than trying to defy their doctors or the law. It is this attempt at self-therapy behind the drug use, if present, that can be harnessed when offering biofeedback-assisted relaxation as an alternate means of coping. Opiates, stimulants, tranquilizers, sedatives, alcohol, and analgesics can all be abused in an attempt to find such relief. Whether the addicting drug is used in an attempt to cope with a problem or in an attempt to escape it seems to be primarily determined by the personality of the user.

Drug and alcohol abuse have historically proved resistant to many well-intentioned and well-reasoned treatments. These problems are frequently secondary to primary psychological or medical disorders. The patient in chronic pain or chronic fear grasps at any source of relief, no matter what the long-term consequences. Pain—physical or emotional—is always in the present and takes precedence. The chronicity of his primary problem leads to addiction. Relaxation therapies can offer such patients an alternative for finding inner quiet and so short-circuit the desperate search for an external, chemical source of calming.

Many patients with a recurrent illness such as migraine use drugs prophylactically to ward off potential pain (29). Fear of helplessness also causes drugs to be taken in anticipation of an attack. This anxious anticipation not only is a major reason for the use of drugs during pain-free intervals, but also accentuates pain perception during attacks, and therefore, increases drug use during them. Biofeedback-enhanced relaxation may blunt this anxiety and alleviate the accompanying feelings of helplessness by offering something active to do.

Both drug and alcohol misuse are complex phenomena indicating a serious difficulty in functioning, and are not amenable to treatment with relaxation therapy alone. Comprehensive therapy requires a patient to appreciate the need for his determined and extended commitment.

A predictable ability to relax on cue is essential to compete with the powerful relief available from drugs, and learning this may be a long-term task. Offhandedly tacking a dozen sessions of feedback onto a standard rehabilitation program has not been found particularly advantageous in a controlled study of inpatient alcoholics (30). On the other hand, relaxation training can be a powerful tool to supplant maladaptive attempts at controlling anxiety or pain when used as described. In a controlled study, anxiety reduction in alcohol and drug addicts was significantly higher for those given biofeedback and relaxation training both at the time of initial hospitalization and 6–9 months after discharge. (31)

Ask the patient to participate in setting up his own schedule for withdrawal. When there is recurrent pain, help him to see the schedule as a gradually evolving replacement process, rather than as deprivation. When the addiction also serves to reduce anxiety about facing social, familial, and vocational problems, direct treatment of the problems or phobias is also attempted. When drugs are used to cope with intrapsychic problems, such as excessive anger, these feelings are also gradually uncovered and talked about, perhaps using the insight-producing capacity of the instrument as a guide. Although not always feasible, for best results, sufficient training in relaxation should be completed before complete withdrawal from the substance is attempted; otherwise, the frustration of not yet having learned to relax adequately is combined with the dysphoria of withdrawal. This can be problematic; among other things, the patient may walk away from treatment.

Relaxation alone will never be a panacea for patients habituated to relieving desperation through chemistry. It will find greatest usefulness with patients who have a fair prognosis by other criteria.

Smoking, overeating, and similar habits are other derivatives of anxiety whose treatment may be less durable if nothing is offered to substitute for their temporarily calming effects. Some attempts to change these habits have relied upon making an uncomfortable patient yet more uncomfortable, frightened, or guilty if he continues to seek relief in the only way he knows how. Other approaches use rewards for stopping the habit, but the "rewards" generally lean toward the superficial, and fall self-defeatingly short of the direct relief afforded by the habit itself. Simple praise and punishment have been used since the first scratchings of history, and by now their advantages and limitations should be known. Biofeedback can assist this treatment by teaching those patients who are vigorously able to adopt it to substitute the relief afforded by relaxation whenever they feel the urge to drink, use drugs, overeat, or smoke.

Psychosomatic Conditions

Several psychosomatic conditions commonly treatable with biofeedback are discussed below. The reader is directed to Chapters 22–29 for information regarding treatment of additional psychosomatic conditions.

Hyperventilation. Hyperventilation is a common symptom of anxiety. In it, anxiety is experienced as a hunger for air. Symptoms can be either acute or chronic, and include lightheadedness, paresthesias in fingers, toes or lips, blurred vision, headache, and precordial discomfort or pain. Hyperventilation is often misdiagnosed and can masquerade as angina pectoris or other disorders. It is a symptom, but also, paradoxically, through the body's own feedback mechanisms of the interpreted sensations of respiratory alkalosis, a cause of, for example, panic attacks. Direct reduction of anxiety with biofeedback-assisted relaxation may be useful in preventing recurrent episodes, but more immediate steps, such as use of ataraxic medication, are indicated for acute episodes. It is a partner of specific pharmacotherapy and psychotherapy in the longer term plan for treating the basic disorder.

Bruxism. Bruxism is the habit of grinding one's teeth, and is usually in response to tension. It sometimes occurs only during sleep, and can lead to headaches, dental problems, or both. Experience (32, 33) suggests that

EMGBF from the masseter or frontalis muscles improves many patient's ability to recognize this insidious, anxiety-driven habit. As with hyperventilation, full relief will require that some patients work through the psychological problems stimulating anxiety or anger.

Phobias

Anxiety is restricted to isolated phobias in certain patients. In others, treatment may need to deal with multiple phobias, and this is typically accomplished sequentially. With isolated phobias, systematic desensitization is the treatment of choice. Biofeedback can expedite systematic desensitization in five ways: (a) it often teaches the patient to relax more rapidly than does progressive relaxation alone; (b) the therapist can feel confident that the patient has learned to relax before he starts desensitization; (c) it can monitor the part of a patient's physiology most sensitive to anxiety; (d) physiological monitoring can be used to accurately rank the anxiogenic potency of items on a systematic desensitization hierarchy; (e) if the patient is then continuously monitored while he envisions those items in the hierarchy, the therapist can determine precisely when to terminate or resume visualization of a scene. (Research has shown that EMG readings, for example, are detected by the instrument before they are detected by the patient.) As a result of these features, biofeedback makes the desensitization process more efficient, less subject to miscalculation, and shorter.

Insomnia

"Insomnia" has many etiologies, and it is understandable why anxiety is prominent among these. Although biofeedback can frequently help treat the insomnia, there is controversy about the extent of this helpfulness and the best technique for maximizing it. This controversy is partly because insomnia is a symptom of many causes, both physical and emotional. One patient will be waking up early from depression; another may have slept fitfully ever since he started a new medicine for his asthma; still another may be addicted to sedatives but is unable to admit it. The fears we have found to be associated with relaxation can also potentially be aroused by the anticipation of sleep—fear of loss of control, of death in the night, of eruption of traumatic memories of noxious feelings. One patient recalled from childhood his father's occasional (but memorable) agitated wanderings through the house all night waving a gun towards vague and rapidly changeable objects of his paranoia. This memory surfaced only well along in treatment; its recollection and the ensuing discussion were followed by rapid relief of insomnia. Treatment that ignored these memories would likely have been ineffective; yet after such revelations, many a patient still needs help with the insomnia habit, with the physiological pattern.

The first job, then, is to diagnose the particular type of insomnia. When emotional conflict seems to be involved, exploratory psychotherapy may need assistance from either relaxation therapies or biofeedback to realign the habitual aspect of insomnia, since resolution of emotional problems alone might not be enough to reset the "biological clock."

Patients with insomnia sometimes improve following biofeedback treatment for other conditions (34, 35) such as headache, and reveal their sleep problems only when they are "cured." Hauri (36) showed that biofeedback usually relieves serious insomnia when the right type of feedback is given for each category of insomniac. He distinguished patients unable to sleep because they are tense from patients who, although seemingly *not* tense, nevertheless cannot sleep. In this study, EMG feedback or relaxation training reduced only the first type of sleeplessness. Wakefulness without anxiety was resolved by teaching the patient to produce what is known as the sensory-motor EEG rhythm using EEG feedback. As the patient learns to increase production of his sensory-motor rhythm, this is followed by the more frequent appearance in his EEG of "sleep spindles," which normally herald sleep onset. Hauri cautions that biofeedback, though in some ways groundbreaking, is no more a panacea for sleep than it is for other symptoms when appraised realistically.

Cardiac Neurosis

In a cardiac neurosis, the patient either experiences cardiac symptoms in the absence of demonstrable cardiac disease or has a disproportionate fear of actual organic symptoms. Biofeedback may assist the patient with cardiac neurosis to become comfortable with awareness of the subjective sensations accompanying his heartbeat.

Both cardiac neurosis and the foremost clinical manifestation of coronary artery disease, angina pectoris, may be helped with relaxation techniques. The autogenic therapy literature is replete with studies indicating that treatment's usefulness in delaying, limiting, and containing these widespread and frightening disorders (37).

The authors were asked to consult on a long-term coronary disease study at Duke Medical School and to reflect upon how self-regulatory interventions could be provided for Type A coronary patients. The Type A personality described by Rosenmann and Friedman (38) is an aggressive, achievement-oriented, time-conscious individual. He is someone struggling to overcome—through action—chronic anxiety, especially, in our opinion, an abiding thanatophobia, and anticipated helplessness. This individual directs his energies toward averting potential harm that he anticipates from aggressive forces within his environment; in this way, he hopes to feel secure. Such a person might be relieved to learn how to directly calm his own internal "environment" instead, or at least first. Young people with Type A personalities are statistically far more likely to suffer coronary disease and myocardial infarction than are their age-matched Type B counterparts. The individual who already has coronary symptoms might find it most rewarding to learn he could control—however slightly—over the heart itself. This can be approximated by teaching him to vary his pulse rate using cardiotachometry feedback.

Sometimes a cardiac patient will be overcome by fear if required to focus on his heart. Such a patient is initially poorly suited for cardiotachometry feedback. It is generally better to start biofeedback using a peripheral, more easily controllable, and less emotionally loaded physiological function. This might be done through a sequence of progressive relaxation, autogenic training, EMGBF, and thermal feedback. After passive concentration has been mastered in this stepwise way, the patient can then begin working with the cardiotachometer. He is thus not suddenly forced to confront his lack of control over this most vital organ. The extent to which someone with a cardiac neurosis will tolerate awareness of his heart rate can be gauged by asking how comfortable he feels taking his own pulse or when he imagines listening to his heart with a stethoscope.

We have seen patients who learned to reduce the frequency of anginal episodes by using temperature feedback. Both anecdotal reports and the autogenic training literature point out the risk that cardiac patients often become overconfident as the result of any success in self-control, and may not respect the organic limits imposed by their disease. As a result, they can overtax their cardiovascular system through strenuous exertion, sometimes enough to develop another infarction.

Character Disorders

Because people with character disorders have, by definition, less anxiety than other psychiatric patients, they are also generally less motivated and less treatable, with self-regulation as much as with alternative therapies. We earlier described reactions to biofeedback of obsessive-compulsive and hysterical personality disordered patients. Theoretically, it would seem that biofeedback could offer little to help transform the person with an antisocial character. Yet, an empirical study using biofeedback to treat prisoners in a penitentiary resulted in improved behavioral measures following treatment (39).

How might this be explained? One type of sociopathy may derive from the patient's insufficient anxiety about engaging in socially deviant behavior. Another variant has been theorized to come from a person's demoralizing expectation that he will never satisfy the excessive demands of his conscience. This second type therefore defends against such failure by refuting his conscience entirely. Biofeedback and psychotherapy might benefit certain patients in the second category, but patients in the first category might find the relaxation leaving even fewer impediments to deviant behavior. Would one really want to help the thief or tyrant lose any of his guilt or apprehension about wrongdoing, as these dysphoric states are all that restrain him from potential mischief? Further empirical studies—large, controlled, well-designed, and with lengthy follow-up are needed to assess the true role, if any, of biofeedback in character disorders.

Organic Brain Syndrome

Biofeedback might help selected organic brain syndrome patients in two ways: first by modulating the anxiety that descends upon the patient with memory loss triggered by constant fear of social humiliation or progression into dependent status; second, if the organic syndrome is accompanied by seizures, biofeedback may be a treatment of last resort for controlling them. The next section concerns how it serves that unlikely function.

Seizure Disorders

Reducing the frequency of several types of seizures remains one of the most promising and exciting areas in biofeedback research. All evidence suggests that a patient's ability to learn to block impending seizures with biofeedback is a specific, repeatable finding that does not depend upon suggestion. Presently, its use is indicated in conjunction with aggressive medication protocols in patients who are insufficiently helped by those anticonvulsants. We refer the reader to the pioneering work of Sterman (40), who first described the sensory-motor EEG rhythm is cats. He found that its appearance time on EEG feedback could be increased by reinforcing this EEG state with operant conditioning—and that a reduction in seizure activity, in patients as well as in cats, ensued. Subsequent well-controlled studies by Lubar, et al. (41) were decisive in confirming this effect and elucidating it further. Training in sensory-motor rhythm enhancement is a fine example of how biofeedback sometimes can teach patients to reach a state unattainable without the specific information the feedback provides, and where the benefits exceed or differ from ones possible using only generalized relaxation. For further details, the reader is referred to Chapter 7 by Lubar.

BIOFEEDBACK NOT INDICATED

At present, there are no indications that either unipolar or bipolar affective disorders can be helped by biofeedback. Unless research convincingly shows otherwise, one can consider acute schizophrenia a contraindication for biofeedback, and chronic schizophrenia a relative contraindication. Recognition of the strength of genetic and biological factors in these conditions doesn't displace biofeedback from active consideration (these elements are equally present in migraine). Nevertheless, these are soul-shaking disorders for which biofeedback would be, at best, a peripheral participant, even with more refined techniques. And it risks drawing some of the more desperately optimistic (i.e., using denial) families away from the essential psychopharmacological treatments available. Paranoid psychoses can distort a patient's view of biofeedback, and the symbolically symbiotic quality of the interaction with the instrument may lead such a patient to incorporate it into a delusion of influence. The normal experience of feeling less clear body boundaries during relaxation could worsen somatoform and identity-related schizophrenic symptoms. In support of this, temporary exacerbation of hallucinatory activity has been reported in some schizophrenics using biofeedback in a loosely structured setting.

On the other hand, Stroebel (42) and his colleagues treated a mixed group of psychiatric inpatients, including some psychotics, for psychophysiological problems with his "quieting response." technique. Although more sessions were required, many of these patients were helped with targeted psychosomatic disorders—but not, it should be emphasized, with the primary psychiatric illnesses for which they were admitted. Factors that boded poorly for the patients in this group included youth and the presence of either depression or passive-aggressive character traits. Findings such as these urge more research—cautious, restrained research—into the applications and limitations of biofeedback with more serious psychiatric conditions.

SOME CAUTIONS

Biofeedback's propensity to evoke feelings of mild dissociation (beneficial for most patients) must be considered with patients who have a history of *pathologic dissociative reactions* such as fugue states or depersonalization, as the training may rekindle these symptoms.

It is hard to see where a significant increased efficiency would come from using biofeedback in groups. Interpersonal problems are typically allowed to arise in group therapy, as its major therapeutic advantage is an ability to evoke and highlight such problems. But this advantage goes unutilized with biofeedback, yet the liabilities of group treatment remain. Depending upon the type of practice and patient goals, there are settings in which group benefits (e.g., convenience) do outweigh drawbacks (e.g., reduced confidentiality). The situation is better when goals are educational rather than clinical.

As we move toward the future, studies not only need to determine whether biofeedback can be used to alter a given dysfunction transiently, but also whether it significantly shortens or improves upon the traditional treatment of that condition, either alone or combined with with more fundamental relaxation techniques—our "detechnologized" brethen. Biofeedback treatments that endure must translate into practical procedures, that in many areas, though not in all which are being explored, biofeedback has surely met this criterion solidly despite it's having to do so in professions not lacking in hegemony, vested institutional interests, and idealized traditions which yield to the backward pull of history as a stone yields to gravity, (though as much devoid of malice as of vision) (43).

Biofeedback is a new tool one can apply to old questions that in the past could not be answered. In addition to generating current hypotheses, if one peruses the old literature on psychosomatic illness, one will be quickly rewarded with previously unanswerable questions and can decide whether our new methods of "extraction" are cause to reopen an abandoned vein of ore. For example, in the first volume of *Psychosomatic Medicine*, Mittleman and Wolff (44) record falling temperatures over the joints of rheumatoid arthritis patients following experimentally induced emotional stress. In 1943, Patterson et al. (45) found that vascular control in rheumatoid arthritics was highly responsive to disturbing emotional experiences and that their peripheral temperatures returned to baseline levels more slowly than did controls. Is thermal feedback a tool that can discover whether temperature feedback from arthritic joints will provide symptomatic help for this painful malady? Such observations, gathered painstakingly into the old literature, can give one a compass for deciding where to direct research efforts.

References

1. Adler, C. S. and Adler, S. M. Biofeedback; interface with the unconscious. *Proceedings of the Biofeedback Research Society*, Boston, 1972.
2. Adler, C. S. and Adler, S. M. The ontogeny of biofeedback. Presented at meeting of the American Orthopsychiatric Association, San Francisco, 1974.
3. Adler, S. M. and Adler, C. S. The headache swamp: pragmatic problems of biofeedback treatment. *Proceedings of the Biofeedback Research Society*, Colorado Springs, 1974.
4. Adler, C. S. and Adler, S. M. *Biofeedback in*

Psychotherapy, vol. 1. Bio-Monitoring Applications, New York. 1975 (cassette tape).

5. Adler, C. S. and Adler, S. M. Biofeedback psychotherapy for the treatment of headaches: a five-year follow-up. Headache, *16*: 189–191, 1976.

6. Adler, C. S. and Adler, S. M. Interface with the unconscious in biofeedback. Presented at meeting of the Am. Acad. Psychoanalysis, Toronto, 1982.

7. Green, E. E. Green, A. M. and Walters, E. D. Voluntary control of internal states: psychological and physiological. J. Transpersonal Psychol., *2*: 1–26, 1970.

8. Adler, C. S., Adler, S. M. Psychodynamics of migraine: A developmental perspective; In *Psychiatric Aspects of Headache*, edited by C.S. Adler, S.M. Adler, and R.C. Packard. Williams & Wilkins, Baltimore, 1987, pp. 158–180.

9. Glucksman, M. Physiological changes and clinical events during psychotherapy. Presented at joint meeting of the American Academy of Psychoanalysis and The American Psychiatric Association, Toronto, 1982.

10. Glucksman, M. Physiological changes and clinical events during psychotherapy (with commentaries by Nemiah, V.C., Michels, R. Horowitz, M.U., Karasu, T.B., Greenspan, K., Alder, C.S., Sedlacek, K.): Integrative Psychiatry, *3*: 168–184, 1985.

11. Green, A. Brain wave training, imagery, creativity and integrative experiences. *Proceedings of the Biofeedback Research Society*, Colorado Springs, 1974.

12. Budzynski, T. H. Some applications of biofeedback produced twilight states. *Fields within Fields ... within Fields, Vol. 5*, Julius Stulman, New York, 1972.

13. Luthe, W. *Autogenic Therapy, vol. 5*. Grune & Stratton, New York, 1969.

14. Jung, C. G. *Memories, Dreams, Reflections*. Pantheon Books, New York, 1969.

15. Levendula, D. Discussion of Adler, C. S. Biofeedback: Exciting New Tool in Psychotherapy, (panel) American Psychiatric Association, Anaheim, 1975.

16. Adler, C. S. and Adler, S. M. A psychodynamic approach to the treatment of headache. Presented at the American Association for the Study of Headache, Dallas, Texas, 1976.

17. Adler, C. S. and Adler, S. M. Biofeedback, evolution, and the tools of mankind. *Proceedings of the Biofeedback Research Society*, Colorado, 1976.

18. Rickles, W. A., Cohen, M. and McArthur, D. A. Psychophysiology study of ANS response patterns in migraine headache patients and their headache-free friends. Read before the American Association for the Study of Headache, San Francisco, Calif., 1977.

19. Toomin, M. GSR biofeedback techniques in psychotherapy. *Proceedings of the Biofeedback Research Society*, Colorado Springs, 1974.

20. Adler, C.S., Adler, S.M. Existential deterrents to headache relief and midlife. In *Advances in Neurology: Headache; Pathological and Clinical Concepts*, edited by M. Critchley, S. Fried-

man, S. Zorini, F. Sicuter. Raven Press, New York, pp. 227–232, 1982.

21. Rickles, W. Some theoretical aspects of the psychodynamics of successful biofeedback treatment. *Proceedings of the Biofeedback Research Society*, Colorado Springs, 1976.

22. Thomas, L. *The Lives of a Cell*. Viking Press, New York, 1974.

23. Stroebel, C. Integrating biofeedback with treatment of depression and severe obsessional states. Proceedings of the twelfth annual meeting, Biofeedback Society of America, Louisville, Ky., 1981.

24. Adler, C. S. and Adler, S. M. Biofeedback and headaches: looking back after five years. *Proceedings of the Scandinavian Migraine Association*. Bergen, Norway, 1975.

25. Adler SM, Adler CS: Physiologic feedback and psychotherapeutic intervention for migraine: A 10-year follow up. In *Updating in Headache*, edited by Pfaffenrath, V. Lundberg, P.O. and O. Sjaastad. *Heidelberg*, Springer-Verlag, 1985, pp. 217–223.

26. Adler CS, Adler SM: An analysis of therapeutic factors seen in a ten-year psychophysiologically and psychodynamically oriented treatment for migraine. In Rose C: *Migraine: Clinical and Research Advances*, edited by Basel, Karger, p. 186, 1985.

27. Giles, S. Separate and combined effect of biofeedback training and brief individual psychotherapy in the treatment of gastrointestinal disorders. *Proceedings of the Biofeedback Society of America*, twelfth annual meeting, Louisville, Ky., 1981.

28. Bosma, W. *The Treatment of Aggression, vol. 2*, No. 4. Audio Digest Psychiatry, 1973 (cassette tape).

29. Adler, C.S. and Adler, S.M. Psychiatric aspects of headache; and Psychological treatment of headache. *Panminerva Medica*, *24*: 145–149, and 167–172, 1982.

30. Bowman, B. and Faust, D. EMG-autogenic training and cognitive-behavior modification: a multimodal strategy for tension reduction for alcoholics. *Proceedings of the Biofeedback Research Society*, Orlando, Fla., 1977.

31. Crabtree, M. and Lacey, R. Effectiveness of biofeedback and relaxation training with drug addicts and alcoholics: a 6 month followup. *Proceedings of the Biofeedback Society of America*, twelfth annual meeting, Louisville, Ky., 1981.

32. Rugh, J. and Solberg, W. The identification of stressful stimuli in natural environments using a portable biofeedback unit. *Proceedings of the Biofeedback Research Society*, Colorado Springs, 1974.

33. Cannistraci, A. *Voluntary Stress Release and Behavior Therapy in the Treatment of Clenching and Bruxism, vol. 1*. Bio-Monitoring Applications, New York, 1975–1976 (cassette tape).

34. Budzynski, T., Stoyva, J. and Adler, C. Feedback-induced muscle relaxation: application to tension headache. Behav. Ther. Exp. Psychiatry, *1*: 205–211, 1970.

35. Budzynski, T., Stoyva, J., Adler, C. and Mullaney, D. EMG biofeedback and tension headache:

a controlled outcome study. *Psychosom. Med.,* 35: 484–496, 1973.

36. Hauri, P. Treating psychophysiologic insomnia with biofeedback. Arch. Gen. Psychiatry, *38:* 752–758, 1981.

37. Luthe, W. and Schultz, J. *Autogenic Therapy,* vol. 2. Grune & Stratton, New York, 1969.

38. Friedman, M. and Rosenmann, R. *Type A Behavior and Your Heart.* Alfred A. Knopf, New York, 1974.

39. Frank, C., Norris, P., Lebow, K. and Allen, B. Applications research of biofeedback in rehabilitation programs in prison settings. *Proceedings of the Biofeedback Research Society,* Monterey, Calif., 1975.

40. Sterman, M. B. Neurophysiological and clinical studies of sensorimotor EEG biofeedback training: Some effects on epilepsy. Semin. Psychiatry, 5: 507–525, 1973.

41. Lubar, J., Shabsin, H., Natelson, S., et al.: EEG operant condition in intractable epileptics. Arch. Neurol., *38:* 700–704, 45 1981.

42. Stroebel, C. F., Ford, M. R., Strong, P. and Szarek, B. L. Quieting response training: treatment of psychophysiological disorders in psychiatric inpatients. *Proceedings of the Biofeedback Society of America,* twelfth annual meeting, 1981.

43. Adler, C. S. Biofeedback, evolution, and the tools of mankind. Presented at the annual meeting of the Biofeedback Society of America, Colorado Springs, 1974.

44. Mittleman, B. and Wolff, H. G. Affective states and skin temperature. Experimental study of subjects with "cold hands" and Raynaud's Syndrome. Psychosom. Med., 1: 271–292, 1939.

45. Patterson, R. M., Craig, J. B., Waggoner, R. W. and Freyberg, R. Studies of the relationship between emotional factors and rheumatoid arthritis. Am. J. Psychiatry, *99:* 775–780, 1943.

CHAPTER 22

Biofeedback and Psychosomatic Disorders

CHARLES SPENCER ADLER
SHEILA MORRISSEY ADLER

"When the spirit is hurt, severe pain ensues; when the body is hurt, there will be swellings. Thus, in those cases where severe pains are felt first and the swellings appear later, one can say that the spirit has injured the body. And in those cases where swellings appear first and severe pains are felt later, one can say that the body has injured the spirit."
—Huang Ti Nei Chin (479–300 B.C.)
The Yellow Emperor's Classic on Internal Medicine (1)

"So this league of mind and body hath these two parts, How one discloseth the other, and how the one worketh upon the other.

For the consideration is double, either how, and how farre, the humours and affects of the bodie, do alter or worke upon the mind; or againe, how and how far the passions or apprehensions of the minde, doe alter or worke upon the bodie . . ."
—Francis Bacon, Lord Verulam (1561–1626)(2)

The hallmark of any era is often less the discovery of new insights than the recovery of old ones recast in a novel light. The intellectual floodlight of present times is inductive scientific confirmation; it can separate empirically derived folk wisdom from common superstition, can transmute the lead of "perhaps" into the gold of fact. Biofeedback is one tool our era can use to illuminate from a fresh perspective the observations of the Yellow Emperor and of Bacon.

The advent of psychoanalysis taught scientists that insight into unconscious motivations could relieve many psychophysiological disorders whose etiology involved pathways that connect a patient's unconscious to his physiology. Thus, science's attention shifted emphasis to uncovering unconscious "trade routes," looking at both their capacity to cause, or, via insight, to relieve psychophysiological disorders.

In contrast, biofeedback is allied with an older tradition, one that focuses on conscious, accessible causes and cures of psychophysiological ills. Overt but exaggerated fears and burdensome amounts of everyday problems can become pathogenic according to current concepts of stress and behavioral medicine.

In fact, patients can get into emotional and physical difficulties from either conscious or unconscious causes; the best treatment will home in on the route that the pathogenic influence took. Unconscious exploration won't help someone deal with poverty; raising one's finger temperature has an undetectable influence on an Oedipal conflict.

The treatment of psychophysiological disorders is one of biofeedback's strongest suits. Here, its unique asset is its capacity to unambiguously reflect to therapist and patient the synchronization between psychological and physiological aspects of disordered functioning which constitutes disease. Its nonverbal but vivid demonstration of the interplay between the mental and the physical lets a patient appreciate how psychosomatic influences actually relate to *his* problem.

Biofeedback is not a treatment but a tool, and a tool can only produce results as good as the skill and judgment of the craftsman who wields it. It is a precise tool, for specialized uses. One of these uses is to aid general relaxation and homeostasis-seeking therapies, but, in itself, it is not one of those therapies. From the earliest years, experienced clinicians have honored this knowledge in their practices by routinely using autogenic therapy or progressive relaxation to initiate and provide an ongoing foundation for treatment.

In the context of such general relaxation therapy, biofeedback is an advanced technique. For most applications, especially those involving anxiety, it will yield uneven results if this basic instruction in relaxation is omitted, as overbroad demands would be placed upon the technique. Because it is so specific, biofeedback has an advantage over generalized relaxation techniques only when used to zero in on a single physiological function and/or anatomical site.

As each part of a patient's physiology functions in equilibrium with his overall physiology and anatomy and his reactions to his psychosocial milieu, even treating the total physiology in isolation can backfire. A man unexpectedly served divorce papers Wednesday morning will not be relaxed Wednesday afternoon no matter what the physiological readings.

Major illnesses have emotional concomitants. One trend in psychosomatic thinking is to view both functional and anatomic components as coexistent manifestations of a single disease. The analogy has been made to a burning log. Neither flame nor wood alone can portray the nature of the phenomenon. Human structure and function, in health or in illness, are flame and log to each other. One may predominate in a given case, but both are always present. Patients with disordered functioning often receive unbalanced treatment because it only deals with one. We now have instruments that can treat both psyche and soma in a single context. They do this by acting as an unbiased electronic consultants to both patient and therapist for conditions in which the interaction between mind and body plays a dominant or elusive role.

Certain disorders *can* be treated using only biofeedback, in concert with traditional medical approaches. Feedback of the sensory-motor rhythm for seizure disorders and EMG for neuromuscular reeducation in poststroke hemiplegia are examples of biofeedback applications where therapeutic improvement is essentially independent of relaxation.

We will first provide, in rough sketch, the cognitive experience of a patient using biofeedback; we will then describe nonspecific benefits that generally accompany biofeedback; follow this with hints for initiating a stable treatment relationship, and finally touch upon some specific psychosomatic disorders which biofeedback might benefit.

MENTAL MANEUVERS

Biofeedback-enhanced relaxation evokes the use of a different mental strategy by the participant than do other relaxation therapies. One aim of all general relaxation treatments is to teach patients to will themselves into a state of psychobiologic harmony which typically facilitates homeostatic functioning.

The first step in such therapies is usually to concentrate one's awareness on the relevant body part, and then to make that attention "passive" rather than "active." Passive attention is not goal-directed, is casual, acceptant, observer-like. Somewhat different mental strategies correspond to different techniques, and these have particular therapeutic implications. Jacobson's progressive relaxation (3) requires the person to actively contract groups of striated muscles in sequence. After each contraction he relaxes the muscle group, and notes the contrast between the two sensations. This involves an active mode of engagement, at least initially. Autogenic training requires that the patient attain a different mental set, that of *passive* concentration, as described earlier. Particular well researched phrases, called "formulae," are attended to. The contrast in mental set means that the two techniques should only be used consecutively, and that the patient should be told about the necessary shift in mental attitude.

A person using biofeedback alternates between the cognitive styles of both methodologies. The active, goal-directed exploration via psychophysiological initiatives characteristic of progressive relaxation is used; but in biofeedback, the initiatives are more often mental than physical. The autogenic training-like attitude of passive, process-oriented attention to the body is also sought. The two attitudes alternate, with attention shifting intermittently from one bodily locus to another. The patient maintains a passive attitude between shifts, but is actively exploring at other times. An analogy can be made to the fisherman moving from spot to spot along a stream, trying out each spot in turn, with peripheral awareness of the gently bobbing float. If a particular spot yields more nibbles than another, he will return there often, and make subtle adjustments in type of bait or depth of hook.

Five stimuli vie for the attention of the patient using biofeedback. By comparing the information gained from each, he moves his physiology in the desired direction. They are: (a) proprioceptive and visceroceptive sensations; (b) fluctuating signals from the biofeedback instrument; (c) a "target sensation" called up from memory of what the desired physiological state feels like; (d) "intermediary images" the patient intentionally calls to mind to make the target sensation more vivid, such as of the sun beating down on his hands to raise their temperature, or similar remembered precursors of the desired physiological state. "Intermediary images" later become unnecessary; a simple, wordless "willing" eventually produces change, much as one "wills" oneself to stand, or reach for a glass, or sign one's name; (e) other images, thoughts, and sensations that drift into awareness seemingly at random. On closer inspection, these spontaneously appearing elaborations turn out not to be random at all, but may be bridges to fears, wishes, or repressed traumata (Chapter 21).

Control of the internal (physiological) world follows a different temporal sequence than control of the outer (environmental) world. When relating to the outer world, fact comes first, and observation follows. In the "inner world," observation can be made first and that observation can induce a (sometimes identical) physiological state to follow. As the hallmark of the scientific mind is strict adherence to *a posteriori* rather than *a priori* reasoning, this simple fact may be difficult for some patients to grasp. In short, *thoughts must be considered as actions*, actions whose target and point of impact is the body itself. Both emotion-laden thoughts and specific thoughts about the state of the body are especially potent in this regard, although the effect will not always be identical to the thought (one is not what, untransformed, one thinks, any more than he is, untransformed, what he eats). The patient must recognize that, even though this way of thinking about his perceptions (as "actions") would be bizarre if he applied it to the external world, things work differently in his body. For example, he should be able to think, "My right arm is warm" even if it feels cold, and, recognizing that it is an "action-observation", not be dismayed by the incongruity. This "action-observation" is then followed by a corresponding change in physiology. Children of a certain age normally believe that through intense concentration they can will clouds to

move one way or the other, but the mentally healthy adult has characteristically abandoned these notions. A perceived return to those days of "magical thinking" can be both exciting and frightening for patients. Thus, the necessity for this curious turnabout in logic to control internal functions is explained to patients at the start of treatment.

NONSPECIFIC BENEFITS OF BIOFEEDBACK

The process of biofeedback allows patient and therapist time to get to know each other. Many patients who need help with emotional problems fear psychotherapy and the trust involved in expressing feelings to another human being. In contrast, they are neither frightened nor ashamed of learning to control their physiology in a setting typically seen as more "medical" in orientation. During the beginning phase of treatment, the patient can get to know the therapist as predictable and helpful. If psychotherapy is indicated, the confidence thus gained may be enough to overcome the patient's resistance. Patients who would otherwise be telling their troubles to a bartender can allow themselves to become involved in a psychotherapeutic encounter. The medical image of biofeedback can also be a face-saving device for patients.

Biofeedback gives a patient an active way to fight his problem. The extent to which problems are aggravated by feelings of helplessness cannot be overstated. Helplessness that continues indefinitely is often followed by hopelessness and despair. Biofeedback can cut into this cycle by offering something concrete, immediate, and active. Being released from a sense of powerlessness can change how a patient relates to chronic illness. With psychotherapy alone, results are often nonapparent early on. In the interim, the patient is left with intangibles, and may even feel worse as his problems are uncovered in all their poignancy. If biofeedback-assisted relaxation is included early in treatment, the patient has something with which to reduce the effects of his problems while he is changing himself in ways that eventually may eliminate them at their source.

Biofeedback introduces the patient to another defense for handling his symptoms; he can view them from a new perspective. He does this by learning to temporarily dissociate from his body's functioning. When a patient is asked to attend to the relationship between sensation and feedback, he is also being asked, by implication, to observe himself—to become both the observer and the observee. And when he learns to maintain a casual, passive, or curious attitude towards the observed "symptomatic self," he also learns how to use that observing function to gain emotional distance from symptoms in general. This defense can then also be used to gain distance from either emotional or physical pain.

Relaxation increases the efficiency of homeostatic functioning, leading to a functional state that has been termed trophotrophic. As is true for other biological systems, the central nervous system participates in self-normalizing activities. Dreaming, which in part functions to reduce the disturbing potency of material from the remote and recent past, is an everyday example of such homeostatic functioning in the central nervous system.

Many patients with somatoform disorders are rigidly defended and fearful of disturbing a tightly guarded psychophysiological equilibrium by any changes of habit. Having a safe experience with trial and error on the feedback may increase such a patient's behavioral flexibility and reduce his need to rely on stereotypes to feel secure. This type of patient is frequently out of contact with his body's internal cues, even those that signal an urgent need for rest, privacy, crying, etc. Because the focus of attention is turned inward during biofeedback, the patient may become aware of this alienation from his own body and be more sensitive to his body's warning cues. In a more extreme form, any patient with a chronic, severe, or terminal illness may feel keenly the lack of control over his body, or feel that his body is turning against him. He refers to bouts with illness as "attacks of ____" rather than "recurrences of ____." This isolation from the body's needs is sometimes reduced when the patient sees on the feedback the quicksilver interplay between his emotions and his physiology. He may then recognize the eerie fact that, unawares, he has been viewing his body as foreign to his innermost sense of self, as a locus of ill health and disturbing affect only, unworthy of the kindly attention he devotes to the needs of others. If this *laissez-faire* attitude toward (or cold retreat from) his body is halted, he may soon reexperience a harmonious contact with it absent since childhood.

BIOFEEDBACK AS A WINDOW ON INFANCY

Few adult treatments shed much light upon childhood psychosomatic functioning. Biofeedback, however, does so to a degree where it qualifies as one of the languages in the Rosetta Stone of infant memories (6, 7). Predisposition to many psychogenic illnesses originates in early childhood, when consciousness is dominated by sensory and motor rather than by intellectual or verbal phenomena. In his "play," the infant makes correlations between sensory-motor and perceptual experiences in the process of learning to manage his internal and external world (8).

In biofeedback treatment, the patient does not talk about this time of life but, in a manner of speaking, returns to it directly. There, he will reenact processes of trial and error that characterized the preverbal stage, but this time he can often view these processes with his adult ego and intellect. As a result, he often makes contact with earliest anlage of his present-day psychosomatic functioning. The "observed self" in biofeedback corresponds in a number of ways to the bodily awareness of infancy. As in infancy, the patient progressing on biofeedback is exploring his internal sensory world in an attempt to master the subtleties of bodily function. Mislearning that occurred during this period has the potential to be restructured, because the sensory-motor phase is functionally reapproximated in treatment, making accessible its rich supply of nonverbal awareness and nonverbal insight, much of which cannot be translated into the verbal language developed at a later age.

EVALUATING THE PATIENT

Whether a disorder turns out to be primarily consequent to emotions or has only minor input from them, the basic psychosomatic philosophy is the most comprehensive approach to patient evaluation and care. It evaluates the interdependence between physical, psychological, and social factors in every illness.

The first step in any treatment is a full diagnostic evaluation. This precedes a decision about what form of therapy, if any, is indicated (Fig. 22.1). In addition to the medical history, physical examination as indicated, review of systems, and relevant laboratory studies, a thorough psychological history, family history, and mental status should be obtained.

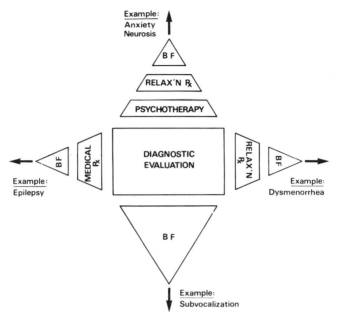

Figure 22.1. The biofeedback star: foundations of biofeedback.

Taking a good history is more than just an evaluation; it is the start of treatment itself. Many psychosomatic patients have been on a long and discouraging pilgrimage from doctor to doctor and from treatment to treatment. The evaluation session is often a critical opportunity to establish rapport with the patient, as it may be the first time he has been asked to reconstruct and share the most important events in his life from his perspective. If the patient leaves feeling it was a worthwhile experience, he may retain a growth-enhancing desire for self-knowledge, and continue to reflect productively upon the meaning of his personal history.

Taking a full psychiatric history also helps the patient make an emotional commitment to treatment. By undertaking the difficult job of sharing personal information, the patient has made an "investment" that he would not want to see wasted. Asking the patient if he has any questions about the therapist's background or qualms about therapy acknowledges that the evaluation is a dual one, with the patient also deciding whether the therapist and therapy are appropriate for him. Then, if he does enter treatment, it is by a personal choice, which reinforces his commitment to it.

The nuances with which questions are phrased can convey to a patient that the thera-

pist will not be sitting in judgment or forever implying that problems are self-generated. Patients are relieved if they pick up that the interviewer's underlying premise is an attitude that the patient has probably coped with problems as best he could on the basis of his past experiences and psychosocial repertoire. What a patient is contending with internally is often unknown or underestimated by both the patient and his family. The schoolteacher whose mother died relatively young from subarachnoid hemorrhage may be abusing narcotics at the earliest indication of a recurrent headache despite her urgent wish to avoid addiction. She may be totally unaware of the intensity or origin of the panic that accompanies the head pain, or that it is more the panic than the pain that can be quelled only by "a shot."

Certain questions and the manner in which they are phrased may stimulate the patient to see himself from an external, more objective perspective; for example, asking how a particular family member would describe the patient's illness or personality, and how this would differ from a self-description. Ask which duties the patient feels most guilty about not being able to fulfill because of the illness, and which chores he most resents. These provide clues to the functioning and contents of the patient's conscience. When one's conscience is overly harsh, illness is sometimes unconsciously needed to justify not meeting its demands.

Diplomacy also facilitates an accurate and thorough evaluation. Asking who in the family becomes most antagonistic when the patient is not feeling well allows the patient to describe such behavior without feeling that he initiated the idea, and is thereby betraying secrets. In the same way, asking which situations stimulate the patient to greatest anger presupposes the inevitability of anger, and may be more revealing than asking, "Do you ever get angry?"

Because unresolved grief is prevalent in the background of patients with psychosomatic illness, losses should be inquired into in detail. Significant losses can include the loss of a goal or a dream, the death of a pet, or the move away from a home. In addition, feelings of loss can often be traced back to a moment in life when the realization crystallizes that a relationship is "ended" or that someone important never loved them. Such recognition is usually experienced as an existential "moment of truth." The therapist who develops the ability to ask these questions with tact and to listen empathically to the many levels on which the patient answers, will experience a growing ability to understand and appreciate patients, their struggles, dignity, and complexity.

Because anxiety is contributory to many illnesses, an inquiry is always made into the subjective experience of it. Questions include how the patient knows when he is anxious, how he knows when he is *not* anxious, and any analogies that he can think of to describe the quality of his anxiety. The patient is also asked what ways he has invented to cope with anxiety. One will spell it out to his diary; another will ride his trail bike for all its worth; yet another will get into a warm bath. These attempts to control anxiety can often be accomplished more directly by using relaxation techniques to supplement them.

Asking which proximal events stimulated the patient to seek biofeedback *now* can illuminate his motivations for treatment. This question is particularly relevant if he has previously avoided help despite difficulties of long duration. For example, a woman might be under pressure from her recently retired husband, who now wishes to travel, to rid herself of long-standing headaches.

Details about the illness' onset should be asked about both initially and later on in treatment. Events precipitating that first episode may be remembered only as treatment progresses and defenses are let down. The patient's impressions and reactions on first becoming aware that "something was wrong" are equally significant. The reason it is useful to trace symptoms back to the first remembered episode is that this experience often influences and capsulizes the qualitative emotional flavor of current symptoms.

Patients should be asked about their worst fears concerning the possible causes of their illness and its prognosis. A surprising number of patients secretly fear cancer or other malign conditions, but have felt too foolish or frightened to tell their doctors about these fears. Such fantasies also often contain metaphoric or symbolic elements related to hidden psychological perceptions of the illness (9). Did anyone close to the patient have an illness similar to the fantasy? The patient may retain a strong identification with that person, even one whose intensity and concreteness show it to be pathological. Features that stand out about the patient's relationship to that person may provide clues to the reasons for this identification. Some patients will fear that because an illness, such as coronary artery disease, "runs in the family," it will be their inevitable destiny.

Ask about the patient's strengths. It is helpful to know what positive resources in the patient can be called upon at critical points in treatment. Most patients feel apprehensive when first meeting a therapist. The typical patient feels some embarrassment that he has been unable, on his own, to get control over his symptoms, and may feel this especially strongly when relating all of his difficulties in an unbroken sequence. If he is encouraged to balance the story of his problems with a description of times and achievements of which he was proud, he leaves the interview with his self-esteem intact.

A complete workup includes a history of injuries, especially head injuries of any sort, of surgeries and other experiences with anesthesia, of childhood memories of witnessing illness or death—indeed, of any seemingly minor traumata that caused significant anxiety. Childhood upsets that seem minor from the vantage point of adulthood, such as being bitten by a dog, or feeling panicked when pressured to first swim or dive, have been found to have significant functional pathogenicity (10). Images, memories, spasms, pains, sensations of disequilibrium, and other discharges that occur during autogenic or biofeedback training are often consequent to these forgotten episodes whose subjective power is camouflaged by "reason." Our observations concur that these incidents can contribute to generalized as well as specific anxiety well into adulthood.

A patient often needs perspective on what has been happening to him. For example, he may be surprisingly unaware that the amount of illness or trauma in his background would deeply disrupt most people's psychological equilibrium. The experienced therapist's objective perspective can reorient how the patient interprets his experience with illness or with life.

Time is reserved at the end of the evaluation to share its conclusions with the patient and to discuss treatment possibilities. This includes summarizing initial impressions of whether underlying problems are contributing to the symptoms, which treatments or alternatives might help, what each might entail in terms of time and expense, and, occasionally (with humility), what the range of prognoses might be. Even though many of these conclusions will undoubtedly be tentative, their summarization helps the patient form a more cohesive picture of the problems from the time they began to a future time when they may diminish. Ground rules of the therapeutic relationship are also gently introduced.

Patients often misinterpret and read unintended meanings into the therapist's description of their condition or its treatment. These are sometimes detected if the patient is asked his thoughts about what has just been conveyed and if he is encouraged to voice any questions or apprehensions he has about treatment. At some point during this conversation, one can point out that initial plans are flexible and can easily be modified in response to relevant new information or developments.

Many patients doubt that they will be able to learn to control their physiology, as the concept is new to them. Such skepticism can be allayed if the therapist explains that doubts are common at the start of treatment, most patients find their negative expectations unfounded. Another hint: point out analogous complex skills that the patient mastered as a child and now takes for granted, such as learning to walk, controlling his bladder, or not crying or falling asleep in inappropriate circumstances. The patient can, nevertheless, expect to encounter plateaus or even temporary setbacks in the progress of learning, and needs to allow sufficient time to relinquish ingrained patterns of reacting and to both acquire and stabilize new ones. If the patient is helped to understand that this progression is inherent in learning any major skill, whether playing the piano or raising his skin temperature, he is less likely to react to setbacks with discouragement.

With some patients it is apparent during the first interview that a psychogenic component is involved in the illness; in many patients, it will be unclear whether psychological difficulties that are uncovered have significant bearing upon presenting symptoms. In the latter case, the patient can be told that it is not yet certain what, role if any, emotions play, either as a result of the symptoms or through the mechanism of adding "stress" to his life. If the patient is asked to help ponder the possibility that the symptoms have an emotional component, rather than putting him on the defensive, each patient's best resources are enlisted into the discovery and treatment of any psychological difficulties.

The diagnostic process does not end with the initial intake, but continues throughout treatment as new material comes to light.

TREATMENT PLANNING CONSIDERATIONS

In planning a patient's therapy, a psychiatric diagnosis such as "generalized anxiety disorder" will broadly categorize a patient only. It is no more useful for understanding him, though, than a book's number in the Dewey Decimal System is for understanding the contents of a book.

Factors to be accounted for in the treatment plan include the patient's: psychopathology, psychophysiology, strengths, weaknesses, character structure, current stressors, chronicity of problems, past experience with therapy, initial reactions to relaxation instructions, and psychological conflicts uncovered in the evaluation.

A history of the "what" and "how" of the patient's medication usage should be taken. Pharmacotherapy is often needed as a partner to self-regulation, and may even be required following successful treatment (11). If excessive drug use is part of the clinical picture, the patient can be gently advised at the start of treatment (or shortly after) that his medication needs to be decreased in a gradual and mutually acceptable manner as he learns other ways to fight the anxiety, pain, or related symptoms.

Individualized goals should always reach higher than the acquisition of visceral dexterity, and may include resolution of impediments to learning relaxation, an increase in psychological-mindedness, enhancement of self-esteem, more compatible functioning within the family, and integration of improvements into social and vocational settings outside the office.

The biofeedback tool itself is capable of great flexibility. Each therapist's technique should be distilled from his own philosophy and personality and especially from his experience with which methods are most successful in his hands. The treatment plan will optimally be a blend of specific patient needs and the particular therapeutic style of the practitioner.

It is advisable to note the patient's impressions of the doctors he has seen, especially of any prior psychotherapists. Adverse therapeutic experiences should be carefully explored to determine whether doctors have been experienced as uncaring or hurtful. When this has been the case, the patient deserves to be praised for his courage in again seeking treatment, and he must be handled with particular delicacy. If he seems to have sabotaged numerous treatments in the past, it is important to learn from these other doctors' experiences before repeating them.

Keep the setting of therapy fairly traditional so that resistances against substantive content of the sessions do not find an ally in the decor of the office or deportment of the therapist. The more secure a patient is about a therapist's unbiased and professional attitude, the more convincing that therapist's words will be when he points out character traits that the patient would wish to deny.

Certain ethnic traditions and socioeconomic class prejudices mitigate against a patient's feeling free to see a psychiatrist or psychologist, to accept a psychosomatic interpretation of a symptom, or to conceive of himself as being wired to an electronic instrument. Because people of diverse backgrounds have disorders treatable with biofeedback, their initial anxie-

ties about entering treatment may center around different things. The fundamentalist Protestant may wince at any procedure he suspects is dominated by Eastern religious philosophy, even if the only apparent connection is the way the treatment is described and the background music in the clinic. When it is necessary to describe the anatomy and functioning of the body to the patient so that he will understand the nature of his disorder or its treatment, use of analogies from the patient's culture or occupation carries the added impact of familiarity.

It is important to make a distinction between the capacity to gain occasional control over tension or other symptoms and the ability to sustain a stable trophotrophic shift to functionally appropriate levels of activation. Most patients with tension-related problems have had them for a long time, and cannot be expected to reap enduring benefits from short-term treatment. Whatmore (12), Jacobson (3), and others have found through extensive experience that it can sometimes take years for patients to unlearn habits of chronic tension. Patients in our 5-year follow-up study of the results of biofeedback-psychotherapy in treating chronic headache (13) still reported finding new ways to improve on their relaxation skills and to integrate them into additional areas of their lives.

Certain patients will require psychological intervention for crisis-type situations prior to any effective biofeedback. Acute states of agitation or depression, for example, must usually be reduced to tolerable levels before patients can focus on feedback. Situational disasters naturally have priority over long-term reactivity patterns, as well.

In our observations of headache patients (14), we became aware that when treating middle-aged or elderly patients who had for years suffered with daily or even weekly headaches, it was imperative to be aware of the existential implications of their symptoms. Often, such a patient had made sacrifices and pivotal life decisions, such as not changing jobs or having children, based on the limitations the illness imposed, and on the anticipation that it would continue. In order for such a patient to learn new patterns of physiology that might eradicate his symptoms, he must not be left with the feeling that these years which cannot be relived and these decisions that cannot be undone were in vain, since the pain had really been remediable all along. If these implications are not handled, he may view his past as wasted or pointless and sink into a depression as symptoms improve; or alternatively, he will just be unable to unravel his symptoms.

The psychological literature (15) contains accounts of patients blind since birth whose vision was restored in midlife through surgery. When the bandages were removed, instead of experiencing a joyous rebirth, many sank into despair, and some committed suicide. The same mechanism can be operative in any disorder of long standing. This pitfall is usually treatable if the clinician anticipates and addresses it when lack of expected progress or lack of pleasure following symptom relief give cause for suspicion.

Certain patients have an unconscious reluctance to be relieved of psychophysiological symptoms. This can be for two reasons: primary gain is an internal, psychodynamic benefit involved in the initiation and maintenance of a psychogenic disorder. A simple example would be a patient who suddenly feels an intense wish to strike her child; she instead develops acute conversion reaction paralysis of the arm with which she would hit the youngster (but now can't because it is "paralyzed"). Removal of the symptom would once again expose her conflict between the urge to strike her child and the wish not to. This type of conflict often needs to be made conscious before the patient will get symptomatic relief. The other potential impediment to letting go of symptoms is called secondary gain. It results from unexpected benefits that have accrued subsequent to development of the disorder and that are contingent upon its continuation. "Compensation neurosis" is an example of this. A patient with low back pain following a minor auto accident, whose insurance suit is still unsettled may be unconsciously reluctant to lose his symptoms because that would put him in a legally disadvantageous position. Secondary gain, when present, is usually a small but overrated component of a patient's problem, and is distinct from malingering. Primary gain is a more common and a more difficult resistance.

When a patient first seeks treatment, all of the ramifications of his problem are rarely apparent. A therapist may need to recruit diverse clinical skills to cope with a complex case, but find that, despite doing so, aspects of it still fall outside of his area of expertise. On these occasions, the treatment relationship is strengthened by asking an associate to consult.

The amount of formal structure that is superimposed upon biofeedback therapy can be varied along a continuum according to the needs of each patient. At the highly structured end of this continuum the therapist provides continual verbal coaching. The patient sits up in the chair with his eyes open, and time devoted to relaxation is decreased or broken up by other activities. Patients are also told that if at any point they feel suddenly and unexplainably uncomfortable, they may resume their former tension level and should communicate their discomfort to the therapist. This degree of structure is best for patients in whom stillness triggers fear, or for cases in which the therapist feels that a precipitous release of disturbing material might occur based upon history and mental status. Borderline patients, patients with brittle defenses, or patients with trauma-laden histories often fall into this category (6). The potential for spontaneous insight with such highly structured sessions is reduced in exchange for needed safeguards.

The other end of the spectrum is the preferred approach for healthier patients. Technically, it uses less active coaching, a recumbent position with the eyes often closed, and increased use of auditory feedback. The patient is asked to experiment, even to engage in open-ended exploration, with the feedback signals, and to share with the therapist any correlations he observes.

Biofeedback can be used in an inpatient setting, but is not in itself sufficient indication for hospitalization. If the patient is in the hospital for other reasons, however, biofeedback treatment can be advantageously begun during his stay.

TECHNIQUES, STEP BY STEP

We are here presenting only one valid protocol for biofeedback; there are many others. Use this approach only if it "fits."

Maintaining Rapport

The therapist remains present throughout the session even if at times only for quiet observation. Although this role appears unexciting when the patient is absorbed in physiological introspection, the therapist who is absent when a patient discovers something novel about himself will not have the gratifying advantage of being able to follow it up immediately. The more the therapist is attuned to the vitality and ever-present potential for insight that characterizes the mental processes of the apparently quiescent patient working his bait and tackle along the biofeedback "stream," the more he will recognize that the time spent quietly keeping these patients company is time well spent. Training patients in biofeedback is especially experienced as an unstimulating routine when the nature of the training itself is viewed as a mechanical process. But just as oversimplification can breed boredom, remaining on guard for the moment that precisely woven intrapsychic events culminate in a shift on the instrument can breed excitement. Furthermore, there are dangers involved in leaving a patient alone. Psychological problems that were undetected during the evaluation can surface, take the patient by surprise, and cause him to panic if he finds that no one is there to help him. It understates the case to note that such occurrences are not propitious.

Careful observation of the patient's physical mannerisms will yield clues to prominent sites of localized tension, as well as ways in which the patient intuitively tries to relax. By identifying key foci of tension in the patient, such as hunched shoulders, erratic respiration, a clenched jaw, anxious foot swinging, or restless hands, the therapist can emphasize techniques designed to relax just those areas.

There are pivotal junctures during the course of biofeedback therapy when most patients can be helped by counseling or will need psychotherapy. Both the length and style of the intervention needed can vary, from spending part of each session working with a sensitive topic to temporarily interrupting the feedback for weeks or months of intensive psychotherapy. In our 5-year follow-up, 80% of the patients required some form of psychological counseling, and the majority of patients for whom biofeedback was not significantly beneficial came from the 20% who did not receive this psychotherapy (13, 16). In a subsequent 10-year follow-up for migraine patients treated with biofeedback, we found a statistically significant benefit ($P = .01$) accruing to those who received some concomitant psychotherapy when compared with controls (see Chapter 21). The need for psychotherapy sometimes becomes apparent when a patient's reaction to the quiet introspection and stillness involved in biofeedback reawakens fears which require intervention with varying degrees of urgency (17, 18). These are described more fully in Chapter 21. In any event, almost without exception, patients require time to discuss how they can best apply what they learn in treatment to their problems.

If psychological problems revealed during the evaluation are moderate in degree and stable in nature, it may be preferable to teach the patient the fundamentals of relaxation while deferring confrontation with psychodynamic material. If relaxation and psychotherapy are pursued together in early sessions, a patient may become too aroused to focus on relaxation; at the same time, the attention he must devote to learning relaxation detracts from any concerted attention to psychological exploration.

A positive rapport can develop more readily if the therapist is clear but nonconfrontative. Also, we find that once a patient can maintain relaxation he becomes better able to focus on problematic images and memories without defensiveness or emotional retreat. He may spontaneously ask the therapist's help in exploring psychological phenomena (7, 19) when his curiosity is piqued by psychophysiological "interpretations" (major reversals in the feedback that repeatedly follow particular images or associations, as described in Chapter 21).

Relaxation and Autogenic Training

Relaxation training can be started by teaching patients progressive relaxation, which immediately gives them a preliminary familiarity with sensations and techniques they will later refine with the help of the feedback. Since this procedure is comparatively simple and usually successful, they begin treatment with a sense of achievement. Shortly thereafter, we start teaching autogenic exercises, with clear instructions to practice the autogenic training separately from progressive relaxation, and to not experiment with altering the autogenic phrases. The patient is told that autogenic phrases act as a shorthand cue to initiate a relaxed state, and can be called on for this purpose whenever needed. One or two standard phrases are introduced at each session, and the patient takes notes describing any "discharges" he becomes aware of during home practice.

Autogenic training typically evokes homeostatically oriented neurological discharges which are experienced as sensations, images, or involuntary motor movements. These phenomena are explained as being of a tension-reducing and self-regulatory nature, which they are, to allay possible anxiety about their meaning. If the patient permits them to continue without interference, he typically feels better after the practice session, and gains confidence that such events are beneficial and self-limiting.

We tell the patient that the best way to gain effective control over visceral processes is to let his active volition "slip to the sidelines." In that way control is returned to those self-regulatory biological mechanisms that have evolved through the millenia to adjust his physiology precisely, much as a thermostat regulates room temperature.

After the patient has acquired basic skill in initiating a relaxed state, biofeedback is begun. We explain that the feedback will show him exactly what works and what does not work for him; whatever preconceptions the therapist or the patient may have, the ultimate arbiter is the direction the feedback takes. Since the feedback can reflect his physiology objectively, he should use this previously "classified information" to guide his efforts at relaxation. On the feedback, patients' distorted concepts of how the body functions may reveal themselves. One patient, whose level of frontal EMG remained fixed and high for most of the session, noticed that it "suddenly dropped," looked up, and said, "When I frown, the feedback goes down." What this gentleman had thought was frowning was in fact the opposite: his "letting go of," that is relaxing, persistently scowling forehead muscles.

The physiological parameter most sensitive to stress in a patient can be ascertained in two ways. The clinician can compare the reactivity of EMG, galvanic skin response (GSR), and peripheral temperature in response to a mild stressor, such as mental arithmetic. A simpler and more practical method is to extrapolate where the greatest trouble is likely to be found by reviewing the patient's history of overt symptoms of anxiety and the most typical physiological patterns accompanying his illness. From this technically uncomplicated approach one can sometimes distinguish two patterns: patients with predominantly muscular and patients with predominantly visceral manifestations of anxiety. The first type is treated with EMG feedback; the second is treated with feedback of autonomic nervous system derivatives, such as peripheral temperature, GSR, or heart rate.

We keep biofeedback instrumentation as simple as possible in order to reserve more attention for observation of the truly complex machinery to which the feedback instrument is attached—the conscious and unconscious psychophysiological apparatus of *Homo sapiens*. Too many dials can interfere with the simple, uncluttered view that the patient needs to have of himself and that the doctor needs to have of the patient. An elaborate polygraph jungle may even frighten some patients and create a set in the patient's mind that does not facilitate "talking," but emphasizes performance.

We have found the frontal, masseter, or paracervical muscles to be convenient and responsive for EMG feedback, but when the history suggests that a patient is experiencing the greatest tension in other muscle groups, those groups also become logical sites for feedback.

It is often advisable to start with EMG feedback even if the basic plan is to eventually use temperature feedback; there have been studies indicating that temperature control is acquired more rapidly if the patient's muscles are first relaxed. One can go directly to temperature feedback when neither signs nor symptoms suggest inordinate muscle tension.

Reasons for Supplementing Basic Relaxation Therapies with Biofeedback

Biofeedback:
- Demonstrates to a patient his ability to control his physiology.
- Treats symptomatic "target organ" more directly and efficiently.
- Helps patient control physiological function most difficult for him to relax.
- Treats specifically vulnerable organ (e.g., heart) prophylactically.
- Treats "silent area," e.g., EEG or partially denervated muscle.
- Accentuates dialogue between psyche and soma.
- Demonstrates relationship between thoughts, feelings and physiology.
- Stimulates spontaneous psychodynamic insights.
- Monitors desensitization for phobias.

The variability of the feedback may be more important than its absolute level in determining which system is most vulnerable. Extremes of variability in either direction—for example, wide and rapid fluctuations in peripheral temperature as well as unvarying "flatness" of temperature response—are both clues to abnormality. The fixed and flat reading, which shows an unwillingness or inability to allow that part of the physiology its natural range of freedom, is more liable to be associated with chronic physiological defenses and a tendency to "overcontrol." An extremely labile response is more characteristic of the symptomatic physiology of undercontrolled affect.

For some patients, a combination of modalities will be optimal, and one's initial strategy often needs to be modified as treatment progresses. Sometimes, instead of using feedback from the most problematic system, the modality chosen is that over which the patient has the greatest control in order to give him an initially nonfrustrating experience with the biofeedback process.

A good rule of thumb for planning the correct feedback sequence is to move from the more general task to the more specific one, and from the easier to the more difficult, in stepwise fashion, always keeping the goal easy enough that the patient feels his overall efforts during the session have been successful.

We have found the number of sessions needed is variable, is rarely predictable at the start of treatment, and usually runs between 20 and 75 visits. Ideally (but not necessarily), therapy should be more concentrated at the beginning, with the patient then being seen for 50 minutes, two or three times a week. The time between appointments can be extended after rapport with the therapist has been solidifed and the patient has progressed enough to not feel frustrated during home practice.

Initially, about 15 minutes of each session are spent discussing developments since the last session and reviewing the home practice. This is followed by about 20 minutes of working with the biofeedback, while the therapist coaches intermittently. The remaining time is devoted to discussing the patient's experience on the biofeedback and correlations he has discovered while experimenting with it. (Patients are instructed to correlate sensations and images that accompay feedback indices of

both tension and relaxation.) This division of time should be modified to suit each patient's needs. The rule of discussion both before and after feedback is always adhered to. Oft, the feedback is left on during the final discussion to allow both patient and therapist to gauge physiological reactions to the content of their conversation.

A patient who finds himself frustrated at one of the inevitable plateaus in therapy can sometimes break the stalemate if he is asked to reverse the feedback (e.g., by tensing his forehead). The contrast enhances the patient's ability to differentiate between relaxed and tensed states and enables him to interpret the full range of his body's language. This maneuver is a form of "paradoxical intention," which is used in a variety of therapies.

The patient is asked to detail his particular plan for how and when he plans to practice relaxation at home and work. He is also asked to carry a small notebook in which to note situations and times when he is tense, for later discussion with the therapist. We suggest that he "reserve" specific times during the day to practice relaxation. It is always important to determine if success on the feedback instrument is also being translated into reduction of the symptoms for which the patient originally sought treatment.

If the patient is not "finding" enough time to practice, this problem should not be ignored. For a variety of reasons, he may seem to lack motivation. If so, the patient can be confronted in a nonaccusatory way, and asked if something is being overlooked.

One possibility: the patient's family might be subtly sabotaging his attempts to relax. They may be frightened of a disruption of familiar patterns of interaction. If true, consider clarifying directly with family members the nature of the therapy, emphasizing the need for their support, and exploring any apprehensions they may have.

MISCELLANEOUS PSYCHOSOMATIC INDICATIONS

Implying to patients that emotions may be affecting their health is often touchy, and making the point in a way that will not offend can fail even if presented with skill and diplomacy. Despite the fact that a psychophysiological explanation of symptoms is alien to many patients' way of thinking, one thing still holds true: seeing is believing. And with the feedback, the relationships are there for them to see. A "psychosomatic" approach to disease is relevant in so many patients that a tool for showing the simultaneous interaction of the somatic and psychological facets of the presenting pathology is one that clinicians should be relieved to have in their armamentarium.

There are diagnostic as well as therapeutic uses of biofeedback. The need for further evaluation or additional types of treatment can become apparent during biofeedback-assisted relaxation. Patients may reveal things unrelated to the presenting symptom in the course of treatment that they had consciously or unconsciously avoided discussing in the diagnostic evaluation. After they have spent some time remaining calm, a symptom (such as a recurrent localized pain) may indicate the need for further medical evaluation. Psychological warning signs, such as depression related to unresolved grief, may also emerge (19, 20). Finally, one should reassess the medical or psychological diagnosis if the patient has "successfully" followed the original treatment plan but his symptoms have not improved.

Biofeedback serves a prophylactic, as well as a therapeutic and diagnostic end. In this context, it is used to help patients correct specific dysfunctional physiology not accessible to change by simpler relaxation approaches. Patients with whom biofeedback might be used in this precautionary fashion include those with family histories of serious disorders exacerbated by tension, such as atherosclerotic cardiovascular disease, those who show strong Type A behavior patterns, or simply with patients who are chronically high-strung and wish to reduce their susceptibility to illness (21). Type A individuals do not tend to be psychologically-minded and, in fact, often feel threatened if their inner feelings are pointed out. Relaxation training is one way to deal with this behavioral pattern without initially "naming it" or dwelling on its roots.

Selye and others have shown that chronic stress activates the pituitary-adrenal-cortical axis, resulting in increased production of corticoids, a psychophysiological condition with multiple pathological sequelae. He termed it the "general adaptation syndrome" (22). Many diseases are accentuated by chronic stress, and they can all be looked at as possible candidates for treatment with biofeedback-assisted relaxation. In a controlled study, autogenic training was found to reduce the level of circulating cortisol (23). The implications of this finding are that other avenues to relaxation may provide a similar defense against the deleterious effects of the general adaptation syndrome.

Asthma

Bronchial asthma is a condition whose etiology has roots in genetic, allergic, and psychological factors. Psychological factors, such as conditions that intensify separation anxiety, often account for flare-ups. Attacks involve increased resistance to airflow through the lungs, accompanied by wheezing, labored breathing, and the anxiety that understandably accompanies feeling unable to breathe adequately. Neural connections from the bronchioles to the brain and back seem to be implicated in psychogenic aspects of the asthma attack. These same neural connections that allow anxiety to initiate or aggravate an attack can potentially be brought under volitional control to ameliorate it.

Bronchial asthma has been studied with two main approaches: the first feeds back specific information about actual resistance to airflow in the pulmonary tree (24); the second uses biofeedback-assisted generalized relaxation to reduce overall difficulty with asthma. Kotses et al. (25) in a well-controlled study, used EMG feedback to teach 36 asthmatic children to relax, with excellent results on their asthmatic problems.

In one creative application of the fundamentals of biofeedback to a novel situation, physicians at the Cleveland Clinic (26) used feedback principles to wean patients from long-term mechanical ventilation. A patient whose breathing has long been regulated by a mechanical respirator will often temporarily lose his capacity to spontaneously synchronize his breathing cycle; when he is disconnected from the respirator, his breathing becomes too fast and too shallow. Anxiety mingles with this confusion to further execerbate inefficient breathing. To reverse this process in a problematic case, the mechanical respirator was turned so that its control panel faced the patient, and he could get continuous visual feedback of his breathing rate (which he was instructed to slow) and his average breath volume (which he was instructed to raise). He was then able to be successfully weaned from the respirator.

In a more formalized study, Feldman (27) used feedback of airway resistance with a small number of asthmatics, and compared it with the effect of isoproterenol (a bronchodilator) on those same children. This form of feedback seems promising, and produced overall improvement in lung function equal to the medication. Nevertheless, following a careful review of biofeedback research on asthma, Kostes and Glaus (28) adopt a conservative position, advising that progress in understanding transfer mechanisms precede large-scale use of specific respiratory feedback techniques. Thus, specific feedback of respiratory resistance is still just emerging from its research cocoon. Although the sophisticated equipment is still expensive and cumbersome, this approach may ultimately capitalize on biofeedback's advantage over general relaxation therapy, via its capacity to home in on on a specific physiological target.

Dysmenorrhea

In 1974, we reported that five patients being treated with temperature feedback for migraine spontaneously described the disappearance of dysmenorrheic symptoms. In two cases, the dysmenorrhea was accompanied, according to their gynecologists, by an anovulatory state, which also remitted (14). Tubbs and Carnahan (29) and Sedlacek (30) have done pilot studies in which they treated dysmenorrheic subjects with EMG and temperature biofeedback. The experience of these researchers suggests that the tophotrophic shift that patients experience during biofeedback training has many salubrious effects upon hypothalamically mediated visceral functioning, one of which may be an easing of dysmenorrhea.

Chronic Pain

Biofeedback has been incorporated into numerous therapies for chronic pain. Pain is a complex phenomenon (31), and involves far more than simply becoming aware of so-called "painful" stimuli impinging upon peripheral receptor sites. Emotional, cognitive, and social factors are as important in determining whether a patient will experience pain and how intense it will be as is noxious stimulation of peripheral receptors, although the extent of their relative influence varies from case to case. Pain may be a manifestation of depression or of anger. Eugene Stead, M.D., in a personal conversation, commented that one must differentiate "pain" from "suffering," as the two are often confused.

The ability to relax can improve a patient's capacity to modulate suffering caused by accentuated attention to painful stimuli. Patients who have a way to fight pain and the fear of pain may not feel as victimized by it.

Alpha EEG feedback has been used to teach patients to gain some distance from pain. The rationale has many similarities to our concept of a defensive "therapeutic dissociation" acquired during experience with all forms of feedback, as it involves putting emotional distance between the perception and the symptom. The technique does not involve directly reducing pain impulses, but changes the way they are attended to. A double-blind study by Melzak and Perry (32) suggests that in those cases where alpha feedback does reduce pain, elements of hypnosis play an important role.

Endocrine Disorders

Certain endocrine disorders are adversely affected by psychological factors and may prove treatable with biofeedback-enhanced relaxation therapies. *Diabetes mellitus* and *hyperthyroidism* may be strongly influenced by overarousal, and are promising areas for research.

Diabetes Mellitus

Surwit et al. (33) treated five noninsulin-dependent diabetics requiring hospitalization with EMG feedback and progressive relaxation. The four who learned to relax increased their insulin production as a result, and showed an improvement in their glucose tolerance tests (although fasting blood glucose did not change). Until such research has thoroughly documented procedural details, there are two grave warnings that apply, especially to diabetes, a volatile condition. First, treating an insulin-dependent diabetic with relaxation therapy without knowledge of his condition might reduce his need for insulin and lead to insulin coma or even, conceivably, to death; second, if a diabetic patient has been intentionally helped to reduce his insulin requirement with biofeedback-assisted relaxation, he may succumb to the very human tendency to become overconfident, neglect regular practice of relaxation and mandatory medical checkups, and revert to a state of uncontrolled diabetes or even diabetic coma. Part of the workup of any patient who may be treated with relaxation technique, therefore, includes asking about his endocrinal history.

Antihypertension Medications

Patients taking strong antihypertensive medications should have their blood pressure monitored periodically during a relaxation treatment program, as one consequence of regular practice may be to lower blood pressure, reduce their need for antihypertensive drugs, and lead to hypotension if dosage is not adjusted.

Other Conditions

An undetermined number of additional disorders may be helped by biofeedback-assisted relaxation, even though the psychophysiological mechanisms which mediate these benefits are unknown. While treating headache patients with biofeedback and psychotherapy we repeatedly heard patients report remission of unrelated afflictions—dermatologic conditions, for example. This was reported by five patients with recurrent herpes simplex, four with postadolescent acne, three with severe seborrhea and four with eczema. These patients further noted that occasional flare-ups usually followed neglecting their relaxation routines, and that the dermatitis would again quiet down when they reinstated home practice.

Still more intriguing are the observations of two multiple sclerosis patients undergoing relaxation training and psychotherapy for anxiety. They began, on their own initiative, to use their relaxation skills to cope with some symptoms. Before treatment, both patients had recurrent numbness, visual problems, and paresthesias in the extremities along with weakness and tiredness, and in one, lasting from a few days to a week. At the onset of these symptoms, they intensified their relaxation practices, and discovered that they could usually abort the attack in one or several days. These improvements were both unexpected and pleasing, even with the knowledge that the disease has a natural history of repeated remissions.

While it would be unwarranted to consider these or other anecdotal observations more than suggestive, it would be equally misleading to offhandedly dismiss them as placebo without study. The observant therapist will find that many such "natural experiments" oc-cur when a patient being treated for one disorder reports improvement or exacerbation of another.

There are many miscellaneous psychosomatic conditions, and these could be dwelt on *ad infinitum*, perhaps *ad tedium*. Most important is the recognition that biofeedback is never used to treat a symptom, or even a disease (34). It is used to treat a patient. No two alcoholics are alike; indeed, no two people are alike, even identical twins. Analysis of two patients diagnosed as having blepharospasm may reveal that one drinks too much coffee and that the other is struggling to hold back tears of an overwhelming depression she has been trying to contain ever since her father's sudden death 8 years before. We can generalize only at great risk about "symptoms" abstracted from the patient who has the symptom. Similarly, a "therapy" for a "symptom" is solely a theoretical construct based on statistics, something that can serve as a guide to general therapeutic directions, but is less likely to lead one completely out of the woods than a 17th-century map.

History teaches us that effective treatment of patients has been done for centuries, even in the most primitive of eras and the most primitive of cultures. If we can draw a conclusion from the lessons of history, it is that there is no more potent and critical element in the treatment of people in distress than the involvement and interest of another human being who is mature, creative, and concerned.

References

1. *The Yellow Emperor's Classic of Internal Medicine*, translated by Veith, I. University of California Press, Berkeley, 1972.
2. Bacon, Sir Francis. Of the proficience and advancement of learning, divine and humane. In *The Roots of Psychology*, edited by S. Diamond, p. 747. Basic Books, Inc., New York, 1974.
3. Jacobson, E. *Progressive Relaxation*, 2nd ed. University of Chicago Press, Chicago, 1938.
4. Schultz, J. H. and Luthe, W. *Autogenic Therapy*, vol. 1. Grune & Stratton, New York, 1969.
5. Luthe, W. *Autogenic Therapy*, vol. 5. Grune & Stratton, New York, 1970.
6. Adler, C. S. and Adler, S. M. *Biofeedback in Psychotherapy*, vol. I. Bio-Monitoring Applications, New York, 1975 (cassette tape).
7. Adler, C. S. and Adler, S. M. Interface with the unconscious in biofeedback. J. Am. Acad. Psychoanal., in press, 1978.
8. Piaget, Jean. *The Origins of Intelligence in Children*. International Universities Press, Inc., New

York, 1952.

9. Adler, S. M. and Adler, C. S. Psychiatric aspects of headache. Panminerva Med., *24:* 167–172, 1982.

10. Luthe, W. *Autogenic Therapy*, vol. 5. Grune & Stratton, New York, 1970.

11. Adler, C. S. and Adler, S. M. Psychiatric treatment of headache. Panminerva Med., *24:* 145–149, 1982.

12. Whatmore, G. B., and Kohli, D. R. *The Physiopathology and Treatment of Functional Disorders.* Grune & Stratton, New York, 1974.

13. Adler, C. S. and Adler, S. M. Biofeedback psychotherapy for the treatment of headaches: a five-year follow-up. Headache, *16:* 189–191, 1976.

14. Adler, C. S. and Adler, S. M. Existential deterrents to headache relief past midlife. In *Advances in Neurology*, vol. 33. Raven Press, New York, 1982.

15. Senden, M. *The Perception of Space and Shape in the Congenitally Blind Before and After Operation*, translated by Heath, P. Methuen, London, 1960.

16. Adler, C. S. and Adler S. M. Headaches, biofeedback and psychotherapy. Read as faculty members for postgraduate course on "Headaches and Other Pains of the Head, Face, and Neck" at Mt. Sinai School of Medicine, New York, N. Y., 1975.

17. Adler, C. S. and Adler, S. M. Ego defenses in biofeedback. Read before the annual meeting of the American Orthopsychiatric Association, San Francisco, Calif., 1974.

18. Adler, C. S. and Adler, S. M. Clinical procedures: private psychoanalytically-oriented practice. In *Handbook of Physiological Feedback*, vol. I, pp. 31–46. Autogenic Systems, Inc., Berkeley, Ca., 1976.

19. Adler, S. M. and Adler, C. S. The headache swamp: pragmatic problems of biofeedback treatment. In *Proceedings of the Biofeedback Research Society*, Colorado Springs, 1974.

20. Adler, C. S. and Adler, S. M. Biofeedback: Interface with the unconscious. In *Proceedings of the Biofeedback Research Society*, Boston, 1972.

21. Friedman, M. and Rosenman, R. *Type A Behavior and Your Heart.* Alfred A. Knopf, New York, 1974.

22. Selye, H. *The Stress of Life*, McGraw-Hill, New York, 1956.

23. Alnaes, R. and Skaug, O. E. Uber veranderungen der cortisonwerte in glut bei heterhypnos e und beii passiver kozentration auf schwere und warformeln des autogenic trainings, In *Autogenic Therapy*, vol. 4, *Research and Theory*, edited by W. Luthe, Grune & Stratton, New York, 1970.

24. Vachon, L. Cited in "Biofeedback in Action," *Medical World News*, March 9, 1973.

25. Kotses, H., Glaus, K. and Bricel, S. Muscle relaxation effects on peak expiratory flow rate in asthmatic children. In *Proceedings of the Biofeedback Research Society*, Orlando, Fla., 1977.

26. Yarnal, J., Herrell, D. and Sivak, E. Routine use of biofeedback in weaning patients from mechanical ventilation (Communications to the Editor). Chest, *79:* 1–127, 1981.

27. Feldman, G. M. The effects of biofeedback training on respiratory resistance of asthmatic children. Psychosom. Med., *38:* 27–34, 1976.

28. Kostes, H. and Glaus, K. Applications of biofeedback to the treatment of asthma: a critical review. Biofeedback Self Regul., *6:* 4, 573–593, 1981.

29. Tubbs, W. and Carnahan, C. Clinical biofeedback for primary dysmenorrhea: a pilot study. In *Proceedings of the Biofeedback Research Society*, Colorado Springs, 1976.

30. Sedlacek, K. and Heczey, M. S. Specific biofeedback treatment for dysmenorrhea. In *Proceedings of the Biofeedback Research Society.* Orlando, Fla., 1977.

31. Adler, C. S., Adler, S. M. and Packard, R. C. *Psychiatric Aspects of Headache*, Williams & Wilkins, Baltimore, 1987.

32. Melzack, R. and Perry, C. Self-regulation of pain: the use of alpha-feedback and hypnotic training for the control of chronic pain. Exp. Neurol., *46:* 452–469, 1975.

33. Surwit, R. S., Feinglos, M. and Scovern, A. Effects of relaxation training on non-insulin dependent diabetes mellitus. In *Proceedings of the Biofeedback Society of America*, twelfth annual meeting, 1981.

34. Adler, C. S. and Adler, S. M. Biofeedback. In *Encyclopedia Britannica Medical and Health Annual, 1986.* Encyclopedia Britannica, Inc. Chicago, pp. 377–382, 1986.

CHAPTER 23

Quieting Reflex (QR): A Conditioned Reflex for Optimizing Applied Psychophysiology, Biofeedback and Self-Regulation Therapies

CHARLES F. STROEBEL

Einstein observed that "Common Sense is that set of prejudices which we acquire prior to the age of eighteen and take for granted." Ironically, intrinsic biofeedback has such obvious and even overwhelming "face validity" that patients and practitioners also take its therapeutic extension, extrinsic biofeedback, for granted as automatic "common sense." Recognition of this erroneous assumption explains why therapeutic biofeedback has encountered resistance, skepticism, and even disdain from traditional health practitioners and the associated insurance-compensation system. This chapter examines relevant background assumptions and presents the rationale, data, and technique for incorporating a simple conditioned reflex training procedure called the Quieting Reflex (QR)® into applied psychophysiology, biofeedback, and self-regulation therapies, permitting the extrinsic therapy to actually become automatic, intrinsic "common sense."

Feedback is one of the most profound and unifying principles governing behavior. It is fundamental in biological adaptation, being the basis of natural selection and evolution. Feedback from the environment about the consequences of one's acts provides the rewards and punishments that are an important part of learning. Maintenance of homeostasis and the neurohumoral regulation of behavior also operate through feedback loops. At whatever level the brain is studied, it is, among other things, an incredible feedback or servomechanism system.

A fundamental principle of cybernetics is that servomechanisms are unable to correct behavior without receiving feedback about performance. Human beings use successive approximation or shaping behavior—termed instrumental, operant, or trial-and-error conditioning—based on whether responses are followed by reward, uncertainty, or punishment. If persons are motivated to improve, the confirmation that they have succeeded in their behavior serves as a reward. If basketball players were blindfolded so that they could not see where their shots went, they would not learn how to play basketball. With many visceral responses and some cases of muscular tension and neuromuscular disorders, patients have a poor perception of what they are doing; they are then in the position of the blindfolded athlete, and thus cannot learn. Biofeedback is a special type of feedback that refers to information provided externally to a person about normally subthreshold bodily processes. With extrinsic biofeedback–measuring devices sensitive to responses in the body beneath the threshold of usual awareness, it is possible to provide moment-to-moment information about those responses, and, by analogy, to remove the blindfold.

INTRINSIC BIOFEEDBACK

Incredibly precise, intrinsic feedback of neuromuscular responses is available to help the conscious brain learn psychomotor skills and perform activities involving the three R's, "reading, 'riting, and 'rithmetic," and such tasks as the test of cerebellar function performed in a neurological exam in which patients are asked to close their eyes and touch the tip of their finger to the tip of their nose. For normally involuntary processes under the control of the autonomic nervous system (ANS), however, there is relatively little conscious feedback, except in conditions of malfunction, where intrinsic feedback is often the relatively imprecise sensation of pain. Neal Miller (1, 2) observed that more precise extrinsic feedback should be useful when (1) the medically desirable direction of change is clear; (2) a response that can produce that change is, in fact, learnable; (3) the desirable learning has been prevented by poor or wrong perception of natural feedback; and (4) moment-to-moment measurement can provide more accurate information. (See also Chapter 2, by Dr. Miller.)

EXTRINSIC (THERAPEUTIC) BIOFEEDBACK

Two types of extrinsic biofeedback therapy may be distinguished. The first is a specific type, in which the patient is provided feedback about the actual condition that needs to be controlled, such as blood pressure or properly timed contraction of the anal sphincters. When it can be demonstrated that voluntary control—that is, the ability to perform the desired response promptly on request—is absent before training but is clearly present after training, the prompt relief of symptoms is often sufficiently rewarding to make further practice with the feedback-augmenting equipment unnecessary.

The second type of biofeedback application is nonspecific. The symptom or condition itself is not directly measured on a moment-to-moment basis; rather, a patient is taught a more general skill, such as electromyographic (EMG) reduction or relaxation, which seems to produce a desirable effect. For example, learning to warm the hands may be used to reduce the frequency of migraine headaches, palpitations of anxiety, or the sensations of angina pectoris. A presumptive mechanism is a lowering of sympathetic activation and voluntary self-regulation of arterial smooth muscle vasoconstrictive tendencies in predisposed persons. In cases of the nonspecific type of biofeedback application, continued frequent practice with or without the biofeedback equipment is critical to maintain therapeutic gains.

The need for continued practice raises the issues of state-dependent learning; of transferring training to the real world from a quiet clinical setting, and of adherence and compliance with home practice strategies, as emphasized in behavioral therapy. As a pragmatic psychobiological procedure, biofeedback actually has heightened awareness of the many contributions from behavioral therapy. These contributions include learning theory, symptom diaries, contracting, desensitization, flooding, reciprocal inhibition, assertiveness training, approach-avoidance gradients, cognitive restructuring, the efficacies of reward and punishment in reinforcing health behaviors, and the crucial issues of adherence and compliance. The bottom line of nonspecific biofeedback therapy is achieving long-term improvement of the clinical symptom in question.

STRESS HYPOTHESIS

Most biofeedback applications incorporate a stress concept, suggesting that somatoform disorders develop when the normal range of homeostatic functioning becomes restricted, whether through stress, isolation, feelings of helplessness and hopelessness, or unconscious conflict. This formulation is becoming increasingly accepted, with estimates that 50–70% of all symptoms presenting in a general medical or gynecologic practice are either induced by stress or exacerbated by a stressful bracing reaction against the primary symptom. According to this logic, acute overactivation of the sympathetic nervous system-adrenal medulla-mediated emergency fight-or-flight response—as described physiologically by Walter Cannon (3) in 1919 and more psychodynamically a half century later by Sandor Rado (4)—may produce symptoms such as essential hypertension, agoraphobia, tension headaches, hyperventilation syndrome, or irritable colon in rather consistent patterns within a given person.

These hierarchical tendencies within indiviuals and families are known as the "principle of psychophysiological response specificity," which is emerging as a predictor of "which illness, how and when," with exciting portent for prevention and intervention, particulary in alexithymic persons. With more chronic stress, the hypothalamic-pituitary-adrenal corticosteroid system is activated in an alarm-resistance-exhaustion defense sequence described as the general adaptation syndrome (GAS) by Selye (5) in 1950 and now being extended by neuropsychoimmunologists with profound implications for onset of conditions as apparently diverse as cancer and depression.

The progenitors of applied psychophysiology envisioned an encompassing treatment model as they struggled to connect soma and symbol with the tools at hand. The basic underlying paradigm of psychobiology, eloquently formalized by Adolf Meyer (6) at Johns Hopkins University in 1913, has progressed relentlessly from the regulatory processes of Claude Bernard's *inner environment* (7)—later Cannon's *homeostasis* and Rado's *adaptational psychodynamics*—to Freud's *project for a scientific psychology* to recent identification of neurotransmitter receptor sites on immune, endocrine, neural, and virtually every body cell, all of which interact with the forces and influences on a person's life as it is lived from conception to death. Psychopharmacology has bridged fundamental molecular biology to behavior with the present-day emerging understanding of the way self-regulation proceeds in its own quiet and lawful ways in health and in many diseases of adaptation.

As a leading psychobiologist, Miller (see Chapter 2) gave credibility to biofeedback and its medical potential for self-regulation by demonstrating that the normally involuntary ANS can be operantly conditioned with appropriate feedback. Through their experiments, Miller and his colleagues (2) challenged a classical doctrine of psychology that instrumental conditioning principles operated only with the voluntary central nervous system and skeletal muscles. He speculated that biofeedback should be well worth trying on any symptom, functional or organic, that is under neural control, that can be continuously monitored by modern intrumentation, and for which a given direction of change is clearly indicated medically ... for example, cardiac arrhythmias, spastic colitis, asthma, and those cases of high blood pressure that are not essential compensation for kidney damage. The implication also seemed clear that instrumental conditioning, through enhanced inner sensory awareness achieved by biofeedback, may be the scientific basis underlying a wide spectrum of poorly understood self-regulation techniques, including the placebo response (both positive and negative), hypnotic phe-

nomena, meditation, autogenic therapy, relaxation, progressive relaxation, and other variants.

Beginning in the 1970s, the mass media began to inflate the "common sense" of biofeedback as a new magic cure for all ills. Entrepreneurs capitalized on this publicity by producing inexpensive over-the-counter biofeedback boxes for unsupervised use at home or by untrained technicians. Controversy and increasing skepticism began to surround the deceptively simple biofeedback concept as reputable clinicians and researchers began to report that initial therapeutic gains with biofeedback often did not significantly transfer outside of the training setting in the long term.

SKILL, NOT PILL

Perspicacious psychophysiologists quickly recognized that biofeedback self-regulation of body functions could not be viewed as a panacea 'pill,' but rather as a skill requiring ongoing practice and activation in virtually all conceivable situations. Many schemes for providing cues for home practice of the skill were tested, including pocket alarms, symptom diaries and cards, stick-on dots, novel reminder jewelry such as mood rings, etc. Most subjects rapidly habituated to such external practice cues or rationalized failure to practice saying, "My life is so busy—I just forget." or, "When I get a headache or feel stressed, I pop a pill—practicing my biofeedback takes too long." This last excuse was reported so often that the need for identifying a cue for practice that would be innate, automatic,' and faster than "popping a pill" began to preoccupy me in 1974. Requisite would be an unconditioned stimulus, which was an early component of the inborn emergency fight-or-flight response to perceived stress—an automatic cue that might be conditioned classically to elicit a biofeedback response at the very moment of stress itself.

IDENTIFYING AN UNCONDITIONED STIMULUS TO OPTIMIZE SKILL ACQUISITION

Polygraph evaluation of 30 subjects' responses to an unexpected loud noise as a stress stimulus produced a consistent vigilance-orienting reflex sequence of body reactions within several seconds as follows:

1. EEG alpha blocking;

2. Pupillary dilation;
3. Increase in frontal EMG-startle reaction;
4. Catch or hold in breathing—progressing to hyperventilation;
5. GSR decrease;
6. Increase in masseter muscle EMG—grim, tense face-jaw clenching;
7. Vasoconstriction as evidenced by cooling of hands and feet.

Of the seven reactions, only one, the catch or hold in breathing, could be recognized quickly and easily by the subject themselves without instrumentation; because it does not habituate and invariably accompanies stress vigilence, it became the obvious candidate as an unconditioned stimulus to initiate a bio-feedback skills practice sequence, which becomes an automatic conditioned response with practice.

THE CONDITIONED RESPONSE

Individuals receiving EMG and thermal bio-feedback experience sensations of heaviness and warmth flowing within their bodies, usu-ally directed toward the hands and feet with exhalation of a diaphragmatic breath—accom-panied by a pleasant sensation of "letting go" of body tension. As they recognize that many of their stress responses are inappropriate, they also develop a sense of inner amusement ("By constantly or accidentally slipping my body into 'passing gear,' I just wear it out.") The same four components—alert inner amusement coupled with easy diaphragmatic breathing, flowing heaviness and warmth—are experienced in most, if not all forms of self-regulation and applied psychophysiology therapies.

The principle of reciprocal inhibition was used to establish a natural and logical se-quence of the four components as a condi-tioned response for practice of biofeedback skills and also to temporarily interrupt pro-gression of the emergency response and, if ap-propriate, to abort it.

The paradigm sequence of steps reciprocally inhibiting the first 6 seconds of the emergency response is labelled the Quieting Response,® which becomes an automatic Quieting Reflex (QR)® through classical, Pavlovian condition-ing with repetition, as summarized in Table 23.1.

CLINICAL APPLICATION

Many clinical psychophysiologists include the 6-second Quieting Reflex® sequences in their training protocols to acheive the follow-ing objectives:

1. QR probably has no equivalent in encourag-ing automaticity in the practice of learning skills associated with biofeedback training.
2. The 6-second response does not interfere with ongoing daily activity. It does not re-quire sitting in a quiet room to practice 20 minutes twice a day (a total of 40 minutes). Most patients experience at least 60 stressor cues eliciting a 6-second QR each day, ac-cumulating a total of 6 minutes' (6 sec. x 60 = 360 seconds) time from their busy sched-ules. QR does not preclude longer practice sessions.
3. Only informal observers can detect practice of a QR, which can occur anyplace, any-time, anywhere—even in a pause in an ath-letic competition.
4. QR encourages state-dependent learning at the very moment of stressors.
5. Adults predictably require $4-6$ months for the Quieting Response® sequence to be-come a consistently automatic Quieting Re-flex.® Automaticity may be operationally tested and is subjectively reported as a sense of self-mastery.

A common criticism of many biofeedback efficacy studies is use of unstandardized, idio-syncratic instructions to accompany biofeed-back training. Contributions of the instruc-tions themselves as opposed to a "biofeedback effect" is difficult to assess. A standardized program that can be administered to a biofeed-back group and a control group *without* bio-feedback offers a distinct advantage.

STANDARDIZED VERSION OF QR

A sequential 8-step instructional program incorporating contracting, diaries and compo-nents of cognitive therapy, autogenic self-sug-gestion, and progressive relaxation "tense-re-lax" contrasts entitled Quieting Reflex Train-ing (8) has been available on audiocassettes with practitioner and personal workbook manuals since 1974, and also in book format in English and Japanese since 1982. Early rec-ognition that children acquire self-regulation skills more rapidly than do adults led Eliza-beth Stroebel to develop two imaginative and

Table 23.1.
Perceived stress, vigilance, sympathetic activation

Emergency Response	Contrary Quieting Response
Conditioned Reflex	
1. Catch or hold breath	1. Inhale easy, deep breath
2. Tensing of Muscles, especially face, mouth,	2. Smile inwardly with mouth, and eyes along with self-suggestion: "Alert Mind, Calm Body"
3. Clench jaw	3. While exhaling breath, let jaw and tongue go limp
4. Constrict blood flow to hands and feet	4. Feeling a wave of heaviness and warmth flowing to hands and feet
5. Threat is real; proceed with emergency response[a]	5. Resume Normal Activity

[a]The steps of the emergency response are highly adaptive when we are faced with bodily physical danger. The breath catch enhances attention, tensing muscles prepares us for fight or flight, jaw clenching may represent a protective defense against a possible blow or a readiness to bite in attack, and peripheral (and gastrointestinal) vasoconstriction directs the flow of blood to deep muscles needed for running or fighting.

effective classroom audiocassette programs, *Kiddie QR* (9) and *QR for Adolescents* (10), which have gained widespread acceptance.

A growing body of research is in preparation for publication as a volume of collected papers documenting the efficacy of the QR paradigm in optimizing applied psychophysiology, biofeedback, and self-regulation therapies.

PHENOMENOLOGY OF THE QR LEARNING EXPERIENCE
THE QR SEQUENCE

As patients experience combined QR-biofeedback learning, many nuances of self-regulation may be easily integrated. The following description of phenomenology for each of the QR steps will serve as an example.

1. Awareness of a Worry, Annoyance, or Anxiety

The first point is to gain a reliable sense of stressful situations as soon as they occur. Many of us have become so accustomed to stress and tension in our lives that we lose the ability to discriminate between a "stressor" that really deserves a "passing- gear" response (that is, greater atttention, energy, and action) and times when such a response is inappropriate when instead, we would better serve our purposes by calming down, or "quieting," ourselves. Learning to recognize stress cues accurately is therefore an essential part of the QR process, giving you a quick pause to ask the question "What is the best response to this situation?" As you proceed with the training, you will discover many personal cues that set

the stage for the succeeding QR components. The most reliable signal is the interruption of your breathing pattern.

2. Inhale an Easy, Natural Breath

Your breathing pattern plays another crucial role in QR training. As mentioned earlier, it provides you with the most reliable, sensitive cue to stressful situations. Therefore, a crucial objective is for you to develop a keen awareness of your breathing patterns to easily identify unwanted tensions as they develop. Equally important is learning, through frequent practice, how to shift your breathing patterns to best meet your immediate needs.

Whether you decide to respond to a stressor by "gearing up" or "gearing down," the way you breathe is an essential part of your response. Breathing is the basic rhythm of life. When regular and easy, it has a profound calming influence on your body and your mind. By taking this step, you exert a powerful influence on the situation, preparing yourself to respond appropriately. If you find that "quieting" is desirable, you can then move easily into the next stage of the technique. If not, you are now ready to "gear up."

3. Smiling Inwardly, Smiling Also with the Eyes, Saying to Yourself, "Alert Mind, Calm Body"

This simple technique is incompatible with tensing face muscles and sets the stage for evaluating the real meaning of a stress cue— that is, whether or not tension is appropriate. It gives you a brief moment to reframe or step back from the situation and experience a constructive sense of alert amusement where you may be otherwise inclined to let your body and mind escape your conscious control. The inner smile helps you to release tension in your mouth and eye muscles, which respond almost immediately to stressors. With practice, this mechanism for release extends to muscles throughout your body.

The concept of self-humor, which is a key part of the 6-second QR technique, is well recognized. Norman Cousins, in his book *The Anatomy of an Illness* (11), provides a superb example. When he contracted an apparently untreatable illness, Cousins's physicians prescribed an elaborate and expensive hospital procedure. After some time passed without positive results, Cousins became fed up, left the hospital, and went to a hotel, where he spent many hours watching classic comedy movies. This "treatment" lifted his spirits, led him to laugh, and kindled a positive attitude about his situation. Using humor, he recovered in a remarkably short period of time.

By learning to laugh again, including at himself, Cousins demonstrated a widely known principle of human behavior. People who can approach difficult or stressful situations with a reasonable sense of humor are much more likely to deal with them constructively.

4. While Exhaling, Let Your Jaw, Tongue, and Shoulders Go Loose, Feeling a Wave of Limpness and Warmth Flowing to the Hands and Toes

This deceptively simple instruction promotes positive release of muscle tension in areas of the body that respond most quickly to stress, including the jaw, tongue, shoulder, and neck. Studies with biofeedback monitoring instruments show that dropping the jaw and "going limp" in this way substantially reduce muscle activity throughout the body, producing a dramatic sense of release. The image of flowing warmth reinforces this experience. Each time you practice this instruction, you are likely to find that you release more residual tension. Don't let this surprise you, since, as pointed out earlier, most people have developed strong "habits" that prevent them from recognizing their potential for tension release.

Here is a simple exercise to increase awareness of how your muscles produce and maintain tension. Gently place your fingertips on your jaw joints, just in front of the ears. Now open and close your mouth several times, feeling the movement of the TMJ where it connects to the skull. Notice the sensations of contraction and release as you do this. Now tighten your jaw muscles as you breathe in, holding that tension for a moment. Then, breathing out, let these muscles go loose and limp. Sense the feeling of release.

As you proceed through QR training, you will learn how to achieve such quieting throughout your entire body. As you will see, the process includes regaining skills you have probably had as a child; children demonstrate an inherent capacity to "let go" when necessary. The combination of jaw limpness and breathing with sensations of flowing warmth and heaviness is designed to accomplish this valuable goal. Remember that the point of QR training is to reestablish full control over your physical and mental responses to stress so that you can in the future deal effectively with daily life situations.

5. Resume Normal Activity

The implication of this instruction is very important. It tells you that the Quieting Reflex® resulting from the previous techniques is entirely compatible with *all* ongoing daily life experiences—every stressful situation. The Quieting Reflex® fosters a constructive state of alert mind and calm, quiet body. Unlike many other so-called "relaxation" exercises that require dropping out, losing touch with immediate activities, or becoming inattentive, this skill lets you stay in full touch with the situation, allowing you to adjust accordingly. As you become proficient through practice, you will be amazed at how this technique provides you with a positive, creative focus for dealing more constructively with all aspects of your daily life.

CONCLUSION

This chapter has examined relevant background assumptions and presented the rationale, data, and technique for incorporating a simple conditioned reflex training procedure called the Quieting Reflex® into applied psychophysiology, biofeedback, and self-regulation therapies. QR permits extrinsic biofeedback therapy to actually become a form of automatic, intrinsic "common sense" (12).

References

1. Miller, N. E. and Dworkin, B. R. Critical issues in therapeutic applications of biofeedback. In *Biofeedback Theory and Research*, edited by Gary E. Schwartz and J. Beatty. Academic Press, New York, 1977.
2. Miller, N. E. *Selected Papers*. Aldine-Atherton, Chicago, 1971.
3. Cannon, W. *The Wisdom of the Body*. W. W. Norton & Co., New York, 1939.
4. Rado, S. *Psychoanalysis of Behavior: Collected Letters*. Grune & Stratton, New York, 1956–62.
5. Selye, H. *The Stress of Life*. McGraw-Hill, New York, 1956.
6. Meyer, A. *Psychobiology: A Science of Man*. Charles C. Thomas, Springfield, MA, 1957.
7. Bernard, C. *An Introduction to the Study of Experimental Medicine*. Macmillan, New York, 1927.
8. Stroebel, C. F. *Quieting Reflex Training. Biomonitoring Applications*. New York, 1977.
9. Stroebel, E. L. and Stroebel, C. F. *Kiddie QR: A Choice for Children*. QR Publications, Wethersfield, CT.
10. Stroebel, E. L. and Stroebel, C. F. *QR for Adolescents*. QR Publications, Wethersfield, CT,
11. Cousins, N. *An Anatomy of an Illness as Perceived by the Patient*. W. W. Norton, New York, 1979.
12. Stroebel, C. F. *QR: The Quieting Reflex*. G. P. Putnam and Sons, New York, 1982.

PART 4
SPECIAL APPLICATIONS

CHAPTER 24

Biofeedback Control
of Gastrointestinal Motility

MARVIN M. SCHUSTER

Biofeedback or operant conditioning connotes both a theory and a technique utilizing instruments to detect physiological responses and to feed back to the subject information concerning these responses so that he can become aware of them and modify them. It is a form of self-regulation (1). The term "operant" refers to the trial and error process by which most learning takes place. Until recently, it was assumed that trial and error learning was applicable only to somatically innervated striated musculature, while visceral autonomically innervated smooth muscle or secretory functions were thought to be accessible only to classical Pavlovian conditioning.

Intestinal motility, absorption, and secretion are autoregulated in an automatic fashion. If voluntary control were required for these functions, little time would be left for other activities. Schwartz (2), emphasizing the protective features of autoregulation, states that "the biological constraints of the homeostatic mechanisms serve not only to protect man against environmental changes and demands, but also to protect man against himself."

Operant conditioning differs from Pavlovian conditioning in that it is voluntary and employs a trial and error process. In this situation, any reward can be utilized to reinforce any immediately preceding spontaneously emitted response. The reward reinforces but does not elicit the response. It simply increases the frequency with which the response

occurs. Miller (3) has effectively challenged the concept that the two types of learning (Pavlovian and operant) operate through different neurophysiological mechanisms. His findings indicate that there may be only one type of learning and that classical conditioning and operant conditioning are variations of the same process.

The present chapter deals with similar achievements in the operant control by man of some gastrointestinal motor functions, both normal and abnormal. Of the major gastrointestinal functions—secretory, digestive and motor—the last would appear to lend itself most readily to the study of instantaneously induced changes. This is important, since conditioning is easiest when there is a short latent period between response and reinforcer or information feedback; conditioning becomes more difficult the longer the delay (4).

Three applications of operant conditioning to gastrointestinal function will be described, each illustrating a specific point.

1. Studies demonstrating man's ability to modify the resting pressure of the lower esophageal sphincter carry immediate theoretical and potential practical implications. They confirm the hypothesis that "involuntary" smooth muscle with a purely autonomic innervation can be controlled by voluntary effort. The clinical potential lies in the possibility that subjects with reflux esophagitis can learn to increase lower esophageal sphincter

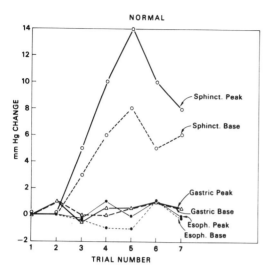

Figure 24.1. Average pressure changes in lower esophageal sphincter, stomach, and esophagus during one session of conditioning for sphincter contraction. Peak and base refer to respiratory excursions. Sphincter contraction (pressure increase) can be effected without altering adjacent stomach and esophageal pressures. An increase of 14 mm Hg is double the normal resting pressure of the lower esophageal sphincter. [Reprinted with permission (5).]

contraction; this provides an effective barrier against reflux. Patients with achalasia due to unrelaxing (often high pressure) sphincters may learn to relax the sphincter.

2. The successful treatment of patients with severe fecal incontinence resulting from neuromuscular impairment firmly establishes operant conditioning as a therapeutic modality in organically determined gastrointestinal motor disorders.

3. The demonstration that patients with irritable bowel syndrome ("spastic colon") can learn to supress abnormal spastic contractions shows the capability of inhibiting abnormal smooth muscle responses in a condition that is thought to be highly susceptible to emotional stress.

LOWER ESOPHAGEAL ("CARDIAC") SPHINCTER CONDITIONING

There are a number of features that make the lower esophageal sphincter attractive for these investigations. First, the lower esophageal sphincter is composed entirely of smooth muscle with exclusively autonomic innervation. Second, the resting pressures of the lower esophageal sphincter are relatively steady. Third, known clinical disorders are associated with abnormal resting pressures, namely reflux esophagitis with diminished pressures and achalasia with increased pressures.

With operant conditioning, normal subjects can learn to contract voluntarily the lower esophageal sphincter to the point that pressure is 100% higher than that of the normal resting pressure (Fig. 24.1). This can be achieved by using standard esophageal motility recording techniques with perfused open-tipped catheters, one catheter resting within the lower esophageal sphincter. When information concerning the intrasphincteric pressure is fed back to the subject by displaying pressures on a meter visible to him, he can learn to control sphincter contraction (Fig. 24.2). The subject is instructed to increase lower esophageal contraction by performing whatever maneuver is necessary to elevate the needle on the meter. He is specifically ordered not to alter his respiration, tighten his abdominal muscles, or utilize skeletal muscles to achieve this effect. To ensure against this possibility, respiration and abdominal muscle contractions are monitored by a pneumograph. Simultaneous pressure measurements from intraesophageal and intragastric pressures provide added safeguards, since they register respirations as well as changes in intraabdominal pressures. The mechanism by which this occurs is unknown, but contraction can be effected without utilizing voluntary musculature or altering intraesophageal or intragastric pressures patients have no cortical awareness of the state of contraction of the lower esophageal sphincter even after they achieve control. It seems likely that the control is effected by a neurological mechanism rather than by humoral means (such as gastrin release) because of the speed with which the response occurs (5, 6).

Patients with heartburn from reflux esophagitis usually have an incompetent lower esophageal sphincter with initial resting pressures that are often one-fifth that of normal. These patients, like normals, can double their initial resting pressure with operant conditioning. However, when impairment is so severe that the pretreatment resting pressures are less than half-normal, a doubling of this pressure does not achieve a normal state and may not be sufficient to provide a continuous-

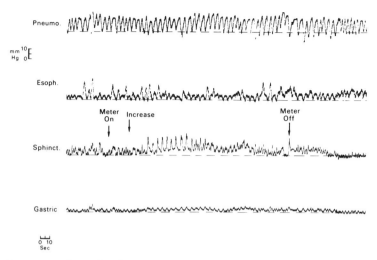

Figure 24.2. Lower esophageal sphincter contraction during operant conditioning. On instructions (second arrow), sphincter pressure increases without alteration of respiration, intraesophageal, or intragastric pressures. "Rebound" contraction occurs as the meter is turned off. [Reprinted with permission (5).]

ly effective barrier against reflux. Further studies are required to determine whether repeated reinforcement over a period of time will raise the pressures to normal levels.

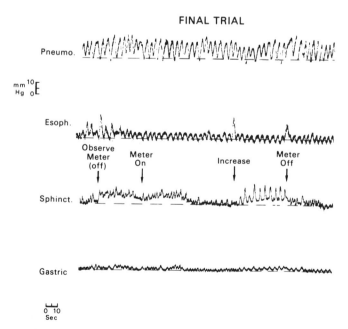

Figure 24.3. "Anticipatory" responses. After successful conditioning, sphincter pressures might automatically increase when subjects were instructed to observe the meter prior to turning the meter on or instructing increase in pressure. In this subject, a second anticipatory increase occurred when the meter was subsequently activated, but before instructions to increase pressure. [Reprinted with permission (5).]

After successful conditioning, anticipatory responses were sometimes noted. These were manifested by the appearance of pressure increases (sphincter contractions) as soon as the subjects were instructed to observe the meter, even though the meter was still turned off. A second anticipatory response sometimes occurred when the meter was subsequently turned on, but before the patient was instructed to increase the pressure (Fig. 24.3). This response is similar to that reported also in classical Pavlovian conditioning.

TREATMENT OF FECAL INCONTINENCE BY BIOFEEDBACK CONTROL OF ANAL SPHINCTER REFLEXES

Of all the clinical disorders that we have studied, fecal incontinence responds most rapidly, completely, and dramatically, especially when the basis for the incontinence is organic. Patients with severe neurosis fared less well. All of our patients presented with gross daily incontinence for many years as their primary complaint. Patients ranged in age from 6 to 87 years. Incontinence resulted from either medical conditions, accidental trauma, or postoperative complications. Medical problems included diabetes, mutiple sclerosis, scleroderma, myelomingocele, and cerebral vascular accidents. Nonmedical incontinence resulted from spinal cord injuries or direct muscle injury from anorectal surgery such as hemorrhoidectomy, and fissurectomy.

Using a specially constructed double balloon device, pressures were measured from the internal anal sphincter (autonomically innervated smooth muscle) and external anal sphincter (somatically innervated striated muscle) (Fig. 24.4). Reflex responses were initiated by momentary distension of a balloon within the rectum. The normal response consists of a momentary reflex relaxation of the internal sphincter and simultaneous contraction of the external sphincter (Fig. 24.5). In patients with fecal incontinence, the external sphincter reflex was absent or markedly impaired. Patients were taught to develop transient reflex contraction of the external sphincter in synchrony with internal sphincter relaxation, which was induced by transient rectal distension (Fig. 24.6). Feedback of responses was provided by permitting the patient to observe the tracing as it was instantaneously produced on a direct writing recorder.

When afferent nerve damage was present and sensory awareness was impaired, conditioning was first directed toward increasing the sensitivity of awareness by decreasing the distending volumes in graded fashion until the normal sensory threshold of 10–15 mm Hg was reached or as near normal as possible. Motor responses also were titrated to the lowest possible distending volume (the motor threshold—normally 10–15 mm Hg). Operant conditioning was successful in inducing reflex contractions in over two-thirds of the patients studied so far, resulting in complete disappearance of incontinence in half of the patients and 90% improvement in the remainder. The results were usually obtained during a single session lasting about 2 hours.

The need to display both internal and extenal sphincter events was dictated by the necessity of developing synchronous responses, since discoordination could result in continued incontinence. The external sphincter contraction must be exquisitely timed to coincide with the relaxation phase in the internal sphincter if incontinence is to be avoided (7–9).

After successful conditioning with feedback, the reflex persisted even when visual feedback was withheld. As a matter of fact, overcompensation occurred, with the amplitudes of sphincter contraction being higher during distensions without feedback than they were during distensions with feedback (Fig. 24.7).

A 6-year-old girl with myelomeningocele, who had been incontinent of urine and stool since birth, had a bladder resection and the construction of an ileal bladder. Prior to operant conditioning, she had neither internal nor external sphincter response. She was able to develop an internal sphincter response with operant conditioning when attention was first devoted to this reflex. Subsequent training focussed on external sphincter response, and this too was successful, with the end result that the patient has been continent over the past 4 years.

Improvement was sustained over a followup period of 4–8 years in all except two of approximately 100 patients. These patients responded to repeat conditioning. Improvement therefore is long-term and may be permanent.

Five factors are important for successful operant conditioning of gastrointestinal functions: (a) The patient must be well-motivated.

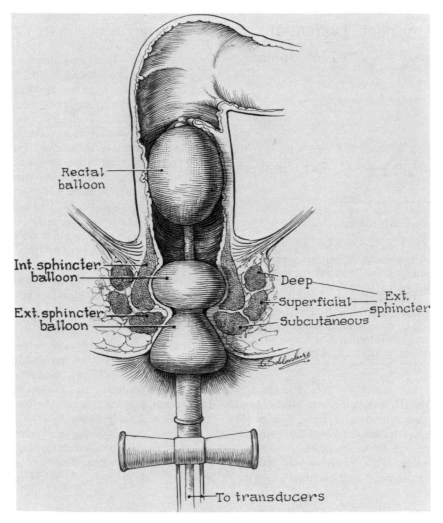

Figure 24.4. Schematic diagram of technique for recording internal and external sphincter reflex response to rectal distension. [Reprinted with permission (5).]

The primary motivating drive in adult patients is the strong desire to overcome severe physical and social disability. More immediate rewards are provided to children by giving them objects such as colored pencils after they have achieved several consecutive correct responses; (b) The subject must be aware of the desired response. This can be achieved by verbal explanations as well as by graphic drawings of normal responses; (c) The patient must be capable of producing a response that can then be strengthened by operant conditioning. For example, those patients who were unable to contract voluntarily the external anal sphincter to a degree that was recordable before conditioning, generally were unable to develop reflex responses, while most of those who could contract voluntarily were also able to incorporate this response into a reflex pattern; (d) There must be a recognizable cue that signals the patient to initiate the response (e.g., pain, heartburn, acid eructation, rectal sensation, urgency, etc); (e) There must be feedback of response.

OPERANT CONTROL OF SPASTIC COLONIC CONTRACTIONS IN IRRITABLE BOWEL SYNDROME

The irritable bowel syndrome is characterized by a triad of abdominal pain, altered bow-

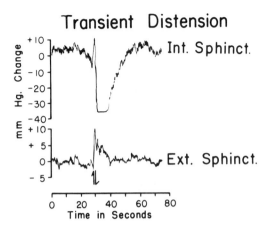

Figure 24.5. Normal rectosphincteric reflexes. Transient rectal distention produces reflex relaxation of the internal sphincter and concomitant reflex relaxation of the external sphincter. [Reprinted with permission from Schuster, M. M., Hookman, P., Hendrix, T. R., and Mendeloff, A. I. Simultaneous manometric recording of internal and external anal sphincter reflexes. Johns Hopkins Med. J., 116: 79, 1965.]

el habits (usually alternating constipation and diarrhea) and absence of organic disease. In contrast to normal subjects, patients with irritable bowel syndrome respond to rectosigmoid distension with diffuse spastic contractions of rectosigmoid and rectum. These responses are elicited by graded increments of distension with 20 ml of air every 2 minutes. These contractions, which encompass a large segment of the colon, are analogous to diffuse esophageal spasm. Threshold for the induction of the spastic response is defined as the lowest cumulative volume of rectal distension that initiates spasm. Feedback was provided by permitting the patient to observe the tracings as they were being recorded. Instructions were given to inhibit this response by preventing the writing pen from rising. With operant conditioning, two-thirds of patients can learn to suppress the spastic responses, and this suppression has been maintained for an 8-week period of follow-up. Studies are now underway to determine whether this objective control persists for long periods of time and whether these objective changes correlate with symptomatic and clinical improvement.

SUMMARY AND CONCLUSIONS

1. Motor responses of autonomically innervated smooth muscle of the gastrointestinal tract can be controlled by operant conditioning, as demonstrated by the studies on the lower esophageal sphincter, the internal anal sphincter and the rectosigmoid.

2. Operant conditioning can be employed as an effective therapeutic tool in the treatment of some gastrointestinal disorders, as demonstrated by the studies on fecal incontinence.

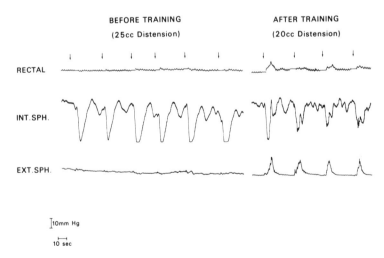

Figure 24.6. Successful operant conditioning of external sphincter reflex in a patient with fecal incontinence. External sphincter reflex was absent before training (tracing on left), but was present after training (tracing on right). [Reprinted with permission (9).]

ALTERNATELY WITH AND WITHOUT FEEDBACK

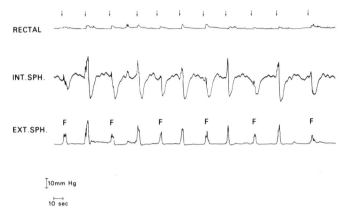

Figure 24.7. "Overcompensation" when feedback was withheld. Amplitudes of external sphincter responses were lower when visual feedback was provided (F) than when feedback was withheld. [Reprinted with permission (9).]

3. Operant control can be developed with a high degree of specificity, as demonstrated by the ability to contract lower esophageal sphincter without affecting the adjacent esophagus or stomach muscle. Anal sphincter specificity is confirmed by the ability to learn to relax one muscle, while contracting the adjacent muscle.

4. Operant conditioning can produce exquisitely synchronized responses (in the case of the internal and external sphincters in opposite directions simultaneously).

5. Because proprioceptive sensation of visceral motor function normally does not reach cortical awareness, instrumental feedback is generally required for visceral conditioning.

References

1. Stoyva, J. Self-regulation: a context for biofeedback. Biofeedback Self Regul., 1:1–6, 1976.
2. Schwartz, G. E. Self-regulation of response patterning: implications for psychophysiological research and therapy. Biofeedback Self Regul., 1: 7–30, 1976.
3. Miller, N. E. Learning of visceral and glandular responses. Science, 163: 434–445, 1969.
4. Schwartz, G. E. Biofeedback, self-regulation, and the patterning of physiological processes. Am. Sci., 63: 314–324, 1975.
5. Schuster, M. M., Nikoomanesh, P., and Wells, D. Biofeedback control of lower esophageal sphincter contraction in man. Fourth International Symposium on Gastrointestinal Motility, edited by E. E. Daniel, pp. 139–144. Mitchell Press, Vancouver, 1974.
6. Schuster, M. M. Operant conditioning in gastrointestinal dysfunction. Hosp. Pract., 9: 135, 1974.
7. Schuster, M. M. Motor action of the rectum and anal sphincters in continence. In Handbook of Physiology, edited by Code, C. and Prosser, C. L., Williams & Wilkins, Baltimore, 1968.
8. Alva, J., Mendeloff, A. I., and Schuster, M. M. Reflex and electromyographic abnormalities associated with fecal incontinence. Gastroenterology, 51: 101, 1967.
9. Engel, B. T., Nikoomanesh, P., and Schuster, M. M. Operant conditioning of rectosphincteric responses in the treatment of fecal incontinence. N. Engl. J. Med., 290: 646, 1974.

CHAPTER 25

Biofeedback Training of the Pelvic Floor and Incontinence

DUGAL CAMPBELL

Human control of evacuation—of liquids or solids—requires a system that can store the material to be disposed of, in increasing amounts, until a convenient moment when the task of storage is replaced by the task of emptying. These tasks are carried out by two different systems: the genitourinary apparatus (the concern of urologists and, in women, of obstetricians) and the anorectal apparatus (the concern of gastroenterologists). The distinctly different requirements—storage and emptying—call for systems that, on the one hand, can silently adapt to increasing quantities, but that can signal changes in the state of the store, and on the other hand, can switch to voluntary control when the signalled quantity and the opportunity to empty the store coincide. These systems must satisfy stringent social demands. Loss of control of evacuation is among the most distressing of social disasters, and training children to control evacuation is high up on the list of a parent's tasks.

Failures of urinary continence are surprisingly common. Wolin (1) found that 51% of young healthy women experienced occasional "stress" incontinence as a result of laughing or sneezing. It is in the elderly or the handicapped that the problem becomes especially acute. Mohide (2) has reviewed the data about urinary incontinence in the elderly, which she points out are based upon a variety of definitions of incontinence and methods of ascertaining the facts. She concludes that in the general elderly population, the prevalence of incontinence may lie between 5 and 10%, and in elderly persons who are being cared for, the rates are substantially higher—10–20% for those receiving home care, and up to 50% for those in institutions. Fecal incontinence is relatively rare in the general population—somewhere in the range of 0.1% to 1.5% (3) but it also increases amongst the elderly, the crippled, and the cognitively impaired (4).

MECHANISMS OF STORAGE, CONTINENCE, AND EVACUATION

As it fills, the bladder maintains a low intravesical pressure due to the elastic properties of the smooth muscle cells of the bladder walls. At the bladder outlet, a higher pressure is maintained by the joint action of smooth muscle in the bladder neck, which suffices to make the system continent if no unusual stress is applied, and the external sphincter of striped muscle, which under voluntary control can add to the outlet pressure. Filling the bladder gives rise to signals that in turn can give rise to conscious awareness of the state of the bladder and the need to void. Evacuation occurs when the following events combine: an increase in intravesical pressure; a decrease in the outlet or urethral pressure; and an alteration in the shape of the bladder as the urethra and bladder neck move downwards as the voluntary muscles of the pelvic floor relax (5–7).

An analogous series of events take place in the colon, rectum, and anus (8). The colon retards the passage of stool by virtue of unorganized motility—greater motility is associated with constipation, diarrhea with an inert colon (9). The two lateral bends and the two anteroposterior turns of the sigmoid colon provide another barrier to the progress of formed stool (10). The rectum is more elastic than the colon and serves as a reservoir; distension of the rectum gives rise to awareness of rectal events and to a wish to pass stool. Gordon (11) emphasizes the sensory capabilities of the anal canal; the rectum can report stretch only, but the more varied anal receptors are responsible for discriminating gas from solid from liquid.

Outlet pressure, usually maintained by the smooth muscle internal sphincter, is reduced following rectal distension, but the passage of stool can be prevented by a reflex contraction of the external sphincter—which can also be contracted or relaxed by voluntary control. Evacuation follows from coordinated contractions in the colon, increased ultraabdominal pressure (straining), alterations in the angles at the turn of the sigmoid colon and rectum (as the pelvic floor relaxes and falls and as the puborectal sling relaxes), and when the external sphincter is relaxed.

When one considers both sets of mechanisms, it is apparent that the passage of stool or urine follows upon an increase in pressure within the storage chamber, a reduction in pressure at the outlet valve, and morphological shifts to permit free passage. No biofeedback treatments have been directed to the alterations in morphology (although it is possible that morphological changes have followed upon biofeedback-induced changes in other targets). But biofeedback has been used to help patients obtain control of storage chamber pressures, to become aware of storage events, and to alter performance of the external sphincter. There are a variety of techniques, and the outcome variables in experiments have most often been alteration in bladder or bowel habit or a reduction in episodes of incontinence. The evidence suggests that biofeedback is an effective treatment for incontinence of both kinds, although no trial has yet been done to estimate the role of nonspecific treatment effects. One should first note in this connection that there are many treatments for incontinence (12) and that many have favorable outcomes (13). The most recent studies, which use EMG feedback from perisphincteric muscles in conjunction with close study of urination or defecation, represent a step forward in the use and analysis of biofeedback. In the sense that they attempt to use signals that monitor specific muscle groups, rather than gross skills, they are a novel development.

FECAL INCONTINENCE AND BIOFEEDBACK: ANAL RECORDING

The method that has become a standard in the treatment of fecal incontinence was developed by Engel, Nikoomanesh, and Schuster (14). (The biofeedback device and similar methods have also been used in the treatment of urinary incontinence.) The device is described fully in Chapter 24. A number of reports, following the original account, show that the method has a good outcome, i.e., a substantial reduction in incontinence, in a variety of patients (3).

Latimer, Campbell, and Kasperski (15) carried out a study in which they attempted to distinguish three possible aspects of biofeedback treatments: sphincter exercise; training synchrony of internal and external sphincters; training discrimination of rectal sensations. Seven of their eight patients improved and were continent at 6 months; however, improvement followed, in several cases, only one of the three varieties of training and, although, at the end of training, patients had improved their ability to detect rectal events and found balloon inflations less "urgent" in signalling for defecation, none had a normal configuration of internal/external sphincter responses following rectal stimulation.

A similar result is reported by Schiller et al. (16), who trained a patient to retain material in the rectum using a method similar to that proposed by Jones (17) for bladder training. The patient watched an infusion reservoir of saline and was told the target was to retain 1500 ml. Despite the continuing diarrhea, the incontinence stopped; yet, measurements of sphincter function showed no changes had taken place in sphincter strength.

The outcome—continence in the presence of sphincter abnormality—shows that although biofeedback produces an effect upon fecal continence, it is by no means clear what the key elements in either normal control or the treatment may be. There may be nonspecific treatment effects arising from attention paid to the patient, paying attention to a problem that has been hidden, coincident alterations in diet and toilet habits; and the relative contributions of discrimination training and sphincter training are not known.

Improvements in continence can be obtained without biofeedback. Tobin and Brockelhurst (18) reported from a geriatric sample that incontinence was eliminated in two-thirds of an experimental group compared with only one-third in controls following the use of enemas and bowel training. In this case, alterations in the patients' attitudes and, perhaps as important, in caretakers' attitudes, provide an important nonspecific aspect of treatment.

The balloon method is hampered by artifacts due, for example, to coughing or moving. An alternative approach is the use of electromyographic signals; these can be made from electrodes mounted on a plug placed in the anus. MacLeod (19) reported the use of this method with 50 patients; he found 72% were improved at 1 year following treatment. In his experimental treatment, MacLeod did not employ rectal stimulation, and therefore sphincter training was the key item.

Whitehead and Schuster (3) argue that, because the control of the external sphincter is voluntary, and because there are no good alternatives, biofeedback and habit training are the treatments of choice for incontinence. However, controlled trials are required to analyze the essential elements in biofeedback treatment, and comparison with a convincing placebo intervention is still needed to show that we are not seeing a nonspecific effect of intervention.

URINARY PROBLEMS AND BIOFEEDBACK

Biofeedback is generally placed among the "behavior" therapies; i.e., the ideas that underly the therapy are taken from an analysis of learning or information processing. In the case of urinary incontinence, the behavior therapies appear to have substantial advantages: surgery for incontinence may be unacceptable to patients or inadvisable in elderly patients; drugs may have unwanted side effects. However, in order to devise the appropriate treatment for a patient, it is necessary to assess each individual's condition and to develop a plan for management that considers behavioral intervention as an option, possibly as an option that can be used in conjunction with medical or other behavioral methods.

The behavioral methods available are: habit training, bladder retraining, reinforcement of "good" toilet habits, staff retraining, and biofeedback. One or more can be used for any patient, and for all methods, good results are claimed by Burgio and Burgio (20). It is important to note that some methods, e.g., combined bladder retraining and reinforcement by Azrin and Foxx (21), can be employed with patients whom many would be inclined to see as unreachable (profoundly retarded adults). In the behavioral techniques mentioned above, the aim of the intervention is the entire pattern of toilet performance. Biofeedback had been aimed at two particular groups of muscles:

those of the bladder wall (smooth muscle), which control intravesical pressure, or the muscles of the pelvic floor, which are linked to the external sphincter (striped muscle). It is argued that incontinence occurs when intravesical pressure exceeds outlet pressure because either the bladder wall fails to relax sufficiently or because the muscles of the pelvic floor fail to contract sufficiently. The first type of failure one tries to counteract by providing the patient with biofeedback information about intravesical pressures and giving training and reinforcement for acquired reductions in pressure ("urge" incontinence), and the second by providing feedback about the pelvic floor and giving training and reinforcement for increasing contractions in the voluntary musculature in the vicinity of the urethra.

Training in the control of intravesical pressure was first reported by Wilson (22) and by Jones (17); a similar technique was used by Campbell and Latimer (23) to treat a patient with urinary retention—biofeedback can be used to train both increases and diminutions of intravesical pressure. A series of patients treated by Cardozo et al. (24) for intravesical control led to cure in 41%. The measurement of intravesical pressure by a device placed in the muscles of the bladder is less convenient for men than for women, and is unlikely to be generally used for men.

The alternative method, biofeedback training of the muscles of the pelvic floor, has been attempted in a number of ways. Kegel (25) developed an exercise plan and a "perineometer," which the patient could use to track improvements in muscular strength; the perineometer is a biofeedback device, but others have used, more simply, the examiners' fingers or the instruction to interrupt the urinary stream. The balloon system devised by Schuster and his colleagues has been used by Burgio et al. (20) to train the pelvic musculature; they found an 82% reduction in incontinence in 19 patients. Shepherd et al. (26) found that the Kegel exercises led to improvement in half of a control group who did not use a perineometer, whereas 91% of an experimental group who did use a perineometer improved. A similar result was obtained by Burgio et al. (20): with feedback, 92% of patients were cured of incontinence, but without it, only 55% were cured or improved. Whitehead, Burgio and Engel (27) also observed that sphincter exercises alone do not lead to continence, whereas biofeedback of sphincter responses led to a 75% decrease in incontinence in 77% of the patients.

The muscles of the pelvic floor contribute to both bladder and anal sphincters; this was shown by Killam et al. (28) who attempted to treat incontinence in eight children with myelomeningocele by means of EMG feedback from perianal surface electrodes and intravesical feedback from a catheter in the bladder. The expected outcome—clinical improvement in urinary incontinence—was obtained in one child; however, four had an improvement in fecal incontinence.

More recently, Barbaree et al. (29) at Queen's University, Kingston, Ontario, have examined the perianal EMG during micturition. They recorded from small disc electrodes placed on the skin while parameters of urine flow were also recorded; this method has the advantage of being noninvasive. Barbaree reports that in patients with "female micturitional syndrome" the symptoms are often, but not always, accompanied by detrusor-sphincter incoordination, i.e., the detrusor muscle contracts, but the external sphincter fails to relax. Biofeedback training of the incoordinated patients led to an increase in volume voided and peak flow, i.e., an EMG-directed alteration from "abnormal" to "normal" during the passage of urine.

Barbaree's work, which is unusual for its close examination of the features of urination by means of urodynamic instruments, gives more precise results than the methods of others who have used EMG, e.g., Maizels et al. (30), Wear et al. (31), and Sugar and Firlit (32). It represents the type of work required if one is to show how biofeedback, assuming it produces favorable clinical results, actually works.

Bleijenberg and Kuijpers (33), who investigated fecal incontinence, have reported an effect analogous to that noted by Barbaree and his colleagues. They trained patients to relax the pelvic floor muscles during straining; in this instance, the problem was constipation due to difficult defecation, and the source of the trouble was found to be that the anorectal angle remained at 90% during attempts to empty the rectum. In 7 of 10 patients, biofeedback training was successful. This paper also illustrates the advantages of an EMG technique allied to a close analysis of the incoordination, which is the cause of the problem.

References

1. Wolin, L.H. Stress incontinence in young, healthy nulliparous female subjects. J. Urol., *101*: 545–549, 1969.
2. Mohide, E.A. The prevalence and scope of urinary incontinence. Clin. Geriat. Med., *2*: 639–655, 1986.
3. Whitehead, W.E. and Schuster, M.M. *Gastrointestinal Disorders: Behavioural and Physiological Basis for Treatment.* Academic Press; New York, pp. 229–275, 1985.
4. Van Nostrand, J.F., Zappolo, A., Hing, E., Bloom, B., Hirsch, B. and Foley, D.J. The national nursing home survey: 1977 summary for the United States. DHEW Publication No. PHS 79-1794., U.S. Govt. Printing Office. Statistics Series 13 (no. 43): Washington, D.C., 1979.
5. Ruch, T.C. The urinary bladder. In *Physiology and Biophysics*, edited by T.C. Ruch and H.D. Patton. W. B. Saunders, Philadelphia, 1966.
6. Tanagho, E.A. and Miller, E.R. Initiation of voiding. Br. J. Urol., *42*: 175–183, 1970.
7. Wein, A.J. and Raezer, D.M. Physiology of micturition. In *Clinical Neuro-urology*, edited by R.J. Krane and M.B. Siroky. Little, Brown, & Co., Boston, 1979.
8. Schuster, M.M. Motor action of rectum and anal sphincters in continence and defecation. In *Handbook of Physiology.* American Psychological Society: Washington, D.C., pp. 2121–2146, 1968.
9. Connell, A.M. The motility of the pelvic colon. II. Paradoxical motility in diarrhoea and constipation. Gut, *3*: 342–348, 1962.
10. Hill, J.R., Kelley, M.L., Schlegel, J.F. and Code, C.F. Pressure profiles of the rectum and anus of healthy persons. Dis. Colon Rectum, *3*: 203–209, 1960.
11. Gordon, P.H. The anorectum: anatomic and physiologic considerations in health and disease Gastroenterology Clinics of North America, *16*: 1–15, 1987.
12. Hilton, P. Urinary incontinence in women: clinical algorithm. Br. Med. J., *295*: 426–432, 1987.
13. Burgio, K.L. and Burgio, L.D. Behaviour therapies for urinary incontinence in the elderly Clin. Geriatr. Med., *2*: 809–827, 1986.
14. Engel, B.T., Nikoomanesh, P. and Schuster, M.M. Operant conditioning of recto-sphincteric reponses in the treatment of fecal incontinence. N. Eng. J. Med., *290*: 646–649, 1974.
15. Latimer, P.R., Campbell, D. and Kasperski, J. A components analysis of biofeedback in the treatment of incontinence. Biofeedback Self Regul., *9*: 311–324, 1984.
16. Schiller, L.R., Santa Ana, C., Davis, G.R. and Fordtran, J.S. Fecal incontinence in chronic diarrhoea: report of a case with improvement after training with rectally infused saline. Gastroenterology, *77*: 751–753, 1979.
17. Jones, H.G. The application of conditioning and learning techniques to the treatment of a psychiatric patient. J. Abnormal Psychol., *52*: 414–419, 1956.
18. Tobin, G.W. and Brockelhurst, J.C. Fecal incon-

tinence in residential homes for the elderly: prevalence, aetiology and management. Age Ageing, 15: 41–46, 1986.

19. MacLeod, J.H. Biofeedback in the management of partial anal incontinence. Dis. Colon Rectum, 26: 244–246, 1983.

20. Burgio, K.L., Whitehead, W.E. and Engel, B.T. Urinary incontinence in the elderly. Ann. Intern. Med., 103: 507–515, 1985.

21. Azrin, N.H. and Foxx, R.M. A rapid method of toilet training the institutionalized retarded. J. Appl. Behav. Anal., 4: 89–99, 1971.

22. Wilson, T.S. Incontinence of urine in the aged. Lancet, ii: 374–377, 1948.

23. Campbell, D. and Latimer, P.R. Biofeedback in the treatment of urinary retention. J. Behav. Ther. Exp. Psychiatry, 11: 27–30, 1980.

24. Cardozo, L.D., Stanton, S.L. and Hafner, J. Biofeedback in the treatment of detrusor instability. Brit. J. Urol., 50: 250–254, 1978.

25. Kegel, A.H. Stress incontinence of urine in women: physiologic treatment. Journal of International College of Surgeons, 25: 487–499, 1956.

26. Shepherd, A.M., Montgomery, E. and Anderson, R.S. Treatment of genuine stress and incontinence with a new perineometer. Physiotherapy, 69: 113, 1983.

27. Whitehead, W.E., Burgio, K.L. and Engel, B.T. Biofeedback treatment of fecal incontinence in geriatric patients. J. Amer. Geriatr. Soc., 33: 320–324, 1985.

28. Killam, P.E., Jefferies, J.S. and Varn, J.W. Urodynamic biofeedback treatment of urinary incontinence in children with myelomeningocele. Biofeedback Self Regul., 10: 161–171, 1985.

29. Barbaree, H.E., Sharp, W.L., Perez-Marrero, R. and Emerson, L. Peri-anal EMG biofeedback as a treatment for female micturitional findings. 1987 (personal communication).

30. Maizels, M. and Firlit, C.F. Pediatric urodynamics: a clinical comparison of surface versus needle pelvic floor/external sphincter electromyography. J. Urol., 122: 518–522, 1979.

31. Wear, J.B., Wear, R.B. and Cleeland, C. Biofeedback in urology using urodynamics: preliminary observations. J. Urol., 121: 464–468, 1979.

32. Sugar, E.C. and Firlit, C.F. Urodynamic feedback: a new therapeutic approach for childhood incontinence/infection. J. Urol., 128: 1253–1258, 1982.

33. Bleijenberg, G. and Kuijpers, H.C. Treatment of the spastic pelvic floor syndrome with biofeedback. Dis. Colon Rectum, 30: 108–111, 1987.

CHAPTER 26

Electromyographic Biofeedback and the Treatment of Communication Disorders

BRENT G. CARMAN AND GARY RYAN

SPEECH-LANGUAGE PATHOLOGY

Speech-language pathology involves the prevention, evaluation, treatment, and management of language, speech, voice, and swallowing disorders. It borrows heavily from the fields of medicine, psychology, linguistics, and others. This is a young profession, however, dealing with its share of "growing pains." Consequently, speech-language pathology has only recently begun to appreciate the significance of electromyographic (EMG) biofeedback as a tool for documenting clinical change objectively.

Speech is an overlaid function (1). That is to say, there is no specific organ for speech. Instead, anatomical structures of the aerodigestive tract must function in a coordinated manner to produce intelligible sounds (2). Normal speech production requires the coordinated activity of respiratory muscles and those muscles responsible for phonation and articulation (3). A controlled delivery of air in expiration is needed to allow the muscles of the larynx and oral pharynx to modulate the vibrations we interpret as voice (4, 5). This is a process that necessarily involves the precise control of muscular functions. As a result, any aberrant muscle activity would naturally cause or contribute to many types of speech disorders (2, 3).

The emphasis in speech therapy and diagnosis is towards improvement, without fully understanding the underlying pathological mechanisms. Direct measurement of the audible characteristics of phonation is possible, but often subject to difficulties in standardization and variations within a given subject (2, 6). More invasive techniques such as needle electrode electromyography (EMG) or fiber op-

tic pharyngoscopy play a useful role but have a limited application because of poor patient tolerance and technical limitations (7, 8). They are better suited to primary diagnosis rather than to monitoring ongoing therapy.

The development of EMG biofeedback as a means of measuring, recording, and displaying the electrical activity of living muscle has significant implications for the assessment and treatment of communication disorders. EMG recording provides a more objective means of measuring and characterizing the nature of muscle activity during speech (7, 9–12), typically focused on a few muscle groups (7, 13). Most studies limited their observation to a single level of the speech mechanism, such as the laryngeal or respiratory muscles (7, 13, 15), and few were designed to record the simultaneous activity of multiple muscle groups in an effort to characterize the patterns present in normal speech (5), especially coordinated activity between synergists and antagonists.

Laryngeal function has been studied using surface electrodes in disorders such as stuttering and dysarthria (16–18). Recordings obtained using this technique have proved to be a reliable measure of vocal fold activity (19, 20). This has been confirmed by measurements using needle electrodes to monitor the laryngeal mechanism during respiration and phonation (21).

The EMG measurement of respiration is somewhat more contentious. The actions of the scalene, intercostal, diaphragm, and abdominal muscles differ, depending on the nature and phase of respiration. Scalene muscle recordings provide an accurate reflection of inspiratory activity (Fig. 26.1). They are thought to act by fix-

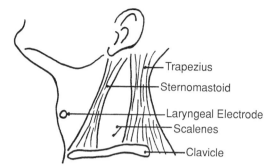

Figure 26.1. Laryngeal electrode placements and location of scalene muscles.

ing the first rib, thereby allowing the intercostals to elevate the remaining ribs during inspiration (19). Scalene muscle recordings using needle electrodes parallel the findings obtained using surface electrodes (22).

The role of intercostal muscles is less well defined. Some feel that they fix the ribs at a constant relative position during both inspiration and expiration (19). Nonrespiratory postural activity may also account for a proportion of intercostal muscle activity. It has also been demonstrated that during quiet breathing, the intercostals are active only during inspiration (23). Other studies have subdivided the intercostals in upper and lower groups, with the former active in both phases of respiration and the latter active in inspiration only (24). It is obvious that the technical factors, such as electrode placement and the structure of the experiment, play a major role in determining these sometimes conflicting results (7, 11). It appears that the intercostals play a significant role in respiration and phonation (25–27), but the procedural difficulties involved in their study make their use of limited value, particularly when using surface electrode techniques (7, 11).

The diaphragm and abdominal muscles also play important respiratory roles. Diaphragmatic contraction is the prime determinant of normal inspiration (7, 28). Unfortunately, the deep location of this muscle makes it difficult for study with surface recording electrodes (7, 29). The abdominal muscles do not contract during either phase of quiet respiration. In addition, it would appear that they do not contract during phonation. They do, however, contribute to the latter phase of forced expiration (30).

THE LOGIC OF EMG BIOFEEDBACK

Neuromuscular reeducation using EMG biofeedback is based on the concept that motor outflow depends on sensory inflow (31, 32). Once behavior becomes observable, even artificially, it can be brought under voluntary control (33–36). Traditionally, the therapist substituted for abnormal proprioceptive information by informing a patient about how a muscle performed, providing information regarding proprioceptive function via audiovisual receptors (32). As a result, temporary external feedback substitutes for abnormal internal feedback. In time, the brain learns to decode and use this information. However, verbal feedback lacks the specifications of being immediate, proportional, and continuous. EMG biofeedback, when correctly employed, meets all the criteria for assisting the central nervous system to correctly interpret incoming signals (7, 32, 37). Once the behavior become observable, it is subject to operant conditioning and can be shaped by the clinician (39).

ELECTROMYOGRAPHIC BIOFEEDBACK— THE POWER

The application of electromyography provides a real time representation of muscular events that can be subsequently analyzed and compared (7, 33, 38). Simultaneous recording from various muscle groups allows a temporal map to be created specifying synergistic and antagonistic muscle activity (7, 39, 40). The technique is comfortable and reproducible if surface landmarks are carefully plotted (33, 38). This technique may be applied to both pediatric and adult populations (2, 12).

The equipment provides a motivational component in excess of that which would be provided by a therapist alone. It monitors the patient's input and may automatically "reward" success or "punish" failure (20, 41). The threshold for success may be continually adjusted by the clinician to promote progressive improvement. The objective documentation of the improvement, or lack thereof, serves to identify limitations, strengths, successes, and needs in treatment (33, 42). By altering reinforcement schedules, the therapist can maintain interest and commitment to treatment (20, 31). Moreover, the greater the number of motoric repetitions, the greater the strength and control the patient establishes over voluntary movement.

The clinical application of EMG biofeedback not only allows for a quantitative change in the therapy process, but also exacts a qualitative change. The conventional dyad of patient-therapist is now superseded by a triad of patient-machine-therapist. The net result of this change is that the patient must accept a more active role in therapy (41). The role of the therapist is altered as well. The application of EMG biofeedback requires that the therapist assume the role of "teacher" or facilitator and not instructor or judge.

TREATMENT OVERVIEW

The three basic applications of EMG biofeedback in the treatment of communicative disorders are:

1. Decreased muscle tone, e.g., lower motor neuron damage;
2. Increased muscle tone, e.g., upper motor neuron damage;
3. Poor volitional control or incoordination, e.g., apraxia.

At a basic physiological level, neuromuscular function of any communication disorders due to any one of these conditions can be improved if enough neuromechanisms are left intact (32, 33). In essence, regardless of the etiology, EMGBF may be an appropriate adjunct to speech-language pathologists and their treatments.

STEPS IN EMGBF TREATMENT

According to Darley, "Speech-language pathologists seek to describe adequately any communication problem with which they deal in order to distinguish it from other problems that it may resemble and to determine its distinctive character. They undertake, that is to diagnose, the problem by making an appropriate examination and placing the data they gather in historical perspective. On the basis of their findings and interpretations of them, they propose a remedial program and attempt to predict its outcome" (42).

It would follow then, that EMG would first impact on the assessment procedure. Once the history has been obtained, the clinician would have had an opportunity to observe the patient and identify any significant problems. At this point, the clinician would prepare a number of sites for electrode placement. Skin preparation consists of rubbing the skin with an alcohol-saturated gauze pad. An optional second step is to rub in some of the electrode gel into the site, for better contact (38). However, this step is time-consuming and may be better left for more formal periodic reassessments. The electrodes are then filled with conductive gel and attached to the skin by an adhesive disc or tape. The most time-effective means of securing electrodes and obtaining accurate recordings may be to use disposable electrodes. Electrode placement involves using two live recording electrodes and one ground electrode to reduce the possibility of obtaining an artifact or signal contamination (38). Finally, electrode placement must be predicated on accurate knowledge of specific muscle location and function.

During the skin preparation phase, it is advisable to explain to the patient what is happening and what is going to happen. This explanation may "demystify" the process and hopefully reduce patient anxiety. In addition, discussing the procedure may help to remind the clinician of each step that is required.

Once the electrodes have been secured, baseline readings of each site should be obtained. Baseline readings are levels of muscle activity at rest measured in microvolts. Normal resting values typically range from .5 to 1.0 microvolts (μV) (7).

Next comes the maximum contraction values. Have the patient contract the muscle and record the peak microvolt level. The resting and maximum contraction levels give the clinician the patient's range for that particular muscle or muscle group. Depending on the nature of the disorder, it may be appropriate to obtain, for example, respiration, pitch range, or conversational speech and corresponding EMG output. The purpose behind recording these values is that they allow the clinician to identify impaired muscle activity, document objectively the degree of severity, and help to characterize the extent of the problem. Note: up to this point the patient has not been exposed to his own EMG output.

Trial Therapy Phase

Allow the patient to appreciate the purpose and power of EMGBF by attaching the electrodes to an unaffected body part and allowing the patient to experiment with the equipment. This provides an opportunity for the patient to slowly become more active in the therapy process and allows the clinician to identify the most effective form of feedback, i.e., auditory, visual, or a combination of both. Once the concept is understood, the electrodes can be reattached to the appropriate areas. The starting point or primary focus for therapy would be those muscles governing the process most amenable to change, the least severely affected, and/or muscles crucial to success.

Once the muscles and behaviors to be changed have been isolated, facilitation techniques such as icing, vibration, yawn-sigh, could be introduced and their effects assessed. The patient's behavior is altered or shaped by conventional therapy techniques and/or supplemented by techniques the patient spontaneously discovers. In fact, any change caused by the patient's experimentation with the instrumentation should be encouraged and accepted. During this phase of therapy, the clinician must be alert to the need to alter threshold in order to maintain a 70 to 90% success rate (42).

The shaping of responses and behavior continues, as do periodic reevaluations. The patient's ability to perform without feedback is periodically assessed by shielding the patient from the feedback while performance is monitored. Progress is measured by changes away from baseline and in the audible characteristics of the patient's speech. Sessions typically run for 40 minutes, twice a week (41).

In many cases, generalization or transfer to outside situations is spontaneous because it is possible to stress the patient and measure the effects of this stress in the clinic (20, 41). As a result, a patient should rarely be discharged before being able to cope with situations outside the clinic. In other words, EMGBF does provide a relatively accurate means of predicting success.

Discharge is considered when patients are able to maintain a good resting level and have the ability to rapidly increase muscle activity to a maximum, i.e., patients should have good control over their entire range (41). In addition, patients should have the ability to sustain the contraction at any given point along the continuum (20, 41). Finally, discharge should be considered only when the patient manifests a corresponding functional change in speech behavior or a plateauing of their performance.

APPLICATION TO STUTTERING

The application of EMGBF to the problem of stuttering has, at time, yielded significant re-

ductions of neuromuscular activity and dysfluency (43–46). Moreover, there are some reports of success in transferring and maintaining the gains made during treatment to the posttreatment environmnet (46, 47). However, the results of EMGBF stuttering therapy have not always been positive or consistent. In fact, there are reports of subjects not responding to therapy or that posttreatment fluency has been accompanied by abnormally slow rates of speech. Some of the reasons for these problems lay with inappropriate application of the technology and/or flawed experimental designs. As a result, although EMGBF has been regarded as one of the most powerful tools available for realizing clinical change, findings to date have not yielded many clinically useful results. Hence, as a clinical tool for the treatment of stuttering, EMGBF has not been fully realized and exploited. However, by concentrating the patient's efforts on altering muscle activity via EMGBF, stuttering can be reduced both quantitatively and qualitatively. The key is that EMGBF must be incorporated into a treatment program, for it is not able to stand alone as an effective treatment for stuttering.

The advantage of EMG biofeedback therapy to stuttering over conventional therapy is that the assessment provides a starting point (and direction) for treatment based or supported by objective data. The assessment should have the patient engage in monologue, dialogue, and reading. The corresponding EMG output for each level of stimuli should be recorded—base line data.

Treatment

I. Trial Therapy Phase

1. Electrode placement is refined. One site has been found to be particularly effective in directly altering laryngeal muscle activity and indirectly altering stuttering behaviors (41). Specifically electrodes are placed on either side of the thyroid cartilage, and one ground electrode is placed midline immediately above the two recording electrodes (41) (Fig. 26.2).

Placement, however, should generally be predicated on the results of the assessment, and different stutters have different sites of tension or trigger points.

2. Facilitation techniques are introduced. For example, the patient uses EMGBF in con-

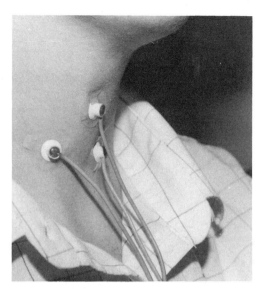

Figure 26.2. Electrode placements related to thyroid prominence.

junction with delayed auditory feedback, and starts with sounds or words that, according to the assessment data, were produced most fluently and easily in an effort to begin to develop the control necessary in order to experience fluency.

II. Therapy Phase

1. Throughout the rest of the treatment phase, the patient should be exposed to progressively more difficult material while still maintaining low EMG outputs and levels of fluency.

2. During the terminal stages of treatment or when the patient is able to engage in fluent conversation, the feedback should be faded. Moreover, the patient could be exposed to spurious feedback readings and their effects assessed. In other words, the patient could be stressed within the clinic and the effects of the stress examined. Patients' ability to resist the stress or rely on internal cues rather than on the equipment with its spurious readings is a good indicator of how well they will perform outside the clinic.

III. Transfer Phase

1. Transfer during EMGBF therapy has been reported to occur spontaneously (41). However, if the fluency does not carry over into extraclinical settings, formal transfer activities

may be necessary: e.g., systematic desensitization (48).

IV. Maintenance Phase

1. Posttreatment regular visits are essential for at least 6 months following treatment. Initially, the visits should be weekly, then biweekly, then, finally, monthly. If problems do arise, immediate steps should be taken to assist patients in regaining control. The maintenance can be formal or informal, depending on the patients' needs. For example, patients may need to borrow the equipment in order to practice at home.

In essence, the instrumentation allows patients to experience fluency within a range of acceptable muscle outputs. If patients exceed those values, stuttering typically occurs. The more successful patients are in identifying and internalizing the range of neuromuscular values that correspond to fluent speech, the more likely patients will be to maintain their fluency.

Things to Consider

The patients' rate of speech and respiratory patterns are not directly addressed in therapy using EMGBF (41).

Absolute EMG values and levels of fluency or dysfluency do not exist. For example, 27 μV of laryngeal neuromuscular activity will not always result in stuttering or blocking behavior in all patients. As a result, patients must act as their own controls, and changes should be measured relative to baseline readings.

Finally, conventional stuttering treatments do not necessarily have to change with the application of EMG biofeedback. EMGBF provides a rationale for their application and objective information regarding their effects.

APPLICATION TO VOICE DISORDERS

Voice disorders are characterized by disturbances in any one or more of the following dimensions: pitch, loudness, vocal quality, and duration. Remediation of the problem typically involves identifying the aberrant elements and attempting to obtain an acoustically acceptable voice (2, 12). Although normal voice production has been well documented, it is difficult to determine what is taking place in patients with voice disorders (49). Clinically, at the muscular level, it is difficult to document the muscle activity subserving voice production. This is where EMGBF has begun to find a direct application for both the assessment and treatment of voice disorders and could soon become more widely used in the management of voice disorders.

Traditionally, in voice therapy, the clinician focuses on the end-product—the voice—and tells patients if the output is within normal limits. It is difficult to identify what muscles are contracting or the sequence of contraction taking place in, for example, a patient recovering from surgery for pharyngeal cancer or from laryngeal trauma. However, EMGBF offers the clinician the opportunity to focus not only on the voice, but also on the muscular activity underlying phonation. Used appropriately, it gives information that could be used by patients to facilitate optimum voice production, as demonstrated by Prosek et al. (50).

Prosek et al. (50) used EMGBF on six adult patients all manifesting excessive laryngeal tension. The patients had voice disorders resulting from different causes such as vocal nodules, carcinoma, recurrent traumatic laryngitis, and spastic dysphonia. Sessions consisted of having the patients use EMGBF to decrease their laryngeal tension during different speaking tasks. No standard voice therapy was provided during the biofeedback sessions. Three patient were able to significantly decrease the level of muscular activity and subsequently improve their voice quality. The three who did not improve voice quality had started with a poor prognosis for change: i.e., spastic dysphonia or structural damage. More recently, Stemple et al. (51) were successful in improving the voice quality in five out of seven patients using EMGBF.

Treatment

I. Trial Therapy Phase

1. Assess and refine electrode placement. There is no one site appropriate for most voice patients.

2. Assess effects of facilitation techniques. For example, patients could use EMGBF in conjuction with pushing techniques to increase the strength of their laryngeal musculature, thereby improving their voice quality. A period of trial therapy may help identify those sites most directly related to improved voice output and those sites most resistant to change. Electromyography is the only objective way of ensuring a qualitatively adequate voice is produced with the least amount of muscular effort.

II. Therapy Phase

As with stuttering therapy, progressively more difficult material must be mastered. Ultimately, EMGBF must be faded.

DYSARTHRIA

Dysarthria refers to a group of speech disorders caused by disturbances in muscle control. The muscles' speed, strength and coordination may be affected. To recover muscle control requires extensive practice. Dysarthria therapy is therefore largely drill therapy (52).

In order to be effective, drill must be enlightened (52). Typically, patients rely on their clinicians to construct drills that are functional and arranged in difficulty to allow maximal treatment gains. They also rely on their clinicians, especially during the initial stages of therapy, to provide the feedback needed for them to learn conscious control of their speech. EMGBF is a tool used by both the clinician and patient to provide the precise, consistent feedback needed for neuromuscular reeducation.

EMGBF allows for patients to practice independently. Where appropriate, patients can spend the extensive time needed to obtain efficacious results in dysarthria therapy without monopolizing the therapists's time. In essence, EMG biofeedback provides the independent practice that can foster a sense of dignity and control. This feeling of control can be a powerful motivator for patients who have, for example, suffered a stroke and lost a significant degree of independent function (41).

The treatment of dysarthria has been shown to be effective in at least some dysarthric patients by a number of researchers (18, 53, 54). No patient should therefore be rejected without some diagnostic or trial therapy. Linebaugh (54) describes his use of EMGBF in the strenghthening of muscle of flaccid dysarthria. He places electrodes on the muscles that elevate and depress the jaw to monitor its opening and closing. He also describes using the EMG equipment to increase lip muscle strength. To strengthen the orbicularis oris superior, he uses a placement just lateral to the philtrum and sets progressively more difficult target levels. Target levels should be altered either by longer sustained contractions or by more forceful contractions.

Alternatively, too much muscle tone can also be treated using EMGBF, as described by Rosenbek et al. (52). They treated a patient with a hemifacial spasm that was severe enough to prevent speech when the spasm occurred. Treatment with EMGBF allowed the patient to reduce the spasm and thus improve his speech output.

An overall approach to the treatment of motor speech disorders should include increasing physiological support for speech to the maximum, and using compensatory speech strategies and alternate means of communication as needed. EMGBF would be one tool to help with increasing physiological support for speech.

Assessment

Quantifying muscle status is possible and helps to determine if the muscles are fully innervated.

Treatment

I. Trial Therapy

Attach the electrodes to an unaffected body part to teach the patient the rationale behind EMGBF/speech therapy.

II. Treatment

Apply the appropriate facilitation technique to increase or decrease muscle tone. For example, techniques such as EMGBF, pushing exercises, and stretching can be used.

Things to Consider

1. EMGBF, if applied properly, may be appropriate for cognitively impaired patients. Specifically, using an unaffected body part, a patient could be conditioned to respond appropriately as defined by EMGBF even when other treatments would require more cognitive knowledge.

2. Encourage patients, if possible, to apply their own electrodes. They should take more control of the process to demystify therapy and to increase independence.

3. Discharge is considered when the patients are their physiological limit.

CASE STUDY

A 14-year-old teenager suffering from mild spastic cerebral palsy was referred to a hospital speech and language department for treatment of a drooling problem. The problem was thought to be due to his neurological condi-tion, which resulted in a mouth-open posture. The posterior fibers of the temporalis muscle are chiefly responsible for maintaining the position of the mandible at rest, i.e., lips together and teeth apart (55, 56).

Muscle recordings from the patients' temporalis muscle at rest were found to be 0 μV, i.e., no activity. However, when the patient achieved a microvolt level of .7 μV, a jaw-closed position was assumed. Consequently, a short course of treatment was instituted to increase resting muscle activity of the temporalis muscles.

The patient was given an increasingly longer period of time to maintain a target level of 9 μV. This value was chosen because it corresponded to a cosmetically acceptable mouth-closed posture. After 5 weeks of twice-weekly 40-minute sessions, the patient was able to achieve a mouth-closed posture with a corresponding EMG level of .4 μV. This posture was accompanied by a functional change in the patient's behavior, i.e., no drooling. In addition, this change was maintained and no problems were reported at the 6-month recheck period.

LOCUS OF CONTROL

Speech-language pathologists will be judged not only on their ability to elicit short-term changes, but also on their skill in helping patients to maintain those changes in the post-treatment environment. For example, virtually all forms of intensive behavioral treatment for stuttering produce rather dramatic increases in fluency only to encounter serious relapse problems later (57). Some research suggests that EMGBF therapy directly addresses the issue of relapse by altering patients' locus of control (41, 58, 59). Stutterers who achieved improvement during EMG biofeedback therapy and maintained fluency following treatment had a commensurate shift in locus of control from external to internal (41, 59). These findings suggest that EMGBF therapy shifts patients' perception of control, thereby allowing for posttreatment gains to be maintained.

References

1. Spriestersbach, D.C. and Morris, L.H. Speech problems of patients with cleft lip and palate. In *Reconstructive Plastic Surgery*, edited by M.J. Converse. W.B. Saunders, New York, 1977.

2. Reed, C.G. Voice therapy: a need for research. J. Speech Hear. Disord., 65:157–67, 1980.

3. Mysak, E.D. Cerebral Palsy Speech Syndromes. In Handbook of Speech Pathology and Audiology, edited by L.E. Travis. Prentice-Hall, Englewood Cliffs, N.J., 1971.

4. Hixon, T.J. Respiratory function in speech. In F.D. Minifie, T.J. Hixon and F. Williams (Eds.) Normal Aspects of Speech, Hearing and Language. Prentice-Hall, Englewood Cliffs, N.J., 1973.

5. Broad, D.J. Phonation. In F.D. Minifie, T.J. Hixon and F. Williams (eds.) Normal Aspects of Speech, Hearing and Language. Prentice-Hall, Englewood Cliffs, N.J., 1973.

6. Morris, H.L. and Spresterbach, D.L. Appraisal of respiration and phonation. In F.L. Darley and D.C. Spriesterbach (eds.) Diagnostic Methods in Speech Pathology. Harper and Row, New York, 1978.

7. Basmajian, J.V. Muscles Alive: Their Functions Revealed by Electromyography, 3rd ed. Williams & Wilkins, Baltimore, 1974.

8. Aronson, A.E. Clinical Voice Disorders: An Interdisciplinary Approach. Thieme-Stratton, New York, 1980.

9. Basmajian, J.V. Clinical use of biofeedback in rehabilitation. Psychosomatics, 23(1): 67–69, 1982.

10. Wolf, S.L. EMG biofeedback applications in physical rehabilitation: an overview. Physiotherapy Canada, 31(2): 65–72, 1979.

11. Basmajian, J.V. and Blumenstein, R. Electrode Placement in EMG Biofeedback. Baltimore: Williams & Wilkins, 1980.

12. Boone, D.R. The Voice and Voice Therapy. Prentice-Hall, Englewood Cliffs, N.J., 1977.

13. O'Dwyer, N.J., Quinn, P.T., Guitar, B.E., Andrews, G. and Nedson, P.D. Procedures for verification of electrode placement in EMG studies of orofacial and mandibular muscles. J. Speech Hear. Res., 24: 273–288, 1981.

14. Floyd, W. F. and Silver, P.H.S. Electromyographic study of patterns of activity of the anterior abdominal wall muscles in man. J. Anat., 84: 132–145, 1950.

15. Jones, D.S., Beargie, R.J. and Pauly, J.E. An electromyographic study of some muscles of costal respiration in man. Anat. Rec., 117: 17–24, 1953.

16. Guitar, B. Reduction of stuttering frequency using analog electromyographic feedback. J. Speech Hear. Res., 18: 672–685, 1975.

17. Moore, W.H., Dunster, J.R. and Lang, M.K. The effects of alpha biofeedback conditioning of laryngeal muscles. Arch. Otolaryngol., 89: 902–907, 1969.

18. Netsell, R. and Cleeland, C.S. Modification in lip hypertonia in dysarthria using EMG biofeedback. J. Speech Hear. Disord., 38: 131–140, 1973.

19. Jones, D.S., Beargie, R.J. and Pauly, J.F. An electromyograhic study of some muscles of costal respiration in man. Anat. Rec., 117: 17–24, 1953.

20. Carman, B.G. An electromyographic comparison between cerebal palsy patients and normals.

Master's Research, Hamilton, 1983.

21. Faaborg-Anderson, K.L. Electromyographic investigation of intrinsic laryngeal muscles in humans: an investigation of subjects with normally moveable vocal cords and patients with vocal cord paresis. Acta Physio. Scand., 41 (suppl 140): 1–148, 1957.

22. Raper, A.J., Thompson Jr., W.T., Shapiro, W. and Patterson Jr., L. Scalene and sternomastoid muscle function. J. Appl. Physiol., 21: 493–502, 1966.

23. Campbell, E.J.M. An electromyographic examination of the role of intercostal muscles in breathing in man. J. Physiol., 129: 12–26, 1955.

24. Koepke, G.H., Smith, E.M., Murphy, A.J. and Dickson, D.G. Sequence of action of the diaphragm and intercostal muscles during respiration. I. inspiration. Arch. Phys. Med., 39: 426–430, 1958.

25. Perlstein, M. and McDonald, E. Nature, recognition and management of neuromuscular disabilities in children. Pediatrics, 11: 166–173, 1953.

26. Peiper, S. Cerebral Function in Infancy and Childhood. Consultants Bureau, New York, 1963.

27. Perlstein, M. and Shere, M. Speech therapy for children with cerebral palsy. American Journal of the Disabled Child, 72: 389–398, 1946.

28. Bahoric, A. and Chernich, V. Electrical activity of phrenic nerve and diaphragm in utero. J. Appl. Physiol., 39: 513–518, 1975.

29. Campbell, E.J.M. The Respiratory Muscles and the Mechanics of Breathing. Lloyd-Luke, (Medical Books) Ltd., London, 1958.

30. Campbell, E.J.M. The function of the abdominal muscles in relaxation to the intra-abdominal pressure and respiration. Archives of Middlesex Hospital, 5: 87–94, 1955.

31. Harris, F.A. Facilitation techniques in therapeutic exercise. In J.V. Basmajian (ed.), Therapeutic Exercise. Williams & Wilkins, Baltimore, 1980.

32. Howson, D. Report on Neuromuscular Re-education. ISIS Medical Instruments Company, Ithaca, New York, 1976.

33. Wolf, S.L. EMG biofeedback applications in physical rehabilitation: an overview. Physiotheraphy Canada, 31(2): 65–72, 1979.

34. Basmajian, J.V. Clinical use of biofeedback in rehabilitation. Psychosomatics, 23(1), 67–69, 1982.

35. Basmajian, J.V., Baeza, J. and Fabrigar, C. Conscious control and training of individual spinal motor neurons in normal human subjects. Journal of New Drugs, 5: 78–85, 1965.

36. Reynolds, G.S. A Primer of Operant Conditioning. Scott, Foresman and Company, Glenview, Illinois, 1968.

37. Smith, W.M. Feedback: real-time delayed vision of one's own tracking behavior. Science, 176: 939–940, 1972.

38. Basmajian, J.V. and Blumenstein, R. Electrode Placement in EMG Biofeedback. Williams & Wilkins, Baltimore, 1980.

39. Costello, J.M. Techniques of therapy based on operant conditioning. In General Principles of Therapy, edited by W.H. Perkins. Thieme-Stratton, New York, 1982.

40. Floyd, W.F. and Silver, P.H.S. Electromyographic study of patterns of activity of the anterior abdominal wall muscles in man. J. Anat., 84: 134–145, 1950.

41. Carman, B.G. An electromyographic biofeedback treatment of stuttering. Doctoral dissertation, Minneapolis, 1985.

42. Darley, F.L. A philosophy of appraisal and diagnosis. In Diagnostic Methods in Speech Pathology, 2nd ed., edited by F.L. Darley and D.C. Spriesterbach. Harper and Row p.5, 1978.

43. Platt, J.R. and Basili, A. Jaw tremor during stuttering block: An EMG study. J. Commun. Disord., 6: 102–109, 1973.

44. Guitar, B. Reduction of stuttering frequency using analog electromyographic biofeedback. J. Speech Hear. Res., 18: 672–685, 1975.

45. Hanna, R., Wilfling, F. and McNeil, B. A biofeedback treatment for stuttering. J. Speech Hear. Disord., 40: 270–273, 1975.

46. Lanyon, R.I. Effect of biofeedback relaxation on stuttering during reading and spontaneous speech. J. Consul. Clin. Psychol., 45: 860–866, 1974.

47. Craig, A.R. and Cleary, P.J. Reduction of stuttering by young male stutterers using EMG feedback. Biofeedback Self Reg., 7(3): 241–255, 1982.

48. Webster, R.L. Evolution of a target-based behavioral therapy for stuttering. Journal of Fluency Disorders, 5: 303–320, 1980.

49. Broad, D.J. Phonation. In Normal Aspects of Speech, Hearing and Language, edited by F.D. Minifie, T.J. Hixon and F. Williams. Prentice-Hall, Englewood Cliffs, N.J., 1967.

50. Prosek, R.A., Montgomery, A.A., Walden, B.E. and Schwartz, D.M. EMG biofeedback in the treatment of hyperfunctional voice disorders. J.

51. Speech Hear. Disord. 43: 282–294, 1978.
Stemple, J.C., Weiler, E., Whitehead, W. and Komray, R. Electromyographic biofeedback training with patients exhibiting a hyperfunctional voice disorder. Laryngoscope, 90: 417–476, 1980.

52. Rosenbek, J.C. and LaPointe, L.L. The Dysarthrias: Description, Diagnosis and Treatment. In Clinical Management of Neurogenic Communicative Disorders, edited by D.F. Johns. Little, Brown & Company, Boston, 1978.

53. Rubow, R.T., Rosenbek, J.C., Collins, M.J. and Celesia, G.G. Reduction of hemifacial spasm and dysarthria following EMG biofeedback. J. Speech Hear. Disord., 49: 26–33, 1984.

54. Linebaugh, C.W. Treatment of flaccid dysarthria. In Current Therapy of Communication Disorders: Dysarthria and Apraxia, edited by W.H. Perkins. Thieme-Stratton, New York, 1983.

55. Latif. An electromyographic study of the temporalis muscle in normal persons during selected positions and movements of the mandible. Am. J. Orthodont., 43: 577–591, 1957.

56. Kawamura, Y. and Fujimoto, J. Some physiologic considerations on measuring post position of the mandible. Med. J. Osaka Univ., 8: 247–255, 1957.

57. Boberg, E., Howie, P. and Woods, L. Maintenance of fluency: A review. Journal of Fluency Disorders, 4: 93–116, 1979.

58. Stern, G.S. and Berrenberg, J.L. Biofeedback training in frontalis muscle relaxation and enhancement of belief in personal control. Biofeedback Self Reg., 2(2): 173–182, 1977.

59. Craig, A.R. and Howie, P.M. Locus of control on maintenance of behavioural therapy skills. Br. J. Clin. Psychol., 21: 65–66, 1982.

CHAPTER 27

Dental Applications of Biofeedback

ANDREW J. CANNISTRACI
GEORGE FRITZ

The diagnosis and treatment of disordered homeostasis of the masticatory system form the basis of this chapter. We shall discuss the dynamic relationship between bruxism and the dental disease process. It is our view that bruxism silently wreaks havoc upon the entire masticatory system. It causes excessive wear of teeth, alveolar bone loss (periodontal disease), or spasm of the masticatory muscles (myofacial pain dysfunction syndrome).

The relationship of dental disease to stress (1, 2) has far-reaching implications, not least of which might be the utility of behavioral and other preventative, stress-management interventions. The treatment of dental anxiety with biofeedback therapy is a worthy topic. Also of interest is management of the stress of the dental profession through biofeedback training. Our theme of disordered homeostasis of the masticatory system seems to us sufficiently important, however, to justify exclusive attention.

THE DENTIST AND THE BIOFEEDBACK PRACTITIONER

The dental patient considers such oral procedures as brushing, flossing, and repair of the teeth to be within the purview of the dentist or the dental hygienist. Advice regarding these behaviors is readily accepted (if not always followed) by the patient.

The professional model represented in behavioral dentistry, on the other hand, recognizes that the dentist is not only a mechanic who adjusts and repairs teeth, but a doctor of dental medicine, who may stand in powerful healing relation to the person seeking dental treatment. By virtue of the role of professional healer, the dentist may make a significant impact on the patient by modeling an effective personal style, by the quality of the attention offered to the patient, as well as through any particular advice.

Consideration of the healing potential of the dentist is not without significance, especially in those instances when the condition of the patient points to deficits in stress management skills and capacity. Here, the attention of any medical specialist must shift from a concern for the specifics of the disorder to an interest in the person. There is a perceptual shift, in gestalt terms, from figure to ground. As Pasteur, father of the germ theory of disease, declared on his deathbed, "The pathogen is nothing; the terrain is everything." The oral habits of interest to the dentist, for instance, must include not only the proper oral hygiene, but the effective management of stress-induced muscle activity of the masticatory system and lifestyle practices that foster health enhancement.

The role of the dentist, as that of any other health specialist treating stress-related problems, is one of diagnosis, treatment of any organic and structural elements of the disorder, and supervision of other medical aspects of the patient's progress. Extremely critical variables are the manner in which the diagnosis is presented to the patient, including the clarity of the explanations given regarding the necessity and nature of the treatment and their understanding and acceptance by the patient, as well as whether a supportive relationship is offered to the patient referred for stress management. These are matters of considerable importance for the ultimate outcome of successful treatment.

ANATOMY OF THE MASTICATORY SYSTEM

The upper teeth, attached to the maxillary bone, are the passive recipients of mandibular action in that their movement can be a function only of the movement of the entire skull. The mandible is a completely separate bone from the rest of the skull and is controlled by a network of muscles and ligaments. Specific

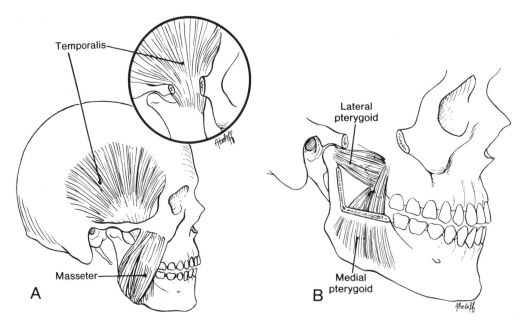

Figure 27.1. *A*, temporalis and masseter muscles. *B*, the pterygoid muscles. (Reprinted with permission from Basmajian, J. V. *Primary Anatomy*, 8th ed. Williams & Wilkins, Baltimore, 1982.)

muscles contract to elevate the mandible, others to lower it, still others to move it from side to side; thus a combination of muscle action is involved in the complex movements and postures of the mandible.

Four major muscle groups are primarily responsible for elevating the mandible: the temporalis, the masseter, and the internal and external pterygoids (Fig. 27.1). The temporalis muscle is a wide fan-shaped muscle, which has its origin on the temporal bone. It elevates the mandible. The masseter muscle originates at the zygomatic arch and inserts at the angle of the mandible. When a person is tense and grits his teeth, the temporalis and masseter are contracted. The internal pterygoid muscle has its origin in the pterygoid fossa and inserts on the internal aspect of the angle of the mandible. The external pterygoid has its origin in the outer border of the lateral pterygoid plate and its insertion on the anterior portion of the condyle or head of the mandible.

The temporomandibular joint (TMJ) (Fig. 27.2) is the condyle of the mandible in the glenoid or mandibular fossa, which is separated by a connective tissue disc. The TMJ has enjoyed great notoriety over the past twenty years, having become the namesake for myofacial pain and dysfunction.

The forceful rubbing together of the teeth when a person is not chewing is defined as bruxism. In individuals who do not engage in bruxing the teeth, the teeth come together relatively infrequently. For instance, they do not come together in speaking. Even in chewing food, the teeth do not truly come together, but rather the upper and lower teeth approach each other to reduce a mass of food. When it is sufficiently reduced to permit swallowing, only then, in the process of swallowing, do the teeth actually come together. It is estimated that in the normal person the teeth come together only 18 minutes per day during chewing and subsequent swallowing (3). The remainder of contact of the teeth is stress-induced.

The mandible closes wherever the teeth happen to interdigitate. The position of the mandible is in this way determined by the occlusion of the teeth. One may say then that the muscles of the masticatory system are slaves of the occlusal relationship of the teeth.

HOMEOSTASIS OF THE MASTICATORY SYSTEM

Ideally, there is a state of harmony and balance between the occlusion of the teeth, the masticatory muscles, and the temporomandibular joints. Under such condition, the

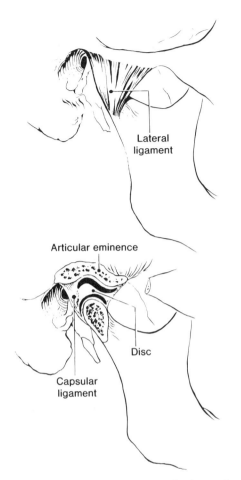

Figure 27.2. Mandibular joint (the lower figure showing the fibrocartilaginous disc that separates joint space into two compartments). (Reprinted with permission from Basmajian, J. V. *Primary Anatomy,* 8th ed. Williams & Wilkins, Baltimore, 1982).

masticatory system can be said to exhibit dynamic equilibrium or homeostasis. Such an ideal condition allows the individual to clench and grind teeth evenly. When the state of equilibrium is lost or altered, a state of imbalance of the parts occurs.

Homeostasis is an active tendency to restore equilibrium, to maintain steady states in the face of constant change (4). In the common case of tooth loss, the teeth adjacent to and opposing the resultant space will drift and rotate, causing abnormal pressures to be exerted on them. The application of such pressure to a tooth initiates a response in the proprioceptors of the periodontal membrane. Through propri-

oception, the resulting stimulus activates the muscles of mastication to move the mandible so that the teeth occlude in a less traumatic position. Dynamic balance or equilibrium has been restored, but it is a disordered homeostasis, leading inevitably to dental pathology.

If the mandible has moved into an abnormal position, certain of its primemover muscles are placed under stress and tension. Any abnormal and sustained contraction of a muscle leads to its overstimulation, with fatigue and waste products building up—which increases stimulation to the muscle, and a vicious cycle ensues. If the adaptive capacity of the muscle is exceeded, a pathologic condition exists. Often, the muscle goes into spasm. Prolonged and sustained hyperactivity of the masticatory muscles past the adaptive capacity of a well-balanced dentition can create the myofacial pain dysfunction (MPD) or TM disorders. Whatever its form and symptoms, myofacial pain dysfunction must be relieved if the patient is to maintain good dental health and associated general comfort.

Traditionally, dentists have employed various methods of overcoming TMJ disorders. The occlusion has been adjusted, or the mandible repositioned with appliances to restore a harmonious relationship between the masticatory components. The muscles have been injected with local anesthetics or sprayed with ethyl chloride, a cooling agent. Muscle relaxants and tranquilizers have been prescribed. In many cases, such "administered" techniques are successful, but they more often mask the underlying symptom by providing incomplete or temporary relief.

Most patients remain unable to cope with tension and emotional stress. They continue to clench and grind, maintaining the muscle spasms and perpetuating the MPD syndrome. Thus, the dentist must consider the psychophysiological process and the best way to deal with it. A voluntary stress control training program, in our experience, offers the best way to accomplish desired results on a lasting basis.

TRIPARTITE TYPOLOGY OF MASTICATORY DYSFUNCTION

Stress-induced muscle activity often results in grinding, clenching, or clicking of the teeth in either conscious or sleep states. There is a forceful rubbing together or application of pressure by opposing teeth. Such force is ex-

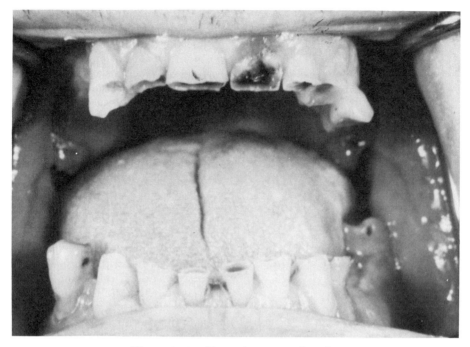

Figure 27.3.   Excessive wear of teeth.

erted by the contraction of the elevator muscles of the mandible. An exerted force affects the recipient of the force. The recipient can be the teeth, which consequently exhibit excessive wear. The force can affect the supporting alveolar bone, contributing to periodontal disease. Excessive and prolonged contraction of the masticatory muscles can cause spasm, in turn causing TMJ disorders.

Something has to give way, usually the weakest part of the system. If a patient has very strong, highly calcified teeth, excessive and prolonged muscle activity may cause breakdown of the alveolar bone or spasm of the masticatory muscles. If the alveolar bone is very strong, the breakdown can occur on the teeth, or the muscles may go into spasm. If the teeth and alveolar bone are both very strong, the destructive effects will be found in the temporomandibular joints and the masticatory muscles.

Type I: Excessive Wear of the Teeth

It is our position that the weakest element of the masticatory triad—teeth, bone, or muscle—succumbs first to the disordered homeostasis of the masticatory system. Figure 27.3 illustrates excessive wear of the teeth, or Type I masticatory dysfunction.

Type II: Periodontal Disease

Manhold (2) observed that a good indicator of the impact of stress upon an individual is the person's periodontal tissue. Periodontal disease may develop from vasomotor changes in the periodontal tissues, breakdown of the alveolar bone caused by stress-induced muscle activity (bruxism), bacterial invasion of the gingival crevice (plaque), probably combined with reduced effectiveness of the immune system.

Immune function is dependent upon many variables. Stress, emotional/attitudinal response, nutritional status, and overall living behavior all play prominent roles in physiological status and host resistance (see Chapters 5 and 6).

Type II masticatory dysfunction, involving periodontal conditions resulting from bruxism, frequently goes unrecognized by the dental professional and patient.

Fig. 27.4 illustrates breakdown of the alveolar bone, resulting in loose teeth and associated periodontal disease.

Type III: Muscle Spasm and Pain

Figure 27.5 presents an individual whose teeth appear in excellent condition, yet she

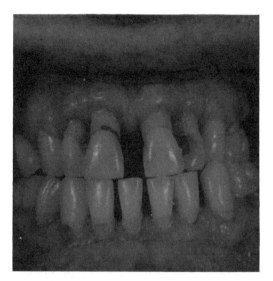

Figure 27.4. Alveolar bone loss (periodontal disease).

complained of myofacial pain. Type III masticatory dysfunction involves spasm of the masticatory musculature.

Mixed Conditions

The tripartite typology of masticatory dysfunction is not meant to suggest that each type only occurs in its pure form. Figure 27.6 presents a mixed condition of occlusal interference, excessive wear of teeth, adverse periodontal condition, and muscle spasm. The

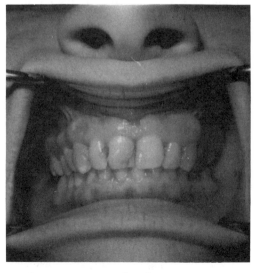

Figure 27.5. Myofacial pain (see text).

components of the masticatory system may all give way more or less equally.

ETIOLOGY OF MYOFACIAL PAIN DYSFUNCTION

The traditional dental view has been that bruxism and related myofacial pain originate in structural anomalies of the masticatory system. In contrast to this traditional structural perspective, Cannistraci (5–8) has argued for an etiology focusing on stress-induced muscular activity. In the former view, structural deficiencies are seen to result in maladaptive compensatory activity of the muscles of mastication, while in the latter, muscle spasm and associated malocclusion reflect inadequate management of life-stress. Treatment strategies have been derived directly from these etiological perspectives: in the *traditional view*, realignment of malocclusion, with biofeedback as a supplementary adjunct only if necessary; in the *stress approach*, biofeedback and relaxation training with occlusal repositioning if necessary.

Rather than focusing only on elements of the masticatory system itself, the following etiological analysis draws also upon higher-order variables of information processing. The attempt is to subsume the skeleton and muscle of the masticatory system under organizational principles of higher level functioning. That is, we consider the bone and sinew of the human masticatory system to reflect the intentionality and purpose of the person as information processor. An information processing hypothesis for the etiology of myofacial pain will be presented as a higher-order synthesis of the malocclusion hypothesis and the stress-induced muscle hypothesis.

THE MALOCCLUSION HYPOTHESIS

The *Task Force Report of the Biofeedback Society of America* on the use of biofeedback in the treatment of dental disorders (9) presents a brief history of the malocclusion hypothesis. Gelb and Siegel (10) cite trauma, as well as genetic, nutritional, and behavioral factors resulting in malposition of the jaws. Their behavioral factors include chewing habits and other bad oral habits. Stress is seen as developing "since the jaws are unbalanced" (p. 20). "The TMJ syndrome's pain can be relieved in only one way; the jaw has to be repositioned properly" (p. 23), according to Gelb and Siegel (10).

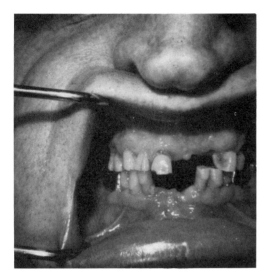

Figure 27.6. Tripartite typology of masticatory dysfunction (see text).

Despite the absolutist position taken by advocates of the malocclusion hypothesis, proper positioning of the jaw is not always sufficient to treat myofacial pain. Although a new homeostatic relationship among the components of the masticatory system is brought about by the rebalancing of the jaw, permitting temporary alleviation of muscle spasticity and related pain, the ultimate causes of the syndrome are not addressed. The healthful homeostatic balance is precarious and liable to subsequent maladaptive adaptations, including muscle spasm, renewed malocclusion, pain, and dental disease.

MUSCLE TENSION HYPOTHESIS

Tengwall (11) has described an etiology of general malposture. Other than structures that have broken down because of disease or trauma, malposture is seen as originating in misdirected effort, which is manifest in dysponetic bracing or inappropriate muscle tension. With specific reference to dental disorders, the mechanical correction of the malocclusion without concern for larger patterns of misdirected effort and related malposture is seen as only reinforcing effortful attentional styles, bad posture and related stress disorders.

In view of Tengwall's discussion of malposture, etiological issues in myofacial pain may be seen as essentially recapitulating that of low back pain. The structural position describes anomalies of the skeleton and spine re-

sulting in muscle tension, while the muscle tension position sees stress-induced muscle activity as precipitating maladaptive structural patterns. The chiropractic and osteopathic practitioners align with the occlusionists, while the stress management specialists see low back and myofacial pain as reflecting similar behavioral response patterns.

Tengwall (11) and Cannistraci (6) share the position that the "startle" or "fight-or-flight" response provides the physiological basis for malposture in general and disorders of the masticatory system in particular. Over thousands of years the human nervous system developed a highly sophisticated fight-or-flight mechanism that went into full gear automatically when danger threatened. This mechanism protected primitive man from the persistent dangers of a physically hostile environment. Contemporary man, however, is not threatened by such persistent dangers. Yet, his nervous system retains this well-developed fight-or-flight response mechanism. Physiological changes are set up by autonomic nerve impulses generated as a result of emotional conflict or tension.

Such nerve responses are a somatic reaction of the body to escape or adapt (cope) to a stress stimulus. A particular stress or stimulus activates sensory receptors. The brain then integrates a particular response, dependent upon interpretations conveyed from the brain's cognitive (cortex) and emotional (limbic) centers. The resulting "threat perception" and hypothalamus-inducing effect on the autonomic nervous system will result in either sympathetic activation (fight-flight) or parasympathetic activation (passive, relaxing).

Today the fight-or-flight response is mobilized when a person feels threatened. The threat may be a thought or an emotional response to some external stimuli. It sets up a chain reaction, first stimulating a response of the autonomic nervous system with resulting physiological responses that, if persistent, tend to eventually produce pathological changes.

Bruxism

Bruxing can be a result of this fight-or-flight reaction. If transient, the activity is harmless. It becomes pathologic in the dental sense when the activity is intense and prolonged. In a psychologic sense, excessive jaw muscle activity is a way of discharging tension in a civilized fashion. Rather than striking out at the environment or fleeing from it, the bruxing patient grinds away, harming no one but himself.

Thus, persistent bruxism is a maladaptive psychological response to stress (12). Part of the hyperactive response can be attributed to the demands of our technological era which taxes our psychological defenses more severely than in the past. However, we have also discovered ways of reducing stress. For the dental profession, this means that most motivated patients can resolve their bruxing problem through biofeedback training, changes in thinking patterns, and living behavior, and counseling.

THE INFORMATION PROCESSING HYPOTHESIS

Schwartz (13) posits a systems theory of disregulation, disordered homestasis, and disease. Disattention is viewed as a neuropsychological disconnection between brain and body, resulting in disregulation of psychophysical systems. Repressive personality styles, wherein persons deny anxiety, are translated into systems theory as involving a neuropsychological process in which negative feedback signals are attenuated and disconnected. In the example of disregulation of the masticatory system, we may suppose gradual loss of attentional contact with muscle activity, exacerbated under conditions of stress, leading to habitual clenching, spasm, and pain. We believe that the hyperattention subsequently given to resulting pain signals a need for a renewal of appropriate attentional contact and consequent restoration of self-regulation of the psychophysical system.

The myofacial tension associated with physical exertion is understood to be normal. The muscular expressions of emotion—the furrowed brow of worry, the grimacing eyes of pain, the grinding mandible of frustration or anger, the clenched jaw of concentration—are also accepted as commonplace. Not as generally acknowledged or understood is the muscular bracing that accompanies goal-oriented, effortful attention, which is chronic and habitual in many individuals in our society. In a phrase, most of us are "trying too hard" most of the time. Depression or learned helplessness and chronic fatigue may be understood as rebound strategies in relation to effortfully focused attention (14, 15). The fact that this effortful attentional style is so rarely objectified

and identified is perhaps due to its ubiquitousness.

The purpose of this chronic effortful attention is control—control over perception and experience. Whereas control over the flux of experience is functional—it renders order out of the chaos of sensation—the overcontrol we are describing is mostly useful for emergency responding. Indeed, this effortful focus of attention may be the attentional concomitant of the "startle," "emergency," or "fight-or-flight" pattern of physiological responding. Like the "fight-or-flight" pattern itself, chronic utilization of this controlling style of attention results in disregulation.

Fehmi and Fritz (14) have proposed an attentional model of mental health disease. Many symptoms reflect problems of attentional rigidity. For example, obsessive-compulsive and perfectionistic personalities represent an attentional state narrowly focused and fixated upon certain thoughts or behavior patterns. Whereas bruxism has been variously ascribed to obsessive-compulsive traits, to perfectionistic expectations, and to expressions of frustration and anger, our perspective is to suggest that a wide variety of stress-related disorders, including bruxism, reflect chronic and rigid deployment of goal-directed attention.

Attention organizes physiology. We are not saying that bruxism is a necessary expression of chronic, goal-oriented attention. In certain individuals, however, bruxism does represent a habitual attentional style.

In the biofeedback setting, goal-directed attention, characterized by "trying hard" to relax, actually interferes with and makes more difficult the production of any psychophysical action that is desired. The treatment of myofacial pain patients, who reflect attentional rigidity through myofacial tension, perforce must involve training in attentional flexibility to circumvent the initial narrowly focused and tense goal orientation towards the subtle task of producing relaxed musculature.

Cacioppo and Petty (16) review the evidence for a relationship between mental processes and focal sites of muscular activity. It has been appreciated for many years that particular mental processes are accompanied by somatovisceral patterns of activity. Darwin (17) described emotions as the cognitive labeling of muscle tension patterns. Indeed, biblical passages refer to the connection between emotion or "wailing and the gnashing of teeth."

An information processing hypothesis is proposed for the etiology of myofacial pain syndrome. Individuals who buttress their primarily goal-directed attentional style with muscle tension in the masticatory system will be more disposed to bruxism and resulting breakdown of healthful homeostatic balance among the components of the masticatory system.

In the instance of genetically derived malocclusion, muscle spasm is not a necessary reaction to the occlusal disharmony. Bruxing will result only if stress-induced muscular activity of the masticatory system reflects that individual's unique way of manifesting overcontrol. An individual's preferred mode of response may involve, instead, disattention and resulting disordered homeostasis at other neuromuscular sites, i.e., tension headaches or low back pain, or may involve a cardiovascular, neurohumoral, or interneuronal stress response (18). Whereas genetically derived malocclusion may predispose a person toward masticatory tension, it is not an inevitable sequela.

DIAGNOSIS OF MYOFACIAL PAIN DYSFUNCTION (MPD)

The diagnostic signs of myofacial pain dysfunction are: (a) pain in the head, neck and/or face; (b) tenderness in the muscles of mastication upon palpation, often radiating elsewhere; (c) limited ability to move the jaw properly; and (d) clicking or popping noise in the temporomandibular joint upon jaw opening (only if present with a and b).

It is not unusual for dental patients to seek a number of consultations, dental, medical, and psychological, before a professional makes a correct diagnosis. The patient may be profoundly relieved to understand the cause of the symptoms. As the philosopher Spinoza observed, "Emotion, which is suffering, ceases to be suffering as soon as we form a clear and precise picture of it."

The diagnosis may itself serve therapeutic purposes. Carlsson and Gale (19) have observed that TMJ patients often respond as effectively to placebo treatments as to occlusal splints and masticatory repositioning. The implication is that the stress associated with the symptom is alleviated considerably upon receiving a plausible explanation for it. The occlusal, muscle tension, and information processing hypotheses may each serve to reduce

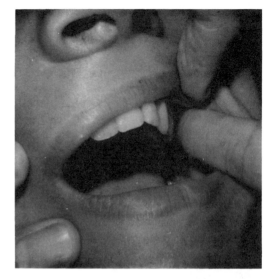

Figure 27.7. Palpating the lateral (external) pterygoid muscle.

anxiety when presented by a credible professional. The high success rates reported by practitioners of occlusal splint therapy are perhaps due to a combination of these placebo effects and the temporary relief from muscle spasm and pain afforded by the occlusal adjustment.

Palpation

Among the diagnostic procedures is palpation of the masticatory muscles. Figures 27.7 to 27.10 illustrate these procedures. In palpating the external pterygoid, one moves the index finger along the muco-buccal fold above the position of the third maxillary molar. If the muscle is in spasm, the patient will feel unmistakable pain. To palpate the internal pterygoid, one moves the index finger along the median raphe directly behind the mandibular third molar. One may also palpate the masseter and temporalis muscles. To palpate for neck muscle spasm, check the posterior cervical, sternocleidomastoid, and hyoid muscles.

Dental Examination

The dentist will examine the oral cavity for signs of clenching and bruxism, such as flatness of contacts, wear facets, erosions, cheek biting, and shiny spots on restorations. To determine the amount and pattern of bruxism, an objective method has been developed by Forgione (20). The *Bruxcore*, a plastic-laminated

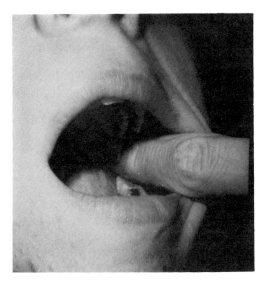

Figure 27.8. Palpating the medial (internal) pterygoid muscle.

mouthguard, may be worn by the patient at night during sleep. The amount of bruxing can then be estimated from the pattern of dots and areas of color obliterated on the Bruxcore. In this manner, not only can a reliable baseline be established, but the results of nocturnal clenching and grinding can be demonstrated convincingly to the patient, motivating participation in a stress management program.

EMG Monitor

A portable electromyographic (EMG) device has been developed to measure bruxism in sleeping subjects in their natural environ-

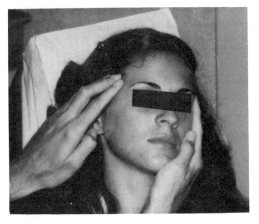

Figure 27.9. Palpating the temporalis muscle.

ments (21). During sleep a miniaturized EMG records clenching and grinding activity and later provides a readout of that activity. The EMG can also be worn during the day to monitor masseter activity continuously during daily routines. The feedback can be set to signal when bruxing is occurring.

An *anterior resistance appliance* may be installed at this point in order to restore the state of balance in the masticatory system. The mandible repositions automatically in response to the appliance, freeing the spastic muscles of mastication to relax. A marked reduction in muscle tonus may be observed on the electromyograph. Harmonious integration of muscle action is temporarily restored by the elimination of the occlusal disharmony. A renewal of uneven clenching suggests that the disordered homeostasis of the system was not due to the occlusal disharmony *per se*, but to habits of goal-oriented attention and associated muscle tension.

THE REFERRAL FOR ATTENTION, BIOFEEDBACK, AND STRESS-MANAGEMENT TRAINING

As mentioned earlier, the manner in which a referral is made for biofeedback training may be crucial to the ultimate success of the program. Though many MPD patients are relieved by their diagnosis, they may not yet be ready to accept responsibility for having precipitated their own dental condition. They may seek, instead, further restorative work and medication to reduce muscle spasms and pain.

A history of destruction of restorative dental work as well as the evidence from the *Bruxcore* and portable EMG devices may convince the patient of the role of stress in the origin of these problems. However, such evidence may still not convince the patient of the nature of the intervention necessary to restore dental health.

At this point, conversation oriented around identifying life stresses can be extremely helpful. The *Social Readjustment Rating Scale* (22) can stimulate discussion of areas of concern. The dentist who displays an empathic and nonjudgmental attitude, who appreciates the role of stress in disease and who personally practices stress management skills will make an effective referral that is pursued by the dental patient.

The practitioner further enhances diagnostic skill by being aware of characteristics common

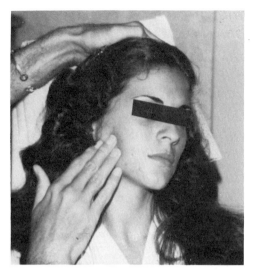

Figure 27.10.   Palpating the masseter muscle.

to individuals manifesting stress-related problems and difficulties.

Some common stress indicators are as follows:

1. Maladjustments to life-change events (personal, social, or professional);
2. Fatigue or sleeping difficulties;
3. Irritability, impatience, aggressive, or competitive behavior;
4. Emotional difficulties;
5. Headaches;
6. Nervousness or emotionally rooted habits or responses (i.e., smoking, substance abuse, tics, etc.);
7. Social or behavioral change (i.e., withdrawal or overinvolvement, maladaptive or antisocial behavior, etc.);
8. Joint or muscle pain, weakness, or stiffness;
9. Obsessive and/or compulsive behavior, rigidity, etc.;
10. Breathing difficulties;
11. Changes in physical appearance, personal hygiene, self-image or self-esteem;
12. Changes in heart rate, rhythm, or blood pressure;
13. Increased, recurrent, or chronic problems (allergies, colds, accidents, sexual problems, etc);
14. Physical or emotional trauma;
15. Inability to relax, do nothing, or "let go" without feeling guilty. (23)

ATTENTION AND BIOFEEDBACK TRAINING

Although progressive muscle relaxation and autogenic training remain as important standard approaches in biofeedback training, other approaches can also provide unique therapeutic applications. In recent years the clinical application of biofeedback training has undergone a paradigm shift from relaxation training to the self-regulation of attention (24). Schwartz and his associates (12) tested and confirmed the hypothesis that the self-regulation of attention involves subtle effects on the self-regulation of specific visceral and somatic responses. Fehmi (25) showed that subjective changes associated with brain rhythm activity are experienced as changes in attention. Clinical observation suggests that physiological activity in general normalizes when individuals are guided to adopt flexible habits of attention.

In our view, the demand characteristic of the training situation created by the relaxation paradigm, regardless of statements made by the biofeedback trainer to mitigate such demands, is an obstacle to achieving relaxed states in biofeedback training. The relaxation paradigm generally pervades trainee expectations regarding biofeedback training. The goal orientation toward lower arousal—"You must relax!"—is, in our opinion, counterproductive. We have observed that the attentional style underlying goal-oriented behavior often maintains and, perhaps, exacerbates tension. A self-regulation of attention paradigm encourages the normalization of physiological activity through strategies of attention training, which do not force change in a particular direction. The salutary effects upon medical symptoms are seen as important side-benefits of this normalization process.

Qualls and Sheehan (26) suggest that EMG training and research have been heretofore compromised by failure to identify patients by attentional propensities. Their research indicates that patients exhibit attentional rigidity in trying to relax during initial biofeedback training sessions. Certain patients are distracted by the biofeedback signal, while others require the signal to attain control. It may be inferred that the relaxation exercises traditionally utilized in biofeedback training are effective in normalizing function to the degree that patterns of attentional rigidity are subtly and indirectly altered during the training process.

In order to more directly guide biofeedback trainees to adopt the attentional disposition or style facilitating normalization of physiological activity and resulting relaxation, a series of exercises, called *open focus training* has been developed (27). Open focus has as its goal an effortless orientation to the biofeedback task, as well as to any wakeful activity. Since narrowness and exclusivity of attention require effort and tension, the prerequisite for establishing this state of open focus involves dropping one's habitual orientation to narrowly focus on certain internal or external events to the exclusion of other events. Ultimately, every perceptible event, whether internal or external, is represented in the nervous system. In order to process information with open focus, one must allow awareness to broaden to include *simultaneously* all those perceptible events that are salient in the nervous system.

Schwartz (13) suggests that ongoing research on the lateralization of brain functions and associated hemispheric differences in styles of information processing may elucidate the neuropsychological mechanisms that regulate and disregulate homeostatic processes. It is our view that attention training to release a chronic goal-oriented style of attention is a prerequisite to the normalization of homeostatic processes, both physiological and psychological.

PAIN MANAGEMENT

The relevance of attention training is especially apparent with regard to management of pain. Rugh and Solberg (28) have observed that for patients with chronic temporomandibular pain and dysfunction the pain itself is of as much clinical importance as the dental disorder. It has been our experience that pain is amplified or exacerbated by narrow and effortfully focused attention. Despite this relationship, the common-sense strategy of pain management consists of narrow focusing away from the experience in order to disassociate pain. Strategies of denial, distraction, and substitution of experience are often as well the only professional strategy offered to the pain patient. In this way the patient perpetuates a vicious cycle of narrow focus → tension → pain → more extreme and effortful narrow focus → increasing tension → more pain. This attention strategy in relation to pain contributes to disregulation in the

long term. A more broadly based attention training offers to the pain patient an alternative. For example, instead of substituting other perceptions for pain, one develops flexibility in how to attend to the pain. We have observed that the inclusion of narrow-focused attention to pain within the context of a more broad open focus can result in the reduction or complete alleviation of pain. In terms of systems theory (13) functional and intact self-regulatory feedback can be restored by appropriate attention to the disordered system. We believe that relaxation exercises may be effective in pain management to the degree that the relaxation permits a more accepting and integrated attention to the pain experience.

RELEASE PHENOMENA

As biofeedback trainees shift attentional disposition from habitual processes of focal attention toward more inclusive attentional styles, the permissive conditions are established for homestatic rebalancing. Associated with this realignment of homeostatic processes are various abreactions known as "release phenomena" (29).

For MPD biofeedback trainees, the release phenomena may take the form of shooting pains, jerks, twitches and tremors; numb or tingling feelings; and thoughts, memories, or emotional experience that spontaneously come to awareness. A common initial reaction to attention and biofeedback training may be an increased awareness of pain and associated muscle tension. The manner in which trainees relate and attend to such experiences is crucial to progress in training. A broad attention by its nature is the permissive condition for the occurrence of releases and for their diffusion once they arise in awareness. Trainees are coached by the biofeedback therapist to accept into open focus any experiential changes which may occur during the progress of biofeedback and attention training, as well as during everyday life.

RESISTANCE AS RELEASE PHENOMENON

It is our view that a chronic style of controlled attention effectively maintains disordered homeostatic equilibrium within a self-regulatory system. Presented with an occasion for release of attentional rigidity during home and clinic biofeedback practice sessions, some individuals may feel compelled to defy instructions to practice or, while complying, to deny or obsess upon emerging phenomena. Such attentional strategies serve to perpetuate disordered homeostasis.

An understanding of the individual as a self-regulatory system permits the therapist to redefine resistance to change and associated strategies of attention as release phenomena. The resistance to practice, i.e., difficulties scheduling the exercises into one's daily routine, need not be viewed by patient and therapist as failure. Rather, the therapist may redefine the patient's struggle with the practice regimen as evidence of the chronicity and rigidity of current attentional habits. Just as muscle tension and associated pain become more apparent as one's muscles become more relaxed, so too one's attentional habits are brought into relief by the opportunity to relax these habits.

The release of tension, whether muscular or attentional, may be interpreted as an initial sign of success. Boredom, restlessness, and racing mind are vestiges of one's habitual narrow-focus habits. When one's resistance is understood in this fashion as a release phenomenon, failure unwittingly becomes success; defiance becomes compliance.

Like other release phenomena, resistance disrupts homeostatic realignment only if it is the occasion for the renewal of effortful and controlling attention. If, on the other hand, one changes how one attends to the release behavior, neither denying nor obsessing, but attending inclusively to the release, then the self-regulatory system can shift toward more healthy homeostatic balance.

In addition to redefining the resistance as a release phenomena and offering an alternative strategy with which to pay attention to the resistance, the biofeedback therapist may directly prescribe the resistance itself. The patient may be asked to monitor the self-statements and emotions associated with resistance to the home practice. Often, direct attention to resistance undercuts the denial processes that maintain it. Moreover, the experiences associated with the resistance—i.e., negative judgments, irrational self-statements, various emotional expressions—may be used as covert cues to change the scope and direction of one's attention. In this way, the covert behaviors that formerly inhibited progress become themselves the occasion for practice of biofeedback and attention skills.

DIAPHRAGMATIC BREATHING

An important aspect of the entire self-regulatory process is proper breathing. Compernolle et al. (30) have described the complaints commonly associated with low-grade hyperventilation syndrome or chronic, shallow, thoracic breathing. Among the symptoms of hyperventilation syndrome that are also present in MPD or TMJ syndrome are dizziness, headache, chest pain, ringing in the ears, and numbness and tingling of the face.

Wilson (18) suggests that the clinician probe for hyperventilation syndrome by tapping the temporomandibular joint. A resulting twitch in the lip is described as Sehastek's phenomenon, a sign of hyperventilation syndrome. Activation of the twitch reflex suggests increased neuromotor activity in the face. The increased reactivity at the myoneural junction is secondary to loss of calcium carbonate in the nerve itself and surrounding tissues, a side effect of chronic, shallow thoracic breathing.

The clinician also observes the rise and fall of the chest during normal breathing. Trainees are taught to facilitate diaphragmatic relaxation, permitting more deep breathing and normalization of blood pCO_2.

Just as with other indices of normalization, such as relaxation, breathing can automatically self-regulate as a side benefit of appropriate attention.

NUTRITIONAL CONSIDERATIONS

Current research is reminding us that nutrition plays an increasingly important role in preventive health care. Health maintenance, immune enhancement, and dental integrity are all similarly dependent upon proper nutritional status. The combined impact of stress and faulty dietary habits are probably two of the most significant considerations in overall health. Part of this concern is the American diet, which tends to be rich in sugar, fats, and processed and convenience food. The shift away from the fresh and more nutrient rich foods of our ancestors, and the high-stress Westernized life-style have been key factors in many nutritional health problems.

Within dentistry, calcium status is of major concern, since about 99% of the average 1200 grams the body stores is used in bone tissue. Proper calcium absorption is critically dependent upon dietary balance. Besides receiving proper calcium, this includes receiving sufficient levels of vitamin D, and limiting fat intake. Additionally, avoiding excess amounts of protein, phosphorus, phytic acid, and oxalic acid are critical to this balance. Calcium status may also be compromised by high levels of stress, which have been reported to create calcium losses of up to 900 mg daily. Stress may also greatly affect other nutrient levels, causing other depletions (i.e., zinc, vitamin C) intimately related to general health, immune, and dental status (31).

SUMMARY

The objective of this chapter has been to illustrate the role of stress and related components in masticatory dysfunction. As a result of disordered homeostatis, masticatory dysfunction will manifest as a breakdown of teeth, muscle, or alveolar bone tissue. The particular, genetically determined, manifestation will depend upon which element is weakest in the individual patient. Although we may identify patients experiencing stress-related problems accurately, a "whole person" or holistic treatment model should be implemented to provide the most comprehensive and successful results. This includes a complete assessment, understanding and considering all the underlying factors that cause or exacerbate the patient's problem.

Based on research and experience, we conclude that mechanical intervention may serve as only an immediate or temporary solution for the bruxing or temporomandibular dysfunctioning patient. For these patients, psychological counseling, biofeedback, stress management, nutritional improvement, and adjunctive life-style modification remain as integral components to successful treatment.

References

1. Manhold, J. H. Extension of a hypothesis: psychosomatic factors in wound healing. Psychosomatics, 19: 143–147, 1978.
2. Manhold, J. H. Mild social stress blocks natural healing process, gum tissues exam reveals. In News from the College of Medicine and Dentistry of New Jersey. 80.0050319.
3. Graf, H. Bruxism. Dent. Clin. of North Am., 13: 659–665, 1969.
4. Green, E. and Green, A. Beyond Biofeedback, Dell, New York, 1977.
5. Cannistraci, A. J. Procedures for voluntary stress release and behavior therapy in the treatment of clenching and bruxism. Bio Monitoring Applications, Inc., New York.
6. Cannistraci, A. J. A method to control bruxism: biofeedback-assisted relaxation therapy. J. Am. Soc. Preventive Dentistry, 6: 12–15, 1976.
7. Cannistraci, A. J. Biofeedback—the treatment of stress-induced muscle activity. In Clinical Management of Head, Neck and TMJ Pain and Dysfunction, edited by Gelb, H. W. B. Saunders, Philadelphia, 1977.
8. Cannistraci, A. J. Myofacial pain and behavioral medicine. In Pain and Anxiety Control in Dentistry, edited by Spiro, S. R. Jack K. Burgess, Inc., Englewood, New Jersey, 1981.
9. Cannistraci, A. J. and Mealiea, N. L. The use of biofeedback in the treatment of dental disorders: the Task Force Report of the Biofeedback Society of America. Published privately by the Society, January 1980 (copies available).
10. Gelb, H. and Siegel, P. M. Killing Pain Without Prescription. Harper and Row, New York, 1980.
11. Tengwall, R. Towards an etiology of malposture. Somatics, Autumn and Winter, 1981.
12. Yunus, M., Masi, A. T., Calabro, J. J., Miller, K. A., and Feigenbaum, S. L. Primary fibromyalgia (fibrositis): clinical study of 50 patients with matched normal controls. Semin. Arthritis Rheum., 11: 151–171, 1981.
13. Schwartz, G. E. Disregulation and systems theory: a biobehavioral framework for biofeedback and behavioral medicine. In Biofeedback and Behavioral Medicine. Aldine Publishing Co., Hawthorne, N. Y., 1981.
14. Fehmi, L. G. and Fritz, G. Open focus: the attentional foundation of health and well-being. Somatics, Spring, 1980.
15. Fritz, G., Selzer, F., and Fehmi, L. G. An attentional strategy for the generalization of biofeedback training skills. A paper presented at the annual meeting of the biofeedback Society of America, Knoxville, Tenn., 1981.
16. Cacioppo, J. T. and Petty, R. E. Electromyograms as measures of extent and affectivity of information processing. Am. Psychol., 36: 441–456, 1981.
17. Darwin, C. The Expression of Emotions in Man and Animals. Watts, London, (reissued) 1948.
18. Wilson, E. How stress makes us ill. An invited address to the New Jersey Biofeedback Society, Rutgers University, December 6, 1981.
19. Carlsson, S. G. and Gale, E. N. Biofeedback in the treatment of long-term temporomandibular joint pain. Biofeedback Self Regul., 2: 161–171, 1977.
20. Forgione, A. Psychological treatments of nocturnal bruxism. Delivered at the eighty-fourth annual convention of the American Psychological Association, Washington, D. C., September 6, 1976.
21. Rugh, J. D. Electromyographic analysis of bruxism in the natural environment. In Advances in Behavioral Research in Dentistry, edited by Weinstein, P. University of Washington Press, Seattle, 1978.
22. Holmes, T. H. and Raye, R. H. The Social Readjustment Rating Scale. J. Psychosom. Res., 11: 213–218, 1967.
23. Cannistraci, A. J. and Friedrich, J. A. A multidimensional approach to bruxism and TMD.

New York State Dental J., *53:* 31–34, 1987.

24. Fritz, G. and Fehmi, L. G. From relaxation to self-regulation: a paradigm shift in biofeedback training. Presented at the annual meeting of the Biofeedback Society of America, March 6, 1982.

25. Fehmi, L. G. EEG biofeedback, multi-channel synchrony training, and attention. In *Expanding Dimensions of Consciousness,* editing by Sugarman, A. and Tarter, R. Springer Verlag, New York, 1978.

26. Qualls, P. J. and Sheehan, P. W. Electromyograph biofeedback as a relaxation technique: a critical appraisal and reassessment. Psychol. Bull., *90:* 21–42, 1981.

27. Fehmi, L. G. Open focus training. Paper presented at the annual meeting of the Biofeedback Society of America, Monterey, Calif., 1975.

28. Rugh, J. D. and Solberg, N. K. Psychological implications in temporomandibular pain and dysfunction. Oral Sci. Rev., *7:* 3–30, 1976.

29. Fritz, G., Fehmi, L. G., and Selzer, F. Psychophysiological release phenomena in the clinical application of biofeedback and attention training. A paper presented at the annual meeting of the Biofeedback Society of America, Colorado Springs, Colo., 1980.

30. Compernolle, T., Hoogduin, K. and Joele, L. Diagnosis and treatment of the hyperventilation syndrome. Psychosomatics, *20:* 612–625, 1979. Fritz, G. and Fehmi, L. G. *Open Focus Handbook: Strategies for Attention Training and Transfer to Everyday Activities.* Biofeedback Computers, Inc., Princeton, N. J., 1982.

31. Garrison, R.H. and Somer, M.A. *The Nutrition Desk Reference.* Keats Publishing, New Canaan, CT, 1985.

CHAPTER 28

Therapeutic Electromyography in Chronic Back Pain

HERBERT E. JOHNSON
VIRGIL HOCKERSMITH

Low back pain affects an estimated 80% of the population, ranks second only to upper respiratory infections as a cause of lost time from work, and remains one of the major causes of long-term disability and loss of earnings. Chronic low back pain (over 6 months' duration) represents a segment of permanently disabled comparable in numbers to those with heart disease or rheumatoid arthritis. In the past, regardless of treatment, less than 50% of such patients returned to gainful employment (1, 2). For nearly a decade, we have used therapeutic electromyography (EMG) in the treatment of more than 500 patients with chronic low back pain as part of a comprehensive rehabilitation program. Completion of the program has resulted in successful vocational restoration in significantly greater than half the patients treated (3).

In this chapter, we will report the rationale, techniques, and results of therapeutic EMG as used in this chronic back pain population. The chronic pain management program is one of several major rehabilitation programs at Casa Colina Hospital for Rehabilitative Medicine, Pomona, California. The treatment model, a cognitive social learning model, consists of a team of clinicians representing rehabilitation medicine, physical therapy, biofeedback therapy, nursing, psychology, and vocational counseling. A self-regulation approach is consistently adhered to in all treatments and social encounters. McArthur et al. reported in detail the favorable short-term outcomes of 702 consecutive admissions to this program (4), and long-term follow-up of 210 patients. (5)

Our reported experience is derived from the treatment of 510 patients from 1973 through 1980. There were 253 female and 257 male patients with a variety of back problems resulting in an average of 1.17 back surgeries and more than 2 years of work disability. The mean age of patients was 42 years with a range between 14 and 69 years. Seventy percent (70%) of the patients were involved in litigation related to their back disability. The average stay in the program was 6 weeks. The basic data are provided in Table 28.1. The goals of the inpatient program, all operationally defined, were: (a) physical reconditioning; (b) effective physiologic relaxation; (c) medication elimination; (d) development of self-regulatory behavior; and (e) return to gainful employment.

RATIONALE

Patients with low back pain are characteristically found to be chronically depressed with strong feelings of helplessness, anger, and resistance to most proposed treatment. Therapeutic EMG is an effective, nonthreatening way to demonstrate quickly to the patient an aspect of his or her own body with which he or she was previously unaware. The patient, on admission, is generally more trusting of machines than of clinicians (6, 7). By setting low initial goals, the patient can usually experience a degree of success. Thereafter, through therapeutic EMG, one can: (a) effectively teach muscle relaxation; (b) monitor the state of relaxation twice within each treament day; and (c) demonstrate graphically to the patient the therapeutic importance of "quiet time." We chose therapeutic EMG, from among several other techniques, for eliciting the "relaxation response" (8), because of its effectiveness, reproducibility, objectivity, and individual applicability in group settings.

Table 28.1.
Patient Characteristics (N = 510)

Sex	Male	50.4%
	Female	49.6%
Age	Average	42 years
	Range	14–69 years
Length of disability	Average	2.7 years
	Range	1–15 years
Back surgeries	Average	1.17
	Range	0–11
Education (years	Average	12.3 years
attended school)	Range	9–17 years
WAIS—full scale	Average	105
	Range	74–135
Medical diagnosis of organic involvement		97%
Prior extensive medical treatment		94%
Moderate to severe psychopathology[a]		94%
Unemployable and incapacitated by pain at admission		100%

[a]Defined by significant deviations from the mean on a battery of standard psychological tests.

PROCEDURE

Training occurred in quiet 8 × 10 foot rooms with appropriate considerations given to external noise and electrical interference. The patient sat or reclined in a well-padded reclining chair (Fig. 28.1). Equipment used for training is Advanced Electro Lab's TriBiosensor.[a]

All biofeedback training was directed by a registered physical therapist, skilled in neuromuscular disorders. During the 6-week program, patients were seen twice daily, 5 days per week, for an average treatment length of 45 minutes each session. Patients generally received 50–60 hours of therapeutic EMG training. The goals of training are to:

1. Achieve a psychophysiological relaxation skill demonstrable without the assistance of feedback.

2. Develop a strong perception of control.

3. Achieve a good appreciation for the relationship of pain-tension-anxiety.

4. Achieve an intimate sensitivity and awareness of stressors and one's response to them with the ability to label such stressors.

---

[a]Manufactured by Advanced Electro Labs, Inc., 366 South Lemon, Walnut, Calif., 91789.

5. Tolerate sitting for 60 minutes.

6. Inhibit pain.

Therapeutic EMG training began with the acquisition of two separate 1-hour baselines. During the baseline sessions, the patient was given no information regarding the details or purpose of sessions. Baselines were obtained with the patient in the sitting position and no feedback was presented. The patient was instructed to sit as relaxed and quiet as possible. Information was gathered by visually recording microvolt readings at minutes 1, 30 and 60 of the two separate 1-hour baseline sessions.

Generalized upper body raw EMG levels were monitored by placing one of two leads on the flexors of each forearm (Fig. 28.2). The generalized sampling of gross upper body motor-unit activity is referred to as upper body tension. The microvolt levels are primarily influenced by the intrinsic and extrinsic muscles of the hands, shoulders and nondiaphragmatic respiratory muscles. Upper body tension levels are defined on a 1–4 scale with four being the optimal goal of training: (1) 9.1 μV and above; (2) 5.2–9.0 μV; (3) 4.0–5.1 μV; and (4) 3.9–0 μV.

Following establishment of baselines, the patient was instructed in relaxation concepts and familiarized with the EMG feedback equipment. This introductory, instructional process was continued individually on a patient-to-therapist level in the early weeks of training. As the patient became fully informed regarding the equipment, task, concepts, etc., the actual one-on-one time diminished. Relaxation, then, became a matter of refining rudimentary skills through practice.

Training often began in the reclining position, noted in data collection, and over time progressed to the full upright sitting position (Fig. 28.1). To achieve a level 4 of performance, one must begin the session at 3.8 μV or below and maintain these levels for 45–60 minutes in the upright position without the assistance of feedback.

Particular care is given to record minute one of each session in an effort to determine carryover of learning. A session on no feedback monitoring occurred after every nine training sessions in an effort to determine true learning. Careful attention is given to threshold settings, allowing the patient to experience success.

Monitoring of specific target areas of spasm, tension, or pain is not done until generalized

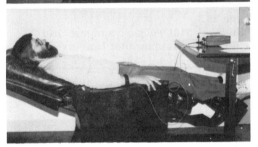

Figure 28.1. Training positions described in text.

muscle tension falls into the moderate-to-low ranges. Frequently, the target areas of complaint fade as one reduces the generalized activity. Approximately one-third of our patients

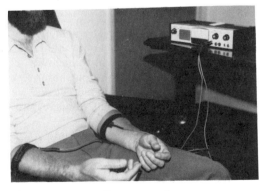

Figure   28.2. Forearm-to-forearm   sensor placement.

demonstrated significant jaw clenching and tension headaches. For reasons clearly stated by Budzynski elsewhere in this book (Chapter 18), frontal EMG training followed upper body training in such patients. Variables, in addition to muscle tension reduction, are also followed and rated by the biofeedback therapist.

Variables Rated

Comprehension (1–4 Scale)

1. Poor—No understanding of relaxation concepts
2. Fair—Receptive to concepts, attempting application
3. Good—Applied skills outside lab setting
4. Excellent—Cites examples of successful skills outside laboratory

Pain-Tension-Anxiety Relationship

1. No understanding or denies relationship
2. Fair intellectual understanding, no incorporation of understanding or observable style change
3. Good intellectual understanding, observable style change, i.e., pacing
4. Good intellectual understanding, observable style change; ability to label stressors and/or tension level with confirmed accuracy

Sitting Tolerance

1. Below 30 minutes
2. 30–45 minutes
3. 45–60 minutes
4. 60 minutes and above

Pain (0–7 Scale)

1. 6–7
2. 4–5
3. 2–3
4. 0–1

Pain reports were gathered before and after each session by the patients' writing on the data-collection sheet their subjective rating on a 0–7 scale. All of the above-mentioned goals were rated on a weekly basis by averaging daily performance.

RATIONALE FOR TECHNIQUE

Upper body monitoring, via forearm-to-forearm sensors, was used for the following reasons:

1. Our experience with sensor placement directly over muscles with greatest palpable tension, i. e., the paraspinals and trapezii, was generally poor.

Table 28.2.
EMG level in microvolts with feedback (N = 510)

		Minute 1	Minute 30	Minute 60
Mean	Admission	11.6	9.6	9.2
	Discharge	5.3	4.4	4.3
	30-day follow-up[a]	5.1	4.2	2.2
Mode	Admission	14.0	7.1	7.1
	Discharge	3.6	3.1	3.1
	30-day follow-up	3.1	3.1	0
Median	Admission	10.0	7.7	7.4
	Discharge	4.1	3.6	3.5
	30-day follow-up	4.8	3.4	2.0
Variance	Admission	50.7	40.7	38.9
	Discharge	24.8	16.5	18.2
	30-day follow-up	21.7	14.8	3.7
Range	Admission	57.0	47.5	46.2
	Discharge	48.9	44.9	52.0
	30-day follow-up	63.5	48.9	9.9

[a]30-day follow-up N = 346.

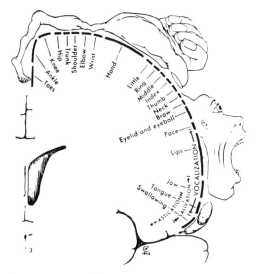

Figure 28.3. The motor homunculus of Penfield and Rasmussen.

Table 28.3.
Pain (N = 510), subjective report, 1 to 7 scale (before training/after training), N = 510

	Before	After
Mean	4.315	2.344
Mode	4.000	0
Median	4.485	2.030
Variance	1.931	3.357
Range	6.830	7.00

2. We have obtained consistently good results with forearm-to-forearm monitoring.

3. The large representation of the forearms and hands on the motor cortex would suggest that relaxation of these areas should have a greater generalized effect than quieting any other single muscle mass, with the exception of the muscles in and about the mouth (Fig. 28.3).

4. As activity decreases in the upper extremities, we are able to monitor nondiaphragmatic respiratory muscles, the quieting of which contributes to general relaxation (9).

5. Finally, when the upper body is quiet, the heartbeat is monitored as an effective and quieting "positive" endpoint. The effect of heart rate monitoring is a complex issue described elsewhere in this book. We feel that such monitoring of heart rate and rhythm provides entry into the autonomic nervous system. Stoyva discusses the role of the autonomic nervous system in general relaxation in Chapter 16.

We used as our feedback the raw EMG activity. This allowed the therapist and/or patient to identify the relative number of motor units firing as well as the source of the activity as being close to or distant from the sensor (10, 11). Through such raw unfiltered signals, we purposefully monitored activity in the respiratory and cardiac musculature.

Reclining chairs were chosen to allow training to occur beginning in the reclining position and gradually progressing to a full sitting position. This allowed training to progress from a more comfortable and tolerable position to a more functional position.

OUTCOME

Objective evidence of learning. is demonstrated by the pre- and posttraining data reported in Table 28.2. Patients generally achieved a significant reduction of baseline EMG levels with improved perception of control and decreased perception of pain (Table 28.3).

Data with feedback were accumulated during training and, as anticipated, showed a steady decrease in muscle tension. We elected to report data baselines obtained without feedback (before and after) to demonstrate actual learned reduction in EMG levels. These data represent the patients' own ability to control tension levels using only their developed internal cues.

RELATIONSHIP TO OTHER THERAPIES

It is important to point out that in the chronic back pain management program, many other therapies are occurring during the treatment day, all of which emphasize the goals stated earlier. Patients are frequently observed in a social setting discussing their therapeutic EMG performances and comparing skills. On a weekly basis, a group biofeedback session is performed in an attempt to stimulate a social setting. Group discussion follows with the participants sharing and comparing experiences to individual training sessions.

Biofeedback therapy is perhaps the most tangible evidence of changes in self-regulation for both patients and clinicians. In many ways, the therapeutic EMG sessions serve to reinforce mind-body relationships. They provide a vehicle allowing all concerned to evaluate patient responses to issues raised throughout the treatment day. Therapists are frequently able to detect a mounting problem through increases in upper body tension levels.

References

1. Nachemson, A. L. The lumbar spine: an orthopaedic challenge. Spine, 1: 59–71, 1976.
2. Grabias, S. L. and Mankin, H. J. Pain in the lower back. Bull. Rheum. Dis., 30: 1040–1045, 1979–80.
3. Gottlieb, H., Strite, L. C., Koller, R., Madorsky, A., Hockersmith, V., Kleeman, M. and Wagner, J. Comprehensive rehabilitation of patients having chronic low back pain. Arch. Phys. Med. Rehabil., 58: 101–108, 1977.
4. McArthur, D. L., Cohen, M. J., Gottlieb, H. J., Naliboff, B. D. and Schandler, S. L. Treating chronic low back pain. I. Admission to initial follow-up. Pain, 29: 1–22, 1987.
5. McArthur, D. L., Cohen, M. J., Gottlieb, H. J., Naliboff, B. D. and Schandler, S. L. Treating chronic low back pain. II. Long-term follow-up. Pain, 29: 23–38, 1987.
6. Gottlieb, H., Strite, L., Koller, R., Hockersmith, V., Madorsky, A., Stanley, J., Adams, B., Wagner, J. and Adams, C. Symposium on Psychologically Oriented Treatment Program for the Chronic Pain Patient. American Psychological Association, Washington, D.C., September 5, 1976.
7. Adler, C. S. and Adler, S. M. Biofeedback and psychosomatic disorders. In Biofeedback—Principles and Practice for Clinicians, edited by J. V. Basmajian. Williams & Wilkins, Baltimore, 1979.
8. Benson, H., Beary, J. F., Carol, M. P. The relaxation response. Psychiatry, 37: 37–46, 1974.
9. Benson, H., Kotch, J. B., Crassweller, K. D. and Greenwood, M. M. Historical and clinical considerations of the relaxation response. J. Holistic Health, 6: 3–9, 1981.
10. Green, E. E., Walters, E. D., Green, A. M. and Murphy, G. Feedback technique of deep relaxation. Psychophysiology, 6: 371–377, 1969.
11. Basmajian, J. V. Muscles Alive: Their Functions Revealed by Electromyography, 4th ed. Williams & Wilkins, Baltimore, 1979.

CHAPTER 29

Biofeedback Treatment of Primary Raynaud's Disease

KEITH SEDLACEK

Three basic treatments have been used for primary Raynaud's: surgical, pharmacological, and, more recently, behavioral techniques, particularly biofeedback. The last has had outstanding success in recent years. The most prevalent suggestion (nontreatment) is avoidance of cold by moving to a warmer climate, or taking long winter vacations in warm areas, and protecting the affected areas with scarves, gloves, caps, etc.

ETIOLOGY AND SYMPTOMS

Raynaud's disease, first described in 1862 (1), usually affects women five times more frequently than men. Its symptoms most commonly consist of a blanching, mottled and cyanotic appearance of the fingers, usually bilaterally (2). The most commonly affected areas are fingers, toes, nose, and earlobes. Sometimes it is progressive in nature and in about 0.5% of cases amputation of a digit or affected area may be necessary (3).

Primary Raynaud's disease is distinguished from secondary Raynaud's by the absence of gangrene, consistent pain, or the presence of an organic change in the arteries or arterioles.

Allen and Brown (4) suggest that emotional or cold factors may trigger the vasomotor activity, and concluded that the uncomplicated primary Raynaud's is due to the hyperactivity of the vasomotor system. The original work by Raynaud (1) also suggested that the symptoms were not organic in etiology.

Secondary Raynaud's, also called Raynaud's phenomenon or syndrome, can be caused by severe injuries to the arteries by trauma, toxic metals, arterial occlusions (such as arterial sclerosis, embolism, or thromboangiitis obliterans), nerve lesions (such as thoracic outlet syndrome and causalgia), intoxication due to ergot and heavy metals, pneumatic and vibratory tools, connective-tissue diseases (scleroderma, disseminated lupus, rheumatoid arthritis, dermatomyositis), and neoplasms (leukemia, myeloma). Secondary Raynaud's can be ruled out by a blood count, erythrocyte rate, urinalysis, blood chemistry, antinuclear antibodies, and hand radiography or arteriography. Some primary Raynaud's patients 5 to 20 years later may progress to become secondary Raynaud's patients.

Variations in skin temperature seem to be correlated with changes in affective states (5), a decrease occurring as a reaction to stress and fear (6, 7). In work using different stressors, there is shown to be a wide variation between each individual in change of skin temperature. Thus, a change of as much as 13°C can be developed using different stresses. Even more important, in terms of the clinical treatment, Mittleman and Wolff (5) found major drops in temperature in subjects who were placed in stressful situations. They demonstrated that subjects who were under emotional stress and who could not relax showed a lower fingertip temperature. While Raynaud's patients did not show a major difference from the controls with regard to the fall in the fingertip temperature with stress, they did show an association under stress of pain and skin color changes (pallor). Lowering the environmental temperature was not sufficient to precipitate the cyanosis and pain. However, emotional stress was sufficient to produce this cluster of symptoms. It is important to note that primary Raynaud's (disease) most often in a combination of both physical stress and emotional stress.

BEHAVIORAL TREATMENT— BIOFEEDBACK

There has been an accumulation of evidence in favor of the use of behavioral self-regulation techniques, particularly biofeedback, as the treatment of choice for primary Raynaud's. Taub and Stroebel (8), Surwit (9), Lynch et al. (10), Taub (11), Taub et al. (12), Freedman et al. (13) and I (14, 15), have demonstrated that subjects can learn to produce voluntary vasodilation. Freedman's impressive controlled group outcome study demonstrated the difference between the use of relaxation and autogenic phrases (33% reduction in attacks) and a biofeedback package of treatment (93% reduction). Experimental subjects and patients can specifically learn to warm the areas involved both in primary and secondary Raynaud's. Taub also demonstrated in work for the armed forces that even with severe cold stresses produced by a body suit, students who are trained with biofeedback and handwarming techniques are more able to maintain peripheral warmth in the hands and fingers. His normal subjects can self-regulate increases in hand temperature, retain the ability for over 1 year, and perform other tasks while maintaining hand temperature increases without temperature feedback.

Stroebel and his group first demonstrated with large numbers of experimental patients and clinical patients that this technique could be learned and maintained at follow-up. At St. Luke's-Roosevelt Hospital and in my private practice, biofeedback treatment for primary and secondary Raynaud's symptoms have had similar success in reducing symptoms of chronic arterial constriction.

I find that a certain intensity of treatment (two sessions a week of 30–60 minutes for 10–30 sessions) is usually necessary. Thus, a 2- or 3-month treatment with specific psychophysiological retraining and awareness training is required, using a "behavioral treatment package" consisting of a biofeedback session in the office or hospital; biofeedback home practice twice a day for 15 minutes; progressive muscle relaxation; autogenic phrases; and mental imagery. I provide a series of 7 home practice tapes for my patients as well as small temperature rings, small thermistors or liquid crystals which "feed back" finger temperature changes. The patients record their finger temperature at home so we can follow their progress in finger and hand warming in home practice sessions and in transferring these learned skills of vasodilation into the home and work environment. As a criterion of having learned handwarming, I require a finger temperature

of 93° in a 72–74° room. Libo (16) has demonstrated the importance of achieving training criteria for successful long-term results.

Since good protocols and equipment are now available, the biofeedback therapist is the other important variable in biofeedback treatment.

An untrained person or a "rigid experimenter" may achieve strikingly different biofeedback treatment results (11). After over 20 years of biofeedback, it is clear that there is no "magic" in the machines.

TREATMENT—PSYCHOPHYSIOLOGICAL RETRAINING

Before starting training, I carefully explain the goals for biofeedback treatment to the patients: they will be taught to self-regulate their vascular spasm and thus relieve the painful symptoms. I explain that many experience relief from their symptoms in 2 or 3 months (10–30 sessions); however, their exercises and attention to their stress reactions must be continued for 8 to 10 months in order to establish a healthy homeostatic balance between the parasympathetic and sympathetic branches of the autonomic nervous system. I explain that the activation of the emergency fight-or-flight response is a link-up to their particular vascular symptoms. Via their cool or cold hands, they can monitor their reactions; with the equipment, the training, and the home practice, they can learn to regulate their physiological disregulation. Thus, the goal is a rebalancing (homeostasis) of the automatic nervous system that affects vasoconstriction.

I begin the retraining with electromyography to relax the skeletal muscles and then proceed to the skin temperature feedback.

For the first 4 sessions, I use electromyographic (EMG) feedback training (forehead placement) and then for the next 4 sessions I use thermal feedback training. This basic 8-session sequence is used for all patients for scientific relaxation or biofeedback training for anxiety. Most patients learn to relax the skeletal muscles and begin to warm their hands by the first 8 to 10 sessions. With Raynaud's patients, I then continue thermal training at the site of the dysfunction, usually with the first finger of the dominant hand. I use the back of the finger since it can be easily taped onto and does not interfere very much with the patient's adjustments of hand position during the 30- to 60-minute session. Right and left finger temperatures may vary during individual sessions. During training I find it prudent to train the nondominant hand for at least two or three sessions, providing a check on the generalization of the treatment. Specific warmth phrases adapted from autogenic training (17) are used, such as, "My right hand is warm and heavy." There are commercially available tapes that are useful to give to the patient (18). I also provide them with a page of these autogenic phrases for their home practice. The physician, nurse, technician, or trainer should be able to warm his own hands as well as repeat the phrases to the patient. This demonstrates that the skill is learnable and effective.

COMMON EXPERIENCE WITH BIOFEEDBACK TREATMENT

One of the purposes of EMG relaxation training is to teach people awareness of deep muscle relaxation. Thus, with 3 or 4 sessions, people are able to notice specific sensations as their muscles relax. In the first stage of skeletal muscle relaxation, a patient's muscles may feel loose, limp, and heavy. In the second state of muscle relaxation, people often report that a limb or their whole body is floating or drifting. They also report having calmer sensations inside their body. As a result of muscle relaxation, our patients often report sleeping better, feeling calmer, and having more energy.

Since the skin temperature biofeedback tells the patients the direction and the speed of changes when they warm their hands, this "warmth" sensation may be used to check their response during home practice sessions and throughout the day. By learning these relaxation skills and having them properly identified, the patient develops a personal biofeedback signal via these checks (rate and depth of breathing, decrease of muscle tension, and "warmth" feelings). I have our patients simply place their fingertips to their foreheads and learn to discriminate reliably between fingertips that are ice cold, cool, lukewarm, warm, or "toasty" warm. (These correspond roughly to skin temperatures of 65–73, 73–80, 80–86, 86–92, and 92–96°F.

One important major difference between biofeedback and other verbal relaxation techniques is that the patient and therapist can confirm the physiological change. Thus, the patient can begin to discriminate and properly identify thoughts, feelings, and physical sensations that accompany muscle and nervous system activation and relaxation. Thus, a verbal technique (relaxation) can become, via the equipment. a biobehavioral treatment (biofeedback).

I have observed differences during training between right and left hand temperatures of up to 15°F. Patients report being aware of this right/left difference. In fact, they often notice that the warmth is easier to feel on one side of the body than the other. In some cases, they notice one area relaxing first on one side and not on the other. The "spotty" effect seems as if they are making contact in a new way with certain parts of their body. When the new "feeling" and contact is made with a bodily area, it is incorporated into a mind/body connection and rarely reappears in as striking a fashion.

CLINICAL RESULTS

Of the original 20 patients (some of whom I have followed for more than 14 years), 80% succeeded in learning self-regulation of the symptoms caused by vascular spasm (15). The number of sessions required for treatment ranged from 12 to 36, with an average of 21. The age range was from 20 to 73 years, and four of the patients were men. All of the men obtained release. The patients practiced home exercise for 15 minutes twice every day with shortened versions of the exercises that are taught to them in the office. I shorten these exercises to 5 minutes, then 2 minutes, and suggest a brief 10-second relaxation exercise at the 3-month follow-up visit. With 42 additional patients, 82% were successfully treated (19). The length of treatment ranged from 12–62 sessions (average—28). The age range was 18–75, and the ratio of female to male patients was 5:1. The criterion for handwarming was achieving a skin temperature above 93°F in an ambient room temperature of 72–74°. Freedman, Stroebel, and I found that with 10–30 treatment sessions, successful results in 80–90% of primary Raynaud's (secondary Raynaud's–50–60%) are possible.

If patients stop their home practice or are overloaded with stressful situations, symptoms often return. One woman stopped her home practice, and her symptoms recurred; she did not return for further treatment. Another woman who had a relapse was treated with an additional six biofeedback sessions and regained self-regulation. (This is very similar to our experience with migraine headaches, in which the headache pain provides reinforcement for patients to return to regular home practice. We find that most patients who return to regular daily practice will regain self-regulation.) Most patients were able to reduce vasospasm from 10–70 attacks per week to 0–7 per week. Skin ulceration showed a reduction in frequency and in the time taken to heal. After treatment, many patients can grasp a cold steering wheel, make a snowball, ski again, or pull frozen foods from the freezer without further attacks.

Patients Who Fail

Some 5–10% of my patients, even after relief of symptoms with the biofeedback technique, will stop their stress management techniques with a return to their symptoms. This group of patients, who choose to return to their symptoms, needs to be studied further, as they seem to be unwilling or unable to maintain a healthy self-regulation of their autonomic nervous systems. Further therapy is a possible answer for them: e.g., assertiveness therapy, psychotherapy, group therapy, movement therapy, psychoanalysis, etc.

CONCLUSION

Biofeedback provides an excellent treatment for primary Raynaud's disease. Biofeedback retraining also suggests that we have all received psychophysiological training from our families, schools, society, and life experiences, and that our overall response to this training may predispose us to a series of disorders or diseases. How personality traits, patterns of cognition, and life stresses are acted out against particular organs or tissues—cranial arteries, coronary arteries, skin, stomach, intestines, and uterus—is still not fully understood.

Biofeedback is also useful adjunctive treatment of secondary Raynaud's. It holds promise as a treatment for other vascular disorders such as angina, claudication, diabetes, frostbite, and Buerger's disease. Some of the real difficulties in the biofeedback treatment of Raynaud's is that the equipment is the simplest part of the treatment. Poor diagnosis, insufficient protocols, insufficient duration of treatment, and poorly trained technicians, nurses, or physicians account for many of the mixed results that are cited in discussions about biofeedback treatment of Raynaud's.

The crucial factors of biofeedback treatment are the biofeedback package, acquisition of handwarming skills, and the awareness training. This awareness training helps the patients transfer the biofeedback skills into everyday living. This transfer and "automatic" response is a necessary endpoint of successful biofeedback treatment.

To summarize, primary Raynaud's is best treated with a trial of approximately 20–30 biofeedback treatment sessions with an experienced clinician. Sympathectomies should be reserved for patients with secondary Raynaud's with demonstrated organic blockage. Vasoconstriction alone is not sufficient evidence for a sympathectomy. Vasodilators may be useful for brief periods in which cold exposure is necessary. There are few negative side-effects of biofeedback treatment, and 80–90% of patients experience a marked reduction of symptoms. Healing of skin ulceration occurs more rapidly, and patients develop new ways of maintaining healthy physical and mental attitudes in their daily life.

References

1. Raynaud, M. *New Researches on the Nature and Treatment of Local Asphyxia of the Extremities* (translated by Barlox, T.). Selected Monographs. The New Sydenham Society, London, 1888.
2. Lewis, T. *Vascular Disorders of the Limbs: Described for Practitioners and Students.* Macmillan, London, 1949.
3. Harrison, T. R. *Principles of Internal Medicine,* 8th ed., p. 276. McGraw-Hill, New York, 1977.
4. Allen, E. V. and Brown, G. E. Raynaud's Disease: a clinical study of one hundred and forty-seven cases. J.A.M.A., 99: 1472–1478, 1932.
5. Mittelmann, B. and Wolff, H. G. Affective states and skin temperature: experimental study of subjects with "cold hands" and Raynaud's disease, Psychosom. Med., 1: 271–292, 1939.
6. Weber, E. *Einfluss Psychischer Vorginge Auf Den Korper.* Springer Verlag, Berlin, 1920.
7. Eng. H. *Experimental Investigations of the Emotional Life of the Child as Compared to That of the Adult* (translated by Morrison, G. H.) Oxford University Press, London, 1925.
8. Taub, E. and Stroebel, C. F. *Task Force Study Section Report: Use of Biofeedback in the Treatment of Vasoconstrictive Syndromes.* Prepared for the Biofeedback Society of America, 10200 West 44th Avenue, #304, Wheat Ridge, Colorado, 80033.
9. Surwit, R. S. Biofeedback: a possible treatment for Raynaud's disease. Semin. Psychiatry, 5: 483–490, 1973.
10. Lynch, W. C., Hama, H., Kohn, S. and Miller, N. E. Instructional control of peripheral vasomotor responses in children. Psychophysiology, 13:

219–221, 1976.

11. Taub, E. Self regulation of human tissue temperature. In *Biofeedback: Theory and Research,* edited by G. E. Schwartz and J. Beatty. Academic Press, New York, 1977.

12. Taub, E. and Emurian, C. S. Feedback aided self-regulation of skin temperature with a single feedback locus. Biofeedback Self Regul., 1: 2, 1976.

13. Freedman, R. Ianna, P. and Wenig, P. Behavioral treatment of Raynaud's disease. J. Consult. Clin. Psychol., 51: 539–549, 1983.

14. Sedlacek, K. EMG and thermal feedback as a treatment for Raynaud's disease. Biofeedback Self Regul., 1: 318, 1976.

15. Sedlacek, K. Biofeedback for Raynaud's disease. Psychosomatics, 20: 537–541, 1979.

16. Libo, L. M. and Arnold, G. E. Does training to criterion influence improvement? A follow-up study of EMG and thermal biofeedback. J. Behav. Med., 6: 397–404, 1983.

17. Luthe, W. and Shultz, J. H. *Autogenic Therapy,* vol. 2. Grune & Stratton, New York, 1969.

18. Stress Regulation Institute, 239 East 79th St., New York, NY, 10021.

19. Sedlacek, K. Biofeedback treatment of Raynaud's. Presented at First International Conference on Bio-Behavioral Self-Regulation and Health, Nov. 18, 1987, Honolulu, Hawaii.

PART 5
TECHNICAL
CONSIDERATIONS

CHAPTER 30

Basic Biofeedback Electronics for the Clinician

BERNARD A. COHEN

Microelectronics now allows the packaging of elaborate circuitry in very compact form. Components made from copper have excellent electrical conductivity. Devices made from carbon resist the flow of electric current. Components made from silicon, germanium, or other semiconductors have electrical properties related to the way in which they are bonded together. Transistors, made from semiconductors, were assembled manually. Now, with the assistance of the electron microscope, many transistors and other components are put on a single device called a chip, smaller in size than the original transistors of 1948. The instrumentation of today is becoming smaller, more portable, and may very well be obsolete in 4 or 5 years.

HYDRAULIC ANALOGY

Let us use an illustrative analogy to demonstrate basic electrical characteristics. Figure 30.1 illustrates water flowing through a system consisting of a large tank with an opening toward the bottom and a valve to control the water flowing out. The pipe leaving the tank goes into a series of other various-sized pipes, and ultimately empties into a pool. This analogy relates the flow of water in the system to the flow of electrons in a conducting medium.

Intuitively, it can be seen that the mass of water in the large container creates a pressure at the point of the valve. The pressure that forces the water through the pipe corresponds to the electrical potential or *electromotive force* (EMF), which causes the flow of electrons. The changes in pressure caused by the varying pipe diameters correspond to the changes in voltages caused by different components within the electrical system. The EMF is measured in volts, or in derived units, such as kilovolts (volts times 1000) or millivolts (volts divided by 1000). The conventional circuit analysis representation for this is E, although frequently the notation V will be used.

Changes in the pressure in the fluid system are caused by the varying constrictions (bends, valves, friction of the fluid against the pipe, etc.). In the electrical system this corresponds to the *resistance* offered to the flow of electrons. The resistance is usually measured in ohms, and in circuit analysis is designated by the letter R. Resistance, which is an opposition to the flow of electrons, is frequently designated by the Greek letter Ω, representing ohms.

The rate of flow of water in the hydraulic system corresponds in the electrical system to the rate of flow of electrons, or the *current*. Current is measured in amperes, or in derived units such as milliamperes (amperes divided by 1000) or microamperes (amperes divided

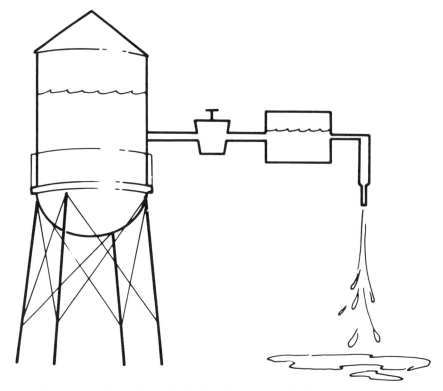

Figure 30.1.   Diagrammatic analogy of a hydraulic system. The level of water in the large tank is controlled by the valve which adjusts the flow through the various-sized connecting tubes and ultimately into the pool.

by 100,000). In circuit analysis, the current is designated by the letter I.

BASIC CIRCUIT PARAMETERS
Ohm's Law

The fundamental law relating the voltage, current, and resistance in an electrical circuit is known as *Ohm's law*. Ohm's law states that the potential drop (E) across any resistance is the product of the resistance (R) and the current (I) flowing through the resistance:

$$E = IR.$$

This equation may be transposed to calculate any of the three parameters if the other two parameters are known. Ohm's law holds accurately for direct current flow in conductors. The extension of Ohm's law to alternating current flow will be discussed later.

When current flows through a conductor, energy is dissipated as heat or light into the environment around the conductor. The resistances used in electrical circuits allow controlling the voltages and currents at prescribed

levels. These values then determine the rate of energy dissipation in the circuit, or power (P). Thus we have:

$$P = I^2R.$$

By appropriate substitution from Ohm's law, this can also be given by the equations

$$P = E^2/R \text{ or } P = EI.$$

Current Flow

The current in an electrical circuit can be *direct current* (d.c.), in which magnitude and polarity remain fixed with relation to time (i.e., the electrons move uniformly in one direction), or *alternating current* (a.c.), which reverses polarity periodically and is constantly changing in magnitude (the electrons oscillate back and forth in the conductor). In an a.c. circuit, both the current and voltage vary with time, and usually in a sinusoidal manner. The rate of oscillation is designated as the frequency, and is expressed in cycles per second, or hertz (Hz). The general equation for either voltage or current in an a.c. circuit can be given by the equation

$$X = X_0 \sin (2\pi ft)$$

where f is the frequency and t is the time. In this equation X_0 is the maximum magnitude of the parameter (X) of interest. The peak-to-peak value would be $2X_0$. Frequently, the specifications of a device will discuss the root-mean-square (rms) value of a parameter, and this may be calculated as X_0 times half the square-root of two; for a pure sine wave

$$\text{rms} = (\sqrt{2}X_0)/2 = 0.707 \ X_0.$$

Resistance

The basic circuit component consists of a device that offers opposition to the flow of current, namely, a *resistor*. Resistors may have a fixed, variable, or time-varying value. They may either be wire-wound or composition. A wire-wound resistor is made by winding wire of the desired size on an insulating core. Molded composition resistors are made from a mixture containing carbon or another relatively poor conductor enclosed in an insulated case. Resistors are made in different current-carrying capacities. Larger resistors, made to carry greater amounts of current, are usually wire-wound. The rating on a resistor is related to the power that can be dissipated by the resistor and is usually given in watts. Thus a 10,000-ohm, 1-watt resistor would have a current-carrying capacity of 0.01 ampere (10 milliamperes) found by the equation given for power previously.

Inductance

If an alternating current passes through a coil of wire, a changing magnetic flux is produced around the wire. Because this magnetic field cuts across adjacent turns of wire, it induces a voltage in them. The induced voltage always has a polarity opposite to that of the applied voltage. The summation of the total voltages induced in all of the turns of the coil is called the back-EMF or back-voltage because it opposes a change in the current. The ability of a circuit to generate such a counter-voltage is known as the *inductance* of a circuit. As the inductance increases, there will be an increase in the circuit's opposition to a change in current flow. The unit of inductance is the henry, and in circuit diagrams the mathematical symbol used is L. The magni-

tude of the opposition to primary current flow offered by the induced counter-voltage is known as inductive reductance. (This is roughly comparable to resistance.) Inductive reactance is designated by the symbol X_L and is calculated by the equation

$$X_L = 2\pi fL$$

where f is the current frequency in cycles per second (Hz) and L is the inductance of the element under consideration. One of the most practical applications of the use of inductors in a circuit is to "block" high-frequency currents, thus allowing d.c. currents to pass freely. Appropriate selection of the inductance of the coil can determine the frequencies to be blocked.

Capacitance

Perhaps the most important circuit component to be used on feedback devices is a device called a *capacitor*. A capacitor consists of two or more parallel plates of conductive material separated by an insulating material. The capacitance of the device is the property that enables storage of electrical energy. A capacitor, or condenser, as it is sometimes called, can be charged by connecting it to a source of direct current such as a battery. Because the electrons have difficulty crossing the nonconducting medium separating the two parallel plates, a charge of electrons is built up on one plate. After a period of time, depending upon the capacity of the condenser and the resistance of the conductors, the condenser becomes fully charged. The time required to charge the condenser is a function of the other parameters in the circuit. Capacitance is measured in farads, and is expressed mathematically as C. When a condenser is connected in a circuit to which a source of alternating voltage is applied, the condenser charges first in one direction and then in the opposite. The electrons in the rest of the circuit will flow to and from the condenser as an alternating current with a frequency of the applied alternating voltage. Consequently, it may be said that the condenser offers opposition to the flow of current. This opposition is known as capacitive reactance and is given by the equation

$$X_c = -1/2\pi fC$$

where f is the frequency in cycles per second (Hz) and C is the capacitance in farads.

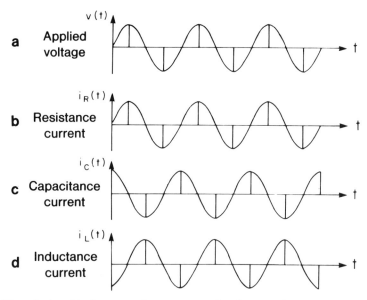

a Applied voltage

b Resistance current

c Capacitance current

d Inductance current

Figure 30.2. The relationship between the current and voltage in the primary circuit component is depicted. Part *a* is the applied voltage, with *b*, *c*, and *d* the currents through a pure resistance, capacitance, and inductance, respectively.

Impedance

Just as resistance represents the total opposition to flow of current in a d.c. circuit, *impedance* is the term used to denote the total opposition to flow of alternating current in a circuit and is also measured in ohms. The circuit may contain elements that are purely resistive, inductive, or capacitive in nature, or the circuit may contain combinations of these elements. The mathematical symbol for impedance is Z. Since impedance in an a.c. circuit is similar to resistance in a d.c. circuit, we may substitute impedance for resistance in Ohm's law and obtain the a.c. equivalent of this equation as being

$$e = iZ$$

Lower case letters (e, i) are used in a.c. circuit equations and the capital letters (E, I) are used in d.c. circuit equations. The total impedance is a function of the resistance, inductive reactance and capacitive reactance, and may be calculated from the equation

$$Z = \sqrt{R^2 + X^2}$$

where R is resistance and X is the total reactance consisting of inductive and capacitive elements. If we substitute the equations previously mentioned, we obtain

$$Z = \sqrt{R^2 + \left(2\pi fL - \frac{1}{2\pi fC}\right)^2}$$

and this equation will then enable us to calculate the total impedance in a circuit.

Voltage-Current Relationships

Figure 30.2 indicates the phase relationships between the voltage and current in a circuit consisting of either resistance, capacitance, or inductance. The top part, *a*, shows the applied voltage v(t) consisting of a pure sine wave applied first to the resistance, then the capacitance, and the inductance. Parts *b*, *c*, and *d* show the current through each of these components, respectively.

If the signal is applied to a resistance, the instantaneous voltage and current vary simultaneously, and they are said to be *in phase*. Thus, if the current and voltage are both 0 at an initial time, t_0, (represented at the start of the coordinate system in the figure), then after a time equal to one-fourth of a full cycle ($2\pi \times$ frequency) they will both reach their peak, with subsequent changes, as shown in the figure.

If, however, the voltage is applied to a capacitor, as the voltage varies as shown in *a*, the current to the capacitor will vary as shown in *c*; it will be 90 degrees *out of phase*. The current and voltage will not have their maximum values at the same time. The current to the capacitor will be greatest when the charge on the capacitor is 0 (i.e., at the beginning of the cycle). When the voltage has reached its peak, the capacitor will be fully charged, and the flow of current into it will be 0.

Similarly, when a voltage is applied to an inductance, the current will also be 90 degrees out of phase, but in the opposite direction, as can be seen in part d. The back-EMF developed by the changing magnetic flux will be greatest when the current is changing most rapidly. As with the capacitor, this is at the beginning of the cycle, where the shape of the curve is the greatest. Since this back-EMF is opposite in sign to the applied voltage, the current will be negative at the beginning of the cycle.

In a circuit containing inductances and capacitances, the phase relationship between voltage and current becomes considerably more complicated. At the point of minimum impedance for a capacitance-inductance combination, the voltage and the current will be exactly in phase; this will occur at what is termed the resonance frequency.

SPECIFICATIONS DEFINED

Perhaps one of the most bewildering aspects of any instrument when first encountered by the novice is the meaning of the various parameters specified by the manufacturers. Working definitions of these parameters will allow the user to more clearly understand their significance with respect to circuit components.

The *range* of the device generally includes all levels of input amplitude and frequency over which the device is expected to operate. The objective should be to provide an instrument that will give a usable reading from the smallest expected value to the largest. The range for a typical EMG biofeedback device may be specified as being 1–250 μV, although this, of course, may vary from one device to another.

The *sensitivity* of a device determines how small a variation of a parameter can be reliably measured. It differs from range in that it is not concerned with the absolute levels of the parameter, but rather with the minute changes that can be detected. The sensitivity directly determines the *resolution* of the device, which is the minimum variation that can accurately be read. Too high a sensitivity often results in nonlinearities or instability. Typical sensitivity values may range from 0-1000 μV, or may be variable.

The *linearity* of the device is the degree to which variations in the output of an instrument follow variations in the input. In a linear system, the sensitivity would be the same for all absolute levels of input, whether in the high, middle, or low portion of the range. In some instruments, a certain form of nonlinearity is purposely introduced to create a desired effect. (A light or tone from a feedback device is actually a nonlinear output that serves a desired purpose.) Linearity should be obtained over the most important segments of the signal, if not over the entire range. Linearity will tell you how well the output reproduces what the input sees. Typically, the linearity will be specified as a percentage of full-scale deflection of a meter, or a percentage of the maximum range.

The *frequency response* of a device is its variation in sensitivity over the frequency range of the measurement. (This specification may be included under the category of "filter characteristics" where parameters such as bandpass and filter roll-off are mentioned.) It is important to display a wave shape that is a faithful reproduction of the original physiological phenomena. A system should be able to respond rapidly enough to reproduce all frequency components of the waveform with equal sensitivity. This condition is referred to as a "flat response" over a given range of the frequencies. The overall band-pass is that area of the frequency response curve which yields a flat response. A typical device may have a band-pass of 50–500 Hz with filter roll-offs of 6 db per octave. The implication is that below 50 and above 500 Hz unwanted signals will be attenuated (suppressed) at a rate specified by the roll-off characteristics of the filter (6 db per octave). The higher the roll-off characteristic number, the better the attenuation, within, of course, practical limitations. Frequencies that are definitely unwanted (e.g., the 60-Hz rejection) should be attenuated greater than 30 db, while those frequencies merely outside of the range of interest can have sufficient attenuation at 6 db.

The *accuracy* of the device is a measure of the system error. Errors can occur in a multitude of ways. Although not always present simultaneously, the following errors should be considered: (a) errors due to tolerance of components; (b) mechanical errors in meter movement; (c) component errors due to drift or temperature variation; (d) errors due to poor frequency response; (e) errors due to change in atmospheric pressure or temperature; (f) reading errors due to parallax, inadequate illumination, or wide ink traces on pen recordings.

The *signal-to-noise ratio* of a device is the ratio of amplification of the signal in relationship to the amount of noise that is encountered in the system being measured. This should be as high as possible. It is possible to have a signal-to-noise ratio that is very high for the device itself, but one may be using it in an environment that is inherently noisy. Power line frequency noise or interference is common, and is usually picked up in long leads. Interference due to electromagnetic, electrostatic, or diathermic equipment is also possible. Signal-to-noise ratios should always be better than 1000 to 1. This will be discussed in greater detail later.

The *stability* of the device is the ability of the system to resume a steady-state condition following a disturbance at the input, rather than being driven into uncontrollable oscillation. This parameter will vary with amplification, filtration, gain, feedback, and so on. The overall system must be stable over the useful range of the device. Baseline stability is the maintenance of a constant baseline value without drift. If the device is not constructed appropriately, movement artifact may drive the system into oscillation. Likewise, d.c. drifting of the baseline is an unstable condition, and equipment not regulated for this parameter should be avoided.

The last specification consideration is that of *isolation*. Measurements should be made on patients in such a way that the instrument does not produce a direct electrical connection between the subject and ground. This can be achieved by using magnetic or optical coupling techniques or radiotelemetry. Telemetry can also be used when the movement of the subject is essential and the encumbrance of connecting leads is to be avoided. Most biofeedback equipment is battery-operated, and this provides another means of isolating the patient from power mains and ground.

THEORY OF CIRCUIT OPERATION

In biological signal applications, we deal with phenomena of relatively small magnitude (usually in the microvolt range). It is desirable to use this information to trigger feedback devices. It is necessary to increase the magnitude of the signal to a range that is more congruent with those necessary for triggering the feedback devices. To do this, we use a device known as an *amplifier*. The *gain* of the amplifier is the factor by which the input signal is multiplied to obtain the output. Mathematically, we have $V_0 = AV_1$, where V_0 is the output voltage, V_1 is the input voltage, and A is the gain of the amplifier. Frequently, A may be as high as 1000. In theory, there is no limitation to the amount of gain we can provide, since all that is necessary is to place several amplifiers back to back, thus increasing the overall gain of the system as desired. Most biofeedback devices have several stages of amplification to achieve the desired output signal.

A specific type of amplifier that we are most concerned with in biological signal monitoring is called a differential amplifier. A *differential amplifier* can be considered as two amplifiers with separate input but with a common output terminal, which delivers the sum of the two amplifier voltages. Both amplifiers have the same voltage gain, but one amplifier is *inverting*, while the other is *noninverting* (Fig. 30.3).

If the two amplifier inputs are connected to the same input source, the resulting *common-mode gain* should be zero, since the signals from the inverting and noninverting amplifiers cancel each other at the common output. In practice, this cancellation is not complete, since the gain of the two amplifiers is never exactly equal. Thus, a small residual common-mode output remains.

When one of the amplifier inputs is grounded, and a voltage is applied only to the other amplifier input, the input voltage appears at the output amplified by the gain of the amplifier. This gain is called the *differential gain* of the differential amplifier.

This leads into an extremely important concept which was alluded to earlier in the discussion of specifications of the devices. The ratio of the differential gain to the common mode gain is called the *common mode rejection ratio* (CMRR) of the differential amplifier. This should be as high as possible, and can be as high as 1,000,000:1. The CMRR is a measure by which signals that are identical are rejected from signals that are nonidentical. For example, if identical noise is applied at both

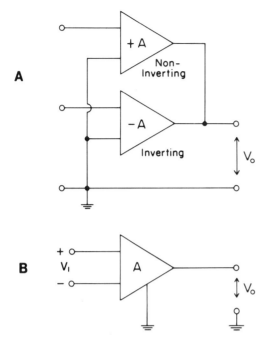

Figure 30.3. Schematic representation of a differential amplifier. The *top sketch* shows an expanded view of how it may be considered as two amplifiers, one inverting (negative gain) and one noninverting (positive gain). The *bottom sketch* shows the conventional circuit representation with its positive input (active), negative input (reference) and ground.

of the inputs, then the noise will cancel. When two electrodes are used (an active and a reference), the biological signal sensed at each is slightly different from the other. The output signal represents the sum (really the difference, since one output is negative) between the two. If the common mode rejection ratio is very high, only the biological signal will be sensed at the output, and the noise will be canceled. In general, when the differential amplifier is used to measure bioelectric signals that occur as a potential difference between two electrodes, the signals are applied between the inverting and noninverting inputs of the amplifier. The signal is thus amplified by the differential gain of the amplifier. For the interference signal, however, both inputs appear as though they were connected together to a common input source. Thus, the common mode interference signal is amplified only by the much smaller common mode gain.

To better understand how the differential amplifier operates and how it is important for

the impedance of the two leads to be matched, it is first necessary to explain the concept of a voltage divider (Fig. 30.4). When a potential difference (voltage) is measured at two points in a circuit, the voltage drop between the two points is dissipated by the resistances between these two points. In the circuit shown, if V_0 is the output voltage and V_1 is the input voltage, then the two quantities are related by the equation

$$V_0 = V_1 \times R_2 \div (R_1 + R_2).$$

This is the general equation for a voltage divider. The output voltage is reduced proportionately by the voltage dropped across the resistances.

An interesting point concerning differential amplifiers can now be illustrated with Figure 30.5. The *electrode impedances* (R_{e+} and R_{e-}) each form a voltage divider with the input impedance of the differential amplifier. If the electrode impedances are not identical, the interference signals at the inverting and noninverting inputs of the differential amplifier may be different, and the desired degree of cancellation does not take place. Because the electrode impedances can never be made exactly equal, the high common-mode-rejection ratio of a differential amplifier can be realized only if the amplifier has an input impedance much higher than the impedance of the electrodes to which it is connected. This input impedance may not be the same for the differential signal as it is for the common-mode signal. Nevertheless, it can be seen from the diagram that to ensure high quality signal reproduction an amplifier with a very high input impedance should be selected.

BASIC BIOFEEDBACK CIRCUIT BLOCK DIAGRAM

The block circuit diagram of Figure 30.6 represents a general circuit configuration of EMG biofeedback devices. Each block depicts a specific element that affects the information retrieved and the type of final output delivered. The first element is the familiar *differential amplifier*. This has already been covered.

The second element is a signal *filter*. The object of filtration is to eliminate unwanted signals. A *high-pass* filter will allow signals above a certain frequency to pass through it. A *low-pass* filter will allow signals below a specific frequency to pass through it. Consequently, with a high-pass filter set at 100 Hz, and a

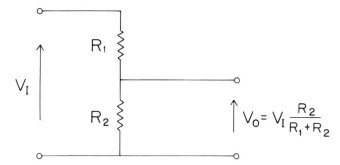

Figure 30.4. Diagrammatic circuit representation of the concept of a voltage divider.

low-pass filter set at 600 Hz, we will reliably reproduce all information between 100 and 600 Hz. In addition to these two types of filter, many instruments have *notch filters* which are used to filter out specific frequency components; for example, a 60-Hz notch filter will be used to eliminate all unwanted signals between approximately 59 and 62 Hz. This enables recording information below and above that point at the same time.

The next element is known as a *rectifier*. A rectifier converts the a.c. signal to a pulsating d.c. signal. Basically, all signals entering the rectifier that are positive remain so, while all signals that are negative are inverted. The output of the rectifier consists of only positive signals. This is necessary because in most feedback instruments, it is desired to relate the output to the collection of all information from the input. If some signals were negative, these would be subtracted, and consequently the collection of all signals would not be complete.

This next element is an *integrator*. An integrator is mainly a device that collects, stores, or sums all of the information entering. It has the capability of allowing some information to be "leaked off" so that the device does not become "overstored." The storage characteristics of an integrator allow the capacitor to serve as an ideal first approximation. The "time constant" of an integrator is the rate at which ex-

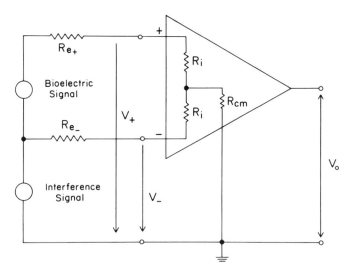

Figure 30.5. Schematic circuit representation of a differential amplifier as used for amplification of the bioelectrical signals. The resistances R_{e+}/R_{e-} represent the total combination of electrode skin and tissue impedance, as would be found when the electrodes are properly applied to a subject. The resistances R_i/R_{cm} represent the internal common mode resistances, respectively, of the differential amplifier.

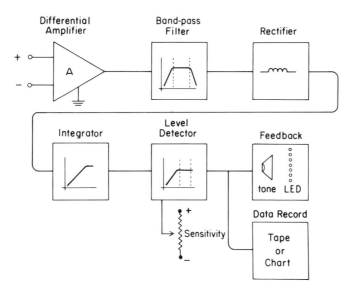

Figure 30.6. Basic block diagram of an EMG biofeedback device. The components include the differential amplifier, band-pass filter, rectifier, integrator, level detector, feedback medium, and recording devices. See text for more elaborate discussion on each component.

cess information is "leaked off." Since the rectifier has assured that all signals entering the integrator are positive, we are confident that integrating these signals will produce a nonzero value. The time constant of the integrator can be set by appropriate selection of the components that go into making up the integrator.

The next element in the basic circuit is the *level detector.* It may be desirable to have a preset level of EMG activity activate the feedback mechanism (e.g., lights, tones, etc.). This preset level may be adjusted externally to the device, and detected internally by the level detector circuitry. When this preset level has been reached, signals beyond that level are allowed to activate the feedback mechanism.

The specific type of feedback selected will depend on the type of information and the manner in which it is to be conveyed to the patient. If it is desired to alert the patient that a preset level has been obtained, a single light may be used to generate that feedback. If more quantitative information is desired to alert to varying levels, then a group of lights may be used. A variable-pitched tone may be used, as can be amplified raw EMG. A meter may be used to display the average EMG output values calibrated in microvolts or "good," "fair," "poor," ranges, etc. The types of output are limitless.

SYSTEM OPERATION

An overview of how the various components in the block diagram affect the signal can be seen in Figures 30.7 and 30.8. Figure 30.7 shows the overall time-compressed effects detailed in Figure 30.8. Here it can be explicitly seen how the level detector rises above the integrated output at the point of feedback activation. This figure also depicts the effects of rectification and integration of the signal.

Figure 30.8 depicts the circuit effects upon both a simulated and an actual EMG signal under contraction strengths ranging from minimum to maximum. In each figure, four traces are shown. Each trace is representative of the outputs from the amplifier, rectifier, integrator, and level detector, respectively, from top to bottom. In following the progress of the effects of varying contraction strengths on the circuit components, the reader should keep in mind that the inclusion of a simulated EMG signal (in actuality, a conventional sine wave) is to enhance one's understanding of the effect of the various circuit components. At each stage, it would be helpful to observe the effect on a simulated signal and then translate that to the effect on the actual EMG.

Under conditions of minimum contraction, the four tracings for both the simulated and

SIMULATED EMG SIGNAL OUTPUTS

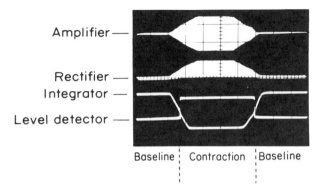

Figure 30.7. Representation of the outputs of the differential amplifier, rectifier, integrator and level detector for varying degrees of contraction strength of a simulated EMG signal. Contraction strength begins at a baseline value, continuing to maximum contraction, and then full relaxation back to baseline.

actual signals show low-amplitude activity. The signal characteristics in the actual tracing may include noise disturbances at the input. Note that while the noise signals may be rectified and possibly integrated, they are well below the level detector preset limits, and consequently, there is no feedback output.

Under conditions of moderate contraction, the sine wave is quite distinct, as is its rectified signal. The integrated level has increased, and the level detector has been triggered. The actual signal shows a small amount of EMG activity in the top trace, as well as its rectified component. This, too, has

been integrated, and the level detector has been triggered.

For a medium contraction, the sine wave is somewhat less discernible because it has increased in both frequency and amplitude. Its rectified component appears as small bumps with intermittent spikes, and the integrated level has risen considerably. The level detector has exceeded the integrated level considerably, indicating that the output has activated some tone or light. In the actual signal, the EMG activity has increased, its rectified component shows the charactistic flattening response, the integrated level is somewhat high

SIMULATED VS ACTUAL EMG FEEDBACK
INSTRUMENT OUTPUTS

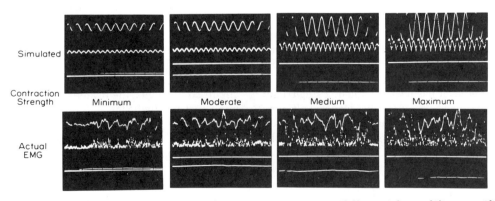

Figure 30.8. Output representation of the circuit parameters (differential amplifier, rectifier, integrator, and level detector) for both simulated and actual EMG signals under contraction conditions ranging from minimum to maximum. See text for more complete discussion.

and exceeded by the level detector, also showing the output activated.

In the final tracing, the simulated signal shows a very active, vigorous sine wave pattern (almost totally discernible because of the increased amplitude and frequency), with the rectified component below, and the integrated level at its maximum saturated point. The level detector, of course, has triggered the output signal. The actual EMG signal shows the characteristic interference pattern with the rectified component showing the peaks in amplitude, the integrated level also saturated, and the level detector activating the output.

ELECTRODES

Although it is not the intent of this chapter to delve into the pros and cons of various electrode configurations, some discussion of the types of electrodes and the effect each may have on the instrumentation is deemed appropriate. Devices that convert ionic potentials into electronic potentials are called *electrodes*. While there are numerous types of electrodes that can be used to measure and record bioelectric events, nearly all, including those used for EMG and biofeedback, can be subcategorized into three major divisions:

1. *Microelectrodes*. These may be used to measure potentials within or near a single cell.

2. *Skin surface electrodes*. These may be used to measure the biopotentials that propagate to the surface of the skin.

3. *Needle electrodes*. These may be used to penetrate the skin to record potentials from a region overlying the particular source of interest.

The measurement of any bioelectric potential requires two electrodes. The voltage measured is the difference between the potentials of the two electrodes. Since there is an inherent voltage associated with the electrode because of the metal-electrolyte interface, it is best to select both electrodes to be made of the same material. The difference measured between them will be relatively small and dependent essentially on the actual difference of ionic potentials measured between the two points. If the two electrodes are different, however, it is possible that a significant d.c. voltage may be produced, which could cause current to flow through the electrodes as well as through the input circuit of the amplifier to which they are attached. This d.c. voltage, due to the electrode potential difference, is called the electrode *offset voltage*. To diminish the effects of this, as well as to assist in elimination of noise, it has been found that the silver/silver chloride electrode is one of the most stable and preferable types of electrodes for measurement of surface potentials.

An electrode may be represented schematically as a combination of resistances and capacitances in a network known as an *equivalent circuit*. This may be represented by constant values of resistance and capacitance. Unfortunately, the total combination of impedance is rarely, if ever, constant, since it varies with frequency. Furthermore, both the electrode potential and the impedance vary by an effect called polarization. *Polarization* is the result of direct current (d.c.) passing through the metal-electrolyte interface. If the amplifier to which the electrodes are connected has an extremely high input impedance, the effects of polarization, or any other change in electrode impedance, are minimized.

The electrode impedance is also related to the size and type of electrode being used. Large electrodes generally have lower impedances. Surface electrodes may have impedances up to 10 kΩ. Fine-wire electrodes, because of their small surface area, have impedances well up into the megaohm range. For this reason, amplifiers with extremely high input impedances (preferably at least 10 times greater than the electrode impedance) are required to avoid loading the circuit and consequently to minimize the effects of small changes in the impedance generated by the interface of the electrode and the tissue.

ARTIFACTS

Electrodes placed over any muscle group record more than just the electrical activity of that muscle. These deflections from all other sources are called *artifacts*. An artifact may be physiological or instrumental. Artifacts may be so similar to real EMG activity that even the expert may occasionally be deceived. A few of the more common artifacts will be discussed briefly.

EEG Artifact

When recording frontal EMG, as may be the case in relaxation therapy, it is not uncommon to detect electrical discharges from the brain tissue underlying the frontalis musculature. Since most EMG of interest will be above the highest frequencies of EEG (somewhere around 35 Hz), appropriate filtration should eliminate this type of interference.

EKG Artifact

This artifact is usually most noticeable when leads are placed in the upper limb and chest regions. It can mimic H-waves of the conventional EMG, though the periodicity of this artifact usually makes it obvious. Care in the attachment of the ground electrode, as well as keeping a watchful eye for rhythmic interference of this nature, can help obviate this problem.

Pulse Artifact

An electrode placed directly over an artery moves in sympathy with the pulse. This may give rise to a potential and has the typical sphygmogram shape. If the R-wave of the EKG also contaminates the EMG, the resulting picture may resemble an H- or F-wave in the EMG. If all EMG leads show the same artifact, while the ground remains constant, it is possible that the ground electrode should be shifted.

Sweat Artifact

Activity of the sweat glands causes significant changes in potential, and the skin resistance is greatly reduced. This results in large, slow deflections in conventional EMG activity. These low sways and waves may be more pronounced in the forehead region, and caution should be exercised when doing relaxation biofeedback.

Movement Artifact

Gross body movements of the subject produce high-voltage artifacts. Any covering over the patient will enhance this type of artifact. A swaying coat, gown, or drape can produce these high-voltage waves. Gross head movements may be associated with a burst of EMG activity. The difficulty of preventing movement artifacts is greatest in young children or mental patients.

Electrode Artifact

Condenser-like "pops" from improperly applied electrodes may be difficult to distinguish from spike or single motor unit waveforms. When they are in all of the different leads used, the ground lead may be at fault.

Sixty-Cycle Interference Artifact

This is probably the most common and easiest to distinguish from any EMG activity. It can usually be eliminated by proper grounding, and takes the characteristic wave shape, which is easily discernible on an oscilloscope. It is unquestionably the most problematic of all interference signals to eliminate. The best general advice for elimination of 60-cycle noise is thorough and appropriate grounding. If this type of noise persists, an individual with some engineering expertise should be consulted.

SAFETY

In the biofeedback instrumentation commercially available today, it is always necessary to connect the patient to the device using electrodes. The physiological signal being monitored should travel through this connection and generally represents no concern for the welfare of the patient. However, it is possible, if the instrumentation is faulty, that electrical currents from other sources may travel from the instrument to the patient. Should this happen, serious shock hazard is possible. Most instrumentation is designed to avoid this possibility, but under certain circumstances, problems of this nature may arise. If the user inappropriately connects the instrumentation, the potential for such shock hazard is increased. For example, if the output of the feedback device is connected to an oscilloscope that happens to be faulty, it is possible for current from the electrical power main to flow back through this pathway to the patient. Consequently, connections not specifically recommended by the manufacturer should be avoided. The user is strongly encouraged to consult a qualified biomedical engineer or the manufacturer of the instrumentation being used for advice on which connections are safe and which are not.

SUMMARY

Every effort has been made to give the reader a general overview of the basic electronics involved in biofeedback instrumentation. No attempt has been made to be totally comprehensive, since that would require a volume in itself. The present "state of the art" in biofeedback electronics involves microprocessor technology, which is covered elsewhere in this volume (Chapter 32). This basic knowledge should serve to give the reader the tools by which appropriate communication with experts in electronics is possible. The reader is encouraged to seek out such an individual within his/her institution and avail himself or herself of his expertise. For those who would like a more thorough background in some of the principles set forth in this chapter, a list of additional readings is included. For specific problems, the author would be happy to correspond with any interested reader.

Additional Reading

Buban, P. and Schmitt, M. L. *Understanding Electricity and Electronics.* McGraw-Hill, New York, 1969.

Camishion, R. C. *Basic Medical Electronics.* Little Brown, Co., Boston, 1964.

DeMaw, D. (ed.). *The Radio Amateur's Handbook,* 50th ed. American Radio Relay League, Newington, Conn., 1973.

Geddes, L. A. and Baker, L. E. *Principles of Applied Biomedical Instrumentation.* John Wiley and Sons, New York, 1968.

Malmstadt, H. V., Enke, C. G. and Toren, E. C. *Electronics for Scientists.* W. A. Benjamin, New York, 1962.

Offner, F. F. *Electronics for Biologists.* McGraw-Hill, New York, 1967.

Smith, B. V. *Simplifying Electricity.* Bantam Unifact, 1966.

Stacy, R. W. *Biological and Medical Electronics.* McGraw-Hill, New York, 1960.

Strong, P. *Biophysical Measurements.* Tektronix, Inc., Beaverton, Oregon, 1971.

Suprynowicz, V. *Introduction to Electronics for Students of Biology, Chemistry, and Medicine.* Addison-Wesley, Reading, Mass., 1966.

Tammes, A. R. *Electronics for Medical and Biology Laboratory Personnel.* Williams & Wilkins, Baltimore, 1971.

Thomas, H. E. *Handbook of Biomedical Instrumentation and Measurement.* Reston Publishing Co., Reston, Va., 1974.

Upton, M. *Electronics for Everyone.* New American Library, New York, 1959.

Whitfield, I. D. *An Introduction to Electronics for Physiological Workers.* Macmillan, London, 1959.

A: Equipment Needs for Psychotherapists

KIRK E. PEFFER

The combining of two widely divergent disciplines, engineering and psychotherapy, into the technique of biofeedback created a unique jargon barrier. Chapter 30 acquaints the therapist with an elementary knowledge of electronic principles; however, the therapist still may require assistance in reading and deciphering the complex specification sheets supplied by various instrument manufacturers.

The evolution of electronic technology over the past decade has produced smaller components performing increasingly complex electronic functions with less distortion and at lower cost. Microelectronic devices, now the essence of the biofeedback systems, permit more faithful reproduction of the particular physiological event monitored within the proportional working range of the instrument.

BASIC PARAMETERS

Most of the physiological signals discussed in this chapter are electrical potentials generated when positive and negative ions concentrate unequally inside and outside the cell wall. A potential difference is established. In the normal resting state of the cell, its inside is negative with respect to the outside. However, when the cell is activated, the outside becomes negative with respect to the inside—*depolarization*. When the cell regains its stable state, the inside is again negative with respect to the outside—*repolarization*. These produce characteristic voltage wave forms that are detected through sensors (electrodes) placed on or below the surface of the body. (The terms *sensor* and *electrode* are synonymous; the former is less emotion-provoking in psychotherapy settings.)

When the physiological signal is nonelectrical, as in temperature, a transducer is employed to convert it to a corresponding electrical signal.

Most equipment manufacturers supply instruction manuals that describe those factors that affect the accuracy of their instruments. These manuals are usually well written and detail the instruments' specifications, operating characteristics, adjustable functions, variations in feedback type, correct use of sensors, and conditions frequently mistaken for malfunctions. Many patients are somewhat apprehensive about having sensors and wires taped or strapped to their bodies, so it is imperative that the therapist become familiar and confident with the use of his instruments beforehand.

Inherent in all biofeedback usage is the problem of artifact, i.e., a distortion in the desired signal. Each type of device has certain problem areas that affect them more significantly than others and will be discussed in separate instrument sections.

Keeping the instruments in top functioning order is of critical importance. In most instances, developing a maintenance schedule that can detect power changes (e.g., battery weakness), sensor or cable breakage is adequate.

THE OBJECTIVE OF BIOFEEDBACK INSTRUMENTATION

The most important characteristic of an instrument is its sensitivity, which refers to the ability to produce an electrical output that is proportional to the input signal. The sensitivity of each biofeedback instrument is specified according to the unique functions of the particular device.

As an instrument's sensitivity is increased, however, it will also increase its sensitivity to unwanted signals, such as line voltage (110 V

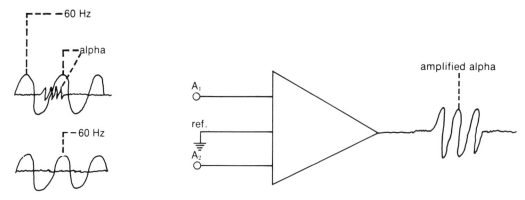

Figure 31.1 The principle of a differential amplifier shown schematically.

or 220 V; 50 or 60 Hz) and artifacts (movement problems, etc.). In order to reduce these problems, the instrument must be highly selective. This means the instrument is capable of discriminating between wanted and unwanted signals. This is accomplished by the use of differential amplifiers with high common-mode rejection ratio (cmrr) and high input impedance (1).

The purpose of a differential amplifier is to reject common-mode signals. Engineers specify common-mode rejection as the ratio of common-mode input to differential input to elicit the same response. Common-mode rejection ratio of 100,000:1 would mean the common-mode signal would have to be 100,000 times as great as a differential signal to produce the same amount of output from the amplifier. Common-mode rejection ratio is usually expressed in decibel (db) rating instead of a ratio. The above example would give a common-mode rejection of -100 db.

A desired physiological signal such as EMG or EEG can be masked by an interference signal, typically EKG and 60 Hz. The goal of the differential amplifier is to reject the interference signal and to amplify the desired signal. Two impedances, Z_1 and Z_2, representing sensor contact impedance, are shown in Figure 31.1. The source of these impedances is the dielectric properties of the skin and the indirect contact of floating electrodes or sensors, which interposes an electrolyte "jelly" or "paste" between the sensor and the skin. Indirect contact sensors produce less movement artifact, and their performance is more predictable than direct contact sensors (1).

Z_1, and Z_2 will usually lie in the range from 1,000–50,000 ohms, and it is typical for the difference between Z_1 and Z_2, with respect to a reference sensor, to be around 10,000 ohms (10 K) (2). Biofeedback instruments have input impedances above 1 megohm, but the sensor impedances Z_1 and Z_2 must be kept low (10 K) and as equal as possible (e.g., $Z_1 = 10$ K, $Z_2 = 9$ K), to allow optimum interference rejection from the differential amplifier. The physiological signal is directed via the sensors to the two input terminals of the differential amplifier and is designated the differential signal. Any interference signal appears on both inputs of the differential amplifier and reference and is referred to as the common-mode signal (Fig. 31.1).

Another important feature required of sophisticated biofeedback instrumentation is linearity, which refers to the ability of an instrument to yield faithful reproduction of a detected signal (2).

The range effectively spans the physiological signal being monitored. For instance, an EEG instrument should have the range to adequately detect all the frequencies the therapist may need in the feedback therapy (2).

Along with the instrument characteristics of sensitivity, selectivity, linearity, and range, an instrument must be stable and reliable.

SURFACE EMG BIOFEEDBACK INSTRUMENTS

The depolarization and repolarization of active muscle and/or nerve cells produce a characteristic voltage wave-form. The voltage appearing between the sensors on the skin is the algebraic sum of all the action potentials (voltages) when the muscle fibers are contracting and recovering near the electrodes. The EMG biofeedback instrument quantifies and gives one or more feedback indications of the amplitude of these complex voltages on the surface of the skin (1).

Sensor or Electrode

The dry outer skin is nonconductive and will not establish an adequate signal-to-sensor continuity unless the skin has been properly prepared to remove the dead horny epidermal layer and body oil. We have found that scrubbing the sites with Brasivol (an acne soap with aluminum oxide particles) reduces the sensor impedance to 10 K or less and makes an excellent connection.

At any sensor-electrolyte-skin interface, the sensor discharges ions into the electrolyte and the ions in the electrolyte combine with the sensor. The result of these reactions is a sensor offset potential (offset voltage) that can adversely affect the performance of the biofeedback unit. Well-designed biofeedback equipment, however, can eliminate the effects of sensor offset potentials (3).

If one changes the sensors supplied with the EMG instrument, one should check with the manufacturer to see if these sensors will be compatible with the particular biofeedback unit.

The sensors consist of a plastic or rubber cup with a metal backing. The cup is filled with an electrolyte "jelly" or "paste" that acts as a bridge between the metal sensor and skin. The sensor is applied to the prepared site and held in place with a rubber strap, length of tape, or adhesive collar.

After the sensors have been securely attached, the effectiveness of the sensor-skin connection can be checked. Some biofeedback units have a built-in sensor impedance test. If not, the connection can be tested with an impedance or ohmmeter. The impedance meter is preferred over an ohmmeter because the ohmmeter introduces a small d.c. voltage and can cause sensor polarization (offset potential) whereas the impedance meter produces an a.c. voltage which eliminates the polarization problem. The cost of an impedance meter, however, is approximately $100 and the ohmmeter can be purchased for under $25. The impedance or ohmmeter test can ensure adequate site preparation and electrical integrity of the sensors and cable.

Manufacturers of EMG instruments typically recommend that the sensor impedance be less than 10 K. This important figure is always stated in the specification sheet of the manufacturer's manual.

The three sensors employed in surface EMG should be closely balanced (e.g., Z_1 10 K, Z_2 = 9 K) to ensure optimum cmrr against unwanted signals (mainly power line voltage at 50 or 60 Hz).

The use of a "dummy subject" that simulates an individual with zero EMG level can be used in place of the sensors to test the clinical environment for strong sources of electrical interference, such as fluorescent lights or other line-operated electrical equipment. Locating the EMG instrument in the lowest (electrical) noise part of the clinic or laboratory will eliminate one of the major interference factors in EMG instrumentation (4). The dummy subject also tests the integrity of the sensor cable. Damaged cable and low battery power are two of the most common equipment difficulties.

Bandwidth

A bandwidth refers to a functional characteristic generated by a filter circuit that eliminates unwanted frequencies and passes the desired frequencies. There is a wide range of bandwidth frequencies currently employed by biofeedback instrument manufacturers.

Although "it is generally agreed that the significant frequency spectrum of muscle action potentials range from 20 Hz to an upper limit of 8,000 to 10,000 Hz . . ." Hayes observed that most of the electrical activity from a number of muscles studied fell in the 30- 100-Hz band and that frequencies above 200 Hz contribute little to the total voltage. He further remarks, however, that the components between 100 and 1000 Hz determine the wave form of the spike potentials sometimes encountered at "low levels of tension" (5).

It would appear then that where 60-Hz, EEG, and EKG artifacts are not paramount, a 30-Hz to 1000-Hz bandwidth is ideal. Where any or all of these artifacts are present to any significant degree, however, a fairly sharp high-pass filter section with a cut-off frequency near 100 Hz has been found to minimize the effects of these artifacts. The roll-off above 1000 Hz can comfortably be 6 db per octave.

Whichever bandwidth is chosen, consistency is most important in order to compare results in one subject, across subjects, and especially if different instruments are used.

Amplitude Quantification

There is a fairly linear correlation between isometric muscle tension and surface EMG voltage amplitude. At least three methods of amplitude measurement are currently being used in biofeedback work:

1. *Average.* The a.c. EMG signal is full-wave rectified and the height of the voltage excursions above 0 are averaged on a short-term or long-term basis. Using a 100–1000 Hz bandwidth, amplitudes around 0.5–1.0 μV average are typical in relaxed muscles while tension headache sufferers may be as high as 10.0 μV before training.

2. *Equivalent Peak-to-Peak Wave* or *Simply "Peak-to-Peak"* (6). If a sine wave is full-wave rectified and averaged, as in Method 1, its average full-wave rectified value will be 0.318 times its peak-to-peak amplitude. If the same bandwidths are used, readings can be converted between methods 1 and 2 by either multiplying or dividing by 0.318. For example, 10 μV p-p × 0.318 = 3.18 μV average.

3. *True RMS (root mean square).* The mathematical process defined by the equation

$$\text{RMS} = \sqrt{1/T \int_0^T e^2 \, dt}$$

is performed on the EMG voltage, e, in the time period O to T. Since e is a nonperiodic, random signal, there is no simple scale factor, which may be to convert RMS to either average or equivalent peak-to-peak amplitude. A scale factor could be arrived at experimentally for a given level of muscle activity, but would most likely be different for a higher or lower level of activity. This is true since the statistics of the EMG voltage vary as a function of tension. An experimental study could be made to determine whether the variation in average to RMS ratio versus EMG level is significant (4).

Input Impedance

It is necessary for the input impedance of the EMG biofeedback instrument to be many times larger than the impedance appearing between the sensors. When a high input impedance is employed, only a small current flows through the sensor impedance, and there is a minimal loss of voltage at the sensor-electrolyte interface. Failure to have high input impedance with respect to the impedance of the small-area sensor can result in a deterioration of the EMG signal. Because of the resistive and reactive components of the sensor-electrolyte impedance, the various components of the EMG signal will not be presented to the EMG biofeedback instrument with the same relative amplitudes and wave forms that they initially possessed (1). A high input impedance helps ensure that the biosignal is not distorted or degraded in any way.

Common-Mode Rejection

Most EMG biofeedback instruments utilize a three-electrode, differential amplifier hookup with the "reference" sensor placed relatively near the two active sensors. The electrical imbalance between either of the actives and the "reference sensor" caused by connecting the sites to an instrument will allow common-mode artifacts of the order of tens of millivolts to be generated by external sources of electrical interference.

A differential amplifier with a cmrr of 80 db or greater will reduce these artifacts to a few tenths of one microvolt as referred to the subject. Cmrrs in the range 70–80 db have been deemed adequate for medical instrumentation of this type. Another source of artifact is the internal (electrical) noise of the instrument that is caused by semiconductor components within the instrument. This noise is somewhat proportional to the noise of the bandwidth. That is, the wider the bandwidth, the greater the noise. For example, a bandwidth of 95–1000 Hz results in noise levels of approximately 1.5 μV peak-to-peak. Since relaxed subjects can attain EMG levels below 2.0 μV peak-to-peak, the noise, unless cancelled, can constitute an error factor in the quantification and in the feedback signal. High-quality EMG systems offer a precise noise measurement cancellation circuit, which separates out the noise factor thus allowing noise-free EMG quantification and feedback (4).

Extremely long input cables, especially if shielded, can degrade the cmrr of the differential amplifier due to capacitive loading. Six-foot input leads are a reasonable compromise between degradation and subject-to-machine distance.

Signal-to-Noise Ratio

It is important to note that as the bandwidth is narrowed, the actual EMG signal level is reduced as well as the noise level i.e., simply reducing the bandwidth in order to decrease the noise level can also degrade the signal-to-noise ratio.

A wider bandwidth such as 95–1000 Hz results in larger noise (electrical), but it also allows a larger EMG signal to be detected and processed. Therefore, a wider bandwidth system can have a better signal-to-noise ratio than some narrow bandwidth systems that have lower noise levels. The signal-to-noise ratio should be specified by db levels in the manufacturer's specification sheets. The higher the db level, the better the signal-to-noise ratio (4).

Accuracy and Resolution

Relaxation training for tension headache patients or even general muscle relaxation require sufficient accuracy to be able to adequately indicate progress from the initial high levels of, say, 20 μV peak-to-peak down to a low-criterion training level of the order 2.0–3.0 μV peak-to-peak. If the subject attained an asymptote training level of 2.6 μV and the machine accuracy was ±10%, the error in the reading would be ±0.26 μV. Much clinical work is carried out with accuracies in the range 50–10%.

Resolution, or the ability of the system to indicate small changes in EMG, should be adequate to give the subject feedback when changes are being made. Here, the numbers may be a few percent. Sometimes too much information received too fast can be unnerving to certain subjects.

Sensitivity

EMG instruments have adjustable sensitivity switches or gain controls to aid in "shaping" the subject from high EMG levels to low-criteria EMG levels (7). These controls allow the EMG instrument to be less or more sensitive to the muscle amplitude so that the subject can discriminate how changes in his muscle physiology correspond to the feedback signal changes and thereby can learn to control muscle tension. The sensitivity control is analogous to the volume control of a television set.

Feedback Modalities

Visual and audible signals are the most widely used feedback modalities, although other possibilities exist. The information conveyed should be meaningful, and the feedback nonaversive. Many subjects find continuous tones above about 1000 Hz displeasing. Sometimes, giving the operators and subjects too

many choices can be confusing. Simplicity in equipment set-up and operation seems to be preferred by most clinicians.

Digital displays require more thinking by the subject in order to interpret trends, but are increasingly popular. They eliminate possible reading errors due to parallax, which is common with meters, and are also generally more accurate (8).

It is my impression that for most low-arousal feedback work, auditory feedback alone is quite effective, and it is usually preferred. There is a variety of auditory analogs used in biofeedback systems. Most instruments provide a click train and/or a tone feedback that increases in frequency as the input signal increases in amplitude.

Safety

Biofeedback units operated from low voltage or battery voltage are quite safe. Low-voltage units employ a "step-down" transformer that plugs into the wall power outlet. Thus, the voltage reaching the unit is stepped down from 120 to 9 V. The larger, more complex units may employ multiple power supplies with the patient-connected circuitry being battery-operated and *electrically isolated* from any nonbattery-operated circuitry. These devices are plugged into wall panels, but the electrical isolation circuitry prevents this high voltage from ever reaching the person.

A good ground rule is: never connect a 120-V a.c.-operated device, such as a tape recorder, to a biofeedback instrument plug or socket that would allow a direct electrical contact to a subject or trainee. An example would be the case where your electronics friend from down the street adds a *tape recorder input* jack to your battery-operated EMG biofeedback unit so that you may play tapes to your subjects along with the audio feedback from the unit. The wall socket-operated tape recorder may develop a short circuit and end up wiring a subject to 120 V! (4)

SKIN-TEMPERATURE BIOFEEDBACK INSTRUMENTS
Definition

A skin-temperature biofeedback instrument quantifies and gives one or more feedback indications of skin temperature at a selected site or sites. The skin temperature is detected by small transducers called thermistors. They convert variations in temperature into signal characteristics that are processed by the biofeedback instrument.

Physiological Substrate

Given an ambient temperature of roughly 72–80°F, the temperature of the skin of the hands and feet is determined primarily by blood flowing through the small arterioles of the skin. The diameter of these small vessels is decreased by increasing sympathetic nervous system activity. Decreasing sympathetic activity increases vasoconstriction and, therefore, lowers skin temperature (9).

Accuracy and Resolution

An absolute accuracy of ±1°F is adequate to indicate progress over a range of possible skin temperatures from 65 to as high as 100°F. A number of users prefer 0.01°F resolution.

Transducer or Probe Response Time

Temperature rates of change as high as 4°F per minute have been observed in good "hand warmers." If the probe response time were 60 seconds, the instrument indication would lag 4°F behind a "super warmer" changing at a continuous 4°F per minute. A small vinyl-type probe, such as the YSI Model 402, with a response time of 3.2 seconds would reduce the tracking error to 3.2/60 × 4 or 0.2°F. A good compromise for most work would appear to be a probe response time in the range of 1 to 2 to 3 seconds (4).

Auditory Feedback of Temperature

Because skin temperature tends to change slowly, the auditory feedback must be such that the ear can detect changes in the sound corresponding to slow changes in the temperature. A unique "chirp" sound produced by one type of temperature feedback unit results from a gated oscillator signal. Both the frequency of the oscillator and the frequency of the gating are proportional to temperature. This "double-wiring" results in a very sensitive type of auditory feedback.

Derivative Feedback

Unlike EMG work, where changes are made faster and can be demonstrated more easily, derivative feedback (or feedback reflecting a rate of change) can be an invaluable aid in temperature training. The subject can make good use of the additional reinforcement received from this form of feedback to get the subtle, slow-moving temperature response under control. Derivative feedback can take the form of either lights, e.g., red for increasing, green for decreasing, or of sound changes.

Digital vs. Analog Displays

The ease of reading a digital display is a definite plus for the operator, while the relaxation-bound subject may relate better to a type of feedback more easily processed, such as auditory feedback. Auditory feedback is an important feature to consider in the purchase of a temperature-feedback instrument. This allows greater flexibility to the therapist.

Safety

Probes are usually electrically isolated from the subject, so battery operation is not a necessity. Battery operation permits a completely portable instrument, although it limits the use of certain power-consuming digital or light-type displays. The use of wall plug-in a.c. to low-voltage d.c. converters (or adapters) affords an additional stage of isolation (via the transformer in the adapter) from 120 V a.c. while allowing more power to be used in the unit without concern about battery drain (4).

EDR BIOFEEDBACK INSTRUMENTS

Definition

An electrodermal-response biofeedback instrument quantifies and gives one or more feedback indications of the electrical conductivity between two selected contact sites on the skin.

Physiological Substrate

Like the peripheral skin "system," the electrodermal response (EDR) is mediated by sympathetic nervous system activity, but, the sweat response, unlike peripheral vasoconstriction, is not maintained by levels of adrenalin in the blood (9).

Measurement Method

Activity of the sweat glands is referred to by one or more of the following terms: electrical skin resistance (ESR), galvanic skin response (GSR), electrodermal response (EDR), or psychogalvanic reflex. "The change in resistance is referred to as the Fere effect on the exosomatic response of the GSR. A decrease in the subject's resistance indicates arousal" (10). GSR measurement by "resistance change" involves the detection of an impedance change between two electrodes on the subject. The GSR primarily changes the resistive (or conversely $1/R = G$, the conductivity) component of this impedance. It is thus important that the measurement technique be insensitive to reactive (usually capacitive) component changes. The simplest technique would appear to be the passage of a d.c. current via the electrodes and the detection of the voltage drop produced between the electrodes due to this current flow. Direct current techniques, however, suffer from artifacts due to electrode polarization. The measurement method, therefore, should be a.c. in nature and as insensitive as possible to the capacitance artifact (11). The parameter sensed is then resistance and may be expressed in the units of resistance, ohms, or megohms (ohms $\times 10^6$), or the reciprocal of resistance, conductance, and its corresponding units, mhos or micromhos (mhos $\times 10^{-6}$). If measured on the palmar surface, between two fingers, with dry, approximately 13 mm-diameter disk electrodes, a relatively dry subject will exhibit about 1 megohm of resistance or 1 micromhos of conductance. A moderately aroused subject will exhibit more than 0.2–0.1 megohm of resistance, and correspondingly 5–10 micromhos of conductance. A subject almost dripping wet will be near 0.04 megohms or 25 micromhos.

Sensors

When recording the GSR or EDR, we record resistance changes due to the action of the sweat glands at the surface of the skin. Thus, electrodes should be used that make direct contact with the skin. The use of any conductive electrode paste would interfere with the action of the sweat glands. The electrodes used should also have no clinical effect on the action of the sweat glands (11).

Parameters Measured

The tonic levels of the EDR is a slow-varying "baseline" from which subjects exhibit spontaneous fluctuations or phasic changes. The changes are bursts of sweating activity followed by refractory periods where the conductivity returns to near the tonic level exhibited before the change. Both the amplitude and time rate of phasic changes may be indications of certain psychological effects (3). A spontaneous fluctuation can be defined in terms of a percentage of change from a given tonic level or an absolute change in ohms or micromhos.

GSR Measurement by Potential Detection

GSR measurement by this technique involves the detection of a d.c. potential between two electrodes on the subject. This d.c. potential will normally be less than 1 mV. An electrode offset potential in excess of 1 mV may be produced at the electrode-subject interface, and any imbalance in the offset potential between the two electrodes cannot be differentiated from GSR potential. Although solid silver electrodes, or perhaps silver-plate electrodes, are used, this offset potential imbalance is difficult to control and will invariably contribute a considerable d.c. potential to the GSR potential. For this reason, GSR measurement by this technique is rarely attempted (3).

The terms EDR (electrodermal response) or EDA (electrodermal activity) are more appropriate designations than the more common term GSR.

Safety

Refer to safety comments under "Surface EMG Biofeedback Instruments" above.

EEG BIOFEEDBACK INSTRUMENTS
Definition

A electroencephalographic biofeedback instrument quantifies and gives one or more feedback indications of the amplitude and/or frequency of complex a.c. voltages on the surface of the scalp in selected frequency bands. The electrical activity within the brain results in various electrical potentials that have been postulated to result from the polarizing effects of the neurons (nerve cells) (12). By placing sensors in various locations around the scalp, a recording of this activity can be obtained. The clinician planning to use EEG should become familiar with the International (10–20) electrode placement as described by Jasper (13). This system gives details of the location for sensor placement over the entire scalp.

Depending on the EEG frequencies of interest to the clinician, the EEG instrument has to amplify the minute surface EEG signals to a level adequate for further processing. The instrument must be capable of rejecting unwanted signals. The input sensors are critical components of the electronic processing and

Table 31.1.
The normal frequency range of the EEG

Hz

0.5–3	=	delta
4–7	=	theta
8–13	=	alpha
12–14	=	sensory motor rhythm
13–28	=	beta
28–40	=	upper beta range

feedback chain. They must conform to rigid electrical specifications if the signals are to be recorded with acceptably low levels of distortion (14).

There may be large sensor offset potentials of the order of many millivolts developed between the scalp and sensor unless suitable sensor-electrolyte material is used. (We have found that Grass or Beckman EEG "paste" applied to silver- or gold-plated sensors is preferable to sponges soaked with an electrolyte.) The high common-mode rejection ratio of the differential amplifier will cancel the common-mode part of the signal, but small movements of the subject's head can cause substantial variations in the sensor potentials. If these potentials are different in each lead, they will appear as differential signals and hence artifact (1).

Another cause of problems in EEG feedback instruments are the electric fields generated by line voltage-driven devices. As was illustrated in the EMG section, the cmrr of the differential amplifier can reduce these signals to an insignificant level—but only if the sensor impedances are low and balanced with respect to the reference (ground) sensor (11).

The EEG signal processing is similar to that discussed in the EMG section.

There is a variety of EEG biofeedback instruments available. Some instruments have set bandwidth filters that detect, quantify, and feed back information only within commonly used frequency bands like alpha (8–13 Hz) and theta (4–7 Hz) (Table 31.1). Other instruments employ adjustable high and low bandwidth filters that can be adjusted by the operator for training in specific frequencies.

The EEG amplitude normally drives a voltage control oscillator that produces an auditory signal that varies as a function of the amplitude. Thus, if a tone is used, the pitch increases or decreases proportionally to the amplitude.

Certain EEG instruments employ a threshold control circuit that can be adjusted to help shape the subject to produce higher amplitude EEG signals (7). The threshold of the instrument is adjusted so that a certain amplitude signal is necessary to activate the feedback signal.

The quantification of the signal is usually in the microvolt range and is read out by a meter, digital display, or percent time meter.

EEG Signal Analysis

Classification and identification of various wave complexes have traditionally been made on the basis of two dimensions, the "frequency" of the signal and its accompanying amplitude. But this definition is clear and most useful for a continuous, periodic signal that has energy in only one part of the frequency spectrum. Since, however, the EEG signal is by nature aperiodic and complex, commonly containing many spectral components at the same time, the strict definition loses meaning in relation to the EEG (11).

Only power-density spectral analysis can provide the total frequency-domain description of a given time segment of an EEG signal sensed between sensors. Such an approach usually requires sophisticated, off-line computer analysis. Current EEG biofeedback instruments are on-stage attempts at obtaining and training specific frequency patterns by means of various types of analog and digital filters, zero-crossing analysis, and frequency-tracking techniques.

Fortunately, some of the applications do not require complex on-line EEG analysis, e.g., some patients may be required to produce energy in the 4- to 7-Hz range with analog bandpass filters (or their digital equivalents). Similarly, some good correlations have been found between the relative energy changes in the alpha bands over left and right hemispheres while subjects are asked to perform tasks that are designed to engage a specific hemisphere.

Epilepsy work with sensorimotor rhythm (SMR) involves the detection of a small (5 V) 14- to 16-Hz signal that must be separated from EMG "noise." These systems also inhibit feedback in the presence of theta (4–7 Hz) frequencies (15).

Some of the "twilight learning" studies by Budzynski and Peffer (16) lean toward the development of adaptive systems. These must not only monitor EEG, but interact with the subject in guiding him through various altered states and present recorded materials based on certain prior conditions.

Noise

Neither 60-Hz interference nor broadband noise is as much a factor in EEG instruments as in EMG. Low-frequency transistor noise, however, can plague an EEG pre-amp that is not properly designed.

Safety

Components regarding safety for EEG were covered under the section on EMG instruments. The connection of EEG instruments to other devices may in some cases be more likely than for EMG or EDR—especially if more sophisticated computer analysis of the composite EEG signal is desired.

CLINICAL SET-UP OF BIOFEEDBACK INSTRUMENTS

Some clinicians prefer to have the biofeedback equipment placed on a table or equipment cart near the client. Other clinicians have the equipment separated from the client by means of separate instrument and client rooms, with communication carried out via an intercom or microphones.

Clinicians may want to feed back more than one modality at a time and/or use voice or taped material. This requires the use of a mixer unit that can combine any selection of auditory signals at the discretion of the clinician.

COMPUTER INTERFACE WITH BIOFEEDBACK INSTRUMENTS

The application of computer interface with biofeedback instrumentation has gained strong interest among clinicians and researchers. The microcomputer and minicomputer have numerous applications with biofeedback instrumentation interfaces. The applications depend on the needs, creativity, and budget requirements of the clinician or researcher. For more details, see Chapter 32, which follows.

References

1. Geddes, L. and Baker, L. *Principles of Applied Biomedical Instrumentation*, 2nd ed. John Wiley and Sons, New York, 1975.
2. Offner, F. *Electronics for Biologists*. McGraw-Hill, New York, 1967.
3. Cromwell, L., Weibell, F., Pfeiffer, E. and Usselman, L. *Biomedical Instrumentation & Measurement*. Prentice-Hall, Englewood Cliffs, N.J., 1973.
4. Picchiottino, J. *Biofeedback Electronics*. Unpublished manuscript, 1977.
5. Grossman, W. I. and Weiner, H. Some factors affecting the reliability of surface electromyography. Psychosom. Med., 28: 78–83, 1966.
6. Budzynski, T., Stoyva, J. and Adler, C. Feedback-induced muscle relaxation: application to tension headache. J. Behav. Ther. Exp. Psychiatry, 1: 205–211, 1970.
7. Budzynski, T. H., Stoyva, J. M. and Peffer, K. E. Biofeedback techniques in psychosomatic disorders. In *Handbook of Behavioral Intervention*, edited by A. Goldstein and E. Foa. John Wiley and Sons, New York, 1980.
8. Brown, J., Jacobs, J. and Stark, L. *Biomedical Engineering*. F. A. Davis, Philadelphia, 1971.
9. Greenfield, N. and Sternback, R. *Handbook of Psychophysiology*. Holt, Rinehart and Winston, New York, 1972.
10. Hastrup, J. and Katkin, E. Electrodermal lability: an attempt to measure its psychological correlates. Psychophysiology, 13: 1976.
11. Strong, P. *Biophysical Measurements*. Tektronix Measurement Concepts, Tektronix, Inc. Part Number 062-1247-00, 1970.
12. Brown, P., Maxfield, B. and Moraff, H. *Electronics for Neurobiologists*. The MIT Press, Cambridge, Mass, 1973.
13. Jasper, H. International Federation of Societies for Electroencephalography and Clinical Neurophysiology. Appendix IV. The 10-20 Electrode System of the International Federation. EEG Clin. Neurophysiol., vol. 10, 1958.
14. Ferris, C. *Introduction to Bioelectrodes*. Plenum Press, New York, 1974.
15. Sterman, M. and Friar, L. Suppression of seizures in an epileptic following sensorimotor EEG feedback training. Electroencephalogr. Clin. Neurophysiol., 33: 89–95, 1972.
16. Budzynski, T. and Peffer, K. Twilight-state learning: A biofeedback approach to creativity and attitude change. Paper presented at the Transformations of Consciousness Conference, sponsored by the R. M. Bucke Memorial Society and the Department of Psychiatry, McGill University, Montreal, Canada, 1973.
17. David J. E. *Digital Circuits and Microcomputer*. Prentice-Hall, Englewood Cliffs, N.J., 1980.

B: Supplementary Equipment Needs in Rehabilitation

C. KUMARLAL FERNANDO

The equipment needs in the rehabilitation setting depend on the kinds of patients seen. We must consider the types of patients, the treatment techniques, and their relation to the equipment needs in this chapter. Patients in a rehabilitation setting generally are stabilized in their vital signs, and they are in this setting for more vigorous and planned rehabilitation therapeutic strategies. Hence, feedback techniques are an adjunct to all the other therapies. The kind of problems to be treated has a bearing on the type of equipment that will be needed.

Patients referred for audiovisual neuromuscular reeducation techniques should not be treated without prior evaluation, as pointed out by Jacobson (1), who called his early technique electroneuromyometry. We use an *evaluation form* to provide a baseline of the patient's status at his first evaluation session. The treatment procedures are designed after this evaluation is complete.

For ideal evaluation, we believe that the electromyography (EMG) unit should have an oscilloscope to verify that motor unit action potentials are recorded and not artifacts. Many therapists have come to erroneous conclusions regarding feedback therapy because they lack an EMG unit with an oscilloscope for the evaluation processes. Errors could have been avoided if the therapist had had an oscilloscope, which allows the therapist to differentiate artifact from muscle action potentials.

ELECTRODES (SENSORS)

There are many different types of surface electrodes. However, the ideal surface electrode is the silver/silver chloride electrode (example—Beckman electrodes). The size may vary from very small to quite large—usually they are about 1 × 2.5 cm (2). This type of silver electrode "minimizes movement artifacts and is excellent for long-term monitoring of activity, i.e., exercises" (2). In our practice, we continue to use this Beckman type of electrode with very good results.

The preparation of the patient for applying the electrodes should be meticulously followed so that the impedance between the electrodes and the skin can be reduced. This is best accomplished by washing and abrading the skin and applying electrode jelly to the electrodes. If properly prepared, the electrical resistance at the electrode-skin interface can be lowered to 3000 ohms (3).

Both pick-up electrodes should be of the same size. The pick-up and the ground electrodes should be made of the same material. This is done for the purpose of keeping the noise levels low. The leads connecting the electrodes to the equipment should be shielded to minimize electrical interference from outside sources.

AMPLIFIER

A differential amplifier is essential in EMG feedback work as it permits amplification of the "minute muscle potentials even in the presence of large interfering voltages of power-line frequency" (4). The other characteristic features of a differential amplifier used for EMG feedback are (a) high and uniform gain for all frequencies within its slated range—usually from 100–1000 Hz; (b) high cmmr—at least 80 db; (c) high input impedance—EMG feedback instrumentation of very high impedance (100–1000 times electrode impedance) is desirable; and (d) low inherent noise—.5 μV or less.

BAND-PASS FILTERING

The frequency range used for EMG feedback in rehabilitation is from 100–1000 Hz. However, modern equipment uses band-pass filters to eliminate on-line frequency. High-pass (low-frequency cutoff) filters of 95 or 100 Hz are used in many commercial devices to reject electrocardiac and 60-Hz artifacts. Another reason to provide band-pass at 100–200 Hz and 400–500 Hz is to improve artifact rejection, signal-to-noise ratio, and to control the radius of transmission characteristics.

These features will lower noise levels of the unit so that deep muscles can be recorded effectively. Different instruments use different bandwidths to optimize the signal-to-noise ratio. However, there is no scientific evidence to determine which bandwidth is more effective for EMG feedback techniques. Generally, it is accepted that a frequency range from 100–1000 Hz is satisfactory.

DATA ACQUISITION CENTER

For baseline studies and research purposes, EMG feedback units incorporated with a data collection center is recommended. We use the Cyborg System R830 with a Q740 for data acquisition. Other more sophisticated systems are available with microprocessors where one can get a printout of the integrated EMG signals over a given period of time.

CLINICAL APPARATUS FOR EVALUATION

For evaluation purposes, the EMG feedback unit should include a single- or, preferably, a double-channel oscilloscope. Our equipment includes a TECA Model B2 and TE4, and a Cyborg R830 Biofeedback, which incorporates a 2-channel Techtronics oscilloscope with storage facilities. These evaluation models can also be used for treatment purposes, although the TECA EMG diagnostic equipment is not designed for treatment. Diagnostic devices have a frequency response range of 20–10,000 Hz and hence a higher sensitivity to ambient electrical interference compared with equipment specially built for feedback techniques. Yet, for many types of patients referred for EMG feedback techniques, diagnostic equipment is adequate.

TWO-CHANNEL SYSTEMS

These systems are really no different from those used for evaluation. They should all incorporate an oscilloscope with two channels, with two different audio signals. The equipment is used with patients who have upper motor neuron lesions resulting in different amounts of tonus in the agonists and the antagonists. Thus, the therapist can monitor the activity of two groups of muscles at the same time and modify treatment accordingly. Patients with spasmodic torticollis and those being trained for use of myoelectric prostheses can also benefit from using this approach.

OTHER TYPES OF FEEDBACK EQUIPMENT

In addition to EMG feedback equipment, there are several other kinds of feedback devices. As Herman (6) pointed out: "A number of sensory aid systems have been designed as therapeutic training devices to assist the patient in the conscious control of locomotion and posture and of abnormal muscle tone (i.e., spasticity)."

LIMB-LOAD MONITOR

Herman (5) described a load-sensing monitor presently being used in patients with both musculoskeletal (e.g., amputations and arthrotomies) and neurological (e.g., cerebrovascular accidents, neuropathies) disorders: (a) for precise monitoring of partial weightbearing, (b) to provide an orderly progression in control of incremental weightbearing, (c) for sustaining maximal weightbearing, and (d) to regulate postural and equilibrium responses. The results suggest that sensory feedback training during locomotion induces more precise and sustained responses that can be attained by traditional methods utilizing patient-therapist interactions. It also provides therapeutic practice (i.e., self-monitoring of performance) for periods of time considerably longer than can be effected or implemented by the therapist.

HEAD-POSITION TRAINER

Various types of head-control units are now available. They are mainly used to gain head position with children diagnosed with cerebral palsy, torticollis, and habitual head tilt. A head-position trainer designed and used by the Hugh MacMillan Children's Rehabilitation Centre in Toronto is commercially available. It consists of a cluster of mercury switches, an electronic buzzer, and a pair of earphones. When the child's head exceeds a preset angle, a mercury switch activates the buzzer—audio-feedback—in one or both earphones. A lateral error activates only one earphone on the appropriate side. Errors forward and backwards activate both earphones. In addition, a radio can also be played through the earphones. An error turns the radio off and activates the appropriate buzzer(s). The buzzer can be kept off by a switch if it is not desired. An output jack, which can be used to control other peripheral devices such as a TV or an electric train for motivational reasons, is provided.

A similar unit called the *head-position monitor (HPM)* has been developed at the Krusen Center for Research and Engineering (Philadelphia) in an attempt to provide augmented sensory feedback information regarding movement and position of the head in relation to the gravitational vertical. The battery-operated unit consists of a transducer, auditory feedback display, and a control box. The transducer is a beam accelerometer that senses the gravitational field to determine the angle of the head with respect to the vertical. It is housed in a lightweight polypropylene helmet that is worn on the head and that also contains the earphones that provide the auditory feedback signal.

The helmet is connected to a control box by a cable. The box provides the circuitry for comparing the actual head position with a preselected desired head position, and for generating the auditory feedback when the head is positioned outside of the threshold area. The threshold can be selected individually for each child. In addition, the control box functions as a portable data collection unit, recording on a visual, digital readout the time spent within the threshold, the number of threshold crossings, and the total operating time. In this manner, objective performance data are available immediately to the child and the therapist, and the information can be used to document current ability and rate of skill improvement.

The HPM can be operated without auditory feedback for assessment purposes. To encourage young children to continue practicing the headrighting and stabilizing skill, the unit may be connected to a television, radio, or electrical toy so that the item operates only when the head is positioned within the threshold area.

JOINT-POSITION TRAINERS

Feedback units designed and used at the Hugh MacMillan Children's Centre, the Krus-

en Center for Research and Engineering, and Emory University's Center for Rehabilitation Medicine are used to provide information about the position of a specific joint. With them in place, one can train patients to overcome hyperextension or excessive flexion of the knees. They also have been used for gait training in cerebrovascular accident patients. Control of jaw closure and drooling in patients with cerebral palsy and abnormal hip rotation are other applications. In essence, the subject is provided with an audible tone, the frequency of which is proportional to the angle of the joint. (This in itself may not be very useful since it is difficult to relate the frequency of an audible tone with a particular joint angle or range of movement.)

The unit developed by the Krusen Center is a knee-angle monitor consisting of two parts: a knee electrogoniometer (Elgon), which detects angular position, and a control box, which provides the auditory signal as a pitch proportional to the angular position. The control box is worn on a belt at the waist and is connected to the electrogoniometer by a coaxial cable. The knee-angle monitor may be used during ambulation, for standing exercise, or during sitting, lying prone, or side-lying positions. The chosen position depends upon the patient's tolerance and the treatment goal.

A dial on the front of the elgon is marked in degrees, and a pointer that rotates around the perimeter of the dial indicates angular position.

References

1. Jacobson, E. *Modern Treatment of Tense Patients,* p. 17. Charles C Thomas, Springfield, Ill., 1970.
2. Goodgold, J. and Eberstein, A. *Electrodiagnosis of Neuromuscular Diseases,* p. 54. Williams & Wilkins, Baltimore, 1972.
3. Basmajian, J. V. *Muscles Alive, Their Functions Revealed by Electromyography,* 3rd ed. p. 58. Williams & Wilkins, Baltimore, 1974.
4. Rogoff, J. B. and Reiner, S. Electrodiagnostic Apparatus. In *Electrodiagnosis and Electromyography,* 3rd ed., edited by S. Licht, p. 48. New Haven, 1971.
5. Herman, R. Augmented sensory feedback in the control of limb movement. Presented at a symposium sponsored by Moss Rehabilitation Hospital, Philadelphia, 1973.

CHAPTER 32

Computers in Biofeedback

DAVID A. PASKEWITZ

Technology has progressed to the point where many individual instruments employ computers within them as part of their circuit design, even though the computers are both invisible and unsuspected by the casual user (1, 2). One of the most pervasive technological breakthroughs has been the availability of high-powered microprocessor circuits on a single chip, a development whose impact is still just beginning to become apparent within the medical and psychophysiological instrumentation field. This chapter will discuss some applications which older, more expensive systems have met, point to some recent trends in the use of microprocessors and microprocessor-based systems, and suggest some practical considerations in the use of computers in biofeedback research and clinical practice.

At present, the issue is less a question of being able to afford a computer than it is a question of getting the most powerful and flexible system one can for the funds available. A second issue, and one to which we will return shortly, concerns the price and availability of the software necessary to fulfill a particular application.

BASIC COMPUTER CONCEPTS

Before discussing applications, it may be useful to discuss briefly some basic computer concepts and terms that will be used later. Computer elements are typically divided into two major categories, hardware and software. The hardware refers to the cabinets, wires, boards, and electronic components that make up the visible part of the computer system. The principal hardware components of any computer system are the central processing unit (CPU), memory (storage), and input or output (I/O) devices.

The CPU is the part of the computer which, as the name implies, processes data from the rest of the system. It typically contains temporary storage locations, called registers, within which and between which data may be manipulated according to some predetermined set of instructions. These manipulations may include storage, retrieval, addition, subtraction, testing the outcome of previous operations, etc. The CPU is responsible for retrieving and interpreting the next instruction, finding and retrieving the data to be manipulated, and, often, changing its order of instructions based on the results of the manipulation. The microprocessor is, in effect, an entire CPU on one small chip of silicon within a single small package.

Storage within a computer system may take several forms. All data (and instructions, too!) within the computer must ultimately be reduced to a pattern of on and off signals, rather like a row of light switches on a wall. This binary (two-state) pattern may be stored in a set of semiconductor memory cells or in magnetic cores, each with a unique address, where it can later be retrieved by the CPU, or the pattern may be written onto various kinds of magnetic tape, spinning magnetic disks, or punched as holes on cards or paper tape. Although semiconductor or magnetic core memories are usually located within the main computer cabinet, the other forms of storage are usually not, and are thus termed "peripheral" storage.

In addition to the storage and manipulation of data, some method must be provided to put data and/or instructions into the computer and to get back the results of computer operations. Input/output devices supply these functions in a computer system. Input may be from a keyboard or switch, where pressing the key generates a recognizable pattern of data. Some intermediate storage may be involved, as in the case of punched paper tape or punched cards. Other inputs may involve pulses indicating the passage of a certain amount of time, coded data representing the voltage at a particular point in a circuit at a particular time (analog-to-digital conversion), or the simple occurrence of an event (heart-beat, switch closure, etc.). In biofeedback situations, the primary data usually involve time, voltage levels, and events, or some combination of these inputs. The results of the computer operations may be reported to the user in a number of ways as well. They may be displayed on a TV-like CRT (cathode ray tube) display, either in alphanumeric or in graphic form. They may similarly be printed out on some type of printer, of which many kinds have been developed. If graphic, the results may be plotted, giving a permanent "hard copy." Using a form of output known as digital-to-analog conversion, the computer may output a constant or changing voltage level that can move a meter needle, or that may be used to modulate the amplitude or frequency of a tone signal. The computer can also put out on-off signals that can turn on or off any number of devices or processes.

Software

Impressive as the computer hardware is, this hardware is absolutely useless without the sequence of instructions that direct the manipulation of data within the computer. These differing sequences of instructions are known as "programs" or, collectively, as "software." Without this software, the computer cannot manipulate data at all; it has no way of knowing the necessary sequence of operations to achieve a desired result. The most basic level of instructions is the various combinations of bits that translate directly into the operations of the CPU registers and data paths, known as the "instruction set" of a particular CPU. Programming a computer at this level of instructions is difficult, and so programs have been written that use the computer itself to decode more easily understood concepts and phrases into a sequence of instructions that the computer can execute. These programming languages range from very simple ones that are close to the computer's instruction set, called "assemblers," to very complex and powerful languages like BASIC, FORTRAN, APL, PASCAL, FORTH, C, ADA, and the like. These higher-level languages let the programmer express his or her desires in broad, English or algebra-like statements. The computer then breaks down these statements into a series of simpler operations that can be sequentially executed. Such large-scale programs will

usually include methods for obtaining and storing a wide variety of data, as well as the means for printing, plotting, or displaying the data.

Computer Systems

The CPU, together with the other hardware, both central and peripheral, form a computer system. In addition, however, it is increasingly common to find that software must be included in considerations of a particular system, both in terms of the operation of the hardware and by virtue of the fact that unlike minicomputers, most microprocessor-based "personal" computer systems contain complete high-level languages (usually BASIC) and/or operating systems—programs to manage disk storage or to interact with a CRT terminal, for instance) in read-only memory (ROM). Although the inclusion of such programs is usually considered a major advantage, it can have drawbacks in biofeedback applications (3).

This need to consider an integrated system can be further extended to include the issue of availability of the kinds of storage and I/O devices needed for a particular application. If, for example, a high resolution analog-to-digital (A/D) converter is necessary to process galvanic skin response (GSR) data, then either such a converter must be available or it must be specially constructed. In the latter case, the ease of interfacing with the basic system, both hardware and software, becomes paramount. Some manufacturers appear to prefer keeping the details of their systems a secret, which makes such interfacing much more difficult.

Basically, the more completely integrated a system is, the easier it is for the inexperienced, novice computer user to successfully apply it to a particular problem without difficulty. This ease of use comes, however, at the expense of flexibility and more general applicability. As an example, a commercially available blood pressure monitor contains a microprocessor with memory, a timer, an A/D converter, several 8-bit parallel inputs and outputs, and software in ROM. The user need only apply the blood pressure cuff and turn on the power switch to operate the device. While simple and effective, the monitor does not store or average the pressures obtained, or, indeed, process the data further than simply displaying three pressure values and heart rate. The same sequence of operations could be performed by a suitably interfaced PDP-11 minicomputer that could, in addition, store the data from one or a large number of subjects, perform summary statistics, and generate graphs or reports. The user of such a system would, however, be faced with the task of becoming familiar with all of the commands and responses necessary to invoke the programs that obtained the blood pressure values, a task somewhat more difficult and error-prone than simply throwing a switch. Both approaches, and many intermediate levels of integration, are valid, and there are many examples of programs written to make flexible, general-purpose systems more "user-friendly" by restricting the number of decisions necessary and by providing recognition of common errors and appropriate responses to them.

COMPUTERS AND BIOFEEDBACK

The use of computers in biofeedback applications began before the term was coined, and has continued until the present time. A number of studies have been conducted with the aid of minicomputers or larger, mainframe computer systems. Much of the work in heart rate control has been computer-based, for example, and much of the work in the analysis and control of EEG activity has used computers, particularly in regard to the more complex multivariate analyses. Computer applications such as these and many others can be conveniently divided into two primary categories: (1) signal processing and experimental control, and (b) data collection and display.

Signal Processing and Experimental Control

One of the most valuable aspects of computer use in the biofeedback context is the ability of the computer to consider sequential and simultaneous values and to evaluate the relationship between those values. Such processing may range from relatively simple decisions such as the question, "Is the voltage on input A greater than zero volts?" all the way to transformations of arrays of data representing varying voltage measurements over time from the time to the frequency domain, such as might occur in the analysis of EEG data.

The vast majority of biofeedback applications involving signal processing intend the processing to take place in "real time," that is, such that the results of the processing are immediately available for use by the individual generating the signals. It is of little use in an experimental or treatment situation to have the processed data available only after a delay of hours or days if the data are to be used as "biological feedback." The principal consideration in real-time signal processing is the relationship between the quantity of data that must be processed within a given time and the speed and power of the computer system to be used. Ideally, the computer system should be chosen to process the data without pressing its abilities to the limit. On the other hand, dedicating a powerful computer to performing very simple signal processing, while possible, is an inefficient use of resources. The considerations that enter into the choice of a computer involve both hardware and software.

In terms of hardware, the speed of the CPU, memory, and data input hardware (A/D conversion time, for instance) all affect the ability of the system to perform signal processing. It may, for example, be possible to use a slow 8-bit microprocessor to produce an output voltage related to the number of milliseconds between successive EKG R-Waves. On the other hand, the production of a similar voltage based on the average amplitude of EEG activity from several sites within a certain frequency range may tax the ability of a much faster 16-bit minicomputer. Obviously, if the data must be stored, displayed, or further manipulated then the capacity and speed of any devices used for these purposes further affect the ability of the system to process signals in real time.

In addition to hardware considerations, the software used to process the signals can drastically affect the ability of the system to deal with real-time data. The ROM-based BASIC languages that come with most of the small computers, and many of the other small computer languages as well, are "interpretive" languages—that is, they read the program and translate it into the processor's instruction set as the program is running. This translation process takes time, however, and these languages are relatively slow in their execution. In addition, because they are included as a permanent part of the system, they often have clumsy ways of dealing with peripheral devices, especially unique or unusual devices. Sometimes, special machine language programs must be furnished to take the place of the BASIC language operations, and even then, certain types of interactions with the peripheral devices may be difficult or impossible unless the entire program is written in machine language. On the other hand, if the requirements for processing are modest, the language furnished with the computer is usually simple and easy to use.

Another sort of language implementation involves the use of what is called a "compiler." This compiling process translates the original program into either machine language or into some intermediate type of code that the computer can execute quickly. These programs run much more rapidly, but are usually more difficult to produce in the first place. The fastest program to execute is one written directly in the computer's own instruction set. Such a program is usually the most difficult by far to produce, however, but such an effort may be justifiable if the signal processing requirements are extensive.

Data Collection and Display

The second principal use for computers in the biofeedback context has involved their use as collectors, averagers, storage managers, and display generators for data that may have been processed by other special-purpose hardware and that may be presented to the computer in a relatively simple and complete form. The hardware that processes the signals initially may be a custom device, a biofeedback instrument in its own right, or even another computer, programmed to process and deliver the data to the central computer for storage or display. Given the low cost of microprocessor hardware, this latter combination is likely to become more prevalent in the future. Additionally, special-purpose display processors and mass storage controllers are increasingly available to perform these functions. In most cases, however, a single microcomputer will suffice to both store and display the incoming data.

When considering the collection and storage of data, the specific quantity and rate of data input are the prime concerns. If data are to be stored in raw form, that is, without averaging or other reduction, then sufficient memory space must be available for all of the data, the program, and any display buffer space needed. The amount of available memory space in some computers is limited, and data may have to be written to some peripheral storage device at regular intervals. Although such a procedure has the added advantage of protecting the data from loss should a power failure occur,

each access to peripheral storage takes a finite amount of time and interrupts the data collection process. If the data are averaged, of course, storage requirements may be greatly reduced. This averaging process may itself take some time, and the time available for storage and/or data reduction depends, in turn, on the rate of data input. Both the rate and quantity of data grow rapidly if several different channels or several different sites are involved.

One of the most exciting aspects of the microcomputer revolution affecting biofeedback is the quality of the displays that can be generated with many of the currently available computer systems. Indeed, some of the earliest applications of "personal" computers to biofeedback were in the area of the simultaneous display of several physiological parameters. The creative use of computer display graphics has also resulted in representations of the feedback data that capture and hold attention and enhance personal involvement. These displays are particularly effective when working with children.

Various types of display options are available, depending on the design of the computer system and the skill of the programmer. The simplest form of display involves the use of the standard alphanumeric character set available from the computer or on an attached video terminal. These displays are usually limited in resolution to the number of character positions on the screen, often 80×24, 40×24, 64×20, or about 1920 characters maximum, and are limited to the characters available on the standard typewriter keyboard. The ability to position the cursor (character pointer) randomly at any character position on the screen (termed "direct cursor addressing") and high-speed character transmission can allow for rather good dynamic display characteristics. Some computer manufacturers have augmented this basic text display ability by allowing additional attributes such as inverse (black on white) or flashing for each character. Many also provide a graphics character set, which is selected just like the standard keyboard characters, but where the character represents a shape that can be incorporated into pictures (a solid square or an upside-down "T," for instance).

A higher-resolution graphics display may be achieved by individually setting each dot on the display screen. If, for example, the screen has 40 × 24, or 960 character positions, each consisting of a 7 × 8 dot matrix, the screen can display up to 280 × 192, or 53,760 individual points. Even if each memory location stores several dots, however, the total memory need for this higher resolution display far exceeds the 960 locations needed to store the equivalent screen full of characters. In addition, software must be available to set and clear the individual bits. The complexity of this software depends on the hardware used to generate the display, as does the speed with which displays may be created and changed. A discrete display processor with its own display memory, separate from the main computer memory, can significantly simplify and speed up the display process.

Color display capability is another enhancement offered by some computer systems. This feature adds to the legibility of complex displays, as well as increases display attractiveness. The addition of color is not without drawbacks, however. An added expense is involved in providing a color monitor rather than the usual black-and-white monitor. Top-quality color demands an RGB (red-green-blue) monitor and special circuitry, although a standard color TV and radio-frequency modulator are adequate for most purposes.

PRACTICAL CONSIDERATIONS

Very few individuals will be prepared to purchase a large minicomputer system, but many are considering or will consider the purchase of one of the smaller "personal" computer systems. The complete hardware system will cost less than $5000, perhaps even less than $3000, and will include an 8-bit CPU with display, one or more 5¼" diskette drives, keyboard, and a printer, probably dot-matrix. The first question asked by most individuals contemplating the purchase of a computer is whether or not they need one. The answer to this question involves several considerations. One consideration is the specific use or uses for the computer. What problems should it solve? Will it allow something to be done that is not possible now? What current method will it replace?

The case in which the computer will significantly enhance or initiate some capability involves the simplest decision. In this case, the need is apparent, and the primary considerations are those of choosing the system that best meets task requirements. Many times, how-

ever, the hope is that the computer will not only add capabilities, but will streamline and simplify current procedures. An example is the purchase of a "personal" microcomputer to collect data from several biofeedback instruments, electromyography (EMG), skin temperature, and skin conductance, for instance, and create a dynamic bar-graph display based on normal levels of activity. A clinician who buys such a system probably hopes to keep track of patient billing, as a word processor to write and maintain patient notes and correspondence, as a storage medium for session summary data, and perhaps even as a means of delivering and scoring psychological tests and inventories. These hopes are not far-fetched, but some realistic appraisal of the range of uses must be made. The capacity of the system needed to meet all these applications and, particularly, the type and number of peripheral devices that will be required are based on this appraisal.

Another important consideration is the need for several independent operations to be carried out simultaneously. This "multi-tasking" or "multi-user" capability seldom comes without the added expense of a larger, more sophisticated, and more expensive system. It is sometimes more effective and less expensive to buy several small systems, each tailored and dedicated to a specific task.

The particular hardware to be purchased will depend on the *maximum* anticipated speed and capacity. Almost any of the popular, low-cost computer systems will meet modest needs for data collection, storage, and display. If dynamic, high-resolution color displays are necessary, some models are better suited than others to this task. Signal processing requirements may demand higher speed and/or greater capacity, in addition to the availability of hardware suitable for signal input. It may be necessary in some cases to step up to a 16-bit micro- or minicomputer with its greater speed, power, and memory capacity to meet storage or signal-processing needs.

Except for the simplest of applications, where a ROM-based microcomputer may be part of a special-purpose device, or when one program may be run again and again and no data are stored, some form of disk storage is a must. This storage will usually consist of one or more 5¼" mini-floppy disk drives, connected to the computer through a programmed interface and some form of DOS (disk operating system). The need for higher speed and/or greater disk capacity may lead to the purchase of 8″ floppy disks or a "hard" disk, which is sealed against contamination and revolves at a much faster speed than the floppies.

In addition to the computer with its terminal or display and some form of disk storage, most users will want a printer. The most cost-effective printers are dot-matrix, where characters are formed by striking a row of wires through the ribbon to the paper as the print head moves along. Many of these printers have added features such as expanded and compressed type styles, alternative character fonts (italic or graphic characters, for example), or dot graphics. If high-quality print is a requirement, formed-character printers such as those using "Daisy wheels" can be added, although the prices for these printers tend to run somewhat higher than for the dot-matrix type, and their speed is somewhat slower (15–45 characters per second vs. 80–120 characters per second).

Important as the hardware aspects of any anticipated computer purchase may be, the software considerations are, if anything, even more important. When standard software packages can be used, in the case of bookkeeping, word processing, or the like, the user need only be aware of what software is available for the intended system to pursue his needs. In this respect, the more popular the system chosen, the more likely there are to be software packages already written for a particular application. The more specialized the application, the more likely it is that the user must at least modify existing software, if not change completely, to produce a unique application software package. In this case, the existence of several language options, including both interpretive and compiled versions of higher-level languages, together with the necessary editing and file-handling utility programs become of relatively high importance.

Software availability is frequently given too little attention in planning for the acquisition of a computer. Even with the current dramatic reduction in hardware costs, a cardinal rule of thumb concerning costs still applies—functioning, effective software will cost at least as much as the hardware, if not in money, certainly in time. When software must be modified or created from the beginning, the question then becomes, Who will write the software?

Relatively simple modifications in existing software packages can often be made by the user, provided the original author made provisions for such modifications, or that the software is sufficiently easy to understand and simple to modify (changing several lines in a BASIC program, for instance). All too frequently, software vendors provide only a machine-language version of the software, and may even resort to disk scrambling or other copy protection schemes to prevent software "pirates" from stealing their work. Unfortunately, such procedures make any customization or minor modification very difficult, although few difficulties exist for those who can use the software as supplied.

Major modifications of existing software or the creation of a new software package is a job that few users are prepared to handle. The effort involved in writing, testing, and documenting software is both exacting and time-consuming. Nevertheless, many users do write their own applications software; you must be prepared to learn a great deal about the hardware and the existing software for your computer.

Another alternative is to hire a programmer to write or modify software. In this case, be sure to get someone familiar both with the language you plan to use and the specific make of your computer. It also helps, of course, if the programmer knows something about your application and how the software will be used. Such programmers range from students to computer professionals, and their services are priced accordingly.

If the computer is replacing another method for collecting data, analysis, carrying out office procedures, etc., you can expect a period of little or no productivity while the computer is being introduced. Even the most reliable computers and the most sophisticated programs require some period of adjustment, and custom software is even more likely to produce initial errors (4, 5).

In spite of all these issues, computers are powerful tools for those who learn to use them effectively. Although a computer alone will not solve problems, and may even create a few new ones, more and more people will use computers to help them solve their problems. For many, computers are either expensive toys or unbelievably complex machines. For others, the choice has been dictated by the complexity of the problems they address, and they cannot accomplish their goals without using a computer. But for many others, the choice is a difficult one. Some helpful references are available (6), but careful research, thought, and planning are the keys to making such decisions wisely.

References

1. Klosterhalfen, W. A. A computer-controlled cardiotachometer. Behav. Res. Methods Instrumentation, *12*: 58–62, 1980.
2. Pottinger, H. J., Hughes, C. W., Schroeder, P., Barefield, A. and Craigmile, J. C. A microcomputer-based cardiotachometer with video display. Behav. Res. Methods Instrumentation, *13*: 227–234, 1981.
3. Kaplan, H. L. Traditional minicomputers: a continuing role in the laboratory. Behav. Res. Methods Instrumentation, *13*: 213–215, 1981.
4. Kieras, D. E. Effective ways to dispose of unwanted time and money with a laboratory computer. Behav. Res. Methods Instrumentation, *13*: 145–148, 1981.
5. Mayer, R. E. My many mistakes with microcomputers (or four years of fun trying to get my computer to run). Behav. Res. Methods Instrumentation, *13*: 141–144, 1981.
6. Reed, A. V. On choosing an inexpensive microcomputer for the experimental psychology laboratory. Behav. Res. Methods Instrumentation, *12*: 607–613, 1980.

CHAPTER 33

Feedback Goniometers for Rehabilitation

GARY DeBACHER

A goniometer is any device for measuring angles. Clinical goniometers are simple hinged devices (Fig. 33.1) useful only for spot measurement of joint angles. The need to measure continuously changing joint angles to analyze complex motion or to correlate joint angle with electromyographic (EMG) activity led to development of electrogoniometers. These usually consist of a hinged mechanical linkage attached to limb segments, which translates joint angle changes into rotation of a potentiometer. Used as a voltage divider, the potentiometer supplies an output voltage linearly proportional to joint angle. This changing voltage can be transmitted to a tape or pen recorder for later analysis.

DEVELOPMENTAL BACKGROUND

The first use of electrogoniometers for motion feedback training cannot be credited with certainty; by 1975, rehabilitation researchers in Seattle (1), Philadelphia (2), Toronto (3), and Atlanta (4) were using feedback goniometry. Harris et al. (1) used elbow joint angle feedback to help athetoid cerebral palsied children learn to flex and extend the arm more smoothly. Wooldridge et al (3) used feedback from a knee joint goniometer to teach two cerebral palsied children appropriate patterns of knee extension during gait. Koheil and Mandel (5) used the same device to train inhibition of knee hyperextension in adult stroke patients. Greenberg and Fowler (6) used a feedback elbow goniometer to help hemiplegic stroke patients practice extension of the elbow.

At Emory University, the first feedback finger electrogoniometers were developed in 1974 as exercise aids for patients recovering from hand trauma and/or surgery. The mechanical linkage was one originally devised by Reswick for studies of the functions of finger musculature (7). Emory researchers added a simple threshold feedback circuit, so that when the joint was flexed or extended to a target angle set by the therapist, a light and a tone were presented to the patient.

Brown et al. (8) subsequently published results of clinical comparisons showing that patients in a thorough and comprehensive hand rehabilitation program after repair of finger flexor tendons would gain active range of motion more rapidly when using feedback finger goniometers. This was also true for rheumatoid arthritic patients undergoing hand rehabilitation after metacarpophalangeal (MP) arthroplasty. Other applications of feedback goniometers in hand rehabilitation are discussed elsewhere in this volume (Chapter 11).

IMPROVING DESIGNS
Finger Goniometers

My involvement with these devices dates from 1976 with the goal of making feedback goniometry more available and affordable to therapists and patients. The result of these efforts (Figure 33.2) is a simplification of Reswick's original finger goniometer (7). Complex electronics are eliminated entirely. The patient can obtain continuous visual joint angle feedback from the pointer and degree wheel. The target angle is marked on the degree wheel with metallic tape. There is a metal wiper pin in the tip of the pointer. When a d.c. buzzer is connected across tape and wiper pin, a simple threshold buzz will occur when the pointer reaches the target angle. Thus the patient can practice joint flexion or extension even during functional activities when attending to the visual feedback display is not feasible. The goniometer reads in true degrees, and

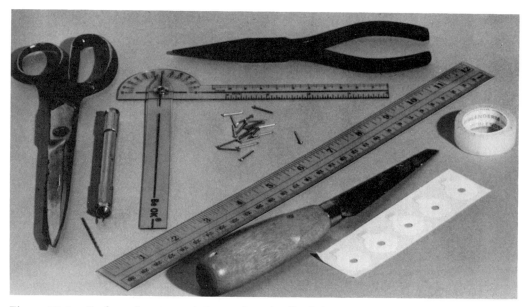

Figure 33.1. Tools and parts needed to make a feedback finger goniometer. The plastic clinical goniometer is seen in the middle of the picture.

the distal base adjusts so it can be used over the MCP or PIP joints.

Therapists can make the device from readily available tools and parts like those shown in Figure 33.1. The rivet of the clinical goniometer is loosened by relieving the pressure washer with a knife blade. The goniometer is then cut up to make the proximal base, the triangular center plate, and the two-piece distal base. The linkage holes are drilled by hand with a pin vise holding a bit slightly smaller than the

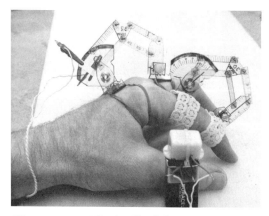

Figure 33.2. The feedback finger goniometer can be attached with tape, electrode patches, rubber bands, or with stretch lace.

No. 18 or 19 escutcheon pins used for the linkage, so these pins will be gripped tightly just beneath their heads and kept from wobbling. The round head of one pin, the lower linkage pin in the degree wheel, is ground thin and flat on sandpaper so it will not interfere with the pointer. The double-parallelogram linkage strips are cut from a thin, flexible ruler, and the linkage holes are drilled with a bit just slighly larger than the escutcheon pins, so the linkage strips will turn freely on the pins. Small retainer washers are cut from the ruler plastic and drilled with the smaller bit; forced down over each pin, they keep the strips in place, and the pins are clipped to within 3 mm of the washers.

The adjustment slots in the distal base can be started with a #28 drill and finished with a chisel preheated on a soldering iron barrel. A nylon 6-32 screw and nut, with #6 toothed lock washers, keeps the distal base where it is set.

The buzzer, metallic sensor tape, battery, wire, alligator clip, etc., needed for audio feedback are available from Radio Shack stores. Outside the United States, electronics distributors can supply everything but the metallic sensor tape. The latter is usually available in stores selling high-fidelity tape recorder supplies.

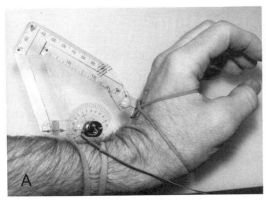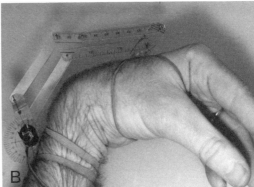

Figure 33.3. The feedback wrist goniometer linkage will follow the complete range of motion.

The goniometer is attached over MP or proximal interphalangeal (PIP) finger joints with double-adhesive miniature surface electrode washers. Tape, rubber bands, or stretch lace can also be used. All goniometer joints are made as friction-free as possible so that the bases do not rock on the flesh and cause hysteresis measurement errors.

If constructed and used properly, these delicate-looking devices will survive many months of clinical use. Care taken during cutting and bending increases device longevity. Only the best scissors should be used, taking very short, slow cutting strokes well back near the hinge of the blades. Most bends can be done without heating, but the acute "dog-leg" bends of the finger goniometer bases will survive longer if the bend-line is heated over the edge of a clothes iron and allowed to cool slowly after bending.

Wrist Goniometer

The feedback wrist goniometer is shown in Figure 33.3. The triangular segment in the linkage allows coverage of the complete range of motion of the wrist. The latest wrist goniometer design also reads in true degrees. Although they must be carefully sized for each patient, rubber bands are superior to straps for secure attachment without restricting motion at the extremes. Contact cement is used to assemble base plates, L-brackets, and the proximal and distal uprights.

The hole spacing in opposite segments of the double parallelogram linkage must be exactly equal for wrist or finger goniometers to function properly. To ensure this, both linkage holes are drilled in one horizontal or vertical

segment, which is then used as a template to drill the remaining segments, pinning the pieces together through the holes at one end while the fourth hole is drilled through the third.

Ankle Goniometer

To adapt the wrist goniometer for the ankle, (Fig. 33.4), two platforms are made from thermoplastic. These platforms span over the tibialis anterior tendon so that it does not rock the goniometer bases as it tightens and relaxes. One base is strapped to the shin with elastic bandage, and the other to the top of the shoe with rubber bands. A wrist goniometer is slipped under the bandage and rubber bands.

The feedback ankle goniometer can be used effectively with stroke patients to help them overcome foot-drop during gait. While EMG feedback is very helpful for initial work with

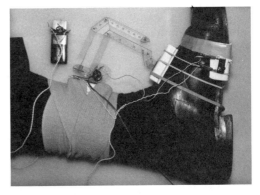

Figure 33.4. The feedback ankle goniometer. Note floor contact switch, which prevents irrelevant feedback during stance phase of gait.

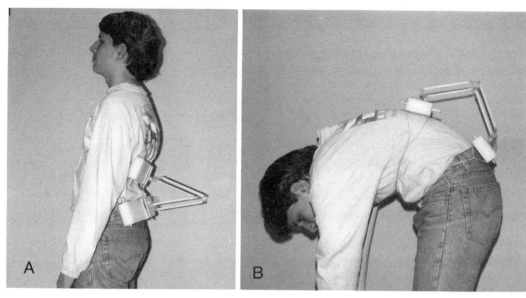

Figure 33.5.   A prototype of a feedback goniometer for lumbar flexion.

such patients in improving control of tibialis anterior, it may be less useful for gait training because the integrated EMG from tibialis is often a poor indication of the extent of dorsiflexion. The ankle goniometer can be set to give a clear audio threshold indication when the foot is dorsiflexed appropriately during the swing phase of gait. In order to eliminate irrelevant feedback when the foot is dorsiflexed during stance phase, a foot switch is added to the circuit in series with the feedback buzzer and degree wheel contact switch. This roller-arm microswitch, available at Radio Shack stores, is mounted near the ball of the foot so that when in contact with the floor, the switch is in the "open" state and eliminates false feedback. As the foot lifts from the floor, the foot switch closes, so that the feedback tone can be activated by sufficient dorsiflexion.

Back Goniometer

In Figure 33.5, the double-parallelogram linkage is further extended to span the substantial length increase of the lower back during forward flexion. This is essentially an expanded wrist goniometer. The light, stiff linkage elements are plastic drinking straws glued to short plastic end tabs. The bases are held with rubber bands to light crossbars cut from semirigid foam. These crossbars are held firmly against the body with chains of rubber bands. This prototype has promise for training

subjects to minimize lumbar flexion during lifting, and with the addition of a potentiometer, will be useful for kinesiological studies.

Elbow Goniometer

The feedback elbow goniometer, pictured in Figure 33.6, uses a sleeve mounting system similar to that of Harris et al. (1) for their elbow electrogoniometer. The sleeve can be made from an over-the-calf sock. Flexible vinyl plastic tabs are contact-cemented to the ends of the sleeve to lie over the medial surfaces of the arm, where they can be taped down to the skin surface to keep the sleeve from shifting or telescoping toward the elbow. Velcro patches are contact-cemented to the lateral surface of the sleeve and to the undersurface of the goniometer. Once the sleeve is in place, the goniometer is stuck on with its axis coinciding as nearly as possible with the elbow's center of rotation.

Visual feedback from the elbow goniometer is possible only in certain positions, or by using a mirror. If single-threshold audio feedback is not sufficient, one can orient the metallic tape crossways rather than radially, and cut several windows in it so that, as the pointer wiper pin passes over the tape, the feedback tone goes on and off every 10 degrees. This can give a good sense of relative motion to a person exercising the elbow over a wider range.

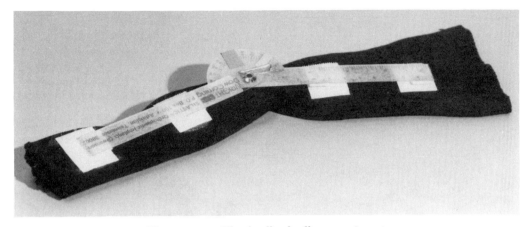

Figure 33.6. The feedback elbow goniometer.

The elbow goniometer can also be used over the knee, if the sleeve is increased in size. The audio threshold tone should suffice as a warning tone for patients who tend to hyperextend during stance. Consider using a heel-mounted footswitch in the circuit if you note irrelevant feedback near toe-off.

Pronation-Supination Goniometer

A feedback pronation-supination goniometer is quite helpful just for measuring the range of forearm pronation and supination (Fig. 33.7). The design consists of a wooden arm-holder, and the goniometer and linkage attached to a slider, allowing adjustment for forearm length. A somewhat larger plastic clinical goniometer can be used for better degree wheel visibility. The twisting motion of the hand is conveyed to the pointer by means of a shaft made from two plastic straws of the kind with the accordion-pleated section, allowing the straw to be bent to convenient angles. To connect the straws, the end of the first is enlarged a bit with a pencil tip or the jaws of long-nose pliers. Then the end of the second straw is pushed in about 8 mm for a swage fit. A straight pin pushed through the joint and clipped off makes the joint permanent. To connect the straw linkage over the goniometer rivet, a small tent-like assemblage is cut and

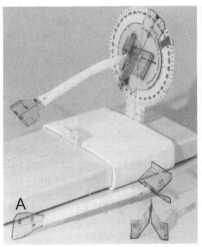
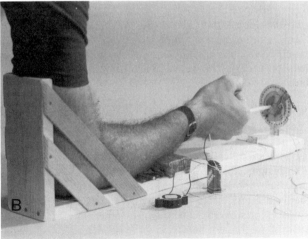

Figure 33.7. Pronation-supination goniometer. The larger plastic clinical goniometer used to make this device is also available from Fred Sammons, Inc., P.O. Box 32, Brookfield, Illinois 60513-0032.

Figure 33.8. Installing a small potentiometer for use with electronic recording devices.

bent from a plastic ruler and glued to the pointer with contact cement. A tapered tab on the assemblage is pushed firmly into the straw end and retained in place by a pin. At the other end of the straw is another pinned tab that the patient grips between the middle and ring fingers of his fisted hand. If the patient's grip is weak, these fingers may be taped together distal to the PIP joints, and the goniometer tab slipped between.

The wooden arm-holder is made from two "stock" lumber sizes—lattice strips and "one by four" (which is actually ¾" × 3½" or about 2 cm × 9 cm). The elbow pocket fits most adult arms well.

Kinesiology

For kinesiological recording or for complex feedback displays, you can easily incorporate a potentiometer into any of these "do-it-yourself" designs. Figure 33.8 shows how this is done. The Spectrol 140 potentiometer (available from many electronics distributors) is an excellent choice for electrogoniometers because of its high linearity, low friction and small size. Also needed are a clear household cement such as Duco, and two sizes of rubber or vinyl grommet. The small size should have

a ⅛-inch (3 mm) inside diameter to grip the Spectrol potentiometer shaft. The large size should have a ¼-inch (6 mm) inside diameter to grip the threads of the potentiometer body. Such grommets can be ordered from the same distributor supplying the Spectrol potentiometers, and are also found in the vinyl grommet assortment sold in Radio Shack stores. Radio Shack can supply everything except suitable potentiometers.

Electrogoniometer conversion is quite simple. First, the rivet is removed from the degree wheel and pointer by nibbling away the rivet flange with the tips of diagonal wire cutters. Using fine sandpaper, the area around the holes in the degree wheel and pointer is roughened. The larger grommet is glued with Duco cement concentrically around the rivet hole of the proximal base of the goniometer. The smaller grommet is glued concentrically to the portion of the goniometer connected to the activating linkage and the distal base. The glue should dry for at least 1 hour.

To install the potentiometer, the threads are screwed into the larger grommet as far as they will go. Then the other half of the goniometer and the small grommet are pushed down over the potentiometer shaft. The potentiometer

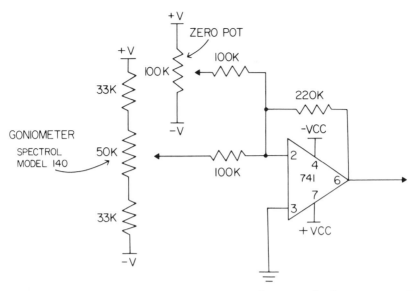

Figure 33.9. A simple circuit for continuous recording of joint angle changes. (A 20K goniometer pot may be substituted if necessary.)

shaft angle can easily be adjusted relative to the degree wheel for calibration purposes, and will remain where it is set unless the linkage is turned so that the pot reaches the limit of its range. If that occurs, the grommet will slip and prevent damage to the pot or the linkage. To give the grommets a little tighter grip on the pot, one can tie some fine string around each. String tension should be modest or the grommets may collapse and crack loose if the potentiometer is withdrawn.

A circuit is shown in Figure 33.9, which will suffice to display joint angle on a meter, an oscilloscope, or pen recorder. The 33K resistors protect the goniometer pot from being damaged by accidental misconnection of wires. For variable pitch auditory feedback, circuitry including a voltage-controlled oscillator, power amplifier, and speaker can be added.

Spectrol 140s sometimes get noisy with age. This noise can be filtered out to some extent by adding a .1 microFarad capacitor in parallel with the 220 kohm resistor shown in the circuit diagram. Sometimes it is necessary to pull out the tiny stop pin, located next to the pot threads, spray in some contact cleaner, and spin the pot shaft for about 10 minutes to clean the wirewound resistive element. This can be done with the pot connected to the circuit while the output signal is monitored on a scope to verify that the noise problem has abated. The stop pin can then be pushed back into place.

Measuring Proprioception

Feedback goniometers may also be used to measure proprioception, in scaling procedures derived from the psychophysical methods of Stevens [10,11]. For example, using a wrist goniometer, tell the subject that full extension is "zero" and full flexion is "100." Then, obstructing the wrist from view, position the wrist passively at random angles, asking the subject to assign a value to each, based on the reference angles. After about 40 trials, quantify performance by calculating the Pearson correlation coefficient r between the stimulus angles and the subject's estimates. Perfect performance would yield $r = 1$, while random guessing by someone without proprioception would yield values around zero. Grigg et al. [12] used this passive scaling procedure to compare proprioception in the normal and operated hips of patients after hip joint replacement. The test was done over a range of only 15° abduction, yet the r values ranged from .78 to .98, with no significant difference between normal and operated hips. The authors also tested active scaling in the same patients. The hip was placed in a neutral starting position, and integers from 1 to 15 were presented in

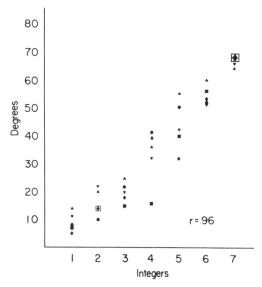

Figure 33.10. A scatterplot of stimulus integers vs. response angles for a patient with an artificial wrist joint. Loss of joint receptors evidently had little or no effect on position sense.

random order. Each patient moved the hip to a position judged subjectively to correspond to the stimulus integer. Again, r values were not significantly different for normal and operated

hips. The authors argued that since removal of joint receptors had so little effect on proprioception, extracapsular receptors in muscles, tendons, or skin must contribute substantially to position sense. Our own test of active scaling in a patient whose wrist joint had been replaced by an artificial insert gave a correlation coefficient of r = .96 (Fig. 33.10), again showing that removal of joint receptors had little effect on proprioception.

Any of the do-it-yourself goniometer designs can be used. For active scaling, a number randomizer of the integers from 1 to 9 is useful (Fig. 33.11). The entire series of integers should be given at least four times for reliable results. The stimulus integers and response angles are recorded in pairs. These can be plotted in a scatterplot as in Figure 33.10, which may highlight special features of individual performance. Calculation of the correlation coefficient can be done easily with a scientific calculator which includes this function.

CONCLUSION

If this overview has convinced you of the utility and feasibility of feedback goniometry for rehabilitation, but you wish more detailed information on construction aspects, please write the author at the address below. A brief

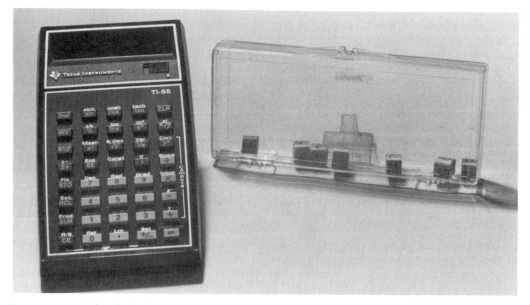

Figure 33.11. The shaker box of numbered cubes of eraser rubber is used to randomize stimulus integers for joint angle magnitude production, a quantitative test of proprioception. The calculator enables rapid computation of test score.

description of your proposed clinical application or research plan will help in providing the information you need.

Gary DeBacher, Ph.D.
Center for Rehabilitation Medicine
Emory University
Atlanta, GA 30322

References

1. Harris, F. A., Spelman, F. A. and Hymer, J. Electronic sensory aids as treatment for cerebral palsied children. Part II. Inappropriception. Phys. Ther., 54: 354–365, 1974.
2. Herman, R. Augmented sensory feedback in the control of limb movement. In *Neural Organization and Its Relevance to Prosthetics*, edited by W. S. Fields, pp. 197–215. Intercontinental Book Corp., New York, 1973.
3. Wooldridge, C. P., Leiper, C. and Ogston, D. Biofeedback training of knee joint position in the cerebral palsied child. Physiotherapy Canada, 28: 138–143, 1976.
4. Kukulka, C. G., Brown, D. M., and Basmajian, J. V. Biofeedback training for early joint mobilization. Am. J. Occupational Ther., 29: 469–470, 1975.
5. Koheil, R., and Mandel, A. R. Joint position feedback facilitation of physical therapy in gait training. Am. J. Phys. Med., 59: 288–297, 1980.
6. Greenberg, S., and Fowler, R. S.: Kinesthetic biofeedback: a treatment modality for elbow range of motion in hemiplegia. Am. J. Occupational Ther., 34: 738–743, 1980.
7. Thomas, D. L. and Long, C. An electrogoniometer for the finger. Am. J. Med. Electronics, 3: 96–100, 1964.
8. Brown, D. M., DeBacher, G. and Basmajian, J. V. Feedback goniometers for hand rehabilitation. Am. J. Occupational Ther., 33: 458–463, 1979.
9. Leiper, C. Comparison of concurrent and terminal auditory feedback as augmentation cues for a joint positioning task. Thesis submitted for Master of Education degree in Physical Education, Temple University, Philadelphia, 1980.
10. Stevens, S. S. The direct estimation of sensory magnitudes-loudness. Am. J. Psychol., 69: 1–25, 1956.
11. Stevens, S. S. The psychophysics of sensory function. In *Sensory Communication*, edited by W. A. Rosenblith, Technology Press and John Wiley, New York, 1961.
12. Grigg, P., Finerman, G. A. and Riley, L. H. Joint position sense after total hip replacement. J. Bone Joint Surg., 55: 1016–1025, 1973.
13. DeBacher, G. The effects of joint angle feedback on accuracy and consistency during range-of-motion exercises to a specified limit. Proceedings of the thirteenth annual meeting of the Biofeedback Society of America, Chicago, Illinois, March 5–8, 1982.

CHAPTER 34

Electrode Placement in Electromyographic Biofeedback

JOHN V. BASMAJIAN
ROBERT BLUMENSTEIN

ANATOMICAL CONSIDERATIONS

Accessible Muscles

Almost all striated muscles of the body are close enough to some overlying skin surface to permit pick-up of myoelectric or electromyographic (EMG) signals through the intervening tissues. But in some cases, precise monitoring of specific muscles is difficult because they: (a) lie deep to others with similar actions; (b) are crowded side-by-side with neighbors having both similar and different actions; and (c) have actions that are not precisely catalogued. For the novice, confusion can result from these conditions even with muscles that are considered "easy" by experienced electromyographers and highly trained anatomist-kinesiologists.

The bulk of our description of electrode placements that follows concentrates on superficial muscles, especially those that can be rather easily discriminated by simple surface electrodes. For special applications, the deeper muscles can be picked up with varying degrees of difficulty. More significantly, their activity often interferes with the pick-up of a target muscle in two ways. They may act as an opposite or antagonist (hence showing fallacious "activity" in the inactive target muscle), or by acting as a synergist, they falsely exaggerate the activity. All our electrode placements are based on experiments comparing surface electrodes with inserted fine-wire electrodes in at least two subjects (sometimes more).

These deeper muscles cannot be ignored. Their influence on precise pick-up can be reduced by "dodging," i.e., placement of electrodes in an eccentric position over a part of the target muscle that is not its very middle. Generally, however, the greatest EMG response is obtained by placing the electrodes as close as possible to the center of the fleshy muscle mass of the specific muscle; this is quite simple with a large, spread-out muscle such as pectoralis major. But even here there are complications because that muscle has two fleshy heads that act in somewhat different ways.

Skin and Fascia

The major electrical insulation of skin, superficial (subcutaneous) fascia ("fat layer"), and the muscle-enclosing deep fascia plays an important role in attenuating myoelectric potentials. Whenever and wherever they are thickened, signals are reduced, sometimes drastically. Thus, pick-up is grossly reduced through the normal thick skin of the back, sole of the foot, etc., and through abnormal layers of fat in a corpulent subject. Deep fascia varies greatly in thickness in different areas; e.g., in the face and arm it is rather thin in contrast to the thick skin of the back, palm, and parts of the thigh, leg, and sole of the foot. When skin, subcutaneous fat, and deep fascia are all thick over a target muscle, the average clinician faces a great challenge.

Raising the sensitivity of the instrument to "solve" the problem simultaneously increases the cross-talk from other muscles and the extraneous artifactive signals. Hence, optimal placement of electrodes becomes a critical issue. Even with the best possible electrode location, the problems may prove to be overwhelming. One final "trick" can be used by those who have solid kinesiologic knowledge, i.e., the use of alternative muscles that are synergistic. An example of this is direct training of the deltoid muscle (which abducts the shoulder joint) to train the scapular rotators indirectly. Those rotators are the synergists of the abductor but are much more difficult to record with surface electrodes, particularly the serratus anterior muscle, which lies in the armpit and deep to the scapula.

Muscle Synergy

Some difficulty arises from confusion among novices over the synergistic roles of muscles. Biceps brachii, a favorite flexor muscle for biomechanical investigations, is not as powerful a flexor muscle as the underlying "workhorse" brachialis. These two muscles usually work together, but there are some functions of the elbow when one is active and the other is not. Slight flexor activity recruits only brachialis; biceps, on the other hand, is also a supinator muscle when strong supination is required.

Bony Landmarks

A number of significant palpable or visible landmarks must be known by the clinician. These include the obvious long bones that are visible or palpable throughout their lengths, e.g., the clavicle. (For details, consult *Surface Anatomy, 2nd ed.,* by J. V. Basmajian, Williams & Wilkins, Baltimore, 1983).

The following landmarks should be identified.

Head and Neck

Orbital margin: easily palpated.

Mastoid process: the lump behind the external ear.

Temporomandibular joint: the lump in front of the external acoustic canal—actually it is the head of the mandible that forms the lump.

Zygomatic arch: the bony ridge that runs horizontally forward from the above joint into the cheek.

Angle of mandible: easily seen and palpated.

Inion (external occipital protuberance): the lump in the midline of the back of the skull above the muscles in the nape of the neck.

Spines of cervical vertebrae: easily palpated down the midline of the neck. The most prominent is C7.

"Adam's apple" (prominence of the thyroid cartilage): obvious in the midline of the front of the neck.

Sternocleidomastoid muscle: the prominent ridge that runs from the mastoid process to the

Sternoclavicular joint, actually the large lump that is the medial end of the clavicle.

Upper Limb

Clavicle: palpable end to end.

Acromion: the flat triangle of bone on the top of the "tip" of the shoulder; it has an

Angle of the acromion posteriorly, from which you can follow medially the

Spine of the scapula.

Inferior angle of the scapula: may be grasped.

Medial and lateral epicondyles of the humerus at the elbow are obvious to palpation, as is the

Olecranon process behind the elbow.

At the Wrist

Styloid processes of the radius and ulna also are palpable.

Distal skin crease of wrist: this constant crease runs through the palpable

Pisiform bone at its medial end, and the

Tubercle of the scaphoid towards its lateral end.

Trunk

Vertebral spinous processes: most are palpable. The 4th lumbar (L4) is at the level of the

Crest of the ilium, palpable from end to end, with the

Anterior superior iliac spine, at its anterior end, an important landmark for the abdominal wall; and the

Posterior superior iliac spine, in an obvious dimple, just over the sacroiliac joint (not palpable).

Pubic tubercle is palpable at the lateral end of the crest of the pubis about 2 fingers' breadths from the midline of the abdomen.

Costal margin and umbilicus are obvious landmarks.

Lower Limb

Several of the aforementioned items are 'lower limb' items. In addition:

Greater trochanter of the femur can be grasped and outlined at the prominence of the hip.

Ischial tuberosity: you can sit on your own and palpate its extent.

At the Knee

The palpable (and sometimes visible) landmarks are the

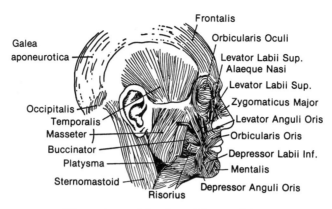

Figure 34.1. Muscles of face and jaw.

Patella—upper and side borders, and the apex below.

Medial and lateral femoral epicondyles (not reliable for purposes of measurements). Use instead the

Adductor tubercle: it is easily palpated above the medial epicondyle by pressing downward with the edge of the hand and index finger.

Head of the fibula: palpated behind the lateral side of the knee as a rounded lump.

Leg and Ankle

Tibial tubercle: the lump 2–3 cm below the patella, from which the sharp

Anterior border of the tibia ('shin') runs its course down to the

Medial malleolus, which can be palpated (and seen) around its entire outline.

Lateral malleolus: is just as obvious on the lateral side of the ankle.

ELECTRODES

Instrumentation has improved significantly over the past few years and can be obtained from a variety of reputable manufacturers. However, even with the finest piece of equipment, a potential source of error exists at the signal collection stage. This stage, which includes the electrodes and their skin attachments, can introduce significant amounts of noise.

Inserted electrodes, which are rarely used in biofeedback therapy, are introduced transcutaneously directly into muscle tissue. Their major advantages include (a) ability to record from deep muscles, (b) precise localization of muscle site, and (c) increased sensitivity when observing single motor units. But inserted

electrodes must be sterile and usually require special training to use.

Surface electrodes are applied to the skin over the muscle of interest. They are commonly used by clinicians for biofeedback application because of their simplicity and convenience. Their major disadvantages are: (a) they are limited to monitoring superficial muscles, and (b) they have decreased specificity. These disadvantages are minimized when small electrodes and proper placement are employed. See figures 34.1–34.45 on the following pages.

SURFACE ELECTRODE PLACEMENT

An EMG biofeedback electrode-assembly generally consists of two active and one inactive (ground) electrode. The active electrodes or sensors are usually placed in a bipolar configuration along the long axis of the muscle. The amount of EMG recorded is the algebraic sum of all action potentials of the contracting muscle fibers between the electrodes. This average value is dependent on (a) size of electrodes and (b) interelectrode distance.

Size of Electrodes

The physical size of electrodes is directly proportional to the amplitude of EMG and volume of muscle monitored. The larger the electrode area, the greater the EMG amplitude and the muscle volume monitored. Conversely, smaller electrodes increase the specificity of placement. The physical size of electrodes is indirectly related to impedance. The larger the electrode, the lower its· impedance. When small electrodes are used with their inherently high impedance, the skin must be meticulously prepared, as already noted.

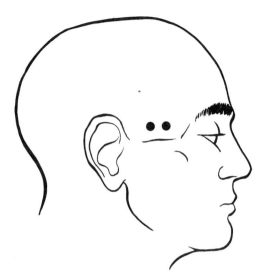

Figure 34.2. Temporalis. For a general pick-up from all temporalis, the best site is just above the zygomatic arch. The exact location is not important; neither is the choice of horizontal or vertical disposition of the pair.

Figure 34.4. Frontalis. For individual (right or left) muscles, the placement is in the midpoint between the eyebrow and hairline. For relaxation therapy, electrodes are widely separated, one on each side, to provide maximum facial muscle pick-up.

Interelectrode Distance

Interelectrode distance will determine the volume of muscle monitored. Large distances will increase the volume of muscle recorded. There is also an increased risk of recording

from muscles not desired. Small interelectrode distances localize EMG pickup and yield the least amount of "cross-talk." Overlapping adhesive discs provides minimal interelec-

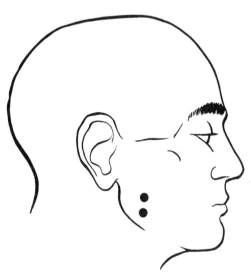

Figure 34.3. Masseter. The angle of the jaw is the landmark. Cross-talk from neighboring facial muscles may interfere. Vertical placement is somewhat better in most cases.

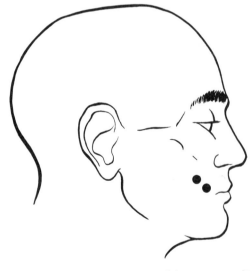

Figure 34.5. Zygomaticus and levator anguli oris. Although this would be the "best" placement for these muscles, these electrodes will also pick up from other nearby muscles, including orbicularis oris.

trode distance, and are preferred to reduce "cross-talk" to a minimum.

GROUND ELECTRODE

The ground electrode places the patient at the same ground potential that exists in the biofeedback unit—which of course is not grounded to the earth in clinical apparatus, which is battery operated. This minimizes susceptibility to electrical artifact. The location of the ground (reference) electrode is not critical, contrary to manufacturers' brochures. There may be some advantage to placing the ground electrode equidistant from the two active electrodes; but this idea is often overemphasized.

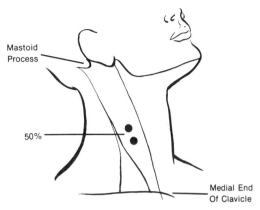

Figure 34.6. Sternomastoid. 1. Draw a line from the mastoid (the bony prominence behind the ear) to the bump on the medial end of the clavicle. 2. Center the electrodes at the 50% point on this line.

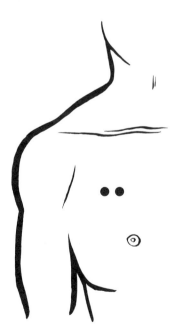

Figure 34.7. Sternocostal head of pectoralis major. Center the electrodes almost anywhere over the breast area. Generally poor pick-up results in any case.

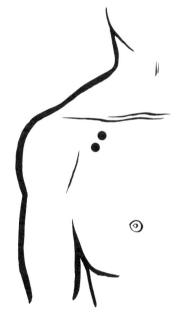

Figure 34.8. Clavicular head of pectoralis major. 1. Place the medial electrode two fingers' breadths below the midpoint of the clavicle. 2. Place the lateral electrode slightly lower and approximately 20 mm from the medial one.

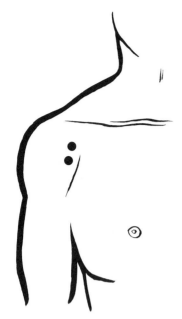

Figure 34.9. Anterior fibers of deltoid. Center the electrodes vertically within an elongated (cigar-shaped) oval below the lateral end of the clavicle.

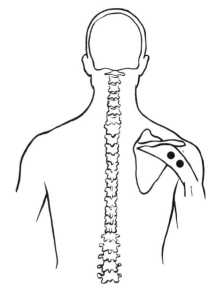

Figure 34.11. Posterior fibers of deltoid. Center the electrodes in the area about two fingers' breadths behind the angle of the acromion.

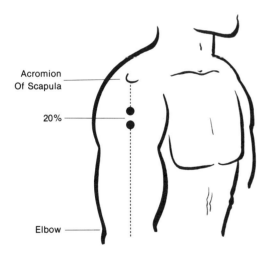

Acromion Of Scapula

20%

Elbow

Figure 34.10. Middle fibers of deltoid. Along the midline of the lateral surface (profile) of the arm, center the electrodes below the lateral margin of the acromion approximately 1/4 of the distance from the acromion to the elbow. This should correspond to the greatest bulge of the muscle.

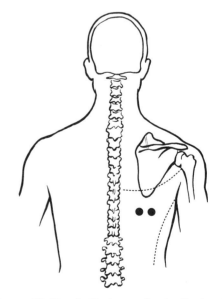

Figure 34.12. Latissimus dorsi. Center the electrodes in the area a short distance below the inferior angle of the scapula.

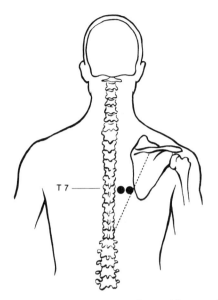

Figure 34.13. Trapezius (inferior fibers). The area immediately medial to the inferior angle of the scapula (lateral to the spine of T7 vertebra).

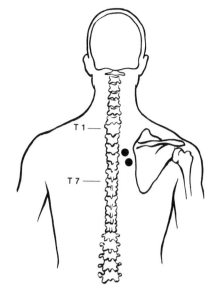

Figure 34.15. Rhomboids and middle fibers of trapezius. Center the electrodes in a long oval (cigar-shaped) area midway between the medial border of the scapula and the spines of the thoracic vertebrae (T1-T6).

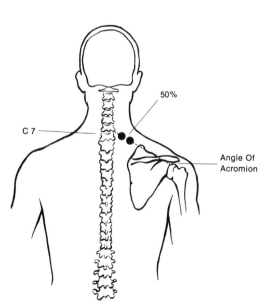

Figure 34.14. Upper fibers of trapezius. Center the electrodes in a small oval area (about 4 cm long) with its long axis horizontal half-way between the angle of the acromion and the easily felt spine on vertebra C7.

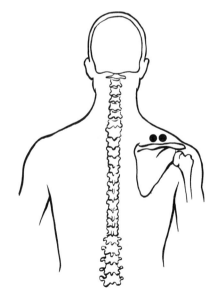

Figure 34.16. Supraspinatus. Center the electrodes in a narrow horizontal strip just along the upper border of the easily palpable spine of the scapula. Note that the supraspinatus is covered by the upper fibers of the trapezius from which considerable cross-talk may be expected, unless specifically inhibited.

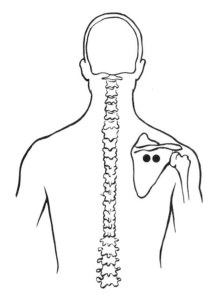

Figure 34.17. Infraspinatus. Center the electrodes in a fairly large circle (about 4 cm in diameter) whose upper edge reaches the spine of the scapula.

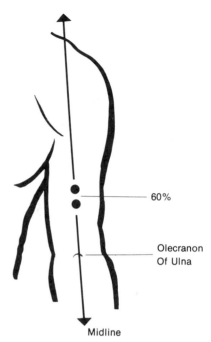

Figure 34.19. Medial head of triceps brachii. Center the electrodes within a small oval area whose center is located 60% of the distance between the angle of the acromion and the olecranon.

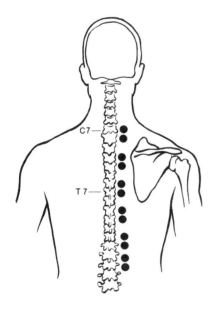

Figure 34.18. Paravertebral muscles (intrinsic). Pairs of electrodes may be placed just lateral to the vertebral spines wherever needed. However, pick-up is poor because of thick skin, fascia, and aponeurosis (especially in the lumbar area where cross-talk is often more easily picked up than the activity of paravertebral muscles).

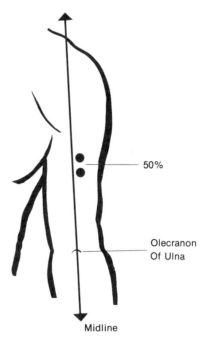

Figure 34.20. Lateral head of triceps brachii. Center the electrodes within a small oval area whose center is located a finger's breadth lateral to the midline and 50% of the distance between the angle of the acromion and the olecranon process.

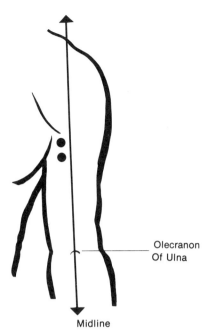

Figure 34.21. Long head of the triceps. Center the electrodes in a small oval area whose center is a finger's breadth medial to the midline just above the 50% mark on the line between the angle of the acromion and the olecranon.

Figure 34.23. Biceps brachii. Center the electrodes over the belly of this obvious target at the greatest bulge of the muscle.

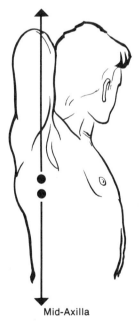

Figure 34.22. Serratus anterior. With the arm raised high, center the electrodes in a vertical oval (about 4 cm long) above the inferior angle of scapula and along the mid-axillary or mid-lateral line (half-way around the torso).

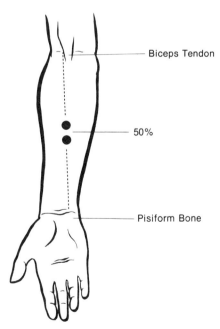

Figure 34.24. Flexor carpi radialis. Center the electrodes around the 50% point on a line from the lateral aspect of the biceps tendon at the elbow crease to the pisiform bone.

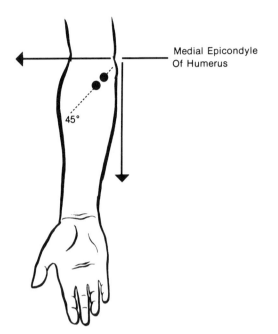

Figure 34.25. Pronator teres. Center the electrodes a short distance (5 cm or 2 inches) along a line that is 45° to a line drawn perpendicular to the medial epicondyle of the humerus.

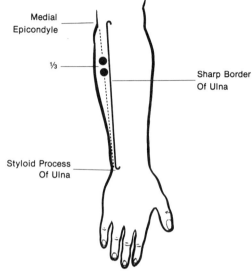

Figure 34.27. Flexor carpi ulnaris. Center the electrodes around the proximal 1/3 point on a line drawn from the posterior portion of the medial epicondyle (groove between the medial epicondyle and the olecranon process of the ulna) to the posterior portion of the styloid process of the ulna.

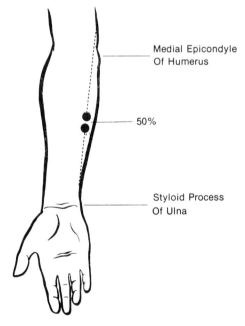

Figure 34.26. Flexors of the fingers. Center the electrodes around the 50% point on a line drawn from the medial epicondyle to the styloid process of the ulna. It is difficult with surface electrodes to separate flexor digitorum profundus from the superficialis.

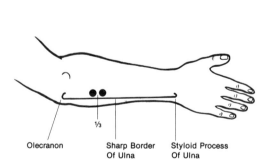

Figure 34.28. Extensor carpi ulnaris. 1. The forearm is flexed and in a semi-prone position. 2. Center the electrodes less than a finger's breadth from the posterior sharp border of the ulna in the region 1/3 the distance between the olecranon process and the styloid process of the ulna.

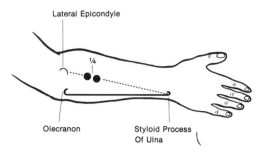

Figure 34.29. Extensor digitorum. Center the electrodes around the 1/4 point on a line drawn from the lateral epicondyle to the styloid process of the ulna.

Figure 34.32. Abductor pollicis brevis. In the oval that begins at the distal skin crease of the wrist and runs down the thumb, center the electrodes over the greatest bulge, at the proximal end of the thumb.

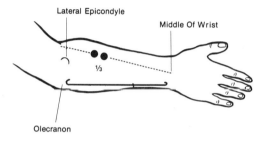

Figure 34.30. Extensores carpi radialis longus and brevis. 1. With the forearm fully pronated, extend a line from the lateral end of the elbow crease to the middle of the wrist. 2. Center the electrodes on this line around the 1/3 point (straight up the middle of the forearm).

Figure 34.33. Flexor pollicis brevis and opponens pollicis. Center the electrodes vertically one finger's breadth inferior and medial to the abductor pollicis brevis site (over the bulk of the thenar group).

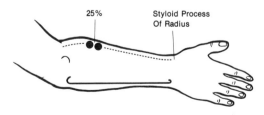

Figure 34.31. Brachioradialis. 1. With the hand pronated and the elbow bent, draw a line from the 3/4 point of the elbow skin crease to the styloid process of the radius (in the snuffbox). 2. Place both electrodes centered in an oval area approximately 25-30% of the distance from the lateral elbow crease to the styloid process of the radius.

Figure 34.34. Adductor pollicis. Center the electrodes within the triangular area whose base is along the skin web.

Figure 34.35. Hypothenar group of muscles. Vertical placement of electrodes along the medial margin of the hand at its greatest bulge will effectively reflect the activity of these three small muscles of the little finger.

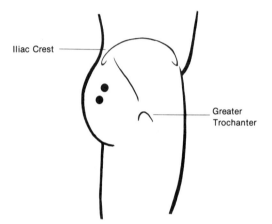

Iliac Crest

Greater Trochanter

Figure 34.36. Gluteus maximus. Center the electrodes over the greatest prominence of the middle of the buttocks well above the visible bulge of the greater trochanter (about midway between the sacral vertebrae and the greater trochanter). Thick skin and subcutaneous fat reduce the pick-up from this huge muscle.

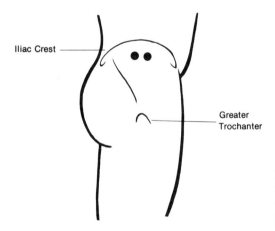

Iliac Crest

Greater Trochanter

Figure 34.37. Gluteus medius and minimus. Center the electrodes in a round area (about 4 cm in diameter) just below the iliac crest, halfway around the body.

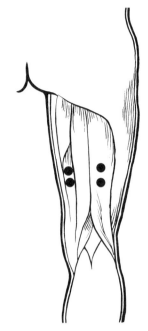

Figure 34.38. Lateral and medial hamstrings. Lateral hamstrings (biceps femoris): center the electrodes in a long vertical oval area (6–8 cm in diameter) on the lateral side of the back of the thigh (near its midpoint). Medial hamstrings (semimembranosus and semitendinosus): center the electrodes in a similar oval area on the medial side.

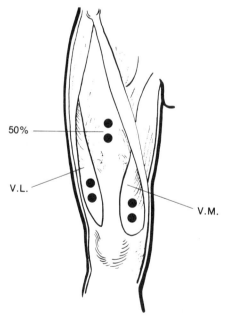

50%

V.L.

V.M.

Figure 34.39. Quadriceps femoris. For maximum pick-up of the whole muscle mass, center the electrodes in the large oval area over rectus femoris, with the lower electrode being a minimum of 10 cm above the patella. For the vastus lateralis choose the area inferolateral to this. For the vastus medialis, the best area is the inferomedial oval, where the muscle is seen to bulge in a well-muscled person.

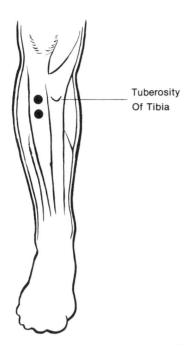

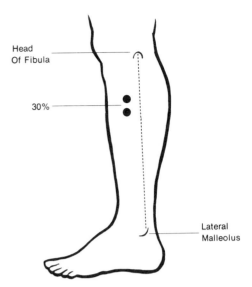

Figure 34.40. Tibialis anterior. Center the electrodes in a long narrow oval area whose upper part is one or two fingers' breadths from the tuberosity of the tibia. It is possible to use placements considerably lower than the above (down to the mid-shaft of the tibia).

Figure 34.42. Extensor digitorum longus and extensor hallucis longus. 1. Draw (or imagine) a line from the head of the fibula to the lateral malleolus. 2. Center the electrodes around the 1/3 point just less than two fingerbreadths anterior to the line. It is very difficult to place surface electrodes for discriminating between these two muscles. Also, cross-talk from the tibialis anterior and the peroneus longus is almost unavoidable.

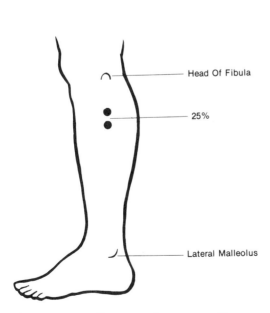

Figure 34.41. Peroneus longus. 1. Draw a line from the head of the fibula to the lateral malleolus. 2. Place both electrodes centered on the proximal 25% mark of this line.

Figure 34.43. Gastrocnemius (medial and lateral heads). Place the electrodes almost anywhere over the bulge of either head of gastrocnemius.

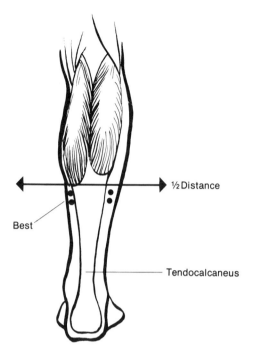

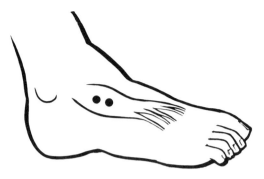

Figure 34.45. Extensor digitorum brevis. Center the electrodes in the oval area on the dorsum of the foot whose posterior end is immediately in front of the lateral malleolus.

Figure 34.44. Soleus. Center the electrodes in a narrow oval area just medial to the edge of the tendon below the half-way mark on back of leg. The lateral placement is usually less effective (but possible).

PART 6
ENVOY

CHAPTER **35**

Research and Feedback in Clinical Practice: A Commentary on Responsible Biofeedback Therapy

GARY E. SCHWARTZ

The purpose of this final chapter is to describe the need for a "research-oriented" perspective in the clinical practice of biofeedback, and to illustrate some ways in which this can be achieved. It is the thesis of this chapter that the fundamental concept underlying the use of feedback in therapy requires a research perspective on the part of the therapist and patient alike. In fact, the nonevaluative use of biofeedback in certain clinical settings is not only irresponsible and potentially unsafe, but is counter to the basic premise regarding the role of information and feedback in the development and maintenance of stable self-regulation (1).

By "research perspective," I do not mean to imply research experimentation in the restricted sense of the term. Typically, research experimentation is often distinguished from clinical practice in that the former is viewed as reflecting tightly controlled conditions in which causal conclusions between inputs (stimuli) and outputs (responses) can be made with some degree of certainty. Clinical practice, on the other hand, usually implies the unsystematic manipulation of numerous inputs (variables) in such a manner as to preclude drawing definitive conclusions regarding the relationship between inputs and outputs. However, these two extremes should at most be seen as poles on a continuum rather than reflecting a dichotomy.

The research perspective emphasized here refers to the more general process or "attitude" involving inquiry, problem solving, and constant evaluation on the part of the potential interventionist. In a real sense, any situation requiring evaluation and intervention can be seen as a problem-solving situation, and therefore as an "experiment." Be the situation one of solving a crime, repairing a television set, learning to play tennis, or helping a person with a stress-related disorder, the specific task in each case requires methods of inquiry, creative problem solving, "tests" or manipulations of one sort of another, and most important, constant evaluation.

Constant evaluation is the key issue here, one that is both at the heart of a general research perspective as well as the nature of biofeedback. The person who constantly evaluates his own hypotheses, and changes his beliefs as a result of his evaluations, reflects the kind of spirit of inquiry that separates the narrow-minded policeman from the effective detective, the blind technician from the creative repairman, or the irresponsible clinician from the responsible scientist/practitioner. I draw these parallels widely with the hope that the more general, systems concepts of evaluation, feedback, and regulation will become self-evident. Modern feedback theorists (e.g., 2) have illustrated the essential component that feedback plays in reducing "noise" as well as in improving "guidance" and effective regulation or control.

What I am suggesting is that biofeedback should not be viewed solely as technique, but rather should be viewed more broadly to reflect a general conceptual approach to intervention and evaluation. By this, I do not mean that the therapist need merely pay lip service to such theoretical concepts as feedback, stability, and self-regulation. Rather, I would argue that the responsible biofeedback therapist must come to recognize and accept the necessity that such a conceptual orientation places on him to adopt a systematic and critical approach to patient and treatment evaluation, and thereby develop improved self-monitoring and self-development. It should be recognized that this perspective on clinical practice is in no way dependent upon whether the application of any specific biofeedback procedure is documented in the formal research literature to be effective. Since it is unlikely that any one technique will be found to be 100% effective for all individuals, it behooves the responsible clinician to develop a research-oriented, problem-solving approach to therapy. This requires that the therapist continually monitor his or her own skills in selecting and administering interventions and evaluate their consequences for specific types of patients.

Most clinicians using biofeedback would agree in principle that therapy should be viewed as a problem-solving and, therefore, research activity. Unfortunately, few clinicians seem to be able to put these ideals into practice, and even fewer recognize that such a perspective is central to the actual use of feedback as a therapeutic modality. Mulholland (2) has recently illustrated how the concept of feedback provides a general scientific framework for studying input/output relationships, and that biofeedback is but a special case of this process. Going one step further, we can argue that *all interventions involve feedback for successful outcome* (3). Therefore, all interventions should be studied and practiced from a general research perspective.

BIOFEEDBACK AS A CENTRAL COMPONENT OF ALL BIOBEHAVIORAL INTERVENTIONS

As shown in Figure 35.1, biofeedback can be seen as the creation of a new feedback loop between the body and brain to aid in self-regulation (4). This feedback loop can be used to help replace one that has been attenuated or injured, or can serve as an additional feedback loop for the purpose of increasing stability.

Biofeedback has been typically viewed as being a psychophysiological procedure for directly modifying specific physiological dysfunctions (e.g., 5). However, there is a broader, more indirect concept of biofeedback, one that emphasizes the use of biofeedback (a Stage 5 process) as a means of helping the patient to modify his environment (Stage 1) or cognitions and emotions (Stage 2) for the sake of his physical health (Stage 3). In certain restricted applications of biofeedback, such as muscle rehabilitation of patients with strokes or other neuromuscular problems, the use of biofeedback as a focused procedure for training a localized psychobiological skill makes theoretical and clinical sense (6). However, to the extent that the patient's disorder is maintained in part by problems at Stages 1 and 2, then theory and practice tell us that biofeedback should be used in a more indirect sense to foster appropriate Stage 1 and Stage 2 modifications for the sake of the peripheral organ's health.

A common illustration of this perspective concerns the role of feedback in the behavioral treatment of obesity (7). For most people, successful weight loss requires a change in diet (decrease in caloric intake) and/or a change in exercise (increase in metabolism). Both of these require changes in a person's behavior, which in comprehensive behavior-change treatment programs involve combinations of environmental (Stage 1) and cognitive (Stage 2) modifications. However, ultimate success in the practice of these changes is defined as reduction in weight, which is assessed by the patient and therapist as a change in pounds recorded on a scale. The scale is an example of a mechanical feedback device that indicates to the patient and therapist that the changes in Stages 1 and 2 were successful in producing the desired change in Stage 3. This is an example of an indirect use of biofeedback.

The more "direct" approach of biofeedback for weight control would be for the patient to stand on the scale, and by thought processes alone (minimal usage of Stage 2), try to voluntarily reduce his weight. Assuming for the moment that some small weight loss was achieved (e.g., through sweating), were the person to reward himself with some desired food morsel, the treatment program would go from impractical to useless. Note that the fault

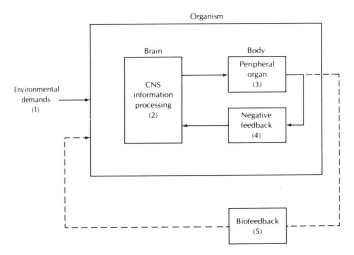

Figure 35.1. Simplified block diagram depicting (1) environmental demands influencing via sensory inputs (not shown), (2), the brain's regulation of its (3) peripheral organs, and (4) negative feedback from the periphery back to the brain. Breakdowns in homeostasis and disregulation can be initiated at each of these stages. Biofeedback (Stage 5) is a parallel feedback loop to Stage 4, detecting the activity of the peripheral organ (Stage 3) and converting it into environmental information (Stage 1) that can be used by the brain (Stage 2) to increase self-regulation [Reprinted with permission (3).]

here is not with the *concept* of a scale as biofeedback, but rather the failure to *use* this feedback to change the relevant causes of the disregulated eating behavior.

As various writers have noted (e.g., 8), feedback is a fundamental aspect of psychotherapy and behavior change. The therapist, in a real sense, is a provider of feedback of the patient's psychobiological state. Furthermore, the therapist hopefully provides corrective feedback that will help the patient change his environment (Stage 1) or behavior (mediated through Stage 2) for the sake of his psychobiological health (combined Stages 2, 3, and 4). From this perspective, the behavior therapist acts as a complex, psychobiologically based biofeedback system, monitoring a patient's psychobiological state as a Stage 5 intervention. If one restricts the use of the term psychophysiology to refer to "method," then the above argument is by definition wrong (since the therapist is not typically defined as a physiological device). However, if one adopts the definition of psychophysiology more broadly to refer to "processes" of intervention, then the psychotherapist is as much a psychophysiological intervention system as is the simple biofeedback device.

Of course, the therapist espousing a more traditional behavioral perspective could turn this perspective around and argue that biofeedback devices are essentially bioelectronic behavior therapists. This, parenthetically, is the underlying rationale for sometimes classifying biofeedback as a behavior therapy rather than as a biological therapy. The point of view of this chapter is that both extreme positions are wrong. Biofeedback, in the general sense, is a psychobiological therapy having psychobiological consequences. From this perspective, the therapist who infers that the patient is embarrassed from a blush on the face and subsequently makes a suitable remark, is essentially practicing a psychobiologically oriented therapy, whether the patient is aware of this fact or not.

The strong form of this position is that *all therapy, be it behavioral, pharmacological, or surgical involves biofeedback as a fundamental component.* Consider various approaches to the treatment of hypertension (9). The most obvious form of biofeedback therapy is to provide blood pressure biofeedback to the patient via a blood pressure monitoring system, and request that the patient use this feedback to lower his blood pressure. However, a less obvious form of biofeedback therapy involves traditional psychotherapy. This would include the older research on psychoanalysis, where free association, insight, emotional expression, and support were provided with the goal of lower blood pressure. Depending upon the therapist, blood pressure would be taken at various phases of therapy to determine how effective the psychotherapy was.

Probably the least obvious form of biofeedback therapy for hypertension involves the use of drugs or surgery. Consider the typical sequence of events in drug therapy. The patient first learns of having high blood pressure because a nurse or doctor takes the pressure and informs him (provides feedback, Stage 5) that the pressure is high. The physician then begins a set of interventions that necessitate *the patient's active, psychobiological cooperation in order for the procedures to influence blood pressure effectively.* For example, the patient must regularly take prescribed medication, despite the negative side effects that may be experienced, in order for lowered levels of blood pressure to be achieved and maintained. However, how does the doctor know whether or not the intervention is effective? The doctor must monitor the pressure in the office, or might have the patient or family members monitor pressure at work or home, to determine the relative effectiveness. Depending upon this feedback, the therapist will alter interactions with the patient (e.g., provide other drugs), so as to ultimately stabilize the pressure.

Hence, in all forms of therapy, Stage 5 feedback processes play an essential role. What vary are the types of inputs or interventions that are being used to effect changes in the desired psychobiological system. Whether one succeeds in lowering pressure by removing environmental stresses (Stage 1), changing the patient's perceptions or reactions to environmental stimuli (Stage 2), giving drugs that *directly* affect the central (Stage 2) and/or peripheral nervous system and organs (Stage 3), or surgically changing the central (Stage 2), peripheral organs (Stage 3) or internal feedback mechanisms (Stage 4), a complex psychobiological feedback loop system (Stage 5) is required to assess and evaluate therapeutic outcome. Note that every therapy involves person-to-person (or machine-to-person) interactions that can activate multi-psychobiological systems affecting the person's response to treatment.

A major change in attitude triggered by research on biofeedback has been to emphasize more of the active monitoring, carrying out of treatment programs, and prevention of disease as the province and responsibility of the individual person. In fact, biofeedback has provided an important demonstration of the potential for psychobiological self-regulation, and the recognition that Stage 1 and 2 processes play a continual role in health and disease.

Emphasizing the fundamental role of feedback in all interventions is not meant to imply that all interventions are the same. On the contrary, current experimental research is continuing to uncover complexities regarding underlying psychobiological' mechanisms in different kinds of behavioral and biological interventions. The purpose of using a general construct (like feedback) and some general properties (like self-regulation and order, and disregulation and disorder) (3) is to provide a foundation for placing behavioral and biological concepts under a common theoretical umbrella. This in turn provides a general framework for viewing the therapeutic setting as a research setting requiring continued hypothesis generation, feedback, and evaluation for successful clinical outcome.

THE INCORPORATION OF RESEARCH IN CLINICAL PRACTICE

The first, and probably major, step in bringing a research perspective to bear on clinical practice is to establish a change in attitude or paradigm (10) regarding health and health care in both the therapist and patient. The general perspective outlined here provides one such rationale. It emphasizes the need for continued assessment, hypothesis testing, and evaluation in therapy provided by feedback. It points out that variables (be they under control of the therapist and patient, or not) *interact* in compact ways, and that continued evaluation using feedback is essential to help establish what combination of variables leads to changes in what patients. This perspective emphasizes that treatment is not a cut and dried affair. Rather, all hypotheses in therapy must be seen to be, in the final analysis, probability statements regarding possible beneficial effects. The patient must come to see that assuming more responsibility for his or her own health necessarily involves the use of feedback for continued evaluation regarding what inputs lead to what outputs. In essence, *self-care is as much a research enterprise requiring feedback as is the delivery of health care to others.*

Having recognized the link between feedback, evaluation, and change, concrete proposals can be offered for improving general clinical practice from a research perspective. The obvious suggestion that therapists keep up with the published literature and attend post-graduate workshops is a necessary but not sufficient component of the perspective emphasized here. Rather, the therapist must come to develop more systematic decision-making skills, and must develop single-subject as well as group-oriented research approaches to evaluating progress in therapy. Systematic procedures can be incorporated into clinics or private practices whereby particular interventions, singularly or in combination, can be continually assessed using evaluation of the feedback provided by the patient.

Both the "software" and "hardware" for such approaches are becoming available. For example, there are now various single-subject case designs described in the literature for assessing biofeedback, behavior therapy, or for that matter, any therapeutic intervention (11). These approaches can readily be incorporated into regular clinical practice, and they emphasize the general research perspective outlined here.

One characteristic of feedback is that the information is usually delayed. In other words, the information occurs after the response has been made, and only then is fed back to the input to help guide or correct the output. Clearly, the more continuous and immediate the feedback process is, the greater the potential for therapist and patient alike to use the feedback effectively. The development of portable psychophysiological monitoring equipment (i.e., biofeedback devices) with built-in computer-based modules for quantifying and displaying the information on-line (such as the development of battery-operated digital integrators) improves the continuity and immediacy of the feedback. However, this is but the first step toward using the concept of feedback to its fullest extent in therapy.

For example, the need for regular and continued follow-up in therapy is essential for valid research, and, therefore, for valid clinical practice. The problem has been that up to now, the hardware to provide this feedback has been lacking to make large-scale follow-up of a clinical practice feasible. However, the recent development of microcomputers costing only a few thousand dollars with associated data base management systems and statistical packages (purchased for the home, office, clinic or laboratory) makes it possible to readily keep track of what patients are in what stage of therapy, and whom should be written to, called, or seen at a particular time to evaluate long-term gains. These microcomputers are programmable in languages designed for the educated layman, and, therefore, should be usable by any person also competent to use the electronic hardware of biofeedback therapy.

These microcomputers can act as the needed feedback device to remind the therapist of the patient's problems, status, and therapy protocol. In addition, the microcomputer makes it possible for individual therapists to obtain group averages across different kinds of patients, and thereby determine what kinds of group trends are occurring. With what kind of patient is the individual therapist most effective? Least effective? What kinds of procedures, with what kinds of problems, seem to be having the greatest effect, both in the short run and the long run? Until quite recently, such questions were not readily answerable for the average clinic or therapist. Neither the software nor hardware was available to make this approach practical. However, theories of feedback, therapy, and evaluation are continuing to evolve, and the hardware necessary to implement these concepts is now available. Their creative and systematic incorporation into clinical practice can make the research aspect of clinical work more stimulating and challenging for the therapist and at the same time improve the quality of care provided for patients.

As mentioned above, clinical practice involves complex problem-solving or decision-making processes on the part of therapist and patient alike. Therefore, procedures for improving decision-making skills using feedback need to be developed. The recent research by Janis and Mann (12) illustrates how decision making can be improved, both in basic and applied settings. Of particular relevance to this chapter is their procedure for improving decision-making skills that emphasizes the use of a "balance" sheet, a paper and pencil feedback device for evaluating the complexities in a decision-making situation. According to Janis and Mann (12):

The "balance-sheet" procedure is a predecisional exercise that requires a decision maker to confront and answer questions about potential risks and gains he had not previously contemplated. Without a systematic procedure, even the most alert and well-motivated person may overlook vital aspects of the alternatives, remaining unaware of some of the losses that will ensue from the preferred course and maintaining false expectations about potential gains (p. 312).

That this issue applies strongly to the historical development and current practice of biofeedback therapy should be self-evident. That the very concept of *feedback as a general process in therapy requires a research perspective in clinical practice* in order to overcome these problems is only just now becoming recognized. Hopefully, the inclusion of this orientation in the present volume will alert the clinician not only to the pressing need to incorporate a research perspective into clinical practice, but that this general perspective is essential to the concept of, and therefore should be applied to, the use of biofeedback in all behavioral as well as biomedical approaches to therapy. It is possible that future clinicians will share clinical data and ideas in a continuous and dynamic manner through research clinic phone networks of modems connected to their microcomputers.

References

1. Wiener, N. *Cybernetics or Control and Communication in the Animal and Machine.* M.I.T. Press, Cambridge, 1948.
2. Mulholland, T. B. Biofeedback as scientific method. In *Biofeedback: Theory and Research,* edited by G. E. Schwartz and J. Beatty. Academic Press, New York, 1977.
3. Schwartz, G. E. Psychobiological foundations of psychotherapy and behavior change. In *Handbook of Psychotherapy and Behavior Change,* 2nd ed., edited by S. L. Garfield and A. E. Bergin. John Wiley & Sons, New York, 1978.
4. Schwartz, G. E. Psychosomatic disorders and biofeedback: a psychobiological model of disregulation. *Psychopathology: Experimental Models,* edited by J. D. Maser and M. E. P. Seligman. W. H. Freeman and Company, San Francisco, 1977.
5. Shapiro, D. and Surwit, R. Learned control of physiological function and disease. In *Handbook of Behavior Modification and Therapy,* edited by H. Leitenberg. Prentice-Hall, Englewood Cliffs, N.J., 1976.
6. Basmajian, J. V. Learned control of single motor units. In *Biofeedback: Theory and Research,* edited by G. E. Schwartz and J. Beatty, Academic Press, New York, 1977.
7. Schwartz, G. E. Biofeedback as therapy: some theoretical and practical issues. Am. Psychol., 28: 666–672, 1973.
8. Lazarus, R. S. A Cognitively-oriented psychologist looks at biofeedback. Psychol., 30: 553–561, 1975.
9. Shapiro, A. P., Schwartz, G. E., Ferguson, D. C. E., Redmond, D. P. and Weiss, S. M. Behavioral methods in the treatment of hypertension: a review of their clinical status. Ann. Intern. Med., 86: 626–636, 1977.
10. Kuhn, T. S. *The Structure of Scientific Revolutions.* University of Chicago Press, Chicago, 1962.
11. Hensen, M. and Barlow, D. H. *Single Case Experimental Designs: Strategies for Studying Behavior Change.* Pergamon Press, New York, 1976.
12. Janis, I. L. and Mann, L. Coping with Decisional Conflict. Am. Sci., 64: 657–667, 1976.

INDEX

Page numbers in *italics* denote figures; those followed by "t" denote tables.